W9-BGF-050

Bolivia

Kate Armstrong
Vesna Maric, Andy Symington

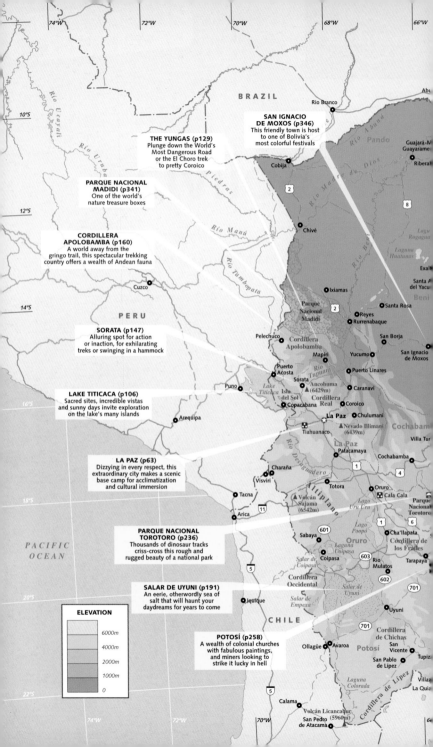

SAN IGNACIO DE MOXOS (p346)
This friendly town is host to one of Bolivia's most colorful festivals

THE YUNGAS (p129)
Plunge down the World's Most Dangerous Road or the El Choro trek to pretty Coroico

PARQUE NACIONAL MADIDI (p341)
One of the world's nature treasure boxes

CORDILLERA APOLOBAMBA (p160)
A world away from the gringo trail, this spectacular trekking country offers a wealth of Andean fauna

SORATA (p147)
Alluring spot for action or inaction, for exhilarating treks or swinging in a hammock

LAKE TITICACA (p106)
Sacred sites, incredible vistas and sunny days invite exploration on the lake's many islands

LA PAZ (p63)
Dizzying in every respect, this extraordinary city makes a scenic base camp for acclimatization and cultural immersion

PARQUE NACIONAL TOROTORO (p236)
Thousands of dinosaur tracks criss-cross this rough and rugged beauty of a national park

SALAR DE UYUNI (p191)
An eerie, otherworldly sea of salt that will haunt your daydreams for years to come

POTOSÍ (p258)
A wealth of colonial churches with fabulous paintings, and miners looking to strike it lucky in hell

ELEVATION

	6000m
	4000m
	2000m
	1000m
	0

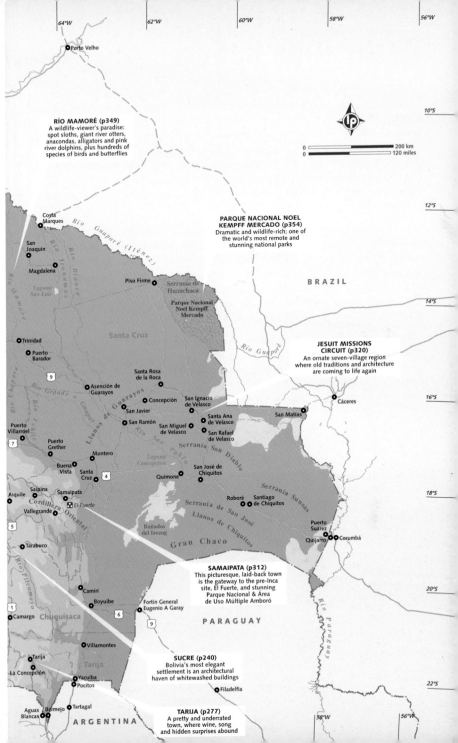

RÍO MAMORÉ (p349)
A wildlife-viewer's paradise: spot sloths, giant river otters, anacondas, alligators and pink river dolphins, plus hundreds of species of birds and butterflies

PARQUE NACIONAL NOEL KEMPFF MERCADO (p354)
Dramatic and wildlife-rich; one of the world's most remote and stunning national parks

JESUIT MISSIONS CIRCUIT (p320)
An ornate seven-village region where old traditions and architecture are coming to life again

SAMAIPATA (p312)
This picturesque, laid-back town is the gateway to the pre-Inca site, El Fuerte, and stunning Parque Nacional & Área de Uso Múltiple Amboró

SUCRE (p240)
Bolivia's most elegant settlement is an architectural haven of whitewashed buildings

TARIJA (p277)
A pretty and underrated town, where wine, song and hidden surprises abound

0 — 200 km
0 — 120 miles

BRAZIL

PARAGUAY

ARGENTINA

Destination Bolivia

Simply superlative – this is Bolivia. It's the hemisphere's highest, most isolated and most rugged nation. It's among the earth's coldest, warmest, windiest and steamiest spots. It boasts among the driest, saltiest and swampiest natural landscapes in the world. Although the poorest country in South America (and boy do Bolivians get tired of hearing that), it's also one of the richest in terms of natural resources. It's also South America's most indigenous country, with over 60% of the population claiming indigenous heritage, including Aymará, Quechua, Guaraní and over 30 other ethnic groups. Bolivia has it all…except, that is, for beaches.

This landlocked country boasts soaring peaks and hallucinogenic salt flats, steamy jungles and wildlife-rich grasslands. Unparalleled beauty is also reflected in its vibrant indigenous cultures, colonial cities, and whispers of ancient civilizations. This is exactly what attracts visitors, and with good reason. Bolivia is now well and truly on travelers' radars; opportunities for cultural and adventure activities and off-the-beaten-path exploration have exploded. But while most travelers stick to the well-worn paths of the Altiplano, there's plenty to be found elsewhere, including the tropical east and the lowland regions in the south.

Bolivia's social and political fronts have been in flux since the appointment of the country's first indigenous president. Optimism is generally high, especially among the indigenous majority, although many changes are afoot. Protests, marches and demonstrations are a perpetual part of the country's mind-boggling landscape. This is a truly extraordinary place. Put on your high-altitude goggles, take a deep breath (or three) and live superlatively.

WOODS WHEATCROFT

Natural Attractions

BRENT WINEBRENNER

Reflect upon the stark beauty of Volcán Licancabur (p196) as you cruise the Southwest Circuit (p190)

RAFAEL ESTEFANIA

Remember your binoculars in Parque Nacional & Área de Uso Múltiple Amboró (p307)

OTHER HIGHLIGHTS

- Drop into remote Parque Nacional Noel Kempff Mercado (p354) for seriously spectacular wildlife-spotting.
- Join an ecotour (p342) for a real appreciation of the Amazon Basin.

Scope the red rock formations in the dramatic countryside around Tupiza (p201)

KRZYSZTOF DYDYNSKI

Historic Architecture

Look heavenward to survey the *mudéjar* (Moorish) domes of Copacabana's cathederal (p111)

RICHARD I'ANSON

ALISON WRIGHT

Have an eye for detail at the Tiahuanaco ruins (p102)

OTHER HIGHLIGHTS

- Enter into the mystery of El Fuerte (p313), the Unesco World Heritage site right on the doorstep of sleepy Samaipata (p312).
- Peruse a wealth of ornate colonial architecture in Potosí (p258), including the National Mint (p261).

Sparkling colonial architecture sees Sucre (p240) reign as Bolivia's most beautiful city

RAFAEL ESTEFANIA

Tradition & Culture

An intricate altarpiece blends traditional indigenous beliefs with Catholicism (p37)

Enjoy the liveliest Aymará New Year celebrations at ancient Tiahuanaco (p104)

OTHER HIGHLIGHTS

- Marvel at the merchandise in La Paz's Mercado de Hechicería (Witches' Market; p71) and possibly purchase a traditional remedy or two.
- Cast an eye over distinctive woven craftwork in a tour of the Jalq'a communities (p257).

Parade your way through riotous festivities in San Ignacio de Moxos (p346)

Outdoor Adventure

WOODS WHEATCROFT

Even beginners can tackle the slopes of majestic Huayna Potosí (p157)

Step back to Inca times via El Choro trek
(p135)

GREG CAIRE

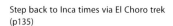

BRENT WINEBRENNER

Glide across the Salar de Uyuni (p191) in the most
surreal 4WD route you're ever likely to encounter

OTHER HIGHLIGHTS

- Take to the road on two wheels, peddling (and
  freewheeling) through some of the country's
  most spectacular scenery (p130).
- Cruise into the Amazon wilderness in a riverboat on the Río Mamoré (p349).

Contents

The Authors	12
Getting Started	14
Itineraries	18
Snapshot	23
History	24
The Culture	34
Environment	44
Outdoors	49
Food & Drink	55

La Paz 63
History	64
Orientation	64
Information	65
Dangers & Annoyances	69
Sights	70
Activities	77
Walking Tour	78
Courses	79
La Paz for Children	80
Tours	80
Festivals & Events	80
Sleeping	82
Eating	85
Drinking & Clubbing	90
Entertainment	91
Shopping	92
Getting There & Away	93
Getting Around	95
AROUND LA PAZ	96
Valle de la Luna	96
Mallasa	97
Valencia & Mecapaca	97
Muela del Diablo	98
Valle de las Ánimas	98
Cañón de Palca (Quebrada Chua Keri)	99
Chacaltaya	100
Milluni & the Zongo Valley	101
Laja	101
Tiahuanaco (Tiwanaku)	102
Urmiri	105

Lake Titicaca 106
Copacabana	108
Copacabana to Yampupata Trek	116
Isla del Sol	118
Isla de la Luna (Koati)	122
Islas de Huyñaymarka	122
Around Lake Titicaca	123
Estrecho de Tiquina	125
Northeastern Shore	125
Guaqui & Desaguadero	125

The Cordilleras & Yungas 127
THE YUNGAS	129
Coroico	129
El Choro Trek	135
Yolosa	137
Takesi (Taquesi) Trek	138
Yanacachi	140
Yunga Cruz Trek	141
Chulumani	143
Around Chulumani	145
Sorata	147
El Camino del Oro (Gold Digger's Trail)	151
Mapiri Trail	153
Consata	155
Aucapata & Iskanwaya	155
Guanay	155
Caranavi	156
CORDILLERA REAL	157
Huayna Potosí	157
Illimani	158
Condoriri Massif	159
Ancohuma	159

CORDILLERA APOLOBAMBA	160
Charazani	160
Área Natural de Manejo Integrado Nacional (Anmin) Apolobamba	162
Lagunillas to Agua Blanca (Curva To Pelechuco) Trek	163
CORDILLERA QUIMSA CRUZ	165
Activities	166
Getting There & Away	166

Southern Altiplano 167

Oruro	169
Around Oruro	177
Parque Nacional Sajama	179
Around Parque Nacional Sajama	182
Parque Nacional Lauca (Chile)	182
SOUTHWESTERN BOLIVIA	184
Uyuni	184
Around Uyuni	190
THE SOUTHWEST CIRCUIT	190
Salar de Uyuni	191
Salar de Coipasa	194
Los Lípez	194
Tupiza	197
Around Tupiza	201
San Vicente	203
Villazón	204
La Quiaca (Argentina)	207

Central Highlands 209

Cochabamba	211
Parque Nacional Tunari	230
Cochabamba Valley	232
Incallajta	234
Totora	235
Mizque	235
Aiquile	236
Parque Nacional Torotoro	236
Sucre	240
Tarabuco	253
Candelaria	254
Cordillera de los Frailes	254
Potosí	258
Lagunas de Kari Kari	272
Hacienda Cayara	272
Betanzos	274
Tarapaya	274
Chaqui	274

South Central Bolivia & The Chaco 275

SOUTH CENTRAL BOLIVIA	277
Tarija	277
San Jacinto Reservoir	285
San Lorenzo	285
El Valle de la Concepción	285
Padcaya	285
Chaguaya	287
Reserva Biológica Cordillera de Sama	287
Reserva Nacional de Flora y Fauna Tariquía	288
Bermejo	288
THE CHACO	289
Yacuiba	289
Villamontes	290
Parque Nacional y Área Natural de Manejo Integrado Aguaragüe	291
Reserva Privada de Patrimonio Natural de Corvalán	291
Boyuibe	291
Camiri	292

Santa Cruz & Eastern Lowlands 293

Santa Cruz	295
Buena Vista	305
Parque Nacional & Área de Uso Múltiple Amboró	307
Santa Cruz to Samaipata	311
Samaipata	312
Around Samaipata	316
Vallegrande	317
Pucará & La Higuera	318
EASTERN LOWLANDS	319
Jesuit Missions Circuit	320
Far Eastern Bolivia	326
Puerto Suárez	327
Quijarro	327
San Matías	328

Amazon Basin 329

CHAPARE REGION	332
Villa Tunari	333
Parque Nacional Carrasco	334
Puerto Villarroel	335
Parque Nacional Isiboro-Sécure	335

WESTERN BOLIVIAN AMAZON	336
Rurrenabaque	336
San Buenaventura	341
Parque Nacional Madidi	341
Reyes & Santa Rosa	343
Yucumo	343
San Borja	344
Reserva Biosférica del Beni	344
San Ignacio de Moxos	346
EASTERN BOLIVIAN AMAZON	347
Trinidad	347
Puertos Almacén & Barador	352
Santuario Chuchini	352
Magdalena	353
Reserva de Vida Silvestre Ríos Blanco y Negro	353
Parque Nacional Noel Kempff Mercado	354
THE NORTHERN FRONTIER	359
Guayaramerín	359
Riberalta	362
Riberalta to Cobija	364
Cobija	364

Directory 366

Accommodations	366
Activities	367
Business Hours	367
Children	368
Climate Charts	368
Customs	368
Dangers & Annoyances	368
Discount Cards	369
Embassies & Consulates	369
Festivals & Events	370
Food	371
Gay & Lesbian Travelers	371
Holidays	371
Insurance	372
Internet Access	372
Legal Matters	372
Maps	372
Money	373
Photography & Video	373
Post	374
Shopping	374
Solo Travelers	374
Telephone	375
Time	377
Toilets	377
Tourist Information	377

Travelers with Disabilities 377
Visas 377
Women Travelers 378
Work & Volunteering 378

Transportation 380

GETTING THERE & AWAY 380
Entering the Country 380
Air 380
Land & River 383
GETTING AROUND 385
Air 385
Bicycle 385
Boat 386
Bus 386
Car & Motorcycle 387
Hitchhiking 388
Local Transportation 388

Train 389
Tours 389

Health 391

BEFORE YOU GO 391
Insurance 391
Medical Checklist 391
Online Resources 391
Further Reading 392
IN TRANSIT 392
Deep Vein Thrombosis 392
Jet Lag & Motion Sickness 392
IN BOLIVIA 393
Availability & Cost of
Healthcare 393
Infectious Diseases 393
Travelers' Diarrhea 396
Environmental Hazards 396

Traveling with Children 398
Women's Health 398

Language 399

Glossary 406

Behind the Scenes 410

Index 420

Map Legend 432

Regional Map Contents

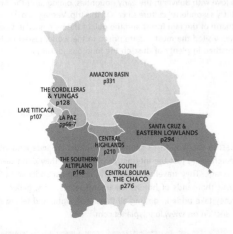

AMAZON BASIN
p331

THE CORDILLERAS
& YUNGAS
p128

LAKE TITICACA
p107

LA PAZ
pp66-7

SANTA CRUZ &
EASTERN LOWLANDS
p294

CENTRAL
HIGHLANDS
p210

THE SOUTHERN
ALTIPLANO
p168

SOUTH
CENTRAL BOLIVIA
& THE CHACO
p276

12

The Authors

KATE ARMSTRONG
Coordinating Author, introductory chapters, La Paz, Lake Titicaca, Directory, Transportation

Kate first wandered to Bolivia during a year-long backpacking trip through South America. Captivated by the country's flavors, she holed up in Sucre to study Spanish and inadvertently joined a folkloric dance troupe after two ungraceful *cueca* lessons in her hiking boots. Her search for the perfect *salteña* and her love of Bolivians and their extraordinary country ensure her regular return. When not marveling at the Altiplano or Amazonian jungle, Kate is a freelance writer in Australia. To research this edition, she ate her way around La Paz, burning off the kilojoules climbing the city's steep market-filled streets. Kate also contributed to Lonely Planet's *South America on a Shoestring*.

My Favorite Trips

Highest, coldest, hottest, slowest, fastest. Superlative moments include sighting a rarely spotted tree anteater in **Parque Nacional Madidi** (p341), yo-yoing the passes on a mountain bike around **Sorata** (p147), the tire blow-out on the road to incredible **Potosí** (p258) and the **yatiri** (p71) who assured me of safe travels. Around La Paz, quirkier moments include the **lucha libre** (free-style wrestling; p76) and **El Alto's market** (p76). Important routines include a daily *salteña* in **La Paz** (p89) and the numerous colorful dance parades in **Sucre** (p240). The sunsets in **Tupiza** (p197) and **Isla del Sol** (p118), flying over the **Cordillera Real** (p157) from La Paz to Rurrenabaque, and the wines of **Tarija** (p277) enriched my experience, as did the kindness of the Bolivians who share so much.

VESNA MARIC
South Central Bolivia, Santa Cruz & Eastern Lowlands, Amazon Basin

Vesna fell in love with Bolivia in the early noughties, pining after the Andes and the country's wonderful culture since. On this trip, Vesna discovered the irresistible charm of the rain forest and the pull of the hammock in tropical Rurrenabaque, visited the most bizarre prison in the world, tasted Bolivian wine and breathed in plenty of dust on the long bus journeys.

LONELY PLANET AUTHORS

Why is our travel information the best in the world? It's simple: our authors are independent, dedicated travellers. They don't research using just the internet or phone, and they don't take freebies in exchange for positive coverage. They travel widely, to all the popular spots and off the beaten track. They personally visit thousands of hotels, restaurants, cafés, bars, galleries, palaces, museums and more – and they take pride in getting all the details right, and telling it how it is. For more, see the authors section on www.lonelyplanet.com.

ANDY SYMINGTON   Cordilleras & Yungas, Southern Altiplano, Central Highlands

Andy first traveled to Bolivia as a child, carried there by his father's voice reading the account of Fawcett's jungle travels. From that moment, South America was a distant but everpresent goal. His first trip to Bolivia didn't disappoint, with some memorable moments in debatable jungle aircraft among the highlights, and he has returned several times since to this much loved country. Andy is the author of several guidebooks and has worked on many Lonely Planet guides. He lives in northern Spain.

CONTRIBUTING AUTHORS

Brian Kluepfel worked in Bolivia for a year as the managing editor of the *Bolivian Times*. He traveled to Paraguay to cover the national team's progress in the 1999 Copa America, and to Chile to attend President Ricardo Lagos' inauguration. His work on Bolivian music and football has since appeared in forums like *Acoustic Guitar* magazine and Major League Soccer's website. Brian contributed boxed texts on football (p36), musical instruments (p40) and Evo Morales (p32).

Dr David Goldberg completed his training in internal medicine and infectious diseases at Columbia-Presbyterian Medical Center in New York City, where he has also served as voluntary faculty. At present, he is an infectious disease specialist in Scarsdale, New York, and the editor-in-chief of the website MDTravelHealth.com. He wrote the Health chapter.

Getting Started

Travelers can no longer be smug about 'discovering' Bolivia; it's well and truly on the traveler's map for those who visit South America. Having said that, most stick to the more accessible and well-worn route and don't give it the attention it warrants. This means that the more curious and motivated traveler will be quickly stimulated if they venture off the tourist track – and this is easy to do. Travelers will be delighted by the multilayered, rich and varied cultures, stunning natural beauty, and unforgettable experiences and characters. Adventure nuts will be well sated: there are plenty of opportunities for outdoor action with a wide variety of luxury levels and travel choices on offer. The going isn't always easy, but the rewards are well worth the effort.

WHEN TO GO

See climate charts (p368) for more information

Travelers will encounter just about every climatic zone, from stifling humidity and heat to arctic cold. Summer (November to April) is the rainy season when overland transportation becomes difficult if not impossible in some areas. The most popular, and arguably most comfortable, time for exploring the whole country is during winter (May to October) with its dry, clear days.

Most of Bolivia lies as near to the equator as Tahiti or Hawaii, but its elevation and unprotected expanses result in unpredictable weather. Bolivia's two poles of climatic extremes are Puerto Suárez with its overwhelming heat, and Uyuni for its icy, cold winds. But there are no absolutes; there are times when you can sunbathe in Uyuni and freeze in Puerto Suárez.

Summer (rainy season) in the lowlands can be utterly miserable, with mud, high humidity, biting insects and relentless tropical downpours. However, washed-out roads necessitate an increase in river transportation, making this the best time to hop on a cargo boat. Winter in the Altiplano means extreme heat during the day, and freezing winds and subzero temperatures at night. The highland valleys are refuges, having a comfortable climate with little rain year round.

DON'T LEAVE HOME WITHOUT

- Checking the visa situation (p377)
- Checking travel advisory warnings (p369)
- Proof of vaccination for yellow fever (p395)
- A copy of your travel insurance policy details (p372)
- Plug adaptor for your camera battery recharge (p367)
- Binoculars for watching wildlife
- Sunscreen and hat for clear skies at 4000m
- First aid kit (p391)
- Ear plugs for disco nights you want to sleep through
- A pack lock or other luggage security for peace of mind
- Your sense of humor – patience and courage will be tested in queues and on bus rides

---

TRAVEL WIDELY, TREAD LIGHTLY, GIVE SUSTAINABLY – THE LONELY PLANET FOUNDATION

The Lonely Planet Foundation proudly supports nimble nonprofit institutions working for change in the world. Each year the foundation donates 5% of Lonely Planet company profits to projects selected by staff and authors. Our partners range from Kabissa, which provides small nonprofits across Africa with access to technology, to the Foundation for Developing Cambodian Orphans, which supports girls at risk of falling victim to sex traffickers.

Our nonprofit partners are linked by a grass-roots approach to the areas of health, education or sustainable tourism. Many – such as Louis Sarno who works with BaAka (Pygmy) children in the forested areas of Central African Republic – choose to focus on women and children as one of the most effective ways to support the whole community. Louis is determined to give options to children who are discriminated against by the majority Bantu population.

Sometimes foundation assistance is as simple as restoring a local ruin like the Minaret of Jam in Afghanistan; this incredible monument now draws intrepid tourists to the area and its restoration has greatly improved options for local people.

Just as travel is often about learning to see with new eyes, so many of the groups we work with aim to change the way people see themselves and the future for their children and communities.

August is the most popular month of the high tourist season, which runs from late June to early September. High season sees the most reliable weather and coincides with European and North American summer holidays. It's when most of Bolivia's major festivals take place, so many Bolivians and South Americans also travel at this time. This can be an advantage if you are looking for people to form a travel group, but prices are generally higher than during the rest of the year.

COSTS & MONEY

Overall, prices are slightly lower here than in neighboring countries. The biggest cost in any trip to Bolivia will be transportation, especially getting to the country (and, to a lesser extent, getting around, as the distances involved are great).

While ultrabudget travelers can get by on less than US$15 per day, most people will spend between US$25 and US$50. Visitors who want to enjoy the best Bolivia has to offer can easily travel comfortably for US$150 a day (this would include hire of private transportation). All prices in this book are quoted in US dollars (US$).

Avoid over-bargaining with local people for goods and services just for the sake of it. While Bolivians themselves might bargain among their friends at markets, bargaining is not a common cultural practice. In any case, be realistic about how much you are actually saving. A few bolivianos can be worth a great deal more to the locals than for you. If you feel uncomfortable about pricing issues, ask locals for a ball-park idea of what you can expect to pay for something, including taxis. Always agree on food, accommodations and transportation prices beforehand to avoid any unpleasant situations.

HOW MUCH?

Dorm bed US$2-5

Set lunch US$1-2

Internet per hour US$0.25-3

Hotel room (double) US$20

City taxi fare US$0.75-1.20

See also the Lonely Planet Index, inside front cover.

TRAVEL LITERATURE

Sitting at the top of the South American travelogue list is the humorous and well-written *Inca-Kola*, by Matthew Parris. It follows the meanderings of several Englishmen on a rollicking circuit throughout Peru and parts of Bolivia.

Marching Powder, by Rusty Young, is the author's account of his four months inside the San Pedro Prison, La Paz, interviewing a British inmate accused of drug smuggling.

TOP TENS

Festivals & Events

Thanks to their rich culture, imbibed with tradition, Bolivians are big on celebrating. There's almost always something fascinating going on, from saints' days in small villages to nationwide events. The following is a list of our favorites. See p370 for more details of festivals and events throughout the country.

- El Gran Poder (La Paz), May/June (p81)
- Carnaval (nationwide, p370; best in Oruro, p173, and Tarija, p282), February/March
- Phujllay (Tarabuco), March (p253)
- Fiesta de la Cruz (Lake Titicaca), May 3 (p113)
- Fiesta del Santo Patrono de Moxos (San Ignacio de Moxos), July 31 (p346)
- Fiesta de San Bartolomé (Chu'tillos; Potosí), August (p267)
- Fiesta del Espíritu (Potosí), June (p266)
- Fiesta de la Virgen de Urkupiña in Quillacollo, August 15–18 (Cochabamba; p225)
- International Theater Festival (Santa Cruz), April (p300)
- International Festival of Baroque Music (Santa Cruz), April (p300)

Extreme Adventures

Bolivia's rugged landscape and outgoing, knowledgeable tour guides offer innumerable and thrilling adventures. Whether you want to hang off a precipice or walk on the wild side in the jungle, Bolivia's got the hot spots.

- Hike the Mapiri Trail, a demanding but superb walking trek (p153)
- Do the tandem mountain bike and raft trip from Sorata to Rurrenabaque (p52)
- Tackle the remote Quimsa Cruz range – not to be missed if you're a serious climber (p165)
- Shoot the rapids from Class II-V in the Yungas (p132)
- Float the Río Mamoré through pristine Amazon jungle (p349)
- Conquer the 6088m Huayna Potosí (p157)
- Soak in hot springs at the base of Nevado Sajama (p179)
- Go wild by heading upriver to a jungle-based community ecolodge (p342)
- Trek the Trans Cordillera route from Sorata to Huayna Potosí and Illimani (p148)
- Head to the most remote of remote national parks, Noel Kempff Mercado, for an awesome nature experience (p354)

Mouth-watering Eats

There are some excellent countrywide eateries, as well as must-try local Bolivian specialties. To tantalize your taste buds, try the following five eateries and five taste sensations.

- El Huerto, Sucre – a classy garden-party eating experience (p251)
- La Estancia, Cochabamba – for lovers of meat, this is hard to beat (p227)
- Casa Típica de Camba, Santa Cruz – for authentic Bolivian eats and atmosphere (p301)
- La Comedie Art-Café Restaurant, La Paz – French/Bolivian fusion cuisine with a touch of class (p88)
- Nayjama, Oruro – renowned for serving the local Oruro specialty, boiled sheep's head (p176)
- Salteñas - heavenly pastry parcels filled with chicken, beef and vegetables (p55 and p89)
- Anticuchos (grilled cow heart on skewers) – a way to reach the heart of the culture, usually served at markets and street stalls (p55)
- Tamales – those from the Tupiza market are especially scrumptious (p200)
- Sopas (soups) – follow the locals to make sure you add the right condiments (p56)
- Trucha (trout) – the famed (and now farmed) Lake Titicaca trout satisfies any fish cravings (p114)

Other travel books that are worth noting include *Chasing Ché – A Motorcycle Journey in Search of the Guevara Legend*, by Patrick Symmes, and *The Incredible Voyage: A Personal Odyssey*, by Tristan Jones, which follows the intrepid sailor's journey through landlocked Bolivia on Lake Titicaca and beyond. An offbeat historical character is portrayed in *Lizzie – A Victorian Lady's Amazon Adventure*, compiled by Anne Rose from the letters of Lizzie Hessel, who lived in the Bolivian Amazon settlement of Colonia Orton during the early 20th-century rubber boom. *Exploration Fawcett*, by Percy Fawcett, is a fabulous jungle travel book from the early 20th century.

Less travelogue and more history book is the comprehensive synthesis of recent Bolivian political history, *Bolivia: Between a Rock and a Hard Place*, by Pete Good, which provides the most up-to-date commentary on Bolivia. You can find copies for sale in many travel agencies and hotels in La Paz. *The Fat Man from La Paz: Contemporary Fiction from Bolivia*, a collection of short stories edited by Rosario Santos, is a widely recommended read.

Some good suggestions for books in general are available on the excellent website www.libreriaboliviana.com (in Spanish).

INTERNET RESOURCES

Bolivia.com (www.boliva.com, in Spanish) Current news and cultural information.

Bolivia web (www.bolivaweb.com) A good starting point, good cultural and artistic links.

Boliviacontact.com (www.boliviacontact.com) A thorough, searchable Spanish-language index of Bolivian sites.

GBT Bolivia (www.gbtbolivia.com) A good commercial site with travel links.

Librería Boliviana (www.libreriaboliviana.com, in Spanish) An excellent place to look for books on all subjects.

Lonely Planet (www.lonelyplanet.com) Succinct summaries of travel in Bolivia, and the Thorn Tree forum for gleaning travel tips.

National Institute of Statistics (www.ine.gov.bo, in Spanish) Contains an excellent summary of the most recent Bolivian census of 2001.

South America Explorers Club (www.samexplo.org) Interesting trip reports and travel bulletins.

Visit Bolivia (www.visitbolivia.com.bo) The tourist office's official website with some good information.

Itineraries

CLASSIC ROUTES

SOUTH-CENTRAL CIRCUIT
Two to Three Weeks

Stimulate your senses around the streets of **La Paz** (p63) before heading by bus to **Sucre** (p240). It's worth going via **Cochabamba** (p211), a great place to eat and get your cultural fill. Sucre is *the* place to visit churches and museums, and offers fascinating short sojourns to nearby villages, famous for their craftworks; try **Tarabuco** (p253). From here, head by bus to **Potosí** (p258), a starkly beautiful Unesco World Heritage city, situated at 4070m. Visit and learn about the cooperative mines, still in operation. You can thaw your chills in the nearby **hot springs** (p274). Jump on an overnight bus to **Tupiza** (p197), former territory of Butch Cassidy and the Sundance Kid. Here, there's a choice of hikes and bike rides among the colored rocks of the surrounding *quebradas* (ravines). Join a tour from here to head to **Uyuni** (p184) and to cruise your way around a three- or four-day Southwest Circuit tour of the **Salar de Uyuni** (p191) and **Reserva Nacional de Fauna Andina Eduardo Avaroa** (p191). From Uyuni make your way up to **Oruro** (p169), famed for its Carnaval. Alternatively, from Tupiza head to **Tarija** (p277) and its surrounds, a relaxing town and region and Bolivia's heart of paleontology and viticulture. From Tarija you can fly or bus to La Paz; from Oruro it's an easy three-hour bus ride.

For those who love a mix of culture and action, Bolivia has it all. A visit to colonial towns, craft centers and mining regions will tantalize your traveling taste buds. You can skate across salt plains one day, and dance with the devils the next.

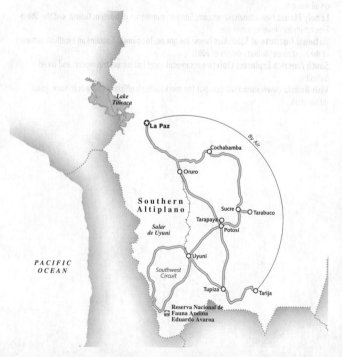

FROM HIGH TO LOW   Two to Three Weeks

The most popular way to enter Bolivia is to come in overland from Peru. This follows the exciting tourist path, with a developed tourist infrastructure. Enjoy the views of Lake Titicaca from white-washed **Copacabana** (p108), eat the local trout dishes, and get some R&R. After a day or two, hike to the tiny port of **Yampupata** (p116) visiting the villages along the way for a reed boat ride. From Yampupata (or nearby villages) or Copacabana you can take a boat across Lake Titicaca to tranquil **Isla del Sol** (p118). Walk from the island's north to south and explore the Inca ruins. Marvel at Illampu in the distance over Isla de la Luna and head back to the mainland.

Back on the mainland, jump on a tourist bus for a trip across the stunning Cordillera Real toward **La Paz** (see p63) For a side trip to the remarkably tranquil **Sorata** (p147), catch another bus at the Sorata turn-off. Chill in this oasis or do some serious hiking or downhill mountain biking. Once in La Paz, spend a few days acclimatizing and absorbing the smells and sights in the hectic markets, fascinating museums and top-class restaurants and cafés. Take a day out at **Tiahuanaco** (p102) or **Chacaltaya** (p100), the world's highest developed (although now seasonal) ski-slope.

From here, the adventurous can take on the **Takesi** (p138) or **Choro Treks** (p135), or ride a bike (or bus) down the **World's Most Dangerous Road** (p78) to **Coroico** (p129) in the Yungas. Alternatively, you could fly to **Rurrenabaque** (p336) and spend a few days chilling in a hammock and exploring the surrounds (add on an extra five to seven days for this to allow for 'plane delays' and jungle visits).

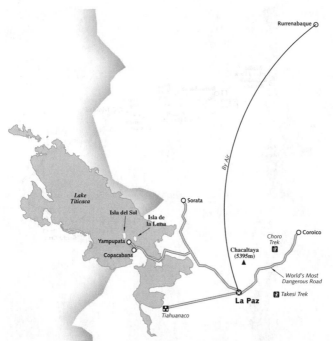

The area around La Paz is jam-packed with highlights and activities, including the sun-filled Lake Titicaca, ancient Inca ruins and tranquil oases. Two weeks will give you a brief taste of adventure and relaxation, and the opportunity to experience a diverse range of environments.

ROADS LESS TRAVELED

AMAZONIAN ADVENTURE   **10 Days to Two Weeks**

A wonderful way to get off the beaten tourist track (but still enjoy an element of comfort) is to start in **Santa Cruz** (p295), a sophisticated and cosmopolitan city with a dreamy (sometimes steamy) climate and tropical atmosphere. From here, fly or catch the overnight bus to **Trinidad** (p347), a sleepy town with a pretty plaza. After whirling around on a *moto*, take a side trip to **Puerto Barador** (p352) for a local fish meal, a visit to a museum or two and a much-needed siesta or three – it gets hot. A three-hour bus ride will take you to the Jesuit mission village of **San Ignacio de Moxos** (p346) – plan your trip around the town's colorful, not-to-be-missed festival in July. Take a side trip into **Reserva Biosférica del Beni** (p344) and then make the long slog via **San Borja** (p344) to **Rurrenabaque** (p336), hammock country, from where you can set out for a couple of days on a jungle or pampas tour. Alternatively, get your jungle fill at the **San Miguel del Bala** (p342) ecoresort, just up-river from Rurrenabaque. Whatever you do, don't miss a trip to **Madidi National Park** (p341), a wild little-trodden utopia and a must for wildlife-watchers. Finally, leave enough time to travel to and stay in the highly regarded, community-run **Chalalán Ecolodge** (p342).

The sights and sounds of the jungle make for a once-in-a-lifetime experience. Start sophisticated and go wild, with a tour from the city to the remote reserves. After a few rough, but adventurous, trips, you can laze away the days in a hammock in tropical temperatures.

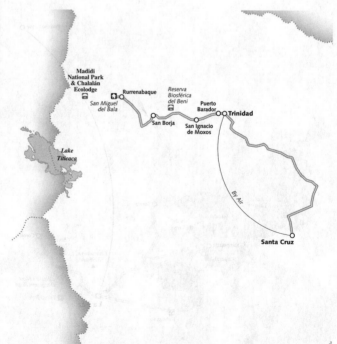

JESUIT MISSIONS CIRCUIT

Six Days

The Oriente's vast expanses are underestimated by the traveler; some of the country's richest cultural and historic accomplishments are found within the seven-town region known as **Las Misiones Jesuíticas (the Jesuit Missions)**; a Unesco-listed World Heritage site. For those with an interest in architecture or history, it's one of Bolivia's most rewarding circuits. The region's magnificent, centuries-old mission churches have been restored to their original splendor. The circuit can be undertaken in a clockwise or counterclockwise direction between **Santa Cruz** (p295) and **San José de Chiquitos** (p324). Mission towns in between include **San Javier** (p320), the region's oldest mission town; **Concepción** (p321), the center of mission restoration projects; and **San Ignacio de Velasco** (p322), the commercial center of the missions. **San Miguel de Velasco** (p323) boasts one of the most accurately restored missions; **Santa Ana de Velasco** (p323) is in a tiny and fascinating Chiquitano village; and **San Rafael de Velasco** (p324) features the first of the country's mission churches.

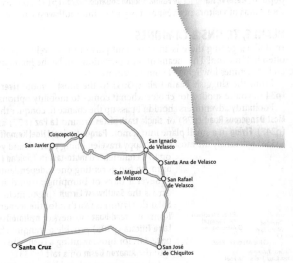

Unesco declared this region a World Heritage site in 1991. Following many years of painstaking restoration work, the churches can be easily accessed and enjoyed by all. Architectural buffs and culture vultures will find this one of Bolivia's most rewarding experiences.

TAILORED TRIPS

NATIONAL PARKS & RESERVES

Bolivia has protected 18% of its territory in 66 national parks and reserves. From **Reserva Biológica Cordillera de Sama's** (p287) slice of the Altiplano and **Kaa-Iya's** (p327) vast chunk of the Gran Chaco, to the inundated savannas of the remote, but spectacular, **Parque Nacional Noel Kempff Mercado** (p354), flora and fauna fans will be in their element. Although some of these protected areas can be difficult to access, not all are difficult, and the following places are worth every ounce of the effort they take to reach.

Parque Nacional Sajama (p179) with its vicuñas, soaring volcanoes (including Bolivia's highest peak) and heavenly hot springs was Bolivia's first reserve. **Parque Nacional Madidi** (p341) is possibly now the best known, encompassing one of the most biodiverse habitats in the world and numerous protected species.

Parque Nacional Carrasco (p334) and **Parque Nacional Tunari** (p230) are two of the more accessible, middle-altitude cloud forests, while **Parque Nacional y Área de Uso Múltiple Amboró** (p307) is a prime place for bird-watching.

Área Natural de Manejo Integrado Nacional Apolobamba (p162) is one of the least visited national parks, while the most popular, **Reserva Nacional de Fauna Andina Eduardo Avaroa** (p191), receives tens of thousands of visitors per year and is part of the Southwest Circuit.

PLANES, TRAINS & CAMIONES

In Bolivia, getting there is an important part of the travel experience, and often half the fun! The means of transportation can be the highlight (okay, and sometimes lowlight) of your adventure.

From the sluggish **Death Train** (p304) to the most remote **river journeys** (p349), you're spoiled for choice when it comes to mobility options.

Foolhardy adventurers shouldn't pass up the chance to conquer the **World's Most Dangerous Road** (p78) or **single track pistes** around **La Paz** (p77) and **Sucre** (p247). **Flying** in a small plane into remote **Parque Nacional Noel Kempff Mercado** (p358) will satisfy the most snap-happy traveler. Piling yourself and your gear on to a chauffeured **moto-taxi** in **Trinidad** (p351) is as much fun as renting one independently.

Several days of bumping around in a **4WD** across the **Southwest Circuit** (p190; including the Salar de Uyuni) is worth it for the scenery alone. Romantic **reed-boat** journeys or **hydrofoil cruises** on **Lake Titicaca** (p108) provide a tranquil change of pace. Or, for those wanting a rush, you can head into the **Amazon Basin** on a **raft** (p333).

Let's not forget our humble feet, the best form of mobility in Bolivia. Awe-inspiring **trekking** includes via Inca trails to the **Yunga Cruz Trek** (p141). As for the inevitable travel on **buses** or **camiones** (flatbed trucks)? This can be as adrenaline-inducing as any mode of transportation, and you'll likely come out with a good travel story or three.

Snapshot

Hear Bolivia, think Evo. Hear Evo, think flux. Bolivia is currently synonymous with former *cocalero* (coca grower) Evo Morales, Bolivia's first indigenous president, who was elected in December 2005, having won 53.72% of the vote for the Movimiento al Socialismo (MAS) party. Whirlwind changes at political, social and economic levels occur on a daily basis. In May 2006 Morales nationalized the country's gas resources in a stance against foreign exploitation. (Bolivia has the second-largest proven reserves in the region after Venezuela and much of its revenue is from gas.) While this process is more about renegotiating contracts than confiscating assets, it is causing ongoing problems.

In July 2006, Bolivian voters elected 255 representatives to the National Constituent Assembly, whose objective is to rewrite the country's constitution in less than one year. As of November 2006 the country was in an uproar over whether changes to the constitution should be decided via a simple majority (51%) or a two-thirds vote. MAS prefers the former; other parties the latter, as a simple majority would mean that MAS would wield power over voting results. Many people went on hunger strikes and marches in protest against the perceived lack of democracy and transparency.

On the whole, however, soccer-enthusiast Morales has a kind of sportsstar status, at least among his faithful who are optimistic that he can make a positive change to the country. His attraction? His demand for indigenous equality, their improved status, and the opportunity for them to share in economic and political power, after centuries of domination by Spanish descendants who have historically controlled the country's wealth. At his inauguration he stated: 'from 500 years of resistance…we pass to another 500 years of power.' Meanwhile, many middle- and upper-class Bolivians are wary of Morales and his anticapitalist stance and socialist ideologies – including his siding with the Venezuelan and Cuban presidents – and more critical about the inexperience of his ministers, who have been hand-selected by Morales himself. Whether these ministers have the know-how to manage a bureaucracy and implement large-scale plans is yet to be seen. Already, several ministers have proposed radical reforms (such as withdrawing religious education from schools), but such plans have been shelved, not surprisingly, following outrage by the Catholic Church.

Discussion of coca eradication has taken a back seat, but Morales continues to tussle with the US. For Bolivia it's simple: coca – for spiritual uses, for chewing, for tea and other coca-based products – should be promoted and is legal in Bolivia, whereas cocaine, the chemical derivative is not. Morales has changed the eradication proponents' battle cry of 'coca zero' to 'cocaine zero' in an effort to distinguish between the plant and its positive uses and the drug derived from the plant. The US points the finger at the illegal excess crops grown by *cocaleros,* while Bolivia blames the US drug consumers.

Morales has other things on his political plate: he is fending off demands by the Santa Cruz department for autonomy; this rebellious state is rich in oil and agricultural lands and is tired of supplementing the country's revenue. At the time of writing, 16 miners had been killed after rival mining groups fought over concession rights. And Chile is still not forgiven for having usurped Bolivia's ocean access. On a positive note, in 2005 the IMF agreed to write off Bolivia's $120 million debt.

Meanwhile, most Bolivians are giving Morales a chance, at least until the outcome of the Constituent Assembly in 2007. Cultural revolution or impending civil war? As the Bolivians themselves say, *vamos a ver…*

FAST FACTS

Population: 8.9 million humans, 3 million llamas

Highest point: Nevado Sajama 6452m

Average annual income: US$2900

Birth rate: 23.3 births/1000

Literacy rate: 87.2%

Population below poverty line: 64%

Merchant marines: 25 ships

Airports with unpaved landing strips: 1068

Annual military spending: US$130 million

History

Tangible history lives on in most of Bolivia's best known destinations. From pre-Hispanic archaeological sites and living indigenous traditions to colonial architecture and the most recent headline-making political upheaval, the country's history reflects influences that have shaped South America as a whole.

The great Altiplano (High Plateau), the largest expanse of arable land in the Andes, extends from present-day Bolivia into southern Peru, northwestern Argentina and northern Chile. It's been inhabited for thousands of years, but the region's early cultures were shaped by the imperial designs of two major forces: the Tiahuanaco culture of Bolivia and the Inca of Peru.

Most archaeologists define the prehistory of the Central Andes in terms of 'horizons' – Early, Middle and Late – each of which was characterized by distinct architectural and artistic trends. Cultural interchanges between early Andean peoples occurred mostly through trade, usually between nomadic tribes, or as a result of the diplomatic expansionist activities of powerful and well-organized societies. These interchanges resulted in the Andes' emergence as the cradle of South America's highest cultural achievements.

During the initial settlement of the Andes, from the arrival of nomads probably from Siberia until about 1400 BC, villages and ceremonial centers were established, and trade emerged between coastal fishing communities and farming villages of the highlands.

History buffs can get stuck into *A Concise History of Bolivia* by Herbert S Klein (Columbia University Press, 2003).

EARLY & MIDDLE HORIZONS

The so-called Early Horizon (1400–400 BC) was an era of architectural innovation and activity, which is most evident in the ruins of Chavín de Huantar, on the eastern slopes of the Andes in Peru. During this period it is postulated that a wave of Aymará Indians, possibly from the mountains of central Peru, swept across the Andes into Alto Perú (Bolivia), driving out most of the Altiplano's original settlers. Chavín influences resounded far and wide, even after the decline of Chavín society, and spilled over into the Early Middle Horizon (400 BC to AD 500).

The Middle Horizon (AD 500–900) was marked by the imperial expansion of the Tiahuanaco and Huari (of the Ayacucho valley of present-day Peru) cultures. The ceremonial center of Tiahuanaco, on the shores of Lake Titicaca, grew and developed into the religious and political capital of the Alto Peruvian Altiplano.

The Tiahuanacans produced technically advanced work, most notably the city itself. They created impressive ceramics, gilded ornamentation, engraved pillars and slabs with calendar markings and designs representing their bearded white leader and deity, Viracocha, as well as other undeciphered hieroglyphs. Over the following centuries wooden boats were constructed to ferry 55,000kg slabs 48km across the lake to the building site, and sandstone blocks weighing 145,000kg were moved from a quarry 10km away.

For more information on the fascinating Tiahuanaco site, read Alan Kolata's *A Valley of Spirits* (Wiley & Sons, 1996).

By 700 BC, Tiahuanaco had developed into a thriving civilization. Considered as advanced as ancient Egypt in many respects, it had an extensive system of roads, irrigation canals and agricultural terraces. Recent

TIMELINE	1400 BC–AD 400	500–800
	Settlement by first peoples in what is now the Bolivian Altiplano	The ceremonial center for the Tiahuanaco people grew and prospered on the shores of Lake Titicaca

archeological findings suggest that these agricultural systems are more sophisticated than previously thought; they were designed to obtain high crop yields from unproductive land. The series of canals were built up with layer upon layer of substances – cobblestone topped with gravel and impermeable clay – designed to keep salt from the lake's brackish waters from seeping into the topsoil. This agricultural system is believed to have supported a population of tens of thousands of people in the 83-sq-km Tiahuanaco Valley.

Tiahuanaco was inhabited from 1500 BC until AD 1200, but its power lasted only from the 6th century BC to the 9th century AD. One theory speculates that Tiahuanaco was uprooted by a drop in Lake Titicaca's water level, which left the lakeside settlement far from shore. Another postulates that it was attacked and its population massacred by the warlike Kollas (sometimes spelt Collas; also known as Aymará) from the west. When the Spanish arrived, they heard an Inca legend about a battle between the Kollas and 'bearded white men' on an island in Lake Titicaca. These men were presumably Tiahuanacans, only a few of whom were able to escape. Some researchers believe that the displaced survivors migrated southward and developed into the Chipaya people of the western Oruro department.

Today the remains of the city lie on the plain between La Paz and the southern shore of Lake Titicaca, and collections of Tiahuanaco relics can be seen in several Bolivian museums. For further information, see p102.

LATE HORIZON – THE INCA

The Late Horizon (AD 1476–1534) marked the zenith of Inca civilization. The Inca, the last of South America's indigenous conquerors, arrived shortly after the fall of Tiahuanaco. They pushed their empire from its seat of power in Cuzco (Peru) eastward into present-day Bolivia, southward to the northern reaches of modern Argentina and Chile, and northward through present-day Ecuador and southern Colombia. However the Inca political state thrived for less than a century before falling to the invading Spanish.

The Inca inhabited the Cuzco region from the 12th century and believed they were led by descendents of the Sun God. The 17th-century Spanish chronicler Fernando Montesinos believed the Inca descended from a lineage of Tiahuanaco sages. There were many similarities between Tiahuanaco and Inca architecture.

Renowned for their great stone cities and skill in working with gold and silver, the Inca also set up a hierarchy of governmental and agricultural overseers, a viable social welfare scheme and a complex road network and communication system that defied the difficult terrain of their far-flung empire. The Inca government could be described as an imperialist socialist dictatorship, with the Sapa Inca, considered a direct descendant of the Sun God, as reigning monarch. The state technically owned all property, taxes were collected in the form of labor and the government organized a system of mutual aid in which relief supplies were collected from prosperous areas and distributed in areas suffering from natural disasters or local misfortune.

Around 1440 the Inca started to expand their political boundaries. The eighth Inca, Viracocha (not to be confused with the Tiahuanaco leader/deity of the same name), believed the mandate from the Sun God was not just to conquer, plunder and enslave, but to organize defeated tribes and absorb

The earliest references to the use of the coca leaf is found in *chulpas* (mummies) in north Peru (2500–1800 BC).

It is believed that between 1200 and 1475 the Incas used the essential oil of the coca plant to remove brain tumors.

800s	1440s
Tiahuanaco's power wanes, its civilization declines and the ceremonial site is largely abandoned	The Inca, based in Cuzco, Peru, extend their political boundaries by pushing eastward into present-day Bolivia

them into the realm of the benevolent Sun God. When the Inca arrived in Kollasuyo (present-day Bolivia), they assimilated local tribes as they had done elsewhere: by imposing taxation, religion and their own Quechua language (the empire's lingua franca) on the region's inhabitants. The Kollas living around the Tiahuanaco site were essentially absorbed by the Inca and their religion was supplanted, but they were permitted to keep their language and social traditions.

By the late 1520s internal rivalries began to take their toll on the empire. In a brief civil war over the division of lands, Atahualpa, the true Inca emperor's half-brother, imprisoned the emperor and assumed the throne himself.

SPANISH CONQUEST

The arrival of the Spanish in Ecuador in 1531 was the ultimate blow. Within a year Francisco Pizarro, Diego de Almagro and their bands of merry conquistadores arrived in Cuzco. Atahualpa was still the emperor, but was not considered the true heir of the Sun God. The Spanish were aided by the Inca belief that the bearded white men had been sent by the great Viracocha Inca as revenge for Atahualpa's breach of established protocol. In fear, Atahualpa ordered the murder of the real king, which not only ended the bloodline of the Inca dynasty, but brought shame on the family and dissolved the psychological power grip of the Inca hierarchy. Within two years the government was conquered, the empire dissolved and the invaders had divided Inca lands and booty between the two leaders of the Spanish forces.

Alto Perú, which would later become Bolivia, fell for a brief time into the possession of Diego de Almagro, who was assassinated in 1538. Three years later Pizarro suffered the same fate at the hands of mutinous subordinates. But the Spanish kept exploring and settling their newly conquered land, and in 1538 La Plata (later known as Sucre) was founded as the Spanish capital of the Charcas region.

The Legacy of Potosí

The first coins in the Americas were minted in Potosí.

By the time the wandering Indian Diego Huallpa revealed his earth-shattering discovery of silver at Cerro Rico (Rich Hill) in Potosí in 1544, Spanish conquerors had already firmly implanted their language, religion and customs on the remnants of Atahualpa's empire.

Spanish Potosí, or the 'Villa Imperial de Carlos V,' was officially founded in 1545 and quickly grew to 160,000 residents, making it the largest city in the western hemisphere. The Potosí mine became the world's most prolific, and the silver extracted from it underwrote the Spanish economy, particularly the extravagance of its monarchy, for at least two centuries.

Atrocious conditions in the gold and silver mines of Potosí guaranteed a short life span for the local indigenous conscripts and African slaves who were herded into work gangs. Those not actually worked to death or killed in accidents succumbed to pulmonary silicosis within a few years. Africans who survived migrated to the more amenable climes of the Yungas northeast of La Paz, and developed into an Aymará-speaking minority (see the boxed text p146). The indigenous peoples became tenant farmers, subservient to the Spanish lords, and were required to supply their conquerors with food and labor in exchange for subsistence-sized plots of land.

1531	1544
The Spanish, led by conquistador Francisco Pizarro, arrive in Ecuador and claim Alto Perú, which would later become Bolivia	Diego Huallpa's discovery of silver in Potosí's Cerro Rico leads to the development of the world's most prolific silver mine

Coca, ace at numbing nerves and once the exclusive privilege of Inca nobles, was introduced among the general populace to keep people working without complaint – see boxed text p140.

INDEPENDENCE

In May 1809 Spanish America's first independence movement – sparked by the criollos (people of Spanish ancestry born in the Americas) and mestizos (people of both indigenous and Spanish ancestry) – had gained momentum and was well underway in Chuquisaca (later renamed Sucre, as it stands today), with other cities quick to follow suit. By the early 1820s General Simón Bolívar succeeded in liberating both Venezuela and Colombia from Spanish domination. In 1822 he dispatched Mariscal (Major General) Antonio José de Sucre to Ecuador to defeat the Royalists at the battle of Pichincha. In 1824 after years of guerrilla action against the Spanish and the victories of Bolívar and Sucre in the battles of Junín (August 6) and Ayacucho (December 9), Peru won its independence.

At this point Sucre incited a declaration of independence for Alto Perú, and exactly one year later the new Republic of Bolivia was born (see p210 for more). The republic was loosely modeled on the US, with legislative, executive and judicial branches of government. Bolívar and Sucre served as Bolivia's first and second presidents, but after a brief attempt by Andrés Santa Cruz, the third president, to form a confederation with Peru, things began to go awry. One military junta after another usurped power from its predecessor, setting a pattern of political strife that haunts the nation to this day.

Few of Bolivia's 192 governments to date have remained in power long enough to have much intentional effect, and some were more than a little eccentric. The bizarre and cruel General Mariano Melgarejo, who ruled from 1865 to 1871, once drunkenly set off with his army on an overland march to aid France at the outset of the Franco-Prussian War. History has it that he was sobered up by a sudden downpour and the project was abandoned (to the immense relief of the Prussians, of course).

A worthwhile read for its articles on history, culture and the environment (but less useful for the practical details which are now out of date) is Peter McFadden's *An Insider's Guide to Bolivia.*

SHRINKING TERRITORY

At the time of independence Bolivia's boundaries encompassed well over two million sq km, but its neighbors soon moved to acquire its territory, removing coastal access and much of its Amazonian rubber trees, as well as attempting to control the potentially oil-rich Chaco; only half the original land area remained.

The coastal loss occurred during the War of the Pacific fought against Chile between 1879 and 1884. Many Bolivians believe that Chile stole the Atacama Desert's copper- and nitrate-rich sands and 850km of coastline from Peru and Bolivia by invading during Carnaval. Chile did attempt to compensate for the loss by building a railroad from La Paz to the ocean and allowing Bolivia free port privileges in Antofagasta, but Bolivians have never forgotten this devastating *enclaustromiento* (landlocked status). In fact the government still uses the issue as a rallying cry to unite people behind a common cause.

The next major loss was in 1903 during the rubber boom when Brazil hacked away at Bolivia's inland expanse. Brazil and Bolivia had been ransacking the forests of the remote Acre territory, which stretched from Bolivia's present Amazonian borders to halfway up Peru's eastern border. The area was so rich

1809	**1824**
Spanish America's first independence movement gains momentum in Chuquisaca (Sucre)	General Sucre incites a declaration of independence for Alto Perú; a year later, the Republic of Bolivia is born

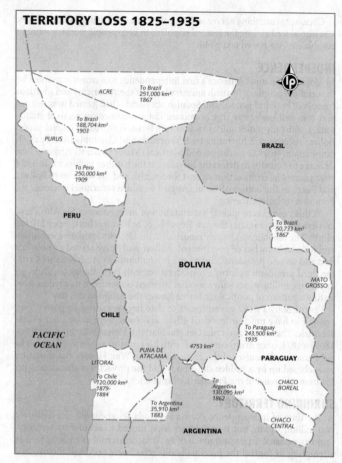

TERRITORY LOSS 1825–1935

(Map showing:)

BRAZIL

ACRE — To Brazil 251,000 km² 1867

PURUS — To Brazil 188,704 km² 1903

To Peru 250,000 km² 1909

PERU

To Brazil 50,733 km² 1867

BOLIVIA

MATO GROSSO

CHILE

PACIFIC OCEAN

PUNA DE ATACAMA

LITORAL

To Chile 120,000 km² 1879–1884

4753 km²

To Paraguay 243,500 km² 1935

PARAGUAY

CHACO BOREAL

To Argentina 130,095 km² 1862

To Argentina 35,910 km² 1883

CHACO CENTRAL

ARGENTINA

In the 1930s, the Chaco War (1932–1935) between Bolivia and Paraguay became a common theme in Bolivian literature, exemplified in *Aluvión de Fuego* (1935) by Oscar Cerruto, *Sangre de Mestizos* (1936) by Augusto Céspedes, and *Laguna* (1938) by Costa Du Rels.

in rubber trees that Brazil engineered a dispute over sovereignty and sent in its army. Brazil convinced the Acre region to secede from the Bolivian republic, and promptly annexed it.

Brazil attempted to compensate Bolivia's loss with a railway, intended to open up the remote northern reaches of the country and provide a coastal outlet for the Amazon Basin. However the tracks never reached Bolivian soil. Construction ended at Guajará-Mirim on the Brazilian bank of the Río Mamoré.

There were two separate territory losses to Argentina. First, Argentina annexed a large slice of the Chaco in 1862. Then, in 1883, the territory of Puna de Atacama went to Argentina. It had been offered to both Chile and Argentina, the former in exchange for return of the Litoral, the latter in exchange for clarification over Bolivia's ownership of Tarija.

1879–1884	1903
War of the Pacific in which Bolivia loses her coastline to Chile	Brazil annexes the Acre area, promising to build a railroad (never completed)

Finally Paraguay went in for the kill. In 1932 a border dispute for control of the potentially huge deposits of oil in the Chaco was revved up by rival foreign oil companies. With Standard Oil backing Bolivia and Shell siding with Paraguay, Bolivia entered into the Chaco War.

Bolivia fell victim to Paraguayan pride and, within three years, lost another 225,000 sq km, 65,000 young men and a dubious outlet to the sea via the Río Paraguai before the dispute was finally settled in 1935 in Paraguay's favor. The anticipated oil reserves were never discovered, but several fields in the area that remained Bolivian territory now keep the country self-sufficient in oil production.

In 1935, just over a century after Bolivia's independence, Bolivia had lost more than half of its territory.

CONTINUING POLITICAL STRIFE

During the 20th century wealthy tin barons and landowners controlled Bolivian farming and mining interests, while the peasantry was relegated to a feudal system of peonage known as *pongaje*. The beating Bolivia took in the Chaco War made way for reformist associations, civil unrest among the *cholos* (indigenous people who dress traditionally but live in cities) and a series of coups by reform-minded military leaders.

The most significant development was the emergence of the Movimiento Nacionalista Revolucionario (MNR) political party, which united the masses behind the common cause of popular reform. It sparked friction between peasant miners and absentee tin bosses. The miners' complaints against outrageous working conditions, pitifully low pay and the export of profits to Europe, raised the political consciousness of all Bolivian workers. Under the leadership of Víctor Paz Estenssoro (commonly referred to as Víctor Paz), the MNR prevailed in the 1951 elections, but a last-minute military coup prevented it from actually taking power. The coup provoked a popular armed revolt by the miners, which became known as the April Revolution of 1952. After heavy fighting the military was defeated and Paz Estenssoro finally took power. He nationalized mines, evicted the tin barons, put an end to *pongaje* and set up Comibol (Corporación Minera de Bolivia), the state entity in charge of mining interests.

The revolutionaries also pressed ahead with a diverse reform program, which included redistribution of land among sharecropping peasants and the restructuring of the education system to include primary education in villages.

The miners and peasants felt they were being represented, which enabled the MNR to stay in power for a notable 12 years under various leaders. But even with US support the MNR was unable to raise the standard of living or increase food production substantially, and its effectiveness and popularity ground to a halt. Víctor Paz Estenssoro was forced to become increasingly autocratic and in 1964 his government was overthrown by a military junta headed by General René Barrientos Ortuño.

Five years later Barrientos died in a helicopter accident and a series of coups, military dictators and juntas followed. Right-wing coalition leader General Hugo Banzer Suárez eventually took over in 1971 and served a turbulent term, punctuated by reactionary extremism and human-rights abuses. In 1978 amid demand for a return to democratic process, he scheduled general elections, lost, ignored the results, accused the opposition of ballot-box tampering and was forced to step down in a coup by General Juan Pereda Asbún.

Keen Ché Guevara fans should definitely grab a copy of Ché Guevara: a Revolutionary Life (Bantam Press, 1997).

The next three years were filled with failed elections, appointed presidents, military coups and hideous regimes, and a rash of tortures, arrests and

1932	1942
Bolivia enters the Chaco War against Paraguay	Hundreds of laborers who had formed a union are shot down by government troops while striking for better wages and conditions

disappearances, as well as a substantial increase in cocaine production and trafficking. One military leader, General Luis García Meza Tejada, eventually fled the country and was convicted in absentia of genocide, treason, human-rights abuses and armed insurrection, and sentenced to 30 years' imprisonment. He was extradited from Brazil to Bolivia in 1995 to serve his sentence.

In 1982 Congress elected Hernán Siles Zuazo, the civilian left-wing leader of the Communist-supported Movimiento de la Izquierda Revolucionaria (MIR). His term was beleaguered with labor disputes, ruthless government spending and monetary devaluation, resulting in a staggering inflation rate that at one point reached 35,000% annually.

When Siles Zuazo gave up after three years and called general elections, Víctor Paz Estenssoro returned to politics to become president for the fourth time (he served his second and third terms between 1960 and 1964, after having changed the constitution to allow himself to run for re-election). He immediately enacted harsh measures to revive the shattered economy: he ousted labor unions, removed government restrictions on internal trade, slashed the government deficit, imposed a wage freeze, eliminated price subsidies, laid off workers at inefficient government-owned companies, allowed the peso to float against the US dollar and deployed armed forces to keep the peace.

Inflation was curtailed within weeks, but spiraling unemployment, especially in the poor Altiplano mining areas, caused enormous suffering and threatened the government's stability. Throughout his term, however, Paz Estenssoro remained committed to programs that would return the government mines to private cooperatives and develop the largely uninhabited lowland regions. To encourage the settlement of the Amazon, he promoted road building (with Japanese aid) in the wilderness and opened up vast indigenous lands and pristine rain forest to logging interests.

The Bolivian congress appointed a woman, Lidia Guellar, as interim president in 1982.

CHAOS PREVAILS

Free from the threat of military intervention, the 1989 presidential elections were characterized mostly by apathy. Hugo Banzer Suárez of the Acción Democrática Nacionalista (ADN) resurfaced, the MIR nominated Jaime Paz Zamora and the MNR put forth mining company president and economic reformist Gonzalo Sánchez de Lozada ('Goni'). Although Banzer and Sánchez were placed ahead of Paz Zamora, no candidate received a majority, so it was left to the National Congress to select a winner. Congress selected Paz Zamora as the new president (meanwhile, rivals Banzer and Paz Zamora formed a coalition).

In the 1993 election Sánchez was elected. Sánchez's Aymará running mate, Victor Hugo Cárdenas, appealed to *cholos* and *campesinos* (subsistence farmers), while European urbanites embraced Sánchez's free-market economic policies. This administration attacked corruption and began implementing *capitalización* by opening up state-owned companies and mining interests to overseas investment. Officials hoped privatization would stabilize and streamline companies, making them profitable. Overseas investors in formerly state-owned companies received 49% equity, total voting control, license to operate in Bolivia and up to 49% of the profits. The remaining 51% of the shares were distributed to Bolivians as pensions and through Participación Popular, which was meant to channel spending away from cities and into rural schools, clinics and other local infrastructure.

1952	1967
A military coup provokes a popular armed revolt by the miners, the April Revolution, and Víctor Paz Estenssoro takes power	Ernesto 'Ché' Guevara, having failed to foment a peasant revolt in Bolivia, is executed by a US-backed military squad

Initially Participación Popular drew widespread disapproval; city dwellers didn't want to lose their advantage, and rural people, who stood to benefit most, feared a hidden agenda or simply didn't understand the program. Most working-class people viewed it as privatization by another name, and believed it would lead to the closure of unprofitable operations that didn't attract investors, resulting in increased unemployment. They had a point: while potential investors clamored for the oil company Yacimientos Petrolíferos Fiscales Bolivianos (YPFB) and the huge agribusinesses of the Santa Cruz department, the antiquated Comibol mining operations and the hopelessly inefficient Empresa Nacional de Ferrocarriles (ENFE) railways drew little more than polite sneers (and many components of these operations have indeed closed down).

In 1995 labor grievances over these new policies resulted in a 90-day state-of-siege declaration and the arrest of 374 labor leaders. By mid-year measures were relaxed, but as the year progressed, reform issues were overshadowed by violence and unrest surrounding US-directed coca eradication in the Chapare. Even the establishment of a Spanish-managed private pension scheme and a subsequent payment of US$248 to each Bolivian pensioner – with the promise of future payments from the less-than-fluid plan – did little to boost the administration's popularity.

In 1997 voters upset by the reforms cast 22.5% of the ballot in favor of comeback king and former dictator General Hugo Banzer Suárez. Congress deemed Banzer the victor, and he was sworn in on August 6 to a five-year term, up from four by a 1996 constitutional amendment.

In the late 1990s Banzer faced swelling public discontent with his coca eradication measures, widespread corruption, unrest in response to increasing gas prices and a serious water shortage and economic downturn in the Cochabamba department. In 2000, public protests over increasing gas prices versus government-controlled transportation fares resulted in the blockade of the Yungas Highway for several weeks, and several issues inspired marches, demonstrations and occasional violence, which sporadically halted all traffic (in some cases even vendor and pedestrian traffic) in La Paz and other cities.

Then in 2000 there was the now-famous Water War in Cochabamba when the World Bank forced the Bolivian Government to sell the province's water utility to the private US-company Bechtel. When there was a water rate hike, the local people took to the streets and Bechtel was forced out (see the boxed text p215).

In August 2002 'Goni' Sánchez de Lozada was appointed president after winning only 22.5% of the vote. In February 2003 his International Monetary Fund (IMF)–endorsed economic policies, including steep tax hikes and the exportation of gas out of Bolivia for processing elsewhere, were met with widespread protests and several days of police lock-down in La Paz. In October 2003, Lozada resigned amidst massive popular protests and fled to Miami, where he lives today in comfort, to the disgruntlement of Bolivians. His vice president and respected historian Carlos Mesa automatically took office.

Tune into Rachel Boynton's interesting documentary *Our Brand in Crisis* (2005), about a band of US political consultants – including much of the Clinton team – hired to market the 2002 election campaign of Gonzalo Sánchez de Lozada.

A NEW ERA

Although the unrest continued, Mesa remained a popular leader during his first two years as president. In 2004 he held a referendum on the future of Bolivia's natural gas reserves. Bolivians overwhelmingly advocated Mesa's proposals to

1982	1985
The Bolivian Congress appointed a woman, Lidia Gueilar, as interim president	Víctor Paz Estenssoro's New Economic Policy promotes spending cuts and privatization, resulting in massive unemployment

EVO MORALES: COCA, SWEATERS AND FUTBÓL FROM THE LEFT WING   *Brian Kluepfel*

As a Solstice sun beamed through the portal of Tiahuanaco in December 2005, and Juan Evo Morales Ayma was crowned as Apu Mallku, the supreme leader of the Aymará worldly realm, a new day dawned, quite literally, for the Bolivian indigenous population. The country has had more than 70 presidents in its tumultuous history, but for the first time, the majority indigenous population had one of their own.

Morales, 56, was born in the outskirts of Oruro and years ago picked a political battle that is dear to the Aymarás and Quechuas – coca cultivation. The culture clash is simple: the West sees coca as a raw product in the manufacture of an addictive drug; the indigenous peoples of the Andes view it as a sacred crop that has sustained them for centuries in its unprocessed form (ie mate).

Morales' hard-line stance against the 1990s' US-led Plan Dignidad (eradication program) won him some political battle scars; intransigence on both sides led to the loss of many lives, cocaleros (coca growers) and soldiers alike, in the Chapare region. Morales continues to claim that the West should confront the demand for cocaine in the developed world (at his first address to the UN, he held up a coca leaf, remarking that it was green, not white).

As the century turned, Morales' power grew, and he rallied cocaleros nationwide, shutting down the country with massive paros (roadblocks). He was expelled from his congressional seat in 2002 for alleged terrorist activities stemming from several deaths in a pro-cocalero protest in Sacaba, but massed enough political capital to run for president. He cleverly used the statements of then-US ambassador Manuel Rocha (who cautioned Bolivia against becoming 'a major cocaine exporter') as a campaign device – posters challenging Bolivians to choose between 'Rocha or the Voice of the People' were instrumental in his Movimiento al Socialismo (MAS) party gaining more than 20% of the vote. Refusing to debate the other presidential candidates, Morales said he preferred to talk directly to Rocha, 'the owner of the circus, not the clowns.'

Although Morales finished second in that election, he would not broker a deal with the ruling coalition, and continued to rail against outside influences in Bolivian affairs, decrying the 'neo-liberal' economic policies that he claimed brought little benefit to Latin America. His rallying cry was heard, and deals to transport natural gas via traditional enemies like Peru, and in particular, Chile, were met with violent protests and, at last, fell through.

With the nation on the brink of collapse again in 2005, Morales' moment arrived, and he won slightly more than 50% of the popular vote in a hastily called election. After the ceremony at Tiahuanaco, he quickly grabbed the lefty spotlight, touring the world and meeting with Venezuela's

exert more control over the foreign-owned gas companies. But in 2005, rising fuel prices led to major protests. Tens of thousands of Bolivians – impoverished miners and farmers – took to the streets. Mesa resigned in June 2005. Supreme Court Judge Eduardo Rodríguez took over as interim president.

In December 2005, Bolivians elected their country's first indigenous president. Former *cocalero* (coca grower) activist Juan Evo Morales Ayma (more commonly known as Evo Morales) of Movimiento al Socialismo (MAS) won nearly 54% of the vote, having promised to alter the traditional political class and to empower the nation's poor (mainly indigenous) majority. Soon after Morales' appointment, the IMF announced a US$2 billion debt-forgiveness plan for Bolivia (along with the debts of 18 other impoverished countries). Morales was quick to set about change, carrying out some hefty initiatives: in May 2006 he nationalized Bolivia's energy industry, and in July 2006 he formed (through local elections) a National Constituent Assembly to set

---

1987

USA begins sending Drug Enforcement Administration anticoca squadrons into the Beni and Chapare regions

1995

Labor grievances over privatization result in a 90-day state-of-siege declaration and the arrest of hundreds of labor leaders

Hugo Chavez, Cuba's Fidel Castro, Brazil's Lula de Silva, and members of South Africa's African National Congress.

His populist rhetoric has stirred the people, as has his distinctive dress-down habits (he wore only a black jacket and button-down shirt to his inauguration). He raised some hackles when he met King Juan Carlos of Spain in one of his favorite chompas (jumpers); given his frequent anti-imperial rants, it is somewhat ironic that the red, white and blue sweater he favors later became a best-selling fashion statement in Bolivia.

Like most populists, President Evo appeals to the common man: Fidel may have his beisbol, but Evo and the Bolivians favor futból (soccer) – a sport the president is so passionate about that he broke his nose in a pick-up game this year. He also capitalized on a topic that gets every Bolivian's nose out of joint, claiming he wants the return of part of the nation's coastline, lost to Chile in the War of the Pacific between 1879 and 1884 (to be fair, nearly every Bolivian president has made political capital of this).

Hearkening back to the Cochabamba water riots of 2000, Evo is trying to consolidate Bolivian resources in Bolivian hands. Symbolically, he nationalized natural gas on May Day 2006. He has chosen to partner with certain nations, however, and teams of Cuban doctors have come to rural Bolivia, bringing free medical attention courtesy of compañero Fidel.

Morales may have near-universal support among the indigenous, but his ascension has raised hackles among other populations. In a land where 'Indio' is still a common insult, the threat of polarization is very real. Santa Cruz province has threatened to secede from Bolivia and culturally has more in common with Miami Beach than the Altiplano.

Thus, in the eastern part of the country, where much of the natural resources lie, Morales may encounter resistance. In October 2006 workers from the Beni, Pando, Tarija and Santa Cruz provinces staged violent strikes against Morales' proposed new constitution. However, Morales has been surprisingly successful in pushing through his initiatives despite this opposition. He was able to convince foreign oil and gas companies to sign over majority control of their operations to the Bolivian state energy firm, and in November 2006, his land reform bill passed the Senate.

What will happen to Bolivia under Evo? It continues to struggle as one of the poorer sisters of the western hemisphere. Will his nationalization policies bring true economic power or ruin to his country? Will the deep pockets of Hugo Chavez be enough to offset loss of support from the US and other former allies? While Morales' power recalls an era when strong indigenous men ruled the southern cone, even his own people's patience may be limited after centuries of ineffectual nonindigenous rule.

about rewriting the country's constitution. The assembly sat for the first time on August 6, 2006 (Independence Day) and will have a year to formulate a new body of law before being ratified in a national referendum. Controversial (at least for the US) is that fact that Morales is challenging the US to rethink its coca eradication efforts. Morales wants to promote the coca leaf and its bi-products, integral to many Bolivians' wellbeing and culture. (Until this time, coca crops – plants, not their chemical derivative of cocaine – were under a zero-tolerance policy, intended to placate the US.)

While Morales is viewed by some as a populist leader, he is seen also to antagonize the US, especially with his ties with the leftist governments of Venezuela and Cuba. Furthermore, he has set about redefining indigenous identity and empowering the underprivileged indigenous majority, fueling what some sociologists and anthropologists are predicting will be the next cultural revolution. For further information see p23.

2002–2003	2005–2006
Gonzalo Sánchez de Lozada ('Goni') wins the presidency with 22.5% of the vote	Bolivia elects the country's first indigenous leader, Evo Morales

The Culture

THE NATIONAL PSYCHE

In Bolivia attitude depends on climate and altitude. Cambas (lowlanders) and Kollas (highlanders) enjoy expounding on what makes them different (ie better) than the other. Lowlanders are said to be warmer, more casual and more generous to strangers; highlanders are supposedly harder working but less open-minded. While the jesting used to be good-natured, regional tensions have increased over the past few years, with Santa Cruz's threats of succession constantly in the news.

Bolivians are extremely proud of their regional foods and cultural practices, including dances, and most Bolivians love any excuse *festejar* (to party).

Over the last 30 years, the Aymará (cultural group of highlanders and descendents of the Tiahuanaco empire) in particular have increasingly embraced their ethnicity with pride and their status has increased with economic success, mostly in the urban areas. In La Paz there has been a resurgence of traditional Aymará dress among some younger women (see the boxed text p38). So strong are the trends that the annual contest to elect a Miss Cholita Paceña is attracting contestants who (the local press claims) have ditched their designer jeans in favor of new-found *cholita* fashions and status. The image of the *chola* (an Aymará woman who lives in the city but wears traditional dress; *'cholita'* is sometimes considered more polite) is altering dramatically. Her traditional image of a market seller is rapidly being superseded by that of a trader, businesswoman and politician (there are even *cholas* in government); her attitudes and behavior are said to represent the contemporary Aymará bourgeoisie. See p38 for more on Bolivian women.

At the time of research, Bolivian identity (and national psyche) was in a state of flux; many Bolivians were 'redefining' and even questioning what it meant to be Bolivian, thanks in part to Bolivia's first indigenous president, Evo Morales. Morales vigorously stressed that Bolivian identity was based on an individual's ethnic origins. Despite his claims that all Bolivians were equal, Morales was quick to espouse the status of indigenous groups. Some accuse him of political maneuvering and of polarizing the country according to race, class, economic status and skin color. He has been seen as favoring indigenous groups over Bolivian and foreign 'Whites' and mestizos who, as descendants of the Spanish colonists and indigenous people, are rightly proud of their Bolivian status.

At a social level, Bolivians are keen on greetings and pleasantries. Every exchange is kicked off with the usual *Buen día* or *Buenos días,* but also with a *¿Cómo está?* or *¿Qué tal?* (How are you?). Bolivian Spanish is also liberally sprinkled with endearing diminutives referring to everyday items such as *sopita* (a little soup) and *pesitos* (little pesos, as in 'it only costs 10 little pesos').

Collectively, Bolivians have a landlocked longing for the sea and unerringly mark El Día del Mar (Day of the Sea) to commemorate the Chilean annexation of Bolivia's only stretch of coastline on March 24, 1879.

LIFESTYLE

Day-to-day life varies from Bolivian to Bolivian, mostly depending on whether they live in the city or in the country. Many *campesinos* (subsistence farmers), including those in the north of Potosí, live without running water, heat or electricity, and some wear clothing that has hardly changed

---

Quechua is spoken by 2.6 million Bolivians, nearly 30% of the population.

Many Bolivians will greet a person – including a stranger being introduced – with a kiss on one cheek (in the country's north) and on two cheeks (in the country's south).

2006 is the year 5514 according to the Aymará calendar.

ARE YOU LOST, MY FRIEND?

Some Bolivians will provide you with incorrect answers or directions rather than give no response at all. They're not being malicious; they merely want to appear helpful and knowledgeable. Furthermore, it's worth remembering that street numbers are hardly used – people give directions by landmarks instead. Sometimes it's best to ask several people the same question – the most common response is likely to be correct.

style since the Spanish arrived. But in cities, especially Santa Cruz (the country's richest city), Cochabamba, Sucre and La Paz, thousands of people enjoy the comforts of contemporary conveniences and live very modern lifestyles.

The Fat Man from La Paz: Contemporary Fiction from Bolivia, edited by Rosario Santos, is a collection of 20 short stories which offer perspectives about typical Bolivians and their lives.

Still, for the vast majority of Bolivians, standards of living are alarmingly low, marked by substandard housing, nutrition, education, sanitation and hygiene. Bolivia suffers from a Third World trifecta: a high infant mortality rate (52 deaths per 1000 births), a reasonably high birth rate (2.3 per woman) and a low female literacy rate (81.6%). Overall 87% of primary school–aged children are enrolled in classes, but attendance isn't necessarily a high priority.

On the higher-education front there are 30 universities in the country, 10 of which are public. The growing ranks of well-educated college graduates are frustrated by the lack of domestic employment opportunities and are increasingly seeking work abroad, especially in Spain, Argentina and the US.

In 2006, US software giant Microsoft launched its Windows and Office software in the Quechua language.

With no social welfare system in place to sustain the elderly, disabled, mentally ill and underemployed, they sometimes take to the streets, hoping to arouse sympathy. (However, most elderly people are cared for by relatives, negating the need for aged-care homes). One ethnic group in Potosí department has even organized a begging syndicate that sends brown-clad older women into larger cities around the country, provides accommodations and supplies them with suitably grubby-looking children.

Homosexuality is legal in Bolivia, but isn't openly flaunted in this machismo society. Despite a growing number of gay bars in some larger cities, gay culture remains fairly subtle. For more details, see p371.

ECONOMY

Despite its rich resources, Bolivia is one of the poorest countries in Latin America. Estimates in 2004 put 64% of the population below the poverty line. The average annual earnings are around US$900 and GDP per capita is around US$2900 (2005 estimate). Current inflation is around 5%.

Bolivia's main exports include gas and zinc. The country's agricultural products include soybeans (also a major export), coffee, sugar, cotton, corn and timber. Coca, sunflower seed (for oil) and organic chocolate are also growing industries.

There is widespread underemployment; a large percentage of the underemployed supplement their income by participating in coca-production, mainly in the Yungas, and in the informal street-market economy.

The recent trend of gold teeth of the indigenous – in the shapes of stars, moons and other symbols – is the sign of wealth and status.

Striking and protests to demand higher salaries and improved conditions and political change are a way of life here, although in more recent years, even some locals have felt that this has been more damaging than constructive to the economy.

The government remains heavily dependent on foreign aid. In December 2005, the G8 announced a US$2 billion debt-forgiveness plan.

See p23 for the latest economic events.

POPULATION

Bolivia is thinly populated with around 8.9 million people occupying approximately 1,098,580 sq km. The Altiplano supports nearly 70% of the population – despite its frigid climate and frequently simmering social and political strife – mostly in the La Paz, Lake Titicaca and Oruro regions.

Bolivia has 36 identified indigenous groups. There are varying figures regarding the indigenous population. According to the 2001 national census, about half of Bolivia's population claims indigenous heritage, while most sociologists and anthropologists cite figures of just over 60%. A mere 1% is of African heritage, mostly descendants of slaves conscripted to work in the Potosí mines (see the boxed text p146). The remainder of Bolivia's citizens are largely of European extraction. Not all are descendants of the early Spanish conquerors; there are some Mennonite colonies, Jewish refugees from Nazi Europe, Eastern European refugees and hordes of researchers, aid workers and missionaries. Small Middle Eastern and Asian minorities, consisting mainly of Palestinians, Punjabis, Japanese and Chinese, have also immigrated.

The vast majority of those who identify as indigenous are Aymará and Quechua (many of whom are located in the highlands), and the remaining groups (including Guaraní and Chiquitano) are located almost entirely in the lowlands.

The Wiphala flag – square-shaped and consisting of 49 small squares in a grid with graduating colors of the rainbow – has been adopted as a symbol of the Aymará people. Whether the colors used originate from Inca times or more recently is cause for debate.

SPORTS

Like its Latin American neighbors, Bolivia's national sport is *futból* (soccer). La Paz's Bolívar and The Strongest usually participate (albeit weakly) in the Copa Libertadores, the annual showdown of Latin America's top clubs. Bolivian teams typically fare well in *futsal* or *futból de salon* (five-vs-five mini-soccer) world championships. Professional *futból* matches are held

---

LA PAZ'S CLÁSICO: HIGH-ALTITUDE DERBY *Brian Kluepfel*

Several times a year *paceñas* (La Paz locals) put aside concerns about the weather, the price of tickets and other worldly matters for a game that's guaranteed to swell the Hernando Siles (Map pp72–3) soccer stadium to its near 50,000 capacity: El Clásico, the showdown between La Paz's (and the nation's) two big *futbol* (soccer) teams, Bolívar and The Strongest.

Everything changes for El Clásico: the streets teem with fans and tickets are harder to come by (but not impossible; as in all of Latin America, walk-up sales are common). There is even a hint of trouble in the air, compelling the local authorities to enforce a policy that's common in Europe but rare in La Paz: a police line forms between the two fan groups before and after the game, forcing rival supporters apart from each other as they enter and exit the stadium. Even so, except for scattered rock-throwing between youth groups, trouble is rare. At worst you may be hit by a water balloon, or if you're lucky, get to buy a slice of chocolate cake from a chap roaming the stands in a vintage Bolivian navy uniform (really).

The intracity rivalry stretches back more than a quarter-century, to Club Bolívar's founding in 1925 (The Strongest are the country's oldest team, begun in 1908). The Strongest (nicknamed the 'Tigres' for their bold yellow-and-black striped uniform) have more support in the working-class and poorer neighborhoods, while the 'Celestes' of Bolívar (dubbed for their sky-blue uniforms) are more of a rich man's team.

Both sides can claim some measure of domination: in the early amateur years of the Bolivian League, The Strongest won the title 14 times to Bolívar's eight. Since the league went semiprofessional and then professional (1977), the Celestes have turned the tables, winning 16 times to The Strongest's eight. But when the two teams meet, as with any other rivalry you can throw out the statistics. It's for the bragging rights of La Paz, and the nation, after all.

Check www.bolivia.com/futbol/to see when the next El Clásico will be held.

every weekend in big cities, and impromptu street games are always happening. While small towns lack many basic services, you can be sure to find a well-tended *cancha* (football field) almost everywhere you go – and you'll be welcomed to join in. Some communities still bar women from the field, but in the Altiplano women's teams have started popping up, where they play clad in *polleras* (skirts) and jerseys. There is a national women's team, and the game is becoming more popular among females.

El Alto is home to the rough-and-ready, athletic and extremely choreographed 'free-style' *lucha libre* (wrestling matches). Less of a sport and more an entertainment for audience voyeurs, 'good guy' and 'bad guy' wrestlers fight it out in the ring wearing outfits that Superman and Spiderman would envy. More recently, much to the delight of the crowds, women have joined the fray, some dressed as innocent looking *cholitas*, others in devilish costumes. Anything goes, from eye gouging to headlocks and occasionally, dwarf-throwing (not for the politically correct or sensitive viewer). You can gauge a crowd's reaction by how much orange peel and plastic bottles it pelts at the contenders. See p76 for more details.

In rural communities volleyball is a sunset affair, with mostly adults playing a couple of times a week. Racquetball, billiards, chess and *cacho* (dice) are also popular. The unofficial national sport, however, has to be feasting and feting – competition between dancers and drinkers knows no bounds.

RELIGION

Roughly 78% of Bolivia's population professes Roman Catholicism and practices it to varying degrees. Around 19% are Protestant and 2.5% are agnostic, while the rest follow other religions. Strong evangelical movements are rapidly gaining followers with their fire-and-brimstone messages of the world's imminent end. Despite the political and economic strength of Western religions, it's clear that most religious activities have mixed Inca and Aymará belief systems with Christianity. Doctrines, rites and superstitions are commonplace, and some *campesinos* still live by a traditional lunar calendar.

Indigenous religions believe in natural gods and spirits, which date back to Inca times and earlier. Pachamama, the ubiquitous earth mother, is the most popular recipient of sacrificial offerings, since she shares herself with human beings, helps bring forth crops and distributes riches to those she favors. She has quite an appetite for coca, alcohol and the blood of animals, particularly llamas. If you're wondering about all the llama fetuses in the markets, they are wrapped up and buried under new constructions, especially homes, as an offering to Pachamama.

Among the Aymará and Quechua, mountain gods, the *apus* and *achachilas*, are important. The *apus*, mountain spirits who provide protection for travelers, are often associated with a particular *nevado* (snow-capped peak). Illimani, for example, is an *apus* who looks over inhabitants of La Paz. *Achachilas* are spirits of the high mountains, who are believed to be ancestors of the people and look after their *ayllu* (native group of people, loosely translated as 'tribe') and provide bounty from the earth.

Ekeko, which means 'dwarf' in Aymará, is the jolly little household god of abundance. Since he's responsible for matchmaking, finding homes for the homeless and ensuring success for businesspeople, he's well looked after, especially during the Alasitas festival in La Paz (p80).

Talismans are also used in daily life to encourage prosperity or to protect a person from evil. A turtle is thought to bring health, a frog or toad carries good fortune, an owl signifies wisdom and success in school, and a condor will ensure a good journey.

The Aymará and Quechua spiritual worlds embrace three levels: Alajpacha (the world above or eternal sky, representing light and life, the center or the earthly world); Akapacha (located between the sky and hell, and between life and death); and Mankapacha (located below, symbolizing death and obscurity).

Despite the high prevalence of llama fetuses in the markets (used for sacrificial offerings), llamas are not killed especially for them. About 3000 llamas are slaughtered daily on the Altiplano for wool and meat; the fetuses are removed from those animals subsequently found to be pregnant.

FIESTA DE LAS ÑATITAS

One of the most bizarre and fascinating Aymará rituals is the **Fiesta de las Ñatitis** (Festival of Skulls), which is celebrated one week after Day of the Dead. *Ñatitas* (skulls) are presented at La Paz cemetery chapel to be blessed by a Catholic priest. Parish priests shy away from associating this rite with mass, but have begrudgingly recognized the custom. The skulls are adorned with offerings of flowers, candles and coca leaves, and many even sport sunglasses and a lit cigarette between their teeth. While some people own the skulls of deceased loved ones and friends (who they believe are watching over them), many anonymous craniums are believed to have been purchased from morgues and (so it is claimed) medical faculties. After the blessings, the decorated *ñatitas* are carted back to the owners' houses to bring good luck and protection. This ancient Aymarán ritual was practiced in secret, but nowadays the chapel's head count is growing every year.

WOMEN IN BOLIVIA

Machismo is alive and well in Bolivia, but women's rights and education organizations are popping up, most notably in El Alto and the strong women's movement Mujeres Creando, in La Paz. The Bolivian congress appointed a woman as interim president in 1982 and many women – including *cholas* under the Morales government – have been elected as members of the 2006 national legislature and as representatives to the Constitutional Assembly.

More recently, new lingo has emerged to describe Bolivian *cholas*, whose status, thanks partly to the support of the indigenous president, is increasing. While the *chola* is a woman who wears traditional dress (see the boxed text, below), the '*chota*' is a woman who has ditched her *chola* dress and converted

CHOLA DRESS

The characteristic dress worn by many Bolivian indigenous women was imposed on them in the 18th century by the Spanish king, and the customary center parting of the hair was the result of a decree by the Viceroy Toledo.

This distinctive ensemble, both colorful and utilitarian, has almost become Bolivia's defining image. The most noticeable characteristic of the traditional Aymará dress is the ubiquitous dark green, black or brown bowler hat. These are not attached with hat pins, but balance on the *cholita*'s heads.

The women normally braid their hair into two long plaits that are joined by a tuft of black wool known as a *pocacha*. The *pollera* skirts they wear are constructed of several horizontal pleats, worn over multiple layers of petticoats. Traditionally, only a married woman's skirt was pleated, while a single female's was not. Today, most of the synthetic materials of these brightly colored *polleras* are imported from South Korea.

The women also wear a factory-made blouse, a woolen *chompa* (sweater/jumper), a short vest-like jacket and a cotton apron, or some combination of these. Usually, they add a shawl known as a *manta*. Fashion dictates subtleties, such as the length of both the skirt and the tassels on the shawl.

Some sling across their backs an *aguayo* (also spelled *ahuayo*), a rectangle of manufactured or handwoven cloth decorated with colorful horizontal bands. It's used as a carryall and is filled with everything from coca or groceries to babies.

The Quechua of the highland valleys wear equally colorful but not so universally recognized attire. The hat, called a *montera*, is a flat-topped affair made of straw or finely woven white wool. It's often taller and broader than the bowlers worn by the Aymará. The felt *monteras* (aka *morriones*), of Tarabuco, patterned after Spanish conquistadores' helmets, are the most striking. Women's skirts are usually made of velour, and are shorter in length.

to Western-style dress, a *'birlocha'* is a Western-style woman who opposes the *chola*, and *'chola* transformers' are females who assume the role of *cholas* when they feel like it, such as in cultural events and fiestas.

ARTS

Bolivia is rich in artistic expression, whether it be music and textiles, or film and literature. While traditional music and textiles are more prevalent than contemporary gallery art, La Paz's Museo de Arte Contemporaneo (p75), opened in 2001, represents a growing appreciation of contemporary art. The **Casa de Cultura** (Map pp72-3; Mariscal Santa Cruz & Potosí) in La Paz is an excellent place to view art exhibits, as well as find out information on the art scene. In the way of performances, formal theater is limited to larger cities and traditional *peñas* (folk-music programs). You can catch lively dance and theatrical performances almost anywhere during festivals and parades.

Artesanía (Textiles)

Weaving methods have changed little in Bolivia for centuries. During the colonial period, woven cloth was one of the most important tribute items (after gold, silver and other minerals) required by the crown. In rural areas girls learn to weave before they reach puberty, and women spend nearly all their spare time with a drop spindle or weaving on heddle looms. Prior to colonization llama and alpaca wool were the materials of choice, although now sheep's wool and synthetic fibers are also prominent.

Bolivian textiles come in diverse patterns. The majority display a degree of skill that results from millennia of artistry and tradition. The most common piece is a *manta* or *aguayo*, a square shawl made of two hand-woven strips joined edge to edge. Also common are the *chuspa* (coca pouch), *chullo* (knitted hat), the *falda* (skirt), woven belts and touristy items such as camera bags made from remnants.

Regional differences are manifest in weaving style, motif and use. Weavings from Tarabuco often feature intricate zoomorphic patterns, while distinctive red-and-black designs come from Potolo, northwest of Sucre. Zoomorphic patterns are also prominent in the wild Charazani country north of Lake Titicaca and in several Altiplano areas outside La Paz, including Lique and Calamarka.

Some extremely fine weavings originate in Sica Sica, one of the many dusty and nondescript villages between La Paz and Oruro, while in Calcha, southeast of Potosí, expert spinning and an extremely tight weave – more than 150 threads per inch – produce Bolivia's finest textiles.

Vicuña fibers, the finest and most expensive in the world, are produced in Apolobamba.

Music

All Andean musical traditions have evolved from a series of pre-Inca, Inca, Spanish, Amazonian and even African influences, but each region of Bolivia has developed distinctive musical traditions, dances and instruments. The strains of the Andean music from the cold and bleak Altiplano are suitably haunting and mournful, while those of warmer Tarija, with its complement of bizarre musical instruments, take on more vibrant and colorful tones.

Original Andean music was exclusively instrumental, but recent trends toward popularization of the melodies has inspired the addition of appropriately tragic, bittersweet or morose lyrics.

In the lowland regions Jesuit influences on Chiquitano, Moxos and Guaraní musical talent left a unique legacy that is still in evidence, and remains particularly strong. Extremely able artists and musicians, the indigenous

---

A common petty crime in La Paz is the theft of bowler hats – valued at around US$8 upwards – from *cholitas'* heads in crowded markets.

Librería Boliviana (www .libreriaboliviana.com in Spanish) stocks an extensive collection of books, videos, traditional instruments and music and ships worldwide.

Los Kjarkas are one of the best-known and -loved Andean music groups in South America. The group has introduced the world to the sounds of the *zampoña*, the *quena* and the *charango*.

JAGUAR-CALLERS TO GOLDEN CHARANGOS:
MUSICAL INSTRUMENTS OF BOLIVIA   Brian Kluepfel

Bolivian traditional music is like the country itself – bigger and broader, deeper and wider than you first imagined. Never mind those pan-pipe and guitar bands you see at every metro station in the world, playing that Simon & Garfunkel cover song about the sparrow and the snail. The national music covers a lot more ground – literally – than those *sarape* (poncho)–clad gentlemen.

One man who has spent a lifetime studying Bolivian music is Ernesto Cavour Aramayo, a multi-instrumentalist from La Paz. Cavour began collecting musical instruments in 1960, but by 1962 he had enough for a museum. Four decades hence, the Museo de Instrumentos Musicales de Bolivia (p76), begun in his home, now has a place of honor on La Paz's street of museums, Calle Jaen.

Cavour's 400-page book, also cleverly titled *Musical Instruments of Bolivia*, is exhaustive. He discusses Bolivia's history and ethnic makeup before classifying its instruments, each category occupying a chapter in the book (and a separate room in the museum).

The *aerofones* (you blow into these) include 'free air' instruments, which only have a chamber of air, and 'flute-like' instruments. The most common, which you can hear in the aforementioned tube stations, are the *quena* and *sicu* (or *zampoña*). *Sicu* (the Aymará name) are those famed pan pipes, a series of reed or cane tubes of various lengths fastened together; each length produces a different note. Names like *chuli*, *malta* and *sanka* denote the length of the tube which generates C major note. Other names are more logical: a '*seis y siete*' *sicu* has one row of six notes and another of seven.

A *jula jula* is a super-*grande sicu*; the longest tube of the largest *jula jula* is a whopping 108cm. Groups of up to 20 players use them to blow out a somewhat martial marching style on holidays like the Day of the Cross and the Feast of San Francisco in Oruro and Potosí.

The *quena*, a small flute made of cane, bone or ceramic, is commonplace in the gringo markets. The instrument predates Europeans by many centuries and the earliest examples, made of stone, were found near Potosí. Cavour lists more than a dozen types of *quenas* in his book. The *pututu* is an animal horn, sometimes played on its own, and sometimes fastened to a longer air tube.

The most curious of the next category, the *membraphones* (a stretched membrane percussion instrument) comes from the Amazon region, and is known as a jaguar-caller. This hollowed-out calabash, with a small hole into which the player inserts his hand, seems to do the trick in calling the big cats to the hunt.

In Cavour's pantheon, the *charango* is king of all *chordophones*, or stringed instruments. Modeled after the Spanish *vihuela* and mandolin, it gained initial popularity in Potosí during the city's mining heyday. It has five courses of two strings and it's not usually picked, but rather is played in a flailing manner, called *rasqueado*, much like a banjo. Thanks to conservation efforts, the *charango* is no longer made of *quirquinchos*, armadillos or tortoises (though examples of each are in Cavour's museum – who knew there were armadillos that big?).

Indeed, the *charango* remains the instrument Bolivia is known by – and well proud of. Noted *charanguista* Pedro Mar sums it up in his instructional booklet: '*el charango es Boliviano.*' Donato Espinoza, a student of Cavour's who has followed his maestro's path to international acclaim with the group Savia Andina, calls the instrument 'the most important instrument of the mestizo cultural period.' Players like Espinoza have taken the little stringed instrument to other styles; he's played throughout Asia, Europe and the Americas, putting a bit of *charango* into jazz fusion and classical pieces.

Bolivia hosts two *charango* festivals: the biannual Encuentro Internacional del Charango, held every other April in different cities, and the annual Sede Nacional del Charango, a competitive event that takes place every November in Aiquile (near Cochabamba). If you're there at the time, stop by to see who wins the Golden Charango. If not, visit Ernesto Cavour's museum and see the *charango*, and a whole lot more.

To learn more about Bolivian music check out www.ernestocavour.com.

people handcrafted musical instruments – the renowned harps and violins featured in contemporary Chaco music – and mastered Italian baroque forms, including opera. In the remotest of settings they gave concerts, dances and theater performances that could have competed on a European scale.

Dance

Traditional Altiplano dances celebrate war, fertility, hunting prowess, marriage and work. After the Spanish arrived, European dances and those of the African slaves were introduced, resulting in the hybrid dances that now characterize many Bolivian celebrations. Several postcolonial dances were traditionally performed as a satire, making fun of the colonists. This includes the dance of the *doctoricitos*, who wear small round glasses and fake hooked noses, imitating the colonial lawyers.

Surf the Bolivian Educational & Cultural network's site www .llajta.org to hear samples of a wide range of traditional and modern Bolivian music.

The country's geography and climate has traditionally influenced the style and costumes of the different dances – those in the highlands are generally more melancholy with more cumbersome costumes than their counterparts in the warmer lowlands. Some costumes can weigh up to 50kg and are worn for more than 10 hours of dancing. Popular pre-Hispanic dances include La Sicuriada, La Morenada, and La Tarqueada. The Spanish introduced their salon dances, the Cueca and Bailecito, still popular in most of Bolivia. They are danced by handkerchief-waving couples, primarily during fiestas.

The most unusual and colorful dances are performed at Altiplano festivals. Oruro's Carnaval draws huge local and international crowds who watch the many *fraternidades* (groups) perform most dances, including the well-known Diablada, and Llamerada, Sicuris and Incas. Huge amounts of money are spent on the costumes and it provides an industry in Oruro (see p173). Potosí is famed for *tinku,* recreating the region's *tinku* fight tradition, while La Paz is renowned for La Morenada, which re-enacts the dance of African slaves brought to the courts of Viceroy Felipe III. The costumes consist of hooped skirts, shoulder mantles and devilish dark-faced masks adorned with plumes.

Architecture

Tiahuanaco's ruined structures and Inca roads, especially around northern La Paz and the Altiplano architecture in Bolivia, are interesting examples of pre-Colombian architecture. The classic Inca polygonal-cut stones that distinguish many Peruvian sites are rare in Bolivia, found only on Isla del Sol and Isla de la Luna in Lake Titicaca.

While modernization, earthquakes and a depressed economy have resulted in the loss of many colonial buildings throughout Bolivia, fine colonial-era houses and street façades survive, notably in Potosí, Sucre and La Paz. Most remaining colonial buildings, however, are religious, and their styles are divided into several major overlapping periods. Look carefully at church fronts as they often possess icons of pagan religions that were incorporated by indigenous artisans trained by European craftsmen.

Renaissance (1550–1650) churches were constructed primarily of adobe, with courtyards and massive buttresses. One of the best surviving examples is in the village of Tiahuanaco (p102). Renaissance churches indicating *mudéjar* (Moorish) influences include San Miguel in Sucre, and the cathedral in Copacabana (p111).

Baroque (1630–1770) churches were constructed in the form of a cross with an elaborate dome. One of the best examples is the San Agustín (p264) in Potosí. Potosí has a long-term renovation project sponsored by the Spanish government to rehabilitate churches and other colonial buildings.

MARINA NÚÑEZ DEL PRADO

Bolivia's foremost sculptor, Marina Núñez del Prado, was born on October 17, 1910 in La Paz. From 1927 to 1929 she studied at the Escuela Nacional de Bellas Artes (National School of Fine Arts), and from 1930 to 1938 worked there as a professor of sculpture and artistic anatomy.

Her early works were in cedar and walnut, and represented the mysteries of the Andes: indigenous faces, groups and dances. From 1943 to 1945 she lived in New York and turned her attentions to Bolivian social themes, including mining and poverty. She later went through a celebration of Bolivian motherhood with pieces depicting indigenous women, pregnant women and mothers protecting their children. Other works dealt largely with Andean themes, some of which took appealing abstract forms. She once wrote, 'I feel the enormous good fortune to have been born under the tutelage of the Andes, which express the richness and the cosmic miracle. My art expresses the spirit of my Andean homeland and the spirit of my Aymará people.'

During her long career she held more than 160 exhibitions, which garnered her numerous awards and she received international acclaim from the likes of Pablo Neruda, Gabriela Mistral, Alexander Archipenko and Guillermo Niño de Guzmán. In her later years Marina lived in Lima, Peru, with her husband, Peruvian writer Jorge Falcón. She died there in September 1995 at the age of 84.

Mestizo style (1690–1790) is defined by whimsical decorative carvings including tropical flora and fauna, Inca deities and designs, and bizarre masks, sirens and gargoyles. See the amazing results at the San Francisco church in La Paz (p74) and San Lorenzo (p264) in Potosí.

In the 18th century the Jesuits in what is now known as the Beni and Santa Cruz lowlands went off on neoclassical tangents, designing churches with Bavarian rococo and Gothic elements. Their most unusual effort was the bizarre mission church at San José de Chiquitos (p324).

Since the 1950s many modern high-rises have appeared in the major cities. Though most are generic, there are some gems. Look for triangular pediments on the rooflines, new versions of the Spanish balcony and the use of hardwoods of differing hues. The cathedral in Riberalta (p362) sings the contemporary gospel of brick and cedar like nobody's business.

Newer modern architecture in La Paz, especially that in Zona Sur, with its reflective glass and anything-goes style, leaves much to be desired.

Visit www.mamani.com to find out more about contemporary Aymará artist Mamani Mamani.

Visual Arts

In the early colonial days Bolivian art was largely inspired by religion, the major contribution being represented by the Escuela Potosina Indígena. Hallmarks of this tradition include gilded highlights and triangular representations of the Virgin Mary.

Notable modern artists include Alejandro Mario Yllanes, an Aymará tin miner turned engraver and muralist, and Miguel Alandia Pantoja who, in the late 1940s, painted scenes of popular revolution.

Contemporary Aymará artist Mamani Mamani from Tiahuanaco village strives to portray the true 'color' of the Altiplano – not the landscape but the images that inspire the people – and it's brilliant. The paceño artist Gil Imana brings out the stark, cold and isolated nature of life in the Andes, using only tiny splashes of color on drab backgrounds to hint at the underlying vibrancy of the culture.

For a comprehensive run down on the history of Bolivian film, see www .embolivia-brasil.org .br/cultura/cine/menu _cine.htm

Film

Bolivian film includes an impressive list of names and titles that cannot be done justice here. Film buffs should make their way to La Paz's Cinemateca Boliviana (p91).

One of the most important films in Bolivian history is the documentary *Vuelve Sebastiana* (The Return of Sebastiana; 1953), directed by Jorge Ruiz. It follows a group of people in the Altiplano who are facing extinction. Later, Ruiz managed the Institute of Cinematography in Bolivia, set up after the 1952 April Revolution to develop national cinema. Between 1953 and 1966 it was one of the top five producers of film in Latin America. In 1964, Jorge Sanjines took over as manager. After making propaganda films for the government, Sanjines then outraged the government by shooting *Ukamau* (And So It Is; 1966), the tale of the rape and murder of an Aymará woman and her mestizo landowner. Today, Sanjines is regarded as the most important director and prolific filmmaker in Bolivian cinema.

As well as the films listed here, look out for: *El Triángulo del Lago* (2000; Mauricio Calderón), *El Atraco* (2004; Paolo Agazzi), and *Di Buen día a Papá* (Say Good Morning to Dad; 2005; Fernando Vargas).

Amargo Mar (1984; Bitter Sea) By highly regarded director Antonio Eguino, looks at the loss of Bolivia's coastline to Chile.

American Visa (2005; Juan Carlos Valdivia) Tells the story of a Bolivian professor who, on being denied a visa to the US, finds himself involved in a web of unsavory activities.

Dependencia Sexual (Sexual Dependency; 2003; Rodrigo Bellot) An award-winning film following five troubled teenagers and shot in an unconventional split-screen double angle.

Jonas y la Ballena Rosada (Jonah & the Pink Whale; 1995; Juan Carlos Valdivia) Deals with the drug trade around the Santa Cruz region.

Sayari (1995; Mela Márques) A breakthrough film, with an all-indigenous cast, and a female director.

Literature

Bolivia has an extraordinarily rich literary tradition, starting with the 19th-century modernist poets, Rubén Dario, Ricardo Jaimes Freyre, Gregorio Reynolds and Franz Tamayo. Other notable poets include the 20th-century poet Oscar Cerruto and feminist poet Adela Zamudi (1854–1928). Award-winning poet and novelist Yolanda Bedregal (1916–1999) is still considered as one of the most prolific and important authors in Bolivia.

In the 1920s, Bolivian literature developed an indigenous theme, with stories such as *La Misk'isimi* ('Sweet Mouth' in Quechua) by Adolfo Costa du Rels and *La Ch'askañawi* (Eyes of Stars) by Carlos Medinaceli. The Chaco War (1932–1935) between Bolivia and Paraguay is examined in *Aluvión de Fuego* (1935), by Oscar Cerruto, *Sangre de Mestizos* (1936), by Augusto Céspedes, and *Laguna*, by Costa Du Rels.

Subversive literature came to the fore in the 1960s, with the death of Ché Guevara in 1967; the best known publication is *Los Fundadores del Alba,* by Renato Prado de Oropeza. By the end of the '60s, fiction, rather than realism, dominated the literature scene. The '70s and '80s saw critical literature restricted by the period's military dictatorships. The 1990s gave rise to urban literature, including *American Visa* (1994) by Juan de Recacochea and *The Fat Man from La Paz* (2000), edited by Rosario Dantos.

One of the best known recent Bolivian films is *Cuestión de Fé* (Marcos Loayza, 1995), the story of three marginalized urbanites transporting a statue of the Virgin Mary from La Paz to the northern Yungas.

Check out www .thedevilsminer.com for information about the award-winning film *The Devil's Miner* (2005), an American-directed film about the life of child miners in current-day Potosí.

Bolivian literature first hit the literary psyche at the end of the 19th century with its modernist poets Ricardo Jaimes Freyre, Gregorio Reynolds and Franz Tamayo.

Environment

When people think of the Bolivian environment, they often think high (La Paz), dry (Altiplano) and salty (Uyuni salt plains). While these cover large regions of the country, there's much more scope to Bolivian landscapes.

The country's varying altitude – between 130m in the jungles of the Amazon Basin and 6542m in the rugged Andes mountain range – means that a huge variety of ecological and geological spheres support a large number of plants and animals. Giant anteaters shelter here, as do anacondas and armadillos, and plants range from the much-lauded mahogany to the palms. In 2005 a new species of monkey, the titi, was discovered in Madidi National Park (see opposite).

The country's 1000 neotropical bird species and 5000 plants species rank among the highest numbers in the world; it's among eight countries with the most diverse range of reptiles (16 of which exist only in Bolivia), and is home to 13 endemic mammals.

The 1990s saw a dramatic surge in international and domestic interest in ecological and environmental issues in the Amazon region. Since the creation of the government-run **Servicio Nacional de Áreas Protegidas** (Sernap; Map pp72-3; ☎ 2-243-4420/243-4472; www.sernap.gov.bo; Edificio Full Office, Loayza btwn Mariscal Santa Cruz & Camacho, La Paz) in 1997, 22 national protected areas have been declared, covering 15% of the national territory. This represents significant strongholds for rarer and regionally threatened wildlife such as spectacled bears, giant otters, Andean condors and jaguar. Local and international nongovernmental organizations (NGOs) have worked with Sernap to craft innovative ways to preserve select habitats.

Unfortunately, however, much of the Bolivian environment is being destroyed or is under threat and many regions risk exhaustion of their forest and wildlife resources; see p46.

THE LAND

Despite the huge loss of territory in wars and concessions (see p27), land-locked Bolivia is South America's fifth-largest country – 1,098,581 sq km or 3½ times the size of the British Isles.

Two Andean mountain chains define the west of the country, with many peaks above 6000m. The western Cordillera Occidental stands between Bolivia and the Pacific coast. The eastern Cordillera Real runs southeast then turns south across central Bolivia, joining the other chain to form the southern Cordillera Central.

The haunting Altiplano, which ranges in altitude from 3500m to 4000m, is boxed in by these two great cordilleras. It's an immense, nearly treeless plain punctuated by mountains and solitary volcanic peaks. At the Altiplano's northern end, straddling the Peruvian border, Lake Titicaca is one of the world's highest navigable lakes. In the far southwestern corner, the land is drier and less populated. Here are the remnants of two vast ancient lakes, the Salar de Uyuni and the Salar de Coipasa.

East of the Cordillera Central are the Central Highlands, a region of scrubby hills, valleys and fertile basins with a Mediterranean-like climate.

North of the Cordillera Real, the Yungas form a transition zone between arid highlands and humid lowlands. More than half of Bolivia's total area is in the Amazon Basin, with sweaty tropical rainforest in the western section, and swamps, flat savannas and scrub in the east.

In the country's southeastern corner is the flat, nearly impenetrable scrubland of the Gran Chaco.

The Altiplano makes up only 10% of Bolivia's land mass, yet is the country's most densely populated zone.

The *bolivianita* is a rare semi-precious stone made up of citrine and amethyst and has a pretty pinky-yellow color.

Bolivia can never forget 1879, the year it lost its outlet to the sea. Each year on March 23 it stages marches and events; discussion is still ongoing as to how it can regain access to the Pacific.

WILDLIFE
Animals

Thanks to its varied geography, sparse human population and lack of extensive development, Bolivia is one of the best places on the continent to observe wildlife. Even the most seasoned wildlife observers will be impressed by Parque Nacional Madidi and Parque Nacional Noel Kempff Mercado.

The distribution of wildlife is largely directed by the country's geography. The Altiplano is home to vicuña, flamingo and condor. The elusive jaguar, tapir and white-lipped and collared peccaries occupy the nearly inaccessible, harsh expanses of the Chaco in relatively healthy numbers. The Amazon Basin contains the richest density of species on earth, featuring an incredible variety of lizards, parrots, monkeys, snakes, butterflies, fish and bugs (by the zillions!).

The southern Altiplano is the exclusive habitat of the James flamingo. The versatile rhea or *ñandú* (the South American ostrich) inhabits the Altiplano to the Beni, the Chaco and the Santa Cruz lowlands. In the highlands lucky observers may see a condor; highly revered by the Inca, these rare vultures are the world's heaviest birds of prey.

River travelers are almost certain to spot capybaras (large amphibious rodents), turtles, alligators, pink dolphins and, occasionally, giant river otters. It's not unusual to see anacondas in the rivers of the Beni department, and overland travelers frequently see armadillos, rheas, sloths and *jochis* (agoutis).

You won't have to travel very far to spot the most common Bolivian fauna – the llama and the alpaca – as these have been domesticated for centuries.

ENDANGERED & RARE SPECIES

The extremity of the landscape has kept many areas uninhabited by people for a long time, preserving pristine habitats for many exotic species.

Vicuñas, which fetch a bundle on the illicit market for their fuzzy coats, are declining in the wild, but in a couple of Bolivian reserves their numbers have been increasing. Other precious wild highland species include foxes and *tarukas* (Andean deer), the mysterious Andean cat and the titi monkey. The best place to see all of these, however, is just across the Chilean border in Parque Nacional Lauca (see p182).

In Bolivia, guanacos are found exclusively in a remote part of the Bolivian Chaco. The viscacha, a longtailed, rabbitlike creature, spends most of its time huddled under rocks in the highlands.

The tracks of puma, native throughout the Americas, are occasionally seen in remote mountain ranges and in the Amazonian regions, but the elusive character of this species means there's little chance of spotting one without mounting a special expedition.

Rarer still, but present in national parks and remote regions, are jaguars, maned wolves, giant anteaters and spectacled bears. These animals can be seen in the Parque Nacional Noel Kempff Mercado.

Amateur birdwatchers should get their binoculars out on *South American Birds: A Photographic Aid to Identification* by John Stewart. Experts will want to spot Jon Fjeldsa's *Birds of the High Andes*.

The Andean condor, the world's heaviest bird of prey, has a 3m wingspan and can effortlessly drag a 20kg carcass.

GOLDEN OPPORTUNITY

When a team of researchers from the Wildlife Conservation Society, led by biologist Dr Robert Wallace, discovered a new species of titi monkey in the park, they came up with a novel idea. As discoverers of the species, they had the rights to name it (it was spotted in 2000, but proceedings were formalized in 2005). Wallace and his team decided to auction the rights to the name, with all proceeds going to Fundesnap, a nonprofit foundation which protects the monkeys' habitat in Madidi National Park. The lucky winner? An online Canadian casino which paid $650,000 for the rights to name the monkey *callicebus avrei palatti* (Golden Palace).

Plants

Because of its enormous range of altitudes, Bolivia enjoys a wealth and diversity of flora rivaled only by its Andean neighbors.

The solstices are important dates for the people of the Andes. Winter (21 June) controls the agriculture and is when the earth is prepared; spring (21 September) is seed-sowing time, and summer (December 21) sees the start of the cropping season.

In the overgrazed highlands, the only remaining vegetable species are those with some defense against grazing livestock or those that are unsuitable for firewood. Much of what does grow in the highlands grows slowly and is endangered. While there's remarkably little forest above 3000m elevation, the rare dwarf *queñua* trees live as high as 5300m. The uncommon giant *Puya raimondii* century plant is found only in Bolivia and southern Peru.

The lower elevations of the temperate highland hills and valleys support vegetation similar to that of Spain or California. Most of southeastern Bolivia is covered by a nearly impenetrable thicket of cactus and thorn scrub, which erupts into colorful bloom in the spring.

The moist upper slopes of the Yungas are characterized by dwarf forest. Further down the slopes is the cloud forest, where the trees grow larger and the vegetation thicker.

Northern Bolivia's lowlands are characterized by true rainforest dotted with vast soaking wetlands and open savannas. The Amazon Basin contains the richest botanical diversity on earth with thousands of endemic species.

NATIONAL PARKS & RESERVES

Bolivia has protected 18% of its total land by declaring 66 parks, reserves and protected areas under what is known as the Sistema Nacional de Áreas Protegidas (SNAP). Although many are just lines drawn on a map, they are home to much of Bolivia's most amazing landscapes and wildlife. The administrative body **Servicio Nacional de Areas Protegidas** (Sernap; Map pp72-3; ☎ 2-243-4420/72; www.sernap.gov.bo, in Spanish; Edificio Full Office, Loayza btwn Mariscal Santa Cruz & Camacho, La Paz) manages 22 national protected areas. Their website has a good overview of each area.

The national flower of Bolivia is the *kantuta*; not only is it aesthetically beautiful, but it reflects the color of the country's national flag.

There have been major changes to Sernap's management recently, with the ousting of one director in favor of an indigenous director, Adrian Nogales. It seems that the idea is to encourage local involvement and co-management of protected areas in an effort to attract tourists to a community-based, ecotourism experience, as well as to produce commercially viable natural products, including medicinal patents. If this works – as has been the case with the success stories of the San José community in Parque Nacional Madidi (p341), and the Izoceño (Guaraní) people in Parque Nacional Kaa-Iya del Gran Chaco (who have co-administered the park since it's inception in 1995; see p327) – then results may be encouraging. On the other hand, should nongovernment organizations (NGOs) and private tourism enterprises feel alienated from the process, it could be detrimental to the communities, the environment and beyond. Things can change overnight, however, so much may have happened on the green front by the time you read this.

ENVIRONMENTAL ISSUES

Bolivian environmental problems are increasing rapidly and, while these have not yet reached apocalyptic proportions, NGOs and environmentalists are concerned that they are not being accompanied by the necessary measures to maintain a sound ecological balance.

Parque Nacional Amboró is under threat by human encroachment and slash-and-burn farming techniques.

While Bolivia lacks the population pressures of Brazil, it is promoting indiscriminate colonization and development of its lowlands. In the past decades, settlers have continued to leave the highlands to clear lowland forest and build homesteads. Slash-and-burn agricultural techniques (see the boxed text p48), overgrazing and soil erosion all serve to create

NATIONAL PARKS, RESERVES & PROTECTED AREAS

Twenty-two national parks, reserves and protected areas administered by **Servicio Nacional de Areas Protegidas (Sernap)** are officially functioning, although in reality some have better infrastructure than others. The following parks vary in their levels of isolation and infrastructure, including the activities on offer. Consult relevant chapters and guides before heading visiting these protected areas on your own.

Protected Area	Features	Activities	Best Time to Visit	Page
Amboró	Home to the rare spectacled bear, jaguars and an astonishing variety of bird life	Hiking, wildlife, waterfalls, endangered species	Any	p307
Apolobamba	Extremely remote park on the Peruvian border, home to typical Andean fauna	Trekking, climbing	May-Sep	p162
Carrasco	Extension to Amboró protects remaining stands of cloud forest in the volatile Chapare region	Bird-watching, hiking, tours	Any	p334
Kaa-Iya	Largest park in Latin America with vast wetlands and few tourist services	Plant- & wildlife-watching	Mar-Oct	p327
Madidi	Protects a wide range of wildlife habitats and over 900 officially registered bird species	Hiking, boating, plant- & wildlife-watching, swimming	Mar-Oct	p341
Noel Kempff Mercado	Remote & spectacular with Amazonian flora & fauna, waterfalls	Hiking, mountain biking, canoeing, wildlife-watching	Mar-Oct	p354
Sajama	Adjoins Chile's magnificent Parque Nacional Lauca; contains Volcán Sajama (6542m), Bolivia's highest peak.	Climbing & mountaineering, hot springs, trekking	Jun-Sep	p179
Torotoro	Rock formations with dinosaur tracks, caves and ancient ruins	Paleontology, hiking, caving (spelunking)	Apr-Oct	p236
Tunari	Within hiking distance of Cochabamba, features the Lagunas de Huarahuara & lovely mountain scenery	Climbing	Apr-Nov	p230
Reserva Nacional de Fauna Andina Eduardo Avaroa	A highlight of the Southwest Circuit tour; wildlife-rich lagoons, pink flamingos, endangered species	4WD tour of Southwest Circuit, climbing	Mar-Oct	p191

serious problems in many areas. In the Madidi National Park, there have been ongoing hydrocarbon exploration and illegal logging in the area outside the park. There is also the possible threat of a new road that will bisect the park.

Further east, particularly around the Santa Cruz and Beni departments, soybean crops continue to cause havoc. Huge tracts of land are cleared for soybean agriculture, without crop rotation programs to ensure the soil can recover. Similarly, cattle ranches are responsible for the destruction of areas of forest. Tracts of the Amazon are being exploited by both companies and individuals to fulfill international demand.

Many water supplies used for irrigation and drinking are polluted, particularly those around La Paz; much of this ends up in the Amazon Basin. Glacial retreat on peaks is an ongoing issue.

EL CHAQUEO: THE BIG SMOKE

Each dry season, from July through September, Bolivia's skies fill with a thick pall of smoke, obscuring the air, occasionally canceling flights, aggravating allergies and causing respiratory strife, especially in the lowlands. Illimani is a blurry blob against the La Paz skyline, visitors to Lake Titicaca are deprived of spectacular views and there is the odd aviation problem.

This is all the result of *el chaqueo*, the slashing and burning of the savannas (and some rainforest) for agricultural and grazing land – including cattle ranches and soy bean crops. A prevailing notion is that the rising smoke forms rain clouds and ensures good rains for the coming season. In reality the hydrological cycle, which depends on transpiration from the forest canopy, is interrupted by the deforestation, resulting in diminished rainfall. In extreme cases deforested zones may be sunbaked into wastelands. The World Bank estimates that each year Bolivia loses thousands of hectares of forest in this manner.

Ranchers in the Beni department have long set fire to the savannas annually to encourage the sprouting of new grass. Now, however, the most dramatic defoliation occurs along the highways in the country's east. In the mid-1980s this was largely virgin wilderness accessible only by river or air, but the new roads connecting the region to La Paz have turned it into a free-for-all. Forest is consumed by expanding cattle ranches; only charred tree stumps remain. Although the burned vegetable matter initially provides rich nutrients for crops, those nutrients aren't replenished. After two or three years the land is exhausted and takes 15 years to become productive again. That's too long for most farmers to wait; most just pull up stakes and burn larger areas.

Ironically all this burning is prohibited by Bolivian forestry statutes, but such laws are impossible to enforce in an area as vast as the Bolivian lowlands. When relatively few people were farming the lowlands, the *chaqueo*'s effects were minimal, but given Bolivia's annual population growth rate of 1.6%, the country must feed an additional 140,000 people each year. Because much of this population growth is rural, more farmers' children are looking for their own lands.

Although the long-term implications aren't yet known (hint: take a look at the devastated Brazilian states of Acre and Rondônia), the Bolivian government has implemented a program aimed at teaching forest-fire control and encouraging lowland farmers to minimize the *chaqueo* in favor of alternatives that don't drain the soil of nutrients. Despite these efforts, it seems that the *chaqueo* will be a fact of life in Bolivia for many years to come.

Many nonprofit groups are working on countrywide environmental conservation efforts. Contact the following for further information.

Armonía (www.birdbolivia.com) Everything you need to know about Bolivian birding and bird conservation.

Conservación Internacional (CI; www.conservation.org.bo) Promotes community-based ecotourism and biodiversity conservation.

Fundación Amigos de la Naturaleza (FAN; www.fan-bo.org, in Spanish; km7.5, Carretera a Samaipata, Santa Cruz) Works in Parques Nacionales Amboró & Noel Kempff Mercado.

Protección del Medioambiente del Tarija (Prometa; www.prometa.org) Works in Gran Chaco, Sama, Tariquía and El Corvalán reserves and Parque Nacional Aguaragüe (p291).

Trópico (www.tropico.org) Works with communities in areas of conservation, sustainable development and environmental and resource management.

Wildlife Conservation Society (WCS; www.wcs.org) Works with local institutions and communities in applied wildlife research, natural resource management, and land use planning and administration through integrated landscape conservation programs in the Madidi and Kaa-Iya regions.

The Andean sacred animals include the condor, titi, puma, guinea pig, llama and frog.

Outdoors

Bolivia is all about getting breathless. If the beauty hasn't already taken your breath away, then the high altitude might, at least when you first arrive. Then there is the outdoor fun; the country offers an awesome mix of activities that get the lungs working and the heart pumping. Adventure companies are entering the market faster than a downhill bike plunge, offering a great mix of trekking, climbing and mountain biking activities. Adventurers can opt for hikes of all levels, from climbs up snow-capped mountains in the Cordillera Real, to low-key wanders along Inca trails or through the jungle. Do you want to retrace the steps of Butch Cassidy and the Sundance Kid on horseback? Cruise in a 4WD across deserts? Shoot down a river in a raft or tube? No problem: it's all here, plus more; basic skiing, wildlife-watching and even canopying are yours for the doing.

HIKING & TREKKING

Hiking and trekking are arguably the most rewarding Andean activities. Bolivia rivals Nepal in trekking potential, but has only relatively recently been discovered by enthusiasts. Some of the most popular hikes and treks in Bolivia begin near La Paz, traverse the Cordillera Real along ancient Inca routes and end in the Yungas. These include the well-known, and well-used, Choro, Takesi and Yunga Cruz treks. Sorata is a trekker's dream-come-true, with a variety of trails, from don't-leave-home-without-a-machete type hikes – the **Mapiri Trail** (p153) amongst them – to more pleasant walks on Inca trails. The **Área Natural de Manejo Integrado Nacional (Anmin) Protegida Apolobamba** (p162) is becoming more popular for medium-standard trekking, including the four- to five-day **Lagunillas to Agua Blanca trek** (p163), thanks to improved access from La Paz and a growing number of accommodations options.

National parks are hikers' paradises, with opportunities in **Parque Nacional & Área de Uso Múltiple Amboró** (p307) and, for anyone who makes it there, in **Parque Nacional Noel Kempff Mercado** (p354). Bird-watching and endemic plants are just part of the magic.

Less hardcore trekkers can enjoy the cultural and historical sites and hot springs around **Cordillera de los Frailes** (p254).

Muggings and robberies continue to be reported in some regions, so be sure to inquire locally about the safety of trails before heading out.

See Lonely Planet's *Trekking in the Central Andes* for more detailed information.

In 1925, Colonel Percy Fawcett disappeared, searching for 'the lost city' of the Incas. Keen treasure hunters should seek out Exploration Fawcett *by the man himself, Lt Col PH Fawcett.*

MOUNTAINEERING & CLIMBING

Climbing in Bolivia is an exercise in extremes – in common with the country itself. In the dry southern winter (May to October) temperatures may fluctuate as much as 105°F in a single day. Once you're acclimatized to the Altiplano's relatively thin air (you'll need at least a week), there are still 2500m of even thinner air lurking above.

A plus for climbers is the access to mountains; although public transportation may not always be available, roads pass within easy striking distance of many fine peaks.

The most accessible and spectacular climbing in the country is along the 160km-long Cordillera Real northeast of La Paz. Six of its peaks rise above 6000m and there are many more gems in the 5000m range. Because of the altitude, glaciers and ice or steep snow, few of the peaks are 'walk-ups,' but some are within the capability of the average climber, and many can be done

A useful website for climbers' logs and accounts on climbs in the Andes is www.andeshandbook.cl.

RESPONSIBLE TREKKING

To help preserve the ecology and beauty of Bolivia, consider the following tips when trekking.

- Carry out all your rubbish. Okay, so many tracks in Bolivia are already littered, but this doesn't mean that you should contribute to it. Don't overlook easily forgotten items, such as silver paper, orange peel, cigarette butts and plastic wrappers.

- Never bury your rubbish: digging disturbs soil and ground cover and encourages erosion. Buried rubbish will likely be dug up by animals, who may be injured or poisoned by it. It may also take years to decompose.

- Contamination of water sources by human feces can lead to the transmission of all sorts of nasties. Where there is a toilet, please use it. Where there is none, bury your waste. Dig a small hole 15cm (6in) deep and at least 100m (320ft) from any watercourse. Cover the waste with soil and a rock. In snow, dig down to the soil.

- Don't use detergents or toothpaste in or near watercourses, even if they are biodegradable.

- Hillsides and mountain slopes, especially at high altitudes, are prone to erosion. Stick to existing trails and avoid short cuts.

- Don't depend on open fires for cooking. The cutting of wood for fires in popular trekking areas can cause rapid deforestation. Cook on a light-weight kerosene, alcohol or Shellite (white gas) stove and avoid those powered by disposable butane gas canisters.

- Do not feed the wildlife as this can lead to animals becoming dependent on handouts, to unbalanced populations and to disease.

- Always seek permission to camp from landowners or villagers.

For further information, contact **Servicio Nacional de Áreas Protegidas** (Sernap; Map pp72-3; ☎ 02-243-4420/243-4472; www.sernap.gov.bo; Loayza, Edificio Full Office, btwn Mariscal Santa Cruz & Camacho, La Paz).

---

by beginners with a competent guide. **Huayna Potosí** (p157) is one of the most popular climbs for nonprofessionals, but be aware that although on the La Paz agency circuit, it's no walk (or climb) in the park! La Paz operators also take climbs up the magnificent **Volcán Sajama** (p179), Bolivia's highest peak.

Around **Cordillera Quimsa Cruz** (p165) there are a variety of lesser known climbing opportunities. **Volcán Illimani** (p158) is for serious climbing expeditions and popular among advanced climbing groups.

The dangers of Bolivian climbing are due to ill-equipped or poorly trained guides, the altitude and the difficulties in mounting any sort of rescue. Mountaineering insurance is essential to cover the high costs of rescue and to ensure medical evacuation out of the country in the event of a serious accident. Note that helicopters cannot fly above 5000m. There is a small but potentially serious avalanche danger. For information on dealing with potentially fatal altitude problems, it's wise to carry the practical and easily transportable *Mountain Sickness*, by Peter Hackett, whenever you ascend to high altitude. See p396 for information regarding altitude sickness.

The **Asociación de Guías de Montaña** (☎ 2-235-0334; La Paz) is an association of registered mountain guides. For climbing opportunities, contact **Club de Montañismo Halcones** (contact Juan Pablo ☎ 2-524-4082; Oruro) or **Club Andino Boliviano** (Map pp72-3; ☎ 2-231-2875; México 1638, La Paz).

> Before you head off on your own into the Amazonian jungle, take heed from Yossi Ginsberg's *Back from Tuichi: the Harrowing Life and Death Story of Survival in the Amazon Rainforest.*

MAPS

Historically, maps of Bolivian climbing areas have been poor in quality and difficult to obtain. Even now, elevations of peaks are murky, with reported altitudes varying as much as 600m – it seems that the rumor that Ancohuma is taller than Aconcagua won't die.

Maps are available in La Paz, Cochabamba and Santa Cruz through Los Amigos del Libro and some book shops. In La Paz try the trekking agents and tourist shops along Sagárnaga, or watch for ambulatory vendors prowling the Prado.

The *Travel Map of Bolivia,* one of the best country maps, and *New Map of the Cordillera Real,* which shows mountains, roads and pre-Hispanic routes, are published by O'Brien Cartographics and are available at various gringo hangouts, including the postcard kiosks within the La Paz central post office.

Government 1:50,000 topographical and specialty sheets are available from the Instituto Geográfico Militar (IGM), which has offices in most major cities, including two offices in La Paz (p65). These sheets cover roughly two-thirds of the country, with notable exceptions including the areas north of Sorata, the Cordillera Apolobamba and Parque Nacional Noel Kempff Mercado. Walter Guzmán Córdova has produced 1:50,000 colorful contour maps of Choro-Takesi-Yunga Cruz, Mururata-Illimani, Huayna Potosí-Condoriri and Sajama, but those other than the Choro-Takesi-Yunga Cruz map are in short supply. The Deutscher Alpenverein (German Alpine Club) produces the excellent and accurate 1:50,000 maps *Alpenvereinskarte Cordillera Real Nord (Illampu),* which includes the Sorata area, and *Alpenvereinskarte Cordillera Real Süd (Illimani),* which centers on Illimani.

> The highest mountain in Bolivia is Sajama at 6542m, followed by Ancohuma at 6427m and Illampu at 6362m.

GUIDEBOOKS

The best mountaineering guide is *Bolivia – A Climbing Guide,* by Yossi Brain; the late author worked as a climbing guide in La Paz and also served as secretary of the Club Andino Boliviano. *Los Andes de Bolivia,* by Alain Mesili, was recently reprinted in Spanish and an English translation is forthcoming.

AGENCIES & GUIDES

Many travel agencies in La Paz and larger cities organize climbing and trekking trips in the Cordillera Real and other areas (see p389 for a list of recommended tour companies). Not all, however, are all they claim to be. Some guides have gotten lost, several have died, and others have practiced less than professional tactics, such as stringing 10 or more climbers on the same rope. Always do your research and go with professionally accredited guides. UIAGM (the IFMGA and IVBV equivalent; see www.uiaa.ch/index .aspx and www.ivbv.info/en/index.asp). **Asoguiatur** (asoguiatur22@hotmail.com; Plaza Alonso de Mendoza, La Paz) provides independent advice on member guides and is a meeting point for guides themselves.

> Sorata Guides & Porters Association (Map p148; ☎ /fax 213-6698; guiasorata@hotmail.com; Jurídica 159) can arrange treks in Sorata.

Specialist agencies can do as much or as little as you want – from just organizing transportation to a full service with guide, cook, mules, porters, a full itinerary and so forth. Trekking guides generally charge US$25 to US$35 per day, plus their food. Mountain guides cost US$50 to US$60 per day plus food. In addition you need your food, technical equipment and clothing and – often the most expensive part of any trip – transportation to and from the base camp or the start of the trek to the mountain. Some people do resort to public transportation or hitchhiking on *camiones* (flatbed trucks), but this requires more time and logistics.

In addition to the agencies, mountain-guide information is available from the Club Andino Boliviano (p78) which is mainly a ski organization but also has a number of top climbers as members.

MOUNTAIN BIKING

Bolivia is blessed with some of the most dramatic mountain-biking terrain in the world, seven months every year of near-perfect weather and relatively easy access to mountain ranges, magnificent lakes, pre-Hispanic ruins and trails, and a myriad of ecozones connected by an extensive network of footpaths and jeep roads.

The Bolivian Andes are full of long and thrilling mountain-biking descents, as well as challenging touring possibilities. One of the world's longest downhill rides will take you from Sajama National Park (p179) down to the Chilean coast at Arica. In the dry season you can even tackle the mostly level roads of the vast Amazon lowlands (though hot, dusty and full of insects). **Parque Nacional Noel Kempff Mercado** (p354) also offers the chance to explore on a treadly.

Some rides from La Paz can be done by riders of any experience level. There are more combinations than a bike lock: trails follow Inca roads, tropical tracks, jeep roads and scree chutes. The best known (but not necessarily the best ride for serious riders as there's lots of traffic and dust) is the thrilling 3600m trip down the **World's Most Dangerous Road** (p78) from La Cumbre to Coroico. Another popular route near La Paz is the lush **Zongo Valley ride** (p130) which can be started at the 5300m Chacaltaya.

The town of Sorata is emerging as the mountain-bike mecca of Bolivia, with scores of single track and jeep road rides near town, including a combination bike-and-boat trip from **Sorata to Rurrenabaque** (see boxed text below). For the hardcore rider, scree chutes to biker-built single track and jump zones abound. Every September Sorata is host to the longest downhill race on a hand-built course, the Jach'a Avalancha (Grand Avalanche) Mountain Bike race. Other epic descents begin in Sorata and head into the hinterland of the Cordillera Muñecas, or start in Copacabana and La Paz and head to Sorata. For descriptions of these routes, see p130.

More and more travelers are taking up the cycling challenge and heading on two wheels from the north of the country to the south, or vice versa. Those with their own bikes need to consider several factors. During part of the rainy season, particularly December to February, some roads become mired in muck, and heavy rain can greatly reduce visibility, creating dangerous conditions. Also worth noting is Bolivia's lack of spare parts and shortage

Each year the Jach'a Avalancha (Grand Avalanche) Mountain Bike race is held in Sorata, attracting local and international participants. Contact Andean Biking (Map p148; ☎ 712-76685; www.andeanbiking.com; Main Plaza, Sorata).

GO WITH THE FLOW

Keen adventurers can experience a double-action whammy – a full-on two-day cycling adventure, followed by three days of floating down a river on a riveting rafting expedition. The cycling component is an exciting 4000m descent on single track and trails from Sorata to Charazani. At Charazani you construct a *balsa de goma* (tube raft with wooden platform) to float downstream on either the Tuichi, Kamata or Aten rivers. The 10-day Tuichi trip heads through the heart of the glorious Madidi National Park, where there are jungle trips, community visits at San José and fishing and swimming opportunities aplenty. Accommodations for all trips is camping in tents on the river banks. This is a class-IV river in one of the most remote and wild areas in South America, so experienced, knowledgeable and responsible guides are vital, as your life is in their hands.

For those more or less keen on the people-powered component of the trip, itineraries can be custom-made; the cycling section can be completed in 4WD and you can choose the length of your trip.

Andean Biking (Map p148; ☎ 712-76685; www.andeanbiking.com; Main Plaza, Sorata) also offers other action-packed trips which are designed to get you off the gringo trail and into the wild areas of the Cordilleras Real, Muñecas and Apolobamba.

of experienced mechanics. Comprehensive repair kits are essential. In the Southern Altiplano and Uyuni regions, water is very scarce; you must be able to carry at least two days worth of water in some places.

4WD

Heading out in 4WD vehicles is becoming an increasingly popular activity. It allows you access to places that are tricky to get to and, although sometimes on the pricier side, may be the only feasible way of visiting a region. As well as the standard Southwest Circuit tours (setting off from Uyuni, Tupiza or La Paz), you can cruise out to the *quebradas* (ravines or washes, usually dry) and beyond around **Tupiza** (p201), visit the **Tarabuco market** (p253, from Sucre; p247) or the **Inca ruins** near Cochabamba (p232).

Tours in 4WDs are a great way to enter some of the country's national parks. Current trips include around **Parques Nacionales Torotoro** (from Cochabamba; p239), **Lauca** (from Arica, Chile; p183) and **Sajama** (from La Paz; see p389), or into the **Cordillera de los Frailes** (from Sucre; p247).

For those keener to arrange trips themselves, consider hiring a driver. This can be an efficient and good-value way of seeing specific areas, especially if you are in a group. See p387 for a list of drivers.

> Before heading out on any adventure trips, make sure you acclimatize in either La Paz or Lake Titicaca. See the Health chapter for advice (p396).

WHITEWATER RAFTING & KAYAKING

One of Bolivia's greatest secrets is the number of whitewater rivers that drain the eastern slopes of the Andes between the Cordillera Apolobamba and the Chapare. Here, avid rafters and kayakers can enjoy thrilling descents. While access will normally require long drives and/or treks – and considerable expense if done independently – there are a few fine rivers that are relatively accessible.

Some La Paz tour agencies can organize day trips on the **Río Coroico** (p132). Other options include the **Río Unduavi** (p146), and numerous wild **Chapare rivers** (p333). Wilderness canoeing is offered in **Parques Nacional Noel Kempff Mercado** (p356) and **Isiboro-Sécure** (p335).

A more gentle but fun rush in the Chuquisaca region is a float downriver in rubber inner-tubes. This trip is often coupled with mountain biking (p247). One of the greatest thrills along the same biathlon idea, is to cruise 4000m downhill on mountain bike to Mapiri and then raft your way for several days, camping en route, to Rurrenabaque (opposite).

HORSEBACK RIDING

For some, a horse saddle sure beats a bus seat. It's a great way to absorb the sights, sounds and smells of a country. Horseback-riding trips are a new and increasingly popular way to see inaccessible wilderness areas. The best place to get your butt into a saddle is in Tupiza, former territory of **Butch Cassidy and the Sundance Kid** (p199). Here, you can bounce, cruise and walk your way through the areas in triathlon tours, where horses, 4WD and foot are the methods of transportation. You get to see the multicolored desertscapes, *quebradas* and cacti-potted countryside. Other pleasant options to trot are through cloud forest in **Coroico** (p132), around La Paz (see Calacoto Tours, p389) and in **Reserva Biosférica del Beni** (p344).

> Bolivia is the 12th most biodiverse country on earth with 2194 known species of amphibians, birds, mammals and reptiles, and more than 14,000 species of plants.

WILDLIFE-WATCHING

Bolivia is the Botswana of South America. Fauna and flora fanatics are spoilt for choice in this extraordinary country; world-class wildlife-watching abounds. The diversity of intact habitats throughout the country account for the huge number of surviving species. Yet surprisingly, tourists have taken a while to catch on to this natural paradise.

The Chacaltaya glacier in Bolivia is expected to completely melt within 15 years if present trends continue.

Parque Nacional Madidi (p341), for example, harbors 1200 bird species, the world's most dense concentration of avifauna species. It is home to wildlife endemic to all Bolivian ecosystems, from tropical rainforest and tropical savanna to cloud forest and alpine tundra. Birding hot spots include the highlands around La Paz and Cochabamba, **Parques Nacional Amboró** (p307) and **Noel Kempff Mercado** (p354), and the **Reserva Biosférica del Beni** (p344).

Agencies – often run by scientists or environmentalists – offering nature trips run out of Santa Cruz, Cochabamba and Samaipata and, to a lesser extent, La Paz. Contact **Asociación Armonía** (www.birdbolivia.com), the Bolivian partner of BirdLife International, for further birding information. Other organizations with birding knowledge include **Fundación Amigos de la Naturaleza** (FAN; ☎ 3-355-6800; www.fan-bo.org, in Spanish; km 7.5, Carretera a Samaipata, Santa Cruz) and **Michael Blendinger Tours** (Map p312; ☎ /fax 3-944-6227; www.discoveringbolivia.com; Bolívar s/n, Samaipata).

OTHER ACTIVITIES

Golf and **tennis** buffs looking for some high-altitude practice must join a club, since public facilities do not exist. For tennis, **racquetball** and **swimming** in a lovely setting, try the Strongest Club at the Achumani Complejo in Zona Sur in La Paz (take any *micro* or minibus labeled 'Achumani Complejo'). Keen golfers can get their fill at **La Paz Golf Club** (Map pp86-7; ☎ 274-5124/5462; www .lapazgolfclub.com; Mallasa, Zona Sur), the world's highest 18-hole course (3318m); Oruro's course is much higher but lacks grass. Green fees are around US$70 and a caddie and rental clubs are US$10 each.

Paragliding is a new activity, so should be done with care – not all local guides are experts of years' standing (or flying!). Most paragliding is done around Sucre (p247) via Cochabamba (p225).

Other hot spots – and far more relaxing ones – are the many **termas (hot springs)** which bubble away in various parts of the country. You don't have to go to the ends of the earth to immerse yourself in this less energetic activity – there are springs just outside of La Paz (p105); Potosí (p274), Charanazi (p160), Chaqui (p274), Talula (p256), San Javier (p320) and Sajama (p179).

Food & Drink

Food-lovers will be well sated in Bolivia. While the Bolivian national cuisine might not have an international profile, it deserves one, not least for its admirable versatility derived from its staple foods. Most Bolivian cuisine uses the freshest of fresh, locally grown ingredients, and unlike many other countries, Bolivia still produces a large share of its food. While pesticide and synthetic fertilizers are on the rise, many growers still cultivate with age-old practices that minimize the use of these substances. We can thank the central Andes for our potatoes and peanuts – it's the center of origin for these important crop plants.

Bolivian diets strongly reflect regional, ecological and cultural diversity – ingredients are particular to where you are. Altiplano fare tends to be starchy and loaded with carbohydrates, while in the tropics, *charque* (jerky), rice and tropical fruits are popular. In the lowlands, fish, fruit and vegetables feature more prominently.

Meat invariably dominates and is usually accompanied by rice, a starchy tuber (usually potato or oca) and shredded lettuce. Often the whole affair is drowned by *llajhua* (fiery tomato-based salsa). The soups are a specialty and must be consumed as a local does – watch how much *llajhua* they do (or don't) add. Learning how to consume Bolivian dishes is integral to their enjoyment.

In the cities, sophisticated world cuisine has well and truly hit the market; many restaurants have created delicious fusions of international dishes and local cuisine. Asian and European restaurants are increasingly prevalent and popular.

STAPLES & SPECIALTIES

Desayuno (breakfast) consists of little more than coffee and a bread roll, and is often followed by a mid-morning street snack such as a *salteña, tucumana* or empanada.

Lunch is the main meal of the day. Most restaurants offer an *almuerzo* (set lunch), which consists of soup, a main course and tea or coffee; sometimes salad and dessert too. Depending on the class of the restaurant, *almuerzos* cost anywhere from US$1 to US$4; meals from the à la carte menu cost roughly twice as much. *La cena,* the evening meal, is served à la carte. Many highlanders prefer a light *te* (tea) instead of an evening meal.

Snacks

Salteñas, tucumanas or empanadas are football-shaped and consist of a pastry shell stuffed with juicy, spiced mixtures of meat and vegetables. Each has a distinct flavor and texture.

Originating from Salta (Argentina), *salteñas* are crammed with beef or chicken, olives, eggs, potatoes, onions, peas, carrots, raisins and sundry spices. The best ones are juicy and dribble all over the place. The *tucumana* has a puffier pastry shell which is filled with a piquant mix of egg, potatoes, chicken and onions. *Salteñas* tend to be sweeter while *tucumanas* pack a spicy punch. Empanadas have a slightly more bready encasement that is sometimes deep-fried rather than baked.

Other scrumptious street snacks include *tamales* (cornmeal dough pockets filled with spiced beef, vegetables, potatoes and/or cheese) and *humintas* (or *humitas;* cornmeal filled with cheese, aniseed and cheese and baked in the oven or boiled). For a hearty snack, try *anticuchos* (grilled cow heart on skewers), served at markets or street stalls.

Cook up a Bolivian storm – browse www .boliviaweb.com/recipes for mouth-watering Bolivian blends of flavors and dishes.

Bolivia is the center of origin for many crops including quinoa, *cañawa,* oca and potato.

The South American Table by Maria Baez Kijac includes hundreds of recipes from Latin America and is flavored with a touch of history as well.

Soup

A large bowl of *sopa* – whether vegetarian or meat-based – is the start of every great Bolivian meal. Two of the most popular soups are the delicious *maní* (peanut) soup and *chairo* (a hearty soup, using many Andean ingredients including *chuños* – freeze-dried potatoes – meat and vegetables, and often topped with crispy fried pigskin). *Chupe*, *cha'que* and *lawa* (aka *lagua*) are the most common thick stew-like soups. Quinoa and *maní* are often used to thicken broth.

Quinoa was baptized 'seed mother' by the Incas. It is renowned not only for its taste and use in cooking, especially soups, but as a high source of protein.

Meat & Fish

Llamas, alpacas and guinea pigs are the only animals domesticated in the Andes for meat production and are generally consumed during feasts and special occasions. Beef, chicken and fish are the backbone to nearly all Bolivian dishes; *carne de chancho* (pork) is considered a delicacy. *Campesinos* (sustainable farmers) eat more *cordero* or *carnero* (mutton), *cabrito* or *chivito* (goat) or llama.

Beef is typically *asado* or *parrillada* (barbecued or grilled) in various cuts (*lomo*, *brazuelo* and *churrasco*). Jerked beef, llama or other red meat is called *charque*. On the Altiplano it's served with *choclo* (corn), corn cob, or *mote* (rehydrated dried kernels); in the lowlands it's served with yuca or mashed plantain. In the Beni, beef may be served as *pacumutus*, enormous chunks of grilled meat accompanied by yuca, onions and other trimmings.

Pollo (chicken) is either *frito* (fried), *al spiedo* or *a la broaster* (cooked on a spit) or *asado* or *dorado* (broiled).

On the Altiplano the most deservedly popular *pescado* (fish) is *trucha* (trout) and *pejerrey* (kingfish), introduced species from Lake Titicaca. The lowlands have a wide variety of other freshwater fish; *surubí*, a catfish caught throughout the lowlands, is arguably the best of the lot. Try to find out which river your lowland fish might have come from, as some rivers may have been polluted with mercury cast-offs from mining. Fish from the Pilcomayo River, for example, is considered to be contaminated and unfit for consumption.

Potato-lovers may enjoy consuming a weighty tome The Potatoes of Bolivia: Their Breeding Value and Evolutionary Relationships by JG Hawkes, an indepth treaty to the humble spud.

Tubers

Tuberous plants are the bulk of the Bolivian diet and are native to the region. There are over 200 potato varieties. C*huños* or *tunta* (freeze-dried potatoes) are rehydrated, cooked and eaten as snacks or with meals. Although bland on their own, in soups such as *chairo* they can be delicious. They are also a testament to the resourcefulness of Andean peoples who developed the complicated freeze-drying process to be able to survive the cold and dry Andean winters. The raw potatoes are left out for several nights to freeze, after which they're stepped upon to squeeze out the water and are then set in the sun to dry further.

Ocas are delicate, purple, potato-like tubers, which taste best roasted or boiled. In the lowlands the potato and its relatives are replaced by plantain or the root of the yuca (manioc or cassava).

The white and pink pasankalla (corn puffs) that you see in giant bags, may be chewy for some, but they use an age-old and sophisticated food preservation technique.

Cereals & Pulses

Other common foods include *choclo*, a large-kernel corn (maize) that's ubiquitous on the Altiplano. *Habas*, similar to the domesticated fava beans, and are eaten roasted or added to stews. In Cochabamba, ask for the delectable *habas con quesillo* (beans with cheese)

Quinoa, a unique Andean grain, is massively high in protein, and is used to make flour and to thicken stews. Recent research has shown that it's the only edible plant that contains all essential amino acids in the same proportions as milk, making it especially appealing to vegans. It's deservedly experiencing a resurgence these days – look for quinoa cookies, cakes, chocolate, croquettes and bread.

Cañawa is another high-protein grain and is roasted and ground into a powder.

Fruit

Many deliciously juicy South American fruits are cultivated in Bolivia. Most notable are the *chirimoya* (custard apple), *tuna* (prickly pear cactus) and *maracuya* and *tumbo* passion fruits.

In the lowlands the range of exotic tropical fruits defies middle-latitude expectations. Among the more unusual are the human-hand shaped *ambaiba;* the small, round, green-and-purple *guaypurú;* the spiny yellow *ocoro;* the lemon-like *guapomo;* the bean-like *cupesi;* the *marayau,* which resembles a bunch of giant grapes; the currant-like *nui;* the scaly onion-looking *sinini;* and the stomach-shaped *paquio.*

> The humble soybean is one of Bolivia's most important exports, but (sadly for vegetarians) is one of the most environmentally unfriendly crops to grow, causing havoc to the Bolivian landscape.

DRINKS
Nonalcoholic Drinks

The most common international drinks like coffee, soda and bottled water are widely available. But don't leave the country without trying any of the local specialty drinks; many are gastronomic highlights.

Api and *mate de coca* are heated morning-time treats. *Api* is made from a ground purple corn while *mate de coca* is an infusion of water and dried coca leaves. A must try is a *mocochinche*, a sugary peach drink made from boiled cane sugar, cinnamon sticks and featuring a floating dried peach (another Andean food preservation marvel). Also popular are the sweet and nutty *tostada*, the corn-based *horchata* and *licuados* (fruit-shakes blended with water or milk).

Throughout most towns and cities juice vendors ply their trade from their fruit carts. For a mere US$0.30 or US$0.40 you can enjoy an orange or grapefruit taste sensation.

Alcoholic Drinks

When Bolivians gather for recreational drinking – beer or harder – they intend to get plastered. Remember altitude increases both froth and effect. Bolivia produces its own wines, lagers and local concoctions of varying qualities.

Enjoyable Bolivian regional lagers include the fizzy and strange-tasting Huari, the good but rather nondescript Paceña (they have also introduced a delicious dark porter), the pleasant but weak-flavored Sureña, the refreshing Taquiña, the robust Potosina, the slightly rough Ducal and the cold and tasty Tropical Extra.

> Beer poured at high altitude, generally has a frothier head. A local superstition is that the frothier your beer, the more money you have. The person with the frothiest lager head must take a pinch of the froth and put it in their pocket.

SPIRITS FOR THE SPIRITS

The world of the original Andean inhabitants is populated by hosts of well-respected supernatural beings, the *apus* and *achachilas* (mountain spirits believed to be ancestors of the people). They mainly pervade wild areas and are prone to both favorable behavior and fits of temper. The people believe they themselves are literally descended from the earth mother, Pachamama, who is also respected and venerated.

The spirits are taken into consideration in facets of everyday life, and certain things are done to keep on their better side. Before a person takes the first sip of alcohol from a glass, it's customary to spill a few drops on the ground as an offering, or *t'inka*, to Pachamama. This demonstrates to Pachamama that she takes precedence over her human subjects (and she likes to drink a drop, too). Alcohol is also splashed or sprinkled over homes and cars as a *cha'lla* (blessing).

Wines are fermented around Tarija and are increasingly being recognized in the world of viticulture. The best – and most expensive – is Bodega La Concepción's Cepas de Altura, from some of the world's highest vineyards, which sells for around US$10 for a 750ml bottle.

Drunk more for effect than flavor and created by fermenting corn, *chicha cochabambina* is favored by the Bolivian masses. It's produced mostly around Cochabamba, where white plastic flags on long poles indicate that the *chichería* is open for business (you can even bring your own bottle for a fill-up).

Campesinos rarely consider taste or personal health when looking for a cheap and direct route to celebration (or inebriation) – thus their willingness to swill the head-pounding *puro* or *aguardiente* (firewater). This burning, gut-wrenching stuff is essentially pure alcohol, so if you're offered a glass, you may wish to make a particularly generous offering to Pachamama (see boxed text p57).

Tarija's vines are grown at high altitude, which speeds up the maturing process of the grape. The wine producers are trying to establish whether the wine deteriorates faster due to these natural factors.

CELEBRATIONS

Bolivians love to eat and drink, and festivals and celebrations provide the perfect excuse. On the Día de los Muertos (Day of the Dead), families prepare the favorite dishes of their loved ones, along with little sweet breads with plaster-cast faces, representing their dead relatives. Very ornate and brightly iced cakes adorn cake shops and are a favorite for birthdays – the fancier the better. *Confites* are a sugar candy (surrounding coconut, dried peach or nuts) made by traditional candy makers, consumed during Carnaval time or for feasts such as Alasitas in La Paz (p80). There are several kinds of *confites*, one of which is brightly colored and not consumed, but instead is used as offerings at a *cha'lla* (blessing).

Maca, a small turnip-type vegetable, is considered the Viagra of the Andes.

WHERE TO EAT & DRINK

Larger towns and cities have a range of eateries, from family-run operations to upscale cloth-napkin restaurants. All towns have cheap food stalls in the market *comedores* (dining halls) that serve filling and tasty meals and snacks.

Disappointingly, there are a growing number of Western-style fast-food joints in the big cities – to eat in these is sometimes seen as a status symbol. Restaurants serving typical European or North American foods are found around larger hotels or in middle-class districts of larger cities. Increasingly popular in larger cities are Italian restaurants, *chifas* (Chinese restaurants), and Mexican, Swiss, and Japanese eateries. Peruvian *cervicherías* (specialized seafood restaurants) and vegetarian options are also increasing. Best of all, are the Bolivian/international restaurants, serving international dishes with a Bolivian twist, using ingredients such as quinoa and the vast range of fresh ingredients that Bolivia should be so famous for. Get your taste buds working, your juices flowing and absorb the wonderfully diverse tastes and flavors of Bolivia. ¡Buen provecho!

Much coca is sprayed with insecticide and other chemicals. There is a strong organic coca movement in Bolivia, promoting the benefits of organic coca for chewing and other consumption. Support the organic movement and seek out the organic types – experts can taste the difference.

Quick Eats

Markets and street stalls are the places for cheap, on-the-go bites and local specialties. Hygiene at some of these places isn't a top priority, so your internal plumbing may need time to adjust. You should be fine if you choose a stall that seems clean and well organized.

Confiterías and *pastelerías* sell little more than snacks and coffee. *Heladerías* (ice-cream parlors) are becoming increasingly worldly, offering pizza, pasta, doughnuts, *salteñas*, coffee specialties and even full (if bland) meals.

COOK UP A BOLIVIAN STORM – THE PLATO PACEÑO

The *plato paceño* is the result of a blend of Spanish and indigenous influence. The Spanish intro-duced lima beans, while the indigenous people added potato, corn on the cob and cheese.

Ingredients
8 fresh corn on the cobs
2.2 pounds (1 kg) peeled lima beans
8 potatoes
4 fresh *quesillos* (fresh cheese – houlumi or any cheese that can be fried is fine), sliced
¼ cup oil or butter to fry the cheese
1 cup *llajwa* (a spicy tomato and chili sauce can be used)

Preparation
Boil water in large pot. Add the corn cobs and the lima beans and boil for 25 minutes or until cooked. Add the washed potatoes and boil for another 20 minutes, or until all vegetables are cooked. In a large pan heat oil over high heat. Fry cheese slices until golden. On each plate, serve one corn on the cob, lima beans, one potato and slices of fried cheese. Add *llajwa* (or any chili or spicy sauce) if desired.

(Serves 8)

VEGETARIANS & VEGANS
Vegetarians may well be delighted by what they find on offer. Many soups are prepared with vegetables and noodles, and often *chuño*. More flexible vegetarians (who can put up with meat stock or pick meat out of a dish) will be fine. Vegans will find themselves eating a lot of potatoes in the highlands, and fresh fruits and vegetables elsewhere. Bigger cities and popular tourist areas have at least one vegetarian restaurant. The typical *plato paceño* (La Paz dish) traditionally is served without meat – just fried cheese, fresh corn and fava bean and, of course, potatoes (see the recipe above). Check first, though, as many restaurants will include a piece of meat with the dish.

Surf www.bolivia
.com/el_sabor_de
_bolivia/ (in Spanish)
for gastronomic delights
and Bolivian bites.

HABITS & CUSTOMS
Nearly everything stops from noon to at least 3pm when families get together and lull over a multihour lunch. It's the main meal of the day and no one rushes through it. *Campesinos* may eat with their fingers among family, but Bolivians in general use Western-style utensils. Tipping up to 10% is standard at upscale restaurants when service is up to snuff; locals leave small change, if anything at all, elsewhere.

EAT YOUR WORDS
Want to know a *pacumutu* from a *pique lo macho*? *Chupe* from *chaque* from *charque*? Get behind the *comida* (food) scene by getting to know the lingo. For pronunciation guidelines, see p399.

Useful Phrases
Do you have a menu in English?
¿Tienen una carta en inglés?   tye·nen oon·a *kar*·ta en een·*gles*
What do you recommend?
¿Qué me recomienda?   ke me re·ko·*myen*·da
Do you have any vegetarian dishes?
¿Tienen algún plato vegetariano?   tye·nen al·*goon* pla·to ve·khe·ta·*rya*·no

Not too spicy please.
No muy picoso/picante, por favor.   no mooy pee·*ko*·so/pee·*kan*·te, por fa·*vor*
I'll try what he/she is having.
Voy a pedir lo que el/ella pedió.   voy ah pe·*deer* lo ke ehl/eh·ya pe·dee·o
I'd like the set lunch.
Quisiera el almuerzo, por favor.   kee·*sye*·ra el al·*mwer*·so, por fa·*vor*
This food is delicious.
Esta comida está exquisita.   es·*ta* ko·*mee*·da es·*ta* eks·kee·*sit*·a
The bill (check), please.
La cuenta, por favor.   la *kwen*·ta por fa·*vor*

Food Glossary

anticuchos	an·tee·*koo*·chos	beef-heart shish-kebabs
ají	a·*hee*	chili condiments
api	a·*pee*	syrupy form of *chicha* made from sweet purple corn, lemon, cinnamon and staggering amounts of white sugar
brazuelo	bra·*zwe*·lo	shoulder
buñuelo	boo·*nwe*·lo	sticky type of doughnut dipped in sugar syrup
cabrito	ka·*bree*·to	goat
carne	*kar*·ne	beef
carne de chancho	*kar*·ne de *chan*·cho	pork
chairo	*chai*·ro	mutton or beef soup with *chuños*, potatoes and *mote*
chajchu	*chakh*·choo	beef with *chuño*, hard-boiled egg, cheese and hot red pepper sauce
chanko	*chan*·ko	chicken with yellow pepper and tomato-and-onion sauce; a Tarija specialty
chaque	cha·*ke*	like *chupe* but much thicker and contains more grain
chirimoya	chee·ree·*moy*·a	custard apple, a green scaly fruit with creamy white flesh
choclo	*chok*·lo	large-grain corn (maize)
chuños	choo·*nyos*	freeze-dried potatoes
camote	ka·*mo*·te	sweet potato
cerveza	ser·*ve*·sa	beer; Taquiña is the best, Huari the fizziest
charque	*char*·ke	jerked meat; the source of the English word 'jerky'
charque kan	*char*·ke kan	meat jerky (often llama meat) served with *choclo*, potato and boiled egg.
chicha	chee·*cha*	popular beverage that is often alcoholic and made from fermented corn; it may also be made from such ingredients as yuca, sweet potato or peanuts
chicharrón de cerdo	chee·char·*on* de ser·do	fried pork
chuflay	choo·*flay*	a blend of *singani* (a distilled grape spirit), lemon-lime soda, ice and lemon
chupe	choo·*pe*	thick meat, vegetable and grain soup with a clear broth flavored with garlic, *ají*, tomato, cumin or onion
churrasco	choo·*ras*·ko	steak
cordero	kor·*de*·ro	lamb or mutton
cuñape	koo·*nya*·pe	cassava and cheese roll
despepitado	des·pe·pee·*ta*·do	aka *mocachinchi*, a dried and shriveled peach in a boiled cane sugar and cinnamon liquid
empanada	em·pa·*na*·da	meat or cheese pasty
escabeche	es·ka·*be*·che	vinegar pickled vegetables, mainly carrots, onion and peppers
fricasé	free·ka·*se*	pork soup, a La Paz specialty
fritanga	free·*tang*·ga	spicy-hot pork with mint and hominy

haba	*a*·ba	bean of the *palqui* plant found on the Altiplano, similar to fava beans
huminta	oo·*min*·ta	(aka *humita*) like a *tamale* but filled with cheese only and normally quite dry
kala purkha	*ka*·la *poor*·ka	soup made from corn that is cooked in a ceramic dish by adding a steaming chunk of heavy pumice; a Potosí and Sucre specialty
lawa	*la*·wa	(aka *lagua*) meat-stew broth thickened with corn starch or wheat flour
licuado	lee·*kwa*·do	fruit shake made with either milk or water
llajhua	*lya*·khwa	spicy-hot tomato sauce
llaucha paceña	*lyow*·cha pa·*ke*·nya	a doughy cheese bread
locoto	lo·*ko*·to	small, hot pepper pods
lomo	*lo*·mo	loin (of meat)
maní	ma·*nee*	peanuts
maracuya	ma·ra·*koo*·ya	a sweet and delicious fruit (aka passion fruit), also see *tumbo*
masaco	ma·sa·ko	*charque* served with mashed plantain, yuca and/or corn, a Bolivian Amazonian staple sometimes served with cheese
mate	*ma*·te	herbal infusion of coca, chamomile, or similar
milanesa	mee·la·*ne*·sa	a fairly greasy type of beef or chicken schnitzel (see *silpancho*)
mote	*mo*·te	freeze-dried corn
oca	*o*·ka	tough edible tuber similar to a potato
pacumutu	pa·koo·*moo*·too	enormous chunks of beef grilled on a skewer, marinated in salt and lime juice, with cassava, onions and other trimmings; a Beni specialty
papas rellenas	*pa*·pas re·*lye*·nas	mashed potatoes stuffed with veggies or meat, and fried; tasty when piping hot and served with hot sauce
panqueques	pan·*ke*·kes	pancakes
parrillada	pa·ree·*lya*·da	meat grill or barbecue
pastel	pas·*tel*	a deep-fried empanada; may be filled with chicken, beef or cheese
pejerrey	pe·*khe*·ray	the most common fish served in Bolivia; it's tasty, and is found everywhere from the Altiplano to the Amazon
pescado	pes·*ka*·do	generic term for fish
pique lo macho	*pee*·ke lo *ma*·cho	chunked grilled beef and sausage heaped over french-fried potatoes, lettuce, tomatoes, onions and *locoto* (chili peppers)
pollo	*po*·lyo	chicken
pomelo	po·*me*·lo	large, pulpy-skinned grapefruit
pucacapa	poo·ka·*ka*·pa	circular empanada filled with cheese, olives, onions and hot pepper sauce and baked in an earth oven
queso	*ke*·so	cheese
quinoa	kee·*no*·a	nutritious grain similar to sorghum
saíce	*sai*·se	hot meat and rice stew
salteña	sal·*te*·nya	delicious, juicy meat and vegetable pasty, originally created in Salta, Argentina; it's now a popular mid-morning snack
silpancho	seel·*pan*·cho	a schnitzel pounded till very thin and able to absorb even more grease than a *milanesa*. A properly prepared *silpancho* is said to be perfect for viewing a solar eclipse!
tallarines	ta·lya·*ree*·nes	long, thin noodles
tamale	ta·*ma*·le	cornmeal dough filled with spiced beef, vegetables and potatoes then wrapped in a corn husk and fried, grilled or baked
tarhui	*tar*·wee	legume from Sucre

thimpu	teem·poo	spicy lamb and vegetable stew
tomatada	to·ma·*ta*·da	lamb stew with tomato sauce
de cordero	de kor·*de*·ro	
witu	wee·to	beef stew with pureed tomatoes
tucumana	too·koo·*ma*·na	empanada-like pastry stuffed till bursting with meat, olives, eggs, raisins and other goodies; originated in Tucuman, Argentina
tumbo	toom·bo	a variety of passion fruit
tuna	too·na	prickly pear cactus
yuca	ee·*oo*·ka	cassava (manioc) tuber

La Paz

La Paz is dizzying in every respect, not only for its well-publicized altitude (3660m), but for its quirky beauty. Most travelers enter this extraordinary city via the flat sparse plains of the sprawling city of El Alto, an approach that hides the sensational surprises of the valley below. The first glimpse of La Paz will, literally, take your breath away. The city's buildings cling to the sides of the canyon and spill spectacularly downwards. On a clear day, the imposing showy, snowy Mt Illimani (6402m) looms in the background.

Although Sucre remains the judicial capital, La Paz – Bolivia's largest city and centre for commerce, finance and industry – is the governmental (some say 'de facto') capital. Meanwhile, El Alto is the Aymará capital of the world. Although in reality an extension of urban La Paz, El Alto's ongoing influx of immigrants – mostly looking for work – means it has morphed into one of Latin America's fastest growing cities.

La Paz must be savored over time, not only to acclimatize to the altitude, but to experience the city's many faces. Wander at leisure through the alleys and lively markets, marvel at the interesting museums, chat to the locals in a *comedor* or relax over a coffee at a trendy café.

Since La Paz is sky-high, warm clothing is desirable most of the year, at least in the evenings. In summer (November to April) the climate can be harsh: rain falls most afternoons, the canyon may fill with clouds and steep streets often become torrents of runoff. In winter (May to October) days can be slightly cooler, but the sun (and its UV rays) is strong and temperatures reach the high 60s, but at night it often dips below freezing.

HIGHLIGHTS

- Head off on a **walking tour** (p80) with a difference, from La Paz's top to its bottom, to consume the city's food, ecology and culture
- Shop till you drop for fine woven wares (or tourist kitsch) in **Calle Linares**, the *artesanía* (locally handcrafted items) alley, and **Calle Sagárnaga** (p92)
- Eat to the beat of a **peña performance** (p91) for a night of traditional dancing and folk music
- Meander through the sprawling markets of **El Alto** (p76) for a taste of indigenous La Paz
- Marvel at the ancient ruins of **Tiahuanaco** (p102)

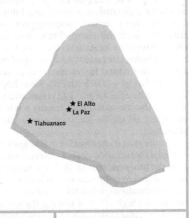

- TELEPHONE CODE: 2
- POPULATION: 829,000 (LA PAZ); 648,400 (EL ALTO)
- ELEVATION: 3660M

HISTORY

La Ciudad de Nuestra Señora de La Paz (the City of Our Lady of Peace) was founded and named on October 20, 1548, by a Spaniard, Captain Alonzo de Mendoza, at present-day Laja situated on the Tiahuanaco road. Soon after, La Paz was shifted to its present location, the valley of the Chuquiago Marka (now called the Río Choqueyapu), which had been occupied by a community of Aymará miners.

The 16th-century Spanish historian Cieza de León remarked of the newfound city: 'This is a good place to pass one's life. Here the climate is mild and the view of the mountains inspires one to think of God.' But despite León's lofty assessment (perhaps he mistakenly got off at Cochabamba), the reason behind the city's founding was much more terrestrial. The Spanish always had a weakness for shiny yellow metal, and the now-fetid Río Choqueyapu, which today flows underneath La Paz, seemed to be full of it.

The Spaniards didn't waste any amount of time in seizing the gold mines, and Captain Mendoza was installed as the new city's first mayor. The conquerors also imposed their religion and their lifestyle on the indigenous people, and since most of the colonists were men, unions between Spanish men and indigenous women eventually gave rise to a primarily mestizo population.

If the founding of La Paz had been based on anything other than gold, its position in the depths of a rugged canyon probably would have dictated an unpromising future. However, the protection this setting provided from the fierce Altiplano climate and the city's convenient location on the main trade route between Lima and Potosí – much of the Potosí silver bound for Pacific ports passed through La Paz – offered the city some hope of prosperity once the gold had played out. By the time the railway was built, the city was well enough established to continue commanding attention.

In spite of its name, the City of Our Lady of Peace has seen a good deal of violence. Since Bolivian independence in 1825, the republic has endured over 190 changes of leadership. An abnormally high mortality rate once accompanied high office in Bolivia; the job of president came with a short life expectancy. In fact, the presidential palace on the plaza is now known as the Palacio Quemado (Burned Palace), owing to its repeated gutting by fire. As recently as 1946 then-president Gualberto Villarroel was publicly hanged in Plaza Murillo.

See the History chapter (p24) for more on Bolivia's history, much of it centered around La Paz, as seat of government and ever-expanding city.

ORIENTATION

It is just about impossible to get yourself lost in La Paz. There is only one major thoroughfare and it follows the Río Choqueyapu canyon (fortunately for your olfactory system, the river flows mostly underground). The main thoroughfare changes names several times from the top to the bottom: Avs Ismael Montes, Mariscal Santa Cruz, 16 de Julio (the Prado) and Villazón. Quite often the section is simply referred to as 'El Prado.' At the lower end of the thoroughfare, the street divides into Avs 6 de Agosto and Aniceto Arce.

The business districts and the wealthier neighborhoods – with their skyscrapers, colonial houses and modern glass constructions – occupy the city's more tranquil lower altitudes (which is the reverse of many US and European cities). The best preserved colonial section of town is near the intersection of Calles Jaén and Sucre, where narrow cobbled streets and colonial churches offer a glimpse of early La Paz. The most prestigious neighborhoods are found further down in the canyon in the Zona Sur (Southern Zone), which includes the neighborhoods of Calacoto, Cotacota, San Miguel, La Florida and Obrajes, as well as a growing throng of other barrios. Numbered streets run perpendicular to the main road in Zona Sur, making navigation easier; the numbers increase from west to east.

Above the city center and the Zona Sur, and still very much part of La Paz, are the cascades of cuboid, mud dwellings and ever-growing neighborhoods, which literally spill over the canyon rim and down the slopes on three sides. This is where most of the daily hustle and bustle takes place, with all sorts of sights, sounds and smells. Above this, stretching for miles away from the canyon's rim across the Altiplano is the city of El Alto. If you find yourself becom disoriented up here and want to return to the center, just head downhill.

LA PAZ IN...

Two Days

Start your day with breakfast on the Prado or a snack (try *salteñas* – filled pastry shells) around Plaza Avaroa – the perfect spots for watching one of the world's highest cities wake up. Stroll the historic cobblestone streets around **Iglesia de San Francisco** (p74), then tie some cultural threads together with a wander through the nearby **artesanía alley** (Calle Linares; p92) and **Witches' Market** (Mercado de Hechicería; p71) while shopping for fine alpaca wear. No visit to Bolivia is complete without a stop at the **Museo de la Coca** (Coca Museum; p71).

Stop for lunch at one of the many delicious cafés in this area, and then head up to **Mercado Negro** (p74) and its surrounding streets, to wander among the people, merchandise and delicious foodstuffs.

Treat yourself to fine dining at an international eatery in Sopocachi or in the trendy Zona Sur (see Eating p85), or sample local cuisine at homely **Casa de los Paceños** (p86). Then head to one of the many popular bars around town (see p90).

On the second day, take a wander along colonial Calle Jaén, the highlight of which is the **Museo de Instrumentos Musicales** (p76). For lunch, head down the Prado to the area of Sopocachi and enjoy a taste of French Bolivian fusion at **La Comédie Art-Café Restaurant** (p88), but leave enough room for your evening meal and taste of traditional music at **Peña Marka Tambo** (p91).

Four Days

Follow the two-day itinerary, then on your third day do a **guided walking tour** (p80) of La Paz or its surrounds getting a taste of local food and its origins. On the fourth day take a day-trip out to **Tiahuanaco** (p102) to explore the excavated ruins. Or depending on the season, you could relax at **Urmiri's rustic hot springs** (p105), visit the **Zongo Valley** (p101) or **Chacaltaya** (p100) or do a day's **bike trip** on the outskirts of La Paz (p77).

Maps

The majority of hotels can offer you free photocopied city maps, but unfortunately good maps to the city are in short supply. The tourist office hands out a free city map *Descubre La Paz* (Discover La Paz). Inside the central post office, opposite the poste restante counter, there are gift shops that sell a range of maps.

La Paz is the place to stock up on maps for the rest of your trip. For information on buying topographic sheets and climbing maps, see also p50 and p372.

Instituto Geográfico Militar (IGM; Map pp72-3; ☎ 237-0118; Oficina 5, Juan XXIII 100) In a blind alley off Rodríguez, IGM offers original 1:50,000 topographic maps (US$6) or photocopies (US$4) if a sheet is unavailable. Another outlet is located at Saavedra, Estadio Mayor, Miraflores.

Librería Olimpia (Map pp72-3; Galería Handal, Mariscal Santa Cruz, Local 14) A stationary store that stocks a small but worthwhile collection of maps.

Los Amigos del Libro (Map pp72-3; ☎ 220-4321; www.librosbolivia.com, in Spanish; Mercado 1315) This place tocks a small collection of maps, including Walter Guzmán Córdova's colorful, mostly accurate 1:50,000 trekking maps.

INFORMATION
Bookstores & Book Exchanges

For used paperbacks in English, check the book section of Mercado Lanza (p74). To trade books, the best library (and we mean *library*) is Oliver's Travels bar (p90), but they are rightly fussy on exchanges. Or try Ángelo Colonial (p86), the side-by-side offices of America Tours (p80) and Gravity Assisted Mountain Biking (p77), or Café Sol y Luna (p90).

et-n-ic (Map pp72-3; ☎ 246-3782; www.visitabolivia .com; Illampu 863) This store (see p93) stocks a large range of Lonely Planet guides.

Gisbert & Co (Map pp72-3; Comercio 1270) Spanish-language literature and maps.

Librería Olimpia (Map pp72-3; ☎ 240-8101; Galería Handal, Mariscal Santa Cruz, Local 14) Stationery store with a good map selection.

Los Amigos del Libro (Map pp72-3; ☎ 220-4321; www.librosbolivia.com, in Spanish; Mercado 1315) Widest selection of foreign-language novels and magazines.

LA PAZ

LA PAZ

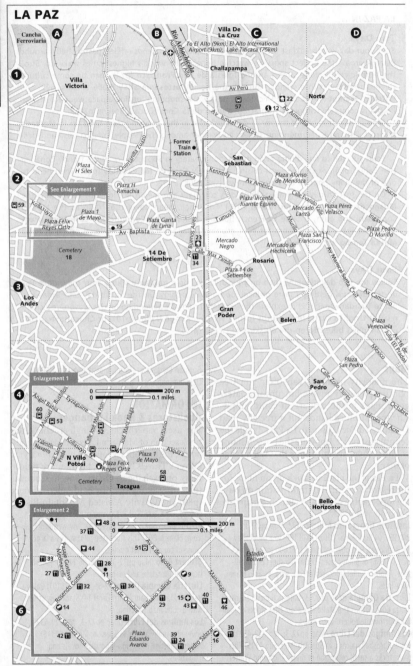

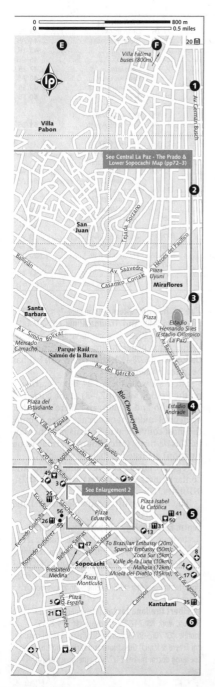

0 — 800 m
0 — 0.5 miles

Cultural Centers
Alianza Francesa (Map pp66–7; ☎ 242-5004; www
.afbolivia.org; Guachalla 399) Offers language classes,
exhibitions and promotes cultural events.
Centro Boliviano-Americano (CBA; ☎ 243-0107;
www.cba.edu.bo; Parque Zenón Iturralde 121) Language
classes and US periodicals library.
Goethe Institut (Map pp72–3; ☎ 244-2453; www
.goethe.de; 6 de Agosto 2118) Films, language classes and
good German-language library.

Emergency
Numbers for emergency services (police, fire
and ambulance) are the same throughout
the country: see the Quick Reference, inside
front cover.
Tourist Police (Policía Turistica; Map pp72–3; ☎ 222-
5016; Plaza del Estadio, Puerta 22, Miraflores) Next to
Disco Love City. English-speaking. Report thefts to obtain
a *denuncia* (affidavit) for insurance purposes – they won't
recover any stolen goods.

Immigration
Migración (Map pp72–3; ☎ 211-0960; Camacho 1468;
⌚ 8:30am-4pm Mon-Fri) With three changes
of directorship in six months, some call this place
'Migraine-ation' but this is where you must obtain
your visa extensions.

Internet Access
La Paz has nearly as many cybercafés as shoeshine boys. Charges range from US$0.15 to
US$0.40 an hour, and connections are gen-
erally fastest in the morning or late evening.
See @ icons on maps for other recommended
places not mentioned here.
Internet Alley (Map pp72–3; Pasaje Iturralde) Just off
the Prado near Plaza del Estudiante. Fast, cheap connections with several places open until late.
Tolomeo's (Map pp72–3; cnr Loayza & Comercio) Fast,
friendly, warm, high-tech and reliably open late.

Internet Resources
Bolivia Travel Guide (www.gbtbolivia.com)
Another privately-run site with excellent coverage of
La Paz.
Visit Bolivia (www.visitbolivia.org) Run by an association
of hotels with good information.
www.lapaz.bo La Paz's municipal website has good
cultural and tourism sections.

Laundry
Lavanderías (laundries) are the cheapest and
most efficient way of ensuring clean (and dry)
clothes in La Paz.

LA PAZ

INFORMATION				
Alianza Francesa	1 A5			
Argentine Embassy	2 E5			
ATM	(see 42)			
Australian Consulate	3 E5			
British Embassy	4 F5			
Canadian Consulate	5 E6			
Centro Epidemiológico				
Departamental La Paz	6 B1			
Dr Elbert Orellana				
Jordan	7 E6			
Dr Fernando Patiño	8 F5			
Dr Jorge Jaime Aguirre	(see 8)			
Dutch Embassy	9 B6			
German Embassy	10 F5			
ie instituto exclusivo	11 A6			
Information Kiosk	12 C1			
Italian Embassy	13 F5			
Japanese Embassy	14 A6			
Medicentro	15 B6			
Paraguayan Embassy	16 C6			
Peruvian Embassy	(see 9)			
US Embassy	17 F6			

SIGHTS & ACTIVITIES	
Cemetery	18 A3
Flower Market	19 B2
Museo de la Revolución	
Nacional	20 F1

SLEEPING	
Alcalá Apart Hotel	21 E6
Hostal Tambo del Oro	22 C1
Hotel La Joya	23 B3
La Loge	(see 33)

EATING	
Alexander Coffee	
& Pub	24 B6
Arco Iris	25 E5
Armonía	26 E5
Boomerang	27 A6
Café La Terraza	28 A6
Chifa New Hong Kong	29 B6
El Arriero	30 C6
Ketal Hipermercado	31 F5
Kuchen Stube	32 A6
La Comédie Art-Cafe	
Restaurant	33 A6
Le Bistrot	(see 1)
Mercado Uruguay	34 B3
New Tokyo	35 F6
Paceña La Salteña	36 B6
Pronto Dalicatessen	37 A5
Salteña Chic	38 B6
Salteña Chiquisaqueña	39 B6
Salteñeria El Hornito	40 B6
Wagamama	41 F5
Zatt	42 A6

DRINKING	
Dead Stroke	43 B6
Diesel Nacional	44 A5
Forum	45 E6
Mongo's	46 C6
Ram Jam	47 E5
Reineke Fuchs	48 A5
Thelonius Jazz Bar	49 E5
Traffic	50 F5

ENTERTAINMENT	
Cine 6 de Agosto	51 B5

TRANSPORT	
Autolíneas Ingavi	52 A4
Buses to Huarina	
& Huatajata	53 A4
Camiones to Zongo Valley	54 A5
Empresa Ferroviaria	
Andina (FCA)	55 F5
Kolla Motors	56 E5
Main Bus Terminal	57 C1
Micros to Center	58 B5
Trans Altiplano	59 A2
Trans-Unificado Sorata	60 A4
Transporte 6 de Junio	(see 61)
Transportes Manco	
Kapac	61 B5
Transtur 2 de Febrero	(see 61)

Calle Illampu, at the top of Sagárnaga, is lined with laundries. Many hotels and some *residenciales* (budget accommodations) offer cheap hand-washing services. For quick, reliable same-day machine wash-and-dry service (US$1 per kilo), try the following:

Lavandería Maya (Map pp72-3; Hostal Maya, Sagárnaga 339)

Limpieza Laverap (Map pp72-3; Aroma) Delivery to nearby hotels with prepaid service.

Limpieza Sucre (Map pp72-3; Nicolás Acosta) Near Plaza San Pedro.

Left Luggage

Most recommended places to stay offer inexpensive or free left-luggage storage, especially if you make a return reservation. The main bus terminal (p94) has a cheap *deposito*, but think twice about leaving anything valuable here.

Media

La Razon (www.la-razon.com), **El Diario** (www.eldiario.net) and *La Prensa* are La Paz's major daily newspapers. National media chains **ATB** (www.bolivia .com) and **Grupo Fides** (www.radiofides.com, in Spanish) host the most up-to-date online news sites.

Medical Services

For medical emergencies, it's best to avoid the hospitals. For serious conditions, ask your embassy for doctor recommendations.

The 24-hour **Medicentro** (Map pp66-7; ☎ 244 1717; 6 de Agosto 2440) and **Trauma Klinik** (☎ 277-1819; Aliaga 1271, San Miguel, Zona Sur) have been recommended for general care. For emergencies, **Clinica Sur** (☎ 278-4001; Hernando Siles, Zona Sur) has been recommended.

There's a well-stocked 24-hour pharmacy on the Prado (Map pp72–3) at the corner of 16 de Julio and Bueno, and there's another open until midnight on circular Plaza Egunio, the most convenient to Sagárnaga. Other *farmacias de turno* (after-hours pharmacies on rotation) are listed in daily newspapers.

A good optical outlet providing glasses and contact lenses is **Pro Lentes** (Map pp72-3; ☎ 231-0937; Potosí 1301).

The following lists reputable medical and dental contacts:

Centro Epidemiológico Departamental La Paz (Centro Pilote; Map pp66-7; ☎ 245-0166; Vásquez 122 at Peru; ☺ 8:30-11:30am Mon-Fri) Off upper Ismael Montes near the brewery. Anyone heading for malarial areas can pick up antimalarials, and rabies and yellow fever vaccinations, for the cost of a sterile needle – bring one from a pharmacy.

Dr Elbert Orellana Jordan (Map pp66-7; Clinica Boston, work ☎ 242-2342, private ☎ 279-8215, mobile ☎ 7065-9743; asistmedbolivia@hotmail.com; cnr Freyre & Mujia) Gregarious and caring English-speaking doctor makes 24/7/365 emergency house calls.

Dr Fernando Patiño (Map pp66-7; ☎ 243-0697/1664, mobile ☎ 7722-5625; fpatino@entelnet.bo; 2nd fl, Edificio Illimani, Arce 1701) US-educated, English-speaking, general practitioner and high-altitude medical expert.

Dr Jorge Jaime Aguirre (Map pp66-7; ☎ 243-2682; 1st fl, Edificio Illimani, Arce 1701) Frequently recommended dentist for routine cleaning to root canals.

High Altitude Pathology Institute (☎ 224-5394, 222-2617; www.altitudeclinic.com; Saavedra 2302, Miraflores) Bolivian member of the International Association for Medical Assistance to Travelers (Iamat). Offers computerized high-altitude medical checkups and maintains a hyperoxygen acclimatization chamber at the summit of Chacaltaya.

Money
ATMS
Cash withdrawals of bolivianos and US dollars are possible at numerous ATMs at major intersections around the city. For cash advances (bolivianos only, amount according to your limit in home country) with no commission and little hassle, try the following:

Banco Mercantil (Map pp72-3; cnr Mercado & Ayacucho)

Banco Nacional de Bolivia (Map pp72-3; cnr Colón & Camacho)

MONEY TRANSFERS
The helpful American Express representative **Magri Turismo** (Map pp72-3; ☎ 244-2727; Ravelo 2101) holds client mail but does not change traveler's checks. Try **DHL/Western Union** (Map pp72-3; ☎ 233-5567; Perez 268), which has other outlets scattered all around town, for urgent international money transfers.

MONEYCHANGERS
Casas de cambio (exchange bureaus) in the city center can be quicker and more convenient than banks. Most places open from 8:30am to noon and 2pm to 6pm weekdays, and on Saturday mornings. If desperate, try Hotel Rosario (p83) or Hotel Gloria (p84).

Be wary of counterfeit US dollars and bolivianos, especially with *cambistas* (street moneychangers) who loiter around the intersections of Colón, Camacho and Santa Cruz. Outside La Paz you'll get 3% to 10% less for checks than for cash. The following places change traveler's checks for minimal commission:

Cambios América (Map pp72-3; Camacho 1223)

Casa de Cambio Sudamer (Map pp72-3; Colón 206 at Camacho) Sells currency from neighboring countries.

Post
Ángelo Colonial (Map pp72-3; Linares 922; ☽ 10am-1pm Jul-Sep) This small post office (in the same building as Ángelo Colonial restaurant, p86) offers an outgoing-only mail service.

Central Post Office (Ecobol; Map pp72-3; Santa Cruz & Oruro; ☽ 8:30am-7pm Mon-Fri, 8:30am-5pm Sat, 9am-noon Sun) A tranquil oasis off the Prado, *lista de correos* (poste restante) mail is held for two months for free here – bring your passport (see p374). A downstairs customs desk facilitates international parcel posting (see p374).

Telephone & Fax
Convenient *puntos* (privately run phone offices) of various carriers – Entel, Cotel, Tigo, Viva etc – are scattered throughout the city. Street kiosks, which are on nearly every corner, also sell phone cards, and offer brief local calls for B$1 (US$0.15). Hawkers with mobiles on a leash offer mobile calls for B$1 per minute.

International calls can be made at low prices from international call centers on Sagárnaga (between Illampu and Murillo) and Calle Linares (between Sagárnaga and Calle Santa Cruz) for around US$0.15 per minute.

Entel office (Map pp72-3; fax 213-2334; Ayacucho 267; ☽ 8:30am-9pm Mon-Fri, 8:30am-8:30pm Sat, 9am-4pm Sun) The main Entel office, it's the best place to receive incoming calls and faxes. There is also internet service.

Tourist Information
Ángelo Colonial (Map pp72-3; Linares 922; ☽ 9am-7pm) Privately run tourist-info office with a book exchange, a notice board, a guidebook reference library and a restaurant (p86).

Information kiosks Main bus terminal (Map pp66-7); Casa de la Cultura (Map pp72-3; Mariscal Santa Crux & Potosí); Mirador Laikakota (Map pp72-3)

Municipal tourist office (Map pp72-3; ☎ 237-1044; Plaza del Estudiante; ☽ 8:30am-noon & 2:30-7pm Mon-Fri) This is your best bet for information, at least of the verbal kind – it's a bit short on printed matter, although it does have good free city maps. Ask to see a copy of *Agenda Cultural*, a listing of the month's activities.

DANGERS & ANNOYANCES
Fake police officers and bogus tourist officials are on the rise. Note: authentic police officers will always be uniformed (undercover police are under strict orders not to hassle foreigners) and will never insist that you show them your passport, get in a taxi with them or allow them to search you in public. If confronted by an imposter, refuse

to show them your valuables (wallet, passport, money etc), or insist on going to the nearest police station on foot. If physically threatened, it is always best to hand over valuables immediately.

Fake 'taxi drivers' are working in conjunction with gangs who steal from or – as has tragically been the case – assault or kidnap unsuspecting travelers (to extort ATM pin details). At the end of 2005 a young Austrian couple was kidnapped and murdered (their bodies were discovered at the beginning of 2006), an event which shocked travelers and locals alike. Although the perpetrators are said to have been caught, always beware of hopping into shared cabs with strangers or of accepting a lift from a driver who approaches you (especially around dodgy bus areas). See p110 for warning on traveling between La Paz and Copacabana.

More annoying than dangerous, *lustrabotes* (shoeshine boys) hound everyone with footwear. Many affect a menacing and anonymous appearance, wearing black ski masks and baseball caps pulled so low you can just make out two eye sockets. It's said that they often do so to avoid social stigma, as many are working hard to support families or pay their way through school – you can support their cause for B$1 (US$0.15).

La Paz is a great city to explore on foot, but take local advice *'camina lentito, come poquito…y duerme solito'* ('walk slowly, eat only a little bit…and sleep by your poor little self') to avoid feeling the effects of *soroche* (altitude sickness).

Scams

Sadly, La Paz seems to have caught on to South America's common ruses. The bogus tourist is a popular one: on engaging you in conversation in English, the 'tourist' is confronted by fake 'tourist police'. The 'tourist' abides by an 'order' to show the tourist police his bag/papers/passport, and 'translates' for you to do the same. During the search, the cohorts strip you of your cash and/or belongings.

Psst my friend! This popular scam involves someone spilling a substance on you or spitting a phlegm ball at you. While you or they are wiping it off, another lifts your wallet or slashes your pack; the perpetrator may be an 'innocent' granny or young girl. Similarly, don't bend over to pick up a valuable item which has been 'dropped'. You risk being accused of theft, or of being pickpocketed. See also p368.

SIGHTS

When the sun shines, La Paz cries out for leisurely exploration. Bolivia's governmental capital has its share of cultural and historical museums, most of which are found in the city center or close surrounds. Yet much of the enjoyment comes from observing the rhythms of local life. Most of the daily action takes place in the upper central regions of La Paz, where a mass of irregular shaped steep streets and alleys wind their way skywards. Here, locals embrace their frenetic daily life. Women, sporting long black plaits, bowler hats and vivid mantas, attend to steaming pots or sell everything from dried llama fetuses to designer shoes, while men, negotiating the frenetic traffic (and its fumes), push overladen trolleys. Keep your eyes peeled for fantastic glimpses of Illimani's triple peak towering between the world's highest high-rises. Many visitors allow another day or two to acclimatize during a day trip to Tiahuanaco (p102) or Lake Titicaca (p106).

Most official sites, including museums, are closed over the Christmas holiday period (December 25 to January 6).

Cathedral & Plaza Murillo

Although it's a relatively recent addition to La Paz's collection of religious structures, the 1835 **cathedral** (Map pp72–3) is an impressive structure – mostly because it is built on a steep hillside. The main entrance is 12m higher than its base on Calle Potosí. The cathedral's sheer immensity, with its high dome, hulking columns, thick stone walls and high ceilings, is overpowering, but the altar is relatively simple. Inside, the main attraction is the profusion of stained-glass work; the windows behind the altar depict a gathering of Bolivian politicos being blessed from above by a flock of heavenly admirers.

Beside the cathedral is the **Presidential Palace** (Map pp72–3), and in the center of Plaza Murillo, opposite, stands a **statue of President Gualberto Villarroel**. In 1946, he was dragged from the palace by vigilantes and hanged from a lamppost in the square. Interestingly enough, Don Pedro Domingo Murillo, for whom the plaza was named, met a similar fate here in 1810.

Museo Nacional de Arqueología

Two blocks east of the Prado, this **museum** (National Archaeology Museum; Map pp72-3; ☎ 231-1621; Tiahuanacu 93; admission US$1.25; ☼ 9am-12:30pm, 3-7pm Mon-Fri, 10am-noon Sat, 10am-3pm Sun) holds a small but well-sorted collection of artifacts that illustrate the most interesting aspects of the Tiahuanaco culture's five stages (see p102). Most of Tiahuanaco's treasures were stolen or damaged during the colonial days, so the extent of the collection isn't overwhelming. Some of the ancient stonework disappeared into Spanish construction projects, while valuable pieces – gold and other metallic relics and artwork – found their way into European museums or were melted down for royal treasuries. Most of what remains in Bolivia – pottery, figurines, trepanned skulls, mummies, textiles and metal objects – is housed in several rooms of this museum. Unfortunately there are no explanations in English, only Spanish.

Mercado de Hechicería (Witches' Market)

The city's most unusual **market** (Map pp72-3) lies along Calles Jiménez and Linares between Sagárnaga and Santa Cruz, amid lively tourist *artesanía* (stores selling locally handcrafted items). What is on sale isn't witchcraft as depicted in horror films and Halloween tales; the merchandise is herbal and folk remedies, plus a few more unorthodox ingredients intended to manipulate and supplicate the various malevolent and benevolent spirits of the Aymará world. An example of these types of ingredients is dried toucan beaks, intended to cure ills and protect supplicants from bad spirits.

If you're building a new house, for example, you can buy a llama fetus to bury beneath the cornerstone as a *cha'lla* (offering) to Pachamama, encouraging her to inspire good luck therein. If someone is feeling ill, or is being pestered by unwelcome or bothersome spooks, they can purchase a plateful of colorful herbs, seeds and assorted critter parts to remedy the problem. As you pass the market stalls, watch for wandering *yatiri* (witch doctors), who wear dark hats and carry coca pouches, and offer (mainly to locals) fortune-telling services.

Photographs taken here may be met with unpleasantness – unless you are a customer and ask politely first.

Museo de la Coca

Chew on some facts inside the **Coca Museum** (Map pp72-3; ☎ 231-1998; Linares 906; admission US$1; ☼ 10am-7pm), which explores the sacred leaf's role in traditional societies, its use by the soft-drink and pharmaceutical industries, and the growth of cocaine as an illicit drug. The displays (ask for a translation in your language) are educational, provocative and evenhanded.

Museo Nacional del Arte

Near Plaza Murillo, this **museum** (National Art Museum; Map pp72-3; ☎ 240-8600; cnr Comercio & Socabaya; admission US$1.25; ☼ 9am-12:30pm & 3-7pm Tue-Fri, 9am-1pm Sat; 10am-1pm Sun) is housed in the former Palacio de Los Condes de Arana. The building was constructed in 1775 of pink Viacha granite and has been restored to its original grandeur. In the center of a huge courtyard, surrounded by three stories of pillared corridors, is a lovely alabaster fountain. The various levels are dedicated to a range of artists: Marina Núñez del Prado's contemporary sculptures, the late-Renaissance paintings of Melchor Pérez de Holguín and students of his Potosí school, and works of other Latin American artists. Modern visiting exhibitions are shown in the outer salon.

Calle Jaén Museums

These four, small, interesting **museums** (Map pp72-3; ☎ 237-8478; combo admission US$0.50; ☼ 9:30am-12:30pm & 3-7pm Mon-Fri, 9am-1pm Sat & Sun) are clustered together along Calle Jaén, La Paz's finest colonial street, and can easily be bundled into one visit. Buy tickets at the Museo Costumbrista (p74).

Also known as Museo del Oro (Gold Museum), the **Museo de Metales Preciosos** (Museum of Precious Metals; Jaén 777) houses three impressively presented salons of pre-Colombian silver, gold and copper works. A fourth salon in the basement has examples of ancient pottery.

Sometimes called the Museo de la Guerra del Pacífico, the diminutive **Museo del Litoral** (Jaén 798) incorporates relics from the 1884 war in which Bolivia became landlocked after losing its Litoral department to Chile. The collection consists mainly of historical maps that defend Bolivia's emotionally charged claims to Antofagasta and Chile's Segunda Región.

Once the home of Don Pedro Domingo Murillo, a leader in the La Paz Revolution of July 16, 1809, the **Casa de Murillo** (Jaén 790) displays

LA PAZ

CENTRAL LA PAZ – THE PRADO & LOWER SOPOCACHI

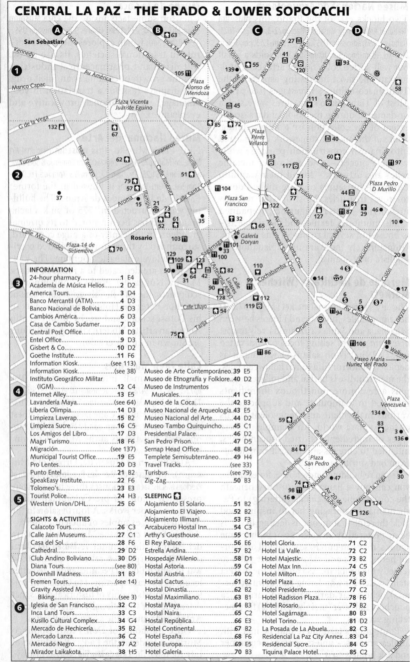

INFORMATION
24-hour pharmacy..........................1 E4
Academia de Música Helios............2 D2
America Tours...............................3 D4
Banco Mercantil (ATM)...................4 D3
Banco Nacional de Bolivia..............5 D3
Cambios América............................6 D3
Casa de Cambio Sudamer...............7 D3
Central Post Office..........................8 D3
Entel Office...................................9 D3
Gisbert & Co................................10 D2
Goethe Institute...........................11 F6
Information Kiosk......................(see 113)
Information Kiosk........................(see 38)
Instituto Geográfico Militar
  (IGM)..12 C4
Internet Alley...............................13 E5
Lavandería Maya.......................(see 64)
Libería Olimpia............................14 D3
Limpieza Laverap..........................15 B2
Limpieza Sucre.............................16 C5
Los Amigos del Libro.....................17 D3
Magri Turismo..............................18 F6
Migración................................(see 137)
Municipal Tourist Office................19 E5
Pro Lentes...................................20 D3
Punto Entel.................................21 B2
SpeakEasy Institute.......................22 F6
Tolomeo's....................................23 E3
Tourist Police...............................24 H3
Western Union/DHL.......................25 E6

SIGHTS & ACTIVITIES
Calacoto Tours.............................26 C3
Calle Jaén Museums......................27 C1
Casa del Sol.................................28 F6
Cathedral....................................29 D2
Club Andino Boliviano...................30 D5
Diana Tours.............................(see 80)
Downhill Madness........................31 B3
Fremen Tours...........................(see 14)
Gravity Assisted Mountain
  Biking...................................(see 3)
Iglesia de San Francisco................32 C2
Inca Land Tours............................33 C3
Kusillo Cultural Complex................34 G4
Mercado de Hechicería..................35 B2
Mercado Lanza............................36 C2
Mercado Negro............................37 A2
Mirador Laikakota.........................38 H5

Museo de Arte Contemporáneo.....39 E5
Museo de Etnografía y Folklore.....40 D2
Museo de Instrumentos
  Musicales.................................41 C1
Museo de la Coca........................42 B3
Museo Nacional de Arqueología....43 E5
Museo Nacional del Arte...............44 D2
Museo Tambo Quirquincho............45 C1
Presidential Palace.......................46 D2
San Pedro Prison..........................47 D5
Sernap Head Office......................48 D4
Templete Semisubterráneo............49 H4
Travel Tracks.............................(see 33)
Turisbus..................................(see 79)
Zig-Zag......................................50 B3

SLEEPING
Alojamiento El Solario....................51 B2
Alojamiento El Viajero....................52 B2
Alojamiento Illimani......................53 F3
Arcabucero Hostal Inn..................54 C3
Arthy's Guesthouse......................55 C1
El Rey Palace...............................56 E6
Estrella Andina.............................57 B2
Hospedaje Milenio........................58 D1
Hostal Astoria..............................59 C4
Hostal Austria..............................60 D2
Hostal Cactus..............................61 B2
Hostal Dinastía............................62 B2
Hostal Maximiliano.......................63 B1
Hostal Maya................................64 B3
Hostal Naira................................65 B2
Hostal República..........................66 E3
Hotel Continental.........................67 B2
Hotel España...............................68 F6
Hotel Europa...............................69 E5
Hotel Galería...............................70 B3

Hotel Gloria................................71 C2
Hotel La Valle..............................72 C2
Hotel Majestic.............................73 B2
Hotel Max Inn..............................74 C5
Hotel Milton................................75 B3
Hotel Plaza.................................76 E5
Hotel Presidente..........................77 C2
Hotel Radisson Plaza.....................78 F6
Hotel Rosario..............................79 B2
Hotel Sagárnaga..........................80 B3
Hotel Torino................................81 D2
La Posada de La Abuela.................82 C3
Residencial La Paz City Annex.........83 D4
Residencial Sucre.........................84 C5
Tiquina Palace Hotel.....................85 C2

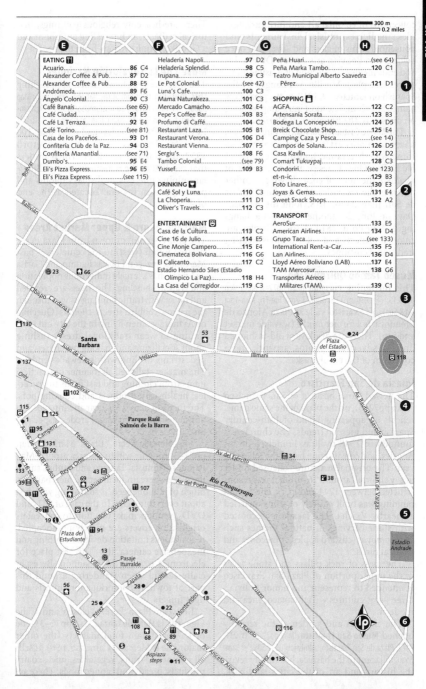

EATING
Acuario...................................86 C4
Alexander Coffee & Pub..........87 D2
Alexander Coffee & Pub..........88 E5
Andrómeda..............................89 F6
Ángelo Colonial.......................90 C3
Café Banaís.........................(see 65)
Café Ciudad...........................91 E5
Café La Terraza......................92 E4
Café Torino.........................(see 81)
Casa de los Paceños.................93 D1
Confitería Club de la Paz..........94 D3
Confitería Manantial............(see 71)
Dumbo's...............................95 E4
Eli's Pizza Express...................96 E5
Eli's Pizza Express...............(see 115)

Heladería Napoli......................97 D2
Heladería Splendid...................98 C5
Irupana..................................99 C3
Le Pot Colonial.....................(see 42)
Luna's Cafe...........................100 C3
Mama Naturakeza...................101 C3
Mercado Camacho..................102 E4
Pepe's Coffee Bar...................103 B3
Profumo di Caffé....................104 C2
Restaurant Laza.....................105 B1
Restaurant Verona..................106 D4
Restaurant Vienna..................107 F5
Sergiu's................................108 F6
Tambo Colonial...................(see 79)
Yussef..................................109 B3

DRINKING
Café Sol y Luna......................110 C3
La Choperia...........................111 D1
Oliver's Travels......................112 C3

ENTERTAINMENT
Casa de la Cultura..................113 C2
Cine 16 de Julio.....................114 E5
Cine Monje Campero...............115 E4
Cinemateca Boliviana..............116 G6
El Calicanto..........................117 C2
Estadio Hernando Siles (Estadio
   Olímpico La Paz)..................118 H4
La Casa del Corregidor...........119 C3

Peña Huari.........................(see 64)
Peña Marka Tambo.................120 C1
Teatro Municipal Alberto Saavedra
   Pérez..............................121 D1

SHOPPING
AGFA...................................122 C2
Artesanía Sorata....................123 B3
Bodega La Concepción.............124 D5
Breick Chocolate Shop.............125 E4
Camping Caza y Pesca..........(see 14)
Campos de Solana...................126 D5
Casa Kavlin...........................127 D2
Comart Tukuypaj....................128 C3
Condoriri..........................(see 123)
et-n-ic.................................129 B3
Foto Linares..........................130 E3
Joyas & Gemas.......................131 E4
Sweet Snack Shops.................132 A2

TRANSPORT
AeroSur................................133 E5
American Airlines....................134 D4
Grupo Taca........................(see 133)
International Rent-a-Car............135 F5
Lan Airlines...........................136 D4
Lloyd Aéreo Boliviano (LAB).....137 E4
TAM Mercosur........................138 G6
Transportes Aéreos
   Militares (TAM)....................139 C1

collections of colonial art and furniture, textiles, medicines, musical instruments and household items of glass and silver that once belonged to Bolivian aristocracy. Other odds and ends include a collection of Alasitas miniatures (see p80). Murillo was hanged by the Spanish on January 29, 1810, in the plaza now named after him. The most intriguing painting on display is *The Execution of Murillo*.

The **Museo Costumbrista Juan de Vargas** (cnr Jaén & Sucre) contains art and photos, as well as some superb ceramic figurine dioramas of old La Paz. One of these is a representation of *akulliko,* the hour of coca-chewing; another portrays the festivities surrounding the Día de San Juan Bautista (St John the Baptist's Day) on June 24; another depicts the hanging of Murillo in 1810. Also on display are colonial artifacts and colorful dolls wearing traditional costumes.

Museo Tambo Quirquincho

This intriguing **museum** (Map pp72-3; admission US$0.15; 9:30am-12:30pm & 3-7pm Tue-Fri; 9am-1pm Sat & Sun), off Evaristo Valle at Plaza Alonzo de Mendoza, is a former *tambo* (wayside market and inn). There are displays of old-fashioned dresses, silverware, photos, artwork and a collection of Carnaval masks.

Iglesia de San Francisco

The hewed stone basilica of San Francisco (Map pp72–3), on the plaza of the same name, reflects an appealing blend of 16th-century Spanish and mestizo trends. The church was founded in 1548 by Fray Francisco de los Ángeles, and construction began the following year. The original structure collapsed under heavy snowfall around 1610, but it was reconstructed between 1744 and 1753. The second building was built entirely of stone quarried at nearby Viacha. The façade is decorated with stone carvings of natural themes such as *chirimoyas* (custard apples), pinecones and tropical birds.

The mass of rock pillars and stone faces in the upper portion of Plaza San Francisco is intended to represent and honor Bolivia's three great cultures – Tiahuanaco, Inca and modern.

The cloisters and garden of the recently opened **Museo San Francisco** (Map pp72-3; 231-8472; Plaza de San Francisco; admission US$2.50; 9am-6pm), adjacent to the basilica, beautifully revive the history and art of the city's landmark.

There are heavenly religious paintings, historical artifacts, an interesting anteroom and a Godlike, if quirky, view from the roof.

Museo de la Revolución Nacional

The first question to ask when approaching this **museum** (Museum of the National Revolution; Map pp66-7; Plaza Villarroel; admission US$0.15; 9:30am-12:30pm & 3-7pm Tue-Fri, 10am-1pm Sat & Sun) is 'Which Revolution?' (Bolivia has had more than 100 of them). The answer is the one of April 1952, the popular revolt of armed miners that resulted in the nationalization of Bolivian mining interests. It displays photos and paintings from the era. Located at the end of Av Busch.

Mercado Negro & Upper Market Areas

The entire section of town from Plaza Pérez Velasco uphill (west) to the cemetery – past Mercado Lanza, and Plazas Eguino and Garita de Lima – has a largely indigenous population and is always bustling. The streets are crowded and noisy with traffic honking its way through the narrow cobbled streets, *cholitas* (Quechua or Aymará women living in the city but continuing to wear traditional dress) rushing about socializing and making purchases, and pedestrians jostling with sidewalk vendors. The market stalls sell all manner of practical items from clothing and fast foods to groceries, health-care products and cooking pots. The focus of activity is near the intersection of Buenos Aires and Max Paredes, especially on Saturdays.

The **Mercado Negro** (Black Market, Map pp72–3) roughly within the area around Max Paredes, Tumusla, Tamayo and Santa Cruz, is the place where undocumented merchandise, much of it bootlegged, is sold along with just about everything else. In the case of CDs and DVDs, vendors make no effort to conceal its origins: the covers are merely photocopied. It also stocks imitation designer clothing and inexpensive camera film. The best place for electronics is along Eloy Salmón. Be especially careful when wandering around this part of town: it's notorious for rip-offs and light fingers.

Between Plaza Pérez Velasco and Calle Figueroa is **Mercado Lanza** (Map pp72–3), one of La Paz's main food markets (the other major one is Mercado Camacho, p90). It sells all manner of fruits, vegetables, juices, dairy products, breads and canned foods. There are also numerous stalls where you can pick up a sandwich, soup, *salteña* (filled pastry shells), empanada or full meal.

The **Flower Market** (Map pp66–7), appropriately located opposite the cemetery at the top of Batista, is a beautiful splash of color amid one of the city's drabber and less safe areas. Unfortunately it also sits alongside a festering open sewer and garbage dump, which make it rather confusing to the nostrils.

Museo de Etnografía y Folklore

This free **museum** (Ethnography & Folklore Museum; Map pp72-3; ☎ 235-8559; cnr Ingavi & Sanjinés; ☼ 9:30am-12:30pm, 3-6:30pm Mon-Sat, 9:30am-12:30pm Sun) is for anthropology buffs. The building, itself a real

treasure, was constructed between 1776 and 1790, and was once the home of the Marqués de Villaverde. The highlight is the Tres Milenios de Tejidos exhibition of 167 stunning weavings from around the country – ask a guide for a look inside the drawers beneath the wall hangings. It also has a fine collection of Chipaya artifacts from western Oruro department, a group whose language, rites and customs have led some experts to suggest that they are descendants of the vanished Tiahuanaco culture.

Museo de Arte Contemporaneo

Better modern art may be found in various other collections around town, but this private **museum** (MAC; Contemporary Art Museum;

SAN PEDRO PRISON – AN INSIGHT INTO THE WORLD'S MOST UNIQUE JAIL *Vesna Maric*

Once the most bizarre hotspot on most travelers' 'must-do' itinerary in La Paz, the infamous prison of San Pedro is now quite a hard place to visit. Tourism was once big business for the prisoners, but the visits were stopped after, apparently, too many came to this place on a 'cocaine shopping spree.'

San Pedro's fame is that it functions unlike any other prison: there are no guards inside, the inmates don't wear uniforms, there are no curfews and the prisoners have to work to be able to pay for their cells, which they have to rent or buy depending on their financial situation (some cost as much as US$150 a month). They work as cooks, carpenters, hairdressers, or sell sweets and food. Richer prisoners have large, almost luxurious cells, with cable TVs and plush amenities. Others are cramped in a tiny place, with a bed, cooker and mirror, or if they are really down in the dumps, a room with a dozen other prisoners. Most inmates (around 80%) are here for cocaine smuggling, and only 25% are serving their sentence. The rest are still awaiting trial.

Inside, it's like a little town. The prison is divided into eight areas, each named and centered around a patio, with small balconies. There is a clear hierarchy between the different areas, and some are richer, brighter and (supposedly) safer, while others are dark, dingy and rough. During the day, the violence is contained and prisoners play cards, football and do their work, but life gets rough at night when misunderstandings are ironed out, robberies take place and prisoners fight with knives.

According to prison figures, there are around four deaths a month here, both from natural causes and 'accidents.' Since there are no guards, problems are solved by the prisoners, who elect their leaders and have unions. Posters of Evo Morales adorn the walls: he's a loved man here, a representative of the underdogs and the poor, Bolivia's marginalized indigenous people.

The prisoners' children live inside and although family members are free to come and go as they please, many children have no one else to live with other than their arrested fathers. There are two crèches and a kindergarten, and though the children play on the community pitch, they are far from carefree: when they go out to school, they are discriminated against, and inside the prison there are reports of child molestation and a high child depression rate, resulting in an occasional suicide attempt.

On the prison football pitch, tournaments are held regularly, with bets exceeding US$20,000 a year. Every sector has a team and good players are sought after. There are even signings by teams from the wealthier sections. When we enquire about how it all works, an inmate laughs: 'It is the same as outside: if you are good, you can make more money with your feet than with your brain!'

Map pp72-3; ☎ 233-5905; www.museoplaza.com; 16 de Julio 1698; admission US$1.25; ☟ 9am-9pm) wins the gold star for the most interesting building: a restored 19th-century mansion (only one of four left on the Prado) with a glass roof and stained-glass panels designed by Gustave Eiffel. The museum's eclectic collection is a mix of reasonable – but not mind-blowing – Bolivian and international work.

Museo de Instrumentos Musicales

The exhaustive, hands-on collection of unique instruments at this **museum** (Museum of Musical Instruments; Map pp72-3; ☎ 240-8177; Jaén 711; admission US$0.60; ☟ 9:30am-1pm & 2:30-6:30pm) is a must for musicians. The brainchild of *charango* master Ernesto Cavour Aramayo, it displays all possible incarnations of *charangos* (a traditional Bolivian ukulele-type instrument) and other indigenous instruments used in Bolivian folk music and beyond. If you don't happen on an impromptu jam session, check out Peña Marka Tambo (p91) across the street. You can also arrange *charango* and wind instrument lessons here for around US$6.25 per hour.

See p40 for more on Cavour and musical instruments.

Museo de Textiles Andinos Bolivianos

Fans of Bolivia's lovely traditional weaving consider this small **textile museum** (☎ 224-3601; Plaza Benito Juárez 488, Miraflores; admission US$1.90; ☟ 9:30am-noon, 3-6:30pm Mon-Sat, 9:30am-12:30pm Sun) a must-see. Examples of the country's finest traditional textiles (including pieces from the Cordillera Apolobamba, and the Jal'qa and Candelaria regions of the Central Highlands) are grouped by region and described in Spanish. The creative process is explained from fiber to finished product. The gift shop sells museum-quality originals; 90% of the sale price goes to the artists. To get there, walk 20 minutes northeast from the Prado or catch *micros* (small buses or minibuses) 131 or 135, or minibuses marked Av Busch.

Templete Semisubterráneo (Museo al Aire Libre)

The open-pit **museum** opposite the stadium (Map pp72-3; admission free) contains replicas of statues found in Tiahuanaco's Templete Semi-subterráneo (p104). The showpiece Megalito Bennetto Pachamama (Bennett monolith) was moved to Tiahuanaco's new site museum to avoid further smog-induced deterioration. This place is only worth seeing if you aren't able to visit the actual site.

El Alto

A billboard proudly announces: 'El Alto is not part of Bolivia's problem. It's part of Bolivia's solution.' Not all would agree, but visiting here is an experience. Having once been a melting pot for *campesinos* (subsistence farmers) and people from all around the country, and with a population of 648,400, El Alto is now a city in its own right. It has a 5% to 6% growth rate per year and is considered the Aymará capital of the world.

If you arrive by air, below you are dozens of white church spires soaring up from the brown earth. These were built by a German priest, Padre Obermaier, renowned in the city for his past and current works (and longevity). From the canyon rim at the top of the El Alto Autopista (toll road) or the top of the free route at Plaza Ballivián, the streets hum with almost perpetual activity. It's hard to distinguish one street from another – the miles of orange brick and adobe houses, shops, factories and *cholita*-filled markets create a hectic atmosphere at every corner.

In the lively La Ceja (Brow) district – which commands one of the highest real-estate prices in the region for its commercial value – you'll find a variety of electronic gadgets and mercantile goods. For an excellent market experience don't miss the massive **Mercado 16 de Julio** (☟ 6am-3pm Thu & Sun), which stretches for many blocks along the main thoroughfare and across Plaza 16 de Julio. This shop-a-holic's paradise has absolutely everything, from food and electronics, to vehicles and animals, all at reasonable prices. You'll have to fight your way through the crowds, though (warning: watch your wallet in both senses of the phrase).

To fighting of a different kind, one of the most popular local attractions in El Alto is the **Lucha Libre** (admission US$1.25; ☟ 4pm Sun), or wrestling matches, where theatrical males and acrobatic *cholitas* play to the crowds. It's on at the Polifuncional de la Ceja de El Alto, a multifunctional sports stadium.

For a great view of La Paz from the El Alto rim, head in a taxi to the Tupac Katari Mirador, situated right on the edge of the rim that plunges down the valley to La Paz. It was – and is – a sacred Inca site and ritual alter where Tupac Katari is believed to have been drawn and quartered by colonialists. The colonialists constructed and interred a statue of Christ on the same site, but that didn't stop locals from performing spiritual rituals here.

Around the *mirador* (lookout) and as far as the eye can see is a long line of small identical blue booths, distinguished only by a number. These house *curanderos* or *yatiris* who provide sage advice. Note: a *yatiri*'s counsel is taken extremely seriously; please be sensitive of this – both photos and tourist appointments are considered inappropriate and are not appreciated.

There's the odd hotel popping up in El Alto, but unless you really need to, it's more pleasant to stay in La Paz and catch a 20-minute ride to the top. Jump in any minibus that says La Ceja or that is heading up Av Montes (US$0.40). Taxis to El Alto charge between US$3 and US$5 from the center.

La Paz Cemetery
As in most Latin American cemeteries, bodies are first buried in the traditional Western way or are placed in a crypt. Then, within 10 years, they are disinterred and cremated. After cremation, families purchase or rent glass-fronted spaces in the cemetery walls for the ashes, and affix plaques and mementos of the deceased, and place flowers behind the glass door. Each wall has hundreds of these doors, and some of the walls have been expanded upward to such an extent that they resemble three- or four-story apartment blocks. As a result the **cemetery** (Map pp66–7) is an active place, full of people passing through to visit relatives and leave or water fresh flowers.

There are also huge family mausoleums, as well as sections dedicated to mine workers and their families, and common graves for soldiers killed in battle. You may even see the black-clad professional mourners who provide suitable wails and tears during burials.

On November 2, the Día de los Muertos (Day of the Dead), half the city turns out to honor their ancestors.

ACTIVITIES
You'll get plenty of exercise hoofing up and down the Prado but you don't have to head far out of town for a real adrenaline rush.

Mountain Biking
For a thrilling experience, zoom down the 'World's Most Dangerous Road' (p78) from La Cumbre to Coroico or from Chacaltaya to Zongo, where extra thrills are the awesome views of La Paz and Cordillera Real. Serious single-track cyclists can choose from a range of great rides in the valleys around La Paz.

Many different operators offer a range of rides. One of the best known is **Gravity Assisted Mountain Biking** (Map pp72-3; ☎ 231-3849; www .gravitybolivia.com; No 10, Edificio Avenida, 16 de Julio 1490), a knowledgeable, highly regarded and professional outfit that has a good reputation among travelers. In addition to the trip to Coroico (per person US$55 to US$75), it offers several rides around La Paz, including road and single-track trips around the Zongo Valley and beyond (from US$65; minimum four people).

Also recommended for the Coroico trip (per person US$50 to US$65) in particular is **Downhill Madness** (Map pp72-3; ☎ 239-1810; www .madnessbolivia.com; Sagárnaga 339), which has superior hand-made, double-suspension Canadian Rocky Mountain bikes.

DEADLY TREADLIES

Many agencies offering the La Cumbre to Coroico mountain-bike plunge give travelers the T-shirts boasting about surviving the road. Keep in mind that the gravel road is just that, plus it's narrow (just over 3.2m wide), with precipitous cliffs with up to 600m drops…and there's traffic. To date, eight people – although numbers vary according to who you talk to – have died doing the 64km trip (with a 3600m vertical drop), and readers have reported close encounters and nasty accidents. Many of these are due to little or no instruction and preparation and poor-quality mountain bikes (beware bogus rebranded bikes). In short, some agencies are less than ideal. Be aware of outfits that deflate prices – cost cutting can mean dodgy brakes, poor-quality parts and, literally, a deadly treadly. Multilingual guides are necessary for coaching and control. Ask agencies for proof of rescue equipment (rope rescue, harnesses, belays, oxygen), and a predeparture briefing.

Skiing, Hiking & Climbing

The world's highest downhill skiing (5320m down to 4900m), which is strictly for enthusiasts (who want to tick off the been-there-done-that list of the world's most unusual ski runs), is on the slopes of Chacaltaya, a rough 35km drive north of La Paz (see p100).

Established in 1939, the **Club Andino Boliviano** (Map pp72-3; México 1638, La Paz; 9:30am-noon & 3-6pm Mon-Fri) runs ski trips (US$10 to US$20 per person, plus transportation) when conditions are suitable. The club operates the lift and the basic lodge, where you can buy snacks, rent ski gear and stay the night (US$5). Make sure you're well acclimatized before setting out, and bring good UV protection. At the time of research, the club was planning to open other ski areas on more snow-covered glaciers.

Many La Paz tour agencies offer daily hiking tours to Chacaltaya, an easy way to bag a high peak.

WALKING TOUR

A good starting point is **Iglesia de San Francisco** (**1**; p74) where it's easy to find snacks on the street. Watch for colorful wedding processions on weekend mornings. From **Plaza San Francisco** (**2**), huff up Calle Sagárnaga, which is lined with stores and stalls selling beautiful weavings, musical instruments, antiques, 'original' Tiahuanaco artifacts and handmade leather bags.

Turn right at Calle Linares for a poke around the **Mercado de Hechicería** (Witches'

THE WORLD'S MOST DANGEROUS ROAD

It's official: the road between La Paz and Coroico is 'The World's Most Dangerous Road' (WMDR), according to an Inter-American Development Bank (IDB) report. Given the number of fatal accidents that occur on it, the moniker is well deserved. An average of 26 vehicles per year disappear over the edge into the great abyss.

Those up for an adrenaline rush will be in their element, but if you're unnerved by a gravel track just 3.2m wide – just enough for one vehicle – sheer 600m drops, hulking rock overhangs and waterfalls that spill across and erode the highway, your best bet is to bury your head and not look until it's over. Conventional wisdom asserts that minibuses traveling by day are safer than larger overnight buses or *camiones* (flatbed trucks).

The trip starts off innocuously enough. On leaving La Paz to cross La Cumbre, you'll notice a most curious phenomenon: dogs stand like sentinels at 100m intervals. *Camión* drivers feed them in the hope that the *achachilas* (ancestor spirits who dwell in the high peaks) will look after them on their way down. At the pass drivers also perform a *cha'lla* (ritual blessing) for the *apus* (ambient mountain spirits), sprinkling the vehicle's tires with alcohol before beginning the descent.

Crosses (aka 'Bolivian caution signs') lining the way testify to the frequency of vehicular tragedies. The most renowned occurred in 1983 when a *camión* plunged over the precipice, killing the driver and 100 passengers in the worst accident in the sordid history of Bolivian transportation.

Accidents along the WMDR stem from several causes. Drunk driving is probably the most prevalent, followed by carelessness and right-of-way disputes. However, these human weaknesses pale in comparison to the undeniable weakness of the earth beneath the precarious turnouts. In 1999 an attempt was made to mitigate the dangers by allowing only downhill traffic in the morning and uphill traffic in the afternoon. However Yungas residents complained that it limited access to their markets, and the plan was scrapped after a few months.

Over the past few years, a new paved route has been constructed on the opposite wall of the valley, thanks to a US$120 million loan from the IDB. It was due to be opened in 2003, but at the time of research only a few smaller vehicles were officially permitted to use it. There is talk that when it does eventually open, the previous road may be for exclusively for cyclists, visiting trekkers and those on foot.

Note: although Bolivian traffic normally keeps to the right, downhill traffic on the Yungas road passes on the outside, whether that's the right or the left side of the road. Vehicles heading downhill must maneuver onto the sliver-like turnout ledges bordering the big drop and wait while uphill traffic squeezes past, hugging the inside wall. This ensures that the risk is taken by the driver with the best possible view of the outside tires.

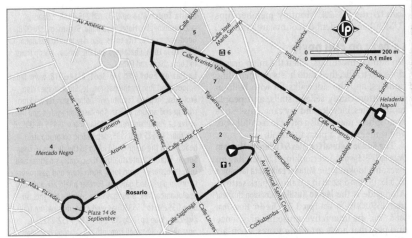

Market; **3**; p71), which is crammed with interesting specimens of herbs and magical potions. If you are lucky, you might convince a *yatiri* to toss the coca leaves and tell your fortune, but they usually refuse gringo customers.

Heading up Calle Santa Cruz toward Plaza 14 de Septiembre and Calle Max Paredes, you'll find the **Mercado Negro (4**; p74), a clogged maze of makeshift stalls that spreads over several blocks. From here, wander downhill, northeast of the markets, through streets choked with people and *micros* to **Plaza Alonso de Mendoza (5)** where you can grab a seat and watch the world go round. Adjacent is the **Museo Tambo Quirquincho (6**; p74) notable for its mask and photography collection. Continue past the bustling **Mercado Lanza (7**; p74) where you can buy a freshly squeezed juice. Amble along pedestrian-only **Calle Comercio (8)**, past street vendors hawking everything imaginable to end at **Plaza Murillo (9)** where ice cream awaits at Heladería Napoli (p89).

COURSES
Language
Note that not everyone advertising language instruction is accredited or even capable of teaching Spanish, however well they speak it, so seek local and personal recommendations, and examine credentials before signing up. Plan on paying around US$6 per hour.
ie instituto exclusivo (Map pp66-7; ☎ 242-1072; 20 de Octubre 2315, Sopocachi) Specialized courses for travelers and professionals.

WALK FACTS

Start: Iglesia de San Francisco
Finish: Heladería Napoli (p89)
Distance: 2.5km
Duration: Two to three hours

Instituto de la Lengua Española (ILE; ☎ 279-6074; www.spanbol.com; Aviador 180, Achumani) Offers private and group lessons.
SpeakEasy Institute (Map pp72-3; ☎ /fax 244-1779; www.speakeasyinstitute.com; Arce 2047) Specialized courses for travelers and professionals (US$100 per month).

The following private teachers have been recommended by readers:
Cecilia C de Ferreira (☎ 248-7458; Camacho 1664, San Pedro)
Isabel Daza Vivado (☎ /fax 231-1471; maria_daza@hotmail.com; 3rd fl, Murillo 1046)
William Ortiz (☎ 231-3721; www.studyspanish-lapaz-bolivia.tk; Linares 980)

Music
For musical instruction (in Spanish) on traditional Andean instruments – *zampoña, quena, charango* etc – see Professor Heliodoro Niña at the **Academía de Música Helios** (Map pp72-3; ☎ 240-6498/99; Indaburo 1166) or inquire at the Museo de Instrumentos Musicales (p76).

Other Courses
Yoga, tai chi and meditation classes are offered at **Casa del Sol** (Map pp72-3; ☎ 244-0928;

Goitia 127; class US$3.20). Monthly memberships (US$30) and student discounts are available.

LA PAZ FOR CHILDREN

On Sunday mornings, when the main drag is closed to traffic, the Prado hosts promenading families, and the sidewalks fill with balloon and cotton-candy sellers, stalls, and people renting kites, bicycles and toy cars. This festive atmosphere may recall a bit of lost childhood, and it makes for a pleasant stroll.

The **Kusillo Cultural Complex & Children's Museum** (Map pp72-3; Ejército) overlooking La Paz has an awesome lookout, the **Mirador Laikakota** (admission US$0.15; 9am-5:30pm) in a tranquil park setting. Alongside is the **Museo Kusillo** (admission children/ adults US$0.80/1; 9am-1pm, 3-7pm Tue-Fri; 10am-7pm Sat & Sun), an interactive museum of science and play that hosts *artesanía* stores, open-air theater and dance programs. The complex is a 20-minute walk east of the Prado along Pérez Zapata, which turns into Av del Ejército.

TOURS

Most of Bolivia's tour agencies are based in La Paz, where there are at least 100 of them. Some are clearly better than others (many are not formally registered) and many specialize in particular interests or areas. Most agencies run day tours (US$10 to US$60 per person) in and around La Paz, to Lake Titicaca, Tiahuanaco, Zongo Valley, Chacaltaya, Valle de la Luna and other sites. See p389 for a list of mostly La Paz–based agencies.

Inexpensive agency transfers to Puno can be the most straightforward way of getting to Peru, and they allow a stopover in Copacabana en route. Agencies are also useful for arranging climbing in the Cordilleras; many rent equipment.

Following is a list of recommended agencies and tour operators.

America Tours (Map pp72-3; 237-4204; www .america-ecotours.com; 16 de Julio 1490, No 9) This warmly recommended English-speaking agency offers a wide range of interesting ecotourism projects and tours around La Paz and Bolivia, including an interesting trip to Tiahuanaco (US$22 to $US45 per person depending on group size – minimum of six), with a stop in Callamarco, an Altiplano village, where you are treated to an explanation of the local culture and village structure, along with a typical lunch. Cost excludes entrance to Tiahuanaco site.

Calacoto Tours (Map pp72-3; 211-5592; office 20, Galería Doryan, Sagárnaga 189) Offers horse rides around La Paz and tours to Lake Titicaca, as well as custom-made tours.

Diana Tours (Map pp72-3; 235-1158; hotsadt@ ceibo.entelnet.bo; Hotel Sagárnaga, Sagárnaga 326-328) Good-value La Paz city tours, plus day trips to Tiahuanaco, Valle de la Luna, Chacaltaya and the Yungas; cheap tours to Copacabana and Puno.

La Paz on Foot (243-3661, 7154-3918; www.lapaz onfoot.com) Run by the passionate, English-speaking ecologist, Stephen Taranto, who offers several walking trips in and around La Paz. The fascinating, fun and inter-active La Paz urban trek (half-day tours US$15 to US$20, day tours US$25 to US$35, depending on group size) heads from the heights of El Alto to the depths of Zona Sur, as Taranto contextualizes the country's natural and cultural history – from food, agriculture and gastronomy to urban parks and gardens. Further afield are a six-day Apolobamba Trek, a Yungas Coca Tour (five nights, six days US$250 to US$350) as well as various nature trails.

Zig-Zag (Map pp72-3; 245-7814, 7152-2822; zigzagbolivia@hotmail.com; office 5, Illampu 867) Run by the extremely professional English-speaking Bolivian, Mario, and offering a range of tours from La Paz (including Tiahuanaco), longer treks and custom-made adventures around Bolivia.

Bus Tours

Viajes Planeta (279-1440, Calle 21, Calacoto, Zona Sur), runs tours of the city and Zona Sur in a red, double-decker, city-tour bus (US$6 per person). Short stops include Mirador Killi Killi, San Miguel in Zona Sur and the Valle de la Luna. The recorded narration is in seven languages and is a bit of a promotional pitch (at one stage it highlights the bonuses of investing in Bolivia) but you'll see a lot in four hours.

FESTIVALS & EVENTS

La Paz is always looking for an excuse to celebrate. Check with the municipal tourist office (p69) for a complete list of what's on.

January

ALASITAS

During Inca times the Alasitas ('Buy From Me' in Aymará, in Spanish it's *Comprame*) fair coincided with the spring equinox (September 21), and was intended to demonstrate the abundance of the fields. The date underwent some shifts during the Spanish colonial period, which the *campesinos* weren't too happy about. In effect they decided to turn the celebration into a kitschy mockery of the original. 'Abundance' was redefined to apply not only to crops, but also to homes, tools, cash, clothing and, lately, cars, trucks, airplanes and even 12-

---

EKEKO

Ekeko is the household god and the keeper and distributor of material possessions. During Alasitas his devotees collect miniatures of those items they'd like to acquire during the following year and heap them onto small plaster images of the god. He's loaded down with household utensils, baskets of coca, wallets full of miniature currency, lottery tickets, liquor, chocolate and other luxury goods. The more optimistic devotees buy miniature souped-up *camiones* (flatbed trucks), first-class airline tickets to Miami and three-story suburban homes! Once purchased, all items must be blessed by a certified *yatiri* (witch doctor) before they can become real. If this apparent greed seems not to be in keeping with Aymará values – the community and balance in all things – it's worth noting that Ekeko is also charged with displaying that which a family is able to share with the community.

---

story buildings. The little god of abundance, Ekeko ('dwarf' in Aymará), made his appearance and modern Alasitas traditions are now celebrated every January 24th.

May/June

EL GRAN PODER

Held in late May or early June, **La Festividad de Nuestro Señor Jesús del Gran Poder** began in 1939 as a candle procession led by an image of Christ through the predominantly *campesino* neighborhoods of upper La Paz.

The following year the local union of embroiderers formed a folkloric group to participate in the event. In subsequent years other festival-inspired folkloric groups joined in, and the celebration grew larger and more lively. It has now developed into a unique La Paz festival, with dancers and folkloric groups from around the city participating. Embroiderers prepare elaborate costumes for the event and upwards of 25,000 performers practice for weeks in advance.

El Gran Poder is a wild and exciting time, and offers a glimpse of Aymará culture at its festive finest. A number of dances are featured, such as the *suri sikuris* (in which the dancers are bedecked in ostrich feathers), the lively *kullasada, morenada, caporales* and the *inkas,* which duplicates Inca ceremonial dances.

If you'd like to catch the procession, go early to stake out a place along the route, keeping a lookout for stray or unruly water balloons. The municipal tourist office (p69) can provide specific dates and details about a particular year's celebration.

AYAMARÁ NEW YEAR & SAN JUAN (WINTER SOLSTICE)

The **Ayamará New Year** is celebrated across the Altiplano around June 21, the longest and

coldest night of the year. Festivities feature huge bonfires and fireworks in the streets, plus lots of drinking to stay warm. **San Juan** (June 24) is the Christian version of the solstice celebration. The solstice celebrations are most lively at Tiahuanaco (p102).

July

FIESTAS DE JULIO

This month-long cultural series at the Teatro Municipal features much folk music.

VIRGEN DEL CARMEN

The patron saint of La Paz department gets her own public holiday (July 16), which includes many dances and parades.

ENTRADA FOLKLÓRICA DE UNIVERSITARIA

Held on the last Saturday in July, and with an atmosphere alluding to Carnaval, hundreds of dance groups made up of students from around the country perform traditional dances through the streets of La Paz.

August

INDEPENDENCE DAY

This lively public holiday (August 6) sees lots of gunfire in the air, parades galore and mortar blasts around the city center.

November & December

DÍA DE LOS MUERTOS (ALL SAINTS DAY)

Colorful celebrations of ancestors fill cemeteries around the city and country.

NEW YEAR'S EVE

Look out for the fireworks – many at eye level – which are best seen from high above the city at a *mirador.*

SLEEPING

Most backpackers beeline for central La Paz to find a bed. The downtown triangle between Plazas Mendoza, Murillo and 14 de Septiembre is full of popular budget and midrange places, and many of the services travelers need. If you want to live closer to movie theaters, a wider array of restaurants and a bar or two, consider staying closer to Sopocachi around Plaza San Pedro. The area around the Witches' Market (between Santa Cruz and Sagárnaga) is about as close as Bolivia gets to a travelers ghetto. For more upmarket luxury look along the lower Prado and further south in Zona Sur.

La Paz has dozens of low-cost hotels and *residenciales,* the vast majority of which are around Sagárnaga and to the east of upper-Montes. A few of the bottom-of-the-barrel places impose a midnight curfew. All places listed below claim to have hot water at least part of the day; few have it all the time.

West of the Prado & Mariscal Santa Cruz

BUDGET

Hostal Cactus (Map pp72-3; ☎ 245-1421; Jiménez 818; r per person US$3.15) This joint could do with a mild cleaning spell or two, but its location, smack in the middle of the Witches' Market, makes up for the saggy beds and shabby student-style digs. The communal kitchen and rooftop 'terrace' appeal to those on a budget.

Alojamiento El Solario (Map pp72-3; ☎ 236-7963; elsolariohotel@yahoo.com; Murillo 776; dm/s/d/tr US$2.50/4/7.50/11.25; 🖳) A mellow and yellow budget hangout with slightly scruffy dormitory-style but adequate rooms, 24/7 hot showers, laundry service, a shared kitchen and luggage storage. Check out the sunny roof terrace. Be aware that travelers have reported missing items.

Hostal Dinastía (Map pp72-3; ☎ 245-1076; hostel dinastia@yahoo.com; Illampu 684; r per person US$4, with bathroom US$7) On a high note, this place is right in the middle of the action. The comedowns are the shabby and slightly soiled semi-carpeted rooms. Some rooms have cable TV.

Hotel Continental (Map pp72-3; ☎ 02-245-1176; hotelcontinental626@hotmail.com; Illampu 626; r per person US$5, s/d with bathroom US$9/15) This older, two-star HI-affiliate is clean, well located and popular among thrifty tour groups. It's hard to meet people due to its unsociable hotel-style design. Lucky, then, that rooms have cable TV.

Hostal Maya (Map pp72-3; ☎ 231-1970; mayahost _in@hotmail.com; Sagárnaga 339; r per person US$6.90, with bathroom US$8.20; 🖳) Some rooms are as smoky and windowless as a witch's den; others, such as those with a front balcony are more appealing, if a little noisy. A *charango*'s strum away from Peña Huari (p91). Breakfast included.

Alojamiento El Viajero (El Lobo; Map pp72-3; ☎ 245-3465; cnr Illampu & Santa Cruz; dm US$3.15; r with bathroom US$8; 🖳) Just like your college dorm, only colder and everything is in Hebrew. The few shared baths are grubby, and rates include all the partying your Israeli neighbors can throw.

MIDRANGE

Hotel Majestic (Map pp72-3; ☎ 245-1628; Santa Cruz 359; s/d/tr with bathroom & breakfast US$11.50/16.50/20) Its pink bathrooms and smart parquetry floors provide some distraction from its nondescript, yet clean surrounds in the heart of things. Excellent value.

Hotel Milton (Map pp72-3; ☎ 235-3511; Illampu 1126-1130; s/d/tr with bathroom & breakfast US$12.50/16.50/20) Tune in, drop out! This '70s pad features red vinyl studded walls, painted murals and funky wallpaper. Darker rooms at the back are a bit dingy, but the higher and lighter front rooms afford stupendous views over La Paz. The associated Milton Tours runs buses to Tiahuanaco and Copacabana.

Hotel Sagárnaga (Map pp72-3; ☎ 235-0252; reservas@hotel-sagarnaga.com; Sagárnaga 326; s/d with bathroom & breakfast US$15/20). The knight in shining armor at the front desk (and no, we're not talking about the receptionist) and the mirrors are the brightest things in this otherwise slightly tarnished, yet perfectly pleasant, '80s-style place. Behind the school dormitory-style corridors you'll find clean rooms with adequate beds.

Arcabucero Hostal Inn (Map pp72-3; ☎ /fax 231-3473; arcabucero-bolivia@hotmail.com; Liluyo 307; s/d/tr with bathroom US$15/24/35) The 10 quiet rooms at this restored antique colonial home are arranged around an ornate indoor courtyard with a glass roof. The electric showers are unpredictable but the rooms have cable TV. Breakfast (US$2.50) is served in the common room. Nicer rooms are upstairs; the downstairs rooms are dark.

Estrella Andina (Map pp72-3; ☎ 245-6421; Illampu 716; s/d with bathroom & breakfast US$18/28) If you're suffering from altitude sickness, amuse yourself at this clean and well-run place. Each room has its own mural (or three) and cable TV. Good value for this price range.

Hotel La Joya (Map pp66-7; ☎ 245-3841; www.hotelajoya.com; Max Paredes 541; s/d/tr US$13/17/23, with bathroom US$20/27/34) A clean, friendly and frilly three-star '80s-style option amid the bustle of the Mercado Negro. It includes a basic breakfast in the disco-lit dining area, cable TV and good hot showers. In the low season, prices are negotiable. Head to the roof-top at night for a sparkling view.

La Posada de la Abuela (Map pp72-3; ☎ 233-2285; Linares 947; s/d US$20/25) This brand-new place is a pleasant oasis in the heart of artesan and tourist mecca. The rooms are sterile and clean, but the plant-filled courtyard adds a colorful, if potentially noisy, touch.

Hotel Galería (Map pp72-3; ☎ 246-1015; hotel galeria@hotmail.com; Santa Cruz 583; s/d/tr with bathroom & breakfast US$20/30/40) This novel, pleasant option rises above the bustling streets overlooking the Mercado Negro. The interior, within a small modern cathedral-like shopping mall, features glass, open balconies and lots of dying greenery. The front rooms overlooking the street are sunny but noisy and some rooms don't have outward-facing windows. Prices can be negotiated for longer stays.

Hostal Naira (Map pp72-3; ☎ 235-5645; www.hostal naira.com; Sagárnaga 161; s/d/tr with bathroom & breakfast US$25/32/42; 🖥) At the bottom of Sagárnaga, near Plaza San Francisco, Naira is repeatedly recommended for its location, cleanliness and heating, which make it quite popular with tour groups. It can be noisy, however. Breakfast is served in the downstairs café.

ourpick **Hotel Rosario** (Map pp72-3; ☎ 245-1658; www.hotelrosario.com; Illampu 704; s/d/tr with bathroom & breakfast US$33/43/57; 🖥) The professional, English-speaking staff at La Paz's best three-star hotel pamper you with five-star treatment. The ultraclean rooms in the well-maintained colonial residence all have solar-powered hot showers, satellite TV and heaters. There is free internet access and the included breakfast buffet at the Tambo Colonial (p86) is worth a trip, even if you can't get a room here. It's base camp for many expeditions, so definitely book ahead. Large family and honeymoon suites fetch US$67 to US$74.

East of the Prado & Mariscal Santa Cruz
BUDGET
Hospedaje Milenio (Map pp72-3; ☎ 228-1263; hospedajemilenio@hotmail.com; Yanacocha 860; r per person

US$3.15) A relaxed joint, run by friendly staff and including kitchen use and hot water. The best rooms are upstairs and outward facing (note: most single rooms have internal windows). There's also a travel agency and a laundry service.

Alojamiento Illimani (Map pp72-3; ☎ 220-2346; Illimani 1817; US$3.15 per person) The religious pictures on the walls of these stark rooms are the most blessed things in this out-of-the way abode… except for the leafy patio where you can cook.

Hostal Austria (Map pp72-3; ☎ 240-8540; Yanacocha 531; dm US$3.15, s/d US$4.50/6.50; 🖥) This shabby, rambling, yet friendly number is a popular traveler's haunt. Despite its 11pm curfew, short beds (some in windowless cells) and dicey shared bathrooms, this old place is good for people contact. Hot showers and cooking facilities available.

Hotel Torino (Map pp72-3; ☎ 02-240-6003; torinonet@hotmail.com; Socabaya 457; s/d/tr US$4/7.50/11.50, s/d/tr with bathroom US$7.50/12.50/19) 'Dark, cold and draughty' is one traveler's view of this modernized (in the '50s) rambling, colonial building. It's more popular for its services – a restaurant, a book exchange and luggage storage – than its comforts.

Hotel La Valle (Map pp72-3; ☎ 245 6085; www.lavallehotel.com; Evaristo Valle 153; s/d with bathroom US$8/12.50) This might as well be called Hotel Value, such are the good basic rooms at fair prices. It's popular among the locals and breakfast is included in one of the hotel's two restaurants. The TV is not cable, but for this price that'd be pushing it. While the front rooms (all double) are the nicest, street traffic can be noisy.

MIDRANGE
Hostal República (Map pp72-3; ☎ 220-2742; www.angelfire.com/wv/hostalrepublica; Comercio 1455; s/d/tr/q US$10/16/21/28, with bathroom US$16/25/36/44; 🖥) Three blocks from the historic heart of the city, this hotel occupies a lovely historic building that was once home to one of Bolivia's first presidents. Its two large courtyards are a pleasant oasis, although it could do with an all-round spruce up. All the rooms are fairly basic (those downstairs can be a little dank) but will make for a pleasant, if unremarkable, stay. Family rooms and a fully equipped and spacious *casita* (separate apartment) are also available (from US$35 for two people).

Tiquina Palace Hotel (Map pp72-3; ☎ 245-7373; Pasaje Tiquina 150; s/d/tr with bathroom & breakfast US$20/23/28) A surprisingly quiet place in the heart of La Paz. Get past the pale-blue, cold corridors to dated, but perfectly passable, carpeted rooms with cable TV, telephone plus a buffet breakfast. Staff are extremely friendly and airport transfers are free for guests staying three or more nights; otherwise they're US$5.50.

Hotel Gloria (Map pp72-3; ☎ 240-7070; www.hotel gloria.com.bo; Potosí 909; s/d/tr with bathroom & breakfast US$36.30/48/55.50; ⊠) At the lower range of the top-end towers, and above the snarling traffic of the Prado. It's got a red-shag pile look and slightly stale smell about it, but the helpful and friendly staff make this place good value.

TOP END

Hotel Europa (Map pp72-3; ☎ 231-5656; www.hotel europa.com.bo; Tiahuanacu 64; s/d with bathroom US$65/105; ⊠ 🖵 ⊠ 🏊) One of the newer and sleeker, biz-focused places in town. All the amenities, like in-room internet, are executive, and thoughtful touches like radiant bathroom heating, a humidification system and telephones in the bathrooms justify the high rack rates. The two suites on the 12th floor have amazing city views. Nonguests can use the spa, heated pool and fitness center for US$10 per day.

Hotel Plaza (Map pp72-3; ☎ 237-8311; www.plazabo livia.com.bo; 16 de Julio 1789; s/d with bathroom US$99/119; ⊠ 🖵 🏊) Friendly, helpful and convenient, but nothing fancy, and with all the amenities: cable TV, a continental buffet breakfast and use of the swimming pool, gym and Jacuzzi.

Hotel Presidente (Map pp72-3; ☎ 240-6666; www .hotelpresidente-bo.com; Potosí 920; s/d/tr/ste US$115/135/155/185; ⊠ 🖵 🏊) This is one of the highest five-star hotels in the world (oxygen tanks are available) with a small casino to chew up your pennies. Once you get past the unconsciously retro furnishings, this venerable grand dame gives a pleasant room-with-a-view experience. You can fine-dine at one of their restaurants – the 16th-floor Bella Vista and the simpler La Kantuta.

San Pedro & Sopocachi

BUDGET

Residencial La Paz City Annex (Map pp72-3; ☎ 236-8380; México 1539; r per person US$3.80) Shabby, but for those on a budget, it has some passable rooms with balconies.

Residencial Sucre (Map pp72-3; ☎ 249-2038; Colombia 340; s/d with bathroom US$10/15) Management

is helpful and the rooms – with the squeakiest of squeaky-clean floors – are around a secure and pleasant courtyard (good for cycle storage). Rooms have cable TV. It's handy to Plaza San Pedro as well as Heladería Splendid (see p89).

MIDRANGE

Hostal Astoria (Map pp72-3; ☎ 215-4081; Almirante Grau 348; s/d with bathroom US$12/18) If the travelers' ghetto around Sagárnaga isn't for you, head to this underrated, excellent-value choice with spotless rooms and cable TV. It's located on a quiet and pleasant plaza, but is close to the bars of Sopocachi.

Hotel España (Map pp72-3; ☎ 244-2643; 6 de Agosto 2074; s/d/tr with bathroom & breakfast US$24/34/40; 🖵) This place is a bit like a great aunt – friendly with a colorful personality but ever-so-slightly worse for wear. It's a slightly overpriced colonial place, with a lovely, sunny courtyard and garden and worn rooms. It's within an easy stroll of many of the city's best restaurants. Rates include cable TV. The attached restaurant also offers inexpensive lunches (US$1.50).

Hotel Max Inn (Map pp72-3; ☎ 249-2247; Plaza San Pedro; s/d with bathroom US$35/47) Possibly the only three-star hotel in the world with views of a 'five-star' prison. (And the guards' moods seemed to have rubbed off onto management.) Rooms are large, bright and carpeted; those at the front face freedom in the plaza below.

Alcalá Apart Hotel (Map pp66-7; ☎ 241 2336; alcalapt@zuper.ent; Víctor Sanjines on Plaza España; s/d/tr apt with bathroom US$50/60/70; ⊠) Come here for an alternative to the standard hotel scene. These good-value, fully-equipped and very roomy apartments overlook leafy Plaza España and are away from the cut and thrust of noisy downtown. You're in walking distance of the Sopocachi cafés.

La Loge (Map pp66-7; ☎ 242 3561; www.lacomedie -lapaz.com; La Comédie Art-Café Restaurant, Pasaje Medinacelli 2234, Sopocachi; apt US$50; 🖵) Oooh la la! This one is tops. The attention to detail in these light, bright and airy self-catering, serviced apartments is French in flavor – and that means bon goût. The four apartments are beautifully designed with modern and stylish trimmings. There's a small kitchen with coffee percolator, microwave and cupboards stocked with basic foodstuffs. Not that you'll want to cook with one of the best restaurants a hop, skip and drink away (see p88). The comfortable rooms include cable TV and your own personal internet (even your clothes are washed for you!).

TOP END

El Rey Palace (Map pp72-3; 241-8541; www.hotel-rey-palace-bolivia.com; 20 de Octubre 1947; s/d with bathroom US$70/80;) This business-oriented and rather over-perfumed four-star boutique hotel has 43 rooms offering European-standard services, including buffet breakfast, telephones and cable TV. Request a room with a private Jacuzzi. The Rey Arturo restaurant serves à la carte dishes and the bar is open nightly.

Hotel Radisson Plaza (Map pp72-3; 244-1111; www.radisson.com/lapazbo; Arce 2177; s/d/ste US$160/180/260;) The Radisson has everything you'd expect in a five-star hotel, but the impersonal atmosphere isn't for everyone. There is also a range of more luxurious options, up to the presidential suite for US$495. The top-floor restaurant affords a superb view over the city and surrounding mountains.

Near the Main Bus Terminal

BUDGET

Hostal Maximiliano (Map pp72-3; 246-2318; hostalmaximiliano@yahoo.com; Inca Mayta 531; s US$5, d with bathroom US$7.50) A lovely older couple run this basic, but clean and secure, place. The beds are a bit saggy, but it has a courtyard and is in a handy location to Plaza San Francisco and the bus terminal. The doubles are more pleasant.

Adventure Brew Hostel (Map pp66-7; 246-1614; www.theadventurebrewhostel.com; Montes 533; dm/r with bathroom & breakfast US$5/8) The name says it all. This brand-new abode offers designer-style rooms, funky communal spaces, pancake breakfasts, BBQs, as well as fun on tap. Yes, there's an authentic microbrewery on site. Best to book via the website.

Hostal Tambo del Oro (Map pp66-7; 228-1565; Armentia 367; s/d US$5/8, with bathroom US$9/12) A pleasantly quiet, cozy and colonial-style place, with good-value, slightly run-down carpeted rooms and gas showers.

Arthy's Guesthouse (Map pp72-3; 228-1439; arthyshouse@gmail.com; Montes 693; r per person US$6.25) This clean and cozy place hidden behind a bright orange door, deservedly receives rave reviews as a 'tranquil oasis,' despite its location on one of La Paz's busiest roads. Chill in the living room over a choice of DVDs. The friendly, English-speaking owners will do all they can do to help you. Kitchen facilities are available.

Zona Sur

MIDRANGE & TOP END

Calacoto Hotel (Map pp86-7; 279-2524; www.hotel-calacoto-bolivia.com; Calle 13 8099, Calacoto; s/d/tr US$32/38/45) The most family-friendly (and pet-welcoming!) place in La Paz is in a tranquil, leafy setting. A large communal garden and choice of rooms, including self-contained apartments, set this place apart from city hotels. The garden is perfect for the kids, and adults may enjoy the spa and small pool. The helpful in-house travel agency offers some alternative takes on traditional sight-seeing trips, including horse-riding tours.

Camino Real (Map pp86-7; 279-2323; www.caminoreal.com.bo; Ballivián 369, cnr Calle 10, Calacoto; s/d suite US$128-168) La Paz's newest five-star hotel and one that deserves an international rating. Modern and luxurious with all the trimmings: pool, business center and restaurants.

EATING

La Paz enjoys an abundance of inexpensive and upmarket eateries offering everything from local treats to more Western-style dishes. For local fare, your cheapest (and sometimes tastiest) bets are the *almuerzos* (set lunches) in the countless hole-in-the-wall restaurants; look for the chalkboard menus out front. As a general rule, the higher you climb from the Prado, the cheaper the meals will be.

Vegetarians are increasingly well catered for and there are some excellent vegetarian restaurants (even *salteñerías* are in on the veggie act, see p89).

Upmarket restaurants are on the rise in La Paz. They serve excellent quality foods with the freshest of fresh ingredients, for which the food of La Paz is famous. Many midrange and upmarket restaurants are concentrated at the lower end of town: on the lower Prado around 16 de Julio and in lower Sopocachi around Avs 20 de Octubre and 6 de Agosto. Zona Sur is considered *the* place to go for a night on the town or a weekend coffee. While there's a good mix of cafés, restaurants and a few eateries which sell Bolivian food, the more upmarket places have a definite Western flavor.

Restaurants

BUDGET

There are heaps of acceptable budget restaurants on Evaristo Valle, near Mercado Lanza (p74); also cheap are the several places along the lower (eastern) end of Calle Rodríguez,

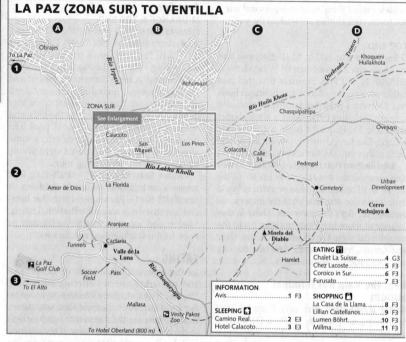

LA PAZ (ZONA SUR) TO VENTILLA

EATING
- Chalet La Suisse...............4 G3
- Chez Lacoste....................5 F3
- Coroico in Sur.................6 F3
- Furusato..........................7 E3

INFORMATION
- Avis.................................1 F3

SLEEPING
- Camino Real....................2 E3
- Hotel Calacoto................3 E3

SHOPPING
- La Casa de la Llama..........8 F3
- Lillian Castellanos............9 F3
- Lumen Böhrt...................10 F3
- Millma...........................11 F3

which also boasts a handful of excellent, cheap Peruvian-style *ceviche* places in the 200 block, including **Acuario** (Map pp72-3; mains under US$3).

Andrómeda (Map pp72-3; Arce; lunch; set menu US$2) Located at the bottom of Aspiazu steps, this is recommended for *almuerzos*.

Coroico in Sur (Map pp86-7; 279-5936; Juli Patino 1526; lunch & dinner Mon-Sat, lunch only Sun; set lunch US$1.80, mains US$1.60-2.50) A great place to join the locals for typical Bolivian lunch dishes of *plato paceño* (see p59) and set lunches in a tranquil garden setting.

Join the locals for a cheap eat at the following.

Restaurant Laza (Map pp72-3; Bozo 244; lunch US$0.75)

Restaurant Verona (Map pp72-3; Colón near Santa Cruz; mains US$2-3)

MIDRANGE

Le Pot Colonial (Map pp72-3; 7154-0082; Linares 906; set lunch US$2.25, mains US$2-4.50) An ambitious menu here features traditional Bolivian dishes that don't always meet their mark and are served at armadillo pace. Pros include an inviting setting above the Coca Museum.

Yussef (Map pp72-3; Sagárnaga 380; lunch & dinner; mains US$2-4.50) Bolivia's best Middle Eastern food. Great mixed vegetarian plate of Lebanese specialties like hummus, falafel, tabouli and *baba ganoush*. The extensive menu also has many meaty choices.

Ángelo Colonial (Map pp72-3; 236-0199; Linares 922; mains US$2.50-5) This quirky, darkened colonial-style restaurant features a ramshackle collection of antiquities – pistols, swords and antique portraits, plus excellent soups, salads and luscious veggie lasagne (US$3).

Casa de los Paceños (Map pp72-3; 228-0955; Sucre 856; lunch & dinner Mon-Sat, lunch only Sun; mains US$3.40-4) Local families and visitors alike love this place for upscale versions of classic *paceño* (local La Paz) dishes like *saice, sajta, chairo* and *fritanga*. It is probably better not to know what some of these dishes are – the menu's translation doesn't do the flavor justice. But to give you a taster: try the *ranga*, boiled cow tongue.

Tambo Colonial (Map pp72-3; 245-1658; Hotel Rosario, Illampu 704; breakfast & dinner; mains US$3-6) Known for its salad bar and excellent mains such as trout in white-wine sauce, llama me-

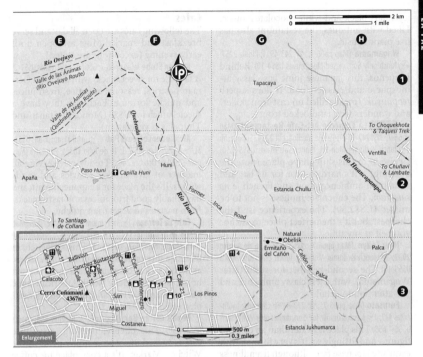

dallions with mushroom sauce, and veggie lasagna. Afterward indulge in what may be the best chocolate mousse south of the equator. Nonguests of Hotel Rosario are welcome to eat at the breakfast buffet (US$3).

Chifa New Hong Kong (Map pp66-7; Salinas 355; ☺ lunch & dinner; mains US$2.80-7.50) Inexpensive, MSG-laden, Chinese grub. '*Sin Agí-no-moto*' is the key phrase to avoid the glutamate. Lunches only US$1.25.

Boomerang (Map pp66-7; ☎ 242-3700; Pasaje Gustavo Medinacelli 2282) A new and appealing bar-come-pizzeria in a bright and open atrium, which has little to do with an Australian icon. That is, unless the slightly soggy but tasty pizzas, Entel cellular phone chargers and Spanish newspapers keep you coming back.

TOP END

El Arriero (Map pp66-7; ☎ 243-5060; 6 de Agosto 2535; ☺ lunch & dinner; mains US$4-7) This Argentine grill restaurant is a spacious, cheery place for a serious protein injection. The chunky meat is kept warm on a tableside grill, while a series of even larger cuts (US$10 to US$12) feed three or four. There's a decent salad bar, but it's no vegetarian hangout! Good, if pricey, wine selection.

Pronto Dalicatessen (Map pp66-7; ☎ 244-1369; Jáuregui 2248; ☺ 7pm-midnight Mon-Sat; mains US$4-8) Eating here is like having sex for the first time: definitely experimental, shockingly foreign, but surprisingly delicious in the end. When the restaurant's name contains an Italian 'Pronto' and a punned '*Dali*catessen,' you know you're in for a surreal fusion. Think goat ravioli with Asian curry sauce or quinoa spaghetti with coca béchamel sauce, and you get the sensation. But the climax has to be the 'Paranoia of textures and tastes of *Dali*ano chocolate' (US$3.15). Coupled with the discreet cover song of Madonna's 'Like a Virgin' (we kid you not), you'll agree that, for a high price, this restaurant is the place to be sated.

Restaurant Vienna (Map pp72-3; ☎ 244-1660; Zuazo 1905; ☺ lunch & dinner Mon-Fri, closed Sat, lunch only Sun; mains US$4-10) Arguably La Paz's best continental restaurant, classy Vienna serves traditional, central European cuisine and unique takes on Bolivian criollo classics. Try the hearty Austrian Farmer's plate or the legendary black-and-white chocolate mousse. Filled with antiques, the restaurant also has live piano music.

Wagamama (Map pp66-7; ☎ 243-4911; Pinilla 2257; ⏰ lunch only Sun, closed Mon; meals US$4-10) Behind Jalapeños, this Japanese joint has classy atmosphere and classier food. It does superb *teppanyaki* (meat grilled on cast-iron skillet) and wonders with landlocked trout.

ourpick La Comédie Art-Café Restaurant (Map pp66-7; ☎ 242-3561; Pasaje Medinacelli 2234, Sopocachi; ⏰ lunch & dinner Mon-Fri, dinner Sat; mains US$5-6.50) Cruise in to this ship-shape place (note the building) – it's hard to beat for its bar and restaurant ambience, food and French *je ne sais quoi*. The chocolate mousse is not to be missed (US$2.50). The experience isn't the cheapest, but it's the perfect place to anchor yourself at any time.

New Tokyo (Map pp66-7; ☎ 243-3654; 6 de Agosto 2932; ⏰ lunch & dinner Mon-Sat, lunch only Sun; meals US$5-10) The second-best bet for sushi (after Wagamama), with a less classy ambience and less attention to detail.

Furusato (Map pp86-7; ☎ 279-6499; Clemente Inofuentes 437; ⏰ lunch & dinner Tue-Sun, dinner only Mon; mains US$5-11.50) This place is neater than an origami figure – and fittingly so. It's very formal, with exquisite Japanese fare, although friendliness isn't always on the menu.

Chalet La Suisse (Map pp86-7; ☎ 279-3160; www .chaletlasuisse.com; Muñoz Reyes, 1710, Calacoto; mains US$7.50-11.50) This Swiss-run restaurant is as upscale as the name sounds – it's seriously expensive (by Bolivian standards), has a very old-style atmosphere and is extremely good. Imported cheeses, top local wines and trout dishes are merely part of the experience. Don't go here if you're after Bolivian atmosphere – it would be as at home in New York or London – but gourmands should splurge.

Chez Lacoste (Map pp86-7; 279-2616; Bustamante 1098, Calacoto; mains US$7-11.50) This is a formal-tablecloth kind of place and haute cuisine in every respect. The Bolivian and French chefs work with beef, llama and fish. And we mean *work*… check out the braid of trout and *pejerry* (kingfish; US$7.50), a pink-and-white checkerboard of delectable fish. Local ingredients – such as quinoa and *huminta* (cornmeal filled with cheese, aniseed and cheese and baked in the oven or boiled)– are on the menu. If you're pining for *pescada*, try the trout fillet with black butter and capers (US$7.50).

Cafés

The following cafés are open all day and serve breakfast and snacks. Most are open until early evening (exceptions are stated).

Kuchen Stube (Map pp66-7; Gutiérrez 461; cakes US$1-2) A favorite for sweet snacks with decadent German pastries, reasonable coffee, fresh juices and quiche lorraine. Each day they have a special lunch for US$3 (Monday is Italian and Thursday is vegetarian).

Alexander Coffee & Pub (⏰ until 11pm; mains US$1-3) the Prado (Map pp72-3; 16 de Julio 1832); Sopocachi (Map pp66-7; 20 de Octubre 2463) Trendy café serving all manner of java drinks, pastries and sandwiches. It's the place for a cappuccino hit, and has reliably good fruit juices and tasty snacks, from pastries to vegetarian quiche.

Café La Terraza (⏰ late; mains US$1-3) the Prado (Map pp72-3; 16 de Julio 1615); Sopocachi (Map pp66-7; 20 de Octubre 2331; Montenegro Bloque US$0.40) This stylish chain offers quality espresso and other coffee treats, as well as rich chocolate cake and cooked breakfasts that include North American–style pancakes and *huevos rancheros* (spicy scrambled eggs).

Pepe's Coffee Bar (Map pp72-3; Jimenez 894; snacks US$1-3.50) This cheery, inviting, arty little café is tucked away on a sunny bend in the Witches' Market. It's a cozy place for coffee or cocktails. Big breakfasts and veggie lunch options go down easy while browsing the library of guidebooks and English-language periodicals.

Profumo di Caffé (Map pp72-3; Museo San Francisco, Plaza San Francisco 503; snacks US$1.25-3.50) In a restored annex to the Museo San Francisco, is this blessed place – imbibe Italian coffee watched over by angels and seduced by cool jazz. It has a rotating selection of tiramisu, cakes, pastries and other snacks.

Confitería Club de La Paz (Map pp72-3; cnr Camacho & Mariscal Santa Cruz; mains US$1.40-3.50) For a quick coffee or empanada, hit this literary café and haunt of politicians (and, formerly, of Nazi war criminals), known for its strong espresso and cakes.

Café Ciudad (Map pp72-3; Plaza del Estudiante 1901; mains US$1.50-3) Slow service and mediocre food but the full menu of burgers, pasta, steak and pizza is available 24/7 every day of the year.

Luna's Café (Map pp72-3; Sagárnaga 289; ⏰ until 11pm; snacks US$1.50-4) A welcoming if gringofied joint with board games, TV, happy hours and snacks. The all-you-can eat breakfast buffet is US$2.80.

Café Banaís (Map pp72-3; Sagárnaga s/n; snacks US$1.50-3) Popular with tourists of all ages for its sunny window seats, handy location next to Plaza San Francisco, and Western-style breakfasts and gourmet sandwiches. Best of all, they know how to make a half-decent coffee.

Café Torino (Map pp72-3; Hotel Torino, Socabaya 457; ☾ until 11pm; snacks US$0.60-2.50) An olde-world café with '80s music and a good selection of snacks including sandwiches, fruit juices and cakes.

Le Bistrot (Map pp66-7; Guachalla 399; ☾ 8:30am-midnight; meals US$1.20-2.50) Hang out with the Sopochachi cool cats at this chic spot below the Alianza Francesa. It's got a smoky atmosphere, art on the walls and funky lighting, and is pleasant for a crêpe and coffee. The food lets it down a little, but it's a lovely place to chill.

Dumbo's (Map pp72-3; 16 de Julio s/n; mains US$2.20-5, ice creams US$2.50) Kids – big and small – with elephant-size appetites will enjoy the massive portions, animal-shaped foods, salads and ice-cream sundaes to drool over.

Quick Eats

Few places that serve breakfast open before 8am or 9am, but early risers desperate for a caffeine jolt before they can face the day will find bread rolls and riveting coffee concentrate at the markets for US$0.35. The *salteñas* and *tucumanas* (like a *salteña*, but with fluffier pastry) sold in the markets and on the streets – even cheaper than those in sit-down cafés – are normally excellent.

Sergiu's (Map pp72-3; 6 de Agosto 2040; ☾ from 5pm; snacks under US$2) Arguably the best pizzas in town come from this rockin', evening-only hole-in-the-wall near the Aspiazu steps. Besides pizza, you'll find gyros, chili and lasagna.

Eli's Pizza Express (Map pp72-3; 16 de Julio 1491 & 1800; mains US$1-2; ☾ lunch & dinner) A Prado fast-food favorite where you can choose between pizza, pasta, pastries and ice cream. The food is not great – but there's no wait.

A good choice for Italian ice cream is **Heladería Napoli** (Map pp72-3; Ballivián; ☾ 8:30am-10:30pm) on Plaza Murillo's north side and **Heladería Splendid** (Map pp66-7; cnr Nicolas Acosta) which has been scooping up splendid ice cream for nearly 50 years. In addition to ice-cream concoctions, it serves breakfasts, pastries, cakes and other snacks. There are also several popular ice-cream parlors along the Prado, such as the circus-like Dumbo's (left).

Mama Naturaleza (Map pp72-3; cnr Sagárnaga & Murillo; ☾ 7:30am-10pm; snacks US$1-3) Get your health kick here at this organic food joint. It's located

---

SAVORING SALTEÑAS

One of the most popular mid-morning (brunch) snacks for Bolivians is the *salteña*, a juicy, pastry-filled parcel of heaven. Originally from Salta in Argentina, these snacks were traditionally filled with a stew of meat or *pollo* (chicken), a piece of egg and an olive. Nowadays, different versions have hit the market, including vegetarian.

These can be bought on-the-run from shops and trolleys around towns, but weekends are the time to savor them in a *salteñería*. Everyone from families to trendy young lovers gather to chew over gossip or flirt over their *jugo con leches* (fruit milkshakes), along with their selection of *salteñas*.

There is strict etiquette to eating these tasty pastries (newcomers can't help but score an armful of juice). Gourmands bite off the end, drink some of the juice and use a spoon to scoop up the insides. Ne'er a drop is spilt. At less than US$0.40 each, these are a great way to fill your stomach without emptying your purse.

The following are what we consider to be among the best *salteñerías* in La Paz.

Salteña Chic (Map pp66-7; Plaza Avaroa, Sopochachi) Your budget option good for take-out only.

Salteñería Chuquisaqueña (Map pp66-7; Plaza Avaroa, Sopochachi; ☾ 7:30am-1:30pm) More modest option with wooden banquette seating and a long queue for take-outs.

Salteñería El Hornito (Map pp66-7; Edificio Hilda, 6 de Agosto 2455, Sopochachi; ☾ 8am-2pm) Vegetarians rave about the high-quality veggie parcels here. What it lacks in size it makes up for in taste.

Paceña La Salteña (Map pp66-7; 20 de Octubre 2379, Sopochachi; ☾ 8:30am-2pm) Peach walls, chintz curtains and gold trimmings give the fare a gilted edge at this award-winning *salteñería*. Vegetarian *salteñas* available on weekends only.

in a small courtyard with a fountain and is surrounded by artisan's stores. If you don't want to sit in the casual outdoor eating area, they do a good take-out.

VEGETARIAN

Armonía (Map pp66-7; Ecuador 2284; ☾ lunch Mon-Sat; buffet US$3) La Paz's best all-you-can-eat vegetarian lunch is found above Liberı́a Armonı́a in Sopocachi. Organic products where possible.

Confitería Manantial (Map pp72-3; Hotel Gloria, Potosí 909; ☾ lunch Mon-Sat; buffet US$3) This place has a popular veggie buffet. Arrive before 12:30pm or you risk missing the best dishes.

GROCERIES

If you don't mind the hectic settings, your cheapest food scene is the markets. For quick eats, head to Mercado Camacho (Map pp72-3), where takeout stalls sell empanadas and chicken sandwiches, and *comedores* (dining halls) dish up filling, set meals. The *comedor* at Mercado Uruguay (Map pp72-3), off Max Paredes selling set meals (of varying standards), including tripe and *ispi* (similar to sardines) for less than US$1. Other areas to look for cheap and informal meals include the street markets around Av Buenos Aires.

In Sopocachi, the northwest border of Plaza Avaroa is lined with *salteña* stands (see the boxed text p89 for more on *salteñas*). Cheap DIY meals can easily be cobbled together from the abundance of fruit, produce and bread at the markets. If you're after sweet snacks, go to Calle Isaac Tamayo (Map pp72-3), near Manco Capac.

Don't go past the Irupana stores (there's one at Murillo 1014, cnr Tarija) which sell locally made organic produce including sugar-free muesli and some of the most delicious chocolate in Bolivia.

If you're headed off for a picnic, load up on everything from olives to cheese, crackers and beer at **Ketal Hipermercado** (Map pp66-7; Arce near Pinilla, Sopocachi). There's also the decent but more basic **Ketal Express** (Plaza España). **Zatt** (Map pp66-7; Sánchez Lima near Plaza Avaroa) is a smaller US-style supermarket option. Opposite Sopocachi Market, **Arco Iris** (Map pp66-7; Guachalla 554; ☾ 8am-8pm Mon-Sat) has an extensive *pastelería* (cake shop) and deli featuring fine specialty regional meat and dairy treats like smoked llama salami, plus products such as fresh palm hearts and dried Beni fruits.

DRINKING & CLUBBING

There are scores of inexpensive, local drinking dens where men go to drink *singani* (distilled grape spirit, or local firewater), play *cacho* (dice) and eventually pass out. Unaccompanied women should steer clear of these dens (even accompanied women may have problems), and only devoted sots will appreciate the drunken marathon that typifies Bolivian partying.

There are plenty of elegant bars, which are frequented by foreigners and middle-class Bolivians. Local, gilded youth mingle with upmarket expats at clubs along 20 de Octubre in lower Sopocachi and in Zona Sur, where US-style bars and discos spread along Av Ballivián and Calle 21. These change as often as fashions, so it's best to ask around for the latest in-spot.

Ram Jam (Map pp66-7; Presbitero Medina 2421; ☾ 6pm-3am) If La Paz had a Paris Hilton, she'd be here. This trendy hot spot has the lot: great food and drinks, mood lighting and live music. There are vegetarian options, English breakfasts and microbrewed beer. After exerting yourself on any of these, you can breathe easy on the bar's first floor in Ozone, the most novel oxygen bar in the world (US$5 for ten minutes).

Oliver's Travels (Map pp72-3; Murillo 1014) The worst (or best?) cultural experience in La Paz is to be had at this pub. It claims to offer 'nothing original – just beer, football, curry, typical English food, cheeky banter and lots of music you've heard before.' But luckily for owner Olly himself, crowds of revelers swallow this stuff. It has one of the best book exchanges around.

Mongo's (Map pp66-7; Manchego 2444; ☾ 6pm-3:30am; free tapas 6pm-7:30pm) La Paz's long-standing hip, hot (it gets crowded) and happening spot. Especially popular with expats and NGO workers. On some nights, you can catch Cuban and Colombian performers.

Café Sol y Luna (Map pp72-3; cnr Murillo & Cochabamba) A low-key, Dutch-run hangout offering cocktails, good coffee but very average meals. It has three cozy levels with a book exchange and an extensive guidebook reference library (many current LP titles), a dart alley and couches downstairs.

Dead Stroke (Map pp66-7; 6 de Agosto 2460; ☾ from 5pm Mon-Sat) An upbeat and marginally sleazy billiards bar with cable TV. It attracts lots of night owls with pool, snooker, darts, chess and dominoes, and also serves standard bar meals.

Thelonious Jazz Bar (Map pp66-7; 20 de Octubre 2172; ☺ 7pm-3am Mon-Sat; cover charge US$3.15) Bebop fans love this charmingly low-key bar for its live performances and great atmosphere.

Reineke Fuchs (Map pp66-7; Jáuregui 2241; ☺ from 6pm Mon-Sat) Sopocachi brewhaus featuring imported German beers, schnapsladen and hearty sausage-based fare. Also in Zona Sur.

La Choperia (Map pp72-3; Pichincha off Ingavi) Opposite the Mormon church, the rustic interior, retro photographs from the '20s and '30s, Western pop music and pitchers/jugs of beer make La Choperia a favorite with middleclass locals.

Forum (Map pp66-7; Víctor Sanjines 2908; cover charge US$2-10) The longstanding and popular granddaddy of La Paz's discos appeals to the young and restless, and offers a different musical theme each night of the week.

Diesel Nacional (Map pp66-7; 20 de Octubre 2271; ☺ from 7:30pm Mon-Sat) The postmodern place to escape reality for an overpriced drink with the rich kids. It doesn't really get going until late.

Traffic (Map pp66-7; Arce 2549; www.trafficsanjorge .com) The cool crowd chills here for cocktails, live music – from world music to disco – and all the attitude and dancing you can muster. You can linger until late.

ENTERTAINMENT

Pick up a copy of the free monthly booklet *Kaos* (available in bars and cafés) for a day-by-day rundown of what's on in La Paz. Otherwise, watch hotel notice boards for bars and live music posters, or check the **Agenda Cultural** (www.utopos.org) for current arts and theater listings. The municipal tourist office (p69) and **Casa de la Cultura** (Map pp72-3; Mariscal Santa Cruz & Potosí) has a free monthly cultural and fine arts schedule, and the **Teatro Municipal** (Map pp72-3; Sanjinés & Indaburo) has an ambitious theater and folk-music program.

Peñas

Typical of La Paz (and most of Bolivia) are folk-music venues known as *peñas*. Most present traditional Andean music, rendered on *zampoñas*, *quenas* and *charangos*, but also often include guitar shows and song recitals. Many *peñas* advertise nightly shows, but in reality most only have shows on Friday and Saturday nights, starting at 9pm or 10pm and

lasting until 1am or 2am. Admission ranges from US$4 to US$7 and usually includes the first drink. Check the daily newspapers for advertisements and details about smaller unscheduled *peñas* and other musical events.

El Calicanto (Map pp72-3; Sanjinés 467; mains US$3-6, dinner buffet US$4) Housed in an old colonial home two blocks from Plaza Murillo, it consists of the café El Molino, which does coffee and lunches, a bar with a nightly *peña*, and the Restaurant Las Tres Parrillas (with reasonably priced and excellent food).

Peña Marka Tambo (Map pp72-3; ☎ 228-0041; Jaén 710; ☺ from 8pm Thu-Sat; cover charge US$4) A less expensive – and some claim more traditional – *peña*. The food is alright, but the music is better.

Peña Huari (Map pp72-3; ☎ 231-6225; Sagárnaga 339; ☺ from 7pm nightly; cover charge US$12; meals US$10) The city's best-known *peña* is aimed at tourists and Bolivian business people. The attached restaurant specializes in Bolivian cuisine, including llama steak, Lake Titicaca trout, *charque kan* (jerky) and salads. The show starts at 8pm.

Peña Parnaso (Map pp72-3; ☎ 231-6827; Sagárnaga 189; ☺ from 8:30pm Mon-Sat; mains US$3.15-5; cover charge US$10) You can sample all sorts of local specialties, including various llama dishes: *charque kan*, shish kebab and even llama fondue. It also features Andean dancing. It's open for lunches (US$2) with no show.

La Casa del Corregidor (Map pp72-3; ☎ 236-3633; Murillo 1040; ☺ 7pm-late Mon-Sat; food & show US$10; cover charge US$3.15) Housed in a beautiful colonial building, this upmarket *peña* is called Rincon Colonial de La Paz, and offers a regular, but enjoyable *peña* experience.

Cinema

Your best chance of catching a quality art film is at the **Cinemateca Boliviana** (Map pp72-3; ☎ 244-4090; cnr Zuazo & Rosendo Gutiérrez), which shows an excellent selection of new art-house Bolivian and subtitled foreign films regularly. (At the time of research the organization's new complex was still being built at the above location; contact them to find out where they're currently showing their releases).

German films are screened regularly at the Goethe Institut (p67). Modern cinemas on the Prado show recent international releases, usually in the original language with Spanish subtitles, for around US$3.15. The following are recommended movie houses:

Cine 6 de Agosto (Map pp66-7; ☎ 244-2629; 6 de Agosto) Between Calles Gutierrez and Salinas.

Cine 16 de Julio (Map pp72-3; ☎ 244-1099; 16 de Julio)

Cine Monje Campero (Map pp72-3; ☎ 212-9033, 212-9034; cnr 16 de Julio & Bueno)

Theater

The **Teatro Municipal Alberto Saavedra Pérez** (Map pp72-3; Sanjinés & Indaburo; tickets US$3-5) has an ambitious program of folklore shows, folk-music concerts and foreign theatrical presentations. It's a great old restored building with a round auditorium, elaborate balconies and a vast ceiling mural. The newspapers and municipal tourist office (p69) have information about what's on here.

Spectator Sports

The popularity of *fútbol* (soccer) in Bolivia is comparable to that in other Latin American countries. Matches are played at Estadio Hernando Siles (Map pp72–3). Sundays (year-round) are the big game days, and Wednesdays and Saturdays also have games. Prices vary according to seats and whether it's a local or international game (US$1.25 to US$12.50). You can imagine what sort of advantage the local teams have over mere lowlanders; players from elsewhere consider the high-altitude La Paz games a suicide attempt! Check newspapers for times and prices. For more on *fútbol*, see the boxed text p36.

SHOPPING
Souvenirs & Artesanía

La Paz is a shopper's paradise; not only are prices very reasonable, but the quality of what's offered can be astounding. The main tourist shopping area lies along the very steep and literally breathtaking Calle Sagárnaga (Map pp72–3) between Santa Cruz and Tamayo, and spreads out along adjoining streets. Here, you'll also find Calle Linares, an alley choc-a-block of artisans' stores.

Some stores specialize in Oriente wood-carvings and ceramics, and Potosí silver. Others deal in rugs, wall-hangings, woven belts and pouches. Amid the lovely weavings and other items of exquisite craftsmanship, you'll find plenty of tourist kitsch, an art form unto itself: Inca-themed ashtrays, fake Tiahuanaco figurines, costume jewelry and mass-produced woolens.

Music recordings are available in small stores along Evaristo Valle and more established places on Linares. Or you can try your luck in the Mercado de Hechicería (p71) where there are figurines and Aymará good-luck charms, including frogs.

For less expensive llama or alpaca sweaters, bowler hats and other non-tourist clothing items, stroll Calles Graneros and Max Paredes.

Comart Tukuypaj (Map pp72-3; ☎ 231-2686; www.comart-tukuypaj.com; Linares 958) Offers export-quality, fair-trade llama, alpaca and *artesanías* from around the country. Upstairs the Inca Pallay women's weaving cooperative has a gallery with justly-famous Jal'qa and Candelaria weavings.

Artesanía Sorata (Map pp72-3; ☎ 239-3041; www.catgen.com/sorata; Sagárnaga 363 & Linares 900) Specializes in export-quality handmade dolls and original alpaca and sheep's wool designs for children.

Waliki (www.waliki.com; Víctor Sanjines 2866, Sopocachi) An alpaca artisan outlet that supports community employment and offers stylish contemporary clothing.

Joyas y Gemas (Map pp72-3; Shop 1, 16 de Julio 1607, near cnr Campero) Below Hungry Jacks, come here for jewelry, including stunning pendants of the Bolivian semiprecious stone, *bolivianita* (a purple and yellow amethyst).

Clothing

Reflecting its status as the more upmarket area, Zona Sur opts for designer clothing. Several stores sell stunning llama and alpaca fashion items. Try the following:

Liliana Castellanos (Map pp86-7; ☎ 212-5770; Montenegro 810, Bloque H, San Miguel)

Millma (Map pp86-7; ☎ 231-1338; www.millma alpaca.com; cnr Sagárnaga 225 & Claudio Aliaga 1202, San Miguel)

La Casa de la Llama (Map pp86-7; ☎ 279-0401; Montenegro, Bloque E, No 2, Calacoto)

Lumen Böhrt (Map pp86-7; ☎ 277-2625; Montenegro 910, San Miguel)

Musical Instruments

Many La Paz artisans specialize in *quenas*, *zampoñas*, *tarkas* and *pinquillos*, among other traditional woodwinds. There's a lot of low-quality or merely decorative tourist rubbish around. Visit a reputable workshop where you'll pay a fraction of gift-shop prices, and contribute directly to the artisan rather than to an intermediary. Clusters of artisans work along Juan Granier near Plaza Garita de Lima. Other recommended stores in La Paz include those on Isaac Tamayo near the top of Sagárnaga, and those at Linares 855 and 859.

Photography & Film

Slide film is widely available for around US$5 per roll; be cautious about buying film at street markets where it is exposed to strong sun all day. Print film costs about US$2.50 per roll of 36 exposures. Lots of photo shops cluster around the intersection of Comercio and Santa Cruz, and in the street stalls along Buenos Aires. It's difficult to find anything over 400 ASA, and, even if you do, it will probably be expired.

For relatively inexpensive cameras and electronics, try the small stores at Eloy Salmón 849 and 929, off the west end of Santa Cruz.

There are many Kodak one-hour developing outlets around the touristy parts of town. Alternatively you could try:

AGFA (Map pp72-3; ☎ 240-7030; Mariscal Santa Cruz 901) Perfect for passport photos in a flash.

Casa Kavlin (Map pp72-3; ☎ 240-6046; Potosí 1130) Good for one-hour slide or print processing.

Foto Linares (Map pp72-3; ☎ 232-7703; Edificio Alborda, Loayza & Juan de la Riva) The best choice for specialist processing.

Tecnología Fotográfica (☎ 242-7402, 7065-0773; 20 de Octubre, 2255). For camera problems, Rolando's your man.

Outdoor Gear

For all kinds of backpack protection – wire mesh, plastic sacks, chains, padlocks and so on – check the street stalls along Calle Isaac Tamayo.

Condoriri (Map pp72-3; ☎ 241-9735; Sagárnaga 343) There is a good selection of new and secondhand climbing, trekking and camping equipment to be found here. Condoriri stocks everything from ropes and backpacks to boots, compasses and headlamp batteries. There is also a selection of high-quality climbing hardware, books and maps. It also rents out equipment and has a repair service.

Camping Caza y Pesca (Map pp72-3; ☎ 240-8095; Galería Handal, Mariscal, Local 9) Visit this place for its range of basic camping equipment, including gas-stove canisters.

et-n-ic (Map pp72-3; ☎ 246-3782; Illampu 863) If you prefer to rent equipment, et-n-ic has some top-quality Swiss-made gear and also sells gas-stove canisters. Ask for Christian – he will kit you out with exactly what you need.

Sarañani (Map pp72-3; ☎ 237-9806; Galería Doryan, Sagárnaga 189, Local 30) This place stocks tents, backpacks, sleeping bags and cooking equipment.

Wine & Food

Breick Chocolate Shop (Map pp72-3; Zuazo at Bueno) Bolivia's best chocolate is for sale here at rock-bottom prices.

Bodega La Concepción (Map pp72-3; ☎ 248-4812; Cañada Strongest 1620 at Otero de la Vega, San Pedro) Award-winning, high-altitude vintages are available at wholesale prices from this outlet of the Tarija-based winery.

Campos de Solana/Casa Real (Map pp72-3; ☎ 249-1776; Otero de la Vega 1427) A Tarija winery best known for its Malbec and Riesling.

GETTING THERE & AWAY

Air

El Alto International Airport (LPB; ☎ 281-0240) is 10km via toll-road from the city center on the Altiplano. At 4050m, it's the world's highest international airport; larger planes need 5km of runway to lift off and must land at twice their sea-level velocity to compensate for the lower atmospheric density. Stopping distance is much greater too, and planes are equipped with special tires to withstand the extreme forces involved.

Airport services include a newsstand, ATMs, internet, souvenir stores, a bookstore, a coffee shop, fast food, a bistro and a duty-free shop in the international terminal. The currency exchange desk outside the international arrivals area gives poor rates on traveler's checks – if possible, wait until you're in town. The domestic departure tax is US$1.30, while the international departure tax is US$25.

AIRLINE OFFICES

AeroSur (Map pp72-3; ☎ 231-1333, 244-4930; www.aerosur.com; Edificio Petrolero, 16 de Julio 1616)

Amaszonas (☎ 222-0840/48; Saavedra 1649, Miraflores)

American Airlines (Map pp72-3; ☎ 235-1360; www.aa.com; Edificio Hernann, Plaza Venezuela 1440)

Grupo Taca (Map pp72-3; ☎ 231-3132; www.taca.com; Edificio Petrolero, 16 de Julio 1616)

Lan Airlines (Map pp72-3; ☎ 235-8377; www.lan
.com; Suite 104, Edificio Ayacucho, 16 de Julio 1566)
Lloyd Aéreo Boliviano (LAB; Map pp72-3; ☎ 237-
1024; Camacho 1460) At the time of research, the company
was headed for a financial crash landing. Check on its
status before booking.
TAM Mercosur (Map pp72-3; ☎ 244-3442; www
.tam.com.py, in Spanish; Gutiérrez 2323)
Transportes Aéreos Militares (TAM; Map pp72-3;
☎ 212-1582, 212-1585, TAM airport ☎ 284-1884;
Montes 738)

Bus

The **main bus terminal** (Terminal de Buses; Map pp66-7;
☎ 228-0551; Plaza Antofagasta; terminal fee US$0.25) is a
15-minute uphill walk north of the city center.
Fares are relatively uniform between companies. This full-service terminal serves all destinations south and east of La Paz, as well as
international destinations. Other destinations
are served mainly by *micros* and minibuses
departing from the cemetery district (right)
and Villa Fátima (right).

MAIN TERMINAL – SOUTHERN & EASTERN
BOLIVIA
Buses to Oruro run about every half hour
(US$2.50 to US$7.50, 3½ hours) between 5am
and 9:30pm. To Uyuni (US$10, 13 hours), Pa-
nasur buses depart every day at 7pm. Several
companies serve Cochabamba (US$3.15 to
US$7.50, seven to eight hours) daily. Buses to
Santa Cruz generally leave in the evening at
5pm or 7pm (US$22.50, 16 hours). El Dorado
runs a direct service.

Most overnight buses to Sucre (US$6.50
to US$11.50, 14 hours) pass through Potosí
(US$7 to US$13, 11 hours) and some require
a layover there. Have warm clothes handy for
this typically chilly trip. Some Potosí buses
continue on to Tarija (US$12.50 to US$27, 24
hours), Tupiza (US$12, 20 hours) or Villazón
(US$12.50 to US$25, 23 hours).

MAIN TERMINAL – INTERNATIONAL
SERVICES
Several companies offer daily departures to
Arica (US$12.50, eight hours) and Iquique
(US$17.50, 11 to 13 hours); to Cusco (US$15
to US$20, 12 to 17 hours) via either Desa-
guadero or Copacabana, with connections to
Puno (US$8 to US$10, eight hours), to Lima
($82, 27 hours) and Arequipa; and to Buenos
Aires (normal/*bus cama* or sleeper US$65/75,
50 hours), via either Villazón or Yacuiba.

CEMETERY DISTRICT – LAKE TITICACA,
TIAHUANACO & PERU
Several bus companies, including **Transportes 6 de Junio** (☎ 245-5258), **Trans Manco Capac**
(☎ 245-9045) and **TransTurs 2 de Febrero** (☎ 245-
3035), run frequent services to Copacabana
(US$2, three hours) between 5am and 8pm
from Calle José María Aliaga (Map pp66–7)
near Plaza Felix Reyes Ortíz (Plaza Tupac
Katari). In Copacabana, you'll find *camiones*
(flatbed trucks) and *colectivos* (minibuses
or shared taxis) to Puno and beyond. Alternatively there are more comfortable tourist
minibuses (US$4 to US$5, 2½ hours) that
do hotel pick-ups; you can book them at
any La Paz travel agency. Most companies
offer daily services to Puno (with a change
in Copacabana) for about US$10, includ-
ing hotel pickup. The trip takes nine to 10
hours, including lunch in Copacabana and
the border-crossing formalities. If a company doesn't fill its bus, passengers may
be shunted to another company so no one
runs half-empty buses. All companies allow
stopovers in Copacabana.

Between 5am and 6pm, **Autolíneas Ingavi**
(Map pp66-7; José María Asín) has departures every
30 minutes to Desaguadero (US$1, two
hours) via Tiahuanaco (US$1, 30 minutes)
and Guaqui. Nearby is **Trans-Unificado Sorata**
(Map pp66-7; ☎ 238-1693; cnr Kollasuyo & Bustillos),
which operates two daily buses to Sorata
(US$1.50, 4½ hours). You need to reserve
buses on weekends, so book your ticket early.
Sit on the left for views. Buses to Huarina
and Huatajata (US$1, two hours) leave
nearby from the corner of Calles Bustillos
and Kollasuyo.

Be sure to watch your bags in this area,
especially while boarding or leaving buses.

VILLA FÁTIMA – YUNGAS & AMAZON
BASIN
Several *flotas* (long-distance bus companies)
offer daily bus and minibus services to the
Yungas and beyond. **Flota Yungueña** (☎ 221-
3513) has two offices; the one at Yanacachi
844, behind the *ex-surtidor* (former gas station), serves Coroico, and the one at Las
Américas 341, just north of the former
gas station, serves Amazon Basin routes.
Nearby **Trans Totaí** (San Borja), and **Trans San Bartolomé** (☎ 221-1674), serve Chulumani. Other
companies serving the region are clustered
along Virgen del Carmen, just west of Av Las

Américas. Except for Rurrenabaque, most Amazon Basin routes only operate during the dry season. For all services, it's wise to reserve seats in advance. *Camiones* depart from behind the gasoline station on Calle San Borja to Riberalta and Caranavi, and from nearby 15 de Abril for Chulumani and Riberalta (although nowadays, with plenty of buses, you'd be doing this for the 'fun' of it only).

Sample fares include Coroico (US$2, four hours), Chulumani (US$2, four hours), Guanay (US$8, eight hours), Rurrenabaque (US$7 to US$10, 18 to 20 hours), Guayaramerín (US$21.50, 35 to 60 hours), Riberalta (US$18.50, 35 to 60 hours) and Cobija (US$26.50, 50 to 80 hours).

Train
La Paz's old train station is now defunct (although rumors of restarting a La Paz to Arica or La Paz to Tiahuanaco *ferrobus* – passenger rail bus – linger). Trains for Chile and the Argentine border, via Uyuni and/or Tupiza, all leave from Oruro (p177). For information and bookings, contact the **Empresa Ferroviaria Andina** (FCA; Map pp66-7; ☎ 241-6545/46; www.fca .com.bo, in Spanish; Guachalla 494; ticket office ☒ 8am-noon Mon-Sat).

For information about rail services within Peru, contact **Peru Rail** (www.perurail.com).

GETTING AROUND
To/From the Airport
There are two access routes to El Alto International Airport: the autopista (US$0.20) toll road and the sinuous free route, which leads into Plaza Ballivián in El Alto.

Minibus 212 (US$0.50) runs frequently between Plaza Isabel la Católica (Map pp72–3) and the airport between around 7am and 8pm. Heading into town from the airport, this service will drop you anywhere along the Prado.

Radio taxis (US$6.25 for up to four passengers) will pick you up at your door; confirm the price with the dispatcher when booking, or ask the driver to verify it when you climb in. For a fifth person, there is an additional US$1 charge. Transportes Aéreos Militares (TAM) flights leave from the **military airport** (☎ 237-9286, 212-1585) in El Alto. Catch a Río Seco *micro* from the upper Prado. Taxi fares should be about the same as for the main El Alto airport.

To/From the Bus Terminals
The main bus terminal is 1km uphill from the center. *Micros* marked 'Prado' and 'Av Arce' pass the main tourist areas but are usually too crowded to accommodate swollen rucksacks. If walking, snake your way down to the main drag, Av Ismael Montes, and keep descending for 15 minutes to the center.

Micros and minibuses run to the cemetery district constantly from the center. Catch them on Av Santa Cruz or grab *micro* No 2 along Av Yanacocha. Heading into the city from the cemetery by day you can catch *micros* along Av Baptista. At night take a radio taxi. Don't accept a ride from anyone who approaches you (see p69).

You can reach Villa Fátima by *micro* or minibus from the Prado or Av Camacho. It's about 1km uphill from Plaza Gualberto Villarroel.

Car & Motorcycle
Driving the steep, winding, one-way streets of La Paz may be intimidating for the uninitiated, but for longer day trips into the immediate hinterlands, you could consider renting a car (but hiring a driver is probably easier and just as economical; see p387). For rental rates and policy details, see p387.

Avis (Map pp86-7; ☎ 211-1870; www.avis.com.bo; office 101, Edificio Tango, Sanchez Lima, Zona Sur)

Kolla Motors (Map pp66-7; ☎ 241-9141; www .kollamotors.com; Gutiérrez 502)

Hertz (☎ 249-4921; www.hertzbolivia.com; Colombia 539)

International Rent-a-Car (Map pp72-3; ☎ 244-1906; Zuazo 1942)

Petita Rent-a-Car (☎ 242-0329; www.rentacarpetita .com; Valentin Abecia 2031, Sopocachi Alto) Swiss-owned and specializing in 4WDs.

Public Transportation
MICRO AND MINIBUS
La Paz's sputtering and smoke-spewing *micros*, the older three-quarter sized buses, mock the law of gravity and defy the principles of brake and transmission mechanics as they grind up and down the city's steep hills. They charge US$0.15 for a trip. Minibuses service most places as well, for a slightly higher cost. In addition to a route number or letter, *micros* plainly display their destination and route on a signboard posted in the front window. Minibuses usually have a young tout screaming the stops. You can simply wave

both down anywhere except for near policed intersections.

TRUFI

Trufis are shared cars that ply set routes. Destinations are identified on placards on the roof or windscreen. They charge US$0.20 around town, US$0.80 to the airport and US$0.40 to Zona Sur.

Taxi

Although most things worth seeing in La Paz lie within manageable walking distance of the center, the bus terminals are all rather steep climbs from the main hotel areas. Especially considering the altitude, struggling up the hills through traffic with bulky luggage isn't fun.

Radio taxis – with roof bubbles advertising their telephone numbers – are recommended as the safer option. They charge about US$0.80 around the center, US$1 from Sagárnaga to Sopocachi, or Sopocachi to the cemetery district and US$1.50 to Zona Sur. Charges are a little higher after 11pm. Radio taxi charges are for up to four passengers and include pickup, if necessary.

Most regular taxis are also collective taxis and charge a per-person rate. This means that the driver may pick up additional passengers, and that you can flag down a taxi already carrying passengers. Regular taxis charge US$0.40 per person around the center (a bit more for long uphill routes).

Taxis can be waved down anywhere, except near intersections or in areas cordoned off by the police. If you're traveling beyond the city center, or your journey involves a long uphill climb, arrange a fare with the driver before climbing in, and try to carry small change at all times.

Pre-ordered or radio taxis to the airport cost between US$5 to US$8.

AROUND LA PAZ

VALLE DE LA LUNA

About 10km down the canyon of the Río Choqueyapu from the city center, **Valle de la Luna** (Valley of the Moon; admission US$2), is a slightly overhyped place, if a pleasant break from urban La Paz. It could be easily visited in a morning or combined with another outing such as a hike to Muela del Diablo (p98) to fill an entire day. It isn't a valley at all, but a bizarre, eroded hillside maze of canyons and pinnacles technically known as badlands. Several species of cactus grow here, including the hallucinogenic *choma,* or San Pedro cactus. Unfortunately, urban growth has caught up to the area, making it less of a viewpoint than it otherwise might be. The area is now fenced off as a tourist attraction and there is a new visitor's centre with shops and bathrooms.

Getting There & Away

If you visit Valle de la Luna as part of an organized tour, you'll have only a five-minute photo stop. On your own, however, you'll have time to explore the area on foot.

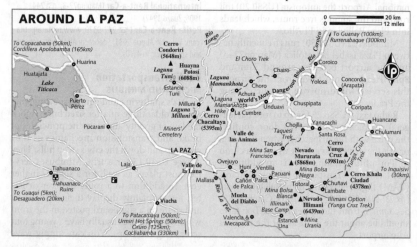

AROUND LA PAZ

0 ——— 20 km
0 ——— 12 miles

RÍO CHOKE

If statistics are anything to go by, the name of the Río Choqueyapu, which flows through La Paz, might as well be shortened to the Río Choke (or 'Omo River,' after the quantity of laundry soap flowing in it). This fetid stream, which provided the gold that gave La Paz its present location, is now utterly dead and beyond help. According to one source, 'the Río Choqueyapu receives annually 132,000 gallons of urine, 200,000 tons of human excrement and millions of tons of garbage, animal carcasses and industrial toxins.' The industrial toxins include cyanide from tanneries and a cocktail of chemicals and dyes from textile and paper industries, which cause the river to flow bright orange in places, or red topped with a layer of white foam.

The Choqueyapu fortunately flows underground through the city, but it emerges in the Zona Sur. Further down, it's used by *campesinos*, who take water for washing, consumption and agriculture. Most people heat the water before drinking it, but few boil it, and even boiling wouldn't eliminate some of the chemical pollutants from industrial wastes. Several years ago there was an outbreak of cholera in La Paz, prompting people to blame the *campesinos* in a nearby valley, who grow vegetables in the fertile valley.

Currently no one can be fined or cited for dumping waste into the river because, incredibly, the city has no laws against it. In 2000 the mayor's Environmental Quality office proposed a raft of projects aimed at controlling water pollution, vehicle emissions, rubbish dumping and noise. As always, the problem with implementation has been funding, and still the foul stream continues to flow, most of it ending up in the Amazon Basin.

From Av México in La Paz, which parallels the Prado, catch any form of transportation marked 'Mallasa' or 'Zoológico.' These will drop you off several meters from the entrance.

For a taxi from the center, you'll pay around US$10 for up to three people, and the driver will wait for an hour or so while you look around.

MALLASA

After a traipse around Valle de la Luna, you can also visit the village of Mallasa, popular among *paceños* on weekends. Just east of Mallasa is La Paz's spacious, but sorely underfunded, **Vesty Pakos Zoo** (Map pp86-7; ☎ 274-5992; admission US$0.40; ⏰ 10am-5pm), where there are photo opportunities aplenty and feeding time (10am) is raucous. Animal lovers may be upset by the poor conditions, however.

From the overlook immediately behind the zoo, you can take the clearly marked walking track that descends to and crosses the fetid Río Choqueyapu, before beginning a lung-bursting 600m climb to the Muela del Diablo (p98).

The Swiss-run **Hotel Restaurant Oberland** (☎ 274-5040; Calle 2, Mallasa; www.h-oberland.com; s/d/ste with bathroom & breakfast US$30/46/47; 🖳 🖭) is a slightly worn but friendly country-style hotel 30 minutes by *trufi* or minibus from the center of La Paz. It sits at an altitude of just 3200m, so

it's a good 40°F warmer than central La Paz. It has a pleasant cactus garden and lots of family features: an indoor pool and sauna, squash and beach-volleyball courts and table tennis. Transfers from La Paz cost US$15 (US$10.50 each for two people). Most pleasant is the outdoor eating area, popular among locals for functions, serving a range of Swiss and local food (US$4 to US$9).

Several stores in Mallasa sell snacks, beer and soft drinks; or you can try your luck at snack stands outside the zoo, but they only function on weekends.

To get to Mallasa from La Paz, take minibus 11 from Sagárnaga, 231, 253 or 379 from Sanchez Lima (San Pedro), or any form of transportation marked 'Mallasa' or 'Zoológico.' From the top of Valle de la Luna, catch a *micro* headed downvalley or continue a couple of kilometers on foot to Mallasa.

VALENCIA & MECAPACA

About 30km from central La Paz, and 15km from Mallasa, are two quaint villages that don't cater to the tourist crowd, but are worth visiting for their authenticity. Mecapaca boasts a beautiful cathedral in its plaza (ask Sra Ninfa Avendaño at the corner store to let you in; if you buy something from her store and add a donation to the church box she'll likely oblige). The church is perched on the hillside of the small plaza with wonderful views of the fertile valley beyond. The color of terracotta is a major feature, thanks to the 'generosity' of the local cement baron, who wanted to prettify the village and had it painted. He resides in La Paz, but has built a large condominium complex for weekend use (look for it down on the right as you enter). On weekends, there are two small super-simple restaurants for lunch (mains US$3.15).

A great treat on the way back to La Paz is to stop for a meal at **Trattoria Sant' Aquilina** (☎ 2-274-5707), an Italian restaurant and part of a Catholic Church training program, 14km on the main road from Valencia. The restaurant is renowned for its wood-fired pizza and is popular among the trendy *paceñan* crowds who converge on a Sunday (bookings advised).

Take minibus 253 from Plaza Belso in San Pedro (US$0.50) or from Mallasa. To return to La Paz take the same minibus 253 from Mecapaca; from anywhere else, catch anything that moves back up the valley.

MUELA DEL DIABLO

The prominent rock outcrop known as the Devil's Molar is actually an extinct volcanic plug which rises between the Río Choqueyapu and the more recent and expanding outer suburb of Pedregal. A hike to its base makes a pleasant, half-day walking trip from La Paz, and can be easily combined with a visit to Valle de la Luna. Warning: several robberies have been reported; inquire locally about safety before heading out.

From the cemetery in Pedregal, the trail climbs steeply (several times crossing the new road that provides access to the hamlet near the base of the *muela*) and affords increasingly fine views over the city and the surrounding tortured landscape. After a breathless hour or so, you'll reach a pleasant grassy swale where the 'tooth' comes into view, as well as some precarious pinnacles further east.

At this point the walking track joins the road and descends through the hamlet. About 300m further along, a side route branches off to the left and climbs toward the *muela*'s base. From the end of this route you can pick your way with extreme caution up to the cleft between the double summit, where there's a large cross. Without technical equipment and expertise, however, it's inadvisable to climb further.

After descending to the main track, you can decide whether to return the way you came, or follow the steep track that circles the *muela* in a counterclockwise direction and descends to the Río Choqueyapu before climbing the other side of the valley to the zoo in Mallasa. The latter option will turn this hike into a full-day trip, as it takes about six hours for the hike between Pedregal and Mallasa.

Getting There & Away

From La Paz the best access to the start of the hike is on minibus 288, marked 'Pedregal,' from the lower Prado. The end of the line is the parking area a couple hundred meters downhill from Pedregal's cemetery. Coming from Valle de la Luna, you can board these minibuses at Zona Sur's Plaza Humboldt or follow the difficult walking track from near the zoo in Mallasa, which involves a descent to the Río Choqueyapu and then a stiff 600m ascent to the eastern side of the Muela. To return to La Paz from Pedregal, catch a 'Prado' minibus from the parking area.

VALLE DE LAS ÁNIMAS

The name Valley of Spirits is used to describe the eerily eroded canyons and fantastic organ-pipe spires to the north and northeast of the *barrios* of Chasquipampa, Ovejuyo and Apaña (which are rapidly being absorbed into the Zona Sur neighborhoods of La Paz). The scenery resembles that of Valle de la Luna, but on a grander scale.

There are two (long-day) walking routes through the valley.

Río Ovejuyo Route

This route (Map pp86–7) begins at Calle 50, near the village of Apaña, accessible from La Paz on *micro* 42 marked 'Chasquipampa' or 'Ovejuyo.' Past Apaña at the police post the road divides to the right and left. Make sure you take the left fork to Palca. Rapidly expanding urban development is the feature here. When you reach the diminutive Río Ovejuyo, turn right and follow its southern bank northeast past the spectacularly eroded formations.

After about 6km, the river valley turns to the north. Make sure you have a compass and 1:50,000 topography sheet *5944-II* and, for a very short section, topo sheet *5944-I* (see p65 for details on where to get maps). Traverse up the slope to your right and head south over Cerro Pararani, until you arrive at the head of Quebrada Negra. From here you can follow the Quebrada Negra route (described below) either back to Ovejuyo or down to the village of Huni. This option can be challenging, especially because of the altitude. Make sure you carry a day's worth of water.

Quebrada Negra Route

The 7km route (Map pp86–7) up Quebrada Negra, over Cerro Pararani and down to Huni is a demanding day hike that requires six to seven hours. It begins at the Quebrada Negra ravine, which crosses the road at the upper (eastern) end of Ovejuyo village. *Micros* and *trufis* marked 'Ovejuyo' stop about half a kilometer short of this ravine, but micro 'Ñ' and minibus 385, marked 'Ovejuyo/Apaña,' or minibus 42, marked 'Apaña,' all travel right past the ravine mouth.

The easy-to-follow 4km route up Quebrada Negra will take you through the most dramatic of the eroded Valle de las Ánimas pinnacles. Near the head of the ravine, you need to traverse southeast around the northern shoulder of Cerro Pararani, until you find the obvious route that descends steeply to Huni village (not Huni chapel, which is also marked on the topo sheet). In fine weather, you'll have good views of Illimani along this section.

To return to La Paz, follow the road for 2km up over Paso Huni and then for another 1.5km downhill to Apaña, where you'll catch up with regular *micros* and *trufis* returning to the city.

For this route you'll need a compass and the 1:50,000 topo sheets *5944-I* and *6044-III*.

CAÑÓN DE PALCA (QUEBRADA CHUA KERI)

The magnificent Palca Canyon (Map pp86–7; marked on topo sheets as Quebrada Chua Kheri) brings a slice of grand canyon country to the dramatic badland peaks and eroded amphitheaters east of La Paz. Although it's now a motorable track, a walk through this gorge makes an ideal day hike from La Paz. Note: go only in groups as assaults on single hikers at the time of research have been reported here. Check the safety status before setting out.

The Route

Heading in an easterly direction from Paso Huni, about 2km above Ovejuyo, you'll pass a small lake just near the point where the road begins to descend the other side. Several hundred meters past the summit, on your left

you'll see some magnificent 'church-choir' formations – rows of standing pinnacles that resemble an ensemble in song.

About 2km beyond the pass, take the right (south) fork of the road into the village of Huni (aka Uni). After less than 1km, the road begins to descend in earnest. Much of this route originally followed an ancient Inca road, with good examples of pre-Hispanic paving, but it was ripped up to make it passable to vehicles.

The route drops slowly toward the gravely canyon floor, and offers sensational views along the way. The approach to the canyon is dominated by a 100m-high natural obelisk, and in the opposite wall is the rock formation Ermitaño del Cañón, which resembles a reclusive human figure hiding in an enormous rock niche. The route then winds alongside the usually diminutive Río Palca for about 2km between spectacular vertical walls. On exiting the canyon you'll have a gentle 3km climb through green farmland to the former gold-mining village of Palca.

Sleeping & Eating

If you don't find transportation back to La Paz on the same day, you can stay at the *alojamiento* (basic accommodations) in Palca or camp around Palca or nearby Ventilla. Beware of the badly polluted surface water, and ask permission before you set your tent up in a field or pasture.

Huni is a small town above the entrance to Cañón de Palca. It has a store selling basic supplies, including bottled water and snack foods, and also provides Bolivian set-menu meals.

Palca is a pleasant but basic town located relatively close to the exit of the canyon. It has a simple **hostal** (per person US$2-4), which offers set meals and is popular with Bolivian tourists on weekends.

Getting There & Away

For the start of this hike, you need to reach Huni, which is served only by *micros* and *trufis* headed for Ventilla and Palca. These leave at least once daily from near the corner of Boquerón and Lara, two blocks north of Plaza Líbano in the San Pedro district of La Paz. There's no set schedule, but most leave in the morning. You'll have the best luck on Saturday and Sunday, when families make excursions into the countryside.

Alternatively take *micro* 42 or minibus 385, marked 'Ovejuyo/Apaña,' get off at the end of the line, and slog the 1.5km up the road to Paso Huni.

From Palca back to La Paz, you'll find occasional *camiones, micros* and minibuses, particularly on Sunday afternoon, but don't count on anything after 3pm or 4pm. Alternatively you can hike to Ventilla, an hour uphill through a pleasant eucalyptus plantation, and try hitchhiking from there.

If you arrive in Palca geared up for more hiking, you can always set off from Ventilla along the Takesi trek (p138).

CHACALTAYA

The 5395m-high Cerro Chacaltaya peak, atop a dying glacier, is a popular day trip. It is also the world's highest developed ski area (the term 'developed' is used loosely). It's a steep 90-minute ride from central La Paz, and the accessible summit is an easy 200m ascent from there.

You can get your thrills, spills (well, hopefully not) and great views on a 60km-plus mountain bike trip from Chacaltaya to Zongo and beyond at descents of up to 4100m (vertical drop). Gravity Assisted (p77) runs trips starting at US$65 per person.

Those who fly into La Paz from the lowlands will want to wait a few days before visiting Chacaltaya or other high-altitude places. For guidelines on avoiding or coping with altitude-related ailments, see p396.

Snacks and hot drinks are available at Club Andino's lodge (right); if you want anything more substantial, bring it from town. Also bring warm (and windproof) clothing, sunglasses (100% UV proof) and sunscreen.

Most La Paz tour agencies take groups to Chacaltaya for around US$10 to US$15 per person. For prospective skiers, Club Andino Boliviano is the best bet.

Skiing

The steep, 700m ski piste runs from 5320m (75m below the summit of the mountain) down to about 4900m. The ski season is from February to March but this is totally dependent on the availability of snow – the glacier is rapidly retreating and the run has been 'broken' as a result. Skiers would go more for the novelty (and beginners be warned – the old lift tow can be tricky to grasp). Wear expendable clothing; it will suffer if you do

manage to hook up to the old-fashioned lift tow (hook and cable).

The **Club Andino Boliviano** (Map pp72-3; ☎ 2-231-2875; México 1638, La Paz; ☀ 9:30am-noon & 3-6pm Mon-Fri) organizes transportation to Chacaltaya on weekends throughout the year when there is sufficient interest, but the ski lift operates only when snow conditions are favorable. Ski trips leave from the club office at around 8:00am and arrive at Chacaltaya around 11am for a two-hour visit before returning at around 2pm. Ring before you pop into the office – hours can be variable.

Whether there's snow or not, the Club will take you to Chacaltaya for around US$10 to US$20 per person (transportation only); if skiing, the equipment rental is an additional US$10, including a *gancho* (hook) for the ski tow.

Hiking

Chacaltaya is popular for visitors and hikers for the spectacular views of La Paz, Illimani, Mururata and 6088m Huayna Potosí. It's a relatively easy (but steep) 1km, high-altitude climb from the lodge to the summit of Chacaltaya. Remember to carry warm clothing and water, and take plenty of rests, say a 30-second stop every 10 steps or so, and longer stops if needed, even if you don't feel tired. If you start to feel light-headed, sit down and rest until the feeling passes. If it doesn't, you may be suffering from mild altitude sickness; the only remedy is to descend.

From Chacaltaya it's possible to walk to Refugio Huayna Potosí, at the base of Huayna Potosí (p157), in half a day. Climb to the second false summit above the ski slope, and then wind your way down past a turquoise lake until you meet up with the road just above the nearly abandoned mining settlement of Milluni. Turn right on the road and follow it past Laguna Zongo to the dam, where you'll see the refuge on your left and the trailhead for Laguna Mamankhota (opposite) on your right.

Sleeping & Eating

For overnight stays at Chacaltaya, you can crash in Club Andino's well-ventilated **mountain hut** (dm US$5). Meals are available. Alternatively you can try the La Paz UMSA research lab, which is heated and just downhill from the warm-up hut.

A warm sleeping bag, food and some sort of headache/*soroche* (altitude sickness) relief are essential for an overnight stay in either location.

Getting There & Away

There's no public transportation to Chacaltaya. You'll have to go with either Club Andino Boliviano or a La Paz tour operator (see p389). The Chacaltaya road may become impassable to 2WD vehicles, especially from March to May, so check the situation before choosing a tour that can't arrive at its destination, or you'll have a long, uphill slog at high altitude.

If you go with Club Andino Boliviano on Saturday, you might be able to catch a lift back to La Paz with their Sunday trip. On other days, tour groups may have space for extra people; they'll charge about half the tour price for the one-way trip.

MILLUNI & THE ZONGO VALLEY

The dramatic Zongo Valley plunges sharply down from the starkly anonymous mining village of Milluni – from 4624m to 1480m within 33km. At its head, between Chacaltaya and the spectacular peak of Huayna Potosí, is the glacial-blue Laguna Zongo, which was created to run the Zongo hydroelectric power station.

Not strictly a town, Milluni is a collection of hydroelectricity company buildings and huts at the head of the Paso Zongo (along the road below Huayna Potosí, which skirts the east side of Laguna Zongo).

Laguna Mamankhota Hike

Once upon a time a lovely set of ice caves high above the valley floor provided a good excuse for day hikes and tours, but in 1992 they melted away, leaving not even an ice cube. Today the best excuse to climb to the former site is the impressive views of Huayna Potosí across Laguna Mamankhota (Laguna Cañada).

To reach the trailhead, take the route northeast of Milluni and continue for about 5km. Along the way Milluni will be visible downhill on your left; stop to have a look at the unusual roadside miners' cemetery overlooking Milluni. If you're traveling by vehicle, you'll reach Laguna Zongo, an artificial lake with milky blue-green water, and the Compañía Minera del Sur gate a few minutes later. On your right you'll see a trail climbing up the hillside. From there the road winds steeply downward into Zongo Valley.

The hike begins at 4600m. From the parking area, strike off uphill to the right. After about 100m, you'll reach an aqueduct, which you should follow for about 50 minutes along a rather treacherous precipice. Watch on your left for the plaque commemorating an Israeli's final motorbike ride along this narrow and vertigo-inspiring route.

About 20m further along you cross a large bridge, then turn right along a vague track leading uphill, following the cairns that mark the way. After a short climb you'll reach Laguna Mamankhota, and stunning views of Huayna Potosí, Tiquimani, Telata and Charquini – if the peaks aren't shrouded in clouds. A further 25 minutes up the vague trail will bring you to the site of the former ice caves.

Sleeping & Eating

Refugio Huayna Potosí (☎ 232-3538; dm low/high season with breakfast US$6/9) At Paso Zongo, above the dam at the head of Zongo Valley, this mountain hut provides basic accommodations for climbers and trekkers. Additional meals cost US$4 to US$5, and there is hot water.

Camping is possible at the seismic station on the western end of Laguna Zongo.

Getting There & Away

Hourly *micros* leave for Zongo Valley, via Paso Zongo, from Kollasuyo in the La Paz cemetery district and from Plaza Ballivián in El Alto when full, normally between 5am and 7am.

The half-day trip by hired taxi costs about US$35 for up to five people. Make sure the driver understands that you want the Zongo Valley via Milluni, as drivers may expect you to ask for Chacaltaya and try to take you there anyway. At the trailhead, the driver will wait while you walk up the mountain to the lake; allow a minimum of three hours for the walk.

To hire a 4WD and driver from La Paz to Paso Zongo costs about US$50 for up to nine people; see p387 for a list of private drivers.

LAJA

This tiny village (formerly known as Llaxa or Laxa) is 38km west of La Paz, or about halfway to Tiahuanaco, and a brief stop here is included on many Tiahuanaco tours.

In 1548 the Spanish captain Alonzo de Mendoza was given the task of founding a city and rest stop along the route from Potosí to the coast at Callao, Peru. On October 20, 1548 he arrived in Laxa and declared it his chosen location. He changed his mind, however, and the site was shifted to the gold-bearing canyon where La Paz now stands.

Over Laja's plaza towers a grand **church** built between the 1580s and 1610 in commemoration of Spanish victories over the Incas. The interior is ornamented with colonial artwork, including lovely wooden carvings adorned with gold and silver. The baroque facade bears the indigenized visages of King Ferdinand and Queen Isabella. Due to looting that has occurred in the past, the church is only open to the public on Sunday mornings (11am to noon) and during festivities every October 20.

TIAHUANACO (TIWANAKU)

Little is actually known about the people who constructed the great Tiahuanaco ceremonial center on the southern shore of Lake Titicaca more than 1000 years ago. Archaeologists generally agree that the civilization which spawned Tiahuanaco rose around 600 BC. Construction on the ceremonial site was under way by about AD 700, but around AD 1200 the group had melted into obscurity, becoming another 'lost' civilization. Evidence of its influence, particularly its religion, has been found throughout the vast area that later became the Inca empire.

The treasures of Tiahuanaco have literally been scattered to the four corners of the earth. Its gold was looted by the Spanish, and early stone and pottery finds were sometimes destroyed by religious zealots who considered them pagan idols. Some of the work found its way to European museums; farmers destroyed pieces of it as they turned the surrounding area into pasture and cropland; the church kept some of the statues or sold them as curios; and the larger stonework went into Spanish construction projects, and even into the bed of the La Paz–Guaqui rail line that passes just south of the site.

Fortunately a portion of the treasure has been preserved, and some of it remains in Bolivia. A few of the larger anthropomorphic stone statues have been left on the site. Others are on display at the Museo Nacional de Arqueología (p71) in La Paz. New finds from the earliest Tiahuanaco periods are being added to the collection of the new onsite **Museo Lítico Monumental** (☉ 9am-5pm; admission US$10). The star of the show is the massive **Megalito Bennetto Pachamama**, rescued in 2002 from its former smoggy home at the outdoor Templete Semi-subterráneo (p76) in La Paz.

Pieces from the three more recent Tiahuanaco periods may be found scattered around Bolivia, but the majority are housed in archaeological museums in La Paz and Cochabamba. The ruins themselves have been so badly looted, however, that much of the information they could have revealed about their builders is now lost forever.

Labeling at the onsite museums is sparse and almost exclusively in Spanish. The single admission ticket includes the site, the **Puma Punku** excavation site (not included in many tours), the new museum and the visitor center. People selling cheap clay trinkets (fortunately all fake; don't pay more than US$0.25 for a small one) are no longer permitted inside the ruins; neither are clientless guides – guides must be registered and can be hired only outside the fence (for up to US$10).

A major research and excavation project is ongoing, which means that some of the main features may be cordoned off during your visit.

History

Although no one is certain whether it was the capital of a nation, Tiahuanaco undoubtedly served as a great ceremonial center. At its height the city had a population of 20,000 inhabitants and encompassed approximately 2.6 sq km. While only a very small percentage of the original site has been excavated – and what remains is less than overwhelming – Tiahuanaco represents the greatest megalithic architectural achievement of pre-Inca South America.

The development of the Tiahuanaco civilization has been divided by researchers into five distinct periods, numbered Tiahuanaco I through V, each of which has its own outstanding attributes.

The Tiahuanaco I period falls between the advent of the Tiahuanaco civilization and the middle of the 5th century BC. Significant finds from this period include multicolored pottery and human or animal effigies in painted clay. Tiahuanaco II, which ended around the beginning of the Christian era, is hallmarked by ceramic vessels with horizontal handles. Tiahuanaco III dominated the next 300 years, and was characterized by tricolor pottery of geometric design, often decorated with images of stylized animals.

Tiahuanaco IV, also known as the Classic Period, developed between AD 300 and 700. The large stone structures that dominate the site today were constructed during this period. The use of bronze and gold is considered evidence of contact with groups further east in the Cochabamba valley and further west on the Peruvian coast. Tiahuanaco IV pottery is largely anthropomorphic. Pieces uncovered by archaeologists include items in the shape of human heads and faces with bulging cheeks, indicating that the coca leaf was already in use at this time.

Tiahuanaco V, or the Expansive Period, is marked by a decline that lasted until Tiahuanaco's population completely disappeared around AD 1200. Pottery grew less elaborate, construction projects slowed and stopped, and no large-scale monuments were added after the early phases of this period.

When the Spaniards arrived in South America, local indigenous legends recounted that Tiahuanaco had been the capital of the bearded white god called Viracocha, and that from his city Viracocha had reigned over the civilization.

Visiting the Ruins

Scattered around the Tiahuanaco site, you'll find heaps of jumbled basalt and sandstone slabs weighing as much as 25 tons each. Oddly enough the nearest quarries that could have produced the basalt megaliths are on the Copacabana peninsula, 40km away beyond the lake. Even the sandstone blocks had to be transported from a site more than 5km away. It's no wonder, then, that when the Spanish asked local Aymará how the buildings were constructed, they replied that it was done with the aid of the leader/deity Viracocha. They could conceive of no other plausible explanation.

Tiahuanaco's most outstanding structure is the **Akapana pyramid**, which was built on an existing geological formation. At its base this roughly square 16m hill covers a surface area of about 200 sq m. In the center of its flat summit is an oval-shaped sunken area, which some sources attribute to early, haphazard, Spanish excavation. The presence of a stone drain in the center, however, has led some archaeologists to believe it was used for water storage. Because much of the original

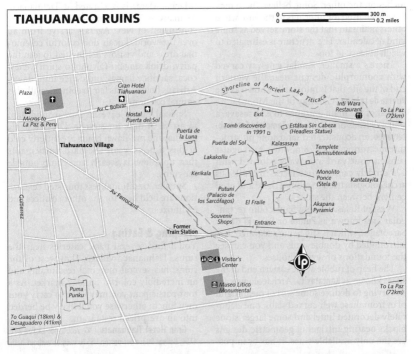

TIAHUANACO RUINS

0 — 300 m
0 — 0.2 miles

Akapana went into the construction of nearby homes and churches, the pyramid is now in a rather sorry state.

North of the pyramid is **Kalasasaya**, a partially reconstructed 130m x 120m ritual-platform compound with walls constructed of huge blocks of red sandstone and andesite. The blocks are precisely fitted to form a platform base 3m high. Monolithic uprights flank the massive entrance steps up to the restored portico of the enclosure, beyond which is an interior courtyard and the ruins of priests' quarters. Note the size of the top stair – a massive single block.

Other stairways lead to secondary platforms, where there are other monoliths including the famous **El Fraile** (priest). At the far northwest corner of Kalasasaya is Tiahuanaco's best-known structure, the **Puerta del Sol** (Gateway of the Sun). This megalithic gateway was carved from a single block of andesite, and archaeologists assume that it was associated in some way with the sun deity. The surface of this fine-grained, gray volcanic rock is ornamented with low-relief designs on one side and a row of four deep niches on the other. Some believe these may have been used for offerings to the sun, while others maintain that the stone served as some kind of calendar. The structure is estimated to weigh at least 44 tons.

There's a smaller, similar gateway carved with zoomorphic designs near the western end of the site that is informally known as the **Puerta de la Luna** (Gateway of the Moon).

East of the main entrance to Kalasasaya, a stairway leads down into the **Templete Semisubterráneo**, an acoustic, red sandstone pit structure measuring 26m x 28m, with a rectangular sunken courtyard and walls adorned with 175 crudely carved stone faces. In the 1960s archaeologists tried to rebuild these and used cement between the stones.

West of Kalasasaya is a 55m x 60m rectangular area known as **Putuni** or Palacio de los Sarcófagos, which is still being excavated. It is surrounded by double walls and you can see the foundations of several houses.

The heap of rubble at the eastern end of the site is known as **Kantatayita**. Archaeologists are still trying to deduce some sort of meaningful plan from these well-carved slabs; one elaborately decorated lintel and some larger stone blocks bearing intriguing geometric designs are the only available clues. It has been postulated – and dubiously 'proven' – that they were derived from universal mathematical constants, such as pi; but some archaeologists simply see the plans for a large and well-designed building.

Across the railway line southwest of the Tiahuanaco site, you'll see the excavation site of **Puma Punku** (Gateway of the Puma). In this temple area megaliths weighing more than 440 tons have been discovered. Like Kalasasaya and Akapana, there is evidence that Puma Punku was begun with one type of material and finished with another; part was constructed of enormous sandstone blocks and, during a later phase of construction, notched and jointed basalt blocks were added.

Note also in the distance of the site's northern boundary, the *sukakollo,* a highly sophisticated system of terraced irrigation.

Festivals & Events

On June 21 (the southern hemisphere's winter solstice), when the rays of the rising sun shine through the temple entrance on the eastern side of the complex, the **Aymará New Year** (Machaj Mara) is celebrated at Tiahuanaco. As many as 5000 people – including a large contingent of New Agers – arrive from all over the world. Locals don colorful ceremonial dress and visitors are invited to join the party, drink *singani* (alcoholic spirit), chew coca, sacrifice llamas and dance until dawn. Artisans hold a crafts fair to coincide with this annual celebration.

Special buses leave La Paz around 4am to arrive in time for sunrise. Dress warmly because the pre-dawn hours are bitterly cold at this time of year. Die-hard participants turn up a few days early and camp outside the ruins.

Smaller, traditional, less touristed celebrations are held here for the other solstices and equinoxes.

Sleeping & Eating

You'll find several basic eateries near the ruins. Tiahuanaco village, 1km west of the ruins, has several marginal restaurants and an incredibly colorful Sunday market. As a tour participant you may want to carry your own lunch; otherwise you'll likely be herded into an overpriced restaurant.

Gran Hotel Tiahuanacu (☎ 289-8548; La Paz 241-4154; Bolívar 903; r per person US$10 with or without bath)

This is the nicest place to stay, with rooms that are clean, breezy and comfortable. There's an Entel phone and a restaurant open daily.

Hostal Puerta del Sol (per person US$2.50) This very basic option, at the La Paz–end of the village, is the closest to the ruins (and looks like it should be part of them). The rather unusual *dueña* (proprietor) offers simple meals.

Inti Wara (☎ 289-8543; ☽ lunch; US$2.50) The best eating option, on the northeastern side of the ruins.

Getting There & Away

Many La Paz agencies offer reasonably priced, guided, full- and half-day Tiahuanaco tours (US$10 to US$20 per person), including transportation and a bilingual guide. These tours are well worth it for the convenience and most travelers visit Tiahuanaco this way.

For those who prefer to go it alone, **Autolíneas Ingavi Autolíneas Ingavi** (Map pp66-7; José María Asín, La Paz) leaves for Tiahuanaco (US$1, 1½ hours) about eight times daily. Most buses continue to Guaqui and Desaguadero. The buses are crowded beyond comfortable capacity – even when passengers are hanging out the windows and doors, drivers are still calling for more.

Buses pass the museum near the entrance to the complex. To return to La Paz, flag down a *micro* along the road south of the ruins. However they'll likely be overflowing, so it may be worth catching one in Tiahuanaco village. *Micros* to Guaqui and the Peruvian border leave from the plaza in Tiahuanaco village, or may be flagged down just west of the village – again, expect crowds.

Taxis to Tiahuanaco from La Paz cost around US$30 to US$40 roundtrip.

URMIRI

Urmiri lies at an elevation of 3800m in the Valle de Sapahaqui, 30km east of the La Paz–Oruro highway and 2½ hours south of La Paz. It features the mineral- and ion-rich **Termas de Urmiri** (Urmiri Hot Springs) which emerge from the source at 72°F, and to which the Hotel Gloria Urmiri owes its existence. This resort-style hotel boasts two outdoor pools, which are allowed to cool to a comfortable temperature.

The Hotel Gloria in La Paz runs the rustic but charming **Hotel Gloria Urmiri** (☎ La Paz 240-7070; per person with/without bathroom from US$22.50/19.50, luxury r with bathroom US$26-250, camping per person US$1.50). Aromatic herbal baths, massage and hydro massage are available. Luxury rooms have their own private Roman bath fed by the hot springs. Off-season, two-night, room-and-board package deals including transportation start at US$19.50 per person during the week and US$16.50 on weekends. Lunch and dinner cost US$12.50 each, and campers and nonguests can use the pools for US$3. Make accommodations and transportation reservations at least two days in advance through the Hotel Gloria in La Paz (p84), and note that the pools are closed on Monday for cleaning.

The easiest way to reach Urmiri from La Paz is with Hotel Gloria's shuttle (per person roundtrip US$6), which leaves the hotel at least a couple of times a week at 8am and returns at 4pm.

Heading there independently is tough. Take a bus or *camión* from La Paz toward Oruro and get off near the bridge in Villa Loza, 70km south of La Paz and 15km north of Patacamaya. From here turn east along the unpaved road and pray for a lift, because if nothing is forthcoming, you're in for a very long walk.

Lake Titicaca

Lake Titicaca is deservedly awash with gushing clichés. This incongruous splash of sapphire amid the stark plains of the Altiplano is one of the most beautiful sights in the region. Although it is often wrongly described as the highest navigable lake in the world (both Peru and Chile have higher navigable bodies of water), it nevertheless sits at a high 3820m. It is more than 230km long and 97km wide, making it South America's second-largest body of freshwater after Venezuela's Lake Maracaibo.

The lake straddles both Peru and Bolivia, and is a remnant of the ancient inland sea known as Lago Ballivián, which covered much of the Altiplano before geological faults and evaporation brought about a drop in the water level.

The traditional Aymarán villages along the lakeshore, with the snow-topped peaks of the Cordillera Real in the background, provide a magical landscape. Even more fascinating for the visitor are the colorful and historical communities that inhabit the lake's many tiny islands. Integral to any visit is learning about the region's ancient legends, which can enhance the travel experience.

Long rumored to be unfathomable, the depth of the lake has now been measured at up to 457m. Trout were introduced into it in 1939, but are now largely farmed in special hatcheries.

HIGHLIGHTS

- Visit the tiny island of **Pariti** (p123), whose new museum features exquisite finds from a recent excavation

- View the sunset over the lake from tranquil **Yumani** (p119) on Isla del Sol

- Check out a baptism (or even a vehicle blessing!) at **Copacabana cathedral** (p111)

- Visit **lakeside villages** (p116) between Copacabana and Sampaya, and take a spin in a reed boat

- Trek **Isla del Sol** (p118) and enjoy spectacular lake views, ancient ruins and landscapes straight out of the Mediterranean

★ Yumani, Isla del Sol
★ Sampaya
★ Copacabana
★ Isla Pariti

| ■ TELEPHONE CODE: 2 | ■ AREA: 9000 sq km | ■ ELEVATION: 3820m |

History

When you first glimpse Lake Titicaca's crystalline, gemlike waters, beneath the looming backdrop of the Cordillera Real in the clear Altiplano light, you'll understand why pre-Inca people connected it with mystical events. Those early inhabitants of the Altiplano believed that both the sun itself and their bearded, white god-king, Viracocha, had risen out of its mysterious depths. The Incas, in turn, believed that it was the birthplace of their civilization.

When the Spanish arrived in the mid-16th century, legends of treasure began to surface, including the tale that some Incas had flung their gold into the lake to prevent the Spanish carting it off. Distinct fluctuations in the water level of the lake have led treasure hunters to speculate that the ruins of ancient cities might lie beneath its surface.

From year to year, changes in the water level of Lake Titicaca are not uncommon; previous fluctuations may even have inundated settlements and ruins. In the floods of 1985 to 1986, highways, docks, fields and streets all disappeared beneath the rising waters, adobe homes turned to mud and collapsed, and 200,000 people were displaced. It took several years for the Río Desaguadero, the lake's only outlet, to drain the flood waters.

Although evidence of submerged cities remains inconclusive, archaeologists are still unearthing exquisite finds around the lake. At Isla Koa, north of Isla del Sol, they found 22 large stone boxes containing a variety of artifacts: a silver llama, some shell figurines and several types of incense burners. And in 2004, the tiny island of Pariti hit world headlines when a team of Finnish and Bolivian archaeologists discovered elaborate and beautiful pottery there, which is now housed in a small museum on the island, and in La Paz.

Climate

From February to November the climate around Lake Titicaca is mostly pleasant and sunny, but there's often a cool wind off the lake and nights can be bitterly cold. Most rainfall occurs in midsummer (December and January).

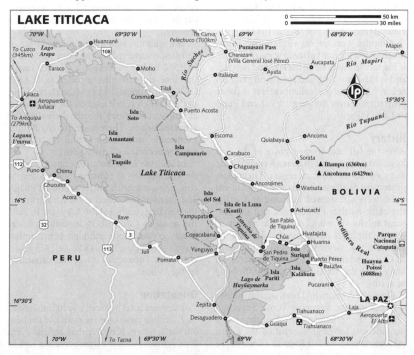

LAKE TITICACA

Getting There & Away

Lake Titicaca is a focal point for visitors from both Peru and Bolivia. The road journey between La Paz and Copacabana – whether in minibus, bus or car – is impressive. It follows a scenic route with the Cordillera Real on one side and, after the Altiplano, the lake shoreline on the other. Vehicles are ferried by barge across the Estrecho de Tiquina (Tiquina Straits) while passengers ride in launches.

If you have limited time, a quick way to 'do' Titicaca is to choose from several La Paz–based companies that offer guided lake excursions on hydrofoils, catamarans or motor boat. The most popular companies are Balsa Tours (p123) which offers motor excursions around the lake; Crillon Tours (p124), an upmarket agency with a hydrofoil service; and Transturin (p124), which runs day and overnight cruises in covered catamarans.

COPACABANA

pop 54,300 / elevation 3800m

Nestled between two hills and perched on the southern shore of Lake Titicaca, Copacabana (Copa), is a small, bright and enchanting town. It was for centuries the site of religious pilgrimages, and today local and visiting Peruvian pilgrims flock to its fiestas (p112).

Although it can appear a little tourist-ready, the town is a pleasant place to wander around. It has scenic walks along the lake and beyond, and is the launching pad for visiting Isla del Sol. With its many excellent cafés it makes a pleasant stopover between La Paz and Puno or Cuzco (Peru).

History

After the fall and disappearance of the Tiahuanaco culture, the Kollas (Aymará) rose to power in the Titicaca region. Their most prominent deities included the sun and moon (who were considered husband and wife), the earth mother Pachamama and the ambient spirits known as *achachilas* and *apus*. Among the idols erected on the shores of the Manco Capac peninsula was Kota Kahuaña, or Copacahuana ('lake view' in Aymará), an image with the head of a human and the body of a fish.

Once the Aymará had been subsumed into the Inca empire, Emperor Tupac Yupanqui founded the settlement of Copacabana as a wayside rest for pilgrims visiting the *huaca* (shrine) known as Titi Khar'ka (Rock of the Puma; p118), a former site of human sacrifice at the northern end of Isla del Sol.

Before the arrival of Spanish priests in the mid-16th century, the Incas had divided local inhabitants into two distinct groups. Those faithful to the empire were known as Haransaya and were assigned positions of power. Those who resisted, the Hurinsaya, were relegated to manual labor. It was a separation which went entirely against the grain of the community-oriented Aymará culture, and the floods and crop failures that befell them in the 1570s were attributed to this social aberration.

This resulted in the rejection of the Inca religion, and the partial adoption of Christianity and establishment of the Santuario de Copacabana, which developed into a syncretic mishmash of both traditional and Christian beliefs. The populace elected La Santísima Virgen de Candelaria as its patron saint, and established a congregation in her honor. Noting the lack of an image for the altar, Francisco Tito Yupanqui, a direct descendant of the Inca emperor, fashioned an image of clay and placed it in the church. However his rude effort was deemed unsuitable to represent the honored patron of the village and was removed.

The sculptor, who was humiliated but not defeated, journeyed to Potosí to study arts. In 1582 he began carving a wooden image that took eight months to complete. In 1583 La Virgen Morena del Lago (the Dark Virgin of the Lake) was installed on the adobe altar at Copacabana, and shortly thereafter the miracles began. There were reportedly 'innumerable' early healings and Copacabana quickly became a pilgrimage site.

In 1605 the Augustinian priesthood advised the community to construct a cathedral to commensurate with the power of the image. The altar was completed in 1614, but work on the building continued for 200 years. In 1805 the *mudéjar* (Moorish-style) cathedral was finally consecrated, although construction wasn't completed until 1820. In 1925 Francisco Tito Yupanqui's image was canonized by the Vatican.

Orientation

Copacabana is set between two hills that offer high altitude views over the town and the lake. All the action in 'Copa centers around Plaza 2 de Febrero, with the transportation hub in

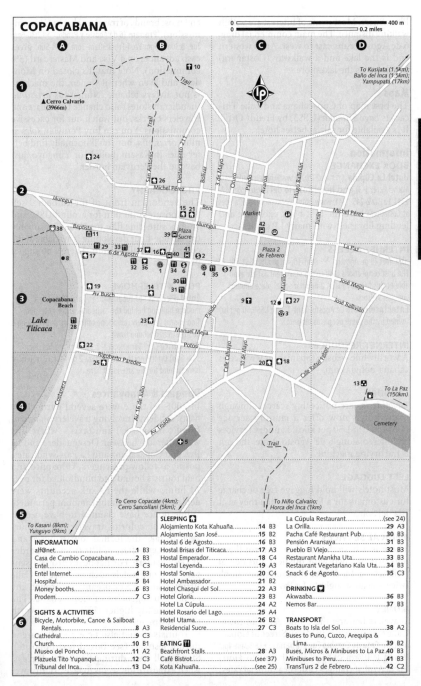

COPACABANA

INFORMATION
alf@net..1 B3
Casa de Cambio Copacabana........2 B3
Entel...3 C3
Entel Internet.................................4 B3
Hospital...5 B4
Money booths.................................6 B3
Prodem...7 C3

SIGHTS & ACTIVITIES
Bicycle, Motorbike, Canoe & Sailboat
   Rentals..8 A3
Cathedral..9 C3
Church...10 B1
Museo del Poncho.........................11 A2
Plazuela Tito Yupanqui..................12 C3
Tribunal del Inca...........................13 D4

SLEEPING
Alojamiento Kota Kahuaña.........14 B3
Alojamiento San José....................15 B2
Hostal 6 de Agosto.......................16 B3
Hostal Brisas del Titicaca..............17 A3
Hostal Emperador.........................18 C4
Hostal Leyenda..............................19 A3
Hostal Sonia...................................20 C4
Hotel Ambassador.........................21 B2
Hotel Chasqui del Sol....................22 A3
Hotel Gloria....................................23 B3
Hotel La Cúpula.............................24 A2
Hotel Rosario del Lago..................25 A4
Hotel Utama...................................26 B3
Residencial Sucre...........................27 C3

EATING
Beachfront Stalls............................28 A3
Café Bistrot................................(see 37)
Kota Kahuaña.............................(see 25)

La Cúpula Restaurant.................(see 24)
La Orilla...29 A3
Pacha Café Restaurant Pub...........30 B3
Pensión Aransaya...........................31 B3
Pueblo El Viejo.............................32 B3
Restaurant Mankha Uta................33 B3
Restaurant Vegetariano Kala Uta..34 B3
Snack 6 de Agosto.......................35 C3

DRINKING
Akwaaba...36 B3
Nemos Bar......................................37 B3

TRANSPORT
Boats to Isla del Sol......................38 A2
Buses to Puno, Cuzco, Arequipa &
   Lima..39 B2
Buses, Micros & Minibuses to La Paz.40 B3
Minibuses to Peru.........................41 B3
TransTurs 2 de Febrero.................42 C2

Plaza Sucre. Most items of interest are within walking distance. The main commercial drag, 6 de Agosto, runs east to west. At its western end is the lake and a walkway (Costañera) which traces the lakeshore.

Maps

The best map of Copacabana and Lake Titicaca is *Lago Titikaka* (US$3) by Freddy Ortiz. It is available for sale at better hotels.

Information

BOOK EXCHANGE

Hotel La Cúpula (☎ 862-2029; www.hotelcupula.com; Michel Peréz 1-3) and **Hotel Rosario del Lago** (☎ 862-2141, La Paz 2-245-1341; www.hotelrosario.com/lago; Paredes at Costañera) have the best book exchange and lending libraries (with many LP guides).

INTERNET ACCESS

alf@net (6 de Agosto; ⏱ 8am-10pm; per hr US$1.50) The best connections (and cheap video rentals) are available at this friendly place, a popular social place among younger visitors.

Entel Internet (6 de Agosto; 7am-11pm; US$1.50 per hr) Owned by the same people as alf@net.

INTERNET RESOURCES

A worthwhile website (Spanish) is www.copacabana-bolivia.com.

LAUNDRY

Lavanderías are noticeably scarce, although many hotels now offer a laundry service (US$1 to US$1.50 per kilo). Laundry services are offered along 6 de Agosto. Note: the sun is the drying machine.

LEFT LUGGAGE

Most hotels will hold luggage free of charge for customers for a few days while they visit Isla del Sol.

MEDICAL SERVICES

There is a basic hospital on the southern outskirts of town with medical and dental facilities, but for serious situations don't think twice – head straight to La Paz.

MONEY

Travelers beware: there's no ATM in town. Calle 6 de Agosto is the Wall Street of Copacabana. **Casa de Cambio Copacabana** (⏱ 8:30am-4pm Mon-Fri, to 1:30pm Sat & Sun) is adjacent to Hotel Playa Azul; it changes cash (near official rates)

and most brands of travelers checks (5% commission). **Prodem** (6 de Agosto y Pando; ⏱ 2:30-6pm Tue, 8:30am-6pm Wed-Fri, 8:30am-3pm Sat & Sun) gives cash advances on a Visa and Mastercard (5% commission). Note that it's closed on Mondays and even when it's open, the machine is not always reliable. Numerous *artesanía* (handicraft stores) also change US dollars and travelers checks, but watch out for excessive commissions. You can buy Peruvian *soles* at most *artesanía*, but you'll normally find better rates in Kasani, Bolivia or Yunguyo, just beyond the Peruvian border.

PHOTOGRAPHY

The vendors in front of the cathedral sell 36-exposure print film for around US$2 and 36-exposure slide film for US$6. Reasonably priced, one-hour developing is available at the color lab on Calle Pando. There's no digital processing.

POST & TELEPHONE

Entel (Plazuela Tito Yupanqui; ⏱ 7am-11pm) In a modern building behind the cathedral. Entel, Cotel and Tigo *puntos* (privately run phone offices) are dotted along 6 de Agosto and around town.

Post office (⏱ 9am-noon & 2:30-6pm Tue-Sat, 9am-3pm Sun) On the north side of Plaza 2 de Febrero, you may have to hunt for the attendant here.

Dangers & Annoyances

In 2005–06 there were several particularly nasty incidents involving travelers on *micros* (public minibuses) and taxis – where lifts were offered – between Desaguadero and La Paz, and Copacabana and La Paz. Syndicates, posing as fellow passengers, kidnapped and held tourists bound and blindfolded for over 24 hours while their bank accounts were depleted to the maximum amount permitted. While police have claimed to have caught most of the culprits, travelers are encouraged to take the formal tourist buses and not to accept offers of lifts from the border at Desaguadero. Formal buses drop passengers at major hotels such as those in Calle Illampu, and can be organized through any of the tour agencies in Copacabana. The cost is slightly higher (US$3) but is worth the investment.

Tourists should also be especially careful during festivals (see boxed text opposite). Stand well back during fireworks displays, when explosive fun seems to take priority over

BEWARE RIOTOUS REVELRY

Copacabana is generally a very safe place. Unfortunately though, during festival time (p112), and especially during the Festival of Independence (first week of August), robberies and muggings are as riotous as the reveling. Local people are quick to point the finger at their Peruvian neighbors, who flood into Copacabana on religious pilgrimages. But whoever the culprits may be is irrelevant to victims of crime, usually tourists. Hotels and businesses display strong warnings to travelers to be extra cautious in the days leading up to and including festivals: don't carry valuables, take only the money you need, and never go out alone at night.

crowd safety, and be wary of light-fingered revelers.

The thin air and characteristically brilliant sunshine in this area combine to admit scorching levels of ultraviolet radiation. To minimize the risk, wear a hat, especially when you're out on the water.

Sights

All of Copacabana's main attractions can be visited in one long but relaxed day.

CATHEDRAL

The sparkling white *mudéjar* cathedral, with its domes and colorful *azulejos* (blue Portuguese-style ceramic tiles), dominates the town. Baptisms take place every Saturday at 4pm; check the notice board in front of the entrance for the mass schedule.

The cathedral's black Virgen de Candelaria statue **Camarín de la Virgen de Candelaria** (8am-noon & 2-6pm; entry by donation), carved by Inca Tupac Yupanqui's grandson, Francisco Yupanqui, is encased above the altar upstairs in the niche or *camarín* (note visiting hours are unreliable). The statue is never moved from the cathedral, as superstition suggests that its disturbance would precipitate a devastating flood of Lake Titicaca.

The cathedral is a repository for both European and local religious art and the **Museo de la Catedral** (8am-11am, 2-5pm; US$0.60) contains some interesting articles. Don't miss the ostrich vases or the hundreds of paper cranes donated by a Japanese woman in the hope of

bearing an intelligent child. There are group tours on demand.

COPACABANA BEACH

While Bolivia's only public beach can't hold a candle to the better-known beach of the same name in Rio de Janeiro, on weekends the festive atmosphere is a magnet for families. You can take a pew at one of the many little eateries along the (unfortunately) drain-ridden shore front. More appealingly, you can soak up sun, trout and beer. Or, you can rent all manner of boating craft (US$4 per hour), bicycles (US$1.25 per hour) and motorbikes (US$5 per hour).

CERRO CALVARIO

The summit of Cerro Calvario can be reached in half an hour and is well worth the climb, especially in the late afternoon to watch the sunset over the lake. The trail to the summit begins near the **church** at the end of Calle Destacamento 211 and climbs past the 14 Stations of the Cross.

NIÑO CALVARIO & HORCA DEL INCA

The small but prominent hill Niño Calvario, southeast of tow (not to be confused with Cerro Calvario west of town), is known variously as Little Calvary, Seroka and by its original name, Kesanani. Its weirdly rugged rock formations merit an hour or so of exploration. From near the end of Calle Murillo, a signposted trail leads uphill to the **Horca del Inca** (admission free), an odd trilithic gate perched on the hillside. This pre-Inca astronomical observatory is surrounded by pierced rocks that permit the sun's rays to pass through onto the lintel during the solstice of 21 June, the Aymará New Year (if it doesn't, it is deemed to be a bad year for agriculture). During this time locals venture up before sunrise to celebrate. A lone guide or three may be at the site – it's worth hearing their explanation for a small donation.

A further 4km down this road toward Kasani, lies **Cerro Copacate**, which features pre-Inca ruins and pictographs. The best known, but difficult to distinguish, is the **Escudo de la Cultura Chiripa**, a unique icon attributed to the pre-Inca Chiripa culture.

TRIBUNAL DEL INCA (INTIKALA)

North of the cemetery on the southeastern outskirts of town is the sadly neglected site of artificially sculpted boulders known as the **Inca Tribunal** (admission free). Its original purpose is unknown, but there are several carved stones with *asientos* (seats), basins and *hornecinos* (niches), which probably once contained idols.

KUSIJATA & BAÑO DEL INCA

A 3km walk northeast along the shoreline from the end of Calles Junín or Hugo Ballivián leads to the community-run colonial manor known as **Kusijata** (admission US$0.60), where there's a small, dusty archaeological display. If you can see in the semi-dark – the lights are not turned on – seek out the long-deceased human sitting in an upright fetal position, as he was buried. A young caretaker should chase after you with the key as you walk up the hill; otherwise ask around. The pre-Columbian tunnel beside the manor was originally used to access the subterranean water supply. The carved-stone water tank and tap are known as the **Baño del Inca** (Inca Bath), although their origins and meanings are a little unclear.

MUSEO DEL PONCHO

The **Museo del Poncho** (🕙 9:30am-12:30pm & 3-6pm Mon-Sat, 9:30am-4:30pm Sun; admission US$1.25) is one of the newest, most professional and lovely museums around. The exhibits, in a modern layout over two floors, help you unravel the mysteries of the regional textiles, particularly ponchos. The labels, in both English and Spanish, give a clear insight into the garments' origins, meanings and the different regions they belong to. The museum was established by *Jiwasax, Culturas y Educación*, a cultural organization set up to conserve and diffuse the Andean textile art, and is a colorful way to tie up some cultural threads.

Tours

A number of tour agencies, most clustered on the corner of 6 de Agosto and 16 de Julio, organize trips around Copacabana's environs. The most popular trip is the half- or full-day visit to Isla del Sol (p118), with departures at 8:30am and 1:30pm daily. Depending on the boat, it may drop you off at a choice of the island's north or south (check with the agency), from where you either walk to the southern end of the island or fill in time in the south before being collected from the Escalera del Inca. A daily return trip costs from US$2.50 to US$3.15; a half day to the south or a one-way trip costs US$2.

Festivals & Events

Copacabana hosts several major annual fiestas. The town also celebrates the **La Paz departmental anniversary** on July 15. Thursdays and Sundays are lively market days.

JANUARY

One local tradition, observed at the **Alasitas festival** (January 24), is the blessing of miniature objects, such as miniature cars or houses. Supplicants pray that the real thing will be obtained in the coming year.

FEBRUARY

From February 2 to 5, the **Fiesta de la Virgen de Candelaria** honors the patron saint of Copacabana and all Bolivia. Copacabana holds an especially big bash, and pilgrims and dancers come from Peru and around Bolivia. There's much music, traditional Aymará dancing, drinking and feasting. On the third day celebrations culminate with the gathering of 100 bulls in a stone corral along the Yampupata road, and the town's braver (and drunker) citizens jump into the arena and try to avoid being attacked.

BENEDICION DE MOVILIDADES

The word *cha'lla* is used for any ritual blessing, toasting or offering to the powers that be, whether Inca, Aymará or Christian. On most mornings during the festival season (above), from around 10am (and reliably on Saturdays and Sundays), cars, trucks and buses hover in front of Copacabana's cathedral decked out in garlands of real or plastic flowers, colored ribbons and flags. They come for a *cha'lla* known as the Benedicion de Movilidades (Blessing of Automobiles). Petitions for protection are made to the Virgin, and a ritual offering of alcohol is poured over the vehicles, thereby consecrating them for the journey home. Between Good Friday and Easter Sunday, the *cha'lla* is especially popular among pilgrims and long-distance bus companies with new fleets. The priest slips owner donations into his vestments faster than you can say Hail Mary, but per vehicle it's still a cheap alternative to insurance!

MARCH/APRIL

As part of the **Semana Santa** festival (p370), on **Good Friday** the town fills with pilgrims – some of whom walk the 158-km journey from La Paz – to do penance at the Stations of the Cross on Cerro Calvario. Beginning at the cathedral at dusk, pilgrims join a solemn candlelit procession through town, led by a statue of Christ in a glass coffin and a replica of the Virgen de Candelaria. Once on the summit they light incense and purchase miniatures representing material possessions in the hope that they will be granted the real things by the Virgin during the year.

MAY

The **Fiesta de la Cruz** (Feast of the Cross) is celebrated over the first weekend in May all around the lake, but the biggest festivities are in Copacabana.

AUGUST

Copacabana stages its biggest event, **Bolivian Independence Day**, during the first week in August. It's characterized by round-the-clock music, parades, brass bands, fireworks and amazing alcohol consumption. This coincides with a traditional pilgrimage that brings thousands of Peruvians into the town to visit the Virgin.

Sleeping

Hotels (many shoddy) are springing up like reeds in Copacabana. During fiestas accommodations fill up quickly and prices increase up to threefold. Ironically given its lakeside position, Copacabana's water supply is unpredictable. Better hotels go to extreme efforts to fill water tanks in the morning (the supply is normally switched off at 11am).

BUDGET

Hostal Emperador (☎ 862-2083, La Paz 2-242 4264; Murillo 235; r per person US$1.25, with bathroom US$2, with bathroom & breakfast US$2.50) This budget travelers' favorite is a great place to meet people. The enthusiastic *señora* runs a lively and colorful joint, with has hot showers and a raft of extras, including laundry service, a small shared kitchen, luggage storage and a sunny mezzanine that's ideal for lounging. A newer wing at the back has bathrooms.

Alojamiento San José (☎ 7150-3760; Jáuregui 146; r per person US$2) This place is as basic but clean as they come – it's always a good sign when the floors smell like a polish factory. Perfectly adequate for a budget traveler, although the claims of constant hot water are a little dubious.

Alojamiento Kotha Kahuaña (Busch 15; r per person US$2, with bathroom US$3) A mini Tiahuanaco awaits you at this cozy and spotless abode. It offers good upstairs rooms, hot water around the clock, and is run by a delightfully caring family.

Hostal Sonia (☎ 7196-8441, 7196-5977; Murillo 256; r per person US$2.50) The rooms here are as bright and cheery as the Dueña Sonia (daughter of the Señora of Hostal Emperador fame). This lively spot's simple and light rooms, kitchen, terrace and laundry service make it an excellent budget choice.

Hostal 6 de Agosto (6 de Agosto; r per person US$3) This rosy place offers a sunny outlook over a garden and clean, if standard, rooms. The only thorn may be its location, almost on top of night spot Diego Pub – you might be boppin' till you're droppin', off to sleep or otherwise. A good restaurant is also on the premises (set lunch menu US$1.50).

Residencial Sucre (☎ 862-2080; Murillo 228; r per person with bathroom US$3.15-4) This option feels more like a midrange hotel than a budget hang-out. It's got color national TV, carpeted rooms, reliable hot water and a restaurant (breakfast costs extra). A sunny courtyard (sometimes a car park) adds to the appeal. Sun abounds in the corner Room 38 – it's frequently shown off to prospective clients – but the other rooms are okay, too.

Hotel Ambassador (☎ 862-2216, La Paz 2-224-3382; Jáuregui at Bolívar; r per person with bathroom US$5) The red shag pile rugs in the entrance set the theme here – it's a slightly chintzy but charming choice, with aging but comfortable rooms. The facilities are a step up from the cheaper places that dominate in town. The colorful restaurant, with possibly one of the town's best outlooks (at least from the town center) and set lunch menus (US$1), is well worth a visit.

Hostal Brisas del Titicaca (☎ 862-2178, La Paz 245-3022; www.hostellingbolivia.org; 6 de Agosto at Costañera; r per person US$5; 🖳) Situated right on the beach, this popular HI-affiliate has amenable (albeit retro 1970s) rooms. A few rooms with shared baths have teeny-weeny windows with no outlook, but several others with private baths have their own lake-view terraces with good vistas. It's hard to get past the front door unless you're serious about taking a room.

For camping, try the summits of both Niño Calvario and Cerro Sancollani. But take care, and if camping near a village always ask permission from the local village authority.

MIDRANGE & TOP END

La Cúpula (☎ 862-2029; www.hotelcupula.com; Michel Pérez 1-3; s US$6-12, d US$8-17, tr US$20, with bathroom s US$14-20, d US$20-32, tr US$18-40) Travelers from around the world rave about this inviting oasis, marked by two gleaming white domes on the slopes of Cerro Calvario, with stupendous lake views. Its popularity is well justified. The 19 individual, creatively-designed rooms (including sweet suites for honeymooners, two with kitchens, and an apartment for families) provide one of Bolivia's best-value and most pleasant stays. Guests can enjoy access to the TV/video room, library and shared kitchen and laundry facilities, and the attached La Cúpula restaurant (opposite) is a favorite for its coziness, vistas and cuisine. Sculptures, hammocks and shady spots are attractive features of its extensive gardens. The helpful staff speak several languages and are full of travel tips. Best to book ahead.

Hotel Utama (☎ 862-2013; cnr Michel Peréz & San Antonio; s US$7-10, d with bath US$10-20) Meaning 'your house' in Aymará, this is indeed a comfortable and good-value hotel, applauded for its breakfasts. It often absorbs the overflow from the nearby La Cúpula and is a popular tour group drop-off. Some cheaper first-floor rooms face into the internal courtyard, but others have external windows. Front rooms with views are slightly more expensive and there are discounts for students with cards.

Hotel Chasqui del Sol (☎ 862-2343; www.chasquidel sol.com; Costañera 55; s/d with bathroom & breakfast US$15/25) An '80s-style frilly number with generous-sized rooms, even larger bathrooms and massive vistas of the lake. Staff are friendly and travelers give good reports.

Hostal Leyenda (☎ 7192-6333, Costañera, esq. Busch; d with bathroom & breakfast US$15) You can overlook the odd crack at this place for its creativity – each room in this small abode has a different creative bent. Room 6 – a double suite – is particularly cozy for its woody interiors. The restaurant is a snore's breath away from the accommodations, which might or might not be a good thing. It's right on the beach front, which can get noisy during busy seasons. Travelers report tepid showers which might dampen the experience.

Hotel Rosario del Lago (☎ 862-2141, La Paz 2-245-1341; www.hotelrosario.com/lago; Paredes at Costañera; s/ d/tr/ste with bathroom US$33/44/59/87; 🖳) It's worth splurging at this neocolonial, three-star sister of Hotel Rosario in La Paz. The charming rooms all have solar-heated showers, double-glazed windows and lake views. The service is worthy of a five-star hotel and extras include magnetic locks and room safes. The Altiplano light streams in, ensuring it as one of the best in town. Included is a breakfast buffet in the classy Kota Kahuaña restaurant (opposite).

Hotel Gloria (☎ 286-2294, La Paz 2-240-7070; 16 de Julio & Manuel Mejía; www.hotelgloriabolivia.com.bo; per person with bathroom & breakfast US$35) This large ex-prefectural hotel has a school boarding house feel, but its institutional atmosphere offers a lovely view of the lake and surrounding mountains. The impersonal rooms are clean and spacious and an upstairs games room will keep the troops occupied. Sometimes good-value all-inclusive packages are available.

Eating

Feeling fishy? You're in luck. The local specialty is *trucha criolla* (rainbow trout) and *pejerrey* (king fish) from Lake Titicaca. The trout were introduced in 1939 to increase protein content in the local diet. Today, trout stocks are mainly grown in hatcheries; *pejerrey* stocks are seriously depleted. The catch of the day is served ad nauseum to varying degrees of taste; some resemble electrocuted sardines, while others are worthy of a Michelin restaurant rating. The best trout dishes seem to be served at La Orilla, La Cúpula Restaurant and Kota Kahuaña.

Nearly every place in town serves breakfast – *Americano* (with an egg or two), *continental* (drink, bread and jams) or muesli with fruit.

RESTAURANTS

Restaurant Vegetariano Kala Uta (6 de Agosto at 16 de Julio; set meals under US$2, mains US$3) An artsy, appealing Andean atmosphere pervades this vegetarian option. Imaginative breakfasts include the *poder Andino* (Andean power), which features quinoa crepes topped with jam, bananas, yogurt, brazil nuts, raisins and coconut, accompanied by an Andean grain drink. Despite the advertised hours (breakfast, lunch & dinner) it seems to keep its own time.

Restaurant Mankha Uta (6 de Agosto; set meals US$2, mains US$2.50-6.50) Laid-back dudes can chill outside, at tables or on couches with the usual dishes, from pizza to *pollo*. Or sink your teeth into the trout special, Trout del Patrón (US$5.50) over a board game and a film or three.

La Cúpula Restaurant (☎ 862-2029; www.hotelcupula.com; Michel Peréz 1-3; mains US$2.50-4; ☺ closed Tue breakfast & lunch) Inventive use of local ingredients make up an extensive international and local menu. The vegetarian range includes a lasagna, and there's plenty for carnivores too. Plan on spending around US$5 for a memorable meal. Dip your way through the cheese fondue with authentic gruyere cheese – it's to die for…which leaves the Bolivian chocolate fondue with fruit platter beyond description. The glassy surroundings admit lots of Altiplano light and maximize the fabulous view of the lake.

La Orilla (☎ 862 2267; 6 de Agosto; mains US$3.50; ☺ 10am-10pm, closed Sundays) This creative winner – decked out with masks and tasteful décor – is a warm, cozy and social experience. And we haven't even got to the food, a more international experience including huge portions of cannelloni, stuffed trout (US$3.50; highly recommended) and coconut fish curry. Vegetarians are well catered for.

Kota Kahuaña (☎ 862-2141, La Paz 245-1341; Paredes at Costañera; mains US$2.50-5) Everything is *¡muy rico!* (delicious!) at Hotel Rosario del Lago's restaurant. It's one of the more expensive in town, but is worth the splurge, especially for the stuffed trout in a romantic atmosphere with lake views. An excellent salad bar, imaginatively prepared main courses and Bolivian wines ensures a fine-dining experience.

Pensión Aransaya (6 de Agosto 121; set meals US$1-2, fish US$3; ☺ lunch & dinner) Super-friendly local favorite for a tall, cold beer and trout heaped with all the trimmings.

Pacha Café Restaurant Pub (Bolívar; mains US$1.90-4; ☺ dinner) There's a bit of everything at this tastefully decorated barn-like place, including a fire place, cocktails and pizzas to *trucha* (trout, prepared in nine ways). Cold when empty, but fun when full.

QUICK EATS
Snack 6 de Agosto (6 de Agosto) Well-prepared meals including the usual breakfast selection (US$1.50) and set dinners (US$1.25). The patio seating is heavenly on a sunny day.

Pueblo El Viejo (6 de Agosto 684; mains US$2-5) Readers love this rustic, cozy and chilled café-bar, with its ethnic décor, hippy lighting and laid-

back atmosphere. It's run by hipsters and is possibly the only place in town where you can get a half-decent coffee (thanks in part due to an imported Italian espresso machine).

Café Bistrot (cnr 6 de Agosto & Zupana; mains US$1.15-2.20) The only thing missing from this place is Oscar from Sesame Street. There are colored tables and 'The Nest' corner for reading, writing or chilling over a drink. There are also musical instruments, including an Australian didgeridoo, and even Vegemite and Marmite (spreads) for Aussies and Brits. Like any preschool, it's a tad messy, and the food takes 20 minutes as the dishes are prepared using fresh ingredients. But with its board games and other distractions, including the English-speaking owner, it's the perfect place for homesick youngsters.

On the waterfront, **beachfront stalls** sell snacks and drinks and, in the busy season, Groundhog Day meals: *trucha* (around US$1.90). Here you can sip a drink and observe the quintessential Bolivian beach life, though the nearby drains detract a little from the experience.

The bargain basement is the market *comedor*, where you can eat a generous meal of *trucha* or beef for a pittance, or an 'insulin shock' breakfast/afternoon tea of hot *api morado* (hot corn drink) and syrupy *buñuelos* (donuts or fritters).

Drinking & Entertainment

New nightspots come and go as frequently as tour boats. Wander along 6 de Agosto to see what's happening.

Akwaaba (6 de Agosto) This Argentine-run joint is the kind of place Miles Davis would have liked – it's as mellow and laid back as you can get. One of the owners is a saxophonist and live music is regularly on the bar menu. The Cuban, salsa and *cumbia* tunes pull in the young (and sometimes not so young) hippy crowds, who squeeze their butts onto the cushioned floor seating.

Nemos Bar (6 de Agosto 684) This warm, dimly-lit, late-night hangout is a popular place for a tipple.

Shopping

Local specialties include handmade miniatures of *totora* reed boats and unusual varieties of Andean potatoes. Massive bags of *pasankalla* (puffed choclo corn with caramel), the South American version of popcorn, abounds.

LAKE TITICACA

Dozens of stores sell llama- and alpaca-wool hats and sweaters; a reasonable alpaca piece will cost around US$10. Vehicle adornments used in the *cha'lla*, miniatures and religious paraphernalia are sold in stalls in front of the cathedral.

Getting There & Away

TO/FROM LA PAZ

Trans Manco Capac (☎ 862-2234, in La Paz 2-245-9045), **TransTurs 2 de Febrero** (☎ 862-2233, in La Paz 2-245-3035) and **Transporte 6 de Junio** (☎ in La Paz 2-245-5258) have several daily connections from La Paz's cemetery district via Tiquina (US$2, 3½ hours). The booking offices are near Plaza 2 de Febrero, but buses sometimes arrive at and depart near Plaza Sucre. More comfortable nonstop tour buses from La Paz to Copacabana cost around US$3.15 in high season and are well worth the investment (see p110). They depart from La Paz at around 8am and leave Copacabana at 1:30pm (3½ hours). Tickets can be purchased from tour agencies.

TO/FROM PERU

Many tour buses go all the way to Puno (Peru), and you can break the journey in Copacabana and then continue with the same agency. You can do just the Copa–Puno leg (US$3.15, three to four hours) or go all the way to Cuzco (US$11 to US$20, 15 hours) – changing buses in Puno. These buses depart and arrive in Copacabana from Av 6 de Agosto.

Alternatively catch a public minibus from Plaza Sucre to the border at Kasani (US$0.40, 15 minutes). Across the border there's frequent, if crowded, onward transportation to Yunguyo (US$0.25, five minutes) and Puno (US$2, 2½ hours). If you're headed straight to Cuzco, many Copacabana agencies offer tickets on the daily buses. They also offer efficient bus journeys to Arequipa (8½ hours, US$11.25), Lima (18 hours, US$50) and other Peruvian destinations. All buses will wait until the last person has completed immigration formalities.

Note that Peruvian time is one hour behind Bolivian time.

TO/FROM ISLA DEL SOL

All agencies sell tickets to Isla Del Sol for boat companies Titicaca and Andes Amazonia. Alternatively, you can buy tickets in the morning of departure (US$2.50-3.15) from one of the beach offices. Local community boats (Mallku

and Sol Tours) also run less frequent trips. For details, see p112.

COPACABANA TO YAMPUPATA TREK

An enjoyable way to reach Isla del Sol is to trek along the lakeshore to the village of Yampupata, which lies just a short boat ride from the ruins of Pilko Kaina on Isla del Sol.

Main Route

This trek is road-bound, making it a fairly hot and hard slog (around seven hours), although with lovely views and interesting village visits.

From Copacabana, head northeast on the road around the lake for around 1½ hours until the **Gruta de Lourdes** (aka Gruta de Fátima), a cave that for locals evokes images of its French and Portuguese namesakes, respectively. For a shortcut, turn right immediately after the small bridge leading to the Virgin and follow the Inca path. When the path peters out head directly uphill to rejoin the main road at the crest of the hill. Note: to save an hour or so and avoid the flat and litter-strewn outskirts of town, you can catch a taxi from Copa to the Gruta de Lourdes (US$6.25 one way, US$7.50 return; 9km), from where the more picturesque hiking begins.

At the fork just below the crest of the hill bear left and descend to the shore and into the village of **Titicachi**, where, if it's open, there's a basic *tienda* (shop) selling soft drinks.

In and around Titicachi are several sites of interest, including some pre-Inca walls and the careworn **Tiahuanacota Inca cemetery**. On the offshore islet of Jiskha Huata perches the **Museo de Aves Acuáticos** (Museum of Aquatic Birds), a small display of Lake Titicaca birdlife which can be reached only by boat (ask around for Sr Quiroga, who will take you over).

At the next village, **Sicuani**, Juan Mamani runs the **Hostal Yampu** (per person US$1.25; meals US$1), which offers basic accommodations with bucket showers. Hikers can pop in for a beer or soft drink. Slightly further on in the same village, don't go past the gregarious, quirky and very photogenic Hilario Paye. Sr Paye will no doubt run through his international post-card collection and, if you're lucky, will take you for a spin around the bay in a *totora* reed boat or via motorboat to the peninsula opposite (prices negotiable), where he's constructed fine walking trails to a 'cave.' For those who want to spend the night in

ISLA DEL SOL & YAMPUPATA

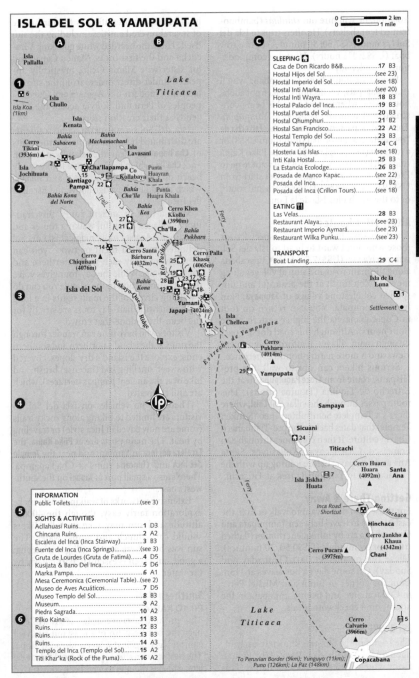

0   2 km
0   1 mile

SLEEPING
Casa de Don Ricardo B&B....................**17** B3
Hostal Hijos del Sol...........................(see 23)
Hostal Imperio del Sol.......................(see 18)
Hostal Inti Marka.............................(see 20)
Hostal Inti Wayra.............................**18** B3
Hostal Palacio del Inca.......................**19** B3
Hostal Puerta del Sol.........................**20** B3
Hostal Qhumphuri............................**21** B2
Hostal San Francisco.........................**22** A2
Hostal Templo del Sol........................**23** B3
Hostal Yampu.................................**24** C4
Hosteria Las Islas............................(see 18)
Inti Kala Hostal...............................**25** B3
La Estancia Ecolodge.........................**26** B3
Posada de Manco Kapac.....................(see 22)
Posada del Inca...............................**27** B2
Posada del Inca (Crillon Tours)..............(see 18)

EATING
Las Velas.....................................**28** B3
Restaurant Alaya.............................(see 23)
Restaurant Imperio Aymará..................(see 23)
Restaurant Wilka Punku.....................(see 23)

TRANSPORT
Boat Landing.................................**29** C4

INFORMATION
Public Toilets.................................(see 3)

SIGHTS & ACTIVITIES
Acllahuasi Ruins..............................**1** D3
Chincana Ruins...............................**2** A2
Escalera del Inca (Inca Stairway).............**3** B3
Fuente del Inca (Inca Springs)................(see 3)
Gruta de Lourdes (Gruta de Fatimá)..........**4** D5
Kusijata & Bano Del Inca......................**5** D6
Marka Pampa..................................**6** A1
Mesa Ceremonica (Ceremonial Table)..(see 2)
Museo de Aves Acuáticos.....................**7** D5
Museo Templo del Sol........................**8** B3
Museum......................................**9** A2
Piedra Sagrada...............................**10** A2
Pilko Kaina...................................**11** B3
Ruins..**12** B3
Ruins..**13** B3
Ruins..**14** A3
Templo del Inca (Templo del Sol).............**15** A2
Titi Khar'ka (Rock of the Puma)..............**16** A2

LAKE TITICACA

Lake Titicaca

To Peruvian Border (9km); Yunguyo (11km);
Puno (126km); La Paz (148km); Copacabana

isolation, he will hire out *chullhas* (bamboo-framed tent shelters). He offers trips to Isla del Sol (around US$7.50; 30 minutes) or in a row boat (US$2; 1½ hours). Hostal accommodations is underway.

Five to six hours from Copacabana, you'll reach **Yampupata**, a collection of lakefront adobe houses, and where a new hostel is being constructed. *Asociación Transporte Yampupata Tours* takes passengers across the **Estrecho de Yampupata** in a motorboat (minimum US$8) or a rowboat (two people US$3) to the Pilko Kaina ruins (right). Specify clearly if you want to go to Escalera del Inca (opposite). Prices start from US$19 to head to the island's north and south, or to the south plus Isla de la Luna.

Alternative Routes

An alternative hiking option, especially for those who don't want to head to Isla del Sol, is to catch a taxi (US$17.50) from Copacabana along the main road and stop at villages along the way. You finish at the beautiful and unspoiled cobblestone village of **Sampaya**, 5km from Yampupata. You can return on foot to Copacabana via the higher eastern route (four hours). Although this road doesn't pass through main villages, it affords magnificent views and a more nature-bound experience.

Serious hikers can opt to walk the pre-Hispanic route from **Cruce Paquipujio**, near the Estrecho de Tiquina (Tiquina Straits). This route passes through the village of **Chisi**, where there's a Templete Semisubterráneo (Sunken Temple) that dates back to the pre-Tiahuanaco Chavín culture. It then continues through San Francisco, Chachacoyas, Kollasuyos, Santa Ana and Sampaya, before joining up with the Copacabana to Yampupata trek at Titicachi.

Getting There & Away

For those who don't want to walk or taxi, the easiest ways to travel between Yampupata and Copacabana are by infrequent *camión* (flatbed truck) or by minibus (US$0.50, 30 minutes). These run on market days (Thursday and Sunday). On some days a bus leaves at 11am from the corner of Junín and Michel Pérez in Copacabana, and from Yampupata in the afternoon – check with locals.

ISLA DEL SOL

The Island of the Sun was known to early inhabitants as Titi Khar'ka (Rock of the Puma), from which Titicaca takes its name. This island has been identified as the birthplace of several revered entities, including the sun itself. There the bearded white god-king Viracocha and the first Incas, Manco Capac and his sister/wife Mama Ocllo, mystically appeared under direct orders from the sun. In fact, most modern-day Aymará and Quechua peoples of Peru and Bolivia accept these legends as their creation story.

Isla del Sol's 2500 permanent residents are distributed between the main settlements of **Cha'llapampa**, near the island's northern end; **Cha'lla**, which backs up to a lovely sandy beach on the central east coast; and **Yumani**, which straddles the ridge above the Escalera del Inca.

With a host of ancient ruins, tiny traditional villages, beautiful walking routes and a distinctly Aegean look, magical Isla del Sol definitely merits a night or two – you can then devote a day each to the northern and southern ends. While the day-tour gives you a decent introduction to the island (you can do a walking circuit of the main sights in a long day), whirlwind half-day tours are strictly for the been-there-done-that crowd.

Visitors who have time can wander through the ruins at the island's northern and southern ends; explore the island's dry slopes, covered with sweet-smelling *koa* (incense) brush; and hike over the ancient *pampas* (terraces), which are still cultivated.

There are no vehicles on Isla del Sol, so visitors are limited to hiking along rocky trails (some are now paved in Inca style) or traveling by boat. The main ports are at **Pilko Kaina**, the **Escalera del Inca** in Yumani and near the **Templo del Inca** and **Chincana** ruins at Cha'llapampa. There's also a small port at **Japapi** on the southwest coast.

Extensive networks of walking tracks make exploration fairly easy, though the 4000m altitude and sun may take its toll. Hikers should carry lunch and ample water. The sun was born here and is still going strong; a good sunscreen is essential, particularly by the water.

Southern Half

PILKO KAINA

This prominent **ruins complex** (admission US$0.60) near the southern tip of the island sits well camouflaged against a steep terraced slope. The best-known site is the two-level **Palacio del Inca**, which is thought to have been constructed

A BOLIVIAN ATLANTIS?

At low tide an innocuous-looking column of rock peeps just a few centimeters above Lake Titicaca's surface, north of Isla del Sol. Most locals dismiss it as a natural, stone column, similar to many others along the shoreline. In 1992 stone boxes containing artifacts (including several made of pure gold) were discovered at the underwater site known as Marka Pampa (aka La Ciudad Submergida). In August 2000 further excavations near the site revealed a massive stone temple, winding pathways and a surrounding wall, all about 8m underwater. Although it remains unclear who was responsible for the structures, it has been postulated that they are of Inca origin. Investigations are ongoing.

by the Incan Emperor Tupac Yupanqui. The rectangular windows and doors taper upward from their sill and thresholds to narrower lintels that cover them on top. The arched roof vault was once covered with flagstone shingles and then reinforced with a layer of mud and straw.

There is a restaurant next door, but you must reserve in advance. At the time of research, the owner was also building hotel rooms with private bathroom.

FUENTE DEL INCA & ESCALERA DEL INCA

About 30 minutes walk north of Pilko Kaina, incongruous streams of fresh water gush from the natural spring Fuente del Inca and pour down three artificial stone channels alongside a beautifully constructed Inca-era staircase, Escalera del Inca; the springs feed a lovely terraced and cultivated water garden.

Early Spaniards believed Yumani's spring was a fountain of youth, and for the Incas the three streams represented their national motto: *Ama sua, Ama llulla, Ama khella,* meaning 'Don't steal, don't lie and don't be lazy.' Today, the fountain is a crucial source of water for locals, who come daily to wash clothes or fetch water and carry it up the steep trail.

YUMANI

Yumani's small church, Iglesia de San Antonio, serves the southern half of the island. Nearby you'll find a growing cluster of guesthouses and fabulous views over the water to Isla de la Luna. You can also climb to the ridge for

a view down to the deep sapphire-colored Bahía Kona on the western shore. From the crest you'll find routes leading downhill to the village of Japapi and north along the ridge to Cha'llapampa and the Chincana ruins.

About midway up the hill between the Fuente del Inca and the ridge, you'll spot the lush grounds of the Inti Wata Cultural Complex, open only to clients of the Transturin catamaran tours (p124). With extra time you can make your way over the isthmus and up onto the prominent Kakayo–Queña Ridge, the island's southwestern extremity. The serene walk along the ridge to the lighthouse on the southern tip takes at least half a day (return) from Yumani.

CHA'LLA

This agreeable little village stretches along a magnificent sandy beach that appears to be taken straight out of a holiday brochure for the Greek islands. Although hidden, the village extends over the hill to the south. There's a small kiosk and a couple of guesthouses (see p121).

In the pastoral flatlands over the low pass between Cha'lla and Yumani is the Museo Templo de Sol (admission US$1.25), with some dusty exhibits including Inca pots. The ticket is also valid for the ruins to the north. It's an hour's walk north of Yumani (or on the western route if coming from the north). It's worth it for the stunning bay and valley views; the museum itself is disappointing.

Northern Half

There are two major routes between the north and south ends of Isla del Sol. The lower route winds scenically through fields, hamlets and villages, and around the bays and headlands above the eastern coast. The more dramatic ridge route begins on the crest in Yumani and heads north, roughly following the uninhabited ridge to the Chincana ruins (see p120). The views down to both coasts of the island are nothing short of spectacular. About half an hour from Yumani, a track to the left leads to the shore at Bahía Kona, the one to the right descends to Bahía Kea. The main track along the ridge to the ruins has been improved, with the route being partially paved in Inca style.

CHA'LLAPAMPA

Most boat tours visiting the northern ruins land at Cha'llapampa, which straddles a slender isthmus.

The main attraction is the **small museum** (admission US$1.25) of artifacts excavated in 1992 from Marka Pampa, fancifully referred to by locals as La Ciudad Submergida (The Sunken City; see boxed text p119).

This museum is the subject of much controversy. Its prized exhibits, Marka Pampa stone boxes and their gold contents, were reportedly stolen by someone from the Cha'lla community as part of an ongoing feud between rights to share funds for the Chincana ruins. The museum's current dusty exhibits include anthropomorphic figurines, animal bones, Tiahuanaco-era artifacts, skull parts, puma-shaped ceramic *koa* censers and cups resembling Monty Python's Holy Grail. Your ticket can be used for entry to the Chincana ruins (and visa versa).

PIEDRA SAGRADA & TEMPLO DEL INCA

From Cha'llapampa, the Chincana route continues parallel to the beach, climbing gently along an ancient route to the isthmus at **Santiago Pampa** (Kasapata).

Immediately east of the trail (turn right at the gate just off the trail) is an odd carved boulder standing upright in a small field. This is known as the **Piedra Sagrada** (Sacred Stone). There are theories that it was used as an execution block for those convicted of wrongdoing.

Over the track and in a field, just southwest of the Piedra Sagrada, are the ancient walls of the complex known as the **Templo del Inca** (or Templo del Sol). Although little remains of this temple, built for an unknown purpose, it contains the only Bolivian examples of expert Inca stonework comparable to the renowned walls found in Cuzco.

CHINCANA RUINS & TITI KHAR'KA

The island's most spectacular ruins complex, the **Chincana ruins** (admission US$1.25), lies near the island's northern tip. Its main feature is the **Palacio del Inca**, a maze of stone walls and tiny doorways, also known as El Laberinto (Labyrinth) or by its Aymará name, Inkanakan Utapa. Within the labyrinth there is a small well, believed by Inca pilgrims to contain sacred water with which they would purify themselves.

About 150m southeast of the ruins is the **Mesa Ceremónica** (Ceremonial Table), which also happens to be a convenient picnic spot. It's thought to have been the site of human and animal sacrifice. East of the table stretches

the large rock known as Titicaca – or more accurately, **Titi Khar'ka**, the Rock of the Puma – which is featured in the Inca creation legend. The name is likely to derive from its shape which, when viewed from the southeast, resembles a crouching puma.

Three natural features on the rock's western face also figure in legend. Near the northern end is one dubbed the **Cara de Viracocha** (Face of Viracocha), which takes some imagination to distinguish – it could be the face of a puma. At the southern end are four distinctive elongated niches. The two on the right are locally called the **Refugio del Sol** (Refuge of the Sun) and those on the left, the **Refugio de la Luna** (Refuge of the Moon). According to tradition it was here during the Chamaj Pacha, or 'times of flood and darkness,' that the sun made its first appearance, and later Manco Capac and Mama Ocllo appeared and founded the Inca Empire.

In the surface stone immediately south of the rock you'll pass the **Huellas del Sol** (Footprints of the Sun). These natural markings resemble footprints and have inspired the notion that they were made by the sun after its birth on Titi Khar'ka.

A ticket from the museum in Cha'llapampa also covers entry to the Chincana ruins and vice versa. If you land in the north at Cha'llapampa you can follow the prominent Inca route past the Piedra Sagrada and Templo del Inca to the Chincana ruins. If coming from the south, veer left as you are at the point above Cha'llapampa. If you've the energy, climb Cerro Uma Qolla for a great view.

Tours

Numerous Copacabana tour agencies offer informal Isla del Sol trips (half day/full day US$2/3.15). Launches embark from the beach around 8:30am. Most full-day trips go directly north to Cha'llapampa. You'll have just enough time to hike up to the Chincana ruins, then return to the Escalera del Inca and Pilko Kaina. Half-day trips generally go to the south only.

Those who wish to hike can get off at Cha'llapampa in the morning and walk south to the Escalera del Inca for the return boat in the afternoon. Alternatively you can opt to stay overnight or longer on the island, then buy a one-way ticket to Copacabana (US$2) with any of the boat companies, including the local boat association.

Turisbus (www.travelperubolivia.com), at the Hotel Rosario del Lago (p114), offers half day tours to the south of Isla del Sol (US$45, minimum two persons) and full day tours (US$75, minimum two persons) to both north and south.

Sleeping

The most scenic place to stay is Yumani – high on the ridge – where guesthouses are growing faster than coca production. Ch'allapampa and Ch'alla have many basic options. You can wild camp just about anywhere on the island. It's best to ask permission from the local authority and then set up away from villages, avoiding cultivated land.

YUMANI
Budget
Hostal Imperio del Sol (☎ 7196-1863; r per person without/with bathroom US$2.50/US$25) This peachy place is hard to beat: central, spotless and with a choice of modern rooms with bathroom, or plainer ones without. The pretty garden and cloth-covered tables will bring back the practice of post-card writing. Meals are available.

Hostal Templo del Sol (☎ 7122-7616; r per person US$3.80) This basic backpackers' favorite is upbeat but rundown, and sits right on the ridge with unsurpassed views down both sides of the island, including a rather haunting vista of the Kakayo–Queña ridge. Meals, staples and cooking facilities are available.

Hostal Inti Wayra (☎ 7194-2015, La Paz 2-246-1765; r per person US$5) The amicable and rambling Inti Wayra affords great views from most rooms; the new rooms upstairs are larger and more open. It seems ever-unfinished, with renovations continually on the go. American breakfasts are US$1, and other meals (including vegetarian options) are US$2.

Other budget options include the **Hosteria Las Islas** (☎ 7128-1710; r per person US$3.15), **Hostal Puerta del Sol** (☎ 7195-5181; r per person US$3.15), and the brand new, great-value **Hostal Palacio del Inca** (☎ 7151-1046; r per person US$3.15), one of the few places with an extraordinary view of both sides of the island.

Midrange & Top End
Casa de Don Ricardo B&B (☎ 7193-4427; birdy zehnder@hotmail.com; s/d with bathroom & breakfast US$12/20) This terracotta place with its domed rooms was once cutting edge, but it seems to have run down a little in recent times. Its front

communal room has an artistic and alternative vibe. More tepid (bordering on cold) is the shower's water supply.

Inti Kala Hostal (☎ 7194-4013; javierintikala@hotmail .com; per person with bathroom & breakfast US$15) The setting is enough to make a grown man weep. This new, clean and ultra popular place has a massive deck, smaller rooms and quirkily angled toilets. Popular with groups.

La Estancia Ecolodge (☎ 7156-7287, La Paz 2-244-2727; www.ecolodge-laketiticaca.com; s/d with bathroom & breakfast US$55/80) Magri Turismo's delightful adobe cottages are set above pre-Inca terraces facing snow-capped Illampu. They are authentically ecological with solar-powered showers, sun-powered hot-boxes for heaters, and Aymará thatched roofs. The price includes breakfast and dinner. La Estancia is a 15-minute walk from Yumani.

Posada del Inca (☎ La Paz 2-233-7533; www.titicaca .com; s/d with bathroom US$49/58) The island's most luxurious accommodations is in a historic colonial compound next to San Antonio Church and is only open to clients of Crillon Tours (p124). Price includes breakfast and dinner.

CHA'LLA
On the hill behind the beach at Cha'lla is the simple, family-run **Hostal Qhumphuri** (prices negotiable), a mustard-colored construction that offers clean rooms, but as yet, no showers. Otherwise, you could bag a bed at the now run-down **Posada del Inca** (r US$1.25) – although it doesn't seem to see much traffic nowadays and is often closed.

CHA'LLAPAMPA
The best options here are **Posada de Manco Kapac** (☎ 7128-8443; r US$2.50) run by the knowledgeable Lucio, or the flowery **Hostal San Francisco** (r US$2.50). Both are to the left of the landing site. Many other budget options are on the beach behind the museum. For boat shuttles around the island, as well as to Isla del la Luna (US$25 min two people), seek out Sr Choque at Restaurant Wara.

Eating
Yumani has the best eating options: there are more cafés than Titicaca has *trucha*. At the top of the Escalera del Inca, Hosteria Las Islas is a convenient place, although its service (and kitchen standards) are as limp as a dead fish (US$3.15 set lunch with trout). On Yumani's hilltop, **Restaurants Imperio Aymará,**

Alaya and Wilka Punku are safe bets for *pejerrey* lunches and dinners. Also on the top perches Las Velas, a small pizzeria with a great view. In Cha'llapampa there are some basic eateries with pleasant sunny settings.

Getting There & Around

BOAT

From the beach in Copacabana, several private *lanchas* (launch, small boat) and tour companies offer transportation to Isla del Sol (US$3.15 per person day return, US$2 one way). In addition to the private tour boats, Mallku community cooperative boats leave several times weekly from Cha'llapampa and the Escalera del Inca.

Tickets may be purchased at the ticket kiosks on the beach or from Copacabana agencies. Boats to the northern end of the island land at Cha'llapampa, while those going to the southern end land at either Pilko Kaina or the Escalera del Inca.

WALKING

You can walk to Yampupata, just across the strait and hire a boat to the north of south of the island. See route info p116.

ISLA DE LA LUNA (KOATI)

Legend has it that the small Island of the Moon was where Viracocha commanded the moon to rise into the sky. A walk up to the eucalyptus grove at the summit, where shepherds graze their flocks, is rewarded by a spectacular vista of aquamarine waters, Cerro Illampu and the entire snow-covered Cordillera Real.

The **ruins** (admission US$0.75) of an Inca nunnery for the Vírgenes del Sol (Virgins of the Sun), also known as Acllahuasi or Iñak Uyu, occupy an amphitheater-like valley on the northeast shore. It's constructed of well-worked stone set in adobe mortar, and was where chosen girls (believed to be around eight years old) were presented as an offering to the sun and moon.

It's possible to camp anywhere away from the settlement, but you should always ask permission and support the locals (around ten families) by buying some local produce. Bring your own water, and plenty of it, as the lake is the island's only supply.

Few tour boats head on to Isla de la Luna from Isla del Sol. You must charter a launch from Yampupata or the Escalera del Inca for around US$19 roundtrip (for up to 12

people), or try your luck from Sampaya in a row boat.

ISLAS DE HUYÑAYMARKA

Lago de Huyñaymarka's most frequented islands – Suriqui, Kalahuta and Pariti – are easily visited in a half day trip. Tourism has become an economic mainstay, but it has not been entirely beneficial to the Kalahuta and Suriqui people who reside on the islands. Please behave sensitively; ask permission before taking photos and refuse requests for money or gifts.

It's possible to camp overnight, particularly on sparsely populated Pariti, however camping is not recommended on Kalahuta – you will probably draw some criticism from locals, who believe in night spirits.

Isla Suriqui

The best known of the Huyñaymarka islands is world renowned for the *totora* reed boats that were, until just a few years ago, used by many islanders in everyday life (see boxed text opposite). Today the island seems tired of tourists: the reed boats have been ditched in favor of the more lucrative wooden boat building, and the only thing floating around the lakeshore are the piles of litter and empty bottles. Consequently, many tour agencies are omitting Suriqui from their itineraries. It's only worth stopping off if you have a few minutes en route to other islands.

Isla Kalahuta

When lake levels are low, Kalahuta ('stone houses' in Aymará) becomes a peninsula. Its shallow shores are lined with beds of *totora* reed, the versatile building material for which Titicaca is famous. By day fisherfolk ply the island's main bay in their wooden boats; just a few years ago you'd also have seen the *totora* reed boats, and men paddling around to gather the reeds to build them, but these boats are no longer used.

ISLA INCAS

It doesn't show up on many maps, but legend has it that this tiny, uninhabited island near Suriqui was part of an Inca network of underground passageways, reputed to link many parts of the Inca empire with the capital at Cuzco.

AFLOAT WITH LOCAL KNOWLEDGE

In the early 1970s Dr Thor Heyerdahl, the unconventional Norwegian adventurer and ethnographer, solicited the help of Suriqui's shipbuilders, the Limachi brothers and Paulino Esteban, to design and construct his vessel *Ra II*. Dr Heyerdahl wanted to test his theory that migration and early contact occurred between the ancient peoples of North Africa and the Americas. He planned to demonstrate the feasibility of traveling great distances using the boats of the period, in this case papyrus. He sought the knowledge of the four Aymará shipbuilders who helped him construct the boat and accompanied him on the successful expedition from Morocco to Barbados.

During Inca times, the island served as a cemetery, and it is still dotted with stone *chullpas* (funerary towers) and abandoned stone houses. Legends abound about the horrible fate that will befall anyone who desecrates the cemetery, and locals have long refused to live in the area surrounding the island's only village, Queguaya.

Isla Pariti

This tiny island, surrounded by *totora* reed marshes, made world news in 2004 when a team of Bolivian and Finnish archaeologist discovered ancient Tiahuanaco ceramics here in a small circular pit. While the American archaeologist Wendell Bennet was the first to excavate the island in 1934, the more recent finds uncovered some extraordinary shards and ceramics, believed to be ritualistic offerings, and many of which are intact. Today, many of these stunning pots and *ch'alladores* (vases) are displayed in the recently opened **Museo de Pariti** (admission US$2), while the remainder are displayed in the Museo Nacional de Arqueología in La Paz (p71). These stunning exhibits reflect the high artistic achievements of Tiahuanaco potters. Don't miss the *Señor de los patos*. For that matter, don't miss a visit here.

Getting There & Around

Calacoto Tours (☎ 2-279-2524; www.hotel-calacoto -bolivia.com; day tour around US$55, minimum 2 people) runs day tours to the islands (excluding Suriqui)

from La Paz, which include knowledgeable guides, luxury bus transportation and a delicious lunch on the shores of the lake. The most experienced guides are the Spanish-speaking Catari brothers (see p124).

On any of these trips you'll get informative commentary (in Spanish) on the legends, customs, people, history and natural features of the lake. You have a generous amount of time on each island, and if you'd like to camp on one of the islands, you can arrange to be picked up the following day by the Catari boat.

Those who aren't pressed for time may want to speak with the Aymará fisherfolk in Huatajata, who may agree to take a day off to informally shuttle visitors around the islands for a negotiated price.

AROUND LAKE TITICACA
Puerto Pérez

Established in the 1800s by English entrepreneurs as a home for the Lake Titicaca steamship service, Puerto Pérez is 67km northwest of La Paz. Today it's the home port of **Balsa Tours** (☎ 2-244-0620; www.turismobalsa.com) and its dated 80s-style five-star (don't hold your breath) lake resort, **Complejo Náutico Las Balsas** (☎ /fax 2-244-0620, La Paz 2-243-3973; r per person US$25-40). The carpeted rooms are large and afford good lake views from your bamboo-headed beds. Using the hotel at the resort as a base, Balsa operates tours to the islands of Kalahuta, Suriqui and Pariti for around US$25 per person.

Most people arrive at the Complejo Náutico Las Balsas on a transfer arranged by Balsa Tours. If you are independent and require public transportation, board anything headed for Copacabana or Sorata and get off at Batallas. From here you may have to walk the last 7km if you can't hitch or connect with the occasional public minibus (US$0.20).

Huarina

This nondescript but pleasant little village, midway between Copacabana and La Paz, serves as a road junction, particularly for the town of Sorata. If you're traveling between Sorata and Copacabana, you'll have to get off at the intersection with the main road (500m from the town itself), and wait here to flag the next bus, usually from La Paz, going in your direction.

Huatajata

This tiny community spread out along the lake's edge and the main road is mostly just a jumping-off point for trips to the Islas de Huyñaymarka (p122) and tourist cruises on Lake Titicaca (right). Life around this part of the lake remains much as it was when the Incas were capturing the imaginations – and the lands – of the Aymará inhabitants with dazzling tales of their origins. Daily life in Huatajata is dominated by age-old fishing routines – in the morning men take out their fishing boats, and each afternoon they return with the day's haul.

The Hotel Inca Utama's **Museo El Altiplano complex** (admission free for hotel guests, US$5 for nonguests) focuses on the anthropology and archaeology of the Altiplano cultures, as well as the natural history of the Lake Titicaca region. It features the traditions, agriculture, medicine and building techniques of the Tiahuanaco, Inca and Spanish empires, as well as the Chipayas and Uros cultures and the Kallawayas medicinal tradition. For hotel guests there's even a traditional healer on staff. Visitors may also get to chat with the Limachi brothers, who helped construct Thor Heyerdahl's *Ra II* (see boxed text p123). The Aymará observatory at the complex, known as *Alajpacha*, was equipped by NASA and presents nighttime stargazing programs.

Paulino Esteban's inaptly named **Museo Paulino Esteban** is more a small artisan's store,

although he has well-thumbed books about *Ra II* and other Heyerdahl expeditions that employed watercraft of ancient design, such as the *Ra I, Tigris* and the *Kon Tiki*. Outside the owner's home sits a large *totora* reed boat (Sr Esteban will request a photo opportunity faster than a jumping trout). A more informative museum is at Hostal Puerto Inti Karka (see below), where boat-builder Maximo Catari has superb reed boat models with excellent summaries of the watercraft expeditions.

TOURS

The **Catari brothers** (☎ 7197-8959; Hostal Puerto Inti Karka) run informative day visits to Isla del Sol, Isla de la Luna and Copacabana for US$150 (min 5 people). More convenient are the tours to Suriqui, Kalahuta and Pariti, which cost US$40 (min two people). See Islas de Huyñaymarka (p122) for details.

The standard **Crillon Tours** (☎ 233-7533; www .titicaca.com; Inca Utama Hotel & Spa; around US$140 per person) trip entails a bus trip from La Paz to Huatajata and a museum visit, before hitting the water in a hydrofoil. The cruise stops at the Urus-Iruitos Islands, Tiquina Straits, Copacabana and Isla de la Luna. From here it proceeds to Isla del Sol for a quick stop at Pilko Kaina and lunch at Yumani before cruising back to Huatajata. At Huatajata, passengers are bused back to La Paz. The company also offers two-day lake tours and one-day transfers by bus and/or hydrofoil between Peru and Bolivia.

A more upmarket option is to take a catamaran tour with **Transturin** (☎ 242-2222; Alfredo Ascarrunz 2518, Sopocachi; www.transturin.com; per person full day US$124, 1½ days US$186), which is based nearby in Chúa. The catamarans can accommodate up to 150 passengers and offer a full-day cruise to Isla del Sol or an overnight cruise (1½ days), stopping at Copacabana, Isla del Sol and the Inti Wata cultural complex.

SLEEPING

Hostal Puerto Inti Karka (☎ 7197-8959; r without/with bathroom US$4/6) Run by the Catari brothers and offering basic rooms; two of the five with a bathroom. It sits right on the shore and enjoys magnificent views of the lake, especially at sunset. It also has a well curated *totora* museum (left). Ask here about excursions to Islas de Huyñaymarka.

CONSTRUCTION OF A TORTORA (REED BOAT)

The construction of *totora* or reed boats is an art form. Green reeds are gathered from the lake shallows and left to dry in the sun. Once free of moisture, they are organized into fat bundles and lashed together with strong grass. In former days, often a sail of reeds was added. These bloated little canoes don't last long as far as watercraft go; after several months of use they become waterlogged and begin to rot and sink. In former times, in order to increase their life span, the canoes were often stored some distance away from the water. Today the boats are made and used mainly for tourism purposes; locals have found that wooden boats are more profitable to make and more practical to use.

Kantuta Hostal (r per person US$4.50) A basic, but decent alternative on the lakefront, next to the gas station.

Inca Utama Hotel & Spa (☎ 213-6614; iutam@entelnet .bo; Camacho 1223; s/d US$60/100) Crillon Tours' five-star (note, this is a regional, not international rating!) hotel is the destination for the agency's Lake Titicaca hydrofoil cruise programs. You can relax in a natural health spa and the float-ing La Choza Nautica bar. Bathrooms and breakfast are standard.

Hotel Titicaca (☎ in La Paz 2-242-2222) Midway between Huatajata and Huarina is this up-market place, which boasts an indoor heated pool, a sauna and racquetball courts.

EATING

Many restaurants here are open only dur-ing the high season or on weekends. On the main road the best bet is **Inti Raymi**, which specializes in trout and typical Bolivian dishes. The slew of similar tourist-oriented and local eateries along the shore all serve trout and standard fare: try **La Playa**, **La Kan-tuta**, **Inti Karka**, **Kala-Uta** or **Panamericano**. On weekends the **Bolivian Yacht Club** is open to nonmembers for lunch.

Getting There & Away

Lakeside communities between La Paz and Copacabana are served by *micros* (US$1, 1½ hours), which leave regularly between 4am and 5pm from the corner of Calles Manuel Bustillos and Kollasuyo in La Paz's cemetery district (see warning p110).

To return to La Paz, flag down a bus heading east along the main highway. The last *micro* passes through Huatajata no later than 6pm.

ESTRECHO DE TIQUINA

The narrow Tiquina Straits separate the main body of Lake Titicaca from the smaller Lago de Huyñaymarka. Flanking the western and eastern shores respectively are the twin villages of San Pedro and San Pablo. Vehicles are shut-tled across the straits on *balsas* (rafts), while passengers travel across in small launches (US$0.20, 10 minutes). It seems unlikely that a bridge will be built as the ferries keep the locals in business. Bus travelers should carry all valuables onto the launch with them.

Small restaurants and food stalls on both sides serve people caught up in the bottleneck of traffic. Note that occasionally, foreign-ers traveling in either direction may have to present their passports for inspection at San Pedro, which is home to Bolivia's largest naval base.

NORTHEASTERN SHORE

There are a couple of sites of minor interest northwest of Huatajata along the seldom-used route to the Peru–Bolivia border beyond Puerto Acosta. About 90km north of La Paz, along the road before the turnoff to Sorata, is the large market town of **Achacachi**, a crucial transportation junction and favorite road-block staging point of the former political boss Felipe Quispe (aka El Mallku). **Ancoraimes**, 20km beyond Achacachi, has a church with a lovely ornamental screen above the altar and sometimes, *cholitas* (local women who wear traditional dress) playing soccer on Sundays. In the colonial township of **Escoma**, where a road strikes off for the Cordillera Apolobamba, there is another vibrant Sunday market.

Getting There & Away

Inexpensive *micros* (see warning p110) run occasionally from La Paz's cemetery district to Puerto Acosta, near the Peruvian border. Be-yond there you'll probably have to rely on the (almost) daily *camiones* that run from Puerto Acosta to Moho (Peru), which has an *alojami-ento* and several onward daily buses. There's also an infrequent *micro* (perhaps three times weekly) between Tilali, near the Peruvian bor-der (a four-hour walk from Puerto Acosta), and the larger town of Huancané, Peru.

Note that to enter Peru by this obscure route, you'll have to check out of Bolivia at immigration in Puerto Acosta. In a hamlet on the Peruvian side of the border, the irritable police will check your documents and order you to beeline for Puno (on the opposite side of the lake), where *migración* will stamp you into Peru. If going by this route, it would be easier to get an exit stamp in La Paz.

GUAQUI & DESAGUADERO

Soporific little **Guaqui** sits beside, and partially beneath, Lago Huyñaymarka, the southern extension of Lake Titicaca. It's 25km beyond Tiahuanaco (p102), and about 30km from the Peruvian frontier at Desaguadero. The town has a truly beautiful church with a silver altar and some colonial artwork, and it sees most of its excitement during the riotous **Fiesta de Santiago** in the final week of July.

Desaguadero's Tuesday and Friday **markets** have been compared by readers to the exotic Sunday market in Kashgar, China.

Residencial Guaqui (r per person US$1.50), near the port, provides Guaqui's only accommodations. Rooms aren't terribly secure, but there's a pleasant courtyard and an attached restaurant. There's also a basic eatery on the plaza.

The Peruvian side of Desaguadero has plenty of small and inexpensive places to stay. If you're stuck on the Bolivian side after the border closes, try the **Hotel Bolivia** (s/d US$6/9), recommended for its clean rooms. It also has a restaurant.

Getting There & Away

Most Tiahuanaco-bound buses from La Paz continue to Guaqui. The first *micros* from Guaqui back to Tiahuanaco and La Paz leave at 5:30am from the main avenue in the lower town, and there's something at least every hour until about 4pm or 5pm.

Direct buses from La Paz to Desaguadero (US$1.50, three hours) leave Transportes Ingavi's office in La Paz's cemetery district.

From Guaqui, minibuses run to Desaguadero (US$0.40, 30 minutes), where you can cross the border on foot and then catch a connecting bus on to Yunguyo (where you can cut back into Bolivia at Copacabana) or Puno.

The Cordilleras & Yungas

Two of South America's icons – the Amazonian jungle and the peaks of the Andes – meet in this fabulously diverse zone of soaring highlands and misty valleys. It offers the traveler unrivalled opportunities for adventure, from serious assaults on 6000m summits to trekking in some of Bolivia's remotest uplands.

The region packs a lot into what isn't, on the map at least, a very large area. However, although some of the attractions are but a short condor flight from La Paz, by the time your bus has twisted and turned its way along the tortuous roads, seeming to detour up every valley, you'll envy the bird. The destinations hereabouts offer an isolated, outpost-like feel, whether buried in the jungle like the riverport Guanay, or lost in the ranges, like sleepy Caranavi.

The Cordillera Real contains most of Bolivia's iconic mountains. Though there are no easy climbs, peaks like Huayna Potosí can be scaled by any reasonably fit person. For the allure of untrodden routes up barely known mountains, head to the Quimsa Cruz.

The drop from the Altiplano to the jungle is an almost sheer one in parts, and the Yungas towns are reached by breathtaking (literally) roads that plunge downwards, losing kilometers in altitude. The trees (remember them?) rush up to meet you, and moisture hangs heavy in the air under the floppy-leaved foliage. It's an exhilarating descent on a bike, and at the bottom, warm, jungly towns await, perfect for hammock-swinging or pool-lounging.

There's phenomenal trekking throughout: Andean scenery and Aymará villages in the majestic Apolobamba; paved Inca roads on the Choro or Takesi trails; leisurely day-strolls out of Coroico or Chulumani; or commando-style physical challenges on the Mapiri route.

THE CORDILLERAS & YUNGAS

HIGHLIGHTS

- Head down the paved paths and plunging scenery on the **Choro** (p135), **Takesi** (p138) or **Yunga Cruz** (p141) treks
- Treat yourself to a hammock and a poolside drink in **Coroico** (p129)
- Swing over to **Sorata** (p147), which offers almost as much trekking as it does relaxing
- Meet delicate wild vicuñas and the re-nowned Kallawaya healers in the remote **Cordillera Apolobamba** (p160)
- Strap on your crampons and swing your ice axe to climb one of the fabulous peaks of the **Cordillera Real** (p157)

★ Cordillera Apolobamba

★ Sorata

★ Cordillera Real

★ Coroico

Choro, Takesi ★ & Yunga Cruz treks

▬ TELEPHONE CODE: 2	▬ POPULATION: 547,600	▬ ELEVATION: 600M TO 6429M

History

The first settlers of the Yungas were inspired by economic opportunity. In the days of the Inca empire, gold was discovered in the Tipuani and Mapiri valleys, and the gold-crazed Spanish immediately got in on the act. To enrich the royal treasury, they forced locals to labor for them, and the region became one of the continent's most prolific sources of gold. Today the rivers of the lower Yungas are ravaged by hordes of wildcat prospectors and bigger mining outfits. A distressing side effect is water pollution from the mercury used to recover fine particles from gold-bearing sediment.

Agriculture has also played a part in the development of the Yungas. Today most farmland occupies the intermediate altitudes, roughly between 600m and 1800m. Sugar, citrus, bananas and coffee are grown in sufficient quantities for export to the highlands. The area centered on the village of Coripata and extending south toward Chulumani is also prime coca-producing country. The sweet Yungas' coca is mostly consumed in Bolivia, while leaves from the Chapare region (p332) generally serve more infamous purposes.

Yungas' coca has also been under fire over the years, but the region's geography (one road in, one road out) has meant that raids are always anticipated. Locals are hoping that the Morales government will let them harvest their crop in peace.

Climate

The Yungas' physical beauty is astonishing, and although the hot, humid and rainy climate may induce lethargy, it's nevertheless more agreeable to most people than the chilly Altiplano. Winter rains are gentle, and the heavy rains occur mainly between November and March. The average year-round temperature hovers in the vicinity of 65°F, but summer daytime temperatures in the 90s aren't uncommon. As a result, the region provides a balmy retreat for chilled highlanders, and is a favorite R&R hangout for foreign travelers. The mountains of the cordilleras, on the other hand, are serious, lofty, beasts and conditions can be extreme.

Getting There & Around

Transportation, commerce and administration focus on Coroico and Chulumani, while such outlying towns as Sorata, Caranavi and Guanay function as regional commercial centers. Access is entirely overland and the region's unpaved roads can get mucky and washed out in the rainy season. Scheduled public transportation is infrequent to many trekking and mountaineering basecamps, so chartered private transportation from La Paz is used more often here than in other regions of the country.

Traveling between towns in the region often necessitates backtracking to La Paz, a frustrating business. If you're adventurous, though, have time on your hands, and don't mind getting a little muddy in the back of a *camión* (flatbed truck), it's usually possible to make up your own routes through remote jungle towns.

THE CORDILLERAS & YUNGAS

0 ━━━ 45 km
0 ━━━ 30 miles

PERU

BOLIVIA

La Paz

TREKS

1 Lagunillas to Agua Blanca (Curva-Pelechuco) Trek

2 Mapiri Trail

3 Illampu Circuit

4 El Camino del Oro

5 El Choro Trek

6 Takesi Trek

7 Yunga Cruz Trek

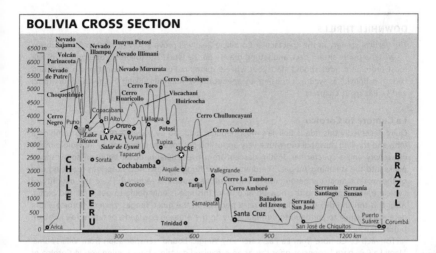

BOLIVIA CROSS SECTION

THE YUNGAS

The Yungas – the transition zone between dry highlands and humid lowlands – is where the Andes fall away into the Amazon Basin. Above the steaming, forested depths rise the near-vertical slopes of the Cordillera Real and the Cordillera Quimsa Cruz, which halt Altiplano-bound clouds, causing them to deposit bounteous rainfall. Vegetation is abundant and tropical fruit, coffee, coca, cacao and tobacco grow with minimal tending. The Yungas is composed of two provinces in La Paz department, Nor and Sud Yungas (oddly, most of Sud Yungas lies well to the north of Nor Yungas), as well as bits of other provinces. Coroico and Chulumani are the main population centers.

COROICO

pop 4500 / elevation 1750m

While Coroico is a metropolis by Yungas standards, it feels like a sleepy hilltop village and maintains a relaxed ambience despite being one of the more popular destinations for weekending *paceños* (La Paz locals) and chilling travelers. Perched aerie-like on the shoulder of Cerro Uchumachi, it commands a far-ranging view across forested canyons, cloud-wreathed mountain peaks, patchwork agricultural lands, citrus orchards, coffee plantations and dozens of small settlements. When the weather clears, the view stretches to the snow-covered summits of Mururata, Huayna

Potosí and Tiquimani, high in the Cordillera Real. The name is derived from *coryguayco*, which is Quechua for 'golden hill.'

The town's biggest attraction is its slow pace, which allows plenty of time for swimming, sunbathing and hammock-swinging. The hill walking around here is more strolling than trekking, which appeals to stiff-legged hikers from the Choro trail or those nursing bruised bottoms after the hectic mountain bike descent from La Paz. Coroico stays relatively warm year-round, but summer storms bring some mighty downpours. Because of its ridgetop position, fog is common, especially in the afternoon when it rises from the deep valleys and swirls through the streets and over the rooftops. The town festival is on October 20, and Saturday and Sunday are market days. On Mondays the town utterly closes down and most stores and restaurants don't reopen until Tuesday morning.

Information

EMERGENCY

There's a basic regional hospital near Hostal El Cafetal, but for serious medical treatment you'll be most happy in La Paz.

INTERNET ACCESS

Únete (Plaza García Lanza; per hr US$1.25; ⊗ 10am-10:30pm) Offers the most reliable access in town.

LAUNDRY

Handwashing services are available at **Lavandería Benedita** (per piece US$0.15), near Hotel

DOWNHILL THRILLS

The vertical scenery in the spectacular Cordillera Real will prove a sort of nirvana for mountain bikers who prefer sitting back and letting gravity do the work! The following descriptions of the most prominent rides should start your wheels spinning. For further information on mountain biking in Bolivia, as well as choosing an operator, see Mountain Biking in the Outdoors (p52) and La Paz (p77) chapters.

La Cumbre to Coroico

Quite deservedly this ride is Bolivia's most popular, made so by travelers wishing to combine a long and thrilling downhill run with a very appealing destination. It features an incredible range of scenery and a spectacular 3600m descent from the Altiplano, down between snowcapped peaks into the steaming Yungas. The dramatic, cliff-hugging descent is notorious for being one of the world's most dangerous roads, and extreme caution is required. Once the majority of vehicle traffic starts using the new Coroico road, this ride is only going to get safer and better. After this thrilling day trip, riders can relax poolside in the quiet Yungas town of Coroico. From here, it's possible to continue to Rurrenabaque, in the Amazon Lowlands, or return to La Paz on public transportation.

To reach La Cumbre from La Paz, catch any Yungas-bound transportation from Villa Fátima. Many La Paz–based agencies offer this as an organized daytrip, either leaving you in Coroico or taking you back to La Paz.

Sorata

Sorata is not only Bolivia's trekking capital but it's also saturated with mountain-biking opportunities, and the fun begins with a descent into the town from the mountains astride Lake Titicaca. From La Paz, take a Sorata-bound bus to the pass north of Achacachi and then choose either the main road or any of the downhill routes along unpaved roads. Most routes eventually lead to Sorata – or at least in view of it (but some don't, so it's wise to have a map). Throughout the ride you're presented with superb views of towering snowcapped peaks, plunging valleys and tiny rural villages. This route and others are organized by Andean Biking (see p149).

Zongo Valley

This ride includes a descent from the base of spectacular Huayna Potosí (6088m) past Zongo Dam, and then along a dramatic 40km, 3600m descent into the lush and humid Yungas. This is a dead-end road that lacks a great destination at its finish, but there's little vehicular traffic, so you tend to have the road to yourself and can open up the throttle a little more.

For further information, including access to the start of this route, see p101.

Chacaltaya to La Paz

This trip begins with a drive up to the world's highest developed ski slope at 5345m. After taking in the incredible view across the Cordillera Real, riders descend along abandoned mine roads. Along the way you'll have marvelous vistas across the mountain ranges, the Altiplano and the city of La Paz nestling in the bottom of the Choqueyapu canyon. This route is nearly all downhill, descending more than 2000m from Chacaltaya back to central La Paz. For more on Chacaltaya, including access from La Paz, see p100.

Gloria (look for the small sign), and at most hotels.

MONEY

There are no foreign-card accepting ATMs in Coroico. **Prodem** (☎ 213-6009; Plaza García Lanza;

🕑 8:30am-noon & 2:30-6pm Tue-Fri, 8:30am-4pm Sat & Sun) changes dollars at a fair rate and does cash advances for 5% commission. You can change traveler's checks at the Banco Unión or at Hostal Kory, which takes a sizable chunk out of them.

TOURIST INFORMATION

There's no tourist office, but the friendly **Cámara Hotelera** (☎ 7157-9438; ✆ Tue-Sat) on the plaza has free town maps and advice. An informative new website for Coroico, www .vivecoroico.com.bo is well worth a look.

Dangers & Annoyances

While Coroico is perfectly tranquil, it's inhabited by some especially vicious biting insects. They don't carry malaria, but the bites itch for days (or weeks!), so don't forget the repellent.

Activities

HIKING

For pretty views head uphill toward Hotel Esmeralda and on up to **El Calvario**, an easy 20-minute hike. At El Calvario the Stations of the Cross lead to a grassy knoll and chapel. There are two good trailheads from El Calvario. The one to the left leads to the **cascadas**, a trio of waterfalls 5km and two hours beyond the chapel. The trail to the right leads to **Cerro Uchumachi** (five hours round-trip), which affords terrific valley views.

A good day's walk will take you to **El Vagante**, an area of natural stone swimming holes in the Río Santa Bárbara. Follow the road toward Coripata to Cruce Miraflores, 750m beyond the Hotel Don Quijote. Here you should turn left at a fork in the road and head steeply downhill past Hacienda Miraflores; at the second fork, bear right (the left fork goes to Santa Ana). After two hours along

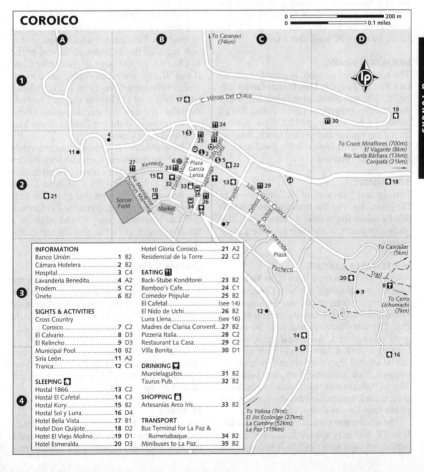

COROICO

0   200 m
0   0.1 miles

To Caranavi (74km)

C. Héroes Del Chaco

To Cruce Miraflores (700m);
El Vagante (8km);
Río Santa Bárbara (13km);
Coripata (21km)

Plaza García Lanza

Soccer Field

Market

Plaza Pacheco

To Cascadas (5km)

Trail

To Cerro Uchumachi (7km)

To Yolosa (7km);
El Jiri Ecolodge (27km);
La Cumbre (52km);
La Paz (119km)

INFORMATION		
Banco Unión	1	B2
Cámara Hotelera	2	B2
Hospital	3	C4
Lavandería Benedita	4	A2
Prodem	5	C2
Únete	6	B2

SIGHTS & ACTIVITIES		
Cross Country Coroico	7	C2
El Calvario	8	D3
El Relincho	9	D3
Municipal Pool	10	B2
Siria León	11	A2
Tranca	12	C3

SLEEPING		
Hostal 1866	13	C2
Hostal El Cafetal	14	C3
Hostal Kory	15	B2
Hostal Sol y Luna	16	B2
Hotel Bella Vista	17	B1
Hotel Don Quijote	18	D2
Hotel El Viejo Molino	19	D1
Hotel Esmeralda	20	D3

Hotel Gloria Coroico	21	A2
Residencial de la Torre	22	C2

EATING		
Back-Stube Konditorei	23	B2
Bamboo's Cafe	24	C1
Comedor Popular	25	B2
El Cafetal	(see 14)	
El Nido de Uchi	26	B2
Luna Llena	(see 16)	
Madres de Clarisa Convent	27	B2
Pizzeria Italia	28	C2
Restaurant La Casa	29	C2
Villa Bonita	30	D1

DRINKING		
Murcielaguitos	31	B2
Taurus Pub	32	B2

SHOPPING		
Artesanías Arco Iris	33	B2

TRANSPORT		
Bus Terminal for La Paz & Rurrenabaque	34	B2
Minibuses to La Paz	35	B2

this route, which features a stretch with some pre-Columbian terraces, you'll reach a cement bridge. Turn right before the bridge and follow the river downstream for 20 minutes to a series of swimming holes and waterfalls. The water isn't drinkable, so carry water or purification tablets – and bear in mind that the return route is uphill all the way.

It can get extremely hot while hiking, so carry plenty of water.

HORSEBACK RIDING

A recommended spot for horseback riding is **El Relincho** (☎ 7192-3814). Equine excursions cost US$6.25 per person per hour, including a guide. Trips sometimes include a good barbecue lunch. The owner, Reynaldo, also offers a two-day trip round Uchumachi for US$150 per person, all-inclusive. El Relincho is between the hotels Esmeralda and Sol y Luna, 10 minutes' walk above town.

MOUNTAIN BIKING

The area around Coroico is great for mountain biking. Friendly **Cross Country Coroico** (CXC; ☎ 7127-3015; www.mtbbolivia.com; Pacheco 2058) offers day-trips to attractions in the region for all levels of rider for around US$20 per person, including a guide and packed lunch. Readers have reported the trips as being good-natured if a little disorganized.

SWIMMING

Feeling lazy? Instead of walking down to the river, dip into the **municipal pool** (admission US$0.65) below the market. Several hotels also allow nonguests to use their pool for a small charge.

WHITEWATER RAFTING

About three hours from town is the **Río Coroico**, which flows through the Nor Yungas. This is the country's most popular commercially rafted river, and is the most convenient to La Paz. The river features well over 30 rapids, great surfing holes, dramatic drops and challenging technical maneuvers (most of these can be scouted from the river and from several bridges). It alternates between calm pools and 50m to 900m rapids, with sharp bends, boils, mean holes, undercurrents, sharp rocks and rather treacherous undercuts.

The whitewater normally ranges from Class II to IV, but may approach Class V during periods of high water (when it becomes too

dangerous to raft). There are few spots to take out and rest, so stay focused and be prepared for surprises.

Access is from the highway between Yolosa and Caranavi; the best put-ins are 20 minutes north of Yolosa and near the confluence with the Río Santa Bárbara, 50 minutes by road north of Yolosa. Just look for any track that winds down from the road toward the river and find one that provides suitable access. Trips average three to five hours. For the take-out, look on the right side of the river for a devastated steel bridge (destroyed in a 1998 flood) across a normally diminutive creek. Don't miss it because after this the climb to the road up the steep jungled slopes is practically impossible, and it's a long, long way to the next possible exit.

The **Río Huarinilla** flows from Huayna Potosí and Tiquimani down into the Yungas to meet the Río Coroico near Yolosa, and is best accessed from Chairo, at the end of the El Choro trek. Although it's normally Class II and III, high water can swell it into a much more challenging Class IV to V. The full-day trip is best suited to kayaks and narrow paddle rafts. The new Yungas Hwy passes right by the take-out at the confluence of the Ríos Huarinilla and Coroico.

The whitewater is great, but unfortunately the high tourist season coincides with the dry season. Several agencies around the plaza offer day-long rafting trips for US$35 to US$50 per person. Several experienced La Paz tour agencies organize daytrips on the Río Coroico and Río Huarinilla (see p80 and p389 for a list of agencies in La Paz and the rest of the country).

Courses & Classes

Coroico is an appealing, relaxed place to learn Spanish. A recommended teacher is **Siria León** (☎ 7195-5431; siria_leon@yahoo.com; Tomás Manning s/n) who lives on the road above Hotel Gloria and charges US$4 an hour for one-to-one lessons.

Ninfa at Villa Bonita (p134) gives yoga classes and meditation sessions, normally on Monday afternoons. They are free, but a gift of fruit is appreciated.

Sleeping

On weekends from June to August hotels are often booked out. It's possible to make advance reservations, but there's no guarantee that all hotels will honor them. On holiday weekends prices may increase by as much as 100%. See also p137 for some appealing choices in the forests of the Coroico area.

BUDGET

Residencial de la Torre (Cuenca s/n; r per person US$2) Sunny and clean, this is the cheapest acceptable accommodations, but don't be jealous when you hear other travelers splashing around in their hotel pools.

Hostal El Cafetal (☎ 7193-3979; danycafétal@hotmail .com; Miranda s/n; r per person US$3.10, Sat & Sun US$4.50; ▣) In addition to the superb eatery here, there are several clean, secure rooms with splendid views. The lush grounds encourage lazing in a hammock or chilling in the pool.

Hostal 1866 (☎ 289-5546; www.hostal1866.fadlan .com; Cuenca s/n; s/d US$3.75/6.25, with bathroom US$6.25/10) This curious building just up from the plaza is a decent choice. The interior rooms are dark and dingy, but the rooms with bathroom are spacious, light and breezy, especially on the higher floors.

Hostal Kory (☎ 7156-4050; Kennedy s/n; s/d US$5.60/11.20, with bathroom US$12.50/20; ▣) Right in the center of town, this is a decent if overpriced choice, built around a good pool. There are fabulous views of the valley and Cordillera peaks. The en suite rooms are particularly good: clean, spacious and modern. Prices are suspiciously flexible; try to negotiate if the quote seems too high. The large pool is available to nonguests for US$1.25, and the restaurant, although usually empty, serves decent food in smallish portions.

MIDRANGE

Hostal Sol y Luna (☎ 7156-1626, in La Paz 244-0588; www.solyluna-bolivia.com; camping US$2, s/d US$5/8, with bathroom from US$7/14, apt/cabaña with bathroom s US$10-20, d US$14-30; ▣) Set on a jungly hill above town, this inspiring spot offers appealingly rustic accommodations in a variety of beautiful *cabañas* (cabins) situated some distance apart on the steep slope. They vary in size and style; palm-thatched Jatata is one of the most charming. There are also apartments (one has a kiln!), comfortable rooms with shared bathroom, and a grassy area to pitch a tent. It's a romantic retreat that feels miles from anywhere, where you can swing in your hammock with just the views (spectacular) and the birds (plentiful) for company. Other

delights include shiatsu massages (US$12), two pools, a small outdoor hot tub (US$6.25 per session), a good restaurant and a book exchange. There's a discount of 20% offered for those learning Spanish in Coroico. Sol y Luna is a 20-minute uphill walk from town, or US$1.90 in a taxi from the plaza.

Hotel Bella Vista (☎/fax 213-6059, ☎ 7156-9237; Héroes del Chaco s/n; r per person US$5, with bathroom US$10) Close to the plaza, this hillside hotel has a racquetball court and video salon but no swimming pool. Rooms are modern and clean, and some have stunning views from the verandas. It also rents bikes.

Hotel Esmeralda (☎ 213-6017; www.hotel-esmeralda .com; Julio Suazo s/n; r per person basic US$5, with balcony US$7, with bathroom US$12, ste US$15; ▣ ▣) A stalwart of the Coroico scene, this hotel complex above town is very popular, and has something of a resort feel, with its pool, sauna and regular tour groups. There's a variety of rooms; the cheapest are tiny and dark, with shared bathrooms, but the suites are stunning, with balconies with great views and hammocks to swing in. The hotel has good facilities – pool table, internet (per hour US$1.10), laundry, wi-fi and a restaurant that does buffet lunches and dinners (US$3 to US$4), as well as pizza nights. You can arrange a transfer to La Paz (US$6) or El Alto airport (US$7.50), and they will pick up free from the plaza in Coroico. Otherwise, it's a seven-minute walk up the hill.

Hotel Gloria Coroico (☎/fax 289-5554, in La Paz 240-7070; www.hotelgloria.com.bo; s/d $6.25/12.50, with bathroom $12.50/25; ▣) At the bottom of town, this faded but attractive old resort hotel has a likeable colonial ambience, with its spacious lounges, high ceilings and grandiose halls. Often spookily empty, it boasts a pool and fine views. The rooms are simple but comfortable enough; the ones with a bathroom boast cunning floor-to-ceiling two-way mirrors for windows. Rooms share a wide veranda; make sure you get a room on the pool/valley side, rather than the car-park side. There's a decent restaurant, also with memorable views. Breakfast is included for rooms with bathroom only.

Hotel Don Quijote (☎ 213-6007; Iturralde s/n; s/d with breakfast $10/15; ▣) A flat 10-minute (1km) walk east of the plaza, this friendly pad is popular with Bolivian families. It looks more expensive than it is and makes a good alternative to staying in town. It's clean and has all the amenities of a solid midrange option – including an inviting pool. They'll pick you up for free from the plaza.

Hotel El Viejo Molino (☎ /fax 220-1519; www.val martour.com; s/d $18/25, superior $25/35; ☒) Coroico's top-end option is a 15-minute downhill walk northeast of town on the road toward the Río Santa Bárbara. All rooms have private bathroom and TV, and include breakfast and access to the temperamental sauna and Jacuzzi, as well as the sizeable pool.

Eating & Drinking

The plaza is ringed by a number of inexpensive local places and pizzerias; all have ordinary menus, acceptable fare and a typically tropical sense of urgency and service. Local volunteers swear that **Pizzeria Italia** (C Ortiz) is the best of the mediocre bunch. If you're in a rush or on a strict budget, there are many food stalls around the mercado municipal and in the Comedor Popular to placate your growling stomach, but you'll need a bit of gastric stamina.

El Nido de Uchi (☎ 289-5539; cnr Sagárnaga & Plaza García Lanza; coffee US$0.40) One of several cafés around the plaza, this stylish set-up, with tables in the form of coffee mills and displays of beans in various stages of processing, is run by the local coffee cooperative.

Villa Bonita (☎ 7192-2917; Héroes del Chaco s/n; mains US$1-2; ☒ 10am-6pm) This delightfully peaceful garden-café is 600m from town and feels a world away. The relaxed, personable owners offer delicious homemade ice-creams and sorbets bursting with fresh fruit, tasty sundaes with unusual local liqueurs, and an eclectic range of vegetarian dishes, served outside where you can appreciate the valley views.

Luna Llena (☎ 7156-1626; mains US$1.50-3; ☒ 8am-10pm) The small outdoor restaurant at the Hostal Sol y Luna is run with a motherly hand by Doña María, and has a well-priced, tasty menu of Bolivian and European dishes including vegetarian options. An extraordinary treat if you have a group – or can muster one – is the Indonesian buffet (US$3.25 per person) for eight to 20 people, which must be booked a day in advance.

Restaurant La Casa (☎ 213-6024; Cuenca s/n; mains US$2-4) While not quite what it was in its glory days, this home-style, candlelit restaurant, in a new location, is still a good choice for its friendly management and selection of fondue and *raclette* meals (per person US$3.75, minimum two). There are also small but tasty

steaks, pasta dishes and a range of scrumptious pancakes. For the sweet of tooth, the sinful chocolate fondue is the way forward.

Back-Stube Konditorei (Kennedy s/n; mains US$2-4.40; ☒ 8:30am-noon Mon, 8:30am-2:30pm & 6:30-10pm Wed-Fri, 8:30am-10pm Sat & Sun) By far the best place to eat in town itself, this welcoming bakery-restaurant is a winner at any time of day. There are excellent breakfasts and coffee, tempting cakes and pastries (applause for the cinnamon rolls), as well as pasta, vegetarian plates and memorable *sauerbraten* (marinated pot-roast beef) with *spätzle* (Swabian dough noodles). There's a great terraced area, and a book exchange.

El Cafetal (☎ 7193-3979; Miranda s/n; mains US$2-5) This great, secluded lean-to has unbeatable views, as well as cane chairs and slate-topped tables where you can enjoy some of the Yungas' finest food. There's a large range of dishes prepared with a French touch. The menu includes sweet and savory crêpes, soufflés, steaks, sandwiches, curries, vegetarian lasagna and regular specials that might include llama goulash. It's near the hospital, a 15-minute walk uphill from the plaza.

Bamboo's Café (Iturralde 1047; mains US$3-4; ☒ food 11am-10pm) This friendly place offers good-value, *picante* (spicy) Mexican food (tacos, burritos and veggie refried beans). Later in the evening it's also a cozy, sociable spot for a candlelit drink or two. The personable owner, José, is always good for a chat.

Madres de Clarisa Convent (☒ 8am-8pm) This place sells homemade brownies, orange cakes, creatively flavored biscuits, and wines. You'll find it down the steps off the southwest corner of the plaza; ring the bell to get into the shop area.

The best places for a drink in town are Bamboo's and the relaxed **Taurus Pub** (☎ 7355-4237; Linares s/n), the name taken from a previous bar of that name, which has a guidebook library and occasional live music. These shut around midnight, after which it's time for **Murcielaguitos** ('Little Bats'; ☎ 7122-9830; Sagárnaga s/n; ☒ Fri & Sat nights), in the Residencial 20 de Octubre, where students from the agricultural college and everybody else crams in to dance to loud Latin music.

Shopping

For quality handmade jewelry visit Artesanías Arco Irís, on the south side of the plaza. It isn't cheap, but most items are unique. During the high season the plaza is frequented by itinerant craftspeople selling a wide range of *artesanía* (locally handcrafted items).

Several cafés around the plaza sell bags of the tasty, nutty, local Yungas coffee.

Getting There & Away

At the risk of appearing foolish (they've been building it for well over a decade), we predict that, by the time you read this, the shiny new La Paz–Coroico road should be open, making the plunge down the mountainside significantly safer and more comfortable.

At the time of research, The World's Most Dangerous Road (see boxed text p78) remained in use: an epic descent along a narrow dirt road that hugs the side of the mountain, and has sheer drops of over a kilometer below it. It plunges more than 3000m in just 75km and is one of the world's most scenic but perilous journeys.

The old road will remain open as a standby (mudslides will frequently block even the new road), and the mountain-bike descent operators (see below) will continue to use it.

BICYCLE

An exhilarating, adrenaline-filled option is to descend by mountain bike from La Paz to Coroico. The thrilling one-day descent from the top at El Cumbre is a memorable experience, but not for the faint-hearted. An ever-increasing number of operators run the trip (see p77). Choose carefully – if your company cuts corners, it's a long way down. There have been many fatalities on this route, the vast majority caused by over-eager bikers going too fast. However, if you're sensible and follow instructions, there's no great risk, and once the new road is open, this route should become a good deal safer, as the amount of vehicle traffic on it will be drastically reduced.

It's also possible to rent a bike in La Paz and do the downhill trip independently, then throw your bike in a *camión* for the long haul back to La Paz.

BUS

From the Villa Fátima area in La Paz, buses and minibuses leave for Coroico (US$2, 3½ hours) at least hourly from 7:30am to 8:30pm, with extra runs on weekends and holidays. In Coroico, they leave from the plaza. **Flota Yungueña** (☎ 289-5513, in La Paz 221-3513) is the best bet. Minibuses stop in Yolosa where you can

catch buses and *camiones* north to Rurrenabaque (US$13, 15 to 18 hours) and further into Bolivian Amazonia.

For Chulumani, the quickest route is to backtrack to La Paz. Although the junction for the Chulumani road is at Unduavi, few passing minibuses have spare seats at this point.

CAMIÓN

Camiones from La Paz to Coroico leave mornings and until mid-afternoon from behind the gas station in Villa Fátima. Expect to get wet on the trip.

To reach the Amazon Basin, you must first get to Yolosa, where drivers always stop for a snack. All downhill vehicles must pass through the *tranca* (highway police post) there, so it's a good place to wait for a lift. When the roads are open, there should be no problem finding transportation to Caranavi, Rurrenabaque or La Paz.

For Chulumani, head back toward La Paz and get off at Unduavi to wait for a passing *camión*. Alternatively, you can make a trip through Bolivia's main coca-growing region: take a *camión* from Coroico to Arapata, another from Arapata to Coripata and yet another to Chulumani. It's a pleasant adventure, but don't be in too much of a hurry and don't try it during the rainy season, as this road features some of the deepest mud ever.

TAXI

To avoid the backbreaking journey in trucks through to Chulumani, it may make sense to arrange a taxi to take you. The going rate is about US$37.50 for up to four passengers.

EL CHORO TREK

The La Cumbre to Coroico (Choro) trek is one of Bolivia's premier hikes. It begins at La Cumbre (4725m), the highest point on the La Paz–Coroico highway, and climbs to 4859m before descending 3250m into the humid Yungas and the village of Chairo. Along the 70km route (which is in the best condition during the April to September dry season), you'll note a rapid change in climate, vegetation and wildlife as you leave the Altiplano and plunge into the forest. You pass through some appealing *campesino* (subsistence farmers) villages, and it's a good opportunity to chat to the local people.

Energetic hikers can finish the trek in two days, but it's more comfortably done in three

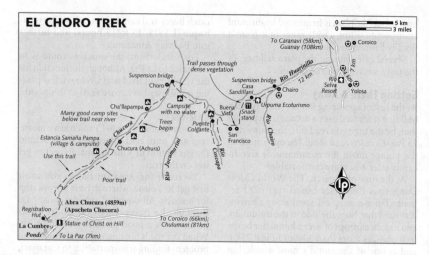

EL CHORO TREK

days. Many people allow even more time, or organize a stay of a few days in the *albergue* (hostel) at Sandillani.

Prepare for a range of climates. It can be pretty cold, even snowy on the first day, but you'll soon be in sweatier climes. For the lower trail, light cotton trousers or something similar will protect your legs from sharp vegetation and biting insects. The Inca paving can be pretty slippery, so make sure you've got shoes with grip.

Dangers & Annoyances

Travelers have occasionally been robbed doing this trek solo. The most thefts are reported below Choro village. These appear to be isolated incidents however, and the trail is not generally deemed unsafe. It's still wise to camp out of sight if possible and do not leave anything outside your tent. It's a good idea to go with a guide.

Tours

A growing number of La Paz outfits offer organized El Choro treks from US$80 to US$120 per person. Most include meals, guides and camping equipment; some include the services of porters. For suggestions of agencies, see p80 and p389.

Access

Once you find the trailhead, the trail is easy to access and follow. From Villa Fátima in La Paz, catch any Yungas-bound transportation. If there's space (Yungas-bound passengers take priority), you'll pay around US$1 in a bus or minibus, or US$0.75 in a *camión* to be dropped at La Cumbre, marked by a statue of Christ, where the trek begins.

The road climbs steeply out of Villa Fátima, and less than an hour out of La Paz at the 4725m crest of the La Paz–Yungas road is La Cumbre. For the best chance of good clear views of the stunning scenery, start as early as possible, before the mist rises out of the Yungas.

You can also take a taxi to the trail (30 minutes). One advantage of this is that they can take you up the first bit to the pass at Abra Chucura, thus avoiding the initial climb if you think it might cause you altitude problems.

The Route

From the **statue of Christ** (there's a registration hut here where you should sign in), follow the well-defined track to your left for 1km. There you should turn off onto the smaller track that turns right and passes between two small ponds (one often dry). Follow it up the hill until it curves to the left and begins to descend.

At this point follow the light track leading up the gravely hill to your right and toward an obvious notch in the barren hill before you. This is **Abra Chucura** (4859m), and from here the trail tends downhill all the way to its end at Chairo. At the high point is a pile of stones called Apacheta Chucura. For centuries travelers have marked their passing by tossing a stone atop it (preferably one that has been carried from a lower elevation) as an offering to the mountain *apus* (spirits). An hour below Abra Chucura lie the remains of a *tambo* (wayside inn) dating from Inca times.

One hour below the *tambo* is the hamlet of Estancia Samaña Pampa, where there's a store selling water, a grassy campsite, a shelter and another registration hut.

A short way further on, basic supplies are available at the village of **Chucura** (3600m). Here you pay a toll of US$1.25 for maintenance of the trail. An hour's walk from here leads to some camp sites (US$1.25), which are found along the river. They are nice, but you might wish to push on down the beautifully paved Inca road to **Cha'llapampa** (2825m), a lovely village with a good roofed camp site (per person US$0.60), an unroofed one (US$0.30) and simple shelters (US$1.25). There are toilets, and water is available from a convenient stream below a bridge close to town.

After two hours following beautiful but slippery stretches of pre-Columbian paving, a **suspension bridge** across the Río Chucura is reached at **Choro** (2200m). The track continues descending steadily along the true left (west) side of the Río Chucura, where there are some small camp sites (US$1) and a store providing drinks and snacks.

From the ridge above Choro, the trail alternately plunges and climbs from sunny hillsides to vegetation-choked valleys, crossing streams and waterfalls. You'll have to ford the **Río Jucumarini**, which can be rather intimidating in the wet season. Further along, the trail crosses the deep gorge of the **Río Coscapa** via the relatively sturdy Puente Colgante suspension bridge.

The trail continues through some tiny hamlets, including **San Francisco** and **Buena Vista**, which are separated by the stiff ascent and descent of the 'Subica del Diablo.' Some five to six hours from Choro is the remarkable **Casa Sandillani** (2050m), a home surrounded by beautifully manicured Japanese gardens with a view. You can camp here (US$1.25). There's also a new community project lodge here, **Urpuma Ecoturismo** (☎ 7355-1377; urpuma@yahoo.com; dm US$7, s/d US$14/24); it's best to book ahead. The rooms are comfortable, rates include breakfast as well as a guided walk, and dinner is also available. The walks take you into the nearby Cotapata national park. Even if you're not staying, you can use the toilets for a nominal

fee. There are also several snack and soft-drink stalls, and a clear water supply is provided by a pipe located diagonally opposite the house (to the right, 20m along the main trail).

From Casa Sandillani it's an easy 7km (2½ hours) downhill to **Chairo**, where camping is possible in a small, flat, grassed area with no facilities, near the bridge above town.

It's possible to walk the relatively level 12km past the Río Selva Resort (p138) or take transportation from Chairo to **Yolosa** (16km) and then catch an onward service the 7km to **Coroico** (p129). A few private vehicles head to Yolosa and Coroico on most days, but beware of being charged scandalous prices. Don't pay more than US$25 – you could call a cab in Coroico to pick you up for less than that. At weekends, there are minibuses running the route (US$0.40).

YOLOSA
elevation 1200m

Traveling between La Paz and the Beni – or from anywhere to Coroico – you'll pass through Yolosa, which guards the Coroico road junction. Yolosa's *tranca* closes between 1am and 4am, impeding overnight traffic between the Yungas and La Paz. Trucks and taxis awaiting passengers to Coroico (20 minutes) line up at the corner by the police checkpoint.

Sleeping & Eating

Restaurant El Conquistador (r per person US$1.40) If you're stuck overnight here, this is your cheapest option.

La Senda Verde Refugio Natural (☎ 7153-2701; www.lasendaverde.com; camping US$5, s/d/q incl breakfast US$18/30/45; ☼) This is a delightful spot, accessed from the Yolosa–La Paz road a short walk from town. It has a verdant setting on the banks of two rivers, and is a great spot to relax. The duplex *cabañas* are excellent, and the camping facilities great – you can also rent a tent. You'll find various friendly rescued animals, a restaurant under a *palapa* (open-sided thatched roundhouse) and a good vibe. It's a favorite lunch stop for the downhill mountain-bike tours, but the rest of the time it's superbly tranquil.

El Jiri Ecolodge (☎ 7155-8215, in La Paz ☎ 2-278-8264; www.eljiri.com; 2-day/1-night program per person US$24; ☼) Near Charobamba, across the valley from Coroico, this lodge is a fun spot to stay, with hanging bridges, a zipline tour, a pool and good meals under a thatched roof. They keep you busy, with walks in the Cotapata national park and plenty of activities. Book ahead via the La Paz number. Ask to see the ruins of an old Jewish settlement nearby.

Río Selva Resort (☎ 241-2281, 241-1561; www .rioselva.com.bo; r/ste/apt/cabin US$50/60/85/100; 🖳 🏊) About 5km from the end of the Choro trek in Pacollo is this posh five-star riverside retreat that can be a welcome deal for larger groups. Peripheral amenities include racquetball courts, a sauna and swimming pool. There's a range of accommodations, from double rooms to cabins sleeping up to six. The owners can arrange transportation from La Paz, but it's much cheaper to head to Coroico or Yolosa and get a taxi from there.

Streetside stalls sell inexpensive snacks and set meals to passing truckers.

TAKESI (TAQUESI) TREK

Also known as the Inca Trail, the Takesi trek is one of the most popular and impressive walks in the Andes. The route was used as a highway by the early Aymará, the Inca and the Spanish, and it still serves as a major route to the humid Yungas over a relatively low pass in the Cordillera Real. Nearly half the trail's 45km consists of expertly engineered pre-Inca paving, more like a highway than a walking track. It has been posited that this paved section was part of a long road that linked the La Paz area with the Alto Beni region.

The walk itself takes only 10 to 15 hours, but plan on two or three days because of transportation uncertainties to and from the trailheads. It's hiked by about 5000 people annually, more than half of whom are Bolivians, and suffers from a litter problem due to its growing popularity.

The May to October dry season is best for this trip. In the rainy season the wet and cold, combined with ankle-deep mud, may contribute to a less-than-optimal experience. Since the trail's end is in the Yungas, however, plan on some rain year-round.

On the first day you ascend to 4700m, so spend a few days acclimatizing in La Paz before heading off.

The entire route appears on a single 1:50,000 IGM topo sheet: *Chojlla – 6044-IV*. A good source of information is **Fundación Pueblo** (☎ 212-4413; www.fundacionpueblo.org; PO Box 9564, La Paz), an NGO that supports rural development projects that encourage rural local self-sufficiency.

The group has done much work with villagers along the trail to improve facilities. The foundation can organize a package that includes transportation to and from the trailheads, meals, accommodations and a guide for $60 to US$100 per person.

Access

If traveling by public transportation, your first destination will be **Ventilla**. A daily *micro* (minibus) leaves from La Paz (US$1.90, three hours) in the market area above Calle Sagárnaga, at the corner of Calles Rodríguez and Luis Lara. Minibus *trufis* (collective transportation) also run this route. Another option for groups is to charter a minibus or taxi (around US$40 for up to four people) to the Choquekhota trailhead. Most La Paz tour agencies can organize this for you or contact Fundación Pueblo.

You can also take an urban *micro* or minibus *trufi* from La Paz to Chasquipampa or Ovejuyo, then trek through the beautiful Palca Canyon (and the Valle de las Ánimas if you like; see p98) to Palca and then to Ventilla. This will add at least one extra day to the trip, but will be a fitting prelude to the longer trek.

Transportation between Ventilla and the San Francisco mine trailhead is sparse. If you're lucky, you may be able to hitch; otherwise you should probably resign yourself to paying a negotiable US$10 to US$15 for a taxi, or slogging three hours uphill to the trailhead.

With a fully serviced lodge two-thirds of the way along the route, the hike is easily done with just a daypack, but agencies and Fundación Pueblo in La Paz can arrange guides and mules if you want them.

The Route

About 150m beyond Ventilla, turn left and take the road uphill, following the Río Palca. After climbing for 60 to 90 minutes, you'll reach the village of **Choquekhota**, where the landscape is reminiscent of the remotest parts of North Wales. Next is a further one to two hours (depending on how the altitude takes you) of uphill hiking along the access road to the **San Francisco mine**; after crossing a stream, you'll see the signpost indicating the trailhead. The mine route veers left here, but hikers should continue along the signposted track. *Campesinos* sometimes offer mules for the ascent from Choquekhota to the trailhead.

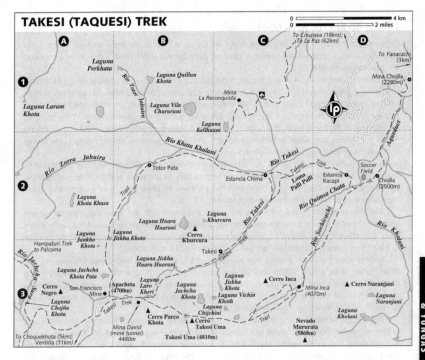

TAKESI (TAQUESI) TREK

After an hour of climbing you'll begin switchbacking for half an hour for the final ascent, partly on superb pre-Inca paving, to the 4700m **Apacheta** (Abra Takesi) pass. There, you'll find the *apacheta* (shrine of stones) and a spectacular view of Nevado Mururata (5868m) to the right and the plunging valleys of the Yungas far below. Just beyond the pass you'll see an abandoned **mine tunnel**; wolfram and tin is mined around here. Entry is not advisable.

From the pass the trail begins to descend into the valley, passing a series of abandoned mining camps and high glacial lakes. If daylight is on your side, look for another lake, **Laguna Jiskha Huara Huarani**, to the left of the trail midway between the pass and Takesi. The trail from here contains some of Bolivia's finest examples of Inca paving. At the ancient-looking thatched village of **Takesi** there's a hut and **camp site** (per person US$0.75); you'll also find meals of potatoes and local trout. When exploring the village, watch out for vicious dogs.

Beyond Takesi the trail winds downhill until it crosses a bridge over the **Río Takesi**

then follows the beautifully churning river before it moves upslope from the river and makes a long traverse around the **Loma Palli Palli**, where you're protected from steep drop-offs by a pre-Columbian wall. As you descend, the country becomes increasingly verdant. Shortly after passing a particularly impressive *mirador* (lookout), you'll enter the village of **Estancia Kacapi**, the heart of the former colonial *estancia* (ranch) that once controlled the entire Takesi valley. Most of the overseers' dwellings have been reclaimed by vegetation, but you can still see the ruins of the Capilla de las Nieves. Kacapi's 10-bed **Albergue Turístico** (dm US$3.10) and camp site are equipped with solar-powered showers. Basic meals are available as well.

After Kacapi the track drops sharply to a bridge over the **Río Quimsa Chata** (which suffers varying degrees of damage each rainy season), then climbs past a soccer field on the left to a pass at the hamlet of **Chojlla**. From there the route descends to the final crossing of the Río Takesi via a concrete bridge. Then it's a 3km, 1½-hour trudge along an **aqueduct** to the ramshackle mining settlement of **Mina**

THINGS GO BETTER WITH COCA

Cocaine, marijuana, hashish and other drugs are illegal in Bolivia, but the coca leaf, which is the source of cocaine and related drugs, is chewed daily by many Bolivians and is even venerated by indigenous peoples.

Both the Quechua and Aymará people make sacrifices of coca leaves when planting or mining to ensure a good harvest or lucky strike. The *yatiri* (traditional Aymará healers) use them in their healing and exorcising rituals, and in some remote rural areas leaves are often used in place of money. People embarking on a journey also place several leaves beneath a rock at the start, as an offering to Pachamama in the hope that she'll smooth their way. Visitors walking or hiking in the mountains may want to hedge their bets and do the same, or at least carry some leaves as a gift for helpful locals (coca is always gratefully received).

The conquering Spanish found that laborers who chewed the leaf became more dedicated to their tasks, so they promoted its use among the peasants. In the wake of the collapse of Bolivian tin mines, many mining families moved to the Chapare to grow coca, a rewarding and easily maintained crop with up to four yearly harvests.

Used therapeutically coca serves as an appetite suppressant and a central nervous system stimulant. Workers use it to lessen the effects of altitude and eliminate the need for a lunch break. They also chew it recreationally and socially in much the same way people smoke cigarettes or drink coffee. Among Bolivian miners the 'coca break' is an institution.

The leaf itself grows on bushes that are cultivated in the Yungas and Upper Chapare regions at altitudes of between 1000m and 2000m. Leaves are sold by the kilogram in nearly every market in Bolivia along with *legía*, an alkaloid usually made of mineral lime, potato and quinoa ash, which is used to draw the drug from the leaves when chewed. There are two kinds of *legía*: *achura*, which is sweet, and *cuta*, which is salty.

The effects of coca chewing are not startling. It will leave the person feeling a little detached, reflective, melancholy and contented. Locals normally chew around 30 to 35 leaves at a time. A beginner places a few leaves, say five to 10, between gum and cheek until they soften. Then the process is repeated with a little *legía* between the leaves. Chewing doesn't start until the desired amount has been stuffed in. Once it has been chewed into a pulpy mess, the bitter-tasting juice is swallowed, which numbs the mouth and throat. (In fact novocaine and related anesthetics are coca derivatives.)

Chojlla (2280m), where there is a cheap *alojamiento* (basic accommodations).

From Mina Chojlla, crowded buses leave for Yanacachi (US$0.15) and La Paz (US$1.25) at 5:30am and around noon daily – buy your ticket on arrival. If you can't endure a night in Mina Chojlla (and few people can), keep hiking 5km (about an hour) down the road past the headquarters of the hydroelectric power project to the more pleasant village of Yanacachi.

YANACACHI

pop 1300 / elevation 2000m

Yanacachi, 87km southeast of La Paz, is near the fringe of the Yungas, and feels tropical, with flitting parrots and humid air. One of the oldest towns in the region, it was an early trading center along the Takesi trail, which was constructed more than 800 years ago as a coca and tropical-produce trade route.

During the colonial period, the town's role as a commercial center expanded as hacienda owners settled there. By 1522 they'd already constructed the **Iglesia de Santa Bárbara**, the Yungas' oldest existing church. The bells in the tower date from 1735 and 1755, and in the lower part of town you can still see traces of the colonial heritage in the balconies and thick stone walls.

Modern amenities include Entel and Cotel telephone offices on Plaza Libertad, as well as a health clinic. For trekking information, contact **Fundación Pueblo** (☎ 288-9524; Plaza Libertad s/n), which has an office on the plaza and can help arrange transportation, as well as guides and mule hire.

Sleeping & Eating

The nicest place to stay is **Hostal Metropoly** (☎ in La Paz 245-6643; per person US$3), which has a good pool table and refurbished rooms.

Alojamiento Tomás (r per person US$2; ▣) has a pool and pleasant gardens – it's across from the big trail map. Ask in the nearby store with the Fanta sign if nobody is home. There's no phone here, but you can make inquiries by calling the Entel office on ☎ 213-7414. The larger **Hostal San Carlos** (☎ in La Paz 223-0088; r per person US$4) has great views from rooms 5, 6 and 7.

The Tomás and San Carlos have reasonable restaurants, while the owners of the Metropoly also run a recommended restaurant on the plaza.

Getting There & Away
Veloz del Norte buses depart Mina Chojlla for La Paz (US$1.25) daily at 5:30am and 1pm, and pass through Yanacachi, stopping in front of Hostal San Carlos at 6am at 1:30pm. It's best to buy tickets in Mina Chojlla, but there's usually little problem getting a seat on the morning bus. Minibuses to La Paz (US$1.50) leave the plaza in Yanacachi less frequently; inquire locally about the departure times. Alternatively, you can walk for an hour and a half down the track out to the main road, where you'll readily find passing transportation to either La Paz or Chulumani.

Veloz del Norte buses leave from their La Paz **office** (☎ 421-7206; Ocabaya 489-495, Villa Fátima) for Yanacachi daily at 8am and 2pm.

YUNGA CRUZ TREK
This is a relatively little-trodden trek with good stretches of pre-Hispanic paving that connects the village of Chuñavi with the Sud Yungas' provincial capital of Chulumani. There are a couple of variations to the standard trek, including a pass over the northern shoulder of Illimani to get you started, as well as an alternative – and considerably more spectacular – route over Cerro Khala Ciudad, which begins beyond Lambate. Some guides even offer the trek backwards, starting at Chulumani, but that's a fairly punishing alternative. Crossing several passes at over 5000m, it's the hardest of the Inca trails and usually takes five or six days. Expect to see lots of condors, eagles, hawks, vultures and hummingbirds along the route.

The map in this book is intended only as a rough guide; you'll need to carry the 1:50,000 topo sheets *Palca – 6044-I, Lambate – 6044-II* and *Chulumani – 6044-III* or arrange a guide. Many agencies in La Paz offer this trek, with

guides, cook and pack animals; see p80 and also p389 for a list of agencies.

Access
There's a good case for hiring a 4WD to take you to the trailhead at Lambate. Otherwise you'll first have to get to Ventilla (p138). Beyond Ventilla, the road is poor and vehicles

YUNGA CRUZ TREK

THE CORDILLERAS & YUNGAS

are scarce but you might be able to hitch a ride on to Lambate with a bit of luck.

A Bolsa Negra *micro* from Plaza Belzu in La Paz will get you all the way to Tres Ríos, 40km beyond Ventilla, where the vehicle turns north toward the Bolsa Negra mine. From Tres Ríos, you can either continue walking along the road toward Ikiko or walk over the northern shoulder of Illimani to Estancia Totoral (not to be confused with Totoral Pampa, 3km west of Tres Ríos). See the Illimani option, below.

Alternatively, you can go straight to Chuñavi by *micro*, which is an all-day trip from La Paz. Buses leave Calle Venancio Burgoa, near Plaza Líbano, at least twice weekly (Friday and Monday are the best bets) at 9am. Advance information is hard to come by and no reservations are taken; you'll just have to turn up early (around 7am) and see if a *micro* is leaving. Failing those options, go to Ventilla and wait for an eastbound *camión*, or begin walking along the road over the Abra Pacuani (4524m).

Taxi access from La Paz (US$70) isn't good owing to the distance and condition of the road; it's at least five hours to the Chuñavi trailhead and six or more to Lambate. It would be preferable to hire a 4WD and driver from La Paz (see the Transportation chapter, p387), cutting the drive to Lambate down to three to four hours.

The return to La Paz is straightforward: catch one of the many daily buses or *camiones* from the *tranca* in Chulumani.

The Route

ILLIMANI OPTION

Once you've made it to **Tres Ríos**, cross the bridge over the **Río Khañuma** and follow the **Río Pasto Grande** uphill toward **Bolsa Blanca mine**, on the skirts of Illimani. After 2km a track leads downhill and across the river (it traverses around the northernmost spur of Illimani), but it's better to continue along the western bank of the river to the **Pasto Grande camp site**, at some abandoned buildings at the head of the valley. Here begins a steep and direct huff-and-puff walk up the valley headwall to the 4900m pass below Bolsa Blanca mine, which is overlooked by the triple-peak of Illimani. It takes the best part of two hours to get from the valley floor to the pass.

From the pass, the route becomes more obvious as it descends steeply into the Quebrada Mal Paso. Once you've entered the valley, cross to the southern bank of the **Río Mal Paso** as soon as possible and follow it down – it's a steep descent – to the village of **Estancia Totoral** back on the Lambate road, where there's a small store.

Even strong hikers will need two days from Tres Ríos to Estancia Totoral because of the altitude as well as the several exhausting climbs and treacherous descents. The best camp site is at the Pasto Grande valley headwall below Bolsa Blanca.

CHUÑAVI TRAILHEAD

Approximately 5km east of Estancia Totoral, turn northeast (left) along the track that descends through the village of **Chuñavi**. There's a *refugio* (mountain hut) here, **Albergue Kala Pukara** (☎ 7253-6943; felixquenta@yahoo.es), where you can also arrange a guide. You'll need to call ahead. Beyond the village the track traverses a long steady slope, high above the **Río Susisa**, and keeps to about 4200m for the next 30km. It passes the westernmost flank of **Cerro Khala Ciudad**, but unfortunately the spectacular views of the mountain's cirques and turrets are hidden from view.

About 2km beyond Cerro Khala Ciudad the Lambate trailhead route joins from the right. There's a good camp site just after a small stream crossing; fill up with water here, because it may well be the last available. Four kilometers after the trails join, the track skirts the peak of **Cerro Yunga Cruz**, before trending downhill along a ridgeline through dense cloud forest. Just below two tree line is a prominent camp site – the last before the trail's end – but unfortunately it's dry, so fill your water bottles at every opportunity. Despite the dampness and the amount of vegetation the track stays above the watershed areas, and running water is scarce unless it has been raining.

After the track narrows and starts to descend steeply, the vegetation thickens and often obscures the way, now marked by green arrows. Three hours below the tree line you reach a small meadow before **Cerro Duraznuni**; continue directly across it, then take the right fork, which climbs the hill but skirts the right side of the peak. At this point you begin a long and occasionally steep descent through increasingly populated countryside to the citrus farm at **Estancia Sikilini**. You can either follow the shortcut across **Huajtata Gorge** – which will seem an excruciating prospect at this stage – or just lumber along the longer but mercifully level road into **Chulumani**.

LAMBATE TRAILHEAD

This route is more difficult but also more beautiful than the Chuñavi route. Lambate is about 2½ hours on foot east of Estancia Totoral, and 2km beyond the Chuñavi cutoff. Lambate, which enjoys a commanding view, has a *tienda* (small store) – the last place to buy a soft drink or pick up snacks.

From Lambate, follow the continuation of the La Paz road toward the village of **San Antonio**, a couple of kilometers beyond, until you reach a small house on the left, set on a precipice. Descend to the house on any of the small paths, and just beyond it turn right to follow a path between some bean fields to an opening in a stone wall. If you take the left fork beyond the wall, you'll descend to a footbridge over the dramatic **Río Chunga Mayu**. Here, you should turn downstream onto a path beside a small house with a cross on top. After crossing the **Río Colani** (collect water here!), head uphill into the village of **Quircoma** (Ranchería).

Follow the main track up through Quircoma; above the village, you'll reach the last possible camp site, but it's waterless. Ascend the only path out of the village. When you reach a gate, cross the pasture – the track continues on the other side. From here the route is fairly straightforward but a real struggle – it's a 10km, 2000m climb past **Laguna Kasiri** to the pass.

After the first couple of hours the heat will ease a bit, and two hours later you'll reach a well-watered meadow with good camp sites beside the Río Kasiri, which you've been following. At this point, the track makes a steep ascent to the prominent mountain spur to the west, then levels off before the final short climb to Laguna Kasiri, which is said to be haunted by an evil spirit. This lovely and mysterious spot lies in a cirque surrounded by the snowy peaks of **Cerro Khala Ciudad**.

Skirt around the right side of the lake; here the path crosses the stream, then switchbacks upward for about 2½ hours to the 4300m pass on Cerro Khala Ciudad, where there's an *apacheta* and an incredible view from the Cordillera Real right down into the Yungas. Immediately after the pass, bear left and pass a narrow section of trail with a vertical drop to the right. After this section, 20 to 30 min-

utes beyond the pass, you should take the left fork between two large rocks over the ridge or you'll descend into the wrong valley.

After this fork the trail descends and deteriorates. About 2km beyond the pass, you'll meet up with the Chuñavi route, where you should turn right. See the Chuñavi Trailhead (opposite) for further details.

CHULUMANI

pop 3000 / elevation 1700m

Perched scenically on the side of a hill, this is the capital of the Sud Yungas and an important centre for the farming communities of the region. The fertile soils hereabouts provide a bumper crop of coca (the country's best for chewing), citrus, bananas, coffee and cacao. The area is also a paradise of birds and butterflies, with clouds of the latter, and several rare species of the former, including types of quetzal. The town used to be the end of the road and it retains that feel. At a subtropically warm and often wet altitude, it's a great trekking base camp and a relaxing weekend retreat with a great view. The only time Chulumani breaks its pervasive tranquility is during the week following August 24, when it stages the riotous **Fiesta de San Bartolomé**. Lots of winter-weary highlanders turn up to join in the festivities.

Rebels during the 1781 La Paz revolt escaped to the Yungas and hid out in the valleys around Chulumani. Today the area is home to a large population of African-Bolivians (see the boxed text, p146). Locals claim the town's name is derived from *cholumanya* (tiger's dew), to commemorate a jaguar's visit to the town; well, it's a good story anyway.

Information

Chulumani's tourist office in the square is being turned into a hamburger stand, so the best sources of local information are hotel owners such as Xavier Sarabia at the Country House (p145). There's no ATM in Chulumani; Banco Unión changes traveler's checks for 5% commission, and Prodem changes US dollars and gives cash advances on credit cards (5% commission). The Cotel office on Plaza Libertad is one of several central phone offices. There's also an Entel near the *tranca* at the top of town. Internet connections are sporadic; on a good day head to **Enternet** (Sucre s/n) or friendly **El Wasquiri** (Bolívar s/n). You can make calls from the Cotel office on the plaza among other places.

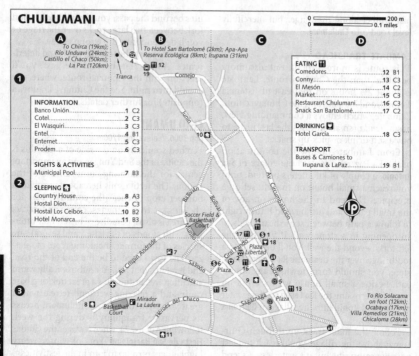

CHULUMANI

0 — 200 m
0 — 0.1 miles

To Chirca (19km);
Río Unduavi (24km);
Castillo el Chaco (50km)
La Paz (120km)

Tranca

To Hotel San Bartolomé (2km); Apa-Apa
Reserva Ecológica (8km); Irupana (31km)

Cornejo

EATING 🍴
Comedores....................12 B1
Conny........................13 C3
El Mesón.....................14 C2
Market.......................15 C3
Restaurant Chulumani.........16 C3
Snack San Bartolomé..........17 C2

DRINKING 🍷
Hotel García.................18 C3

TRANSPORT
Buses & Camiones to
Irupana & LaPaz..............19 B1

INFORMATION
Banco Unión..................1 C2
Cotel........................2 C3
El Wasquiri..................3 C3
Entel........................4 B1
Enternet.....................5 C3
Prodem.......................6 C3

SIGHTS & ACTIVITIES
Municipal Pool...............7 B3

SLEEPING 🛏
Country House................8 A3
Hostal Dion..................9 C3
Hostal Los Ceibos...........10 B2
Hotel Monarca...............11 B3

Soccer Field &
Basketball Court

Plaza
Libertad

Plaza

Mirador
La Ladera

Basketball
Court

Heroes del Chaco

Plaza

To Río Solacama
on foot (12km);
Ocabaya (17km);
Villa Remedios (21km);
Chicaloma (28km)

Sights & Activities

Chulumani sees few visitors, yet it is a good base for several worthwhile excursions. The **municipal pool** was dry at the time of research; several hotels allow nonguests to take a dip for US$1.25.

An interesting day trip is to the **Apa-Apa Reserva Ecológica** (☎ 213-6106, 7202-1285; apapayungas@hotmail.com), 8km from Chulumani. The private 500-hectare property has dry forest and one of the last remnants of primary cloud forest in the Yungas, and is rich in trees, orchids, butterflies and birds; the 300-plus species sighted include two types of quetzal. You can also stay in the beautiful historic hacienda or camp at the well-equipped site above it (see opposite). The reserve runs four-hour guided forest walks (US$5 per person with a US$25 minimum) and has a café serving meals and homemade ice-cream. A taxi from Chulumani to the reserve costs US$3.10.

There are several lovely walks in the Chulumani area. A butterfly-clouded, five-hour (one-way) downhill hike will take you from Chulumani down to the Río Solacama; you can easily get a bus or *micro* back. In three to

four hours you can also walk to Ocabaya, while other walks take you from the higher village of Villa Remedios to the lower one, or from Chicaloma down to Ocabaya. Another beautiful hike is the four-hour walk from Chulumani to Chirca, where there's the church of a revered local virgin. See opposite for more details.

Sleeping

Hostal Los Ceibos (☎ 7301-9213; Junín s/n; r per person without/with bathroom US$3.10/4.40) Between the *tranca* and the plaza, this decent place has a motherly figure who runs a good tight ship. There are appealing views over the valley, and tempting sweets and pastries in the café out front.

Hostal Dion (☎ 213-6070; Bolívar s/n; r per person without/with bathroom US$3.75/5) The best of the cheapish options catering mostly to the market trade, this is a friendly, clean and well-maintained choice just off the plaza. It can be noisy at weekends when the nearby karaoke bar cranks up. Rates include a simple breakfast.

Hotel Monarca (☎ 213-6121; in La Paz 235-1019; r per person US$6.90; 🏊) Like most ex-prefectural holiday camps, the Monarca is a bit run down and lacks character, but it's run by nice people and is pretty good value. The enormous pool is open to nonguests for US$1.50.

Apa-Apa Reserva Ecológica (☎ 213-6106, 7202-1285; apapayungas@hotmail.com; r incl breakfast US$7.50, camping one-off fee US$10 plus US$1.25 per person per night; 🐾) This beautiful old adobe hacienda makes a good place to stay, set in elegant grounds 8km from Chulumani. The cordial owners maintain the property with care and thought; there's an excellent grassy camping area with palm-thatched tables, barbecues and good bathroom facilities, as well as five rooms, a café-restaurant and a lovely pool.

Country House (Tolopata 13; s/d US$8/12; 🐾) This welcoming home in a beautiful setting 10 minutes' walk (on the flat) from the plaza is a cozy and relaxing place to stay. The owner Xavier is a colorful character who loves this part of the Yungas and appreciates a good chat. The rooms are decorated in an attractively rustic style, are spotless, and have hot-water bathrooms and fresh flowers. Great breakfasts (US$3), abundant birdlife, a pool table, an extensive video collection and a peaceful setting are other highlights, as are the delicious homecooked dinners and relaxing mineral pool. Xavier can organize all sorts of local excursions too. To get there, head out of the plaza along Calle Lanza; you'll reach the guesthouse a couple of minutes after passing a basketball court.

Castillo el Chaco (☎ in La Paz 241-0579; r per person US$20-30; 🐾) Along the Chulumani road (20km beyond Unduavi) at 1934m, this place is a unique riverfront castle that is a real surprise for the eyes; it looks very out of place in the Yungas! It functions as a hotel and restaurant; call ahead to check that it's open. It's only a couple of hours from La Paz, and its swimming pool, waterfalls and subtropical climate make it an appealing weekend getaway.

Hotel San Bartolomé (☎ 213-6114, in La Paz 244-0208; d from US$30; 🐾) Owned by the upscale Plaza Hotel in La Paz, this relatively posh pad is notable for its odd Z-shaped swimming pool. Deals include four-person *cabañas* for US$60 and all-inclusive weekend packages from US$60 per person. For weekend guests the hotel organizes minibus transportation from La Paz. It's 2km out of town on the road to Irupana.

Eating & Drinking

Food choices are limited. For cheap and cheerful fried chicken, **Snack San Bartolomé** (per serve US$0.90) on the plaza is a friendly choice.

There are also basic *comedores* (dining halls) near the *tranca*.

The best *almuerzos* (set lunches) can be had at **El Mesón** (Plaza Libertad s/n; lunch US$0.90; 🕑 lunch) and **Conny** (Sucre s/n; lunch US$0.90, mains US$1.50-3), which has a pleasant dining room with views and is also open in the evenings. Also on the plaza, Restaurant Chulumani has an upstairs dining terrace. The spick 'n' span market also has good cheap meals.

The Country House and Apa-Apa Reserva do tasty dinners with a few hours' notice, and a few of the hotels have mediocre restaurants.

Nightlife options are limited; on Friday and Saturday nights **Hotel García** (Plaza Libertad) spins karaoke at its cacophonous disco.

Getting There & Away

The beautiful route from La Paz to Chulumani, which extends on to Irupana, is wider, less unnerving and statistically safer than the road to Coroico. Yunga Cruz trekkers finish in Chulumani, and the town is readily accessed from Yanacachi at the end of the Takesi trek. From Yanacachi walk down to the main road and wait for transportation headed downhill; it's about 1½ hours to Chulumani.

From Villa Fátima in La Paz, around the corner of Calles San Borja and 15 de Abril (two blocks north of the ex-petrol station), different companies depart when full for Chulumani (US$2.25, four hours) from 8am to 4pm. *Camiones* (US$1.25, nine hours) leave between 5am and 2pm. From Chulumani, La Paz–bound buses wait around the *tranca* until they fill up; it's sometimes a long wait.

If you're coming from Coroico or Guanay, get off at Unduavi and wait for another vehicle. It will likely be standing room only; if a seat is a priority, you'll have to go all the way back to La Paz.

It's also possible to go to Coroico via Coripata; take a La Paz–bound bus and get off at the crossroads just after Puente Villa at Km 93. Here, wait for a bus or *camión* to Coripata and then change again for a lift to Coroico. It's a lo-o-o-ng and dusty but worthwhile trip. An easier option is to hire a taxi; expect to pay US$37.50 for the trip to Coroico for up to four people.

AROUND CHULUMANI

The area around Chulumani is a beautiful, fertile zone comprised of both patches of forest and of farms producing coca, coffee, bananas and citrus fruits. Some of the villages are remote colonial gems. Another interesting aspect of the region is the presence of a significant population of Afro-Bolivians (see the boxed text, below), the descendants of slaves who once were forced to work the Potosí mines.

An intriguing circuit takes you from Chulumani past the **Apa-Apa reserve** (see p144) toward the humble fruit-farming hamlets of **Villa Remedios** (there are two hamlets, a higher and a lower one; the latter has a pretty little church). You'll likely see coca leaves being harvested and dried.

The main road winds its way down to the **Río Solacama**, whose banks are populated by numerous butterflies; it's a lovely spot for a bathe on a hot day. Just after the bridge, a left turn heads away from the main road up a steep hill to **Laza**. A *via crucis* (Stations of the Cross) leads up to the pretty square and its church, where there's an appealing dark-wood and gold altarpiece and baldachin. The much-revered statue of Christ, the Señor de la Exaltación, is the destination of an important *romería* (pilgrimage-fiesta) on September 14.

The main settlement over this side of the river is **Irupana**, an attractive, sleepy colonial town founded in the 18th century on one of the few bits of flat ground in the area. It became an important fortress, as the nearby ruins of **Pasto Grande** had once been in Tiwanaku and Inca times.

From Irupana, you can head back to Chulumani a different way, fording the Río Puri and passing through the principal Afro-Bolivian town, dusty **Chicaloma** – known for

its annual town festival on May 27, which features lots of traditional *saya* music – before crossing the Solacama river again. On the way back, you pass through tiny, postcard-pretty **Ocabaya**, which has one of the oldest churches in Bolivia, fronted by a liberty bell and a memorial to two local martyrs to the struggle for *campesino* rights. Locals may well offer food in their homes here.

Xavier Sarabia at Country House in Chulumani will happily give walking information (even for nonguests) and can help arrange taxi drop-offs or pick-ups.

Whitewater Rafting

The road to Chulumani follows part of another good whitewater river, the **Río Unduavi**. The upper section ranges from essentially unnavigable Class V to VI, with steep chutes, powerful currents, large boulder gardens, blind corners and waterfalls. Beyond this section it mellows out into some challenging Class IV whitewater followed by Class II and III rapids. Access is limited, but the Chulumani road does offer several put-ins and take-outs. The best access points have been left by construction crews who've mined the riverbanks for sand and gravel. A good take-out point is Puente Villa, which is three to four hours below the best put-ins. See p80 and p389 for details of tour agencies.

Sleeping

As well as a few cheap *alojamientos* (the Sarita on the main street is the cleanest), Irupana has a couple of interesting accommodations options. The **Hotel Bouganvillea** (☎ 213-6155; Sucre 243; r per person US$10; ⊠) is an attractive,

---

AFRO-BOLIVIANS

The hill villages of the Chulumani region are home to a high proportion of the country's Afro-Bolivian people. At a rough estimate, there are some 35,000 Bolivians descended from African slaves who were brought over to work the Potosí silver mines (where an astronomical number of them died). One of the traditional Bolivian dances, the *morenada*, has its roots in a portrayal of an African slave train arriving at the mines.

Slavery in Bolivia was abolished in 1851, and the Afro-Bolivians of the Yungas live as farmers, growing coca and other typical local products. Seeing them dressed in typical *cholita* costumes, you might assume total integration, but they are a community somewhat apart; while relations with the Aymará community are friendly, there is little intermarriage. At a political level, their existence as a people has fundamentally been ignored.

Although there is increasing awareness of their roots among Afro-Bolivians, most people in the villages around Chulumani have no idea of their origins. In their haunting *saya* music and distinct funerary rites, however, are many echoes from the other side of the ocean.

modernized, whitewashed building built around a pool. Its rooms are clean and appealing, although management is not overly welcoming.

One of the most memorable places to stay in the Yungas is **Nirvana Inn** (☎ 213-6154; www .posadanirvanainn.cjb.net; cabañas per person US$20; ☑) in the barrio of Chiriaca at the top of Irupana (go past the soccer field and turn right). It consists of five sublime *cabañas* in an immaculate hillside garden full of orange and mandarin trees (help yourself!). There are top views over the valley, it's run by kind and considerate hosts, and the rooms are new, comfortable and romantic. All rooms have a log fire and optional kitchen facilities. There's also a swimming pool and sauna. Breakfast is included, and other meals, as well as forest walks, can be arranged.

Getting There & Away

There are regular buses that drive the 31km from Chulumani to Irupana (US$0.40, one hour). There are also some direct connections to Irupana from La Paz. Minibuses run to the smaller villages from Chulumani and Irupana.

One of the most comfortable ways to see these places is to hire a taxi from Chulumani (although not in the rainy season, December to February). For the whole circuit, expect to pay around US$30 to US$40 for a day's hire. It's worth getting hold of a driver who can also act as a guide; recommended are **Walter Haybar Escobar** (☎ 7208-1972) and **David Monte Villa** (☎ 7252-2364).

SORATA

pop 2500 / elevation 2670m

Sorata wins many travelers' votes as the most relaxing spot in Bolivia. This laid-back place preserves a crumbling colonial atmosphere in a spectacular natural setting, perched on a hillside in a valley beneath the towering snowcapped peaks of Illampu and Ancohuma. It's a great spot to chill for a few days, and also a popular base camp for hikers and mountaineers.

In colonial days Sorata provided a link to the Alto Beni's goldfields and rubber plantations, and a gateway to the Amazon Basin. In 1791 it was the site of a distinctly unorthodox siege by indigenous leader Andrés Tupac Amaru and his 16,000 soldiers. They constructed dikes above the town, and when these had filled with runoff from the

slopes of Illampu, they opened the floodgates and the town was washed away.

In September 2003, Sorata hit the national headlines. A blockade further up the La Paz road, expression of an overwhelming wave of *campesino* dissatisfaction that eventually led to the downfall of the government, trapped hundreds of Bolivian and foreign tourists in Sorata (hardly a nightmare). In a misplaced show of force, the army busted them out, killing a *campesino* and inducing a riot. The town suffered in the wake of this, as tourism abandoned it, but it is now picking up again.

The main **town fiesta**, a great time to visit, is held on September 14.

Information

Sunday is market day, and Tuesday, when many businesses are closed, is considered *domingo sorateño* (Sorata's Sunday). There's no tourist information centre; the best resource is Pete's Place (p150) or your hotel.

There are no ATMs in Sorata. **Prodem** (☎ 213-6679; Plaza Enrique Peñaranda 136; ☑ 2:30-6pm Tue, 8:30am-noon & 2:30-6pm Wed-Fri, 8:30am-4pm Sat, 8:30am-3pm Sun) changes US dollars and does cash advances with a 5% commission. For slow internet access, head for **Buho's Internet & Café** (per hr US$2.50) on the south side of the plaza.

Sights

There isn't much of specific interest in Sorata itself – its main attractions are its historic ambience and its maze of steep stairways and narrow cobbled lanes. It's worth taking a look at **Casa Günther**, a historic mansion that now houses the Residencial Sorata (p149). It was built in 1895 as the home of the Richters, a quinine-trading family, and was later taken over by the Günthers, who were involved in rubber extraction until 1955.

The main square **Plaza General Enrique Peñaranda** is Sorata's showcase. With the town's best view of the *nevados* (snowcapped mountain peaks), it's graced by towering date palms and immaculate gardens. Upstairs in the town hall on the plaza is the free **Alcaldía museum** (☑ 8am-noon & 2-5pm Wed-Mon), containing a number of artifacts from the Inca Marka site near Laguna Chillata and an exhibit of old festival clothing.

GRUTA DE SAN PEDRO

Although it's not the most spectacular of caves, a popular excursion is to the **Gruta de San Pedro** (San Pedro Cave; admission US$1.25; ☑ 8am-5pm), 12km

THE CORDILLERAS & YUNGAS

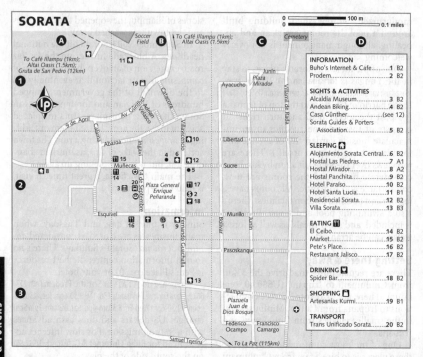

SORATA

INFORMATION
Buho's Internet & Cafe..........1 B2
Prodem.............................2 B2

SIGHTS & ACTIVITIES
Alcaldía Museum...................3 B2
Andean Biking.....................4 B2
Casa Günther.................(see 12)
Sorata Guides & Porters
Association.......................5 B2

SLEEPING 🏠
Alojamiento Sorata Central....6 B2
Hostal Las Piedras...............7 A1
Hostal Mirador....................8 A2
Hostal Panchita...................9 B2
Hotel Paraíso....................10 B2
Hotel Santa Lucia...............11 B1
Residencial Sorata.............12 B2
Villa Sorata.....................13 B3

EATING 🍴
El Ceibo.........................14 B2
Market...........................15 B2
Pete's Place.....................16 B2
Restaurant Jalisco.............17 B2

DRINKING 🍸
Spider Bar.......................18 B2

SHOPPING 🛍
Artesanías Kurmi...............19 B1

TRANSPORT
Trans Unificado Sorata........20 B2

from town. You can swim in a lagoon inside the cave; it's not as cold as you might think. Although the attendant supplies a lamp, it's worth taking a torch, particularly if there are several of you. Insect repellent and plenty of water are also good ideas.

It's a scenic 12km hike to the cave along a dirt road (2½ to three hours each way). Taxis will do the return trip for US$5 to US$6, including waiting time. At the time of research, the San Pedro community was constructing two simple *albergues* to overnight in.

Activities
HIKING
Sorata is best known as a convenient base for hikers and climbers pursuing some of Bolivia's finest landscapes. The peak hiking season is May to September.

The most popular walk is the hike to **Laguna Chillata**, a pretty spot with great views of the surrounding sierra and Lake Titicaca. It's a fairly stiff five-hour climb, ascending some 1500m, and, while you can get there and back in a day, it's a pleasant and popular spot to camp. It's worthwhile taking a guide, as it's

easy to get lost. If you're going to overnight there, a beast of burden is a sound investment; let the mule do the carrying while you enjoy the views.

An optional third day can be built into this hike. Leaving the tent and your gear at Laguna Chillata (it'll get nicked if you haven't brought a guide, who can detail someone to watch over it), a steep ascent takes you up to **Laguna Glacial**, a top spot where you can watch big chunks of ice cracking off into the water. It's at 5100m, so take it easy; the altitude can make it a tough climb.

Ambitious adventurers can do the seven-day **El Camino del Oro trek** (p151), an ancient trading route between the Altiplano and the Río Tipuani gold fields. Otherwise there's the challenging **Mapiri trail** (five days; p153) or the Illampu circuit (seven days); however, armed robbers have made this latter route risky in recent years – although guides can get you through with a bit of night hiking, we recommend insisting on a detour around the trouble area.

The ultimate hardcore challenge is the 20-day **Trans Cordillera route**: eight days gets you from Sorata to Lago Sistaña, with possible four-day (to Huayna Potosí) and eight-day (to Illimani) extensions.

Basic information on climbing some of the region's peaks is included under Cordillera Real (p157). For detailed trekking information, pick up Lonely Planet's *Trekking in the Central Andes*. Hikers should carry the *Alpenvereinskarte Cordillera Real Nord* (Illampu) 1:50,000 map; this can be bought at Buho's Internet Café.

While it's possible to hike independently, hikes are best done with a guide, mainly because of the need to be aware of local sensibilities and the difficulty of finding the routes.

The most economical authorized option is to hire an independent, Spanish-speaking guide from the **Sorata Guides & Porters Association** (☎/fax 213-6698; guiasorata@hotmail.com; Jurídica 159), which also rents equipment of varying quality and arranges many different treks. Expect to pay from US$10 to US$20 per day for a guide; it costs around US$5 extra to hire a mule too. Cooking equipment is included in these prices, but food is extra. Clients are expected to pay for the guide's food too.

Louis Demers, the boss of the Residencial Sorata, is worth speaking to before embarking on a trek; he's an expert on the region's routes.

MOUNTAIN BIKING

The Sorata area, with its thrillingly steep descents and spectacular mountain scenery makes it a top two-wheel destination. The Jach'a Avalancha (Grand Avalanche) Mountain Bike race takes place in Sorata each year. 'Jach'a' is Aymará for 'grand,' and this is the biggest downhill race course in South America based on the MegaAvalanche format. It is a 2000m descent using a mass start and draws riders from across Bolivia and the world.

Andean Biking (Ciclismo Andino; ☎ 7127-6685; www .andeanbiking.com; Plaza Peñaranda s/n) is a professional and enthusiastic set-up that offers a range of great mountain-bike trips for riders of all levels. These range from sedate half-day excursions to awesome multi-day adventures in the surrounding sierras. Owner Travis is always plotting out new routes; one of his specialties is a five-day trip from Sorata to Rurrenabaque, starting with a two-day ride from Sorata to Mapiri via Consata (descending almost 4000m from the starting point in the mountains), followed by a three-day boat

journey with hikes as side-trips. A minimum of four people is required for the longer rides; prices are from US$50 to US$70 per ride. The season is from April to November – it's too muddy at other times.

Sleeping

Alojamiento Sorata Central (r per person US$1.35) This is the cheapest place in town; it's basic but friendly, with plaza views and shared cold showers. You'll find it on the north side of the plaza.

Hostal Mirador (☎ 289-5008; hostellingbolivia@yahoo .com; Muñecas 400; s/d US$1.90/3.80) Sorata's pleasant Hostelling International affiliate has a sunny terrace, a café, decent rooms with shared bathroom and lovely views down the valley. Members get a 10% discount.

Residencial Sorata (☎ 279-3459; r per person US$1.90-5) On the northeast corner of the plaza, this ultra-characterful colonial-style mansion makes a romantic place to stay. Do your eyes a favor and ask to see the old-style rooms; do your back a favor and ask to stay in one of the new ones (with private bathroom). There's a restaurant, laundry service, spacious lounge, ping pong table and a friendly welcome. Manager Louis Demers speaks several languages and is a mine of information on local trekking routes.

Hostal Las Piedras (☎ 7191-6341; Ascarrunz s/n; r per person US$2.50, s/d with bathroom US$5/7.50) The most pleasant and homelike of Sorata's *hostales*, this recommendable spot offers very pretty rooms with attractive wooden furniture, a cozy feel and comfy beds with duvets. Some have great valley views, and the optional breakfast (US$1 to US$2) includes homemade wholemeal bread and yoghurt. The owner Petra will make you feel very welcome. It's near the town soccer oval, a seven-minute walk from the plaza down Calle Ascarrunz (a rough track) off the shortcut to the cave.

Hostal Panchita (☎ 213-4242; s/d US$2.50/5) Built around a clean and sunny courtyard on the south side of the plaza, the pleasant, atmospheric Panchita has spacious rooms with shared bath. Some of the mattresses are newer than others, so you might want to see a couple of rooms. The management is friendly, there's hot water, and the attached café-restaurant does arguably the best of the town's pizzas.

Hotel Santa Lucia (☎ 213-6861; r per person US$2.50, with bathroom US$5) This cheerful, bright yellow place with carpeted rooms and laundry sinks has a friendly owner, Serafín, who'll do his utmost to make your stay comfortable. It's across from the soccer field off the shortcut to the caves.

Villa Sorata (Guachalla 238; r per person without/with bathroom US$3.10/4.75) An appealing if neglected option, this appealing colonial house is built around a courtyard and boasts a roof terrace for stargazing and Illampu views. The rooms are cool and attractive; most have decent hot-water bathrooms. Although the sign claims B&B, there is no breakfast – the owner is seldom present – but you can use the kitchen, and there's a good dining/lounge area. If nobody's about, you can ask at the Hotel Paraíso; the caretaker family looks after both places.

Altai Oasis (☎ 7151-9856; www.altaioasis.lobopages .com; camping US$1.90, s/d US$3.10/7.50, r with bathroom US$10-13, cabins for 2-5 people US$45-60) This really does feel like an oasis, with a lush garden, hammocks, caged macaws, a pretty balcony café-restaurant and a range of accommodations options. Welcoming hosts Johny and Roxana run this beautiful riverside retreat, and offer grassy camp sites, rooms with and without bathroom, and romantic accommodations in appealingly rustic *cabañas*, one intricately and fancifully painted. There are also cuddly farm animals, a book exchange, laundry service, hot showers and a communal kitchen. To get there, follow the downhill track past the soccer field to the river, climb back up to the road and turn left before reaching Café Illampu. More direct but steeper is the descent at the end of Calle Muñecas and back up the other side; even more direct is a taxi (US$1.90).

Hotel Paraíso (☎ 213-6671; Villavicencio s/n; r per person US$4.40) This central spot has a bright flowery patio, a terrace and decent rooms with bathroom, although the mattresses might be a little thin for some tastes. There's also a restaurant, which at the time of research opened only on request.

Camping is also available at the friendly Café Illampu.

Eating & Drinking

Small, inexpensive restaurants around the market and the plaza sell cheap and filling *almuerzos*. A curiosity of Sorata is that it's bristling with almost identical pizza restaurants, some of which share a kitchen. There was once a real Italian pizzeria here; once it closed up, locals rushed to grab the business. They are all much of a muchness, charging US$2.50/3.75/5 for a small/medium/large pizza.

Café Illampu (snacks US$1-2; 9am-7pm Wed-Mon) A 15-minute down-and-up walk from town, this lovely relaxing spot is en route to the San Pedro cave. Leave it for the return journey, for if you stop here on the way to the cave, you might not make it as the place is exceedingly tranquil (vistas, garden, llamas), and there's good coffee, sandwiches on homemade bread and great cakes – the Swiss owner is a master baker. You can camp here too (US$1 per person).

Pete's Place (Esquivel s/n; set lunch/dinner US$1.75/2.10, mains US$2-5; 8:30am-10pm) In new premises above a *hostal* just off the plaza, this is a great place to eat. Big breakfasts set you up for a day's hiking, while there's a large selection of well-prepared and presented vegetarian fare, as well as chicken curry and tasty steaks, served in a cheerful, comfortable setting. The knowledgeable owner keeps an extensive library of maps and guidebooks, as well as the latest *Guardian Weekly*, and also provides up-to-date trekking information. It's well worth picking up a copy of his recent book *Bolivia – Between a Rock and a Hard Place*, which provides an accessible and comprehensive synthesis of Bolivian political history.

El Ceibo (Muñecas 339; mains US$2-3) This is one of a row of simple Bolivian eateries serving hearty portions of typical Bolivian dishes.

Restaurant Jalisco (mains US$2-4) On the east side of the plaza, Jalisco delivers an ambitious menu of pizzas, Bolivian choices, pasta and creditable attempts at Mexican food – tacos and burritos.

Altai Oasis (☎ 7151-9856; mains US$3-6.25; 8am-8:30pm) The peaceful balcony restaurant at this loveable spot 15 minutes' walk from town (see left) serves coffee, drinks and a range of vegetarian dishes. There are also T-bone steaks and an Eastern European touch, with Polish borscht and tasty goulash. It's a great place to just sit with a drink too, with views over the valley and the tinkle of wind chimes.

Drinking & Entertainment

Not a lot goes on in Sorata at night. The Spider Bar on the plaza (name taken from a former bar of that name) has a decent drinks selection and outdoor seating, but shuts fairly early. A couple of earthy local bars on Calle

Muñecas offer no frills, but are friendly places to drink a beer or two.

Shopping

For local handiwork look for the friendly **Artesanías Kurmi** (Günther 107), in a rustic two-story white house. Here Wilma Velasco sells wonderful homemade and hand-dyed clothing, hats, dolls, bags and wall-hangings for excellent prices; also ask to try the homemade orange wine! There's no sign, but if you ring the bell, she'll open up.

Getting There & Away

Sorata is a long way from the other Yungas towns, and there's no road connecting it directly with Coroico, so you must go through La Paz. The rough route to La Paz was being asphalted at the time of research, but it will take a while to complete.

From La Paz, **Trans Unificado Sorata** (Map pp66-7; ☎ 238-1693; cnr Kollasuyo & Bustillos) departs the cemetery district 10 times daily (US$1.60, four hours). From Sorata, La Paz–bound buses depart from the plaza hourly from 4am to 5pm. For Copacabana you must get off at the junction town of Huarina and wait for another, probably packed, bus. Similarly, for Charazani you should change at Achacachi, but you'll need to start out from Sorata very early. There are also minibuses running between La Paz and Sorata (US$1.75), which can be quicker and more comfortable.

The only road route between Sorata and the lowlands is a rough 4WD track that leads to the gold-mining settlement of Mapiri. It strikes out from Sorata and passes through Quiabaya, Tacacoma, Itulaya and Consata, roughly following the courses of the Ríos Llica, Consata and Mapiri all the way. The biggest drawbacks are the horrendous mud, the road construction and some river crossings that are passable only with 4WD. *Camionetas* (pickup trucks) leave Sorata daily for the grueling journey to Consata (US$3.50, four hours) and on to the Sorata Limitada mine (US$5, seven hours). From Sorata Limitada, you'll find *camionetas* to Mapiri, which is another three hours away.

EL CAMINO DEL ORO (GOLD DIGGER'S TRAIL)

This was once a classic, demanding trek along a paved Inca transportation route, but over recent years it has been degraded by road building and indiscriminate gold-mining activity.

If the current road-building trend continues, this popular hike between Sorata and the Río Tipuani goldfields may soon disappear.

For nearly 1000 years this Inca road has been used as a commerce and trade link between the Altiplano and the lowland goldfields. Indeed, the Tipuani and Mapiri valleys were major sources of the gold that once adorned the Inca capital, Cuzco.

Today, however, the fields are worked primarily by bulldozers and dredges owned by mining cooperatives. They scour and scrape the landscape for the shiny stuff and dump the detritus, which is picked over by out-of-work Aymará refugees from the highlands. Squalid settlements of plastic, banana leaves and sheet aluminum have sprung up along the rivers, the banks of which are staked out for panning by wildcat miners. It's projected that gold will soon replace tin as Bolivia's greatest source of mineral export income.

Fortunately the upper part of the route remains magnificent, and almost everything between Ancoma and Chusi has been left alone, including some wonderfully exhausting Inca staircases and dilapidated ancient highway engineering.

This trek is more challenging than the Takesi or El Choro routes; if you want to get the most from it, plan on six or seven days to walk between Sorata and Llipi, less if you opt for a jeep to Ancoma. At Llipi, find transportation to Tipuani or Guanay to avoid a walking-pace tour through the worst of the destruction.

Access

Nearly everyone does the route from Sorata down the valley to Tipuani and Guanay, simply because it's generally downhill. If you don't mind a climb, however, you might prefer to do it in reverse, thus leaving the prettiest bits to last.

There are three options for the route between Sorata and Ancoma. First, you can rent a 4WD in Sorata and cut two days off the trek. After bargaining, you'll pay US$3.50 per person or around US$40 to rent the entire vehicle. A challenging alternative is the steep route that begins near the cemetery in Sorata. The route roughly follows the Río Challasuyo, passing through the village of Chillkani and winding up on the road just below the Abra Chuchu (4658m) – this is also the access to the Mapiri trail (p153), a four-hour walk from Ancoma. The third option, which

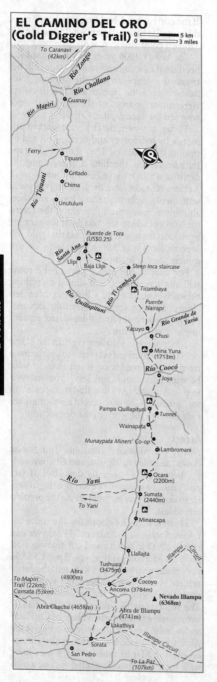

EL CAMINO DEL ORO
(Gold Digger's Trail)

is shorter and more scenic, is to follow the route through the village of Lakathiya and over the Abra de Illampu (4741m) to meet up with the road about 1½ hours above Ancoma. Foreigners are charged US$1.25 per person to camp anywhere in the vicinity of Ancoma, and US$0.40 to cross the bridge there.

Allow two days for either of the *abras* (mountain passes), and before setting out speak to Louis Demers at the Residencial Sorata for advice on routes and conditions. You're better off going with a guide.

The Route

Once you're in **Ancoma**, the route is fairly straightforward. Leave the 4WD track and follow the southern bank of the **Río Quillapituni** (which eventually becomes the Río Tipuani). At a wide spot called **Llallajta**, 4½ hours from Ancoma, the route crosses a bridge and briefly follows the north bank before recrossing the river and heading toward Sumata. Another Inca-engineered diversion to the north bank has been destroyed by bridge washouts, forcing a spontaneously constructed, but thankfully brief, detour above the southern bank.

Just past the detour is the village of **Sumata**; just beyond, a trail turns off to the north across the river and heads for **Yani** (which is the start of the Mapiri trail). A short distance further along from the trail junction is **Ocara**. From here, the path goes up the slope – don't follow the river. After 1½ hours you'll reach **Lambromani**, where a local may ask foreigners to pay US$0.40 per person to pass. Here you can camp in the schoolyard.

An hour past Lambromani you'll reach **Wainapata**, where the vegetation grows more thick and lush. Here, the route splits (to rejoin at Pampa Quillapituni); the upper route is very steep and dangerous, so the lower one is preferable. A short distance along, the lower route passes through an interesting tunnel drilled through the rock. There's a popular myth that it dates from Inca times, but it was actually made with dynamite and likely blasted out by the Aramayo mining company early in the 20th century to improve the access to the Tipuani goldfields. At **Pampa Quillapituni**, half an hour beyond, is a favorable camp site. Just east of this spot, a trail branches off to the right toward Calzada Pass, several days away on the Illampu circuit.

Four hours after crossing the swinging bridge at the **Río Coocó**, you'll reach the little settlement of **Mina Yuna**, where you can pick up basic supplies, and it's possible to **camp** on the soccer field.

An hour further down is **Chusi**, which is four hours before your first encounter with the road. There's no place to camp here, but you can stay in the school. **Puente Nairapi**, over the Río Grande de Yavia, is a good place for a swim to take the edge off the increasing heat.

Once you reach the road, the scene grows increasingly depressing. For a final look at relatively unaffected landscape, follow the shortcut trail, which begins with a steep **Inca staircase** and winds up at **Baja Llipi** and the **Puente de Tora** toll bridge (US$0.25) over the **Río Santa Ana**.

After crossing the bridge, climb up the hill and hope for a *camioneta* or 4WD to take you to **Tipuani** and **Guanay**. *Camionetas* between the Río Santa Ana bridge and **Unutuluni** cost US$0.75 per person; to continue on to Tipuani or Guanay costs an additional US$2.

You can pick up basic supplies at Ancoma, Wainapata, Mina Yuna, Chusi and Llipi, as well as all the lower settlements along the road. Spartan accommodations may be found in Unutuluni, Chima (rough-and-ready and not recommended), Tipuani and Guanay, all of which are along the road.

MAPIRI TRAIL

A longer and more adventurous alternative to the Camino del Oro trek is the six- to seven-day pre-Hispanic Mapiri trail, which was upgraded 100 years ago by the Richter family in Sorata to connect their headquarters with the *cinchona* (quinine) plantations of the upper Amazon Basin.

It's a tough, demanding trek with a lot of physical exertion besides mere walking – expect to clamber over and under logs, hack at vegetation with a machete, get assaulted by insects and destroy formerly decent clothing! That said, it's an amazing experience; the nature is unspoilt, and for the large part you are out on your own miles from any roads or villages.

While the trailhead is technically at the village of Ingenio, you can also begin this unspoilt route by climbing from Sorata over the 4658m Abra Chuchu, then ascending and descending through the open grassy flanks of the Illampu massif to Ingenio. For the next three days it descends along one long ridge through grassland, dense cloud forest and pampa to the village of Mapiri. With the Sorata approach, the entire route takes anywhere from six to eight days, depending on the weather, your fitness and whether you reach the trailhead at Ingenio on foot or by motor vehicle.

An excellent side trip before you get started will take you from Ingenio up to the lovely and medieval, cloud-wrapped village of **Yani**, where there's a basic *alojamiento*. Bolivia doesn't get much more enigmatic than this and adventurers won't regret a visit.

No maps are available for this route, due to government sensitivity on mining issues, and landslides often cause changes to the paths,

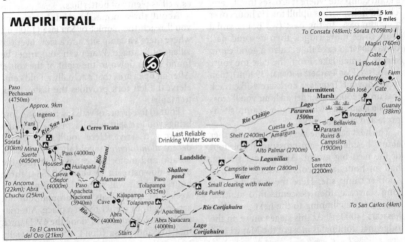

MAPIRI TRAIL

which in some parts are heavily overgrown – a machete will be necessary. Therefore, it is strongly recommended to take a guide from Sorata (p149). Guides for this trek charge around US$100 per group, and porters are US$70 each. You'll thank yourself for every kilo you're not carrying if you opt for the porter.

Access

The Mapiri trail begins at the village of **Ingenio**, which has basic *alojamientos*. It can be reached either by 4WD from Sorata (US$35 to US$50 for five people, three to four hours) or on foot over Abra Chuchu (4658m). For the latter, start at the cemetery in Sorata and follow the track up past the tiny settlements of Manzanani and Huaca Milluni to the larger village of Chillkani, about three hours beyond Sorata. From there you have five hours of fairly relentless climbing of the semiforested slopes to the Abra Chuchu. You'll meet up with the road twisting 4km below the pass.

Shortly after the crest, take the left turn (the route straight on leads to Ancoma and the Camino del Oro trek) down toward a small lake. This route will take you over Paso Pechasani Pass (4750m) and down past Mina Suerte to Ingenio and the start of the Mapiri trail at 3550m.

The Route

Past Ingenio you'll cross the **Río Yani**. Here the trail starts downstream, but half an hour later it cuts uphill along a side stream; there's a good camp site where it crosses the stream. The path then twists uphill for 1½ hours over a 4000m pass. In the next two hours you'll cross three more ridges, then descend past **Cueva Cóndor**, a cave that is also a good camp site, to a small lake. From the lake the route ascends to **Paso Apacheta Nacional** (3940m), then twists down **El Tornillo**, a corkscrew-like track that drops 150m. In under an hour you'll cross the **Río Mamarani**, where a good camp site is protected by large rocks.

The next camp site lies three hours further along, beside a stream-crossing at the foot of the next big ascent. At the next stream, half an hour later (collect water here!), is another camp site. Here the trail climbs a long staircase, then descends into another valley before climbing to the next pass, **Abra Nasacara** (4000m). At this stage you're on the ridge that dominates most of the Mapiri trail

route, with great views of the Illampu massif. For the next three days, you'll follow this ridge up and down, slowly losing altitude and passing through mostly lush jungle vegetation; fill your water bottles at every opportunity here. The first water along this stretch is at **Tolapampa**, which would also make a good camp site.

The next stretch passes through thick forest and may require a bit of bush bashing with a machete; plan on getting good and wet from mud and all the soaked vegetation. Six hours beyond Abra Nasacara is a very pleasant ridgetop camp site, **Koka Punku**, with water in a shallow pond 50m away. About three hours later, just before a prominent landslide, watch for the water 3m off the track to the right. Four hours and three crests later is the last permanent water source and camp site at **Lagunillas**. An hour later you'll find good (but dry) camp sites on the hill, **Alto Palmar**.

From Alto Palmar, the trail tunnels through dense vegetation along the **Cuesta de Amargura** (Bitterness Ridge). After three hours the jungle gives way to merely thick bush. Six hours later you'll reach **Pararaní** (1900m), where there's water (which needs to be purified) in a small pond near the ruins of an old house. An hour later there's a semipermanent lake, and just beyond it the trail leaves the dense vegetation and issues onto a grassy ridge flanked by thick forest. It's then 4½ hours to **Incapampa**, with a semipermanent marsh and a camp site. Along this stretch, wildlife is rife – mainly in the form of bees, ants, ticks, flies and mosquitoes, as well as plenty of butterflies.

About three hours beyond Incapampa you'll reach the hamlet of **San José** (1400m), where there's a camp site and a view over the village of Santiago. Water can sometimes be found 300m down to the right of the route. After an open area that's actually an old cemetery, the left fork provides the faster track to Mapiri.

Four to five hours of walking from San José brings you to **Mapiri**, which is visible 1½ hours before you arrive. Here you'll find several decent *alojamientos* (avoid the Alojamiento Sorata) and motorized canoes that race the 80km downstream to **Guanay** (US$4, three hours), which will seem like a city after a week of isolation! Boats leave around 9am, but arrive an hour earlier to get a place. Alternatively, catch a *camioneta* along the 4WD track first to Santa Rosa (don't attempt to walk, because there are two large river crossings), which has a decent *hostal* with a swimming pool, and then 175km uphill back to Sorata (US$6, 12 hours).

CONSATA

The semi-abandoned gold-mining town of Consata, which looks like a holdover from the Old West is accessible every couple of days by vehicle from Sorata (US$7.50, seven hours). This lovely village, characterized by rambling tropical gardens, hasn't yet been discovered by tourists. There's a hotel here, the cheap and rather charming **Hotel de Don Beto** (r per person US$2.50); the eponymous owner is going on 90 and a man of strong opinions.

AUCAPATA & ISKANWAYA
elevation 2850m

The tiny and remote village of **Aucapata** is truly an undiscovered gem. Perched on a ledge, on the shoulder of a dramatic peak, it's a great place to hole up for a couple of days' reading, hiking and relaxing. While most of Aucapata's very few visitors want to see Iskanwaya – somewhat optimistically dubbed 'Bolivia's Machu Picchu' – they may well take one look at the 1500m descent to the ruins (and the corresponding climb back up) and seek out the small Iskanwaya museum, in the village itself, which contains artifacts from the site. Admission is free but donations are expected.

The major but near-forgotten ruins of **Iskanwaya**, on the western slopes of the Cordillera Real, sit in a cactus-filled canyon, perched 250m above the Río Llica. Thought to date from between 1145 and 1425, the site is attributed to the Mollu culture.

While Iskanwaya isn't exactly another Machu Picchu, the 13-hectare site is outwardly more impressive than Tiahuanaco. This large city-citadel was built on two platforms and flanked by agricultural terraces and networks of irrigation canals. It contains more than 70 buildings, plus delicate walls, narrow streets, small plazas, storerooms, burial sites and niches.

Note that there's no accurate map of the area, and in the rainy season hiking is dangerous on this exposed route and not recommended.

For more information ask around for Señor Jorge Albarracín, a local who is passionate about the area and the Iskanwaya ruins, or Marcelo Calamani, who can guide you down to the ruins and speaks a little English. You can get in touch on the village telephone (☎ 213-5519). You could also look for the book *Iskanwaya: La Ciudadela que Solo Vivía de Noche,* by Hugo Boero Roja (Los Amigos del Libro, 1992), which contains photos, maps and diagrams of the site, plus background information on nearby villages.

Sleeping & Eating

Hotel Iskanwaya (r per person US$2.50) Aucapata's one smart-looking, little hotel has clean rooms and hot showers. There is no phone, but you can try to reserve a room via the village Entel point, ☎ 213-5519.

There's also a small **alojamiento** (r per person US$1.25) behind the church. For meals there's only a small eatery on the corner of the plaza where you'll get whatever happens to be available. Be sure to bring small change or you're likely to clean out the town!

Getting There & Away

Aucapata lies about 20km northeast of Quiabaya and 50km northwest of Sorata, but is most easily reached from La Paz. A weekly *camión* leaves from Calle Reyes Cardona in the cemetery district of La Paz on Friday and returns on Sunday. You'll probably pay around US$4 for this spectacular (and grueling) trip, which may well take more than 24 hours. You might have better luck getting transportation from more accessible Charazani (p160), or getting off a Charazani-bound bus at the *cruce* (turnoff) for Aucapata.

There's also a rather difficult access from Sorata, which involves a four-day hike via Payayunga. Guides are available from Sorata Guides & Porters (p149). One other access route, which is quite challenging and very interesting, is a little-known trek from the village of Amarete, in the Cordillera Apolobamba. A guide is essential; you may be able to hire one by asking around Amarete, Curva or Charazani.

GUANAY

Isolated Guanay makes a good base for visits to the gold-mining operations along the Ríos Mapiri and Tipuani. If you can excuse the utter rape of the landscape for the sake of gold, chatting with the down-to-earth miners and *barranquilleros* (panners) can make for a particularly interesting experience. This area and points upriver are frontier territory that may be reminiscent of the USA's legendary Old West. Gold is legal tender in shops and saloons, and the foundations of the local culture appear to be gambling, prostitutes and large hunks of beef.

Information

There's no place to change traveler's checks, but everyone displaying 'Compro Oro' signs (just about everyone in town) changes US dollars. The Entel office is in the entrance to the Hotel Minero.

River Trips

Access to the mining areas is by jeep along the Llipi road, or by motorized dugout canoes up the Río Mapiri. The Mapiri trip is easier to organize because boats leave more or less daily. The trip to Mapiri takes five hours upstream and costs around US$5 per person; if the river is low this is replaced by a jeep service. The exhilarating three-hour downstream run back to Guanay costs US$3.50. The forest has been largely decimated, and bugs are a nuisance, so bring repellent. If you want to spend the night, Mapiri has several *alojamientos* that will put you up for around US$1.25 per person.

Sleeping & Eating

Hotel Pahuichi (r per person US$2.50) A block downhill from the plaza, this is fairly primitive but probably the best value in town, and it also has Guanay's best and most popular restaurant.

Hotel Minero (r per person US$2.50) A good alternative to Pahuichi and right next door.

Hospedaje Los Pinos (d with bathroom & fan US$4.50) This friendly place is near the dock.

Around the plaza are several cheap *alojamientos*, charging the standard US$1.25 per person; Alojamiento Plaza and Alojamiento Santos have been recommended. For large steaks and fresh juices try Las Parrilladas on the road leading to the port. The Fuente de Soda Mariel on the plaza offers empanadas, cakes, ice cream, *licuados* (fruitshakes blended with water or milk) and other snacks.

Getting There & Away

For information on walking routes from Sorata, see the El Camino del Oro (p151) and Mapiri trek (p153) descriptions. A rough and seasonally unreliable 4WD track connects Mapiri with Sorata, via Consata.

BOAT

Boats to Mapiri leave daily at 9am (three to four hours) from Puerto Mapiri. When the river is too low (August to September) departures are by jeep (US$5, five hours).

Charter boats take travelers to Rurre, but these are pricey (US$300 for a 10- to 15-person boat, eight to 10 hours when high water levels). Bear in mind the boat owners face a three-day return trip with no income and a hefty fuel bill. Stock up on equipment and food. Some agencies in La Paz offer this trip (see p80 and p389 for agency listings).

BUS & CAMIÓN

The bus offices are all around the plaza, but buses actually depart from a block away toward the river. Four companies offer daily runs to and from La Paz via Caranavi and Yolosa (US$5, 10 hours). For Coroico, get off at Yolosa and catch a lift up the hill. If you're heading to Rurrenabaque (US$7.50, 14 hours), get off in Caranavi and connect with a northbound bus. *Camiones* to Caranavi, Yolosa and La Paz are plentiful and cheaper, but the trip takes longer.

CARANAVI

elevation 976m

All buses between La Paz and the lowlands pass through uninspiring Caranavi, midway between Coroico and Guanay. Travelers love to knock this place, but it doesn't deserve their scorn. If you're passing time here, take a look at the **Untucala suspension bridge**, which spans a crossing used since Inca times. Get online at **DumboNet** (☎ 823-2071; cnr Santa Cruz & Ingenieros).

Caranavi has several inexpensive hotels, all near the highway. **Hotel Landivar** (☎ 823-2052; Calama 15; r per person US$5; 🏊) is one of the better ones and has a pleasant pool. More sophisticated is the recommended **Hostal Caturra Inn** (☎ 823-2209; www.hostalcaturra.cjb.net; s/d with bathroom & breakfast US$15/20; 🏊), which has hot showers, fans, lovely gardens, a good restaurant and a clean pool; a really unexpected treat if you've just climbed out of a muddy *camión*! **Hotel Avenida** (Santa Cruz s/n; r per person US$2.50) and the basic but economical **Residencial Caranavi** (r per person US$2.50) are also decent choices. El Tigre does basic meals for less than US$1.

CORDILLERA REAL

Bolivia's Royal Range has more than 600 peaks over 5000m, most of which are relatively accessible. They're also still free of the growing bureaucracy attached to climbing and trekking in the Himalayas. The following section is a rundown of the more popular climbs in the Cordillera Real, but it is by no means an exhaustive list. There are many other peaks to entice the experienced climber, and whether you choose one of those described here or one of the lesser known, climbing in the Bolivian Andes is always an adventure.

The best season for climbing in the Cordillera Real is May to September. Note that most of the climbs described here are technical and require climbing experience, a reputable climbing guide and proper technical equipment. You should be fully acclimatized to the altitude before attempting any of these ascents. For information on Bolivian mountaineering, see p49. A good website to consult is www.andeshandbook.cl; it offers route information on several of the peaks in the Cordillera Real in Spanish, with English to come.

Guides & Equipment

By far the easiest way of tackling these mountains is to go on a guided climb. Several La Paz agencies offer trips that include transportation, *refugio* accommodations, equipment hire and a guide. Some of the same agencies will rent you equipment on its own if you want to tackle the peaks without taking the tour. Prices start at around US$120 for an ascent of Huayna Potosí, but are significantly more for the more technical climbs – say US$400-plus for Illimani. Several agencies, and foreign climbing tour agents, offer packages that combine ascents of several of the Cordillera Real peaks. See p389 for more information.

You can also contract a guide independently. The **Club Andino Boliviano** (Map pp72-3; ☎ 2-231-2875; México 1638, La Paz; ☷ 9:30am-noon & 3-6pm Mon-Fri) can provide a list of recommended guides. The **Asociación de Guías de Montaña** (☎ 2-235-0334; Chaco 1063, La Paz) is an association of registered mountain guides.

If you are in a group, it's worth paying extra to make sure that there are two guides accompanying you, so that if one member of the group succumbs to altitude sickness the ascent isn't compromised.

HUAYNA POTOSÍ

This is Bolivia's most popular major peak because of its imposing beauty and ease of access, as well as the fact that it's 88m over the magic 6000m figure (but 26ft under the magic 20,000ft figure). It's also appealing because it can be climbed by beginners with a competent guide and technical equipment. Beginners yes, but fit beginners; it's quite steep toward the end and it's a tough climb.

Some people attempt to climb Huayna Potosí in one day; this cannot be recommended. It's a 1500m vertical climb from Paso Zongo (the trailhead, and a mountain pass, situated at 4700m) and a 2500m vertical altitude gain from La Paz to the summit, and to ascend in one day would pose a great risk of potentially fatal cerebral edema. It's far better to spend a night at the trailhead, head up to the base camp (5200m) the next day, then start the summit climb that next night.

There are two *refugios* in the Paso Zongo area; the better-equipped is **Huayna Potosí Refugio** (☎ in La Paz 2-232-3584; www.huayna.com; dm low/high season with breakfast US$6/9). Run by a La Paz tour company, it's a comfortable, heated spot and a fine place to acclimatize – there's pretty walking to be done hereabouts and plenty of advice and good cheer. Reserve ahead. The other, **Refugio San Calixto** (Casa Blanca; dm $1.90), is right by the La Paz–Zongo road (buses will let you off outside) and is a simpler, but very hospitable spot. You can also camp here. Transportation to the *refugio*, guides, rations and porters can be arranged.

Access

A 4WD from La Paz to the trailhead at Paso Zongo costs around US$40 for up to five people. A taxi should be a bit less with haggling – make sure your driver knows the way. Daily buses also leave at 6am from Plaza Ballivián in El Alto (US$2, two hours).

As Huayna Potosí is so popular, lots of climbers are headed out that way during the climbing season. If you only want a lift, check with specialist climbing agencies. Someone will probably have a 4WD going on the day you want, and you can share costs for the trip.

The Route

From the *refugio*, cross the dam and follow the aqueduct until you reach the third path taking off to your left. Follow this to a glacial stream where a signpost points the way. Take this path through and across the rocks to reach the ridge of a moraine. Near the end of the moraine descend slightly to your right and then ascend the steep scree gullies. At the top you should bear left and follow the cairns to reach the glacier. At the glacier is **Campamento Rocas**, situated at 5200m. There's a hut to sleep in, and dry spots to camp. Most tours stop here for the night, before commencing the ascent at around 2am. Other people choose to continue to Campo Argentino.

The glacier is crevassed, especially after July, so rope up while crossing it. Ascend the initial slopes then follow a long, gradually ascending traverse to the right, before turning left and climbing steeply to a flat area between 5500m and 5700m known as **Campo Argentino**. It will take you about four hours to reach this point. Camp on the right of the path, but note that the area further to the right is heavily crevassed, especially later in the season.

The following morning you should leave from here between 4am and 6am. Follow the path/trench out of Campo Argentino, and head uphill to your right until you join a ridge. Turn left here and cross a flat stretch to reach the steep and exposed **Polish Ridge** (named in honor of the Pole who fell off it and died while soloing in 1994). Here you cross a series of rolling glacial hills and crevasses to arrive below the summit face. Either climb straight up the face to the summit or cross along the base of it to join the ridge that rises to the left. This ridge provides thrilling views down the 1000m-high west face. Either route will bring you to the summit in five to seven hours from Campo Argentino.

Descent to Campo Argentino from the summit takes a couple of hours; from there, it's another three hours or so back to the *refugio* at Paso Zongo.

ILLIMANI

Illimani, the 6439m giant overlooking La Paz, was first climbed in 1898 by a party led by WM Conway, a pioneer 19th-century alpinist. Although it's not a difficult climb technically, the combination of altitude and ice conditions warrants serious consideration and caution. Technical equipment is essential above the snow line; caution is especially needed on the exposed section immediately above Nido de Cóndores where several climbers have perished.

Access

The easiest way to reach the Illimani first camp, **Puente Roto**, is via Estancia Una, a three-hour trip by 4WD from La Paz (about US$125). From there, it's three to four hours' walk to Puente Roto. At **Estancia Una** you can hire mules to carry your gear to Puente Roto for around US$5. You can hire porters in Estancia Una or Pinaya for US$10 to carry rucksacks from Puente Roto to the high camp at Nido de Cóndores.

A daily 5am bus (US$1.25) goes from near La Paz's Mercado Rodríguez to the village of **Quilihuaya**, from where you'll have a two-hour slog to Estancia Una – complete with a 400m elevation gain. Buses return from Quilihuaya to La Paz several days a week at around 8:30am, but if you're relying on public transportation you should carry extra food just in case.

An alternative route to the base camp is via Cohoni. Buses and *camiones* leave La Paz for Cohoni (US$1.50, four hours) in the early afternoon Monday to Saturday from the corner of General Luis Lara and Calle Boquerón. They leave Cohoni to return to La Paz around 8:30am and may take anywhere from four hours to all day depending on which route is followed.

The Route

The normal route to Pico Sur, the highest of Illimani's five summits, is straightforward but heavily crevassed. If you don't have technical glacier experience, hire a competent professional guide.

The route to **Nido de Cóndores**, a rock platform beside the glacier, is a four- to six-hour slog up a rock ridge from Puente Roto. There's no water at Nido de Cóndores, so you'll have to melt snow – bring sufficient stove fuel.

From Nido de Cóndores you need to set off at about 2am. Follow the path in the snow leading uphill from the camp; the path grows narrower and steeper, then flattens out a bit before becoming steeper again. It then crosses a series of crevasses before ascending to the right to reach a level section. From here aim for the large break in the skyline to the left of the summit, taking care to avoid the two major crevasses, and cross one steep section that is iced over from July onwards. After you pass through the skyline break, turn right and continue up onto the summit ridge. The final three vertical meters involve walking 400m along the ridge at over 6400m elevation.

Plan on six to 10 hours for the climb from Nido de Cóndores to the summit and three to four hours to descend back to camp.

If possible continue down from Nido de Cóndores to Puente Roto on the same day. The 1000m descent is not appreciated after a long day, but your body will thank you the following day and will recover more quickly at the lower altitude. You'll also avoid having to melt snow for a second night.

On the fourth day you can walk from Puente Roto back out to Estancia Una in about two to three hours.

CONDORIRI MASSIF

The massif known as Condoriri is actually a cluster of 13 peaks ranging in height from 5100m to 5648m. The highest of these is **Cabeza del Cóndor** (Head of the Condor), which has twin winglike ridges flowing from either side of the summit pyramid. Known as Las Alas (The Wings), these ridges cause the peak to resemble a condor lifting its wings on takeoff.

Cabeza del Cóndor is a challenging climb following an exposed ridge, and should be attempted only by experienced climbers. However a number of other peaks in the Condoriri Massif, including the beautiful Pequeño Alpamayo, can be attempted by beginners with a competent guide.

Access

There is no public transportation from La Paz to Condoriri. A 4WD to the start of the walk-in at the dam at **Laguna Tuni** costs around US$55. If you don't want to use a 4WD transfer, you can trek the 24km from Milluni to Laguna Tuni dam on the road to Paso Zongo (see Huayna Potosí, p157).

From Laguna Tuni follow the rough road that circles south around the lake and continues up a drainage trending north. Once you're in this valley, you'll have a view of the Cabeza del Cóndor and Las Alas.

It isn't possible to drive beyond the dam because there's a locked gate across the road. Some drivers know a way around it, but if you need to hire pack animals you'll have to do so before the dam anyway. Locals charge US$7 per day for mules, and a bit less for llamas, which can carry less. You might have to sign into the Parque Nacional Condoriri.

The Route

From the end of the road, follow the obvious paths up along the right side of the valley until you reach a large lake. Follow the right shore of the lake to arrive at the **base camp**, which is three hours from Laguna Tuni.

Leave base camp at about 8am and follow the path up the north-trending valley through boulders and up the slope of a moraine. Bear to the left here and descend slightly to reach the flat part of the glacier above the seriously crevassed section. You should reach this point in about 1½ hours from base camp.

Here you should rope up and put on crampons. Climb left across the glacier before rising to the col (lowest point of the ridge), taking care to avoid the crevasses. Climb to the right up the rock-topped summit called **Tarija** – which affords impressive views of Pequeño Alpamayo – before dropping down a scree and rock slope to rejoin a glacier on the other side. From there either climb directly up the ridge to the summit or follow a climbing traverse to the left before cutting back to the right and up to the summit. The summit ridge is very exposed.

ANCOHUMA

Ancohuma is the highest peak in the Sorata massif, towering on the remote northern edge of the Cordillera Real. It was not climbed until 1919 and remains a challenging climb.

For a long time, various sources put Ancohuma at around 7000m, which would have made it higher than Argentina's Aconcagua, but in 2002 an American student lugged GPS equipment to the top and determined that its true height is 6425m, a few meters short of Bolivia's highest mountain, Sajama.

Access

The peak is accessed via Sorata (p147). From this lovely little town you can hire a 4WD for the long traverse to **Cocoyo**, where the fun begins. (It's also possible to hire a 4WD all the way from La Paz to Cocoyo, which is convenient but expensive.) If you have a serious amount of gear, you can hire a mule train to carry it from Sorata to base camp, which is in the lake basin east of the peaks at about 4500m. Plan on at least two days for these various transportation arrangements to get you to the lakes. Alternatively Ancohuma can be climbed from the west, using **Laguna Glacial** as a base camp (p148). Further advice and information is available in Sorata.

The Routes

From the lakes head west up to the glacier following the drainage up through loose moraine. Make camp below the north ridge, the normal route. After a circuitous path through a crevasse field, a steep pitch or two of ice will gain the north ridge. An exposed but fairly easy ridge walk will take you to the summit.

If you have opted for the more easily accessed western route, hike from Sorata to the base camp at Laguna Glacial. From here the route climbs the obvious moraine and then ascends the glacier, over fields of extremely dangerous crevasses to a bivouac at 5800m. It then climbs to the bergschrund and across a relatively level ice plateau to the summit pyramid. This is most easily climbed via the north ridge; the first part is quite steep and icy, but then gets easier toward the summit.

CORDILLERA APOLOBAMBA

The remote Cordillera Apolobamba, flush against the Peruvian border north of Lake Titicaca, is becoming a popular hiking, trekking and climbing venue. Mountaineers, in particular, will find a wonderland of tempting peaks, first ascents and new routes to discover, and the trek from Lagunillas to Agua Blanca is one of the most memorable in the country, with overpowering Andean landscapes.

While access is improving, it must be emphasized that this is an isolated region, and far from set up for tourism. There are few services, transportation isn't reliable and the people maintain a fragile traditional lifestyle. Comparatively few locals – mostly men – speak more than rudimentary Spanish. Sensitivity to the local sentiments of this highly traditional Aymará- and Quechua-speaking area will help keep its distinctive character intact.

Every town and village in the region holds an annual festival, most of which fall between June and September. The **Fiesta de La Virgen de las Nieves**, one of the best, takes place in Italaque, northeast of Escoma, around August 5. It features a potpourri of traditional Andean dances.

CHARAZANI

elevation 3250m

Charazani is the administrative and commercial center and transportation axis of Bautista Saavedra province and by far the largest town in the area. You can hike from here to the trailhead for the Lagunillas–Agua Blanca trek. Services in Charazani have increased exponentially in recent years, and several NGOs are working in the area on sustainable development projects, including solar power, textile production and the promotion of responsible tourism. As a town, it's a relaxed spot to visit, and weary hikers will enjoy the hot springs.

Two **fiestas** are held, the biggest around July 16 and a smaller one on August 6. There's also a wonderful **children's dance festival** (around November 16).

Information

There are telephones at the **Transportes Altiplano** (☎ 213-7439) office on the plaza and in the **alcaldía** (town hall; ☎ 213-7282), a block below the plaza. The **gas station** (a *tienda* opposite the church selling fuel out of plastic jugs) exchanges cash dollars at good rates. If you happen to find it open, the public **Nawiriywasi Library** has books on medicinal plants and the Kallawaya culture, and maps and information for hikers, trekkers and climbers. Market day is Sunday.

Sights & Activities

Along the river about 10 minutes' walk upstream from town, you'll pass the **Termas de Charazani Phutina** (US$0.60; ⏲ 7am-9pm, closed Mon to 2pm for cleaning), a hot springs complex where you can bathe and enjoy a hot shower. Other **natural thermal baths**, complete with a steaming hot waterfall, are found a two-hour hike away down the valley from Charazani along the Apolo road alongside the Río Kamata. It's a lovely spot.

The traditional Kallawaya village of **Chari**, 1½ hours' walk from Charazani, is a lovely blend of terraces, flowers and vegetable gardens. A German anthropologist started the Tuwans textile project, which is designed to market the local hand-dyed weavings. The town is also home to a **Kallawaya cultural museum**, a stone and thatch structure with exhibits pertaining to medicinal plants and textile arts. About an hours' walk outside the village are some **pre-Incan ruins**, reached by

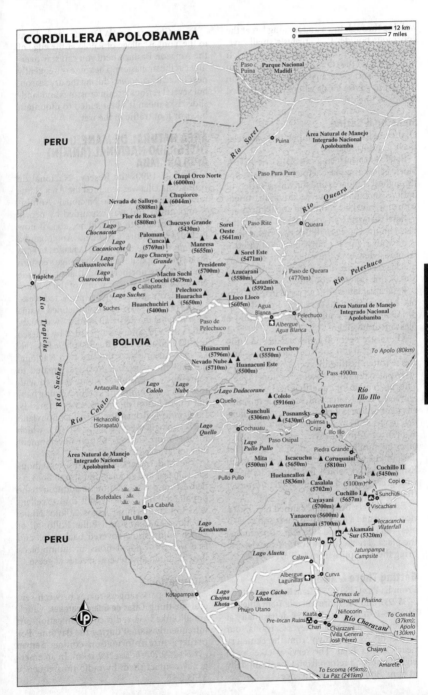

CORDILLERA APOLOBAMBA

0   12 km
0   7 miles

PERU

Paso Puina

Parque Nacional Madidi

Río Sorel

Puina

Área Natural de Manejo Integrado Nacional Apolobamba

Paso Pura Pura

Río Queara

Chupi Orco Norte (6000m)

Chupiorco (6044m)

Nevada de Salluyo (5808m)

Flor de Roca (5808m)

Lago Chocnacota

Palomani Cunca (5769m)

Lago Cacanicoche

Lago Chucuyo Grande

Lago Saihuanlcocha

Lago Churococha

Chucuyo Grande (5430m)

Sorel Oeste (5641m)

Manresa (5655m)

Sorel Este (5471m)

Paso Rite

Queara

Presidente (5700m)

Azucarani (5580m)

Katantica (5592m)

Paso de Queara (4770m)

Río Pelechuco

Machu Suchi Coochi (5679m)

Pelechuco Huaracha (5650m)

Lloco Lloco (5605m)

Agua Blanca

Pelechuco

Área Natural de Manejo Integrado Nacional Apolobamba

Calliapata

Lago Suches

Huanchuchiri (5400m)

Suches

Trapiche

Río Trapiche

BOLIVIA

Paso de Pelechuco

Albergue Agua Blanca

To Apolo (80km)

Huanacuni (5796m)

Cerro Cerebro (5550m)

Nevado Nube (5710m)

Huanacuni Este (5500m)

Pass 4900m

Río Suches

Antaquilla

Lago Cololo

Lago Nube

Lago Dadacorane

Cololo (5916m)

Río Illo Illo

Hichacollo (Sorapata)

Quello

Lavaererani

Sunchuli (5306m)

Posnansky (5430m)

Quimsa Cruz

Río Cololo

Cochauau

Lago Quello

Lago Pullo Pullo

Paso Osipal

Illo Illo

Piedra Grande

Área Natural de Manejo Integrado Nacional Apolobamba

Mita (5500m)

Iscacuchu (5650m)

Coruqunini (5810m)

Cuchillo II (5450m)

Copi

Pullo Pullo

Huelancallos (5836m)

Casalala (5702m)

Pass (5100m)

Cuchillo I (5657m)

Sunchuli

Bofedales

La Cabaña

Cayayani (5700m)

Viscachani

Ulla Ulla

Yanaorco (5600m)

Akamani (5700m)

Akamani Sur (5320m)

Incacancha Waterfall

PERU

Lago Kanahuma

Canizaya

Jatunpampa Campsite

Lago Alueta

Calaya

Curva

Albergue Lagunillas

Termas de Charazani Phutina

Kotapampa

Lago Chojna Khota

Lago Cacho Khota

Phujro Utano

Kaata

Niñocorin

Pre-Incan Ruins

Chari

To Comata (37km); Apolo (130km)

Río Charazani

Charazani (Villa General José Pérez)

Chajaya

Amarete

To Escoma (45km); La Paz (241km)

walking through town and turning left at the enormous boulder that creates a small cave. Follow this path to the cemetery, keep left until you gain the ridge, then continue 200m up to the ruins. Because of local suspicion it's best to advise locals where you're headed before setting off.

Sleeping & Eating

Of the five lodging possibilities, three are relatively comfortable.

Hotel Akhamani (r per person US$1.25, apt US$5) A block below the plaza, Hotel Akhamani has the highest standards and the widest variety of options, including a four-bed mini-apartment with a private bathroom and small kitchen.

Hotel Charazani (r per person US$1.25) Just off the plaza on the Curva road this two-room hotel is on your right. It's fairly basic but offers a fabulous view over the valley, and, crucially, quicker access to *dueña* (proprietor) Doña Sofia's fine Bolivian cooking.

Residencial Inti Wasi (r per person US$2.65) This place is nearby and is arranged around a traditional cobbled courtyard that provides a pleasant atmosphere.

There are several *pensiones* around the plaza that dish out soup, a main course and coffee (often tasting like *chuño* – traditional dehydrated potatoes – water) for under US$1. The aforementioned efficient but quick-tempered Doña Sofia, who has made the most eminent anthropologists cower, serves *almuerzos* at 12:30pm sharp and *cenas* (dinners) at 6pm or 7pm; reserve early, don't arrive late, stay humble and clean your plate. After dark follow your nose just off the plaza to Tu Esnack Kiosko, which lives up to its name with greasy, esnackalicious *pollo al broaster* (fried chicken).

Essentials (wheat, oats, canned fish, pasta, rice, bread and a few bruised fruits and vegetables) can be purchased at *tiendas* surrounding the plaza. Trekkers, however, are advised to bring their supplies from La Paz.

Getting There & Away

From La Paz (US$3.25), **Trans Norte** (☎ in La Paz 2-238-2239) and the more reliable **Trans Altiplano** (Map pp66-7; ☎ in La Paz 2-238-0859) depart daily at 6:30am from along Calle Reyes Cardona, four blocks up Av Kollasuyo from the cemetery near Cancha Tejar. The services take six to eight hours and return from Charazani daily at 6pm. Book tickets in advance.

From Charazani, a 4WD route winds down to the Yungas village of Apolo at the edge of the Amazon Basin, where you can stay overnight at the monastery. The route is frequently negotiated by *camiones* during the dry season, but several serious stream crossings and landslide risks mean it's best suited to mountain bikes or foot traffic in the wet.

ÁREA NATURAL DE MANEJO INTEGRADO NACIONAL (ANMIN) APOLOBAMBA

In the late 1990s the Reserva Nacional de Fauna Ulla Ulla was renamed the Área Natural de Manejo Integrado Nacional (Anmin) Apolobamba and was expanded by nearly 300,000 hectares to 484,000 hectares. It now includes the entire Cordillera Apolobamba and most of the renowned **Lagunillas to Agua Blanca trek** (opposite) along the range's eastern slopes. At its northern end it abuts Parque Nacional Madidi to form one of the western hemisphere's most extensive protected areas.

The original park – a loosely defined vicuña reserve along the Peruvian border – was established in 1972, and was upgraded by Unesco in 1977 into a Man and the Biosphere Reserve. Later that same year the Instituto Nacional de Fomento Lanero (Infol) was created to represent wool producers and charged with researching, monitoring and preventing habitat degradation of the reserve's camelids. Infol morphed into the Instituto Boliviano de Tecnología Agropecuaria (IBTA), which focuses more on agricultural development and social services.

The modern park is home to several thousand alpacas and vicuñas, and also to Bolivia's densest condor population. In addition to the popular hiking routes you'll find excellent wild trekking around Lagos Cololo, Nube, Quello, Kanahuma and Pullo Pullo, all of which enjoy snow-covered backdrops and rich waterbird populations, including black ibis, flamingo and several species of geese.

Information

A team of park rangers roams between several far-flung **Casas de Guardaparques**, which are all linked via radio communication but infrequently staffed during the daytime. For predeparture information contact **Sernap** (☎ 244-2870; 20 de Octubre 2782, La Paz). In an emergency contact them by radio on frequency 8335 USB.

THE KALLAWAYA

Originating in six villages around Curva in the Apolobamba region, the Kallawaya is a group of healers who pass ancient traditions down the generations, usually from father to son. Around a quarter of the inhabitants of these villages become involved in the healing tradition, although there are many more people throughout the Andes that pass themselves off as authentic Kallawayas when they are nothing of the kind.

The origins and age of the Kallawaya tradition are unknown, although some Kallawaya claim to be descended from the vanished people of Tiahuanaco. The Kallawaya language, however, which is used exclusively for healing, is derived from Quechua, the language of the Inca. Knowledge and skills are passed down through generations, although it's sometimes possible for aspiring healers to study under acknowledged masters.

The early Kallawaya were known for their wanderings and traveled all over the continent in search of medicinal herbs. The most capable of today's practitioners will have memorized the properties and uses of 600 to 1000 different healing herbs, but their practices also involve magic and charms. They believe that sickness and disease are the result of a displaced or imbalanced *ajallu* (life force). The incantations and amulets are intended to encourage it back into a state of equilibrium within the body.

Hallmarks of the Kallawaya include the *alforja* (medicine pouch) carried by the men. While women don't become healers, they still play an important part in the gathering of herbs.

In Lagunillas, there's a small exhibition about the Kallawaya in the Museo Interpretátivo. The Kallawaya's legacy has also been recorded by several anthropologists and medical professionals; German university psychiatrist Ina Rössing has produced an immense four-volume work called *El Mundo de los Kallahuaya* about her ongoing research, and Frenchman Louis Girault has compiled an encyclopedia of herbal remedies employed by the Kallawaya, entitled *Kallahuaya, Curanderos Itinerantes de los Andes*.

The village of **Curva** (3780m) has a few basic stores, and at nearby Lagunillas there's the **Museo Interpretátivo center**, which provides limited local information and an exhibition on the Kallawaya traditions. As part of the same project, Agua Blanca, near Pelechuco, has a small **museum** and **weaving workshop**. Curva's main festival is a colorful affair that takes place on June 29.

Sleeping & Eating

Noncampers can normally find accommodations in local homes for US$2 per person *más o menos* – just ask around. The biggest *tienda* is in Ulla Ulla. At **La Cabaña**, 5km from Ulla Ulla village, IBTA has a small hostel where you may be able to stay, but it's suggested that you reserve via Sernap in La Paz.

The best accommodations in the area are two associated **albergues** (☎ 241-3432; per person US$2.50) at Lagunillas and Agua Blanca. They offer dorm beds, hot showers, kitchen facilities and a fireplace, and can also arrange simple meals (per person US$2.50). Reserve ahead, or hunt around to find the keeper of the keys. There are **ranger stations** at Antaquilla, Charazani, Curva, Kotapampa, Pelechuco,

Pullo Pullo, Suches and Hichacollo; the last three were designed by a La Paz architect and blend adobe construction, domed thatched roofs and passive solar walls to reflect both modern and traditional styles.

Hikers can camp at any of these sites – or can even stay inside, space and Spanish skills permitting.

LAGUNILLAS TO AGUA BLANCA (CURVA TO PELECHUCO) TREK

This fantastic four- to five-day hike (115km) passes through splendid and largely uninhabited wilderness. The track stays mostly above 4000m and includes five high passes. There's arguably no better scenery in the Andes, and along the way you're sure to see llamas and alpacas, as well as more elusive Andean wildlife, such as viscachas, vicuñas, condors and perhaps even a spectacled bear. (The Wildlife Conservation Society runs a bear research center five hours on foot from Pelechuco, where a couple of bears have been tagged and are occasionally observed.)

The trek may be done in either direction, as both ends have relatively reliable – albeit limited – public transportation links with La

THE CORDILLERAS & YUNGAS

Paz. Most people do the route from south to north, but starting in Agua Blanca would mean an additional day of downhill walking and could include a grand finale at Charazani's hot springs.

Pack animals and guides are available at both ends for the following prices: llamas (US$3 to US$4 per day), mules (US$5 to US$7 per day) and guides/muleteers (US$5 to US$7 per day). Clients must often carry their own food and stove, and are also often expected to provide meals for their guides, porters and muleteers. If possible bring all your trekking food from La Paz, as Curva and Pelechuco have only basics at inflated prices.

Access

Because of the sensitive nature of this frontier territory, no good maps exist. **Trans Altiplano** (Map pp66-7; ☎ in La Paz 2-238-0859) runs four weekly buses to Lagunillas from La Paz. They leave from Reyes Cardona in the cemetery district at 6:30am on Tuesday, Wednesday, Friday and Saturday (US$3, eight hours), returning at 4pm on Wednesday, Thursday, Saturday and Sunday. **Trans Norte** (☎ in La Paz 2-238-2239) runs a service to Agua Blanca and Pelechuco from El Alto (at the ex-*tranco* Río Seco) on Wednesday, Thursday and Sunday at 7am (US$3.15, 12 hours). The bus may stop en route – depending on the driver's mood – at the market in Huancasaya on the Peruvian border, before continuing to Ulla Ulla, Agua Blanca and Pelechuco. Buses return at odd hours – midnight on Monday, 3am on Friday and 8am on Saturday. Check all these schedules before leaving La Paz, as they change often. See p162 for services to Charazani.

A more expensive but considerably easier and more comfortable way to go is by 4WD. A vehicle and driver from La Paz to Lagunillas (US$250, seven hours) or Agua Blanca (US$250 to US$300, 10 hours) may be worthwhile because it allows daylight travel through the incomparable scenery. Alternatively you can pay to leave the logistics to someone else and do the trek with an agency (see p389).

The Route

Because most people do the trek from south to north – from Lagunillas (also known as Tilinhuaya) to Agua Blanca – that's how it's described here. If you want to start from **Charazani**, you can either follow the long and winding road for four to five hours or take the 3½- to four-hour shortcut. Cross the river at the thermal baths, then climb the other bank and back to the road. After about an hour you should follow a path that climbs to a white-and-yellow church on your left. Beyond the church, descend the other side of the hill, to just above the community of **Niñocorín**. After a short distance you'll strike an obvious path; turn left onto it and follow it as it contours through the fields and then descends to cross a river, where it starts the steep climb into Curva.

Most people choose to start in **Lagunillas**, with its pretty lake bristling with waterbirds. The *albergue* here (see Sleeping, p163) can arrange beasts of burden and guides. From here, it's a short walk to the village of **Curva**, centre of the Kallawaya community. From Curva, head toward the cross on the hill north of the village and skirt around the right side of the hill. About an hour out of Curva, you'll go across a stream. Continue uphill along the right bank of the stream. At a cultivated patch about 200m before the valley descending from the right flank of the snow peak, cross the stream to join a well-defined path entering from your left. If you continue along this path, you'll reach an excellent flat streamside camp site. Alternatively, keep following this trail for another 1½ hours to an ideal camp site at **Jatunpampa** (4200m).

From Jatunpampa, head up the valley and across a small flat to the col with a cairn, about two hours along. From this **4700m pass**, you'll have fabulous views of Akamani off to the northwest. One to two hours further along you'll arrive at a good camp site (4100m) near the **Incacancha** (aka Incachani) waterfall.

The following morning's ascent appears a bit daunting, but it isn't that bad. Cross the bridge below the waterfall and follow the switchbacks up the scree gully. As you ascend, enjoy distant views of Ancohuma and Illampu. After two hours or so you'll reach a **4800m pass**.

From the pass, traverse gently uphill to the left until you gain the ridge, which affords great views of the Cordillera Real to the south and Cuchillo II to the north. At this point the obvious trail descends past a small lake before arriving at a larger lake with a good view of Akamani.

Climb up to the next ridge before descending an hour to the small mining settlement of

Viscachani, where you'll strike the 4WD track toward Illo Illo (aka Hilo Hilo). In another hour this road ascends to a **4900m pass**, which also provides superb views of the Cordillera Real to the south and the Sunchuli Valley to the north and west.

At the pass the road drops into the valley; at the point where it bears right, look for a path turning off to the left. This will take you to a point above the **Sunchuli gold mine**. From Sunchuli, follow a contour line above the aqueduct for about an hour, until you see an idyllic camp site (4600m) below Cuchillo I.

The fourth day of the hike is probably the finest, as it includes sections that have been used for centuries by miners and *campesinos*. From the camp site, the road ascends for about two hours via a series of switchbacks to a **5100m pass**. From the pass, you can scramble up to a cairn above the road for excellent views dominated by **Cololo** (5916m), the southern Cordillera Apolobamba's highest peak.

Descend along the road for a few minutes, then jog right down a steep but obvious path that crosses a stream opposite the glacier lake below Cuchillo II before descending to the valley floor. If you follow the valley floor, you'll rejoin the road a couple of minutes above the picturesque stone-and-thatch village of **Piedra Grande**, three hours from the pass.

Follow the road for about an hour, then join the pre-Hispanic road turning off downhill to your right. After you cross a bridge, you should follow the obvious path to the right, leading you up into the village of **Illo Illo** in about an hour. Here you'll find small stores selling the basics – perhaps even beer and batteries.

When leaving Illo Illo don't be tempted onto the path to the left, which leads west to Ulla Ulla (although this is also a viable trek). The correct route leaves the village above the new school, between the public facilities and the cemetery. From there, cross the llama pastures until the path becomes clear again. After crossing a bridge (about an hour out of Illo Illo) and beginning up a valley with a sharp rock peak at its head (if it's too overcast to see the rock, look for several small houses on your left and turn there), you'll stumble onto an ideal camp site set in a bend in the valley, where there are a number of large fallen rocks.

From the camp site, head up the valley for about 1½ hours until you reach a bridge over the stream. At this point the route begins to ascend to the **final pass** (4900m), which you should reach in another 1½ hours. From the pass, descend past a lake, crossing camelid pastures and follow some pre-Columbian paving. In less than two hours you'll arrive in **Pelechuco**, a quaint colonial village founded by Jesuits in 1560. It's got an **Entel** (☎ 213-7283) office.

There are a couple of simple *alojamientos* in Pelechuco, but half an hour's walk further, passing two intriguing pre-Columbian settlements, takes you to the mining village of **Agua Blanca**, where there's a well-deserved *albergue* (see Sleeping, p163).

CORDILLERA QUIMSA CRUZ

The Cordillera Quimsa Cruz, although close to La Paz, is a largely undiscovered wilderness of 5000m-plus peaks, some of which have only been climbed for the first time in the last few years. Basque climbing magazine *Pyrenaica* once labeled it a 'South American Karakoram.' In 1999, near the summit of Santa Veracruz, the Spaniard Javier Sánchez discovered the remains of an 800-year-old ceremonial burial site with ancient artifacts and weavings.

The Quimsa Cruz is not a large range – it's only some 50km from end to end – and the peaks are lower than in other Bolivian ranges. The highest peak, Jacha Cuno Collo, rises to 5800m, and the other glaciated peaks range from 4500m to 5300m. Granite peaks, glaciers and lakeside camping make the Quimsa Cruz an unforgettable, untouristed Andean experience. It lies to the southeast of Illimani, separated from the Cordillera Real by the Río La Paz, and geologically speaking it's actually a southern outlier of that range.

The Quimsa Cruz lies at the northern end of Bolivia's tin belt, and tin reserves have been exploited here since the late 1800s. However, with the replacement of tin by plastics and aluminum, the current tin prices mean that it isn't viable to extract it from such remote sites. The few miners who've stayed on and continue to work some of the mines here either take their chances with cooperatives or are employed as caretakers for mining companies who don't want to abandon their holdings, and are presumably hoping for better days. In any case all the major mining areas in the region – which includes every valley along the western face of the Quimsa Cruz – are still populated.

ACTIVITIES

The Quimsa Cruz offers some of the finest adventure climbing in all of Bolivia, and in every valley mining roads provide access to the impressively glaciated peaks. Although all of the *nevados* of the Quimsa Cruz have now been climbed, there are still plenty of unclimbed routes, and expeditions are unlikely to encounter other climbing groups. Without climbing experience you're better off with a guide from a La Paz agency if you want to tackle any of the peaks here (make sure that they really know the area and aren't just winging it).

Trekking is also possible throughout the range, which is covered by IGM mapping (see p65). The main route is the two- to three-day **Mina Viloco to Mina Caracoles trek**, which crosses the range from west to east. Of interest along this route is the renowned site of a 1971 airplane crash, which had already been stripped by local miners before rescue teams arrived at the scene two days later! Mina Viloco is 70km southeast of La Paz, and is centered on what was once quite a major tin mine. Mina Caracoles is still worked by cooperatives, and is 13km northwest of Quime.

Staples are available in both Mina Viloco and Quime, but it's still best to carry everything you'll need (food, fuel and other supplies) from La Paz.

GETTING THERE & AWAY

Road access is relatively easy because of the number of mines in the area, and it's possible to drive within 30 minutes' walk of some glaciers. Others, however, are up to a four-hour hike from the nearest road. The easiest access is provided by Flota Trans-Inquisivi, which leaves daily from La Paz's main bus terminal for the eastern side of the range (to Quime, Inquisivi, Cajuata, Circuato, Suri, Mina Caracoles, and, less often, Yacopampa and Frutillani). Alternatively take any bus toward Oruro and get off at the *tranca* at Khonani, 70km short of Oruro. This is the turnoff for the main road into the Quimsa Cruz, and here you can wait for a truck or bus heading into the Cordillera.

A bus service is also available to the communities and mines on the western side of the range. To Mina Viloco, Araca or Cairoma, buses leave most days of the week, but the biggest challenge can be finding its office in El Alto, as it seems to shift around with some frequency; you'll just have to ask locally.

Those with a bit more ready cash can hire a 4WD and driver for the five- to seven-hour journey (between US$150 and US$250); any of the services used by mountaineers and trekkers can organize the trip.

Southern Altiplano

The harsh, at times almost primeval geography of the Southern Altiplano will tug at the heart-strings of those with a deep love of bleak and solitary places. Stretching southwards from La Paz to the limits of the country, it encompasses majestic volcanic peaks, wide treeless wilder-nesses and the white emptiness of the *salares*, eerie salt deserts almost devoid of life.

There's something really otherworldly about the zone, enhanced by shimmering heat hazes and bizarre rock formations. At night, the starscapes are truly incredible, worth enduring the bitter after-dark temperatures for. For it can get seriously cold here; the altitude combined with scouring winds and lack of shelter or vegetation can sometimes make traveling here something of an endurance test, particularly when few of the accommodations are heated.

The region has traditionally lived off mining, backed up by agriculture (corn, potatoes) and llama herding. Oruro is a mining city par excellence: gritty, honest and straight-talking, a place of meat, carbohydrates and hard work. It's well worth a visit, but many travelers only pass through, heading with bated breath for Uyuni and the surreal landscapes of the southwest. This is the domain of the Landcruiser, in which people head out on multi-day adventures into the rugged, unforgettable terrain.

Southeast of Uyuni is Tupiza, where the jagged, eroded cactus-studded scenery evokes memories of Sergio Leone films and lone gunslingers on fading horses. It's a great place to jump in the saddle yourself. The western associations are further enhanced by Butch Cassidy and the Sundance Kid, whose last stand took place in the remote village of San Vicente.

SOUTHERN ALTIPLANO

HIGHLIGHTS

- Gorge your senses with the almost extra-terrestrial landscapes of **Los Lípez** (p194) region in the country's extreme southwest
- Explore the **Parque Nacional Sajama** (p179) with its towering snow-coned volcano, Bolivia's loftiest peak
- Strap on some serious sunglasses and wonder at the salty expanse of the **Salar de Uyuni** (p191)
- Marvel at the stunning costumes of Oruro's boisterous **Carnaval** (p173)
- Whistle the theme from your favorite western as you guide your horse up the narrow gullies around **Tupiza** (p197)

Parque Nacional Sajama ★

★ Oruro

★ Salar de Uyuni

Tupiza ★

Los Lípez ★

■ TELEPHONE CODE: 2	■ POPULATION: 623,800	■ ELEVATION: 3500M TO 6542M

THE SOUTHERN ALTIPLANO

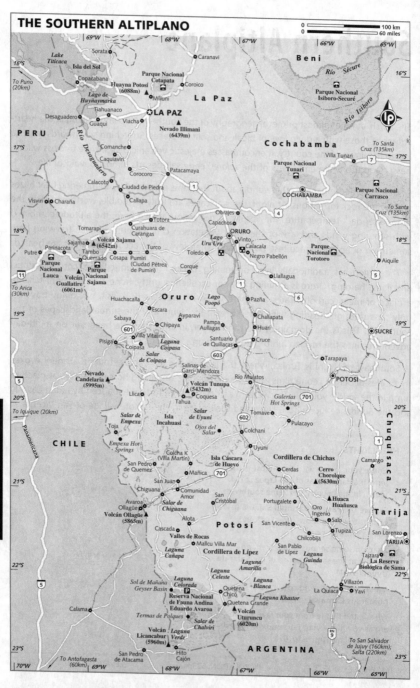

History

The prehistoric lakes Minchín and Tauca, which once covered most of this highland plateau, evaporated around 10,000 years ago, leaving behind a parched landscape of brackish puddles and salt deserts. Humans haven't left much of a mark on the region; some time in the mid-15th century, the Inca ruler sent his son Tupac Inca Yupanqui southward to conquer all the lands he encountered. Yupanqui and his gang marched on across the wastelands to the northern bank of Chile's Río Maule, where a fierce band of Araucanian people inspired them to stake out the southern boundary of the Inca empire and turn back toward Cuzco.

These days, outside the major towns, most of the people cluster around mining camps. Mining has been fundamental to most of the area, and although many of the major operations closed down in the crisis period of Bolivian mining, miners continue to operate on a local cooperative basis.

Climate

Climatically, the best months to visit are August, September and October, after the worst of the winter chills and before the summer rains. From May to early July, nighttime temperatures combined with stiff winds can lower the windchill temperature to –105°F. Summer is warmer but, for an arid area, there's quite a lot of rainfall between November and March. At any time of year you'll need protection against sun, wind and cold.

National Parks

Parque Nacional Sajama (p179), Bolivia's first national park, adjoins Chile's Parque Nacional Lauca (p182), preserving a stretch of magnificent peaks, plains and wildlife habitat. Sajama is home to the world's highest forest and some of South America's loftiest hot springs. Even if you're not into superlatives or hardcore mountaineering, an evening dip in the clear springs at the base of Volcán Sajama in the company of a few camelids is worth the trek. The Reserva Nacional de Fauna Andina Eduardo Avaroa (p191) is a highlight of Southwest Circuit tours and the gateway to Chile for those headed for the desert oasis of San Pedro Atacama.

Getting There & Away

From La Paz, the Southern Altiplano is easily accessed by bus, although off the paved main roads it can be a long and bumpy ride. The route from the central highland cities of Potosí and Sucre is rough on the back, bum and bladder. The overland route from Chile is a scenic mountain traverse on a good road from Arica, and Villazón has an easy border crossing with Argentina.

The train between Oruro and Villazón, which stops in Uyuni and Tupiza, provides a fine alternative to grueling overland travel. Rumors of flights starting up to Uyuni linger, but tricky Altiplano wind conditions have so far kept regularly scheduled flights grounded.

ORURO

pop 216,600 / elevation 3702m

By far the largest settlement of the southern Altiplano, palindromic Oruro is a miners' city with a tough climate. In many ways it's the most Bolivian of Bolivia's nine provincial capitals. It's an intriguing place where 90% of the inhabitants are of pure indigenous heritage. Locals refer to themselves as *quirquinchos* (armadillos), after the carapaces used in their *charangos* (traditional Bolivian ukulele-type instruments). *Orureños* are salty, hard-working and upfront people who have done it tough over the years with the decline of Bolivian mining and the extreme climate.

Oruro, whose name means 'where the sun is born,' sits against a range of mineral-rich low hills at the northern end of the salty lakes Uru Uru and Poopó, linked by river to Titicaca. While many visitors slate Oruro, it's got good museums and restaurants and there's plenty to see in the surrounding area. It's also culturally very colorful, with a rich dance and musical heritage that culminates in the riotous Carnaval celebrations, famous throughout South America for the lavish costumes and elaborate traditions on display.

History

Founded in the early 17th century, Oruro owes its existence to the mineral-rich 10-sq-km range of hills rising 350m behind the city. Chock-full of copper, silver and tin, these hills still form the city's economic backbone.

By the 1920s Bolivia's thriving tin-mining industry rested in the hands of three powerful capitalists. The most renowned was Simón Patiño, a mestizo from the Cochabamba valley who became one of the world's wealthiest men. In 1897 Patiño purchased La Salvadora

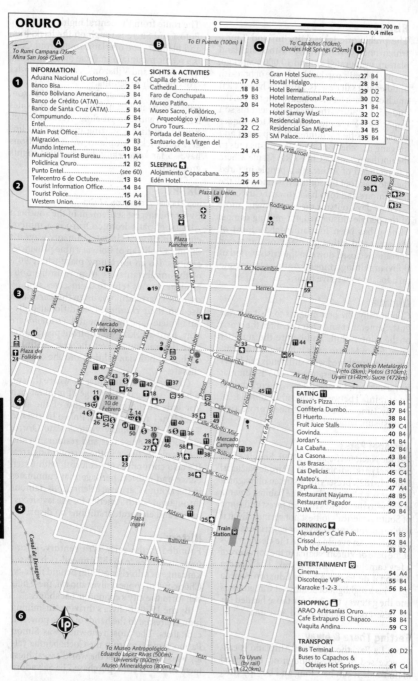

ORURO

0   700 m
0   0.4 miles

INFORMATION
Aduana Nacional (Customs)........1 C4
Banco Bisa..................................2 B4
Banco Boliviano Americano........3 B4
Banco de Crédito (ATM)..............4 A4
Banco de Santa Cruz (ATM).........5 B4
Compumundo.............................6 B4
Entel..7 B4
Main Post Office.........................8 A4
Migración...................................9 B3
Mundo Internet........................10 B4
Municipal Tourist Bureau..........11 A4
Policlínica Oruro.......................12 B2
Punto Entel.........................(see 60)
Telecentro 6 de Octubre...........13 B4
Tourist Information Office..........14 A4
Tourist Police...........................15 A4
Western Union..........................16 B4

SIGHTS & ACTIVITIES
Capilla de Serrato.....................17 A3
Cathedral..................................18 B4
Faro de Conchupata..................19 B3
Museo Patiño............................20 B4
Museo Sacro, Folklórico,
   Arqueológico y Minero...........21 A3
Oruro Tours..............................22 C2
Portada del Beaterio.................23 B5
Santuario de la Virgen del
   Socavón................................24 A4

SLEEPING 🏠
Alojamiento Copacabana............25 B5
Edén Hotel................................26 A4

Gran Hotel Sucre.......................27 B4
Hostal Hidalgo..........................28 B4
Hotel Bernal..............................29 D2
Hotel International Park.............30 D2
Hotel Repostero........................31 B4
Hotel Samay Wasi.....................32 D2
Residencial Boston....................33 C3
Residencial San Miguel.............34 B5
SM Palace.................................35 B4

EATING 🍴
Bravo's Pizza............................36 B4
Confitería Dumbo......................37 B4
El Huerto..................................38 B4
Fruit Juice Stalls.......................39 C4
Govinda....................................40 B4
Jordan's....................................41 B4
La Cabaña.................................42 B4
La Casona.................................43 B4
Las Brasas................................44 C3
Las Delicias..............................45 C4
Mateo's....................................46 B4
Paprika.....................................47 A4
Restaurant Nayjama..................48 B5
Restaurant Pagador..................49 C4
SUM...50 B4

DRINKING 🍷
Alexander's Café Pub................51 B3
Crissol......................................52 B4
Pub the Alpaca.........................53 B2

ENTERTAINMENT 🎭
Cinema.....................................54 A4
Discoteque VIP's.......................55 B4
Karaoke 1-2-3...........................56 B4

SHOPPING 🛍
ARAO Artesanías Oruro.............57 B4
Cafe Extrapuro El Chapaco........58 B4
Vaquita Andina.........................59 C3

TRANSPORT
Bus Terminal............................60 D2
Buses to Capachos &
   Obrajes Hot Springs..............61 C4

To Rumi Campana (2km);
Mina San José (2km)

To El Puente (100m)

To Capachos (10km);
Obrajes Hot Springs (25km)

To Complejo Metalúrgico
Vinto (8km); Potosí (310km);
Uyuni (314km); Sucre (472km)

To Museo Antropológico
Eduardo López Rivas (500m);
University (800m);
Museo Mineralógico (800m)

To Uyuni
(by rail)
(320km)

mine near the village of Uncia, east of Oruro, which eventually became the world's most productive tin source. Patiño's fortunes snowballed and by 1924 he had gained control of about 50% of the nation's tin output.

Once secure in his wealth, Patiño migrated to Britain, where he started buying up European and North American smelters and tin interests. As a consequence Bolivia found itself exporting both its precious metal and its profits. Public outcry launched a series of labor uprisings, and set the stage for nationalization of the mines in 1952 and the subsequent creation of the government-run Corporación Minera de Bolivia (Comibol).

Decades of government inefficiency, corruption and low world tin prices proceeded the push for *capitalización* (a variation on privatization), which eventually brought about the dissolution of Comibol in the mid-1980s.

Most of the mines in the area closed down, although they are still worked by local cooperatives. The Morales government is now seeking investment to reopen some of the mines, with higher commodities prices on the global market making this a potential reality. It's an important symbolic step too, as Bolivia's mineral wealth has long been linked to feelings of national pride. *Orureños* are also proud that Morales is from their province; he was born in Isallavi, a tiny Aymará village on the western side of Lake Poopó, and went to secondary school in Oruro.

Information

EMERGENCY
Tourist police (☎ 525-1923; Plaza 10 de Febrero) There's another office at the bus station.

IMMIGRATION
Migración (☎ 527-0239; S Galvarro btwn Ayacucho & Cochabamba; ☽ 8:30am-4:30pm Mon-Fri) Extend your stay here (last door on the left).

INTERNET ACCESS
Every second building in Oruro seems to be an internet place. The going rate is US$0.25 to US$0.40 per hour. Many offer cheap international calls too.
Compumundo (6 de Octubre) One of plenty on 6 de Octubre, catering to university students.
Mundo Internet (Bolívar 573) One of the better connections in town.
Telecentro 6 de Octubre (cnr Junín & La Plata)

LAUNDRY
Gran Hotel Sucre (cnr Sucre & 6 de Octubre) Charges US$1.90 per dozen for hand wash and dry service.

MAPS
The best city map is the *Plano Turístico* (US$0.65), sold around town before and after Carnaval (until supplies run out). The rest of the year, the tourist information offices hand out an adequate free map.

MEDICAL SERVICES
Policlínica Oruro (☎ 524-2871; Rodríguez) Near Plaza la Unión, this is Oruro's best hospital.

MONEY
There are several banks with ATMs in town, as well as change kiosks at the bus and train stations, which will change several currencies, including euros at a poorish rate. There are several Western Union offices, including one half a block north of the plaza. Banks listed below change cash and traveler's checks (for 4% to 6% commission).
Banco Bisa (Plaza 10 de Febrero) Cashes Amex traveler's checks into B$ without commission (or 6% commission for US dollars).
Banco Boliviano Americano (cnr Bolívar & S Galvarro)
Banco de Crédito (Plaza 10 de Febrero) ATM issues US dollars or bolivianos.
Banco de Santa Cruz (Bolívar 460)

POST & TELEPHONE
The main post office is just north of Plaza 10 de Febrero. Parcels must first be inspected by the **Aduana Nacional** (Customs; Velasco Galvarro at Junín), located where the city's fort once stood. The modern Entel office is west of the corner of Soña Galvarro and Bolívar. There are numerous other call centers around town, plus there is also a Punto Entel and a last-minute postal kiosk downstairs at the bus station.

TOURIST INFORMATION
The great little booklet *Oruro – Destino Turístico*, by Juan Carlos Vargas, is sometimes sold at the tourist office.
Municipal tourist bureau (☎ 525-0144; Plaza 10 de Febrero) Can be helpful, but not really designed for walk-ins. Inside the Galería Prefectural.
Tourist information office (Caseta de Información Turística; ☎ 525-7881; cnr Bolívar & S Galvarro; ☽ 8am-noon & 2-6pm Mon-Fri) A friendly kiosk located next to Entel; it is also open on weekends for two weeks before Carnaval.

Dangers & Annoyances

Watch your cash stash, especially around the train and bus stations. Readers have reported groups of young men pretending to help buy tickets or transfer luggage to a bus, and then taking off with backpacks. Carnaval is a godsend for competent pickpockets, bag-slashers and con artists.

Sights

MUSEUMS

The **Museo Sacro, Folklórico, Arqueológico y Minero** (☎ 525-0616; Plaza del Folklore s/n; admission both museums US$1.25, camera use US$0.40; ☟ 9am-1pm & 3-6pm, last tour 5:30pm) is an excellent double museum attached to the Santuario de la Virgen del Socavón. You descend from the church itself down to an old mining tunnel, which exhibits various methods and equipment from both the colonial and modern mining eras. There are also two representations of the devilish El Tío, spirit of the underground. The tour then goes upstairs to the other part of the museum, which has a variety of exhibits, from Wankarani-period stone llama heads to Diablada costumes and an interesting cutaway of the hill behind town, showing the numerous mining tunnels. Entry is by guided tour; the guides are knowledgeable and some speak English. Outside the sanctuary is a monument to miners in socialist-heroic style.

At the south end of town adjacent to the zoo, the **Museo Antropológico Eduardo López Rivas** (☎ 527-4020; España s/n; admission US$0.40; ☟ 8am-noon & 2-6pm) is a fascinating anthropological and archaeological museum that is well worth a visit. Like many such museums, there's something of a hodgepodge of exhibits, from mastodons to Carnaval costumes. There are several excellent stonecarved llama heads; other finds from a multitude of sites include various mummies from the *chullpares* (funerary towers) that dot the region, as well as skulls exhibiting the horrific cranial deformations once practiced on children. Take any *micro* (minibus) marked 'Sud' from the northwest corner of Plaza 10 de Febrero or opposite the train station, and get off just beyond the old tin-foundry compound.

A university-administered cultural complex, the **Museo Patiño** (☎ 525-4015; S Galvarro 5755; admission US$1; ☟ 9am-noon & 3-6pm Mon-Fri) is a former residence of tin baron Simón Patiño. Exhibits include his furniture, personal effects, fine toys and an ornate Art Nouveau stairway. Visiting exhibitions are featured in the downstairs

lobby. Entry is by guided tour only; they leave on the hour (last morning tour 11am, last evening tour 5pm).

On the university campus south of town, the **Museo Mineralógico** (☎ 526-1250; Ciudad Universitaria; admission US$1; ☟ 8am-noon & 2-7pm Mon-Fri, 8am-noon Sat) houses a remarkable collection of more than 5000 minerals, precious stones, fossils and crystals from around the world. Hop on minibus 102 or any *micro* marked 'Sud' or 'Ciudad Universitaria' from opposite the train station or Plaza 10 de Febrero.

CHURCHES

Just east of the main plaza, the **cathedral** has fine stained-glass above the altar. The adjacent tower was constructed by the Jesuits as part of a church before Oruro was founded. When the Jesuits were expelled, it was designated as the cathedral of the Oruro bishopric. In 1994, the original baroque entrance was moved and reconstructed at the **Santuario de la Virgen del Socavón** (Virgin of the Grotto), which presents a grand city view. It was here that 16th-century miners began worshipping the Virgen de Candelaria, the patron of Oruro miners. The present church, which is a 19th-century reconstruction of the 1781 original, figures prominently in Oruro's Carnaval as the site where good ultimately defeats evil (see the boxed text opposite).

Capilla de Serrato, a steep climb from the end of Calle Washington, also offers impressive city views. A couple of blocks southeast of the main plaza, it's worth checking out the **Portada del Beaterio**, the facade of a convent church carved with ornate vegetal and bird motifs.

FARO DE CONCHUPATA

On November 17, 1851 Bolivia's red, gold and green flag was first raised at **Faro de Conchupata**: red for the courage of the Bolivian army, gold for the country's mineral wealth and green for its agricultural wealth. The spot is now marked by a platform and column topped by an enormous glass globe, illuminated at night. It provides a fine vista over the town.

MINES

There are numerous mines in the Oruro area, most of which are abandoned or operated by *cooperativos* (small groups of miners who purchase temporary rights). One of the most important is **Mina San José**, which has operated for over 450 years. You can hike around the

A DEVIL OF A GOOD TIME

Oruro's **Carnaval** has become Bolivia's most renowned and largest annual celebration. It's a great time to visit, when this somewhat unfashionable mining city becomes the focus of the nation's attention. In a broad sense, these festivities can be described as re-enactments of the triumph of good over evil, but the festival is so interlaced with threads of both Christian and indigenous myths, fables, deities and traditions that it would be inaccurate to oversimplify it in this way.

The origins of a similar festival may be traced back to the medieval kingdom of Aragón, these days part of Spain, although *orureños* (Oruro locals) maintain that it commemorates an event that occurred during the early days of their own fair city. Legend has it that one night a thief called Chiruchiru was seriously wounded by a traveler he'd attempted to rob. Taking pity on the wrongdoer, the Virgin of Candelaria gently helped him reach his home near the mine at the base of Cerro Pié del Gallo and succored him until he died. When the miners found him there, an image of the Virgin hung over his head. Today, the mine is known as the Socavón de la Virgen (Grotto of the Virgin), and a large church, the Santuario de la Virgen del Socavón (see opposite), has been built over it to house the Virgin. The Virgen del Socavón, as she is also now known, is the city's patron. This legend has been combined with the ancient Uru tale of Huari and the struggle of Archangel Michael (San Miguel) against the seven deadly sins into the spectacle that is presented during the Oruro Carnaval.

Ceremonies begin several weeks before Carnaval itself, with a solemn pledge of loyalty to the Virgin in the sanctuary. From this date on, there are various candlelit processions, and dance groups practice boisterously in the city's streets.

As well as traditional Bolivian dance groups, such as the Caporales, Llameradas, Morenadas and Tinkus, Oruro's Carnaval features **La Diablada** (Dance of the Devils). These demonic dancers are dressed in extravagant garb. The design and creation of Diablada costumes has become an art form in Oruro, and several Diablada clubs – consisting of members from all levels of Oruro society – are sponsored by local businesses. There are anywhere from 40 to 300 dancing participants, whose costumes may cost several hundred dollars each.

The main event kicks off on the Saturday before Ash Wednesday with the spectacular *entrada* (entrance procession) led by the brightly costumed San Miguel character. Behind him, dancing and marching, come the famous devils and a host of bears and condors. The chief devil Lucifer wears the most extravagant costume, complete with a velvet cape and an ornate mask. Faithfully at his side are two other devils, including Supay, an Andean god of evil that inhabits the hills and mineshafts. The procession is followed by other dance groups, vehicles adorned with jewels, coins and silverware (in commemoration of the *achura* rites in which the Inca offered their treasures to Inti – the sun – in the festival of Inti Raymi), and the miners offer the year's highest-quality mineral to El Tío, the demonic character who is owner of all underground minerals and precious metals. Behind them follow Inca characters and a group of conquistadores, including Francisco Pizarro and Diego de Almagro.

When the archangel and the devils arrive at the soccer stadium, they engage in a series of dances that tell the story of the ultimate battle between good and evil. After it becomes apparent that good has triumphed over evil, the dancers retire to the Santuario de la Virgen del Socavón at dawn on the Sunday, and a mass is held in honor of the Virgin, who pronounces that good has prevailed.

There's another, less spectacular *entrada* on the Sunday afternoon, and more dance displays on the Monday. The next day, Shrove Tuesday, is marked by family reunions and *cha'lla* libations, in which alcohol is sprinkled over worldly goods to invoke a blessing. The next day people make their way into the surrounding countryside where four rock formations – the Toad, the Viper, the Condor and the Lizard, are also subjected to *cha'lla* as an offering to Pachamama. Plenty of the spirit is sprinkled down the revelers' throats as well.

Thursday is a big party day, with fairground rides and general merriment, and the Saturday sees a final performance of the dance groups in the stadium. On Sunday, the 'burial' of Carnaval is celebrated with a children's procession.

colorful tailing heaps; if you want to enter the mine, ask one of the miners or contact Oruro Tours (below). To get there take a yellow *micro* (marked 'San José') from the northwest corner of Plaza 10 de Febrero.

The US$12 million **Complejo Metalúrgico Vinto** (☎ 527-8078, 527-8091; admission free; ☑ 9am-noon Mon-Fri) tin smelter was constructed in the early 1970s during the presidency of General Hugo Banzer Suárez. By the time it was put into operation, the Bolivian tin industry was already experiencing a steady decline, but it still processes up to 20,000 tons of ore annually. Vinto is 8km east of Oruro. It's wise to phone in advance for permission to tour the operation. To get here, take *micros* marked 'Vinto ENAF' from the northwest corner of Plaza 10 de Febrero or Calle Bolívar.

Activities

Rumi Campana (Bell Rock), named after an unusual acoustic phenomenon, is a climber's playground just 2km northwest of town. On weekends you can practice your skills with the friendly local climbing club, **Club de Montañismo Halcones** (cmh_oruro@yahoo.com). There's a range of routes with protection already in place. Try your hand at the challenging overhanging route Mujer Amante, or the wonderful 7-rated route known as Sueño.

Tours

There's a wealth of things to explore in the wild reaches of Oruro department. Tour operators can arrange custom excursions or simpler trips to nearby sites such as Calacala (p178) or the Obrajes hot springs (p177).

Oruro Tours (☎ 524-2274; orurotours@hotmail.com; Pagador 659) is a decent set-up that runs tailored trips in comfortable 4WDs; if it's closed, ring the top bell. A day's excursion should cost US$15 to US$25 per person depending on the itinerary.

Sleeping

Accommodations are often booked solid during Carnaval, so make your reservation (usually three days minimum) early or ask the tourist office about rooms in local homes. Expect to pay up to five or six times the normal price for a room.

There are good lodging options by the bus station, and less appealing ones by the train station, but by far the most interesting place to be is in the centre.

BUDGET

Alojamiento Copacabana (☎ 525-4184; V Galvarro 6352; r per person US$2, with bathroom US$2.50) There's a row of budget *alojamientos* (basic accommodations) opposite the train station on Velasco Galvarro. Most are pretty dire, but this is a significant step above. It's bright, clean, secure and used to dealing with traveling types.

Pub the Alpaca (☎ 527-5715; wcamargo_gallegos@hotmail.com; La Paz 690; r per person US$3.75) Marked only by a wooden alpaca sign by the door, this is one of the best budget options in town. There are three simple but sunny and spacious rooms and a shared kitchen. Plus, you've got the city's best pub in your front room (p176)! Ring ahead.

Hotel Bernal (☎ 527-9468; Brasil 701; s/d US$3.75/5.65, with bathroom US$7.50/11.30) Opposite the bus terminal, this is a good-value and friendly place, and has appealing rooms (with or without bathroom) with back-friendly beds. Try to avoid the front rooms; the noise is a bronze-medal annoyance after the smell of diesel and the cold. There are decent hot showers and cable TV.

Residencial San Miguel (☎ 527-2132; Sucre 331; s/d US$3.75/7.50, with bathroom US$5/10) This is handy for both the train station and the centre. Run by friendly folk, it's a curious place that you can almost get lost in, with warmish rooms scattered around. It's quiet and has hot water – if you don't shower before 10am.

Residencial Boston (☎ 527-4708; Pagador 1159; s/d US$4.40/6.25, with bathroom US$6.25/8.75) A class above most Oruro *residenciales*, this welcoming place is built around a courtyard and cheerfully tiled in blue and yellow. The rooms are darkish but stylish and comfortable, with particularly comfortable beds.

MIDRANGE

Hotel Repostero (☎ 525-8001; Sucre 370; s/d US$10/15) Although probably not the best value in town, there's something likeable about this faded old place run by solicitous people. There's a variety of rooms, most with somewhat concave beds and all with hot showers and cable TV; try for one of the renovated ones. There's private parking alongside.

Hostal Hidalgo (☎ 525-7516; 6 de Octubre 1616; s/d US$10/17) This place is very central, with spacious modern rooms that, although some are a little on the dark side, are a reasonable bet. There are cheaper rooms without bathroom available (US$5), although these are scheduled for conversion.

Hotel Samay Wasi (☎ 527-6737; samay wasioruro@ hotmail.com; Brasil 232; s/d US$18.75/26.25; ☐) This European-style hotel is right by the bus station and is an attractive option. The rooms have tiled floors, firm beds and decent bathrooms, as well as cable TV. There's also a pretty salon where you can watch the nonstop action around the station. The staff is helpful and professional and the hotel is HI-affiliated, so members theoretically get a 15% discount. Parking is available.

Hotel International Park (☎ 527-6227; Bakovic s/n; s/d/ste with breakfast US$20/35/45; ☐) This modern hotel is literally on top of the bus terminal, and entered from it. It's pleasant enough in a loungey sort of style and is comfortable, heated and helpful. There are magnificent views from many of the rooms, and there's a decent restaurant and parking. A sauna has been in the pipeline for years but don't bet on it being ready.

SM Palace (☎ 527-2121; Mier 392; s/d with bathroom & breakfast US$25/30) This central, modernish hotel has pleasant light rooms with TV and, despite its name, is painless. It's friendly and fairly bland.

Gran Hotel Sucre (☎ 527-6320, 527-6800; hotelsucre oruro@hotmail.com; Sucre 510; s/d/ste US$25/35/45; ☐) This noble old lodging is Oruro's most characterful hotel, combining modern conveniences with an appealing sense of past grandeur. The rooms have all been recently renovated, and have decent hot-water bathrooms and comfortable-enough beds. The suites are excellent; one has an internet terminal. The ballroom restaurant, Pukara, decorated with Carnaval murals and a fountain, serves an abundant buffet breakfast as well as good lunches and dinners. There's private parking available.

TOP END

Look out for the Edén Hotel, a spectacular modern hotel being built on the plaza. It is scheduled to open in mid-2007, but don't put the smallest fraction of a boliviano on it being ready on time.

Eating

As ever, the markets are an interesting eating option; Mercado Campero and Mercado Fermín López have rows of lunch spots as well as drinks stalls serving *mate* (a herbal infusion of coca, chamomile or similar) and coffee. Local specialties include *thimpu de cordero* (a mutton and vegetable concoction smothered with *llajhua*, a hot tomato-based sauce) and *charquekan* (sun-dried llama meat with corn, potatoes, eggs and cheese). On hot days, locals flock to the row of excellent fruit juice stalls on Av Velasco Galvarro opposite the Mercado Campero.

The cheapest set-lunch specials are around the train station and Mercado Campero. Recommended is **Restaurant Pagador** (Pagador 1440; set lunch US$0.80), deservedly popular with locals. If you want to try *charquekan*, head to one of the eateries around the bus station or, better, to **El Puente** (cnr Teniente Villa & 6 de Octubre), near Plaza Pagador, where US$2 gets you a plate of staggering proportions.

Confitería Dumbo (Junín, near 6 de Octubre; snacks US$0.15-0.50) This is a decent quick stop for cakes, empanadas, *salteñas* (meat and vegetable pasties), hot drinks and *helados* (ice creams).

SUM (cnr Bolívar & S Galvarro; snacks US$0.25-0.75) This upstairs café is opposite the tourist kiosk – you enter through a small *salteñería* (an eatery specializing in *salteñas*). It's a peaceful spot more used to locals than tourists. What's on offer is very limited, but it's friendly.

Jordan's (☎ 525-5268; Bolívar 380; coffee US$0.75; ☙ Mon-Sat; ☐) There's a bit of everything here, with a clothes store at the front, internet terminals upstairs and a wi-fi zone in the café. Best is the café, which serves pricy but excellent coffee and moist, tasty cakes in a stylish modern space.

El Huerto (Bolívar near Pagador; burgers US$0.50, lunch US$1.25; ☙ closed Sat) This tiny spot does snacks and cooked-to-order lunches. It's friendly if a little wacky. Don't be alarmed by the list of 'kills'; we think they mean *mates*!

Mateo's (cnr Bolívar & 6 de Octubre; meals US$0.50-2) This traditional café-restaurant on a busy corner in the heart of town has a range of adequate snacks, light meals, decent coffee and cold beer.

Govinda (6 de Octubre 6089; mains US$1-2) Forget you're in Bolivia for a meal or two at this Hare Krishna-devoted restaurant where vegetarian meals are fresh, cheap and creative.

La Casona (Montes 5969; salteñas US$0.25-0.40, pizzas from US$3) This great little spot has a friendly buzz. Hot-out-of-the-oven *salteñas* by day, quick sandwiches for lunch and pizza by night keep this place busy.

Paprika (Junín 821; set lunch US$1.25) This smart upstairs restaurant is popular with local business workers for their lunch. It's a light, comparatively formal place by Oruro standards, and the service and food are of good quality.

Las Brasas (6 de Agosto 1050; mains US$2-3) Another decent grilled-meat restaurant is this down-to-earth place, where tasty *churrasco* (steak) is grilled on the street to the envy of passers-by.

Las Delicias (☎ 527-7256; 6 de Agosto 1278; set meals US$1, mains US$2-4) There are several popular grilled-meat restaurants on this long street. This is perhaps the best, with attentive service and sizzling tableside *parrilladas* (plates of mixed grilled meats). *Almuerzos* (set lunches) are served outside on the covered patio.

La Cabaña (Junín 609; mains US$2.50-3.50) This attractive bamboo-clad restaurant is an attentive, amiable place that serves Oruro's best steaks; they are all delicious. Go for the half portions unless you are seriously hungry. There are also omelettes, and pasta and fish dishes.

Bravo's Pizza (Bolívar near Potosí; small/large pizzas US$2/4.50) A cozy hideaway – when the big screen isn't on the Latin music channel – with something for everyone, this place does decent breakfasts (US$2), good coffee and very tasty chunky pizzas. It's child friendly (there's even a playroom) and popular with both visitors and locals.

Nayjama (☎ 527-7699; Aldana at Pagador; mains US$3-5.50) This appealing upstairs choice is run by well-traveled chef Roberto, who presides over a kitchen that turns out high-quality food in huge portions. It's Oruro traditional cooking with a dash of innovation and a very high standard. There's a cracking vegetarian plate (ask for more veggie choices), but the restaurant's specialty is *colita,* the exquisitely tender and tasty back end of a lamb. You can also snack on the other end of the animal here – *cabeza* (the sheep's head) is a traditional Oruro plate served with salad and dehydrated potatoes.

Drinking & Entertainment

Pub the Alpaca (☎ 527-5715; La Paz 690) A surprising and worthwhile option, this Finnish- and Bolivian-run pub is an attractive, white intimate spot set up in a front room. There are more-than-decent mixed drinks and there's a good-mood feel. If the door is locked, just knock or ring the bell; the bar normally opens at 8:30pm but don't plan your evening around it, as opening is at the whim of the owners.

Alexander's Café Pub (☎ 525-0693; 6 de Octubre, near Montecinos) This is a favorite with romancing Bolivians; moody and low-lit, it does beer, coffee and a range of decent mixed drinks until late.

Crissol (☎ 525-3449; Plaza 10 de Febrero) This car-themed popular spot has a pool table, full restaurant, decent bar, live music and dancing after hours on weekends.

Cinema (Plaza 10 de Febrero) Housed in an opulent baroque-style colonial-era concert hall, this no-name cinema screens first-run films nightly for US$1.

For karaoke, **Discoteque VIP's** (Junín at 6 de Octubre) and **Karaoke 1-2-3** (Potosí at Junín) are tough to beat.

Shopping

The design, creation and production of artistic Diablada masks and costumes is Oruro's main cottage industry. Av La Paz, between León and Villarroel, is lined with small workshops offering devil masks, headdresses, costumes and other devilish things from US$2 to more than US$200.

ARAO Artesanías Oruro (☎ 525-0331; arao@coteor .net.bo; cnr S Galvarro & Mier) This place offers the best selection of high-quality, cooperatively produced handicrafts from Oruro department and beyond. The naturally dyed wool rugs and wall hangings and Challapata shoulder bags are especially notable.

Llama and alpaca wool bags and clothing are sold at *artesanías* (stores selling locally handcrafted items) in the center and at the bus terminal, while the cheapest articles are found around the northeast corner of Mercado Campero. Hawkers sell cheap *zampoñas* (pan flutes made of hollow reeds), *charangos* and other indigenous musical instruments near the train station.

Tucked away in the middle row of the Mercado Fermín López is the impressive Mercado Tradicional, which has more dried llama fetuses and flamingo wings than a voodoo master has pins. The affable vendors are more than happy to explain the usage of their wares.

Cafe Extrapuro El Chapaco (Potosí near Bolívar) sells Yungas beans – to taste them brewed, visit Mateo's (p175). **Vaquita Andina** (☎ 528-2233; 6 de Agosto) sells tasty traditional local cheeses.

Getting There & Away

BUS

All long-distance buses use the **bus terminal** (☎ 527-9535; terminal fee US$0.20), a 15-minute walk or short cab ride northeast of the center. There's a *cambio* (money-changing office), luggage storage and an office of the tourist police, who can sometimes provide maps and other information.

Numerous companies run buses to La Paz (US$1.25 to US$3, three hours) every half-hour or so. There are also several daily buses to Cochabamba (US$2.50, four hours), Potosí (normal/*bus cama,* sleeper, US$3.75/8.20, eight hours) and Sucre (US$5.75/12, 10 hours). Several nighttime services depart daily for Uyuni (US$3.20, eight hours) along a rough, cold route that is often impassable after rains. For Santa Cruz (US$12, 18 to 20 hours) you must make a connection in Cochabamba.

There are at least five daily services to Arica, Chile (US$10 to US$12, eight to 10 hours), via Tambo Quemado and Chungará (Parque Nacional Lauca). These continue to Iquique, but there are also several (quicker but less comfortable) services (US$10 to US$14, 12 to 14 hours) via the Pisiga border crossing.

TRAIN

Thanks to its mines, Oruro has one of Bolivia's most organized train stations, but only has southbound services to Uyuni and beyond. Since 1996, the railway has been run by the Chilean **Empresa Ferroviaria Andina** (FCA; www.fca.com.bo). They run a relatively tight ship timetable-wise, but were a possible candidate for nationalization at the time of research, so check timetable information closely. Buy tickets from the **station** (☎ 527-4605; ☼ 8:15-11:30am & 2:30-6pm Mon & Thu, 8:15am-6pm Tue & Fri, 8:15am-noon & 2:30-7pm Wed, 8:15-11am & 3-7pm Sun); bring your passport, and try to buy them a day ahead. There's baggage storage here.

The principal service runs south to Uyuni and on to Tupiza and Villazón on the Argentine border. It's the most popular way of reaching Uyuni, as it avoids the cold, bumpy journey on the night bus. From Uyuni, there are slow rail services to Chile (see p189).

The *Expreso del Sur* offers reclining seats, heaters, videos, a dining car and a choice of *popular, salón* and *ejecutivo* classes. It departs Oruro at 3:30pm Tuesday and Friday to Uyuni (*popular/salón/ejecutivo* US$4.15/6.50/12.60,

seven hours), Tupiza (US$7.25/11.50/25.25, 12½ hours) and Villazón (US$9/13.60/29.50, 16½ hours). It returns from Villazón at 3:30pm Wednesday and Saturday. A connecting bus service from La Paz leaves El Alto at 10am to meet this train.

The *Wara Wara del Sur* runs Wednesday and Sunday at 7pm to Uyuni (*popular/salón/ejecutivo* US$4/5/10.75, 7½ hours), Tupiza (US$6.75/8.60/19, 13½ hours) and Villazón (US$8/10.75/23.10, 17 hours). It returns from Villazón at 3:30pm Monday and Thursday.

Getting Around

Micros (US$0.15) and minibuses (US$0.20) connect the city center with outlying areas. Their routes are designated by their letters, colors and signs (and in the case of minibuses, numbers). It's a fairly confusing system, so check with the driver before boarding. Note that *micros* and minibuses are small and crowded, so if possible, avoid carrying luggage aboard.

Taxis around the center, including to and from the terminals, cost a non-negotiable US$0.40 per person. A **radio taxi** (☎ 527-6222, 527-3399) costs US$0.75.

AROUND ORURO

There's plenty to see around Oruro, particularly along the road south towards Uyuni, where bleak and epic scenery holds old mines and the remnants of ancient lakeside cultures. These areas can be visited by bus from Oruro or on a tour (see p174).

Termas de Obrajes

These **hot springs** (admission US$1.25), 25km northeast of town, are a popular destination. It's a well-run complex, with a pool and, around the edge, private bathrooms, which you reserve for half an hour and gradually fill up with the magnesium-rich water. You can buy (but not rent) towels here; make sure you have a swimming costume to enter the public pool.

There's also **accommodations** (☎ 525-0646, 513-6106; r per person US$10.60, luxury d US$27.50) with a choice of comfortable but unadorned rooms around the grassy courtyard, or smarter rooms in the hotel building itself that come with their own private thermal bath. There's also a slightly disappointing restaurant. On the hill above is an impressive *chullpa.*

From the corner of Caro and Av 6 de Agosto, catch an Obrajes *micro* (US$0.75, 30 minutes) from 7:30am to 5pm daily, which also passes the grungier **Capachos hot springs**, 10km east of town.

Calacala

This atmospheric **site** (admission per person US$2) makes a worthwhile trip from Oruro. It consists of a series of **rock paintings** under an overhang 2.5km beyond the village of Calacala, which is 15km southeast of Oruro: fork left off the main road just before reaching the smelting works of Vinto.

Stop in the village to locate the guard, who has the keys; she can often be found in the small café marked only by a rusted Pepsi sign. The site itself is a 30-minute walk past the village, near the old brewery.

The paintings are mainly of llamas in red and orange tones, but you can also identify humans and a puma. Some of the figures are in white, and others in black. Archaeologists suggest that they date to the first millennium BC, but their meaning remains unclear.

The views from the site are spectacular; the valley is exceptionally beautiful, and provides some of Oruro's water. On the way to Calacala you pass through **Sepulturas**, which has a crumbling but picturesque colonial-era church.

On weekends, *micros* run from Oruro to Calacala; at other times, you'll have to take a taxi (US$9 round-trip) or tour.

On September 14, Calacala hosts a pilgrimage and fiesta in honor of Señor de la Laguna (Lord of the Lake).

South of Oruro

The picturesque asphalted main road heads south from Oruro towards Uyuni, and roughly follows the eastern shores of Lago Uru Uru and the even larger Lago Poopó. The lakes are shallow and much smaller than they once were; you can see fishing piers and boat ramps from the main road in places where the lakeshore is 10 or more kilometers away.

The road (in excellent condition) passes numerous abandoned mining operations and spectacular bare hills, on many of which you can still see remains of Inca-period terraces.

PAZÑA & CHALLAPATA

At **Pazña**, 80km south of Oruro, there are some hot springs (look for the green building on your left as you enter the village). A further 38km brings you to **Challapata**, the largest town on this stretch. It was once an important center for lime extraction; now, smuggling cars from Chile is what keeps people in the money.

Challapata's fiesta is in mid-July, and celebrates the feast day of the Virgen del Carmen.

A good place to stay and eat is **Restaurant Potosí** (☎ 557-2359; Beneméritos de la Patria & Alto de Alianza; r per person US$2.50). The rather grand dining room is a reminder of wealthier days, and serves up local specialties as well as more elaborate dishes. There's also simple but decent accommodations.

There are six daily buses from Oruro bus station to Challapata (US$0.80), and many more *micros*. Southbound trains also make a brief stop.

HUARI & BEYOND

Thirteen kilometers beyond Challapata is **Huari**, a small town with a big brewery that keeps the whole province in Huari beer. There's a small but lovable **museum** (US$1; ☾ 9am-4pm Mon-Fri) behind the *alcaldía* (town hall) on the main square; it details the local Uru-Llapallapari culture. There's also a posh tourist office in the square but it's rarely open.

There are many ruined *chullpares* along the road between Challapata and Huari, and

---

CHULLPA TOMBS

A *chullpa* is a funerary tower or mausoleum that various Aymará groups built to house the mummified remains of some members of their society, presumably people of high rank or esteem within the community. Oruro province is particularly rich in *chullpares*, especially along the shores of Lago Poopó and around the Sajama area. A *chullpa* was constructed of stone or adobe, and typically had a beehive-shaped opening, which nearly always faced east towards the rising sun. The body (in some cases, bodies) was placed in the fetal position along with various possessions. Some communities would ritually open the *chullpares* on feast days and make offerings to the mummified ancestors; the Chipaya (see boxed text p193) still do. Most of the tombs, however, have been looted, and the mummies can now be found in museums, such as the Museo Antropológico Eduardo López Rivas in Oruro (p172).

a particularly good one 7km beyond Huari on the Uyuni road; you'll see it on the left.

Thirty kilometers beyond Huari (where the asphalted road stops), the road divides at Cruce. The main road heads south to Uyuni, 150km beyond. Heading west, you eventually reach the Salar de Coipasa (p194) or Chipaya (p193).

Twenty-four kilometers west of Cruce, the village of **Santuario de Quillacas** nestles between rocky hills and subsists on cultivating quinoa and herding llamas. It has a beautiful and unusual church, the Santuario, and a small museum. You can stay at the **Albergue Quillacas** (☎ 513-4701; Plaza Avaroa; r per person US$3), which has decent beds with colorful blankets, and a restaurant. Ring ahead as it only opens when booked.

A further 14km northwest of Quillacas (take the Orinoca/Andamarca road) is tiny **Pampa Aullagas**. Here, some pre-Inca fortifications and canals have led one potty theorist to name it the historical location of the kingdom of Atlantis. Check out www.geocities.com/ webatlantis for more info.

There are six daily buses from Oruro bus station to Huari (US$1.50, two hours). For Santuario de Quillacas (US$2, 3½ hours), minibuses leave from the corner of Caro and Tejerina in Oruro (destination Salinas). There's no public transportation from Quillacas on to Pampa Aullagas, but you may be able to hitch on a truck.

PARQUE NACIONAL SAJAMA

Bolivia's first national park occupies 80,000 hectares abutting the Chilean border. It was created on November 5, 1945 for the protection of the rare wildlife that inhabits this northern extension of the Atacama Desert. Unfortunately, depredation has already eliminated several species, and only limited numbers of vicuña, condor, flamingo, rhea and armadillo survive.

The world's highest forest covers the foothills flanking the hulking **Volcán Sajama** (Nevado Sajama volcano), which at 6542m is Bolivia's highest peak. The forest consists of dwarf *queñua* trees, an endemic Altiplano species, but while technically a forest, it's a little underwhelming – the 'trees' have the size and appearance of creosote bushes!

Orientation & Information

The best map of the park is the glossy 1:50,000 *Nevado Sajama* published by Walter Guzmán Córdova; it can be found in better La Paz bookstores.

Admission (US$1.90) is payable at the Sernap headquarters in Sajama village (4200m), one of two main settlements in the park – the other is Tomarapi. The fee applies to all foreigners, including those just visiting the village. Sernap will help climbing expeditions organize mules and porters to carry equipment to the base camp. Señor Telmo Nina, in Sajama village, keeps a log of routes up the mountain. If you're planning to climb it, consider reading Yossi Brain's *Bolivia – A Climbing Guide* (Mountaineers, 1999), which describes several routes.

Sajama itself is a sleepy place with a couple of *alojamientos* and some nice walks in the surrounding area. Further on, Tomarapi has an enticing new ecolodge for more comfortable accommodations (see p181).

Volcán Sajama

This volcano is unquestionably the centerpiece of all it surveys, a majestic snow-capped peak that's an awe-inspiring sight. It's a popular mountain to climb, and also offers challenging hiking on its lower slopes.

Although it's a relatively straightforward climb, Sajama's altitude and ice conditions make the peak more challenging than it initially appears. Most of the glaciers are receding, turning much of the route into a sloppy and crevasse-ridden mess. Quite a few La Paz agencies offer organized climbs of Sajama; see p389 for a list of recommended tour agencies. Only consider going without a guide if you have experience of high-altitude climbing.

In 2001, the summit joined the record books as the pitch for the highest ever game of soccer; check out www.geocities.com/zubie taippa/sajamasoccer.html for details of this crazy but mightily impressive endeavor!

The easiest access to the mountain is from the village of Sajama, 18km north of the Arica–La Paz highway. From here, it's about a three-hour walk to the base camp at Río Aychuta. From there a six-hour ascent will get you to a reasonably sheltered camp site at 5700m from where you can assault the summit. Prepare for extremely cold and windy conditions. Carry lots of water, though once on the snow cap, there will be plenty in the form of ice and snow.

Hot Springs & Geysers

For a relaxing warm soak, there are some lovely 95°F hot springs 7km north of Sajama village. The springs are relatively easy to find;

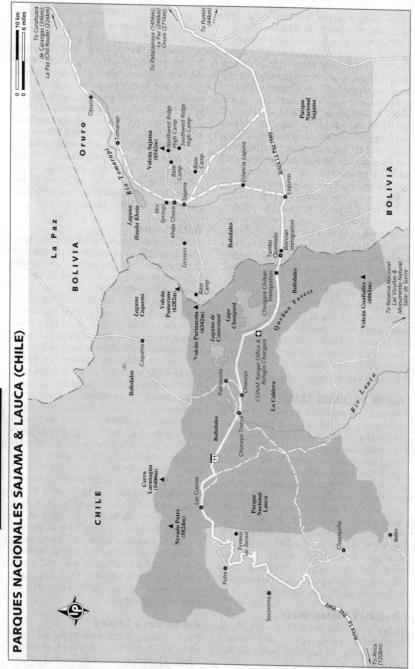

PARQUES NACIONALES SAJAMA & LAUCA (CHILE)

locals can point you in the right direction. About 1½ hours on foot due west of Sajama is an interesting spouting geyser field.

Sleeping & Eating

Camping is fine just about anywhere in this sparsely populated region, so a tent and a good cold-weather sleeping bag are recommended. Otherwise, contact the **Junta de Vecinos** (☎ via Entel office 513-5525; Cruz s/n, Sajama) about homestays with local families (per person US$1.25), which are organized on a rotation basis between 14 homes; most are very modest, so you'll still need a sleeping bag and many layers of clothing for the typically cold, windy nights.

Albergue Ecoturístico Tomarapi (☎ in La Paz 2-241-4753; ecotomarapi@hotmail.com; s/d US$25/50) In Tomarapi, on the northern border of the park, and 12km beyond Sajama, this community-run ecolodge has won many plaudits, having been cited as an ideal model for community involvement in tourism projects. Occupying a lovely thatched building, it boasts simple, comfortable rooms with private baths and hot water, a very welcome log fire and excellent food. The employees, who work on a rotational basis, are from the village and are very welcoming. The rates include breakfast and an abundant dinner; cut lunches can be arranged.

Getting There & Away

All La Paz–Arica buses pass through Sajama National Park, but you'll most likely be expected to pay the entire fare. Get off at Tambo Quemado, from where it's easy to find onward transportation to Sajama village.

Once you've come this far, a visit to Chile's Parque Nacional Lauca (p182) is highly recommended. For onward travel to La Paz or into Chile, go to the paved road

---

ANDEAN CAMELIDS

Unlike the Old World, the western hemisphere had few grazing mammals after the Pleistocene era, when mammoths, horses and other large herbivores disappeared from North and South America. For millennia, the Andean people relied on the New World camelids – the wild guanaco and vicuña and the domesticated llama and alpaca – for food and fiber.

Guanaco (*Lama guanicoe*) and vicuña (*Vicugna vicugna*) are relatively rare today but are the likely ancestors of the domesticated llama (*L. glama*) and alpaca (*L. pacos*). In fact they were among few potential New World domestic animals – contrast them with the Old World cattle, horses, sheep, goats, donkeys and pigs that have filled so many vacant niches in the Americas. While the New World camels have lost ground to sheep and cattle in some areas, they are not likely to disappear.

The rust-colored guanaco ranges from sea level up to 4000m or higher. There's only a small population in Bolivia; the animals can be seen in the highland plains of the Reserva Nacional de Fauna Andina Eduardo Avaroa (p191).

The vicuña occupies a much smaller zone, well above 4000m in the highlands from southern Peru to northwestern Argentina. Although not as numerous as the guanaco, it played a critical role in the cultural life of pre-Columbian Peru. Its very fine golden wool was the exclusive property of the Inca emperors.

Strict Inca authority protected the vicuña, but the Spanish invasion destroyed that authority. By the middle of last century, poaching reduced vicuña numbers from two million to perhaps 10,000 and caused it to become endangered. Conservation efforts in Chile's Parque Nacional Lauca and Bolivia's Parque Nacional Apolobamba have been so successful that economic exploitation of the species is now being allowed in some communities.

The Altiplano's indigenous communities still depend on llamas and alpacas for their livelihood. The two species appear very similar but they differ in several important respects. The taller, rangier and hardier llama has relatively coarse wool that is used for blankets, ropes and other household goods. It also works as a pack animal, but thanks to the introduction of the *camión*, llama trains are increasingly rare in Bolivia.

Llamas can survive and even flourish on relatively poor, dry pastures, whereas the smaller, more delicate alpacas require well-watered grasslands to produce their much finer wool, which has a higher commercial value than that of llamas. Both llama and alpaca meat are consumed by Andean households and are sold in urban markets all over Bolivia.

(Arica–La Paz Hwy) and flag down a bus or *camión* (flat-bed truck); most of the traffic passes after midday. Be aware that the buses are often full; you may need patience or powers of persuasion to get onboard. The border crossing between Tambo Quemado (Bolivia) and Chungará (Chile) is straightforward.

AROUND PARQUE NACIONAL SAJAMA

Curahuara de Carangas, at the foot of the Jank'l Khollo (Beautiful Little Heaven) mountains, was the site of the final battle between indigenous Paka Jakhes (Eagle Men) and conquering forces of Tupac Inca Yupanqui. After a diligent fight, the defenders were eventually defeated at the terraced hill fortress of **Pukara Monterani** (where several warriors are buried), and the Inca leader declared his victory by thrusting a golden rod into the summit of the hill. The Quechua for 'golden rod' is *kori wara*, hence the Hispanicized name, Curahuara. You can climb up to the fortress, where there's ongoing archaeological investigation. It preserves sections of its walls and several *chullpares* are also in the vicinity.

The village's lovely adobe-and-thatch **church** has rather hopefully been dubbed 'the Sistine chapel of the Altiplano.' While that's rather overblown, the charming little structure does contain a wealth of lovely naive 16th-century frescoes depicting typical mestizo-style themes and Biblical scenes. Along the route eastward toward Totora lies the **Yaraque archaeological site**, with several stone ruins, numerous rock paintings and an Inca-era *chullpa* constructed in fine stonework comparable to that of Cuzco. The site is open and free to visit.

The signposted turnoff is 100km west of Patacamaya, accessible on any bus between Oruro and Arica, Chile. Get off at the turnoff and walk 5km south to the village, which has a small **alojamiento** (per person US$1.25) and eateries. The area also offers some fabulous rock-climbing. Many tours to Parque Nacional Sajama from La Paz include a visit to Curahuara. There is also direct transportation from Patacamaya to Curahuara (US$1).

A remote but fascinating spot to visit is the **Ciudad Pétrea de Pumiri**, a bizarre complex of stone caves and eroded rock formations 185km west of Oruro. It's named the 'Stone City' because it resembles a prehistoric village. It's 20km west of the village of Turco, near the Thica Utha Cameloid Research Station, and about 80km southeast of Sajama. Getting here is quite an adventure. There are *camiones* and buses that head to Turco from Oruro; some go on to the *cruce* (turnoff) for Pumiri, about 4km from the site. You should be able to arrange basic accommodations in **private homes** ($1.25 per person) in Turco, which also has a simple restaurant.

PARQUE NACIONAL LAUCA (CHILE)

Across the frontier from Sajama is Chile's poodle-shaped Parque Nacional Lauca – 138,000 hectares of marvelously intact Andean ecosystems bisected by the La Paz–Arica highway. It was declared a national park in 1970 to protect its profusion of wildlife: flamingos, coots, Andean gulls, Andean geese, condors, vicuñas, guanacos, llamas, alpacas, rheas, viscachas, Andean foxes, armadillos, Andean deer and even pumas, as well as unusual vegetation such as the bizarre shaggy-barked *queñua* trees and the rock-hard moss known as *llareta*. Adjacent to the park, but more difficult to access, are Reserva Nacional Las Vicuñas and Monumento Natural Salar de Surire. See www.conaf.cl for details (in Spanish); Lonely Planet's *Chile & Easter Island* book also has more information.

Lago Chungará

Near the Bolivian border beneath the spectacular volcanoes Pomerane and Parinacota, both over 6000m, is the lovely alpine Lago Chungará. At 4517m, it's one of the world's highest bodies of water and was formed when a lava flow dammed a snowmelt stream. Visitors may walk at will, but will have to reckon with the high altitude and swampy ground, as well as frequently fierce climatic conditions. Nevertheless, it's a hauntingly beautiful place, particularly in the late afternoon as the angled sun lights up the landscape with vibrant lucidity.

Parinacota

This lovely pre-Columbian stone village (4400m) sits along the old silver route from Potosí to the coast. In the background stretches the Laguna de Cotacotani and its surrounding *bofedales* (shallow marshes dotted with tussocks of vegetation). Conaf operates a **visitors center** (⊙ 9am-12:30pm & 1-5:30pm) here, which has an exhibition, nature trails and also functions as a high-altitude genetic research station.

The imposing whitewashed stone **church** was originally built in the 1600s but was reconstructed in 1789. Inside, surreal 17th-century frescoes, the work of artists from

ARICA, CHILE

Arica is a pleasant seaside and port city, the northernmost in Chile, and a useful point of access from Bolivia for both Chile and Peru, which is just 20km away.

In the center, there's plenty of budget accommodations on and around Av 21 de Mayo, the partly pedestrianized central street, and the parallel Calle Sotomayor, two streets north. **Hotel Savona** (☎ 058-231-000; www.hotelsavona.cl; Yungay 380; s/d US$50/60; ⚏ ⚐) is the nicest central hotel, with huge comfortable beds and wi-fi. Just down the road from here, friendly **Terra Amata** (☎ 058-259-057; Yungay 201; mains US$7-14; ⏱ 11:30am-3:30pm & 7pm-1am Mon-Sat) is a new, beautiful restaurant with a Moorish feel to the décor, a Mediterranean feel to the classy cuisine and a great wine list.

Most buses arrive at the terminal, which is a kilometer northeast of the centre. From here, companies run morning services to La Paz (US$13, nine hours); you can change at Patacamaya for southbound buses to Oruro. There are also regular services to points further south in Chile. Next door is the terminal for minibuses heading to Tacna in Peru (US$3.50, one hour). In the center there's a train station that also has services to Tacna (US$1.50). A taxi around the center should cost US$1.50 to US$2.50; it's US$8 to US$10 to the airport, 18km north.

the Cuzco school, recall Hieronymus Bosch's *The Last Judgment*. To gain entrance ask the caretaker for the key, and leave a small donation to the church.

Tours

Several Arica tour operators, including **Turismo Lauca** (☎ 058-252-322; turismolauca@gmail.com; Thompson 200) run long single-day trips to Lauca from US$30 per person, but owing to the rapid elevation gain, participants are highly subject to altitude sickness. A better option can be to head to Putre, acclimatize a little, and take a tour from there. Several companies run tours, such as **Cali Tours** (☎ 8-856-6091; krios_team@hotmail.com; Baquedano 399, Putre). A more in-depth choice is the American-run **Alto Andino Nature Tours** (☎ 9-282-6195; www.birdingaltoandino.com; Baquedano 294, Putre), which offers excellent personalized trips in the national park; advance reservations are required.

Sleeping & Eating

Putre is at 3500m, well below most of the park, so it makes a comfortable base.

Hostal Cali (☎ 8-856-6091; Baquedano 399; per person US$7) This is one of a few cheap options, but has decent rooms with private hot-water bathroom.

Residencial La Paloma (Baquedano s/n; r per person US$8) You'll find hot showers here; it also does good simple meals at its restaurant on parallel Av O'Higgins.

Casa Barbarita (☎ 9-282-6195; www.birdingaltoandino.com; Baquedano 294; d without/with breakfast US$55/60; ⚏) Alto Andino Nature Tours runs this comfort-

able B&B accommodations in a pretty Putre house equipped with kitchen and nature library. You get the house to yourself (which sleeps up to five at a pinch), but it must be reserved in advance. There's a two-night minimum stay.

Hostería Las Vicuñas (☎ 058-224-997; s/d incl meals US$55/80) This large hotel sprawls by the approach to town, and was originally built for mining interests. It has more than a hundred carpeted, well-heated bungalows.

Inside the park, Conaf runs the following: **Refugio Chungará** (beds US$6, camp sites US$8) on Lago Chungará, which has six beds a warm stove, camp sites and picnic tables, and the basic **Refugio Parinacota** (beds US$6, camp sites US$8) at Parinacota village. Pack food and a warm sleeping bag. Families in Parinacota also rent out basic rooms and welcome campers.

Getting There & Away

The entire route from Arica to La Paz (via Tambo Quemado) is paved. Outside Arica it follows the lovely oasis-like Lluta Valley and climbs into the Atacama hills with a prolific belt of candelabra cactus, which grows just 5mm annually and flowers for only 24 hours.

Independent access to Lauca isn't inordinately difficult. From Arica, several companies leave the main bus terminal in the morning and pass Chungará (US$6 to US$8, 3½ hours), in Lauca National Park, en route to La Paz (US$10 to US$17, eight hours). Any of these buses will drop you at the Putre *cruce*, from where it's a half-hour walk to the village.

La Paloma (☎ 058-222-710) runs one daily bus direct to Putre (US$4, 2½ hours), leaving from German Riesco 2071 at 6:30am, and returning to Arica at 1pm. See p177 and La Paz (p94) for buses from Bolivia to Arica.

SOUTHWESTERN BOLIVIA

The southwest of Bolivia is perhaps its most magical corner, a wilderness of harsh hill-scapes, bubbling geysers and psychedelic mineral colors. Although it gets plenty of visitors, in many ways it's still a remote wilderness, with rough dirt roads, scattered settlements centered around mines, and little public transportation.

The main town, Uyuni, is a military outpost with a real frontier feel; at times you expect the harsh temperatures and biting winds to do away with it altogether. It's the launching point for expeditions into the region, from the desolate expanses of the *salares* to the craggy hills of Los Lípez, which rise into the high Andean peaks along the Chilean frontier. Many of these are active volcanoes, and they preside over a surreal landscape of geothermal features and flamingo-filled lakes.

UYUNI

pop 14,000 / elevation 3669m

Seemingly built in defiance of the desert-like landscape, Uyuni stands desolate yet undaunted in Bolivia's southwestern corner. Mention Uyuni to a Bolivian and they will whistle and emphasize '*harto frío*' – extreme cold. Yet despite the icy conditions, which are compounded by the fact that, no matter how you plan it, you always seem to arrive at 2am, Uyuni's got a cheerful buzz about it. Travelers arrive and eagerly plan a trip around the Southwest Circuit; those who return see Uyuni with new eyes, as a sort of paradise filled with much-missed daily comforts.

Although there's not much to see here, and the wind chill can strip your soul bare as you pace the wide streets, Uyuni's isolated position and outlook elicit an affectionate respect from both Bolivians and foreign travelers.

The town was founded in 1889 by Bolivian president Aniceto Arce. It remains an important military base; tourism and mining are the other major sources of employment.

Information

IMMIGRATION

Migración (cnr Sucre & Potosí; ☒ 8:30am-noon & 2-7:30pm Mon-Fri)

INTERNET ACCESS

There are several internet places around the center. One of the more reliable is **Cibernet** (Potosí btwn Bolívar & Arce; per hr US$0.60), opposite the Ranking information center.

LAUNDRY

Most hotels offer some sort of laundry service, costing from US$0.50 to US$1 per kilo. **Lavarap** (Ferroviaria 253) does laundry for US$1 per kilo.

MONEY

At the time of research there was no ATM in Uyuni, but the **Banco de Crédito** (cnr Potosí & Bolívar) was eagerly awaiting the delivery of one. It also gives cash advances on credit cards at the best rate, and changes US dollars. **Prodem** (Plaza Arce; ☒ Mon-Fri & Sat morning) and several similar places also change dollars and give cash advances; for traveler's checks, head to **Manaco** (Potosí near Arce) by the Wiphala pub. Several places on Potosí buy Chilean and Argentine pesos.

TOURIST INFORMATION

Office of Reserva Nacional de Fauna Andina Eduardo Avaroa (REA; ☎ 693-2400; www.bolivia-rea .com; Avaroa 584; ☒ 9am-12:30pm & 2-7pm Mon-Fri) Helpful administrative office for the park of the same name. You can buy your park entry here if going under your own steam.

Ranking Bolivia (☎ 693-2102; rankingbolivia@ hotmail.com; Potosí 9; ☒ 8:30am-8pm) By far the best choice for general or specific info, this mightily impressive set-up collects data from travelers to help you choose a tour that fits your requirements. It is impartial and independent, and has an astonishing amount of information on the region and the country as a whole. It also runs a great bar-café (see p188).

Sights & Activities

In town the **Museo Arqueología y Antropológico de los Andes Meridionales** (Arce at Colón; admission US$0.60; ☒ 8:30am-noon & 2-6pm Tue-Fri, 9am-1pm Sat & Sun) features mummies and long skulls. There are also Spanish descriptions of the practices of mummification and cranial deformation.

Uyuni's only other real tourist attraction is the **Cemeterio de Trenes** (Train Cemetery), a large collection of historic steam locomotives and rail cars, which are decaying in the yards

UYUNI

0 ————— 400 m
0 ————— 0.2 miles

To Expediciones Tayka/
Fremen Tours (100m)

To Salar de Uyuni (30km);
Colchani (30km);
Oruro (314km)

Mercado
Antofagasta

To Pulacayo (22km);
Potosí (219km);
La Paz (by train) (552km)

Plaza
de Armas

Clock
Tower

Plaza
Arce

Workers'
Monument

Street
Market

Train
Station

Monumento a
Los Héroes
del Chaco

Military
Base

To Cementerio
de Trenes (3km);
Ollagüe (147km);
Tupiza (215km);
Villazón (310km)

INFORMATION	
Banco de Crédito............................1	A2
Cibernet..2	B2
Lavarap..3	B2
Manaco.................................(see 33)	
Migración......................................4	C2
Office of Reserva Nacional de Fauna	
Andina Eduardo Avaroa (REA)......5	A2
Prodem...6	B2
Ranking Bolivia.............................7	B2

SIGHTS & ACTIVITIES	
Blue Line Service............................8	B2
Expediciones Empexsa.....................9	B2
Expediciones Lípez........................10	A1
Huaynuma Tours....................(see 9)	
Kantuta Tours.........................(see 9)	
Museo Arqueología y Antropológico de	
los Andes Meridionales................11	B2
Oasis Odyssey..............................12	B2

Reli Tours....................................13	B2
Toñito Tours................................14	B3
Turismo El Desierto................(see 13)	
Uyuni Bike Hire............................15	C2

SLEEPING	
El Cactu......................................16	B2
HI-Salar de Uyuni.........................17	C2
Hostal La Magia de Uyuni...............18	C1
Hostal Marith..............................19	A3
Hotel Avenida..............................20	C2
Hotel Kory Wasy...........................21	B2
Hotel Kutimuy..............................22	A3
Jardines de Uyuni.........................23	D1
Los Girasoles Hotel........................24	C1
Residencial Sucre..........................25	B1
Toñito Hotel................................26	A3

EATING	
Arco Iris......................................27	B2
Café Bar Ranking....................(see 7)	
Kactus..28	B2
La Loco.......................................29	C2
Market Comedor...........................30	A3
Minuteman Revolutionary	
Pizza................................(see 26)	
Place of Colors.............................31	C2
Restaurant 16 de Julio...................32	B2
Salteña Cart...........................(see 1)	

DRINKING	
Wiphala Pub................................33	B2

TRANSPORT	
Bus Offices..................................34	A1
Todo Turismo...............................35	A1

about 3km southwest of the station along Av
Ferroviaria. There have long been plans to turn
the collection into a railway museum, but that
seems a pipe dream and they'll most likely just
keep on rusting. Many tours visit the train
cemetery as a first or last stop on the four-day
salar circuit.

You can hire bikes in Uyuni to explore the
surrounding area, or even the Salar if you are
hardy. Head to **Uyuni Bike Hire** (☎ 693-2731; Ferroviaria btwn Sucre & Camacho; ♡ 8am-7pm).

Tours

While you can visit the Salar de Uyuni and the
attractions of the Southwest Circuit yourself,
the vast majority of people take an organized
tour from either Uyuni or Tupiza (p199).

The most popular tour is the four-day circuit around the Salar de Uyuni, Laguna Colorada, Sol de Mañana, Laguna Verde and points
in between. Expect to pay from US$80 to
US$130 for this trip, going with six people in
the jeep. The main advantages of this trip are
that it takes in many stunning natural sights
and that, because it is so popular, you'll have
little trouble finding companions to make up
the numbers on a tour. The disadvantages are
that it is very much a 'trail' – it's not unusual
to see a couple of dozen Landcruisers parked
up alongside some of the major attractions –
and that the fourth day involves a very long
return trip to Uyuni.

Another option offered by a variety of agencies is to do the first three days of the four-day

SOUTHERN ALTIPLANO

CHOOSING A SOUTHWEST CIRCUIT AGENCY

Uyuni is a far-flung outpost, and tourism is what keeps it viable these days. So it's little wonder that everyone wants a piece of the pie. A mushrooming number of agencies – nearly 80 at last count – offer *salar* (salt pan or salt desert) tours. While this means you have more choice, the flipside is that there are many fairly shonky operators who have neither the best interests of their customers nor the environment at heart.

The agency market in Uyuni is volatile, and it's impossible to recommend operators with confidence. The best option is to get information on arrival in Uyuni. Travelers who've just returned from a tour are an obvious source, and Ranking Bolivia (p184) keeps an impressive database of travelers' opinions of various facets of their trip. A visit to its office before choosing your tour is highly recommended.

The database is a set of statistics rather than a league table. Choose various aspects of the trip that are important to you, and plug them into the system to see what comes out. Think carefully about what your priorities are – is an English-speaking guide, for example, crucial given that the guide spends most of the time driving, and much of what there is to see is self-explanatory?

Especially significant is the condition of the vehicle. The *salar* is super-tough on cars, so maintenance is crucial. That said, even the most reliable companies have frequent breakdowns; how they deal with them (and you) is the crux of the matter.

Of course, an important criterion for many travelers is price. But, while it's often possible to negotiate a cheaper rate, you're often only cutting off your own options. Due to the competition, the agencies make a very small profit on these tours. So if you manage to chop US$20 off the price, think about where it'll be made up – a seventh person squeezed in next to you perhaps, part of the circuit skipped, or much simpler, smaller meals. Think carefully about whether you want to wreck a once-in-a-lifetime experience for the sake of a few dollars. The cheapest operators also tend to be those with least knowledge of, and respect for, the unique environment of the southwest.

The best operators have written itineraries outlining meals, accommodations and other trip details. Get any verbally agreed changes written down, as it's a common complaint that agencies don't adhere to promised 'extras.'

Trips are cheaper if you form a group of four to six. While agencies will do this for you, in practice it works better if you can do it yourself. This avoids the problem of one company sending you off as a filler for another company's tour (it's common to book with one company but end up going with another), and means that you can really plan your own custom itinerary around the region, rather than just going with the standard trip. This is highly recommended, as there are many places of interest around the *salar* that are not on the standard trip, and many interesting choices emerging with regard to accommodations. Another benefit is that you avoid the underwhelming experience of seeing one of the world's great wildernesses in a convoy of a couple of dozen 4WDs all on the same route.

It's impossible for us to reliably recommend Uyuni agencies, and we strongly suggest that you speak to several companies after doing some research of your own in town. The following companies were performing well in travelers' eyes when this guide was researched:

Blue Line Service (☎ 693-2415; blueday_54@hotmail.com; Ferroviaria s/n)

Expediciones Empexsa (☎ 7241-3728; expedicion_empexsa@hotmail.com; Arce s/n) Good guides.

Expediciones Lípez (☎ 693-2388; Arce s/n)

Expediciones Tayka/Fremen Tours (☎ 693-3543; www.andes-amazonia.com; Sucre s/n) Offers tailored excursions to lesser-known corners, with accommodations in high-quality hotels that are part of a community tourism initiative.

Hidalgo Tours (☎ 693-3089; www.salardeuyuni.net) Potosí-based agency that owns several classy accommodations around the Southwest Circuit. Book in the Jardines de Uyuni hotel.

Huaynuma Tours (☎ 693-2428; huaynumatours@hotmail.com; Arce s/n) Recently established.

Kantuta Tours (☎ 693-3084; kantutatours@hotmail.com; Arce s/n)

Oasis Odyssey (☎ 693-2308; oasistours2002@yahoo.com; Arce s/n)

Reli Tours (☎ 693-3209; relitours@relitours.com; Arce 42)

Toñito Tours (☎ 693-2094; tonitotours@yahoo.com; Ferroviaria 162) Experienced, more upmarket operator.

Tupiza Tours (☎ 694-3003; www.tupizatours.com) Based in Tupiza, runs reliable tours from there to Uyuni or vice versa (see p199).

Turismo El Desierto (☎ 693-3087; turismoeldesiertouyuni@bolivia.com; Arce 42)

circuit and then connect at Laguna Verde with an onward transfer to the pretty town of San Pedro de Atacama in northeast Chile. This is now a popular means of crossing between Bolivia and Chile. Check that the price of the transfer to San Pedro is included when booking.

Shorter visits, basically taking in just the *salar*, cost from US$45 to US$60 per person for two days and one night. Single-day trips also run, but these have angered the locals around the *salar*, who feel that their community gains nothing from these visits.

With the increasing numbers of people on the standard trail, and a growing number of interesting choices of accommodations around the Salar de Uyuni and Southwest Circuit, it's an appealing prospect to customize your own tour, striking off into lesser-known areas, or incorporating some climbing or walking opportunities. Some agencies are more willing to do this than others; be especially wary when they've got a 'standard' tour to fill and will promise you any route you want just to sign you up!

The typical tour is in a 4WD of variable health holding up to six (or, inadvisably, seven) passengers, a cook and a driver/guide who may or may not speak English.

Accommodations tend to be in basic hostels that are icy at night. If you don't have a warm sleeping bag, make absolutely certain that the agency provides one; no one should make these trips without one. There are now several more enticing lodging choices around the *salar*, however, and some companies can arrange stays in these. Always check whether things like accommodations and national park entry are included in the price you are quoted.

Food varies in quality and quantity, but has improved in recent years. Vegetarian catering is much better by some agencies than others.

Note that only larger Uyuni agencies accept credit cards. Since there's no ATM in town, it's best to bring enough cash to cover your tour.

Your choice of tour operator is an important one; a well-run trip might well be a highlight of your traveling life, while a surly, shonky *salar* disaster could wreck your trip. See the boxed text on opposite for advice.

Festivals & Events

Uyuni's big **annual festival** falls on July 11 and marks the founding of the town. Celebrations entail parades, speeches, dancing, music and naturally, lots of drinking.

Sleeping

Uyuni's tourism boom means new hotels are opening all the time. The best hotels fill up fast in the high season so reservations are recommended, especially if you're chugging in on the train at 2am! Cheap places near the station come in handy as most trains arrive and depart at these sort of ungodly hours (if you're not shipping out, however, all the comings and goings can be sleep-depriving). Few hotels offer heating.

BUDGET

Hostal Marith (☎ 693-2174; Potosí 61; r per person US$2.50, with bathroom US$5) This quiet no-nonsense cheapie is a backpackers' favorite and hence is often full. It's set around a courtyard and has decent shared showers with hot water all day. Some rooms are on the dark side, and service varies.

Hotel Avenida (☎ 693-2078; Ferroviaria 11; s/d US$3/5, with bathroom US$5/10) Near the train station, this place is popular for its clean, renovated rooms, laundry sinks and hot showers (available 7am to 1pm). If you get off the train and they don't answer the door, it means they're full.

HI-Salar de Uyuni (☎ 693-2228; www.hostelling bolivia.org; cnr Potosí & Sucre; dm/d US$3.10/7.50; 🖳) This HI affiliate offers good beds and all the typical hostel amenities. It's on the dark side (physically not morally) and the rooms vary significantly; check out a few. It belongs to a tour company, but the owners aren't pushy about it.

Other options:

El Cactu (☎ 693-2032; Arce 46; r per person US$2.50) Friendly, handy, recently refurbished shelter near the train station. Plenty of blankets.

Residencial Sucre (☎ 693-2047; Sucre 132; r per person US$2.50) Marginal with basic but sanitary rooms.

MIDRANGE

Toñito Hotel (☎ 693-3186; www.bolivianexpeditions.com; Ferroviaria 60; r per person US$5, s/d/ste with bathroom & breakfast US$20/30/40) An appealing choice built around a central courtyard, the Toñito has colorful rooms with spacious beds. There's a variety on offer – including some promising-looking new rooms out the back that were being built at the time of research – but it tends to get pretty full with tour groups, so try to book ahead.

Hostal La Magia de Uyuni (☎ 693-2541; magia_ uyuni@yahoo.es; Colón 432; s/d with bathroom & breakfast US$20/30) This solid choice has cozy rooms that are simple for the price but comfortable; they're arranged around an indoor courtyard featuring a weird pair of stuffed armadillos. It's one of the nicer places in town, and thus is popular with upmarket tour groups. The management is very helpful, and arriving at night is no problem.

Jardines de Uyuni (☎ 693-3089; hidalgohuyuni@ entelnet.bo; Potosí 113; s/d US$35/55; 🖥 🖭) Uyuni's most distinctive hotel is extremely visually appealing; it's built around a courtyard in a delightful rustic style. Adobe walls and beds, wall paintings and all sorts of intriguing tools and curios abound, but it can feel that a little comfort has been sacrificed for the ambience – rooms are darkish and feel a mite overpriced. Nonetheless, it's got many attractions, including a pretty bar area, hammocks, a Jacuzzi, a sauna and an indoor pool.

Los Girasoles Hotel (☎ 693-3323; girasoleshotel@ hotmail.com; Santa Cruz 155; s/d US$35/60) This spacious and handsome new hotel offers helpful service and particularly attractive rooms with big comfortable beds, cactus-wood paneling and excellent gas-heated bathrooms. Although a couple of quirks (no telephones, and US$5 extra for a room with a TV) could be improved, it's Uyuni's best all-round choice.

Two mediocre but popular hotels offer prices somewhat lower than the previous midrange choices:

Hotel Kory Wasy (☎ 693-2670; Potosí 304; r per person US$10) Friendly management but somewhat poky rooms. All with private bath, but some are external to room.

Hotel Kutimuy (☎ 693-2391; cnr Potosí & Avaroa; r US$25) Poor service but spacious rooms.

Eating & Drinking

For quick eats, cheap meals are on offer at the market *comedor* (dining hall) and nearby street food stalls. Our intensively researched 'Best Uyuni Salteña' award goes to the small cart that you can find mornings on Potosí outside the Banco de Crédito near the corner of Bolívar.

Wiphala Pub (☎ 693-3545; Potosí 325; dishes US$2-3; 🕓 4-11pm) Named after the multicolored Aymará flag, this place has a welcoming feel with its wooden tables, good attitude and board games. It's a popular spot for a drink, and also serves tasty Bolivian dishes.

Place of Colors (Potosí btwn Sucre & Arce; mains US$2.50-3; 🕓 9am-1pm & 4-11pm) This friendly café wins points for its charming name and keeps visitors happy with various breakfasts, sand-

wiches and baguettes, a great *pique* (hearty Bolivian favorite of chopped beef, sausages, chips and a spicy sauce) in the evening, and hot wine for that cold you caught on the *salar* tour. Small, simple and pleasing.

Kactus (☎ 7242-6864; cnr Potosí & Arce; mains US$3) In a new upstairs location, this is a popular restaurant with tasty pastas, simple soups, international dishes and a few typical Bolivian choices, which are comfortably the best bet. It's let down somewhat by poor service, and it's hard not to feel sorry for the ragged macaw in the corner.

Restaurant 16 de Julio (☎ 693-2171; Arce 35; lunch US$1.90, mains US$2-5) This place is better than it looks from the outside – the upstairs dining room is pleasant and a good choice for lunch or, in the evenings, pizza and pasta.

La Loco (☎ 693-3105; Potosí btwn Sucre & Camacho; snacks US$1.25, mains US$3-4; 🕓 4pm-2am) This friendly French-run restaurant and pub is a barn-like space that's lit low and furnished with comfortingly chunky wooden furniture around a log fire. There are plenty of drinks and a short but classy menu that offers *croques monsieur* (grilled ham and cheese sandwiches), crepes and llama steaks with a gourmet touch. There's better service from the boss than the staff.

Café Bar Ranking (☎ 693-2102; Potosí 9; mains US$3-4; 🕓 8:30am-late) This relaxed spot, which funds the adjacent Ranking information office, is a very enticing place for a tea or coffee (it has a huge range), meal or sociable late night drink – try the 'llama sperm' shooter. It's very atmospheric with a salt floor, friendly service and some of the best *salar* photos you are likely to see. It's also a good place to learn the classic Bolivian dice games.

Arco Iris (☎ 693-3177; Arce 27; pizzas US$3-6) Something of an Uyuni classic for pizza and drinks, this place is busy, popular and friendly, but the service is fairly slow. It's a fine place to socialize and to link up with other travelers to form a tour group.

Minuteman Revolutionary Pizza (☎ 693-2094; Ferroviaria 60; 🕓 7:30-10am & 5-10pm; pizzas US$3.75-7.50, pasta US$2.50-3, breakfast US$2-2.50) This convivial spot is a deserved travelers' favorite, and a real center for welcome human comforts after the sometimes harsh conditions around the *salar*. The pizzas are generously proportioned and extremely tasty, and it's also a cozy spot for a candlelit glass of wine or a hearty pre-tour breakfast. Enter through the Toñito Hotel.

Getting There & Away

Getting out of isolated Uyuni can be problematic. Buy your bus ticket the day before and your train ticket as far in advance as you can. An air service is constantly being mooted, but it's a sketchy prospect due to the cost of construction of high-altitude runways and treacherous Altiplano wind conditions.

If you're heading on to Chile, it can be a wise idea to pick up a Bolivian exit stamp at *migración* (p184), since the hours of the Bolivian border post at Hito Cajón (just beyond Laguna Verde) are somewhat unreliable. Although it's rarely enforced, you're expected to leave Bolivia within three days of getting the stamp.

BUS & JEEP

There's supposedly a new bus terminal in the works (funded by the US$0.20 terminal fee), but at last look all buses were still leaving from the west end of Av Arce, a couple of minutes' walk from the plaza. There's a choice of services to most destinations, so ask around to get the best price or service. Ranking Bolivia (p184) keeps an updated timetable of all services.

Several companies offer daily evening buses to Oruro (US$2 to US$3, eight hours), where you can change for La Paz. It's a chilly, bone-shaking trip, so you might prefer the train or **Todo Turismo** (☎ 693-3337; www.touringbolivia.com; Cabrera s/n, btwn Bolívar & Arce), which runs what is surely the best bus in Bolivia, a luxury affair with friendly staff and an onboard meal. It heads between Uyuni and La Paz (US$25, 10 hours) via Oruro (US$20, seven hours), leaving at 8pm Tuesday, Thursday and Saturday. While it's expensive, there are two advantages to this service: it's heated, and you avoid having to deal with freezing Oruro in the middle of the night – travelers have reported being robbed while waiting there for a connection to La Paz.

There are several departures around 10am and 7pm for Potosí (US$3, six hours), with connections to Sucre (US$5, nine hours) and Tarija. There's also a 3pm direct service to Tarija (US$12, 18 hours) if conditions permit.

There are daily 4WD services to Tupiza (US$6.25, six to eight hours), leaving around 10:30am. Although it's a tight fit for 10 in the back of the Landcruiser, it's a spectacular, memorable trip via Atocha, where you can expect to spend at least an hour. Buses also run the same route a couple of times a week, as does the odd *camión*.

There are services at 3:30am on Monday and Thursday to the Chilean border at Avaroa (US$3.75, five hours), where you can connect to a service to Calama.

An alternative route to Chile is with an organized tour, which will leave you in San Pedro de Atacama. Some of the tour companies, including **Turismo El Desierto** (☎ 693-3087; turismoeldesiertouy uni@bolivia.com; Arce 42) and **Colque Tours** (☎ 693-2199; www.colquetours.com; Potosí 56), offer direct jeep transfers to San Pedro. These leave around 3pm and take seven to 10 hours. The disadvantage is that the agencies never know if they are sending a jeep until shortly before departure, as it depends on whether someone has booked a tour in San Pedro. It costs US$15 to US$30 per person.

TRAIN

Uyuni has a modern, well-organized **train station** (☎ 693-2153). Buy your ticket several days in advance or get an agency to do it for you.

Comfortable *Expreso del Sur* trains ramble to Oruro (*popular/salón/ejecutivo* US$4.15/ 6.50/12.60, seven hours) on Thursday and Sunday at 12:05am (that's Wednesday and Saturday nights folks) and southeast to Tupiza (US$3.10/5/12.60, 5½ hours) and Villazón (US$4.75/7/16.90, 8½ hours) on Tuesday and Friday at 10:40pm.

Chronically late *Wara Wara del Sur* trains are supposed to chug out of the station at 1:45am on Tuesday and Friday (ie Monday and Thursday nights) for Oruro (*popular/ salón/ejecutivo* US$4/5/10.75, 7½ hours) and on Monday and Thursday at 2:50am for Tupiza (US$2.75/3.60/8.25, six hours) and Villazón (US$4.25/5.75/12.40, 10 hours); these engines always seem to be chanting 'I think I can… I think I can…'

Depending on size, you may have to check your backpack/case into the luggage van. Look out for snatch thieves on the train just before it pulls out.

If tickets sell out on these trains, take a bus 111km south to Atocha, where there are bus connections and where the train stops two hours before/after Uyuni. There are often tickets available there even though the Uyuni station has sold out their allocation.

On Monday at 3:30am a train trundles west for Avaroa (US$3.90, five hours) on the Chilean border, where you cross to Ollagüe and may have to wait a few hours to clear Chilean customs. From here, another train continues to Calama (US$11.40 from Uyuni, six hours from Ollagüe). The whole trip can take up to 24 hours but it's a spectacular, if uncomfortable journey.

AROUND UYUNI
Pulacayo

At this semighost town, 22km northeast of Uyuni, brilliantly colored rocks rise beside the road and a mineral-rich stream reveals streaks of blue, yellow, red and green. The **Pulacayo mines** north of the village, which yielded mainly silver, were first opened in the late 17th century (the grave of the company founder A Mariano Ramírez can still be seen), but they closed in 1832 on account of the Independence war. In 1873, however, Compañía Huanchaca de Bolivia (CHB) took over operations and resumed silver extraction. At the time of its final closure in 1959, it employed 20,000 miners, but today, only a few hundred hardy souls remain.

There are several kilometers of **mine tunnels** to explore. Also worthwhile is the **mill** that spins llama wool into cloth, and the **mansion** of the 22nd president of Bolivia, Aniceto Arce Ruíz.

Pulacayo is also home to several decaying **steam locomotives** that were originally imported to transport ore. They include Bolivia's first steam engine, *El Chiripa*, which dates from 1890, and others with such names as *El Burro, El Torito* and *Mauricio Hothschild*. There's also the ore train that was robbed by legendary bandits Butch Cassidy and the Sundance Kid, including a wooden railcar that bears the bullet holes from the attack.

Pulacayo has an important place in Bolivian history, and an active community of residents and expats that is trying to establish a tourist infrastructure. At present, however, none of this is in place. Nonetheless, it remains a picturesque place to visit, and you might be able to find a local to guide you around the mine tunnels. Guided tours to Pulacayo from Uyuni have run in the past – check the current situation when you visit. Otherwise, all transportation between Uyuni and Potosí passes through Pulacayo, and a return taxi trip from Uyuni should cost from US$8 to US$12.

There are a couple of simple hotels in town, but both were closed at time of research; check in Uyuni.

Colchani

Right on the edge of the Salar de Uyuni (see opposite), Colchani is the easiest point to access that great salt flat, and the place to go if you just want a glimpse of it without going on a tour. There remain at least 10 billion tons of salt in the Salar de Uyuni, and around Colchani *campesinos* (subsistence farmers) hack it out with picks and shovels and pile it into small conical mounds that characterize the *salar* landscape in this area.

Most of the salt is sold to refiners and hauled off by rail, but some is exchanged with local villages for wool, meat and grease. At the time of research, locals were developing a new **museum** dealing with the *salar*, the salt trade and the now practically extinct llama caravans.

Southwest of Colchani is the extraordinary **Cooperativa Rosario workshop**, also called the Bloques de Sal (Salt Blocks). Here, blocks of salt are cut from the *salar* and made into furniture and lively works of art. The operation has become a solid attraction on Salar de Uyuni tourist circuits.

Right on the edge of the salt, the **Hotel Palacio de Sal** (☎ 622-5186; www.palaciodesal.com; r per person US$80; ⌨) is a luxurious complex built almost completely out of the white condiment. It's very luxurious, and boasts all sorts of facilities ranging from a pool and sauna to a salt golf course (don't bring your favorite white balls). Breakfast and dinner are included in the rates. The hotel is booked through Hidalgo Tours in Potosí (see boxed text, p186) or at the Jardines de Uyuni hotel (p188); it comes cheaper as part of a package.

GETTING THERE & AWAY

Colchani is 20km north of Uyuni, and passed through by all buses traveling between Uyuni and Oruro. Daily *camiones* also leave for Colchani from Av Ferroviaria in Uyuni. You'll have the most luck between 7am and 9am. Some salt workers living in Uyuni commute daily to Colchani in private vehicles or on motorcycles, and for a small fee you may be able to hitch along. Otherwise, a taxi there will cost from US$5 to US$7.

THE SOUTHWEST CIRCUIT

Bolivia's southwestern corner is an awe-inspiring collection of harsh, diverse landscapes ranging from the blinding white Salar de Uyuni salt flat to the geothermal hotbed of Los Lípez, one of the world's harshest wilderness regions and an important refuge for many Andean wildlife species. The ground here literally boils with minerals, and the spectrum of colors produced is extraordinary. A circuit from Uyuni takes you through absolutely unforgettable, literally breathtaking landscapes and is the highlight of many people's visit to Bolivia.

Much of the region is nominally protected in the **Reserva Nacional de Fauna Andina Eduardo Avaroa** (REA; www.bolivia-rea.com; admission US$3.75), which was created in 1973 and receives in excess of 50,000 visitors annually. Its emphasis is on preserving the vicuña and the *llareta* plant, both of which are threatened in Bolivia, as well as other unique ecosystems and endemic species. It covers an area of 7150 sq km.

Most people visit the region on an organized trip from Uyuni (p185) or Tupiza (p199); see the boxed text below for some alternative places to visit.

Apart from a couple of Entel points, there are no phones out in the Southwest Circuit. All communication is by radio. Any phone numbers listed in this section are for offices located in Uyuni.

SALAR DE UYUNI

One of the globe's most evocative and eerie sights, this, the world's largest salt flat (12,106 sq km) sits at 3653m and covers nearly all of Daniel Campos province. When the surface is dry, the *salar* is a blinding white expanse of the greatest nothing imaginable. It's just the blue sky, the white ground and you. When there's a little water, the surface perfectly reflects the clouds and the blue Altiplano sky, and the horizon disappears. If you're driving across the surface at such times, the effect is positively

---

SALT HOTELS

There are several hotels around the *salar* (salt pan or salt desert) that are built of salt, including the luxurious Palacio de Sal in Colchani (opposite) and Ecohotel de Sal in Tahua (p194). These are unique and comfortable places to stay, and nearly everything is constructed of blocks of salt (with a few obvious exceptions). Note that it is illegal to actually construct buildings on the *salar* itself – Playa Blanca salt hotel, a morning stop on many tours, falls into this category. Local environmentalists strongly recommend that you don't give them any business.

---

eerie, and it's hard to believe that you're not actually flying through the clouds.

The Salar de Uyuni is now a center of salt extraction and processing, particularly around the settlement of Colchani (opposite). The estimated annual output of the Colchani operation is nearly 20,000 tons, 18,000 tons of which is for human consumption while the rest is for livestock.

Formation

From 40,000 to 25,000 years ago, Lago Minchín, whose highest level reached 3760m, occupied much of southwestern Bolivia. When it evaporated, the area lay dry for 14,000 years before the appearance of short-lived Lago Tauca, which lasted for only about 1000 years and rose to 3720m. When it dried up, it left two large puddles, Lagos Poopó and Uru Uru, and two major salt concentrations, the Salares de Uyuni and Coipasa.

SOUTHERN ALTIPLANO

GET OUT OF THE LANDCRUISER

There are plenty of opportunities for getting out of the Landcruiser and doing something active throughout the southwest region. There are various mountains to climb, with guides easily available in the region's settlements. The climbs are challenging for the altitude rather than being technically difficult. Taking a guide is a good idea, and contributes something to the local community, so often bypassed by the Uyuni-based tours. The most frequently climbed is the **Volcán Licancabur** (see p196), but **Nevado Candelaria** (5995m) west of the Salar de Coipasa is exhilarating. The active **Volcán Ollagüe** (5865m) on the Chilean border southwest of San Pedro de Quemez is another interesting option – you can get pretty close to the crater if there's no wind, and the views are spectacular.

Various locals are trying to organize interesting alternatives to the standard trips – at the time of research, **Mateo Huayllani** (☎ 613-7290), based in Mañica, was about to start offering three-day trips with a traditional llama salt caravan in the western part of the Salar – a fascinating prospect.

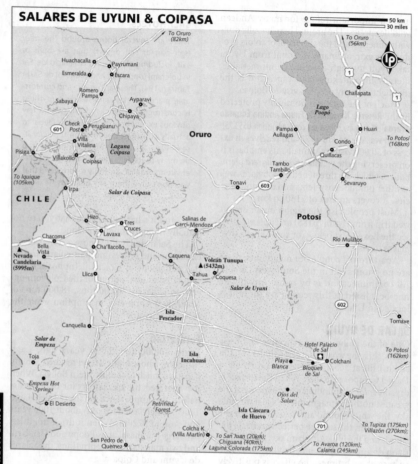

This part of the Altiplano is drained internally, with no outlet to the sea; the salt deposits are the result of the minerals leached from the mountains and deposited at the lowest available point.

Isla Incahuasi

For most Salar de Uyuni tours, the main destination is the lovely Isla Incahuasi (erroneously known as Isla del Pescado, which is further west), in the heart of the *salar* 80km west of Colchani.

Isla Incahuasi is a hilly outpost in the middle of the *salar,* covered in Trichoreus cactus and surrounded by a flat, white sea of hexagonal salt tiles. It was once a remarkably lonely, otherworldly place. However, to the horror

of some and the delight of others, there's now a café-restaurant run by Mongo's of La Paz, and the island is normally very busy, as all the tour groups arrive at the same time and swarm over the trails chasing the perfect photo.

The island is administered by Daniel Campos Province and there's an admission charge of US$1.25, which may or may not be included in your tour.

Isla Cáscara de Huevo

The small **Eggshell Island** was named for the broken shells of birds' eggs that litter it. It lies near the southern end of the Salar de Uyuni and is visited mainly to see the strange patterns of salt crystallization in the area, some of which resemble roses.

SOUTHERN ALTIPLANO

Volcán Tunupa, Coquesa & Tahua

Diagonally opposite Colchani, a rounded promontory juts into the Salar de Uyuni and on it rises **Volcán Tunupa** (5432m). One legend states that Atahualpa slashed the breast of a woman called Tunupa on its slopes, and the milk that spilled out formed the *salar*. Altitude aside, this hulking yellow mountain is a relatively easy climb.

At the foot of the volcano is the village of **Coquesa** in an area specked with ruined ancient villages and burial grounds. Articles of clothing and artifacts in ceramic, gold and copper have been discovered at some of the sites, indicating the presence of an advanced but little-known culture. Unfortunately, its remoteness has left it vulnerable to amateur treasure hunters who have plundered several items of archaeological value.

At simple **Hospedaje Chatahuana** (r per person US$1.25), one of four places to stay in this little settlement, you can ask for the keys to the **Museo Coquesa** (admission US$1.25), which has a collection of ceramics and mummies. In Coquesa, you can also arrange a nighttime visit to the nearby **observatory**, to really

---

CHIPAYA

Immediately north of the Salar de Coipasa, on the Río Sabaya delta, live the Chipaya people. They occupy two desert villages (Chipaya and Ayparavi) of unique circular mud huts known as *khuyas* or *putucus*, which have doors made from cactus wood and always face east. Chipayas are best recognized by their earth-colored clothing and the women's unique hairstyle, which is plaited African-style into 60 small braids. These are, in turn, joined into two large braids and decorated with a *laurake* (barrette) at each temple.

Some researchers believe the Chipaya were the Altiplano's first inhabitants, and that they may in fact be a remnant of the lost Tiahuanaco civilization. Much of this speculation is based on the fact that their language is vastly different from both Quechua and Aymará, and is probably a surviving form of Uru.

Chipaya tradition maintains that they came into the world when it was still dark, and that they are descended from the 'Men of Water' – perhaps the Uru. Their religion, which is nature-based, is complex and symbolic, deifying phallic images, stones, rivers, mountains, animal carcasses and ancestors. The village church tower is worshipped as a demon – one of 40 named demons who represent hate, ire, vengeance, gluttony and other deadly sins. These are believed to inhabit the whitewashed mudcones that exist within a 15km radius of the village, where they're appeased with libations, sacrifices and rituals to prevent their evil from invading the village.

The reverent commemoration of dead ancestors culminates on November 2, **Día de los Muertos** (Day of the Dead), when bodies are disinterred from *chullpares* (funerary towers). They're feted with a feast, copious drink and coca leaves, and informed about recent village events and the needs of the living. Those who were chiefs, healers and other luminaries are carried to the church where they're honored with animal sacrifices.

Visiting Chipaya

In general, tourists aren't especially welcome, and are expected to pay a fee for entering the Chipaya 'nation' (visitors have been charged anything from US$1 to US$50 per person; you'll pay a lot less if you don't turn up in a 4WD!). The Chipayas don't like to be photographed. There's a simple *alojamiento* (basic accommodations) in Chipaya village, and a small shop.

Chipaya can be reached from Llica, across the Salar de Coipasa, or from Oruro via Huachacalla. On most days, *micros* from Uyuni to Llica (US$2.50, four hours) leave daily around noon. From Llica, you can wait for a *camión* (flatbed truck) or hire a motorcycle taxi to Pisiga (around US$15); there you'll find Iquique–Oruro buses headed for Sabaya (where you'll find an *alojamiento* and basic meals), Huachacalla and Oruro.

From Oruro, buses leave daily for Huachacalla, 30km beyond. Alternatively, you can reach Sabaya or Huachacalla on any bus between Oruro and Iquique. In addition, a few tour companies organize visits to the village; check with **Viajeros del Tiempo** (☎ 527-1166; S Galvarro 1232, Oruro).

appreciate the starry skies. Ask at the Chatahuana; prices vary from US$1.25 to US$5 per person depending on how many in the group and whether you walk (25 minutes) or take a car. Plenty of much-needed hot drinks are provided!

More upmarket lodgings are available in nearby **Tahua**, to the west on the edge of the *salar*. The beautiful **Ecohotel de Sal** (☎ in Uyuni 693-3543; d/t/q US$75/80/85) is part of a joint business-community project and will eventually devolve entirely to the village. Built entirely of salt, apart from the thatched roof and the black stone bathrooms, it offers plenty of comfort and makes a good base for excursions into the *salar* or to climb peaks like Nevado Candelaria. Rooms have heaters and solar-powered hot water. Tasty typical meals (perhaps llama meat with quinoa and dehydrated potatoes) are available (US$6), as is breakfast (US$3).

Other accommodations include Jardines de Tahua, usually only bookable as part of a package with **Hidalgo Tours** (☎ 693-3089; www .salardeuyuni.net) in Potosí, and a hotel owned by Mongo's of La Paz (see p90), which was due to open shortly after research on this book was completed.

Llica

On the opposite side of the *salar* from Colchani is the village of Llica, the unlikely site of a teachers' college. There are a couple of very basic places to stay, each charging a couple of dollars a day; ask in the *alcaldía's* office. For meals, the *pensiones* Inca Wasi, Bolívar and El Viajero serve soup for US$0.20 and full meals for US$0.90. *Micros* (US$2.50, four hours) leave Uyuni for Llica more or less daily at noon. *Camiones* make this trip, and sometimes continue further into the southwest region; an adventurous way to go, but come well prepared with food, water and camping gear.

San Pedro de Quemez

At the southwestern tip of the *salar*, off the regular beaten track, this is a remote spot and home to another appealing hotel, the **Ecohotel de Piedra** (☎ in Uyuni 693-3543; d/t/q US$75/80/85). Part of the same project as the Ecohotel de Sal in Tahua (above), it offers the same facilities, but is instead built of rugged local stone. Hotel staff can organize intriguing local excursions to little-known points of interest.

SALAR DE COIPASA

This great 2218-sq-km remote salt desert, northwest of the Salar de Uyuni at an elevation of 3786m, was part of the same system of prehistoric lakes as the Salar de Uyuni – a system that covered the area over 10,000 years ago. The 4WD-only road to the Salar de Coipasa is extremely poor. The salt-mining village of Coipasa, which (not surprisingly) is constructed mainly of salt, occupies an island in the middle of the *salar*. You can also reach the Salar de Coipasa from Oruro province (see p178).

LOS LÍPEZ
Salar de Uyuni to Laguna Colorada

The normal tour route from Uyuni is via Colchani, then 80km west across the *salar* to Isla Incahuasi (p192). After a stop to explore the island, the route turns south and 45km later, reaches the edge of the *salar*. Here, at Atulcha, is the **Hotel de Sal Marith** (r per person US$10), one of the cheaper choices if you want to bed down in a salt hotel.

After another 22km, you'll pass through a military checkpoint at the village of **Colcha K** (*col*-cha *kah*). In the village, there's a pleasant adobe church and a series of fairly rudimentary dormitory accommodations.

About 15km further along is the quinoa-growing village of **San Juan** at an elevation of 3660m. It has a lovely adobe church, a population of 1000, and several volcanic-rock tombs and burial *chullpas* in the vicinity. Budget accommodations are provided in private homes and basic *alojamientos*. All charge around US$2.50 per person. Upmarket tours stay at **Magia de San Juan** (barronhumberto@hotmail.com; s/d with bathroom & breakfast US$15/20), where the cozy pub has a fireplace and is open to nonguests. There's even an Entel cabin nearby; one of few phones in the region. The community-run **Museo Kausay Wasi** (admission US$1.25) displays regional archaeological finds.

At this point the route turns west and starts across the borax-producing **Salar de Chiguana**, where the landscape opens up and snow-capped **Ollagüe** (5865m), an active volcano straddling the Chilean border, appears in the distance.

The route then turns south and climbs into high and increasingly wild terrain, past the several mineral-rich lakes filled with flamingos (see boxed text, opposite). Several of the lakes are backed by hills resembling spilled chocolate sundaes. After approximately 170km of rough bumping through marvelous landscapes, the road winds down to the much-photographed **Árbol de Piedra** (Stone Tree) in the Desierto Siloli, 18km north of Laguna Colorada.

About half an hour before reaching the tree, you'll pass the **Ecohotel del Desierto** (☎ in Uyuni 693-3543; d/t/q US$75/80/85), set in a landscape of stupendous ocher colors. It's part of a four-hotel community/business project and features an excellent standard of accommodations, heating, hot water and tasty local meals.

Laguna Colorada

This fiery red lake (4278m) covers approximately 60 sq km and reaches a depth of just 80cm. The rich red coloration is derived from algae and plankton that thrive in the mineral-rich water, and the shoreline is fringed with brilliant white deposits of sodium, magnesium, borax and gypsum. The lake sediments are also rich in diatoms, tiny microfossils used in the production of fertilizer, paint, toothpaste and plastics, and as a filtering agent for oil, pharmaceuticals, aviation fuel, beer and wine. More apparent are the flamingos that breed here; all three South American species are present (see the boxed text below).

The sprawling **Huayllajara Hostal Altiplano** (dm US$2.50), 6km from the lake, provides beer, snacks and basic insulation from the cold in clean six-bed dorms with plenty of blankets. At the lake itself, **Señor Eustaquio Berna's refugio** (US$2.50) is basic but popular. At the time of research, new accommodations were being built here, with double rooms and en suite bathrooms.

The most upmarket option is Hidalgo Tours' Hospedería Hidalgo Laguna Colorada, usually only bookable with a tour from the same company (see p186). It has rustic rooms with heating, hot water and private bathrooms.

The clear air is bitterly cold and winter nighttime temperatures can drop below −68°F. Just as well; if it ever increased much above freezing, the stench would probably make the place unbearable. Instead, the air is perfumed with llareta smoke, which seems ironic given the proximity to potentially limitless solar, geothermal and wind power.

Sol de Mañana Geyser Basin

Apart from tour groups, most vehicles along the tracks around Laguna Colorada will be supplying or servicing mining and military camps or the geothermal project 50km south at Sol de Mañana. The main interest here is the 4850m-high geyser basin with bubbling mud pots, hellish fumaroles and the thick and nauseating aroma of sulfur fumes. Approach the site cautiously; any damp or cracked earth is potentially dangerous and cave-ins do occur, sometimes causing serious burns.

FROZEN FLAMINGOS

Three species of flamingo breed in the bleak high country of southwestern Bolivia, and once you've seen these posers strutting through icy mineral lagoons at 5000m elevation, you'll abandon time-worn associations between flamingos, coconut palms and the steamy tropics. The sight of these pinky-white birds with their black bills and tails adds yet another color to the already spectacular palette hereabouts.

Flamingos have a complicated and sophisticated system for filtering the foodstuffs from highly alkaline brackish lakes. They filter algae and diatoms from the water by sucking in and vigorously expelling water from the bill several times per second. The minute particles are caught on fine hairlike protrusions that line the inside of the mandibles. The suction is created by the thick fleshy tongue, which rests in a groove in the lower mandible and pumps back and forth like a piston.

The Chilean flamingo reaches heights of just over 1m and has a black-tipped white bill, dirty blue legs, red knees and salmon-colored plumage. The James flamingo is the smallest of the three species and has dark-red legs and a yellow-and-black bill. It's locally known as jututu. The Andean flamingo is the largest of the three and has pink plumage, yellow legs and a yellow-and-black bill.

Environmentalists have been particularly concerned for the birds in recent years, as tourism has affected the flamingos' breeding. Don't try to creep up to them to get a better photo; above all don't put them to flight or encourage any guide that suggests doing this.

Termas de Polques & Salar de Chalviri

At the foot of Cerro Polques lies the **Termas de Polques**, a small 85°F hot spring pool, and an absolute paradise after the chilly *salar* nights. Although they're not boiling by any means, they're suitable for bathing and the mineral-rich waters are thought to relieve the symptoms of arthritis and rheumatism. There's a new restaurant here, and changing sheds with toilet facilities (US$0.40).

To the east, the adjacent **Salar de Chalviri** supports populations of flamingos and ducks. A mining operation extracts borax in the middle of the *salar*.

Laguna Verde

This stunning blue-green **lake** (4400m) is tucked into the southwestern corner of Bolivian territory, 52km south of Sol de Mañana. The incredible green color comes from high concentrations of lead, sulfur, arsenic and calcium carbonates. In this exposed position, an icy wind blows almost incessantly, whipping the water into a brilliant green-and-white froth. This surface agitation combined with the high mineral content means that it can remain liquid at temperatures as low as –70°F.

Behind the lake rises the cone of **Volcán Licancabur** (5960m), whose summit is said to have once sheltered an ancient Inca crypt. Some tours include an ascent of Licancabur, and although it presents no technical difficulties, the wind, temperature, altitude and ball-bearing volcanic pumice underfoot make it quite grueling. Several Uyuni and Tupiza agencies are happy to include a guided climb of the volcano in a Southwest Circuit route, adding an extra day to the trip. You can normally find a guide somewhere around Laguna Verde – they tend to charge about US$25 to US$30 for an ascent of the mountain, which can be done comfortably (if you handle the altitude) in a day.

Where the route splits about 20km south of Sol de Mañana, the more scenic left fork climbs up and over a 5000m pass, then up a stark hillside resembling a freshly raked Zen garden dotted with the enormous **Rocas de Dalí**, which appear to have been meticulously placed by the surrealist master Salvador himself.

Down the far slope are two sulfur mines, a military camp and an attractive new **albergue** (dm US$5), with comfortable six-to-a-room accommodations, decent beds and tasty meals.

There are no showers, but behind the complex there's a hot spring in a creek where you can have a welcome bath.

GETTING THERE & AWAY

Most agencies now offer cross-border connections to San Pedro de Atacama by arrangement with Chilean operators. It's wise to check out of Bolivia at immigration in Uyuni; the exit stamp allows three days to leave the country. The Hito Cajón border post near Laguna Verde is much more reliable than it used to be, but has been known to take unpaid leave.

Laguna Celeste

This 'blue lake' or – more romantically – 'heaven lake,' is still very much a peripheral trip for most Uyuni agencies, but it's gaining popularity with adventurous travelers as a one-day detour. A local legend suggests the presence of a submerged ruin, possibly a *chullpa*, in the lake. Behind the lake, a road winds its way up Volcán Uturuncu (6020m) to the Uturuncu sulfur mine, in a 5900m pass between the mountain's twin cones. That means it's more than 200m higher than the road over the Khardung La in Ladakh, India, making it quite possibly the highest motorable pass in the world.

Other Lakes

In the vast eastern reaches of Sud Lípez are numerous other fascinating mineral-rich lakes that are informally named for their odd coloration and have so far escaped much attention. Various milky-looking lakes are known as **Laguna Blanca**, sulfur-colored lakes are **Laguna Amarilla** and wine-colored ones are known as **Laguna Guinda**. You can negotiate to add these to a tailored circuit.

Quetena Chico & Around

About 120km northeast of Laguna Verde and 30km southwest of Laguna Celeste is the small mining settlement of Quetena Chico, which has a few basic services and supplies, a military post and the **Centro de Ecología Ch'aska** (admission US$1.25), which has an exhibition on the geology and biology of the Los Lípez region, and the lives of the local llama herders. There's a couple of simple *albergues* here.

Southeast of here, 6km away, is the picturesque abandoned village of **Barrancas**, which nestles against a craggy cliff.

To the northeast, and well off the standard circuit (although visited by some of the tours from Tupiza), the village of **San Pablo de Lípez** is building a hotel, the Ecohotel de Barro, which will have the same contact details, facilities and pricing as the Ecohotel de Sal in Tahua (p194). It's due to open in mid-2007.

Heading back toward Uyuni, the village of **Mallcu Villa Mar** has an interesting *mercado artesanal* (craft market) that's worth a visit. Stretch your legs by strolling the 4km to some of the area's most spectacular *pinturas rupestres* (rock paintings), with impressive human figures wearing headdresses, and incised animals. There are several simple *albergues* in Mallcu, and also an upmarket hotel run by Hidalgo Tours (p186).

Valles de Rocas & San Cristóbal

The route back to Uyuni turns northeast a few kilometers north of Laguna Colorada and winds through more high, lonesome country and several valleys of bizarre eroded rock formations known as **Valles de Rocas**. From the village of Alota it's a trying, six-hour jostle back to Uyuni.

If you can still cope with sightseeing at this stage, a short side trip leads to the village of **San Cristóbal**, in a little valley northeast of Alota. Here you'll find a lovely 350-year-old church constructed on an age-old Pachamama ritual site. The walls bear a series of paintings from the life of Christ, and the altar is made of pure silver and backed up by a beautifully preserved 17th-century organ. A strange angel spreads its metallic wings outside.

The **Hotel San Cristóbal** (s/d US$6/8) offers electricity and hot solar-powered showers, and a unique restaurant structure. The complex, built with mitigation funds from the massive mining project nearby, also includes a medical and communications center.

Uyuni to Tupiza

The rough track south of Uyuni initially heads out across the high desert. Immediately north of the market village of Cerdas are several impressive sand-dune fields. After the road drops dramatically off the Altiplano, it descends into a riverbed filled with bizarrely colorful, unusual and mineral-rich geology.

Just north of the active mining town of **Atocha**, which retains an Old West feel, you'll pass a picturesque miners' cemetery. In the center of Atocha, don't miss the Cessna that is impaled on a post along the main street. If you fancy overnighting here, there are three cheap *residenciales* on the plaza. Atocha is serviced by the Oruro–Uyuni–Tupiza train services.

Beyond Atocha, the road enters increasingly scenic country, with excellent views of the stunning cone of **Cerro Chorolque** (5630m). For the next four hours, the road twists through seriously mountainous country, past **Huaca Huañusca** (p203), Butch and Sundance country, then plummets into the fertile **Río Tupiza Valley**, flanked by cactus and brilliant red rock.

TUPIZA

pop 20,000 / elevation 2950m

> In the background looms the Tupizan range, very red, or better, a ruddy sepia; and very distinct, resembling a landscape painted by an artist with the animated brilliance of Delacroix or by an Impressionist like Renoir… In the tranquil translucent air, flows the breath of smiling grace…
> *Carlos Medinaceli, Bolivian writer*

The pace of things in tranquil Tupiza seems a few beats slower than in other Bolivian towns, which makes it a top spot to hang out for a while. Set in spectacular countryside, it's the capital of Sud Chichas. The city lies in the valley of the Río Tupiza, and is surrounded by rugged scenery – weird eroded rainbow-colored rocks cut by tortuous, gravelly *quebradas* (ravines, usually dry) whose slopes are studded with cactus.

The climate is mild year-round, with most of the rain falling between November and March. From June to August, days are hot, dry and clear, but nighttime temperatures can drop to below freezing.

Economically, the town depends on agriculture and mining. A refinery south of town provides employment, and the country's only antimony (a flame-retardant metallic element) smelter operates sporadically.

Tupiza has a lot to offer the traveler. Explore the surrounding hills and canyons on horseback, check out where the Butch Cassidy & the Sundance Kid story ended (see boxed text, p204) or just take a few days out to read novels in the pretty central square or by the

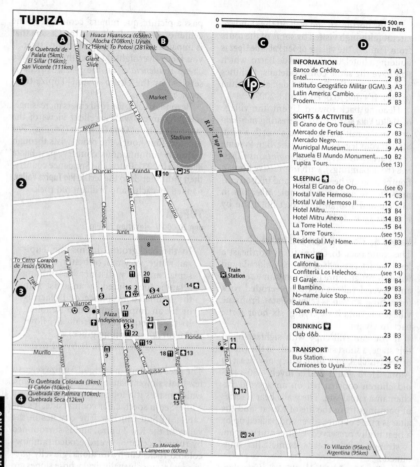

TUPIZA

0 .... 500 m
0 .... 0.3 miles

INFORMATION
Banco de Crédito **1** A3
Entel **2** B3
Instituto Geográfico Militar (IGM) **3** A3
Latin America Cambio **4** B3
Prodem **5** B3

SIGHTS & ACTIVITIES
El Grano de Oro Tours **6** C3
Mercado de Ferias **7** B3
Mercado Negro **8** B3
Municipal Museum **9** A4
Plazuela El Mundo Monument ... **10** B2
Tupiza Tours .... (see 13)

SLEEPING
Hostal El Grano de Oro .... (see 6)
Hostal Valle Hermoso **11** C3
Hostal Valle Hermoso II **12** C4
Hotel Mitru **13** B4
Hotel Mitru Anexo **14** B3
La Torre Hotel **15** B4
La Torre Tours .... (see 15)
Residencial My Home **16** B3

EATING
California **17** B3
Confitería Los Helechos ...... (see 14)
El Garaje **18** B4
Il Bambino **19** B3
No-name Juice Stop **20** B3
Sauna **21** B3
¡Quee Pizza! **22** B3

DRINKING
Club d&b **23** B3

TRANSPORT
Bus Station **24** C4
Camiones to Uyuni **25** B2

hotel pool. Tupiza is also an excellent place to embark on a tour of the Southwest Circuit to Uyuni, a route that's attracting growing numbers of travelers.

History

The tribe that originally inhabited the region called themselves Chichas and left archaeological evidence of their existence. Despite this, little is known of their culture or language, and it's assumed they were ethnically separate from the tribes in neighboring areas of southern Bolivia and northern Argentina. Unfortunately, anything unique about them was destroyed between 1471 and 1488 when Tupac Inca Yupanqui annexed the region to the Inca empire.

Once the Inca empire had fallen to the Spanish, the entire southern half of the Viceroyalty of Alto Peru was awarded to Diego de Almagro by decree of Spain's King Carlos V. When Almagro arrived on a familiarization expedition in 1535, the Chichas culture had been entirely subsumed. Officially, Tupiza was founded on June 4, 1574, by Captain Luis de Fuentes (who was also the founder of Tarija), however this date is pure conjecture.

During the tumultuous 1781 Campesino Rebellion, the peasants' champion, Luis de la Vega, mobilized the local militia, proclaimed himself governor and encouraged resistance against Spanish authorities. The rebellion was squashed early on, but the mob was success-

SOUTHERN ALTIPLANO

ful in executing the Spanish *corregidor* (chief magistrate) of Tupiza.

From Tupiza's founding through the War of Independence, its Spanish population grew steadily, lured by the favorable climate and suitable agricultural lands. Later, the discovery of minerals attracted even more settlers. More recently, *campesinos* have drifted in from the countryside and many unemployed miners have settled.

Information

INTERNET & TELEPHONE

There are several places on the plaza that charge US$0.40 per hour for internet access, as does **Entel** (cnr Avaroa & Santa Cruz), where you can also make calls.

LAUNDRY

All accommodations can do a load of washing for you, tending to charge around US$0.80 per kilo.

MAPS

For maps, try the **Instituto Geográfico Militar** (IGM; ☎ 694-2785), upstairs inside the Municipalidad on the plaza.

MONEY

You can change cash or get cash advances at Banco de Crédito or Prodem on the plaza. Another place for cash is the **Latin America Cambio** (Avaroa 160), which accepts several currencies. Hotel Mitru charges 6% commission to change traveler's checks.

TOURIST INFORMATION

There's no tourist office, so the hotels and agencies are your main source of information.

Sights & Activities

Tupiza's main attraction is the surrounding countryside, best seen on foot or horseback. The short hike up **Cerro Corazón de Jesús**, flanked by the Stations of the Cross, is a pleasant morning or evening outing when the low sun brings out the fiery reds of the surrounding countryside.

The permanent **Mercado Negro**, where you'll encounter a mishmash of consumer goods, occupies an entire block between Santa Cruz and Chichas. Lively **street markets** convene Thursday and Saturday mornings near the train station. A kilometer south of town, the **Mercado Campesino** features more of the same

on Thursday and Saturday. The central **Mercado de Ferias** has lots of produce stalls and *comedores* upstairs.

Tupiza's **municipal museum** (Sucre near plaza) houses a dusty mix of historical and cultural artifacts, including an antique cart, old photographs, archaeological relics, old weapons and historic farming implements. It was closed for renovation at the time of research.

Nonguests can enjoy Hotel Mitru's sparkling, solar-heated **swimming pool** all day for US$1.25. Several agencies, including Tupiza Tours, rent **bikes** for around US$8 per day.

See Around Tupiza (p201) for hiking options.

Tours

There's an ever-increasing number of operators in Tupiza offering trips through the Southwest Circuit, ending in Uyuni or back in Tupiza (or, in some cases, San Pedro de Atacama in Chile). Tupiza is a great place to do this trip from, as you get to explore the lesser-known wild lands of Sud López as well as seeing the well-established highlights at different times to the large convoys of 4WDs that visit them out of Uyuni. The downside is that you may have to wait a while in Tupiza to get a group together (although the larger outfits have departures almost daily). Expect to pay US$100 to US$160 per person for the standard four-day trip, depending on group size and season.

While most tour operators display enthusiastic comments from satisfied customers, the truth is that standards vary widely. Many people end up choosing the agency based on their accommodations choice, but it's well worth getting out there and chatting to a few different operators. Professionalism, honesty and flexibility are the things to look for, rather than willingness to haggle on the price.

Recommended operators:

El Grano de Oro Tours (☎ 694-4763; elgranodeoro tours@hotmail.com; Arraya 492) This newly established company has good personal service and local knowledge. It offers flexible tailored tours of the Southwest Circuit, which can include climbing options, and an appealing two-day horseback route with a night in a pretty *hostal* on a working farm (US$35), as well as biking and jeep options.

Tupiza Tours (☎ 694-3003, in La Paz 2-224-4282; www.tupizatours.com; Hotel Mitru, Chichas 187) This professional, well-run outfit pioneered many of the Tupiza-area routes now also offered by competitors. Its Southwest

Circuit tours are consistently recommended by readers and depart daily in the high season. As well as horseback trips, it offers a 'triathlon' (per person US$25 to US$30), which is an active full-day tour of the surrounding area by jeep, horse and mountain bike. Butch and Sundance fans are catered for by trips to Huaca Huañusca or San Vicente or, better still, a circuit taking in both, overnighting in the atmospheric crumbling colonial village of Portugalete (per person US$45 to US$80).

Sleeping

You'll often be quoted cheaper rates for rooms in the hope that you'll then take a tour with their agency. The cheapest options are several basic *residenciales* opposite the train station.

Hostal Valle Hermoso (☎ 694-2370; www.bolivia .freehosting.net; Arraya 478 & Arraya 554; r per person US$2.50, with bathroom US$4.40) This is actually set across two separate buildings a block apart. The one nearer the bus station is a little more modern, with significantly more spacious rooms. It's HI-affiliated, clean and convenient, and guests have use of a kitchen. Readers have been kinder about the *hostal* than about its tours.

Hotel Mitru Anexo (☎ 694-3002; Avaroa at Serrano; r per person US$3.10, with bathroom US$5.60) An offshoot of the Hotel Mitru, this place offers very good value, with solid rooms with cable TV and phone. The bathrooms are modern, and guests have use of a kitchen, as well as the pool at the Mitru.

Hostal El Grano de Oro (☎ 694-4763; elgranodeorotours@hotmail.com; Arraya 492; r per person US$3.10) Run by a friendly family, this place offers four simple and sunny rooms with comfortable new mattresses, cactus furniture, shared bathrooms with reliable hot water and a welcoming feel. Guests have use of a garden area.

Residencial My Home (☎ 694-2947; Avaroa 288; r per person US$3.10, with bathroom US$4.40) Bright, clean and cheerful, this place is a good-value option run by kind, interesting people.

Hotel Mitru (☎ 694-3001; www.tupizatours.com; Chichas 187; r per person US$3.75, with bathroom US$5-8, ste US$15-25; ☐ ☑ ☑) The best hotel in town, the busy, friendly Mitru has been run by the same family for generations and is a reliable, relaxing choice built around a swimming pool that's just the ticket after a dusty day out on horseback. There's a variety of rooms – the new suites with minibar are particularly appealing, but all are good, and include a tasty breakfast. Facilities include currency exchange, laundry service and a book exchange.

La Torre Hotel (☎ 694-2633; latorrehotel@yahoo.es; Chichas 220; s/d US$5/10, with bathroom US$10/15) This sound, central choice offers clean, spacious rooms with good beds and clean hot-water bathrooms. Rooms at the front are much lighter but chillier, and have no curtains. Guests have use of a kitchen and a TV lounge, and there's a decent breakfast. You can easily negotiate lower room prices.

Eating

Tupiza's accommodations are much more inviting than its eateries, but there are a couple of decent places.

For a real morning treat, head for Mercado Negro after 8am, when the renowned Doña Wala starts serving up her fabulous *charque*-filled *tamales* (cornmeal dough filled with jerky; US$0.15) – go early because she always sells out. Her stall is outside just to the right of the entrance. A couple of no-name **juice stops** (Santa Cruz) blend refreshing juices and milkshakes from carrots and papaya. In the afternoon, stalls outside the train station serve filling meals of rice, salad, potatoes and a main dish for under US$1.

El Garaje (Chichas; light meals US$1-2.50) A relaxed space that was indeed once a garage, this place is trying hard to offer the standard gringo menu of omelettes, pastas, fruit salads, burgers and juices. Some days it seems to work better than others, but it's a peaceful spot to hang out. It's opposite Hotel Mitru.

Il Bambino (Florida & Santa Cruz; almuerzos US$1.25) This friendly corner eatery offers excellent *salteñas* in the morning, and is a popular spot with locals for its filling *almuerzos* at high noon.

California (Plaza Independencia s/n; mains US$2-3) On the plaza, this is a popular choice for a drink, a game of cards or a meal. The vegetarian choices are OK but overpriced; there's also llama steak, burgers, pizzas and beer.

Sauna (Santa Cruz 318; mains US$2-3) This tucked-away spot is better than it looks from the street, has a no-nonsense boss and specializes in good solid meat cooked on the *parrilla* (barbecue).

Confitería Los Helechos (Avaroa s/n; mains US$2-3; ☾ 7am-10pm) Attached to the Mitru Anexo, this spacious spot offers especially tasty breakfasts, a salad bar, burgers and vegetarian dishes, as well as refreshing juices. The atmosphere is sedate, and the service on the slow side.

¡Quee Pizza! (Florida near Plaza Independencia; pizzas US$2-6.30) The best of several pizza choices, this place features a cozy interior and delicious thin-crusted beauties coming out of its wood-fired oven. There are also meat dishes, Chinese choices and pasta available.

Drinking & Entertainment

Club d&b (Santa Cruz & Florida; 10pm-late) This is the place to be in town after hours. It's a very Bolivian spot whose welcoming boss has done a great job of creating a sleazy '70s vibe with aluminum foil. He tends to kick the evening off with rock and pop classics, but once the comfy booths are full, it's karaoke time.

Getting There & Away

BUS, CAMIÓN & JEEP

Several *flota* (long-distance bus company) buses leave the **bus station** (terminal tax US$0.20) in the morning and evening for Potosí (US$4 to US$6, at least eight hours) and Villazón (US$1.25, 2½ hours), and at night for Tarija (US$4, eight hours), with connections for Villamontes and Santa Cruz. There are daily departures to La Paz (US$12, 16 hours) via Potosí and Oruro at 10am and 3:30pm. **O Globo** (624-3364) leaves for Cochabamba at 10am and 8:30pm daily.

There are daily 4WD services to Uyuni (US$6.25, six to eight hours), leaving around 10:30am. Although it's a tight fit for 10 in the back of the Landcruiser, it's a spectacular, memorable trip via Atocha, where you can expect to spend at least an hour. Buses also run the same route a couple of times a week (US$5), and *camiones* sometimes leave in the early morning from just east of Plazuela El Mundo, a traffic circle around an enormous globe.

TRAIN

Unfortunately, if you travel by train you miss most of the brilliant scenery on the route to Uyuni, so you might consider the less comfortable jeep service from the bus station. The **ticket window** (694-2529) at the train station opens irregularly on days when there's a train, so it can be easier to have an agency buy your tickets for a small surcharge.

The *Expreso del Sur* trundles north to Uyuni (*popular/salón/ejecutivo* US$3.10/5/12.60, 5½ hours) and Oruro (US$7.25/11.50/25.25, 12½ hours) at 6:25pm on Wednesday and Saturday. At 4:10am on Wednesday and Sat-urday the *Expreso* speeds south to Villazón (US$1.60/2.10/4.25, 2¾ hours).

The *Wara Wara del Sur*, which is often late, leaves at 7:05pm on Monday and Thursday evenings for Uyuni (*popular/salón/ejecutivo* US$2.75/3.60/8.25, six hours) and Oruro (US$6.75/8.60/19, 13½ hours), and at 9:05am on Monday and Thursday for Villazón (US$1.40/2.10/4, three hours).

AROUND TUPIZA

Much of Tupiza's appeal lies in the surrounding landscape, a visually stunning wilderness of *quebradas*, thirsty riverbeds and thriving cactus that'll have you whistling a Morricone theme tune in no time. It's great hiking country and also perfect for exploration on horseback – several Tupiza operators offer these excursions (see p199 for Tupiza operators) – or 4WD.

If you're hiking without a guide, it's not easy to get lost, but take a map anyway – you can get them from the IGM office on the plaza in Tupiza. Carry at least 3L of water per day in this dry desert climate. It's wise to wear shoes that can withstand assault by prickly desert vegetation, and to carry a compass or GPS if you're venturing away from the tracks. Flash flooding is also a danger, particularly in the summer months; avoid camping in the *quebradas*, especially if it looks like rain.

Note that most trips from Tupiza to Uyuni include the Quebrada de Palala and El Sillar on the first morning. To hire a taxi to explore the surrounding area (where there's road access, that is) costs about US$4 an hour for up to four people.

Quebrada de Palala

Just northwest of Tupiza, this broad wash is lined with some very impressive red formations known as fins. During the rainy season it becomes a tributary of the Río Tupiza, but in the winter months it serves as a highway into the back country and part of the salt route from the Salar de Uyuni to Tarija. Beyond the dramatic red rocks, the wash rises very gently into hills colored greenish-blue and violet by lead and other mineral deposits.

To get here, head north on Tupiza's Av La Paz from Plazuela El Mundo past the giant slide; 2km ahead, along the railroad line, you'll see the mouth of the *quebrada*. About 5km further along, the route passes some obvious

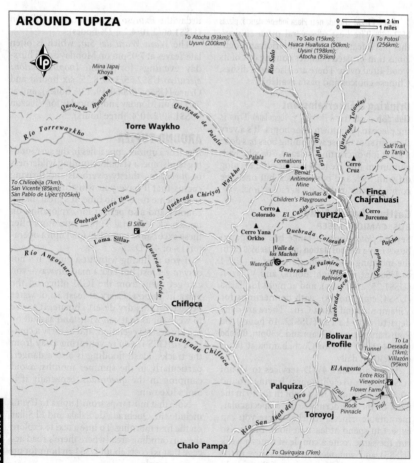

AROUND TUPIZA

To Atocha (93km);
Uyuni (200km)

To Salo (15km);
Huaca Huañusca (50km);
Uyuni (198km);
Atocha (93km)

To Potosí
(256km)

Río Salo

Mina Japaj
Khoya

Quebrada Huattoyo

Río Torrewaykho

Quebrada de Palala

Torre Waykho

Río Tupiza

Quebrada Totonias

Salt Trail
to Tarija

Palala

Fin
Formations

Bernal
Antimony
Mine

Cerro
Cruz

To Chilcobija (7km);
San Vicente (85km);
San Pablo de Lípez (105km)

Quebrada Chiriyoj Waykho

Vicuñas &
Children's Playground

**Finca
Chajrahuasi**

Quebrada Fierro Unu

El Sillar

Cerro
Colorado

El Cañón

TUPIZA

Cerro
Jurcuma

Loma Sillar

Cerro Yana
Orkho

Quebrada Colorada

Pajcha

Río Angostura

Quebrada Volcán

Valle de
los Machos

Waterfall

Quebrada de Palmira

YPFB
Refinery

Quebrada Seca

Quebrada

Chifloca

**Bolivar
Profile**

Quebrada Chifloca

Tunnel

To La
Deseada (1km);
Villazón (95km)

El Angosto

Entre Ríos
Viewpoint

Palquiza

Trail

Flower Farm

Toroyoj

Río San Juan del Oro

Rock
Pinnacle

Trail

Chalo Pampa

To Quiriquiza (7km)

---

fin formations and continues up the broad *quebrada* into increasingly lonely country, past scrub brush and cacti stands.

El Cañón

A lovely walk leads west of Tupiza through a narrow twisting canyon past dramatic fin formations and makes a great half-day stroll from town. It gently ascends for 2.5km along a sandy riverbed, to end at a waterfall.

From town, the route begins along Calle Chuquisaca, heading west past the military barracks and cemetery (the route is obvious from the summit of Cerro Corazón de Jesús). The road then narrows to a sandy track running parallel to the mountains. From here you'll have good views of some

spectacular fin formations and steep cactus-filled ravines, backed by red hills. Then bear left and follow the narrowing *quebrada* into the hills.

El Sillar (The Saddle)

About 2.5km past the first large fin formations in the Quebrada de Palala, the road turns sharply left and begins to climb up the steeper and narrower **Quebrada Chiriyoj Waykho**. After another 10km of winding and ascending, you'll reach **El Sillar**, where the road straddles a narrow ridge between two peaks and two valleys. Throughout this area, rugged amphitheaters have been gouged out of the mountainsides and eroded into spires that resemble a stone forest.

El Sillar is 15km from Tupiza; if you follow this road for another 95km you'll reach **San Vicente** (right), of Butch and Sundance fame. This entire route is part of a centuries-old trade route. From May to early July you may see a trickle of llama, alpaca and donkey trains (nowadays more likely *camiones*) humping salt blocks 300km from the Salar de Uyuni to trade in Tarija.

Quebrada de Palmira

Between Tupiza and Quebrada Seca lies a wonderful, normally dry wash flanked by tall and precarious fin formations. The right fork of the wash is rather comically known as Valle de los Machos (Valley of Males) or Valle de los Penes (Valley of Penises). The names stem from the clusters of exceptionally phallic pedestal formations.

At the head of the main fork of the *quebrada*, you can ascend along a trickle of calcium-rich fresh water, up over boulders and through rock grottoes, into a hidden world beneath steep canyon walls. About 300m up the canyon you'll find several excellent camp sites with some water available most of the year.

Quebrada Seca (Dry Wash)

Near the refinery 9km south of town, a road turns southwest into a dry wash. Unfortunately, Quebrada Seca's lower reaches serve as a garbage dump, but if you continue up the wash, the trash thins out and the route passes into some spectacular red-rock country. At the intersection, the right fork climbs the hill toward the village of Palquiza and the left fork crosses the Río San Juan del Oro, eventually losing itself in the side canyons opening into the main channel. This particularly beautiful route is a good place to see condors.

During the dry season, hikers can turn left just before the Río San Rafael bridge (10km south of Tupiza) and follow the river's northern bank to Entre Ríos. If you wade the Río Tupiza at this point, you can return to town via the road coming from Villazón.

Huaca Huañusca

On November 4, 1908, Butch Cassidy and the Sundance Kid pulled off the last robbery of their careers when they politely and peacefully relieved Carlos Peró of the Aramayo company payroll, which amounted to US$90,000, at the foot of a hill called Huaca Huañusca

(Dead Cow). The name was apparently applied because of the hill's resemblance to a fallen bovine.

From an obvious pass on the ridge, a walking track descends the steep slopes to the west for about 2km to the river, where there's a small meadow, a tiny cave and some rugged rock outcrops where the bandits probably holed up while waiting for the payroll to pass.

Of special interest along the 65km route from Tupiza is the village of **Salo**, where a local woman produces the Altiplano's best cheese and onion empanadas – coming from Tupiza, it's the first house on the right; also delicious is the local *asado de chivo* (charbroiled goat). Along the way, you can marvel at red spires, pinnacles (the most prominent is known as La Poronga, a crude Argentine expression denoting a feature of male anatomy), canyons, tall cacti and tiny adobe villages.

Several Tupiza agencies offer jeep trips to Huaca Huañusca.

SAN VICENTE
elevation 4800m

> Kid, the next time I say let's go someplace like Bolivia, let's go someplace like Bolivia!
> *Paul Newman, in the film* Butch Cassidy & the Sundance Kid

This remote one-mule village wouldn't even rate a mention were it not the legendary spot where the outlaws Robert LeRoy Parker and Harry Alonzo Longabaugh – better known as Butch Cassidy and the Sundance Kid – met their untimely demise (see boxed text, p204). The mine in San Vicente is now closed and the place has declined to little more than a ghost town. Most of those remaining are military people, mine security guards and their families.

To be honest, even hardcore Butch and Sundance fans are sometimes a little disappointed by the place, a dusty spot with little tourist infrastructure. Bring your imagination: you can still see the adobe house where the bandits holed up and eventually died, the cemetery where they were buried and the sign welcoming visitors to the town: 'Here death's Butch Kasidy Sundance the Kid.'

The **El Rancho Hotel** (r per person US$1.90) and the adjoining restaurant are the only game in

---

THE LAST DAYS OF BUTCH CASSIDY & THE SUNDANCE KID *Anne Meadows & Daniel Buck*

Butch and Sundance came to southern Bolivia in August 1908 and took up residence with the Briton AG Francis, who was transporting a gold dredge on the Río San Juan del Oro. While casing banks to finance their retirement, the outlaws learned of an even sweeter target: a poorly guarded US$480,000 mine-company payroll to be hauled by mule from Tupiza to Quechisla.

On November 3, 1908, manager Carlos Peró picked up a packet of cash from Aramayo, Francke & Compañía in Tupiza and headed north with his 10-year-old son and a servant, but they were discreetly tailed by Butch and Sundance. Peró's party overnighted in Salo, then set off again at dawn. As the trio ascended the hill called Huaca Huañusca, the bandits watched from above with binoculars. In a rugged spot on the far side of the hill, they relieved Peró of a handsome mule and the remittance, which turned out to be a mere US$90,000 – the prized payroll had been slated for shipment the following week.

Dispirited, Butch and Sundance returned to Francis' headquarters at Tomahuaico. The following day, Francis guided them to Estarca, where the three of them spent the night. On the morning of November 6, the bandits bade farewell to Francis and headed west to San Vicente.

Meanwhile, Peró had sounded the alarm, and posses were scouring southern Bolivia. A four-man contingent from Uyuni reached San Vicente that afternoon. Butch and Sundance arrived at dusk, rented a room from Bonifacio Casasola and sent him to fetch supper. The posse came to investigate and had scarcely entered the courtyard when Butch shot and killed a soldier. During the brief gunfight that ensued, Sundance was badly wounded. Realizing that escape was impossible, Butch ended Sundance's misery with a shot between the eyes, then fired a bullet into his own temple.

At the inquest, Carlos Peró identified the corpses as those of the men who had robbed him. Although buried as *desconocidos* (unknowns) in the cemetery, the outlaws fit descriptions of Butch and Sundance, and a mountain of circumstantial evidence points to their having met their doom in San Vicente. For example, Santiago Lowe, Butch's well-known alias, was recently found among the hotel guest list published in the Tupiza newspaper just a few days before the Aramayo holdup, which confirms eyewitness accounts that he was there. Nonetheless, rumors of their return to the USA have made their fate one of the great mysteries of the American West.

In 1991, a team led by forensic anthropologist Clyde Snow attempted to settle the question by excavating the bandits' grave. No one in the village had any knowledge of its location, except one elderly – and as it turned out, imaginative – gentleman, who led them to a specific tombstone. The grave's sole occupant turned out to be a German miner named Gustav Zimmer.

See http://ourworld.compuserve.com/homepages/danne for an exhaustive Butch and Sundance bibliography.

Anne Meadows is the author of Digging Up Butch and Sundance, *University of Nebraska Press, 2003*

---

town. Otherwise, come prepared for camping at this high, cold altitude. There are a few shops, but don't rely on them, as food is brought in by truck and disappears quickly. Occasionally, you can get hearty llama fricassee from a stall on the plaza.

Getting There & Away

There's no regular public transportation between Tupiza and San Vicente. Occasionally, a *camión* departs for San Vicente early on Thursday morning from Tupiza's Plazuela El Mundo, but it's dependent on San Vicente's current economic situation. The route runs via El Sillar, turning north at the village of Nazarenito.

The easiest way to go is with a Tupiza agency. While the one-day trips to San Vicente and back are a long, expensive slog, Tupiza Tours (p199) runs a more interesting two-day excursion, taking in Huaca Huañusca and an overnight stop in atmospheric Portugalete.

VILLAZÓN

pop 28,000 / elevation 3440m

The Bolivian side of the main border crossing to Argentina is a sprawling, dusty, chaotic sort of place crammed full of stalls selling cut-price goods, many of which are contraband. Around the railway station are numerous warehouses stocking smuggled produce; it tends to be brought across by *campesinos*, who form a human cargo train across the border. The frontier and bus station are always busy, for numerous Bolivians work in Argentina.

Despite the smuggling, Villazón is a bustling rather than sinister place, but watch out for the usual shysters who tend to congregate at borders; dodgy banknotes and petty theft are not unknown.

From October to April Bolivian time lags one hour behind Argentine time. The rest of the year, Argentina operates on Bolivian time (only a bit more efficiently).

Information

The **Argentine consulate** (Plaza 6 de Agosto 123; 10am-1pm Mon-Fri) is on the main square. Numerous *casas de cambio* near the bridge along Av República Argentina offer reasonable rates of exchange for US dollars and Argentine pesos, less for bolivianos. Casa de Cambio Beto changes traveler's checks at similar rates, minus 5% commission. **Banco Mercantil** (JM Deheza 423) changes cash and has an ATM dispensing US dollars and bolivianos. **Prodem** (Plaza 6 de Agosto 125) changes dollars and gives cash advances on credit cards. There are several internet places, including **ChatMania** (20 de Mayo 130; per hr US$0.40) and **Punto Entel** (cnr La Paz & 20 de Mayo), which also has telephone cabins.

Sleeping

If you're traveling through, you might as well sleep on the Argentine side (see La Quiaca, p207), which has a better choice and a less chaotic feel.

Residencial Martínez (596-3353; 25 de Mayo 13; r per person US$2) Right opposite the bus terminal, this friendly place has gas-heated showers, making it the best deal in Villazón. There's one room with private bathroom too.

Grand Palace Hotel (596-5333; 25 de Mayo 52; r per person US$2.50, with bathroom US$5.60) Neither grand nor a palace, this somewhat institutional option is handy for the bus station. It's got acceptable, clean rooms and a level of service that depends on which member of the family you get. Enter down the side street.

Residencial El Cortijo (596-2093; 20 de Mayo 338; r per person US$2.50, d with bathroom US$10.50) This clean and reliable option is a couple of blocks north of the bus terminal on a quiet street behind the Entel complex. The pool, alas, is never filled, but the rooms are decent and have cable TV.

Hot showers cost an extra US$0.65 for rooms without bath.

Hostal Plaza (596-3535; Plaza 6 de Agosto 138; s/d US$4.40/6.25, with bathroom US$6.25/12.50) While it's no paradise, this decent modern option is well-located on the square and has reasonable rooms with bathroom and cable TV. The simpler rooms without en suite are OK, but the shared bathrooms might leave you postponing your shower for a day or two.

Eating

Villazón is no garden of gourmet delights; a walk across the bridge to La Quiaca (p207) is your best bet. In Villazón, there are cheap chicken places opposite the bus station, and a clutch of mediocre restaurants nearby on Calle La Paz. The best option is **Snack Pizzeria Don Vicco** (25 de Mayo 56; pizzas US$2-3; 6-11pm), done out diner-style in red vinyl; it's an OK spot for burgers, beer and pizza. The stalls upstairs in the main market near the plaza make up in price what they lack in variety. Don't miss the delicious *licuados* (fruit shakes) and juices.

Getting There & Away

BUS

All northbound buses depart from the **Villazón bus terminal** (fee US$0.25). All except those bound for Tarija pass through Tupiza (US$1.25, 2¼ hours); it's a beautiful trip, so try to go in the daylight and grab a window seat. Regular services also head to La Paz (US$20 to US$30, around 20 hours) via Potosí (US$9, 10 hours) and Oruro.

Daily services along the rough but amazing route to Tarija (US$3.15, seven to eight hours) continue to Bermejo and Yacuiba at 11am and 8pm. Argentine bus companies have ticket offices opposite Villazón's terminal, but all Argentine buses leave from the La Quiaca bus terminal.

You'll be hassled by ticket sellers for both Argentine and Bolivian bus services; don't be rushed into buying a ticket, as there may be a service leaving sooner. You can easily bargain down the price on longer routes; conversely, the sellers may try and overcharge you on shorter journeys.

TRAIN

The Villazón train station is 1.5km north of the border crossing – a taxi costs US$2. The *Expreso del Sur* departs Wednesday and Saturday at 3:30pm for Tupiza (*popular/salón/*

SOUTHERN ALTIPLANO

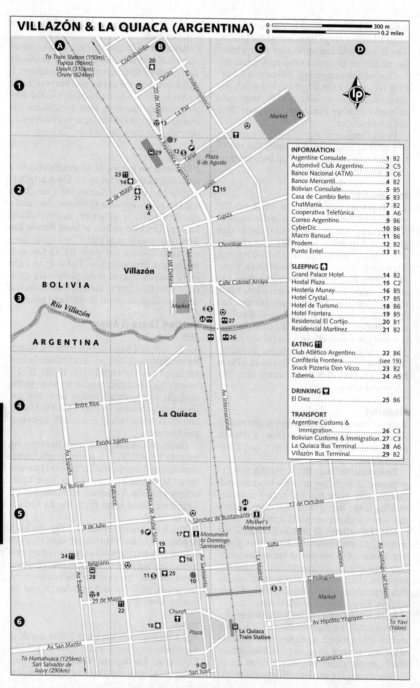

VILLAZÓN & LA QUIACA (ARGENTINA)

INFORMATION
Argentine Consulate	1 B2
Automóvil Club Argentino	2 C5
Banco Nacional (ATM)	3 C6
Banco Mercantil	4 B2
Bolivian Consulate	5 B5
Casa de Cambio Beto	6 B3
ChatMania	7 B2
Cooperativa Telefónica	8 A6
Correo Argentino	9 B6
CyberDic	10 B6
Macro Bansud	11 B6
Prodem	12 B2
Punto Entel	13 B1

SLEEPING 🛏
Grand Palace Hotel	14 B2
Hostal Plaza	15 C2
Hostería Munay	16 B5
Hotel Crystal	17 B5
Hotel de Turismo	18 B6
Hotel Frontera	19 B5
Residencial El Cortijo	20 B1
Residencial Martínez	21 B2

EATING 🍴
Club Atlético Argentino	22 B6
Confitería Frontera	(see 19)
Snack Pizzeria Don Vicco	23 B2
Taberna	24 A5

DRINKING 🍷
El Diez	25 B6

TRANSPORT
Argentine Customs & Immigration	26 C3
Bolivian Customs & Immigration	27 C3
La Quiaca Bus Terminal	28 A6
Villazón Bus Terminal	29 B2

SOUTHERN ALTIPLANO

ejecutivo US$1.60/2.10/4.25, 2¾ hours), Uyuni (US$4.75/7/16.90, 8½ hours) and Oruro (US$9/13.60/29.50, 16½ hours). This is an enjoyable trip with superb scenery for the first few hours. The more crowded and basic *Wara Wara del Sur* departs Monday and Thursday at 3:30pm for Tupiza (*popular/salón/ejecutivo* US$1.40/2.10/4, three hours), Uyuni (US$4.25/5.75/12.40, 10 hours) and Oruro (US$8/10.75/23.10, 17½ hours). It's a good option as far as Tupiza, but after dark it turns tedious.

TO/FROM ARGENTINA

To just visit La Quiaca briefly, there's no need to visit immigration; just walk straight across the bridge. Crossing the border is usually no problem, but avoid the line of traders getting their goods searched; otherwise it may take you hours to clear customs.

On the north side of the international bridge, **Bolivian customs & immigration** (24hr) issues exit and entry stamps (the latter normally only for 30 days) – there is no official charge for these services. Argentine immigration is open 24/7, but Argentine customs is only open from 7am to midnight. Formalities are minimal, but those entering Argentina may be held up at several control points further south of the border by exhaustive customs searches.

LA QUIACA (ARGENTINA)

☎ (54) 03885

Villazón's twin town of La Quiaca (3442m) is just across the Río Villazón and *only* 5121km north of Ushuaia, Tierra del Fuego. In contrast to the frenetic Bolivian side, La Quiaca is a neat sort of place, with tree-lined avenues and quiet streets. Apart from the turmoil around the bus station, almost nothing goes on here, but it has some decent places to stay and eat. La Quiaca's centenary is in 2007, so perhaps it will be a little more lively than usual…

Information

There's no tourist office, but you can sometimes find Argentine maps at the **Automóvil Club Argentino** (ACA; cnr Internacional (RN9) y Sánchez de Bustamante). There is also Lonely Planet's *Argentina* guide for information.

The **Bolivian consulate** (☎ 422-283; Árabe Siria 531; 7am-6:30pm Mon-Fri) also opens irregularly on Saturday morning and issues visas for US$15.

Banco Nacional (La Madrid & Pellegrini) exchanges US dollars and has an ATM. **Macro Bansud** (Árabe Siria near Belgrano) also has an ATM. It's easy to buy pesos with dollars at good rates.

Services at the post office **Correo Argentino** (San Juan at Sarmiento; 8am-1pm & 5-8pm Mon-Fri, 9am-1pm Sat) and the **Cooperativa Telefónica** (España at 25 de Mayo) are generally more reliable in Argentina than in Bolivia. There are many late-opening internet places; one is **CyberDic** (Sarmiento 439; per hr US$0.30).

Sleeping

Hotel Frontera (Belgrano at Árabe Siria; s/d/tr US$4.50/8/12) A basic but friendly *hostal*-restaurant, Frontera has chilly rooms with shared bathrooms that have electric showers.

Hostería Munay (☎ 42-3924; www.munayhotel.jujuy.com; Belgrano 51-61; r per person US$5, with bathroom US$6.50) La Quiaca's most appealing choice, this place is set back from the road. Rooms are spacious and modern, and breakfast is included.

Hotel Crystal (☎ 45-2255; Sarmiento 543; s/d/t with bathroom US$6.50/9.90/13) This slightly run-down hotel is in a shopping arcade and has a loungey feel with decorative mirrors and a wraparound bar in the lobby. More spartan rooms out the back (without bath) fetch US$3.25 per person.

Hotel de Turismo (☎ /fax 42-2243, ☎ 42-3390; Árabe Siria at San Martín; s/d with bathroom & breakfast US$10/16;) This comfortable but slightly institutional place is the tourism ministry hotel and the fanciest place in town. Rooms with TV.

Eating

While it ain't one of Argentina's best places to dine, La Quiaca has more to offer than Villazón. The Hotel de Turismo has a high-ceilinged, draughty dining room with a fireplace; *bife de chorizo* (rump steak) with chips and fried eggs goes for around US$4. There is a fast-food café at the bus terminal.

Confitería Frontera (Belgrano at Árabe Siria; mains US$2-5) Hotel Frontera's cheap and cheerful café has good-value meat plates, Spanish omelettes and decent *tallarines al pesto* (noodles with pesto), plus a four-course set *menu económico* for US$3. Service is friendly and it's popular with locals.

Taberna (España at Belgrano; mains US$3-4) Across the way from the bus station, this place does decent *parrillada*.

Club Atlético Argentino (Balcarce & 25 de Mayo; lunch) This is worth a try for pizza, *parrillada*, *panchos* (hot dogs) and ice cream.

Drinking & Entertainment

There isn't a hell of a lot going on in La Quiaca at night, but **El Diez** (Árabe Siria near Belgrano), a nightspot with some reasonably up-to-date music, can get fairly lively.

Getting There & Away

Buses depart from the mobbed **La Quiaca bus terminal** (Terminal de Omnibuses; left luggage US$0.35) at the corner of España and Belgrano. Argentine bus services are among the world's best;

most offer heating, air-conditioning, videos, meals *and* bladder-friendly facilities. Several southbound services depart almost hourly for Humahuaca (US$2.20; two hours) and San Salvador de Jujuy (US$4.80, five to six hours). The route passes through some stunningly colorful, cactus-studded landscapes. There are also regular direct services to Buenos Aires (US$38, about 24 hours). The short taxi ride to the *frontera* (border) should cost no more than US$0.50.

SOUTHERN ALTIPLANO

Central Highlands

True to their name, the Central Highlands occupy the heart of the country, and in many ways are the spiritual heart of the Bolivian nation. Gorgeous whitewashed Sucre, whose elegant patioed houses and noble churches make it the nation's handsomest city, is still the judicial capital of the country. It was here that Bolivian independence was declared in 1825, and it's still known as the 'Cradle of Liberty.'

Potosí, on the other hand, is a powerful symbol of the natural wealth of the country. The Cerro Rico mountain looms over the city; so much silver has been extracted from it over the centuries, it's a wonder it still stands. These days, co-operative miners eke a living in its cramped tunnels in some of the most appalling working conditions still extant in the 21st century.

At a much lower altitude, Cochabamba is one of Bolivia's most livable cities, with a perfect climate, and surrounded by fertile valleys. It's got a more modern feel, with cinema centers and Americanized chain restaurants popping up, but it still preserves much character, and has excellent restaurants and nightlife.

But it's not all about cities here. Throughout the region, there are lovely, little-known colonial towns gently crumbling with age. It's well worth eschewing the city-to-city mode of travel to give you time to explore them. A more distant past is evoked by the Inca ruins in the Cochabamba valley, but Parque Nacional Torotoro has the last laugh on the age front. A rugged, geologically-fascinating wilderness, it's bristling with dinosaur footprints and fossils, some of which date back 300 million years.

HIGHLIGHTS

- Admire the churches of **Potosí** (p258), filled with evocative religious artworks
- Goggle at the colonial beauty of **Sucre** (p240), Bolivia's most beautiful city
- Pack on the pounds or party hard in **Cochabamba** (p211), which boasts some of the country's best restaurants and bars
- Home in on remote, wild **Parque Nacional Torotoro** (p236), literal stomping ground of dinosaurs
- Roam the **Cordillera de los Frailes** (p254), home to the intriguing Jalq'a weaving culture

★ Cochabamba

★ Parque Nacional Torotoro

★ Cordillera los Frailes
★ Sucre

★ Potosí

| TELEPHONE CODE: 4 | POPULATION: 2,573,000 | ELEVATION: 1600M TO 5400M |

History

Prior to Spanish domination, the town of Charcas, where Sucre now stands, was the indigenous capital of the valley of Choque-Chaca. It served as the residence of local religious, military and political leaders, and its jurisdiction extended to several thousand inhabitants. When the Spanish arrived, the entire area from Southern Peru to the Río de la Plata in present-day Argentina came to be known as Charcas.

In the early 1530s Francisco Pizarro, the conquistador who felled the Inca empire, sent his brother Gonzalo to the Charcas region to oversee indigenous mining activities that might prove to be valuable to the Spanish realm. He was not interested in the Altiplano, and concentrated on the highlands east of the main Andean cordilleras. As a direct result, in 1538 a new Spanish capital of the Charcas was founded. Following in the conquered population's footsteps, he chose the warm, fertile valley of Choque-Chaca for its site. The city, later to become Sucre, was named La Plata – silver was god in those days.

Whereas previously all territories in the region had been governed from Lima, in 1559 King Felipe II (Philip II) created the Audiencia (Royal Court) of Charcas, with its headquarters in the young city, to help administer the eastern territories. Governmental subdivisions within the district came under the jurisdiction of royal officers known as *corregidores*.

CENTRAL HIGHLANDS

In 1776, a new Viceroyalty was established in what is now Buenos Aires, and the Charcas came under its control. The city became known as Chuquisaca (a Spanish corruption of Choque-Chaca, as there were too many La Platas around for comfort.

The city had received an archbishopric in 1609, according it theological autonomy. That, along with the establishment of the University of San Xavier in 1622 and the 1681 opening of the Academía Carolina law school, fostered continued development of liberal and revolutionary ideas and set the stage for 'the first cry of Independence in the Americas' on May 25, 1809. The minirevolution set off the alarm throughout Spanish America and, like ninepins, the northwestern South American republics were liberated by the armies of the military genius Simón Bolívar (see boxed text p244).

After the definitive liberation of Peru at the battles of Junín and Ayacucho, on August 6 and December 9, 1824, Alto Peru, historically tied to the Lima government, was technically free of Spanish rule. In practice, however, it had been administered from Buenos Aires and disputes arose about what to do with the territory.

On February 9, 1825 Bolívar's second-in-command, General Antonio José de Sucre, drafted and delivered a declaration that rejected Buenos Aires authority and suggested that the political future of the region should be determined by the provinces themselves.

Bolívar, unhappy with this unauthorized act of sovereignty, rejected the idea, but de Sucre stood his ground, convinced that there was sufficient separatist sentiment in Alto Peru to back him up. As he expected, the people of the region refused to wait for a decision from the new congress, to be installed in Lima the following year, and rejected subsequent invitations to join the Buenos Aires government.

On August 6, the first anniversary of the Battle of Junín, independence was declared in the Casa de la Libertad at Chuquisaca and the new republic was christened Bolivia, after its liberator. On August 11 the city's name was changed for the final time to Sucre, in honor of the general who'd promoted the independence movement.

Difficult years followed in the young republic, and Bolívar commented on his namesake, 'Hapless Bolivia has had four different leaders in less than two weeks! Only the kingdom of Hell could offer so appalling a picture discrediting humanity!'

For more on the region's fascinating past, see the History sections under Cochabamba (p213) and Potosí (p258).

Climate

The saying 'Las golondrinas nunca migran de Cochabamba' ('The swallows never migrate from Cochabamba') aptly describes what cochabambinos believe is the world's most comfortable climate, with warm, dry, sunny days and cool nights. Sucre residents rightfully maintain that their climate is just as salubrious. The coolest time of year is winter (June–August), with clear skies and mild temperatures, but chilly Potosí is one of Bolivia's few big cities to see snow.

National Parks

The region's protected areas include the remote Parque Nacional Torotoro (p236), peppered with thousands of dinosaur footprints and Parque Nacional Tunari (p230), easily accessible from the city of Cochabamba

Getting There & Away

The Central Highlands' major population centers are well served by intercity buses. Getting between towns in the region is a bit more of a challenge if venturing beyond the Potosí–Sucre paved highway; the route between Cochabamba and Sucre is a particularly slow one.

Cochabamba has the busiest airport, while for Potosí you must fly into Sucre, not too far away.

COCHABAMBA
pop 586,800 / elevation 2558m

Busy, buzzy Cochabamba is one of Bolivia's boom cities, and has a distinct, almost Mediterranean vitality that perhaps owes something to its clement climate. While much of the city's population is typically poor, parts of town have a notably prosperous feel. The spacious new-town avenues have a wide choice of restaurants, eagerly grazed by the food-crazy cochabambinos, and the bar life is lively, driven by students and young professionals. Despite this, Cochabamba remains a very affordable city, with prices far below those in Sucre or La Paz.

The city's name is derived from the Quechua khocha pampa, meaning 'swampy

CENTRAL HIGHLANDS

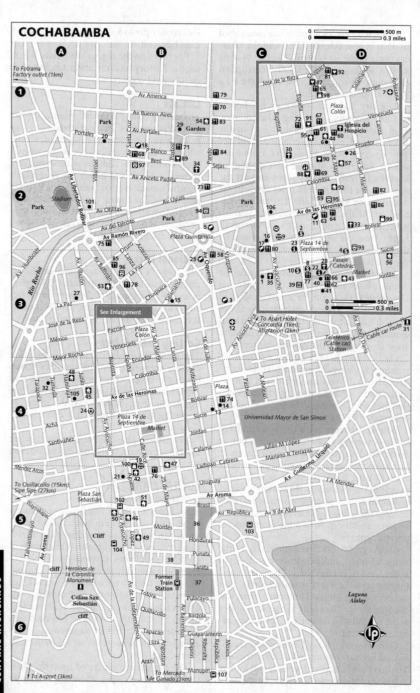

INFORMATION
Alliance Française......................**1** C3
American.................................**2** C2
Argentine Consulate.................**3** C3
Banco Unión............................**4** D2
Brazilian Consulate...................**5** B2
Centro Boliviano-Americano......**6** D1
Centro Medico Boliviano Belga...**7** D1
Efex.......................................**8** C3
Entel......................................**9** C2
Exprint-Bol.............................**10** C3
German Consulate...................**11** D2
Hospital Viedma.....................**12** C3
Instituto Cultural Boliviano-Alemán
(ICBA)................................**13** C4
Instituto Geográfico Militar
(IGM)................................**14** C4
Lavaya...................................**15** B3
Los Amigos del Libro...............**16** C2
Paraguayan Consulate.............**17** C2
Peruvian Consulate.................**18** B2
Punto Viva Estación................**19** B4
Sernap office..........................**20** A1
Tintorería...............................**21** B5
Tourist Information Kiosk.........**22** D3
Tourist Office.........................**23** C2
Tourist Police.........................**24** A4
US Consulate..........................**25** B3
Volunteer Bolivia....................**26** D2

SIGHTS & ACTIVITIES
AndesXtremo..........................**27** A3
Cathedral...............................**28** D3
Centro Cultural Simón Patiño...**29** B1
Convento de Santa Teresa.......**30** C2
Cristo de la Concordia.............**31** D3
Fremen Tours.........................**32** A4
Iglesia & Convento de San
Francisco...........................**33** D2
Iglesia de la Recoleta..............**34** B2
Iglesia de Santo Domingo........**35** C3
Mercado Cancha Calatayud......**36** B5
Mercado de Ferias..................**37** B6
Mercado Incallacta.................**38** B5
Museo Arqueológico...............**39** C3

Sol Viajes..............................**40** D3
Todo Turismo.........................**41** D3

SLEEPING ⊕
Alojamiento Cochabamba........**42** B5
City Hotel...............................**43** D3
Hostal Buenos Aires................**44** D1
Hostal Colonial.......................**45** A4
Hostal Elisa............................**46** B5
Hostal Florida.........................**47** B4
Hostal Jardín..........................**48** A4
Hostal Oruro.....................(see 46)
Hostal Ossil...........................**49** B5
Hostal Versalles......................**50** B5
Hotel Americana.....................**51** B5
Hotel Boston..........................**52** D2
Hotel Diplomat.......................**53** A3
Hotel Portales........................**54** B1
Monserrat Hotel.....................**55** C1
Residencial Familiar.................**56** D3
Residencial Familiar Anexo.......**57** D2

EATING ⊞
Búfalo's Rodizio......................**58** C3
Café Francés...........................**59** D2
Café La Republica...............(see 90)
Casa de Campo...................(see 73)
Casablanca.............................**60** D1
Co Café Arte..........................**61** D1
Cochalita...............................**62** D3
Cristal...................................**63** D2
Dumbo..................................**64** D2
Dumbo..................................**65** D1
Espresso Café Bar...................**66** D3
Ganesha Comida Vegetariana...**67** D1
Globo's..................................**68** B2
Gopal....................................**69** D2
IC Norte................................**70** C1
Kabbab..................................**71** B2
La Cantonata.........................**72** C1
La Estancia.............................**73** B2
Mosoj Yan.............................**74** C4
Paprika..................................**75** A2
Restaurant Marvi....................**76** B5
Rodizio Grill Americano.........(see 51)

Sabor Limeño.........................**77** C3
Savarín..................................**78** B3
Sole Mio................................**79** C1
Street Vendors.......................**80** C2
Sucremanta............................**81** D1
Sucremanta.......................(see 62)
Super Haas............................**82** D2
Super Natural.........................**83** C1
Tea Room Zürich.....................**84** C2
Tunari...................................**85** B3
Uno's....................................**86** D2

DRINKING ⊟
Brazilian Coffee Bar.................**87** D1
Cerebritos..............................**88** C2
Ecla......................................**89** B2
La Republika......................(see 90)
Marka...................................**90** D2
Prikafé..................................**91** C1
Top Chopp.............................**92** D1

ENTERTAINMENT ⊡
Cine Astor..............................**93** D2
Cine Center............................**94** B2
Cine Heroínas.........................**95** D2
La Pimienta Verde...................**96** B3
Lujos Discoteca y Karaoke.......**97** B2

SHOPPING ⊞
Arte Andino.......................(see 77)
Asarti....................................**98** D1
Fotrama.................................**99** D2
La Concepción........................**100** B4

TRANSPORT
AeroSur.................................**101** A2
Localiza Rent-a-Car.............(see 102)
Main Bus Terminal..................**102** B5
Micros & Buses to Chapare......**103** C5
Micros to Quillacollo, Payrumani &
Sipi Sipe............................**104** B5
TAM......................................**105** A4
TAM Mercosur........................**106** C2
Trufis & micros to Cochabamba Valley
& Torotoro.........................**107** C6

plain.' Cochabamba lies in a fertile green bowl, 25km long by 10km wide, set in a landscape of fields and low hills. To the northwest rises Cerro Tunari (5035m), the highest peak in central Bolivia. The area's rich soil yields abundant crops of maize, barley, wheat, alfalfa, and orchard and citrus fruits. Cochabamba is famous for its *chicha*, a refreshing fermented drink made from maize. It gets drunk in liberal quantities by *campesinos* (subsistence farmers) at village fiestas.

History

Cochabamba was founded in January 1574 by Sebastián Barba de Padilla. It was originally named Villa de Oropeza in honor of the Count and Countess of Oropeza, parents of Viceroy Francisco de Toledo, who chartered and promoted its settlement.

During the height of Potosí's silver boom, the Cochabamba Valley developed into the primary source of food for the miners in agriculturally unproductive Potosí. Thanks to its maize and wheat production, Cochabamba came to be called the 'breadbasket of Bolivia.' As Potosí's importance declined during the early 18th century, so did Cochabamba's, and grain production in the Chuquisaca (Sucre) area, much closer to Potosí, was sufficient to supply the decreasing demand.

By the mid-19th century, however, the city had reassumed its position as the nation's granary. Elite landowners in the valley grew wealthy and began investing in highland mining ventures. Before long, the Altiplano

CENTRAL HIGHLANDS

mines were attracting international capital, and the focus of Bolivian mining shifted from Potosí to southwestern Bolivia. As a result, Cochabamba thrived and its European-mestizo population gained a reputation for affluence and prosperity.

In 2000, the eyes of the world turned to Cochabamba as its citizens protested against rises in water rates – a struggle that, for many, highlighted a growing global problem (see boxed text opposite).

Orientation

Cochabamba is a large, sprawling city, but its central business district is compact. It lies roughly between the Río Rocha in the north, Colina San Sebastián in the southwest and weedy Laguna Alalay in the southeast.

The largest market areas are on, or south of, Av Aroma, sandwiched between Colina San Sebastián and Laguna Alalay. The long-distance bus terminal and most of the intravalley bus terminals are also in this vicinity.

The central square, Plaza 14 de Septiembre, is a hive of daytime activity, and home to the tourist office and the cathedral.

Cochabamba addresses are measured relative to the crossroads of two main avenues, Heroínas (running east–west) and Ayacucho (north–south). Street numbers are preceded by 'N' (*norte*; north), 'S' (*sud*; south), 'E' (*este*; east) or 'O'(*oeste*; west – although to avoid alphanumeric confusion, a 'W' is sometimes used instead). Addresses north of Av de las Heroínas take an N, those below take an S. Addresses east of Av Ayacucho take an E and those west an O. The number immediately following the letter tells you how many blocks away from these division streets the address falls.

MAPS
The tourist office gives out a good free city map. See the **Instituto Geográfico Militar** (IGM; ☎ 425-5563; 16 de Julio S-237) for topo sheets covering Cochabamba department.

Information
BOOKSTORES
There's an alleyway behind the post office full of vendors of Spanish-language literature and other books for reasonable and negotiable prices.
Los Amigos del Libro (☎ 425-4114; Ayacucho near Bolívar; ☎ 425-6471; Oquendo E-654; also at airport) Stocks

the best range of English, French and German paperbacks, plus Bolivian literature and Lonely Planet guides.

CONSULATES
See p369 for details of foreign consulates in Cochabamba.

CULTURAL CENTERS
The following centers sponsor cultural activities and language classes:
Alliance Française (☎ 425-2997; Santiváñez O-187)
Centro Boliviano-Americano (CBA; ☎ 422-1288; www.cbacoch.org; 25 de Mayo N-365) Can recommend private language teachers.
Instituto Cultural Boliviano-Alemán (ICBA; ☎ 422-8431; icbacbba@supernet.com.bo; Lanza 727, btwn La Paz & Chuquisaca) Offers group Spanish lessons.
Volunteer Bolivia (☎ 452-6028; www.volunteer bolivia.org; Ecuador 342) Runs the Café La Republika cultural center and arranges short- and long-term volunteer work, study and homestay programs throughout Bolivia. Also offers language courses.

EMERGENCY
Tourist police (☎ 120 or 222-1793; Achá O-142)

IMMIGRATION
Migración (☎ 422-5553; General Galindo at Torrez; ☽ 8:30am-4pm Mon-Fri) For visa and length-of-stay extensions. In the northeast of town a couple of kilometers from the centre. Ignore the queues; they are for a separate department.

INTERNET ACCESS
If you spot a city block without an internet place let us know; they are everywhere. Most charge US$0.25 to US$0.40 per hour.

LAUNDRY
Most hotels offer laundry services.
Lavaya (Salamanca & Antezana)
Tintorería (Cabrera E-163) No-name spot which dry-cleans and does bagwashes by the kilo.

MEDICAL SERVICES
Centro Medico Boliviano Belga (☎ 422-9407; Antezana N-455) Private clinic.
Hospital Viedma (☎ 422-0223) Full-service public hospital.

MONEY
Moneychangers powwow around the Entel office and along Av de las Heroínas. Their rates are competitive but they only accept US cash. There are numerous ATMs; cash advances are

also available at major banks. **Banco Unión** (25 de Mayo & Sucre) has one of several Western Union offices. The best places to change cash or traveler's checks (2% to 3% commission) are:

American (☎ 422-2307; Baptista S-159)

Efex (☎ 412-8963; Plaza 14 de Septiembre; ☺ 9am-6pm Mon-Fri) Handy location, but don't change traveler's checks (despite the sign).

Exprint-Bol (☎ 425-4413; Plaza 14 de Septiembre 0-252) Slow but friendly.

POST & TELEPHONE
The main **post** and **Entel** (Ayacucho & Heroínas; ☺ 6:30am-10pm) offices are together in a large complex. The postal service from Cochabamba is reliable and the facilities are among the country's finest. Downstairs from the main lobby is an express post office. In the alleyway behind, the customs office is a good place to send packages; it stamps them so that they won't be opened later on, and offers a cheaper rate than the post office itself.

There are numerous places to make cheap international calls. Often it's as cheap as US$0.05 a minute to the USA, and US$0.10 or less to Europe. One such is **Punto Viva Estación** (Arce nr Cabrera).

TOURIST INFORMATION
Sernap office (☎ 448-6452/53; Portales 353) Has information about Parques Nacionales Torotoro, Carrasco and Isiboro Sécure.

Tourist office (☎ 425-8030; Plaza 14 de Septiembre; ☺ 8am-noon, 2:30-6:30pm Mon-Fri) One floor up in the town hall, on the plaza side. Very welcoming, and hands out good material. There are several information kiosks, which also open Saturday mornings. One is behind the cathedral on Pasaje Catedral; there are others at the bus station and airport.

Dangers & Annoyances
Several Cochabamba scams are widely reported. False police may ask for documents – insist that you will only comply at a police station – while ingenious bogus tourists (camera and Lonely Planet in hand) may ask to accompany you because they are lost. Once they have your confidence, they will try to maneuver you into a situation where an accomplice can take advantage.

The Colina San Sebastián is now regarded (even by locals) as dangerous throughout the day, so it is inadvisable to walk on any part of it.

Sights
MARKETS
Cochabamba is Bolivia's biggest market town. The main market is the enormous **La Cancha**, which is one of the most crowded, chaotic, claustrophobic, and exhilarating spots in the country. Around the markets you'll find just about everything imaginable, but keep an eye out for pickpockets.

THE WATER WAR
With the rapid growth of Cochabamba in the late 20th century, water shortages became acute, and the city sought financing for a tunnel that would bring water through the mountains from another zone. But the World Bank, then more or less controlling Bolivia's economy, refused to countenance the government spending money on the project and forced them to sell the province's water utility to the US giant Bechtel, who rapidly put the rates up.

But the company hadn't reckoned with the citizens, who rapidly established an organization to oppose the sale. With the people furious at the rate hike, strikes were called in February 2000. The citizenry took to the streets and, after violent clashes with police, forced the government to negotiate. Arrogantly, the government refused to deal with the people's organization, and suggested a gradual price rise. This was angrily rejected, and a general strike called for early April. Nearly a hundred thousand people from all walks of life occupied the streets; when the police foolishly arrested the movement's leader, the situation rapidly deteriorated, and one man was shot by an army sniper. Things then quietened, but a massive march two days later finally forced Bechtel out, submitting a huge compensation claim in the process. Anti-globalization campaigners around the world saw it as a highly symbolic popular victory over a multinational that had bullied the Bolivian government with World Bank complicity.

These days, the water rates are back at pre-privatization levels, but, although the community water company is gradually increasing service, the money for the much-needed pipeline is as far away as ever. Still, *cochabambinos* remain justly proud of their victory.

The largest and most accessible area is **Mercado Cancha Calatayud**, which sprawls across a wide area along Av Aroma and south toward the former railway station. Here is your best opportunity to see local dress, which differs strikingly from that of the Altiplano. The **Mercado Incallacta** and **Mercado de Ferias** spill out around the old railway station. *Artesanías* (stores selling locally handcrafted items) are concentrated near the junction of Tarata and Calle Arce, near the southern end of the market area, where alleys are stuffed with friendly, reasonably priced stalls.

Due to overcrowding, the fruit and vegetable section has now moved to the shore of Laguna Alalay in the southeast of town. The fascinating **Mercado de Ganado** livestock market operates Wednesdays and Sundays at the end of Avenida Panaméricana, far to the south of the centre; it's worth taking a taxi out there to see it in operation. As always, it pays to get there earlyish.

MUSEUMS

The **Museo Arqueológico** (☎ 425-0010; Jordán E-199, cnr Aguirre; admission US$1.90; 🕙 8am-6pm Mon-Fri, 8am-noon Sat) has an excellent overview of various of Bolivia's indigenous cultures. There's an intriguing range of artifacts: funerary urns with characteristic bat and snake motifs, impressive fossils, painted ceramics, and spooky mummies and trepanned skulls. Look out for the Tiwanaku section; their shamans used to snort lines of hallucinogenic powder through elegant bone tubes. There's good information in Spanish, and an English-speaking guide is usually available from 1:30pm to 6pm Mondays to Fridays.

The **Centro Cultural Simón Patiño** (☎ 424-3137; Potosí 1450; admission US$1.25 with guide; 🕙 gardens 2:30-6:30pm Mon-Fri, 10:30am-12:30pm Sat & Sun; 🕙 tours Spanish/English 5/5:30pm Mon-Fri, 11/11:30am Sat) in the barrio of Queru Queru provides evidence of the extravagance of tin baron Simón Patiño. Construction of this opulent French-style mansion began in 1915 and was finalized in 1927. The fireplaces were constructed of flawless Carrara marble, the furniture and woodwork were carved in French wood and the walls were covered with silk brocade – one intricate 'painting' is actually a woven silk tapestry. The gardens and exterior, which were inspired by the palace at Versailles, also reflect inconceivable affluence. In spite of all this extravagance, the house was never occupied, and today it is used as an arts and cultural complex and as a teaching center. Take *micro* E north from east of Av San Martín.

CHURCHES

The most interesting building in town is the noble, timeworn **Convento de Santa Teresa** (Baptista & Ecuador; US$2.50; 🕙 9am-noon, 3-6pm, tours approx every hour). The city has hopes that the convent will be converted into a museum. At time of research, guided tours of the beautiful complex were being taken by students from the restoration school here. You see the peaceful cloister, fine altarpieces and sculptures (from Spanish and Potosí schools), the convent church, and even get to ascend to the roof. The convent was founded in 1760, then destroyed in an earthquake; the new church was built with an excess of ambition, and was too big to be domed. The existing church was built inside it in 1790. There's still a Carmelite community here, but its 13 nuns are now housed in more comfortable modern quarters next door. It's a fascinating visit; pacing the convent's corridors, you could be in a García Márquez novel.

On the arcaded Plaza 14 de Septiembre, the **cathedral** (🕙 8am-noon, 5-7pm Mon-Fri, 8am-noon Sat & Sun) is the valley's oldest religious structure, begun in 1571. Later additions and renovations have removed some character, but it preserves a fine eastern portal. Inside it's light and airy, with various mediocre ceiling paintings. There are statues of several saints, a gilded altarpiece and a grotto for the ever-popular *Inmaculada* (Virgin of the Immaculate Conception).

Constructed in 1581, the **Iglesia & Convento de San Francisco** (25 de Mayo & Bolívar; 🕙 7:30-11am) is Cochabamba's second-oldest church. Major revisions and renovation occurred in 1782 and 1925, however, and little of the original structure remains. The attached convent and cloister were added in the 1600s. The cloister was constructed of wood rather than the stone that was customary at the time. The pulpit displays fine examples of mestizo design, and there's a fine gold retable.

The Rococo **Iglesia de Santo Domingo** (Santivañez & Ayacucho) was founded in 1612 but construction didn't begin until 1778. The intriguing main facade is made of brick, with anthropomorphic columns. The interior, with a much-revered Trinity, is less interesting.

North of the river, the Baroque **Iglesia de la Recoleta** was started in 1654. It contains the attractive wooden Cristo de la Recoleta.

(Continued on page 225)

MARGIE POLITZER

A family affair, Amazon Basin (p329)

ALISON WRIGHT

An Aymará New Year celebrator,
Tiahuanaco (p104)

Snack time, La Paz (p63)

BRENT WINEBRENNER

A *charango* player backs up a violinist; the *charango* is a traditional Bolivian ukelele-
type instrument (p40)

BRENT WINEBRENNER

The thriving shopping intersection of Calles Linares and Sagárnaga, La Paz (p92)

View of La Paz from the heights of El Alto (p76)

Detail of Iglesia de San Francisco, La Paz (p74)

The Prado at night, La Paz (p64)

A fresh fruit and veggie fix, La Paz (p63)

View of Lake Titicaca from atop Cerro Calvario (p111)

Chincana ruins (p120), Isla del Sol, Lake Titicaca

Laguna Glacial (p148), Cordillera Real

The Zongo Valley (p101) rising to the southern ridge of Huayna Potosí (p157)

Ancohuma (p159), Cordillera Real

GRANT DIXON

Volcán Sajama, Parque Nacional Sajama (p179)

RYAN FO

Vicuñas graze below Volcán Tunupa (p193)

Sunrise, Sol de Mañana geyser (p195)

BRENT WINEBRENNER

RAFAEL ESTEFANIA

Casa Nacional de Moneda (p261), Potosí

Phujllay festival (p253), Tarabuco

ERIC L WHEATER

RAFAEL ESTEFANIA

Artesanía (locally handcrafted items) for sale,
Sucre (p240)

River crossing, Rurrenabaque (p336)

RAFAEL ESTEFANI

Parque Nacional Madidi (p341)

RAFAEL ESTEFANI

(Continued from page 216)

CRISTO DE LA CONCORDIA

This immense statue stands atop Cerro de San Pedro behind Cochabamba. It's a few centimeters higher than the famous Cristo Redentor in Rio de Janeiro, which stands 33m high, or 1m for each year of Christ's life. *Cochabambinos* justify the one-upmanship by claiming that Christ actually lived *33 años y un poquito* (33 years and a bit…).

There's a footpath from the base of the mountain (1250 steps) but several robberies have been reported, particularly around sunset. Safer and sweatless is the *teleférico* (cable car), which costs US$0.80 for the round-trip (closed Monday). On Sunday, for another US$0.20, you can climb right to the top of the statue and get an even better overview of the city.

The closest public transportation access is on *micro* LL, which leaves from the corner of Heroínas and 25 de Mayo. Taxis charge US$4.50 for the round-trip to the top, including a half-hour wait while you look around.

Courses

Cochabamba is a popular place to hole up for a few weeks of Spanish or Quechua lessons. Several cultural centers offer courses for around US$5 per hour. See also Cultural Centers (p214) for organizations running courses.

The **Escuela Runawasi** (☎ /fax 424-8923; www.runawasi.org; Blanco s/n, Barrio Juan XXIII) offers a recommended program that involves linguistic and cultural immersion. It also includes a trip to a relaxing Chapare rain forest hideout.

There are plenty of private teachers who offer instruction (most around US$5 per hour), but not all are experienced. You may have to try several before finding one that brings out the best of your abilities. The **Centro Boliviano-Americano** (p214) has a list of recommended teachers.

Tours

There are various agents running a variety of activities, particularly excursions to spots of interest in the province:

AndesXtremo (☎ 452-3392; www.andesxtremo.com; La Paz 138) Offers climbing, rafting, canyoning, trekking and paragliding excursions.

Fremen Tours (☎ 425-9392; www.andes-amazonia.com; Tumusla N-245). Recommended agency who can organize local excursions or high-quality trips to the Chapare, Amazon and Salar de Uyuni. Try to deal with the boss.

Sol Viajes (☎ 450-8451; Pasaje Catedral) Can organize trips to Incallajta and the surrounding area. Helpful and friendly.

Todo Turismo (☎ 450-5292; tturismo@entelnet.bo; Jordán E-280) Excursions to Incallajta at US$80 per person for two to three people, US$60 for four people or more.

Villa Etelvina (☎ 424-2636; www.villaetelvina.com; Juan de la Rosa 908, Torotoro; see p239) The best operator for trips to Torotoro National Park.

Festivals & Events

A major annual event is the **Heroínas de la Coronilla** (May 27), a solemn commemoration in honor of the women and children who defended the city in the battle of 1812. At the fiesta of **Santa Veracruz Tatala** (May 2), farmers gather at a chapel 7km down the Sucre road to pray for fertility of the soil during the coming season. Their petitions are accompanied by folk music, dancing and lots of merrymaking. The **Fiesta de la Virgen de Urkupiña** (August 15 to 18) is the valley's biggest, with pilgrims converging on the village of Quillacollo, 13km west of Cochabamba.

Sleeping

BUDGET

There are several basic, mostly shabby, rock-bottom *alojamientos* (basic accommodations) strung out along the gritty Av Aroma. For a bed, shower and little else, you'll pay around US$2 per person. The best of them is the basic but decent **Alojamiento Cochabamba** (☎ 422-5067; Aguirre S-591), which is popular with budget travelers and has hot water (in the morning only).

Hostal Oruro (☎ 424-1047; López S-864; r US$3.15 per person) Marginally cheaper than the Elisa next door, this solid family-run business has spacious rooms with solar-heated showers that seem to provide hot water more than half the time. It's safe and close to the bus station.

Hostal Ossil (☎ 425-4476; López S-915; s/d US$3.15/5) A cheerful, modern place near the bus station, this has adequate rooms with cleanish shared bathroom. There are better rooms with private bathroom, and all are spacious and light.

Hostal Versalles (☎ 422-1096; Ayacucho S-714; r per person US$3.25, with bathroom US$4.40) The best budget choice near the bus terminal is this clean, friendly HI-affiliate where breakfast is included. Rooms are clean and quiet (if you're not facing the street). You pay a little extra to have cable TV. HI members get a 15% discount.

Hostal Elisa (☎ 425-4406; www.hostalelisa.com; López S-834; s/d US$3.75/6.25, with bathroom US$7.50/12.50) Although it's got a fairly downbeat location near the bus station, this place is a real treasure. You leave the dusty street and emerge in a peaceful garden courtyard that seems somewhere else entirely. The management is friendly and the rooms are decent. There's a communal cable TV, and you can use the fridges; there's also a laundry service. Breakfast is also available.

Hostal Florida (☎ /fax 425-7911; floridahostal@latinmail .com; 25 de Mayo S-583; r per person US$3.75, with bathroom, phone & cable TV US$6.25) A charismatic and popular option, this has a quiet patio and lawn furniture downstairs plus a sun deck upstairs. It's well situated between the center and the bus terminal and is a good place to meet other travelers. The friendly staff will give you plenty of advice on what to do and not to do in Cochabamba. A good breakfast is available for US$1 to US$2.

Residencial Familiar (☎ 422-7988; Sucre E-554; r US$3.75, s/d with bathroom US$6.25/10) Set in a lovely old building, this worn but recommendable place has plenty of character. It's built around a pretty patio, complete with nude sculpture in the fountain. The downside is that the mattresses are fairly thin.

Residencial Familiar Anexo (☎ 422-7986; 25 de Mayo N-234; r US$3.75, s/d with bathroom US$6.25/10) Similar to Residencial Familiar, but slightly more comfortable and slightly less charming.

Hostal Buenos Aires (☎ 425-3911; hostalbuenosaires@ yahoo.com; 25 de Mayo N-329; s/d US$4.40/7.50, with bathroom US$8.75/12.50) This exceptionally friendly spot is in a handy location for the central sights and the nightlife. It's set around a cool, enclosed courtyard and has decent if darkish rooms – the superior ones have cable TV and phone.

Hostal Colonial (☎ 422-1791; Junín N-134; s/d US$5/8.80) Friendly, clean and secure, this is a traveler's favorite, despite less-than-firm mattresses. The best rooms are upstairs overlooking the leafy courtyard gardens.

Hostal Jardín (☎ 424-7844; Hamiraya N-248; s/d US$5/10) In a quiet part of town, this longtime favorite is centered around a likeably chaotic garden with an enormous starfruit tree. Rooms come with bathroom and hot water. The welcome is occasionally surly though.

MIDRANGE & TOP END
Apart Hotel Concordia (☎ 422-1518; hotelconcordia@ hotmail.com; Arce 690; apt per person US$10; 🖳) This fading but likeable place is family-run and

family-oriented. Three- and four-person apartments include a bath, kitchenette (dishes available on request) and phone. Guests have access to the pool and laundry service. It's north of town near the university and accessible on *micro* B.

City Hotel (☎ 422-2993; cityhotel42@hotmail.com; Jordán E-341; s/d/family r US$12.50/17.50/22.50; 🖳) This spotless, friendly, and central hotel is an excellent choice. Rooms are bright and well-equipped – are these Bolivia's best showers? – and the beds are firm and enticing. There's a laundry service, cable TV and breakfast included. It's close to the best value in town.

Monserrat Hotel (☎ 452-1011; hotelmonse@supernet .com.bo; España N-342; s/d US$15/25; 🖳) An exceptional renovation of an historic building has resulted in this, Cochabamba's most charming hotel, opened in mid-2006. It's right in the heart of the eating and café scene but is a quiet, relaxing retreat, built around a shady courtyard. The rooms are elegant, comfortable and beautifully decorated in soft ocher colors. Some may find them dark, but South American houses were traditionally built this way to escape the heat. The service is extremely personable and enthusiastic; the place is a real gem.

Hotel Boston (☎ 422-4421; hboston@supernet.com.bo; 25 de Mayo N-167; s/d with bathroom & breakfast US$16/26) The reliable old Boston has been surpassed in recent years by other hotels in this price category, but still offers a central location, cable TV, breakfast and a warm welcome if other places are booked up.

Hotel Americana (☎ 425-0552; www.americana hotel.net; Arce S-788; s/d/ste with bathroom & breakfast US$25/35/35-65) This friendly three-star option is a sound choice. The service is good, and the spotless rooms have plenty of natural light and pleasing facilities, including cable TV. Only the location leaves a little to be desired.

Hotel Diplomat (☎ 425-0687; www.hdiplomat .com; Ballivián 611; s/d US$63/73; 🖳) One of several upmarket business hotels in Cochabamba, the Diplomat combines decent service with a location right on Av Ballivián, known as the Prado, and a centre for shopping or bar-hopping. There are great views from some of the well-appointed rooms, and the hotel's facilities are the best in town.

Hotel Portales (☎ 448-5150; www.hotel-portales.com; Pando 1271; s/d/ste US$77/95/155; 🏊 🖳 🐕) In the wealthy Recoleta district, this smart hotel is set around a pool and replete with elegant busts and chandeliers. It has fine grounds, but it isn't the five-star establishment it claims to be by any stretch of the imagination. The rooms are comfortable enough, and service is willing (although more valium than espresso in nature). There's also a restaurant and bar, but on our visit they seemed a little moribund. Check the website for discount package deals.

Eating

Cochabambinos pride themselves on being the most food-loving of Bolivians, and are forever stopping to grab a pavement juice or snack, or discussing where the finest empanadas (savory pastries) can be had.

Markets (p215) are cheap for simple but varied and tasty meals – don't miss the huge, mouth-watering fruit salads. They're also the cheapest places to find coffee – and the tasty local breakfast specialty, *arroz con leche* (rice with milk). Watch out for bagsnatchers and pickpockets though.

RESTAURANTS – LOCAL

Sabor Limeño (Pasaje Catedral; lunch US$1) This quiet spot is tucked away on an alleyway behind the cathedral, and boasts a very pleasant enclosed terrace. The food is mostly Peruvian – including a decent ceviche.

Restaurant Marvi (Cabrera at 25 de Mayo; lunch US$1.50) This decent family-run place offers one of the best typical *almuerzos* (set lunches) around. At dinnertime, solid plates of *comida criolla* (criollo food) set you back around US$2 to US$3.

Savarín (☎ 425-7051; Ballivián 626; lunch US$1.65) This popular, well-established barn on Ballivián has a wide streetside terrace where people congregate for filling *almuerzos* and, in the evening, for a beer or two.

Sucremanta (☎ 422-2839; Esteban Arce 340 & Ballivián 560; mains from US$1; ☻ 11am-4pm) These two cheerful daytime locals offer traditional Sucre food; hearty soups and meat dishes, including *mondongo* (pork ribs) and *menudito* (pork, chicken and beef stew). Good for both traditional *almuerzos* and à la carte dishes.

Tunari (☎ 452-8588; Ballivián 676; mains US$2-4) This longstanding local favorite specializes in the sort of things you either love or hate: grilled kidneys (a patent local hangover cure), tripe and tasty chorizo. But if innards aren't your thing, there are other typical Cochabamba plates. Not to be confused with the mediocre

Tunari Churrasquería, which (like this) has several branches.

Paprika (Ramón Rivero & Lanza; mains US$3-5) One of the 'in' spots, this is a block removed from the roar of Av Ballivián, and is a quiet leafy place popular for its food – both Bolivian and international, including tasty baked potatoes and fondues. Later, it becomes a trendy spot for an after-dinner drink, and is a good place to meet young Bolivians.

Casa de Campo (☎ 424-3937; Pasaje Boulevar 618; mains US$4-5) A Cochabamba classic, this loud and cheerful partly open-air restaurant is a traditional spot to meet, eat, and play *cacho* (dice). There's a big range of Bolivian dishes and grilled meats; the food is fine (and piled high on the plates), but the lively, unpretentious atmosphere is better.

RESTAURANTS – INTERNATIONAL

Kabbab (☎ 424-9149; Potosí N-1392; ☻ 6pm-midnight; mains US$1.50-3) A thousand and one variations on Persian kebabs served in an intimate space adjacent to the Palacio de Portales. Highlights include clay-oven flat bread, Turkish coffee and decent baklava.

Rodizio Grill Americano (beside Hotel Americana; lunch US$2, mains US$2-4) Steak-oriented Rodizio is a carnivore's delight, but also serves great soups and has a full salad bar for vegetarians. It serves three meals daily, including good-value *almuerzos*.

Casablanca (☎ 452-9328; 25 de Mayo btwn Ecuador & Venezuela; mains US$2-5) Both restaurant and bar, this spot is popular with both locals and visitors and always has a busy buzz. As one might expect, there are dodgy Bogart murals on the walls. The place also offers a large range of international dishes, and drinks until late. Service is very poor.

La Estancia (☎ 424-9262; Uyuni E-786, near Plaza Recoleta; mains US$3-5) One of a knot of spacious restaurants just across the river in Recoleta, this Argentine-style grill is a fine place. There are thick, juicy steaks (it's worth upgrading to the Argentine meat), ribs, and kidneys, as well as fish and chicken, all sizzled on the blazing grill in the middle. There's also a decent salad bar and very good service.

Sole Mio (☎ 428-3379; América E-826; ☻ dinner only Mon-Fri, lunch & dinner Sat & Sun; pizzas US$3-6) The best pizzas in Cochabamba are to be found here. The owners, encouragingly, are from Napoli, and import the ingredients for their robust wood-fired pizzas – thin crust, light on the sauce. Soft opera music, rich Italian wines and excellent service make this a comfortable place to linger over a meal. They also serve a range of meat and pasta entrées.

La Cantonata (☎ 425-9222; España & Rocha; ✆ closed Mon; mains US$4-5) This classy Italian place is one of the city's better places to eat. The cozy interior has a roaring fire, and there's a long menu of fresh pasta dishes and plenty of wine choice. The meat dishes are particularly tasty; the starters are a bit more hit-and-miss.

Búfalo's Rodizio (☎ 425-1597; Torres Sofer, Oquendo N-654; buffet US$5; ✆ lunch only Sun, dinner only Mon) This all-you-can-eat Brazilian-style grill has smart waiters bringing huge hunks of delicious meat to your table faster than you can pick up your fork. There's a large salad bar, but, let's face it, it's designed for the carnivore. It's on the 2nd floor of a shopping arcade; take the lift.

CAFÉS

Along Calle España, near Ecuador and Venezuela/Major Rocha, you'll find an ever-changing assortment of trendy cafés, whose names seem to change every fortnight or so.

Mosoj Yan (☎ 450-7536; Bolívar at Plaza Busch; set lunch US$0.90; ✆ 10:30am-6pm Mon-Fri) This attractive, light and airy café is a very pleasant spot, and as well as serving delicious desserts, decent coffees and cheap lunches, your bolivianos go to a good cause. It's part of a support centre for teenage prostitutes; the girls run the place and make the food; they also create some of the handicrafts in the store next door. There's a decent book exchange here too.

Espresso Café Bar (☎ 425-6861; Esteban Arce 340) Just behind the cathedral, this wins the 'best coffee in town' award. It's an attractive, traditional-looking place with pleasant staff. It also serves good juices. A word of advice – don't order a 'large' espresso unless caffeine is more of a compulsion than a pleasure.

Café Frances (España N-140; ✆ 8am-8:30pm Mon-Sat) This intimate and popular option serves excellent coffee, tea, cakes, quiche and both sweet and savory crêpes in a Paris-like setting.

Co Café Arte (Venezuela, near España; ✆ 6-11pm) A relaxed café with wooden tables and repro art on the walls. The cordial owner does decent coffee, juices and a few snacks.

Tea Room Zürich (☎ 448-5820; Pando 1182; ✆ closed Tue) This upmarket, old-fashioned place is *the* place in the Recoleta district to take tea, strudels and éclairs.

QUICK EATS

There's tasty street food and snacks all over Cochabamba, with the *papas rellenas* (potatoes filled with meat or cheese) at the corner of Achá and Villazón particularly delicious. Great *salteñas* (filled pastry shells) and empanadas are ubiquitous; for the latter, try **Cochalita** (Esteban Arce S-362; empanadas US$0.30), which has a range of delicious fillings and also does ice creams. Locals swear by the *anticuchos* (beef-heart shish kebabs) that sizzle all night at the corner of Av Villaroel and Av América.

The jumbo-size **Dumbo** (dishes US$2-5); Heroínas E-345 (☎ 450-1300); Ballivián 55 (☎ 423-4223) and **Cristal** (Heroínas E-352, American breakfast US$2) serve a range of eats throughout the day, from pancakes to bland but decent burgers and main dishes, and are particularly popular for a late-afternoon *helado* (ice cream) and coffee. A similar place that's a real fun palace for children is **Globo's** (cnr Beni & Santa Cruz). Balloons, ice creams, juices and kid-friendly meals – it's got the lot.

VEGETARIAN

Uno's (Heroínas & San Martín; lunch US$1.10) Probably Cochabamba's best vegetarian food; a simple four-course lunch includes a super-fresh salad bar. They also do good fruit salads and soy burgers, but there's no alcohol. It's open from breakfast through to dinner time.

Ganesha Comida Vegetariana (☎ 452-2534; Mayor Rocha 375; set lunch US$1.10; ✆ noon-3pm) Popular lunchtime vegetarian spot just off Plaza Colón, with a range of tasty choices that diminish the later you get there.

Gopal (España N-250; mains US$1.50-2; ✆ lunch daily, dinner Mon-Fri) This friendly vegetarian place has a great setting at the end of a quiet arcade; the terrace is a tranquil spot. The location is better than the food, which includes soy-based conversions of Bolivian dishes and a few curries.

GROCERIES

IC Norte (América at Pando) Well-stocked US-style supermarket with imported and unique export-quality Bolivian products.

Super Haas (Heroínas E-585) Convenient if expensive mini-market with a deli and snack counter.

Super Natural (Pando 1270) Great eco-mercado, full of local natural and organic products.

Drinking

There's plenty of drinking action along El Prado (Avenida Ballivián), where Top Chopp is a typical Bolivian beerhall. Calle España is also fertile territory, with an everchanging parade of appealing, bohemian café-bars.

Cerebritos (España N-251; ☺ 8pm-late) A grungy, likeable bar with cabledrums for tables and loud rock and hip-hop music. The house special is a mixed platter of colorful shooters; local students down them as *cacho* forfeits.

Prikafé (España & Rocha) This cozy corner spot is an intimate, candlelit place popular with romancing couples. It's better for drinks – coffee, wine, cocktails – than the additive-laden food (US$2 to US$3.75).

Ecla (☎ 448-5406; Beni 558; ☺ 4pm-2am Wed-Sat, noon-10pm Sun) A very welcoming bar in the Recoleta district with a good vibe and live music on Friday nights. They also do decent food. They sometimes put on club nights at the Club Social, just off Plaza Colón.

Brazilian Coffee Bar (Ballivián 55) This Brazilian chain spot does a weird mixture of coffee, sushi and alcohol. Head elsewhere for the first two, but it has to be said that they pour fine, if pricy, mixed drinks. It claims to be open 24 hours.

Marka (☎ 7271-7935; Ecuador 342) This tucked-away bar set back off Calle Ecuador next to La Republika is a fine, relaxed spot to enjoy low-key music, friendly service and good mixed drinks. There's live music – jazz and blues – every now and then.

La Republika (☎ 945-2459; Ecuador 342) This comfortable café-bar is part of the Volunteer Bolivia set-up. It's a friendly spot, firmly on the gringo circuit, and offers a book exchange, Mexican dishes (US$2) and a leafy courtyard with regular live music.

Entertainment

For information about what's on, see the newspaper entertainment listings. The huge new multiplex, **Cine Center** (Ramón Rivero s/n) has several screens; nicer are bright **Cine Heroínas** (Heroínas s/n) and smaller **Cine Astor** (Sucre & 25 de Mayo).

Popular dancing spots include **Lujo's Discoteca y Karaoke** (Beni E-330), which operates Wednesday to Sunday night. There are several spots on Av Ballivián, including **La Pimienta Verde** (Ballivián s/n) a subterranean dance den.

Shopping

Locally made woolens are available at a few outlets: the long-standing co-op **Fotrama** (☎ 422-2980; Bolívar 439), its bargain **Fotrama factory outlet** (☎ 424-0567; Circunvalación 1412) and the more expensive **Asarti** (☎ 425-0455; Edificio Colón No 5,

Paccieri at 25 de Mayo), which makes export-quality alpaca. **Arte Andino** (Pasaje Catedral s/n) has a good selection of woolens too. Cheaper alpaca- and llama-wool *chompas* (sweaters) are found in the markets. For inexpensive souvenirs, scour the *artesanía* stalls behind the main post office.

For wine, visit the retail store of **La Concepción** (☎ 412-1967; Aguirre 577), one of Bolivia's more famous wineries. Try to taste what you are going to buy; if not, spend up, as some of the cheaper reds are pretty astringent.

Getting There & Away

AIR

Cochabamba's **Jorge Wilstermann Airport** (CBB; domestic/international departure tax US$1.90/3.10) is served daily by **AeroSur** (☎ 440-0909/0910; Villarroel 105) and **LAB** (☎ 425-0750; office at airport) from La Paz (US$48.50), Santa Cruz and Sucre. The flight between La Paz and Cochabamba must be one of the world's most incredible (sit on the left coming from La Paz, the right from Cochabamba), with fabulous views of the dramatic Cordillera Quimsa Cruz, and a (disconcertingly) close-up view of the peak of Illimani. **AeroCon** (☎ 448-7665; office at airport) has a daily flight to Trinidad.

TAM (☎ 458-1552; Hamiraya N-122) lifts off from the military airport to Santa Cruz on Tuesday mornings and La Paz (US$27) on Tuesday afternoons. **TAM Mercosur** (☎ 458-2166; Heroínas 0-130) connects Cochabamba with Asunción, Buenos Aires and São Paulo daily except Sunday, while AeroSur flies three times a week to Miami via Santa Cruz.

BUS

Cochabamba's **main bus terminal** (☎ 155; Ayacucho near Aroma; US$0.40 terminal fee) has an information kiosk, a branch of the tourist police, ATMs, luggage storage and a *cambio* (money exchange bureau).

Bus cama (sleeper) service is available on most long-distance routes for about twice the price of those listed below.

There are at least 20 buses daily to La Paz (US$5, seven hours). Most leave between 7am and 9pm. A baker's dozen of *flotas* (long-distance bus companies) have daily services to Oruro (US$2.50, four hours) between 7am and 10pm. Most Santa Cruz buses (US$6 to US$8, 10 to 13 hours) depart before 9am or after 5pm; some take the old Chapare road, some the new. *Flotas* go to Trinidad (US$8, 24 to 30 hours) via Santa Cruz, at 6:30am and 7:30pm.

Frequent buses leave for Sucre (US$5.70, 10 hours) between 4:30pm and 6:30pm daily. Some then continue on to Potosí (US$7, 15 hours). *Micros* and buses to Villa Tunari (US$1.90, three to four hours) and less frequently to Puerto Villarroel (US$2, seven hours) in the Chapare region leave every hour or so from the corner of 9 de Abril and Oquendo.

Flechabus and Almirante Brown offer a marathon international service to Buenos Aires (US$68, 72 hours) leaving at 5:30am and 6:30pm daily.

Trufis and *micros* to eastern Cochabamba Valley villages leave from the corner of República and 6 de Agosto. To the western part of the valley they leave from the corner of Ayacucho and Aroma. Torotoro *micros* leave on Thursday and Sunday at around 6am from República and 6 de Agosto.

Getting Around

TO/FROM THE AIRPORT
Micro B (US$0.20) shuttles between the airport and the main plaza. Taxis to or from the center cost US$2.50.

BUS
Convenient lettered *micros* and *trufis* (collective taxis) display their destinations and run to all corners of the city (US$0.20).

CAR
Localiza Rent-a-Car (Avis; ☎ 428-3132; Pando 1187), next to Hotel Portales, isn't the cheapest, but it's the best. It's also at Jorge Wilstermann Airport.

TAXI
The taxi fare around the centre is US$0.50 per person. An extra boliviano is charged if you cross the river or go far to the south. For a radio taxi, ring **CBA** (☎ 422-8856).

PARQUE NACIONAL TUNARI

This easily accessible, 300,000-hectare park was created in 1962 to protect the forested slopes above Cochabamba, as well as the wild summit of Cerro Tunari. You can get simple walking maps of the park from the Sernap office in Cochabamba (p215).

Cochabamba Area

A good dirt road zigzags its way from the park gate (open until 4pm) up the steep mountain face. After 3km from the gate, you'll reach a **picnic site** with BBQs and a playground. Be-

yond here is a *sendero ecológico* (nature trail). Don't expect too much in the way of *ecología*, but it's a well-made path that gains altitude rapidly, winding into thickening mature woodland. The views are tremendous, with Cochabamba spread out below, and in the opposite direction, Cerro Tunari and other hills in the Cordillera. With an early start and plenty of water, you should be able to make it up to some of the nearer peaks on a long day hike.

Coming from town, take *micro* F2 or *trufi* No 35 from Av San Martín, which will drop you three minutes from the park entrance, a big wooden archway with a fire-risk indicator. You may have to show ID and sign into the park. From the gate, turn right, then turn left after 100m; the road zigzags up past the playground to the lakes.

Cerro Tunari Area

Snow-dusted Cerro Tunari (5035m) is the highest peak in central Bolivia (it's the second peak from the left on the Taquiña beer label). Its flanks are 25km west of Cochabamba along the road to Independencia. This spectacular area offers excellent hiking and camping, but access is less than straightforward. For climbs, pick up the 1:50,000 map *Cordillera de Tunari* (sheet 6342III) from the IGM (p214).

The first step is to catch a *micro* to Quillacollo (p232), then walk or take *trufi* No 35 from Plaza Bolívar to Cruce Liriuni, 5km north of Quillacollo. From there it's a complicated four- to five-hour ascent to the summit, with some sections requiring technical equipment. Experienced climbers can manage the round-trip in a long day, but the high-altitude ascent will be more pleasant if you allow two days and camp overnight. A guide will be very useful to find the best route.

An easier route ascends from Estancia Chaqueri or Tawa Cruz, 12km beyond Cruce Liriuni (which has accommodations at the village school) at 4200m. *Micros* and *camiones* (flatbed trucks) toward Morochata leave on Monday, Thursday and Saturday at 7am from three blocks off the main plaza in Quillacollo; they return to Cochabamba in the afternoon on Tuesday, Friday and Sunday. The relatively easy path, which takes around five hours, ascends the north face of the peak.

Another option is Fremen Tours (p225). It leads all-inclusive two-day excursions using the northern route.

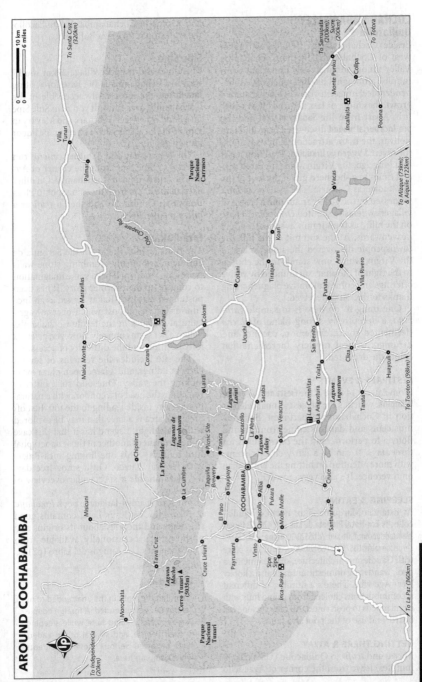

AROUND COCHABAMBA

COCHABAMBA VALLEY
Quillacollo

Besides Cochabamba itself, Quillacollo (13km west of Cochabamba) is the Cochabamba Valley's most commercially important community, although it has lost much of its independent feel in recent years, as Cochabamba's growth has more or less absorbed it as a suburb. Apart from the **Sunday market** and the **pre-Inca burial mound** discovered beneath Plaza Bolívar, the main attraction is in its church, the revered **Virgen de Urkupiña**. Tradition has it that long ago, the Virgin Mary appeared several times to a shepherd girl at the foot of the hill known as Calvario. The visits were later witnessed by the girl's parents and a crowd of villagers when she shouted *Orkopiña* ('There on the hill!') as the Virgin was seen ascending heavenwards. At the summit of the hill, the townspeople discovered the stone image of the Virgin, which now stands in the church to the right of the altar, surrounded by votive offerings and commemorative plaques giving thanks for blessings received.

One thing to do here is to sample *garapiña*, a deceptively strong blend of *chicha* (fermented corn), cinnamon, coconut and *ayrampo*, a local mystery ingredient that colors the drink red.

FESTIVALS & EVENTS
From August 14 to 18 is the **Fiesta de la Virgen de Urkupiña**, which is the biggest annual celebration in Cochabamba department. Folkloric musicians and dancers come from around Bolivia to perform, and the *chicha* flows for three days. It can be a fairly chaotic scene, with more attention on hitting the bottle than on reverence. It's also very crowded.

SLEEPING & EATING
At Estancia Marquina, 5km north of Quillacollo, is **Eco-Hotel Planeta de Luz** (☎ 426-1234; www .planetadeluz.com; full board s/d US$20/30, deluxe s/d US$65/75, 3-4 person cabins US$75, ste US$120; ▨), a curious place with Gaudíesque architecture, spa treatments, a pool, wandering domestic animals and a kooky New Age vibe. There's a number of different accommodations choices, from round huts with circular beds to posh suites. All rates include full board, and use of the pool and sauna.

GETTING THERE & AWAY
Micros and *trufis* to Quillacollo (US$0.20, 30 minutes) leave from the corner of Ayacucho and Aroma in Cochabamba. In Quillacollo, the *trufi* stop is on Plaza Bolívar.

Sipe Sipe

This quiet and friendly village 27km southwest of Cochabamba is the base for visiting **Inca-Rakay**, the most easily accessible of the Cochabamba area ruins. If you're in Sipe Sipe on a Sunday between February and May try to sample the local specialty, a sweet grape liquor known as *guarapo*.

On Wednesday and Saturday, *micros* run directly to Sipe Sipe from the corner of Ayacucho and Aroma in Cochabamba. On other days, take a *micro* from the same spot to Plaza Bolívar in Quillacollo and then a *trufi* or a *micro* to Sipe Sipe.

Inca-Rakay

The ruins of Inca-Rakay, in the Serranía de Tarhuani, are mostly crumbling stone walls these days, and you'll need some imagination to conjure up their former glory. It has been postulated that Inca-Rakay served as an Inca administrative outpost which oversaw agricultural colonies in the fertile Cochabamba Valley. That seems unlikely, however, given its lofty position and the difficulty of access.

The site includes the remains of several hefty buildings, and a large open plaza overlooking the valley. One odd rock outcrop resembles the head of a condor, with a natural passageway inside leading to the top. Just off the plaza area is a cave that may be explored with a flashlight. Legend has it that this cave is the remnant of another of those apocryphal Inca tunnels – this one linking Inca-Rakay with faraway Cuzco. On a smog-free day, the plaza affords a spectacular overview of the valley.

The rare Spanish-language book *Inkallajta & Inkaraqay*, by Jesús Lara, contains good site maps and theories about its origins and purposes; it's occasionally available from Cochabamba's Los Amigos del Libro (p214).

WARNING

Spending the night in the unattended ruins cannot be recommended. A foreign couple was reportedly killed here while sleeping in their vehicle, and several other readers have reported serious violent incidents while camping here.

GETTING THERE & AWAY

Inca-Rakay is accessed on foot from Sipe Sipe. Since staying overnight is not a safe option, you must get an early start out of Cochabamba; the trip takes the better part of a day and you'll need time to explore the ruins.

It's a 5km, 2½ hour cross-country (but well-signed) walk up a steep hill from Sipe Sipe to the site. From the southwest corner of Sipe Sipe's main plaza, follow the road past the secondary school. From there the road narrows into a path and crosses a small ditch. Across the ditch, turn left onto the wider road. Starting several hundred meters up the road from town, follow a water pipeline uphill to the first major ridge; there'll be a large ravine on your left. From there, bear to the right, following the ridge until you see a smaller ravine on the right. At this point you're actually able to see Inca-Rakay atop a reddish hill in the distance, but from so far away it's hard to distinguish.

Cross the small ravine and follow it until you can see a couple of adobe houses on the other side. In front you'll see a little hill with some minor ruins at the top. Climb the hill, cross the large flat area, and then climb up two more false ridges until you see Inca-Rakay.

Tiquipaya

The town of Tiquipaya, 11km northwest of Cochabamba, is known for its **Sunday market** and its array of unusual festivals. In late April or early May there's an annual **Chicha Festival**; the second week in September sees the **Trout Festival**; around September 24 is the **Flower Festival**; and in the first week of November there's the **Festival de la Wallunk'a**, which attracts colorfully dressed traditional women from around the Cochabamba department.

The classy **Cabañas Tolavi** (☎ 428-8370; s/d/tw with breakfast buffet US$30/38/48, cabañas US$55-85; 🐟) has chalet-style *cabañas* constructed of perfumed wood, which occupy a gardenlike setting among the trees. Nonguests can enjoy German-style meals, including a buffet breakfast. It's 500m downhill from the *trufi* stop in Tiquipaya.

Micros leave half-hourly from the corner of Avs Ladislao Cabrera and Oquendo in Cochabamba.

Villa Albina

If you haven't already had your fill of Simón Patiño's legacy in Oruro and Cochabamba, in the village of Pairumani you can visit **Villa Albina** (☎ 424-3137; admission free by guided tour; 🕑 3-3:45pm Mon-Fri, 9am-1pm Sat) and tour the home the tin baron actually occupied. This enormous white mansion, which could have inspired the TV home of the Beverly Hillbillies, was named for his wife. Albina was presumably as fussy as her husband when it came to the finer things in life, and the elegant French décor of the main house and the Carrara-marble mausoleum seem typical of royalty anywhere in the world. There's a formal garden, complete with topiary – you would never guess you were in Bolivia.

To reach Pairumani, take *trufi* 211Z or *micro* No 7 or 38 from Av Aroma in Cochabamba, or from Plaza Bolívar in Quillacollo, and get off at Villa Albina. It's only 18km from Cochabamba, but the trip may take a couple of hours, so you might consider a taxi.

La Angostura

This village sits on the shores on the artificial lake of the same name, and is a popular spot for *cochabambinos* to head to fill up on fish. It's on the route to Tarata, 18km from Cochabamba. There are many places to eat along the lake shore, which feed you up with enormous plates of *trucha* or *pejerrey* (trout or king fish) with rice, salad and potato for US$3 to US$4. Las Gaviotas is one of the best. There are also places to hire rowboats and kayaks at weekends. From near the corner of Barrientos and 6 de Agosto in Cochabamba, take any *micro* (US$0.15) toward Tarata or Cliza and get off at the Angostura bridge; if you see the dam on your right, you've gone too far (just). Nearby, on the highway, is the famous open-air **Las Carmelitas**, where Señora Carmen López bakes delicious cheese and onion empanadas (US$0.40) in a large beehive oven.

Punata

This small market town 50km east of Cochabamba is said to produce Bolivia's finest *chicha*. Tuesday is market day and May 18 is the riotous **town festival**. Access from Cochabamba is via *micros* (US$0.40) that depart frequently when full from the corner of República (the southern extension of Antezana) and Pulacayo, at Plaza Villa Bella.

If you have been hunting for the perfect alpaca sweater, contact the *alcaldía* (town hall) about **Alpaca Works** (☎ 457-7922; Bolivia 180; www.geocities.com/alpacaworks/home.html), a women's cooperative where you can browse their existing stock or order a customized Western-style sweater.

Tarata & Huayculi

Tarata, 35km southeast of Cochabamba, is one of the region's loveliest towns, a picturesquely decayed beauty that's well worth a visit for its noble buildings, cobbled streets and gorgeous plaza, filled with palm trees and jacarandas. It's famous as the birthplace of the mad president General Mariano Melgarejo, who held office from 1866 to 1871. While the citizens aren't necessarily proud of his achievements, they're pretty proud of producing presidents (populist military leader René Barrientos, who ruled from 1964 to 1969, was also born here) from such a small town, so there's a huge horseback statue of him on the main road.

The town's name is derived from the abundant *tara* trees, whose fruit is used in curing leather. The enormous neoclassical **Iglesia de San Pedro** was constructed in 1788 and restored between 1983 and 1985; several of the interior panels include mestizo-style details carved in cedar. The 1792 **Franciscan Convent of San José**, which contains lovely colonial furniture and an 8000-volume library, was founded as a missionary training school. It now contains the ashes of San Severino, Tarata's patron saint, whose feast day is celebrated in grand style on November 30.

The village also has several other **historic buildings**: the Palacio Consistorial (government palace) of President Melgarejo (built in 1872) and the homes of President Melgarejo, General Don Esteban Arce and General René Barrientos. There's a small tourist information office on the square.

Huayculi, 7km from Tarata, is a village of potters and glaziers. The air is thick with the scent of eucalyptus being burned in cylindrical firing kilns. The local style and technique are passed down from generation to generation and remain unique.

Trufis leave Cochabamba hourly from Av Barrientos and Manuripi (US$0.45; 1½ hrs). There are no *micros* to Huayculi, but minibuses running between Tarata and Anzaldo can drop you here.

Cliza

Cliza's **Sunday market** is a good alternative to the total Sunday shutdown in Cochabamba, and it's a good place to sample *pichón* (squab),

a local specialty. On other days, there's not much happening, but it's a pleasant enough town to stroll. **Restaurant El Conquistador** (Plaza de Granos s/n) is near the bus stop and has a pleasant open patio. They serve traditional dishes and a decent US$1 *almuerzo*. Micros make the 30–60 minute trip to Cliza from Av República and 6 de Agosto in Cochabamba (US$0.45).

Other notable times to visit include the **bread festival** (the second week of April) and the festival of the **Virgen del Carmen** on July 16.

INCALLAJTA

The nearest thing Bolivia has to Peru's Machu Picchu is the remote and rarely visited site of Incallajta (meaning 'land of the Inca'), 132km east of Cochabamba on a flat mountain spur above the Río Machajmarka. This was the easternmost outpost of the Inca empire and after Tiahuanaco it's the country's most significant archaeological site. The most prominent feature is the immense stone fortification that sprawls across alluvial terraces above the river, but at least 50 other structures are also scattered around the site, which covers over 12 hectares.

Incallajta was probably founded by Inca Emperor Tupac Yupanqui, the commander who had previously marched into present-day Chile to demarcate the southern limits of the Inca empire. It's estimated that Incallajta was constructed in the 1460s as a measure of protection against attack by the Chiriguanos to the southeast. In 1525, the last year of Emperor Huayna Capac's rule, the outpost was abandoned. This may have been due to a Chiriguano attack, but was more likely the result of increasing Spanish pressure and the unraveling of the empire, which fell seven years later.

The site is on a monumental scale; some researchers believe that, as well as serving a defensive purpose, it was designed as a sort of ceremonial replica of Cuzco, the Inca capital. The site's most significant building, the *kallanka*, measures a colossal 80m x 25m. The roof was supported by immense columns. Outside it is a large boulder, probably a speakers' platform. At the western end of the site is a curious six-sided tower, perhaps used for astronomical observation. On the hilltop, a huge zigzag defensive wall has a baffled defensive entrance.

The ruins were made known to the world in 1914 by Swedish zoologist and ethnologist Ernest Nordenskiöld, who spent a week at the ruins, measuring and mapping them. However, they were largely ignored – except by ruthless treasure hunters – for the next 50 years, until the University of San Simón in Cochabamba launched its investigations. They are hoping that the site will be recognized by Unesco.

At Pocona, 17km from the ruins, there's an information centre and a small exhibition of archaeological finds from the site.

Tours

Cochabamba agencies run day-long tours to Incallajta when they have a group large enough to make it worthwhile. Fremen Tours (p225) is recommended. Beware of tours that seem suspiciously cheap or that involve 'trekking.' These generally involve getting a cab to the *cruce* (turnoff) and walking up to the site – you can do that yourself.

Sleeping & Eating

Without your own transportation, visiting Incallajta will prove inconvenient at best. Additionally, if you can't arrange lodging in private homes you'll probably have to camp for two or three nights, so be sure to take plenty of water, food, warm clothing and camping gear. Camping and basic shelters are available at the Centro de Investigaciones in Pocona.

Getting There & Away

From Cochabamba, take the daily *micro* to Pocona (US$1.90, three hours), which leaves from the corner of República and Manuripi at 6am, and get off at the turnoff for the site at Collpa. From here it's an 8km uphill walk. Pocona is a further 9km past Collpa. You may be lucky and get a lift with archaeologists traveling between Pocona and the site.

TOTORA

Totora, 142km east of Cochabamba, huddles in a valley at the foot of Cerro Sutuchira. It is on the main route between Cochabamba and Sucre, but few travelers ever see it because most buses pass through at night. Nevertheless it is a lovely colonial village, built around a postcard-pretty plaza with colorful buildings and arcades. In May 1998 the town was struck by an earthquake measuring 6.7 on the Richter scale. While there's still plenty of damage visible, much of the town has since been lovingly restored. The parish church was reopened to great rejoicing in November 2006.

The annual **town festival** on February 2 features bullfights. There's a **piano festival** at the end of September, but Totora's most charming and famous festival is that of **San Andrés**. On November 2, giant swings are erected on the streets, and throughout the month young women that are hoping for marriage are swung high on them. They are also believed to be helping the wandering souls, who descended to earth on All Souls Day, return to heaven.

The **Hotel Municipal** (☎ 413-6464; Plaza Ladislao Cabrera s/n; r per person US$3.75) is an attractive reconstruction of what was once the town's hospital, and is one of two good hotels in town. It's got spacious, comfortable rooms in an old-fashioned style. There's also a couple of simple *alojamientos*.

Micros (US$1, 3½ hours) leave daily for Totora between 1pm and 4pm from the corner of República and 6 de Agosto in Cochabamba.

MIZQUE

This pretty colonial village enjoys a lovely pastoral setting on the Río Mizque. Founded as the Villa de Salinas del Río Pisuerga in 1549, it soon came to be known as the Ciudad de las 500 Quitasoles (City of 500 Parasols), after the sunshields used by the locals. It makes a great escape from the cities and main tourist sights, and the few visitors who pass through on trips between Sucre and Cochabamba are impressed by the beauty of the Mizque and Tucuna Valleys, where you may spot the flocks of endangered scarlet macaws, which squawk and frolic in the early morning.

Sights & Activities

The lovely restored **Iglesia Matríz**, which was slightly damaged in a 1998 earthquake, once served as the seat of the Santa Cruz bishopric (until the seat was shifted to Arani in 1767). There's also a small archaeological and historical **museum**. Monday is **market day**.

With the help of Peace Corps volunteers, the *alcaldía* (on the north side of the plaza) is organizing **self-guided hiking circuits** and **guided trips** to several local sites of natural and historic interest. Moises Cardozo at the Entel office or Restaurant Plaza will arrange an interesting visit to his **apiary** just outside of town.

Besides its cheese and honey, Mizque is best known for its **Fería de la Fruta** (April 19), which coincides with the *chirimoya* (custard apple) harvest and **Semana Santa**. From September 8 to 14, Mizque holds the lively **Fiesta del Señor de Burgos**, which features much revelry and bull- and cockfighting.

Sleeping & Eating

Hotel Bolivia (r per person US$1.90, with bathroom US$2.50) Next to the *campesino* market on the road to the river, the Hotel Bolivia has firm beds and is probably the nicest place in town. There's no phone, but they can be reached through the **Entel** (☎ 413-4512/14) office.

Residencial Mizque (☎ 413-5617; US$1.50) Set amid gardens, this clean place is the easiest to find if you arrive at night – look for the Prodem sign.

Hospedaje Graciela (☎ 413-5616; r per person with bathroom US$2.50) A good option with rooms with decks; it's affiliated with the recommended Restaurant Plaza.

Mizque has several cheap Taquiña-sponsored *pensiones* that serve typical Bolivian meals. They're all within a block of the plaza. Alternatively, you can eat at the street stalls beside the church.

Getting There & Away

A daily *micro* (US$2, four hours) leaves Cochabamba from the corner of Avs 6 de Agosto and República at noon; from Mizque they depart for Cochabamba at 8am on Tuesday and Friday and for Aiquile at 3pm daily. There are also occasional *micros* that travel between here and Totora – 31km on a rough road.

AIQUILE

Thriving, cheerful little Aiquile, which was decimated by the same 1998 earthquake that damaged Totora, is known for some of Bolivia's finest *charangos* (traditional Bolivian ukulele-type instrument). In late November it holds the **Feria del Charango**. Every Sunday is a busy market day.

The small **Museo del Charango** (admission US$1.25) holds a collection of the instruments, including the ones that won prizes at the festival, and also has some archaeological pieces. The **cathedral** is quite spectacular, with a freeform central building flanked by two free-standing towers.

Accommodations are available at the pleasant **Hostal Campero** (r per person US$1.90) and the basic **Hotel Los Escudos** (r per person US$2.50), which both serve simple meals. The Campero is in an old colonial building surrounding a pleasant courtyard, and the personable owner likes to chat with guests. The cost of accommodations rises during the *charango* festival.

Aiquile lies on the main route between Cochabamba and Sucre, but most buses pass in the wee hours of the night when this already soporific settlement is sound asleep. Buses to Aiquile (US$2.50) depart daily at around 3pm from Av 6 de Agosto between Barrientos and República in Cochabamba.

It's about a 1½ hours between Aiquile and Mizque. There are a couple of *micros* a day, or you can readily thumb a ride on passing *camiones*, but be prepared for a real dust bath.

PARQUE NACIONAL TOROTORO

One of Bolivia's most memorable national parks, Torotoro at times can seem like a practical demonstration of geology on an awe-inspiring scale. Beds of sedimentary mudstone, sandstone and limestone, bristling with marine fossils and – from drier periods – dinosaur footprints, have been muscled and twisted into the sharp, inhospitable hillscapes of the Serranía de Huayllas and Serranía de Cóndor Khaka. In places, the immensity of geological time is showcased, with exposed layers revealing fossils below a hundred meters or more of sedimentary strata.

Amidst it all, the characterful, impoverished colonial village of Torotoro itself (2720m) is one of the region's most remote settlements (although road access is steadily improving).

Information & Registration

Information about the park is available from the Sernap office in Cochabamba (p215). On the main street in the village of Torotoro, the **tourist office** (Charcas s/n; ☑ daily) is housed in the entrance of the *alcaldía*. This is where you contract guides and register for your visit to the park (US$2.50). Hang on to your ticket at all times as it will be inspected by park rangers.

There's an Entel office on the main street in Torotoro, which also has internet access. This is the only place in the village with a **phone** (☎ 413-5736).

GUIDES

In order to protect the park's geological wonders, it is compulsory to take a guide on any excursion outside the village. The best place

to find a guide is at the park office – ask for *'un guía confiable'* (a reliable guide), as your visit will be greatly enhanced. One of the best around is Félix González, but make sure you specify it's the *guide* you want, as the mayor shares the same name!

The going rate for a guide is around US$6 for a half-day excursion for up to four people, more for a visit to the Gruta de Umajalanta. For dinosaur footprints, it can be very helpful if the guide has a brush (otherwise buy one) to whisk the dust out of the hollows. If you are going to the cave, the guide should have head-lanterns and rope.

Guides are unlikely to speak any English.

Dinosaur Tracks

Most visitors to Torotoro come for the paleontology. The village, which sits in a wide section of a 20km-long valley at a 2600m elevation, is flanked by enormous inclined mudstone rock formations, bearing bipedal and quadrupedal dinosaur tracks from the Cretaceous period (spanning 145 million to 65 million years ago).

There are numerous tracks *(huellas)* all over the place, and much work remains to be done on their interpretation. Many different dinosaur species are represented, both herbivorous and carnivorous.

The closest tracks are just at the entrance to the village, on the other side of the river. Above the water but below the road are the area's largest tracks, made by an enormous quadruped dinosaur (diplodocus or similar),

and they measure 35cm wide, 50cm long and 20cm deep. Near here, just above the road, the angled plane of rock reveals a multitude of different tracks, including a long set of a heavy quadrupedal dinosaur that some have posited are those of the armadillo-like anklyosaurus.

Along the route to Umajalanta cave, the flat area known as the Carreras Pampa site, has several excellent sets of footprints (on both sides of the path). These were made by three-toed bipedal dinosaurs, both herbivores (with rounded toes) and carnivores (pointed toes, sometimes with the claw visible).

All the tracks in the Torotoro area were made in soft mud which then solidified into mudstone. They were later lifted and tilted by tectonic forces. For that reason, many of the tracks appear to lead uphill. Many local guides, however, believe that the footprints were made in lava as the dinosaurs fled a volcanic eruption.

Sea Fossils

In a small side gully, an hour's walk southwest of Torotoro, on the Cerro de las Siete Vueltas (Mountain of Seven Turns – so called because the trail twists seven times before reaching the peak), is a major sea-fossil deposit. At the base of the ravine you may see petrified shark teeth, while higher up, the limestone and sedimentary layers are set with fossils of ancient trilobites, echinoderms, gastropods, arthropods, cephalopods and brachiopods. The site is thought to date back about 350 million years. There's another major sea-fossil site in the **Quebrada Thajo Khasa**, southeast of Torotoro.

Pachamama Wasi

This astonishing and beautiful **house-museum** (Sucre s/n; admission US$0.40) is the quirky home of a man who has spent years of his life pacing the cerros (hills) with a rockhound's eye. The house is like a botanic garden, but of stones: fossils, geological quirks and unusually shaped rocks form a unique, soothing ensemble. It's uphill from the main street but only open when the owner or his family are at home.

Cañón de Torotoro & El Vergel

Three kilometers from Torotoro, the ground suddenly drops away into an immense and spectacularly beautiful canyon, over 250m deep. From the *mirador* (viewpoint) at the top, you can gaze along it, watching vultures wheeling. The cliffside here is also home to the rare paraba frente roja (red-browed macaw), which you are a good chance of seeing, or at least hearing.

From here, following the diminishing canyon along to the left, you come to a flight of 800 stairs that lead down to El Vergel (or Huacasenq'a – 'cow's nostrils' in Quechua), which always has water and is filled with incongruous moss, vines and other tropical vegetation. At the bottom a crystal-clear river tumbles down through cascades and waterfalls, forming idyllic swimming pools.

Batea Cocha Rock Paintings

Above the third bend of the Río Torotoro, 1.5km downstream from the village, are several panels of ancient rock paintings collectively called Batea Cocha because the pools below them resemble troughs for pounding laundry. The paintings were executed in red pigments and depict anthropomorphic and geometric designs as well as fanciful representations of serpents, turtles and other creatures.

Gruta de Umajalanta

The Río Umajalanta, which disappears beneath a layer of limestone approximately 22m thick, has formed the impressive Umajalanta Cavern, of which 4.5km of passages have been explored.

The exciting descent is moderately physical, and you must expect to get both wet and dirty, as there are several parts where you must crawl and wriggle to get through, and a couple of short roped descents. Make sure you have good non-slip shoes on.

Inside are some spectacular stalagmite and stalactite formations, as well as a resident population of vampire bats (don't worry, they don't attack humans and stay well out of reach), who have produced an impressively large pile of steaming dung over the years.

You eventually descend to an underground lake and river, which is populated by small white, completely blind, catfish. The ascent from here is fairly easy, as it takes a more direct route.

The 8km one-way walk to the cavern entrance takes two hours from the village, with plenty of dinosaur footprints to inspect on the way.

There are numerous other caverns in the area, many of which are substantially unexplored.

Llama Chaqui

A challenging 19km hike around the Cerro Huayllas Orkho from Torotoro will take you to the ruins known as the Llama Chaqui (Foot of the Llama). The multilevel complex, which dates from Inca times, rambles over distinctive terraces and includes a maze of rectangular and semicircular walls, plus a fairly well-preserved watchtower. Given its strategic vantage point, it probably served as a military fortification, and may have been somehow related to Incallajta (p234), further north.

Tours

A few Cochabamba agencies (p225) run trips, including visits to the major sights, from town. The best is Villa Etelvina, who are experts in the Torotoro area, and passionate about the national park and the local community. They arrange comfortable 4WD transfers from Cochabamba, and put visitors up in their excellent lodge (opposite) in Torotoro village. Fremen Tours also runs good trips.

Festivals & Events

From July 24 to 27, the village stages the **Fiesta del Señor Santiago**, which features sheep sacrifices, dynamite explosions, colorful costumes, much chicha and some light *tinku* (traditional Bolivian fighting; see boxed text p271). This is an interesting time to visit – and there's much more public transportation – but the natural attractions are very crowded.

Sleeping & Eating

There are several downmarket *residenciales* (simple accommodations) in Torotoro, but few that are much more than huts with signs. One that's substantially better is **Hostal Las Hermanas** (Cochabamba; r US$4.40), which is simple but clean and comfortable, with hot water; it's on the street that enters the village, on the left.

Villa Etelvina (☎ 424-2636, 7072-1587; www.villaetelvina.com; Sucre s/n; r per person US$15, plus full board US$8 extra) The best option in town, this is a comfortable and welcoming oasis owned by a delightful couple who love the area. As well as having extremely comfortable and stylish bungalowstyle rooms, which can sleep a group or family, they put on some of the most delicious home cooking you're likely to find on your travels in Bolivia. Vegetarian fare is available on request, and is particularly good. As well as transfers from Cochabamba, they will arrange visits in the area (try to get Ramiro to accompany you, as he knows substantially more than most guides about the geology, and speaks English) and can also offer a mountain-bike descent as part of the trip. Book ahead, as they need notice to be able to accompany guests.

You can also camp at Villa Etelvina, but if you wish to camp elsewhere, locals will expect you to pay. It's important to set a mutually agreeable price (perhaps US$1 per group per night) and pay only the family in control of the land.

Getting There & Away

Parque Nacional Torotoro is 138km southeast of Cochabamba in Potosí department. The road has been substantially improved in recent years, and works are continuing. It is envisaged that, within a few years, the whole route will be either asphalt or cobblestone, but in the meantime, access in the rainy season (November to February) can be problematic – flying can be the best way to arrive.

AIR

No air services are scheduled to Torotoro, but you can sometimes charter a plane. This costs about US$140 for up to five passengers one-way and takes 30 minutes. A spectacular flight.

Eugenio Arbinsona (☎ 422-7042, 424-6289) Private pilot.

Grupo Aéreo 34 (☎ 423-5244) Local airforce, sometimes will comply if not busy.

Misión Nuevas Tribus (☎ 424-2057, 424-7489, 425-7875) Mission with a plane.

BUS & CAMIÓN

Buses (US$2.50, six to eight hours) depart on Thursday and Sunday around 6am from the corner of Avs República and 6 de Agosto in Cochabamba. They return early Monday and Friday morning from near the plaza in Torotoro. They are run by **Trans del Norte** (☎ 456-1496); it's worth ringing, as there are often additional departures, particularly during the holiday season.

Camiones ply the same route during the dry season, leaving at around the same time. It's cheap but not very comfortable (US$1.25) unless you get a seat in the cab (US$2).

CAR & MOTORCYCLE

By far the most comfortable terrestrial way to get to Torotoro is by 4WD or motorbike. Tour agencies (see opposite) arrange transfers from Cochabamba; the journey takes around five hours.

You can rent 4WDs in Cochabamba (p230). Fill the tank in Cochabamba, as there's no petrol in Torotoro itself. To reach Torotoro, head out on the Sucre road. Once you see the signs advertising La Angostura, take the uphill right turn that follows the lake above the village. If you reach the Angostura dam on your right, you have gone too far by a couple of hundred meters.

Follow this road until you reach the town of Totora (you'll know it by the large equestrian statue). Cross one bridge, then take a right turn immediately before a second bridge. About 500m along this road, you need to cut across the riverbed to your left; on the other side, a good cobblestone road starts and soon reaches the potters' village of Huaycalí. Continue on this road past the town of Anzaldo; this is the last possible refueling place. About 10km beyond here, you turn left onto a dirt road; this is signposted, but easy to miss. This spectacular road descends into a river valley, and finally makes a precipitous switchback ascent to Torotoro itself.

The road is in the process of being upgraded, so make sure you find out the state of play in Cochabamba before leaving.

MOUNTAIN BIKE

Villa Etelvina (see left) offers an exciting option to ride a good part of the journey by mountain bike. While not quite as heartin-mouth as the more famous Coroico descent, it's a memorable downhill run through spectacular scenery, and with almost no traffic. The bikes are in good condition and much care is taken.

SUCRE

pop 247,300 / elevation 2790m

Proud, genteel Sucre is Bolivia's most beautiful city, and the symbolic heart of the nation. It was here that independence was proclaimed, and while La Paz is now the seat of government and treasury, Sucre is still Bolivia's judicial capital . A glorious ensemble of whitewashed buildings sheltering pretty patios, it's a spruce place that preserves a wealth of colonial architecture. Sensibly, there are strict controls on development (don't even think about painting your house black, for example), which have kept Sucre as a real showpiece of Bolivia. It was declared a Unesco World Heritage site in 1991. See p210 for an overview of Sucre's history.

Set in a valley surrounded by low mountains, Sucre enjoys a mild and comfortable climate. It's still a center of learning, and both the city and its university enjoy reputations as focal points of progressive thought within the country. It was no coincidence that it was chosen as the seat of the Asamblea Constituyente, a committee who gathered in 2006 to thrash out a new, more representative constitution for Bolivia.

With a selection of excellent accommodations, a wealth of churches and museums, and plenty to see and do in the surrounding area, it's no surprise that visitors end up spending much longer in Sucre than they bargained on.

Orientation & Maps

Sucre is compact and laid out in an easily negotiated grid pattern. Tourist offices give out a good town map and better hotels and tour agencies include maps on the back of their brochures.

Instituto Geográfico Militar (☎ 645-5514; Arce 172) has topographic maps of Chuquisaca department.

Information

CULTURAL CENTERS

There's a monthly brochure detailing Sucre's cultural events; look for it at tourist offices or in bars and restaurants.

Alliance Française (☎ 645-3599; Arce 35) French-language library, foreign films and La Taverne restaurant (p250).

Casa de la Cultura (☎ 645-1083; Argentina 65) Hosts art exhibitions and music recitals and runs a café and public library.

Centro Boliviano-Americano (CBA; ☎ 644-1608; cba@mara.scr.entelnet.bo; Calvo 301) English-language library. Referrals for private Spanish-language teachers.

Instituto Cultural Boliviano Alemán (ICBA; ☎ 645-2091; www.icba-sucre.edu.bo; Avaroa 326) German-language library, listings of rooms for rent, Kulturcafé Berlin (p251). Also offers Spanish lessons (see p247).

IMMIGRATION

Migración (☎ 645-3647; Pasaje Argandoña 4; ⏰ 8:30am-4:30pm Mon-Fri) A no-fuss place to extend visas and lengths of stay.

INTERNET ACCESS

Sucre is full to the brim with internet places, most with reasonable connections, and charging US$0.25 to US$0.40 per hour.

LAUNDRY

Hostal Charcas (☎ 645-3972; hostalcharcas@yahoo .com; Ravelo 62; nonguests US$0.90 per kilo) Offers same-day service if you drop off early.

Lavandería Laverap (☎ 644-2598; Bolívar 617; US$2.50 for up to 4.5kg; ⏰ 8:30am-8pm Mon-Sat, 9am-1pm Sun) Full-service laundry in 90 minutes.

Lavandería LG (☎ 642-1243; Loa 407; US$1 per kilo; ⏰ Mon-Sun) Delivers to hotels.

MEDICAL SERVICES

Hospital Santa Bárbara (☎ 646-0133; Destacamento 111) Good hospital.

MONEY

There are numerous ATMs around the city center (but not at the airport or bus station). **Casa de Cambio Ambar** (☎ 646-0984; San Alberto 7) and **Casa de Cambio El Arca** (☎ 646-0189; España 134) both change traveler's checks – the latter normally at better rates. **Banco Nacional de Bolivia** (España & San Alberto) changes traveler's checks to dollars for 3% commission. Many businesses display 'Compro Dólares' signs, but they only change cash. Street moneychangers, who operate outside the market along Av Hernando Siles, are handy on weekends when banks are closed. Cash advances are available for a fee at the Banco Nacional de Bolivia.

POST & TELEPHONE

The tranquil main **post office** (Estudiantes & Junín) has an *aduana* (customs) office downstairs for *encomiendas* (parcels). It doesn't close for lunch and is open late. There are numerous Entel and Punto Viva call centers around, charging competitive rates for international calls. One is at **Arenales 117** (per minute to international landlines US$0.13). The main **Entel office** (España & Urcullo) opens at 8am.

TOURIST INFORMATION

In addition to the following, there are tourist offices at the airport and bus terminal, which are actually often the most useful.

Municipal tourist kiosk (Plazuela Zudáñez, Bustillos & Olañeta) Open at times of high demand.

Municipal Tourist Office (☎ 643-5240; Argentina 65) In the Casa de la Cultura. Not terribly helpful, but staff can usually answer specific questions.

Oficina Universitaria de Turismo (☎ 644-7644; Estudiantes 49) Information office run by university students; sometimes provides student guides for city tours (US$10 for groups of up to four). It's the best for general city info.

Regional Tourist Office (☎ 645-5983; Argentina 50) Down the side of the Prefectura building, and upstairs. Can help with information about the Chuquisaca region.

Dangers & Annoyances

Sucre long enjoyed a reputation as one of Bolivia's safest towns, but occasionally visitors are harassed by bogus police or 'fake tourists.' If you have a problem, report it to the **tourist police** (☎ 648-0467; Plazuela Zudáñez).

You can't sit down on the plaza without being surrounded by eager shoeshine boys. They are persistent but good-natured; one boliviano is the going rate for a polish.

Sights

Sucre boasts several impressive museums and colonial churches, as well as the shiny new Parque Cretácico for dinosaur lovers. For the best view in town, inquire at the national police office inside the wedding cake–like **Prefectura de Chuquisaca** (State Government Building), next to the cathedral. If they're in a good mood, they might take you up to the cupola of the building for free. Note the murals depicting the struggle for Bolivian independence as you come upstairs.

CASA DE LA LIBERTAD

For a dose of Bolivian history, it's hard to beat this **house** (☎ 645-4200; www.casadelalibertad.com.bo; Plaza 25 de Mayo 11; admission US$1.25; ۞ 9am-12:30pm & 2:30-6pm Mon-Fri, 9:30am-12:30pm Sat & Sun) where the Bolivian declaration of independence was signed on August 6, 1825. It's been designated a national memorial, and is the symbolic heart of the nation.

The first score of Bolivian congresses were held in the Salón de la Independencia, originally a Jesuit chapel. Doctoral candidates were also examined here. Behind the pulpit hang portraits of Simón Bolívar, Hugo Ballivián and Antonio José de Sucre. General Bolívar claimed that this portrait, by Peruvian artist José Gil de Castro, was the most lifelike representation ever done of him. The charter of independence takes pride of place, mounted on a granite plinth. A fine *artesonado* (inlaid wooden) ceiling and elaborate choir stalls are also noteworthy.

The museum also includes portraits of presidents, military decorations, war- and independence-related art and relics, and old governmental documents. The most memorable is a huge wooden bust of Bolívar carved by artist and musician Mauro Núñez. Guided tours are available in English, French, German or Spanish.

MUSEO TEXTIL-ETNOGRÁFICO

This superb **museum of indigenous arts** (ASUR; ☎ 645-3841; www.bolivianet.com/asur; San Alberto 413; admission US$2; ۞ 8:30am-noon & 2:30-6pm Mon-Fri, 8:30am-noon Sat) is a must for anyone interested in the indigenous groups of the Sucre area. Run by an anthropological foundation, it focuses particularly on the woven textiles of the Jalq'a and Candelaria (Tarabuco) cultures. It's a fascinating display, and has an interesting subtext: the rediscovery of forgotten ancestral weaving practices has contributed to increased community pride and revitalization.

There's information in English available, and you can observe the weavers at their patient work. The contiguous store markets ceramics and weavings, but it's a more satisfying experience to buy them direct from the villages where they are made (see p254 and p257).

PARQUE CRETÁCICO (CAL ORCK'O)

It seems that 65 million years ago the site of Sucre's Fancesa cement quarry, 6km from the centre, was the place to be for large, scaly types. When the grounds were being cleared in 1994, plant employees uncovered a nearly vertical mudstone face bearing over 6000 tracks – some of which measure up to 80cm in diameter – from over 150 different species of dinosaur.

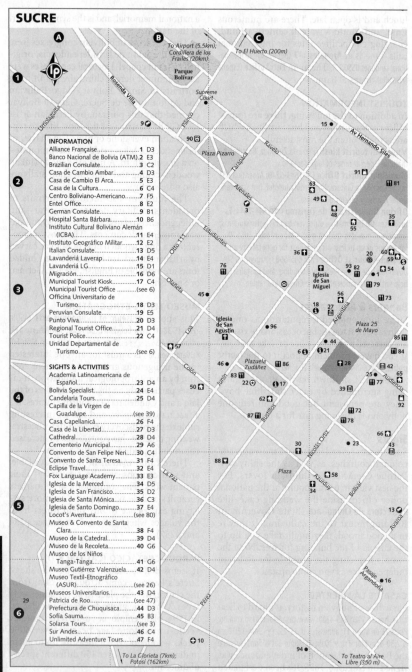

SUCRE

INFORMATION
Alliance Française...........................1	D3
Banco Nacional de Bolivia (ATM).2	E3
Brazilian Consulate.......................3	C2
Casa de Cambio Ambar..............4	D3
Casa de Cambio El Arca..............5	E3
Casa de la Cultura........................6	C4
Centro Boliviano-Americano.........7	F5
Entel Office....................................8	E2
German Consulate.........................9	B1
Hospital Santa Bárbara...............10	B6
Instituto Cultural Boliviano Alemán	
(ICBA)..11	E4
Instituto Geográfico Militar........12	E2
Italian Consulate.........................13	D5
Lavandería Laverap.....................14	E4
Lavandería LG.............................15	D1
Migración....................................16	D6
Municipal Tourist Kiosk...............17	C4
Municipal Tourist Office ....(see 6)	
Officina Universitario de	
Turismo.....................................18	D3
Peruvian Consulate......................19	E5
Punto Viva..................................20	D3
Regional Tourist Office...............21	D4
Tourist Police..............................22	C4
Unidad Departamental de	
Turismo..................................(see 6)	

SIGHTS & ACTIVITIES
Academia Latinoamericana de	
Español......................................23	D4
Bolivia Specialist.........................24	E4
Candelaria Tours..........................25	D4
Capilla de la Virgen de	
Guadalupe..............................(see 39)	
Casa Capellanicá..........................26	F4
Casa de la Libertad.....................27	D3
Cathedral.....................................28	D4
Cementerio Municipal..................29	A6
Convento de San Felipe Neri.......30	C4
Convento de Santa Teresa...........31	F4
Eclipse Travel...............................32	E4
Fox Language Academy................33	E3
Iglesia de la Merced....................34	D5
Iglesia de San Francisco..............35	D2
Iglesia de Santa Mónica..............36	C3
Iglesia de Santo Domingo...........37	E4
Locot's Aventura......................(see 80)	
Museo & Convento de Santa	
Clara...38	F4
Museo de la Catedral..................39	D4
Museo de la Recoleta...................40	G6
Museo de los Niños	
Tanga-Tanga.............................41	G6
Museo Gutiérrez Valenzuela........42	D4
Museo Textil-Etnográfico	
(ASUR)..................................(see 26)	
Museos Universitarios..................43	D4
Patricia de Roo........................(see 47)	
Prefectura de Chuquisaca............44	D3
Sofía Sauma.................................45	B3
Solarsa Tours...........................(see 3)	
Sur Andes....................................46	C4
Unlimited Adventure Tours..........47	F4

To Airport (5.5km);
Cordillera de los
Frailes (20km)

To El Huerto (200m)

Parque
Bolívar

Supreme
Court

Av Hernando Siles

Rosenda Villa

Urriolagoitia

Plaza Pizarro

Pilinco

Tarabuco

Ravelo

Avenales

Estudantes

Otto 111

Olañeta

Loa

Colón

Junín

La Paz

Pérez

Iglesia
de San
Agustín

Iglesia
de San
Miguel

Argentina

Plaza 25
de Mayo

Plazuela
Zudáñez

Bustillos

Nicolás Ortiz

Plaza

Azurduy

Bolívar

Audiencia

Avaroa

Pasaje
Argandoña

To La Glorieta (7km);
Potosí (162km)

To Teatro al Aire
Libre (350 m)

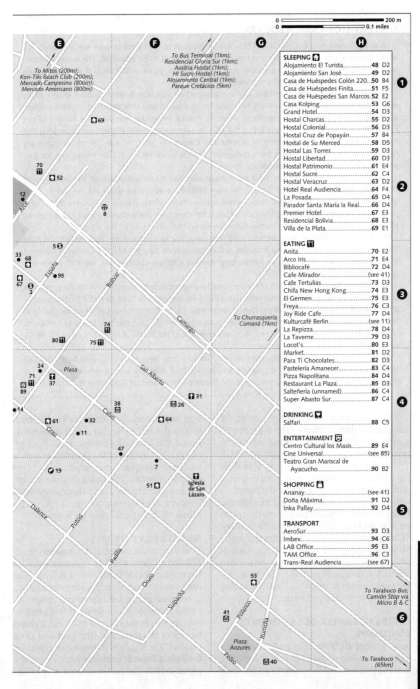

0 ——————— 200 m
0 ——————— 0.1 miles

SLEEPING 🏠
Alojamiento El Turista	48	D2
Alojamiento San José	49	D2
Casa de Huéspedes Colón 220	50	B4
Casa de Huéspedes Finita	51	F5
Casa de Huéspedes San Marcos	52	E2
Casa Kolping	53	G6
Grand Hotel	54	D3
Hostal Charcas	55	D2
Hostal Colonial	56	D3
Hostal Cruz de Popayán	57	B4
Hostal de Su Merced	58	D5
Hostal Las Torres	59	D3
Hostal Libertad	60	D3
Hostal Patrimonio	61	E4
Hostal Sucre	62	C4
Hostal Veracruz	63	D2
Hotel Real Audiencia	64	F4
La Posada	65	D4
Parador Santa María la Real	66	D4
Premier Hotel	67	E3
Residencial Bolivia	68	E3
Villa de la Plata	69	E1

EATING 🍴
Anita	70	E2
Arco Iris	71	E4
Bibliocafé	72	D4
Cafe Mirador	(see 41)	
Cafe Tertulias	73	D3
Chifa New Hong Kong	74	E3
El Germen	75	E3
Freya	76	C3
Joy Ride Cafe	77	D4
Kulturcafé Berlín	(see 11)	
La Repizza	78	D4
La Taverne	79	D3
Locot's	80	E3
Market	81	D2
Para Ti Chocolates	82	D3
Pastelería Amanecer	83	C4
Pizza Napolitana	84	D4
Restaurant La Plaza	85	D3
Salteñería (unnamed)	86	C4
Super Abasto Sur	87	C4

DRINKING 🍸
Salfari	88	C5

ENTERTAINMENT 🎭
Centro Cultural los Masis	89	E4
Cine Universal	(see 85)	
Teatro Gran Mariscal de Ayacucho	90	B2

SHOPPING 🛍
Ananay	(see 41)	
Doña Máxima	91	D2
Inka Pallay	92	D4

TRANSPORT
AeroSur	93	D3
Imbex	94	C6
LAB Office	95	E3
TAM Office	96	C3
Trans-Real Audiencia	(see 67)	

THE LIBERATOR – SIMÓN BOLÍVAR

Born of Basque parents in Caracas in 1783, Bolívar, greatest of the Libertadores – the liberators – of South America, was sent to Spain and France as a 15-year-old to be educated. The works of Rousseau and Voltaire imbued in the young man notions of progressive liberalism that would shape his entire life and the destiny of a continent.

Bolívar married a Spaniard in 1802, but she succumbed to yellow fever in Caracas shortly afterwards. Although he had many lovers, he could never again marry. The death of his wife marked a drastic shift in Bolívar's destiny. He returned to France, where he met with the leaders of the French Revolution and then traveled to the USA to take a close look at the new order after the American Revolution. By the time he returned to Caracas in 1807, he was full of revolutionary theories and experiences taken from these two successful examples. It didn't take him long to join the clandestine pro-independence circles.

Spain at the time was in a terrible mess. Napoleon had taken advantage of the weakness of Carlos IV, beset by family strife, to put his own brother, a notorious drunkard, on the Spanish throne. In 1808 Spain revolted; French troops were sent in, which started the Guerra de la Independencia (Peninsular War). Fighting desperately for their own freedom, they were in no state to effectively counter any independence movements on the other side of the Atlantic.

At the time, disillusionment with Spanish rule was close to breaking into open revolt. On April 19, 1810 the Junta Suprema was installed in Caracas, and on July 5, 1811 the Congress declared independence. This turned out to be the beginning of a long and bitter war, most of which was to be orchestrated by Bolívar.

His military career began with the Venezuelan independence movement, which he soon took command of. Battle followed battle with astonishing frequency until 1824. Of those battles personally directed by Bolívar, the independence forces won 35, including a few key ones: the Battle of Boyacá (August 7, 1819), which secured the independence of Colombia; the Battle of Carabobo (June 24, 1821), which brought freedom to Venezuela; and the Battle of Pichincha (May 24, 1822), which led to the liberation of Ecuador.

In September 1822 the Argentine liberator General José de San Martín, who had occupied Lima, abandoned the city to the Spanish, and Bolívar took over the task of winning in Peru. On August 6, 1824 his army was victorious at the Battle of Junín, and on December 9, 1824 General

While you once could go right up to the tracks, these days you have to be content with gazing at them from the brand-new **Cretaceous Park** (www.parquecretacico.com; admission US$3.75, ☻ 10am-6pm Mon-Fri, 10am-3pm Sat-Sun). This slick, family-friendly visitors centre has a couple of dozen scary life-size models of dinosaurs, as well as an audiovisual display and a restaurant. From the terrace, you can examine the tracks on the rockface opposite with binoculars. While plans for a shuttle bus from the centre of Sucre were in the pipeline, at the time of research the only way to get there was to catch *micro* A and walk 2km to the site. A taxi for the 6km journey costs about US$7, including waiting time to take you back.

CATEDRAL, CAPILLA DE LA VIRGEN DE GUADALUPE

Sucre's **cathedral** (☎ 645-2257; Plaza 25 de Mayo) dates from the middle of the 16th century and is a harmonious blend of Renaissance architecture with later Baroque additions. It's a noble structure, with a bell tower that is a local landmark. Inside, the white single-naved space has a series of oil paintings of the apostles, as well as an ornate altarpiece and pulpit. Some might find the interior a little saccharine, particularly the hanging angels. The cathedral opens on Sundays; otherwise you can enter as part of the Museo de la Catedral visit, see below.

MUSEO DE LA CATEDRAL

Next door to the cathedral this **museum** (☎ 645-2257; Ortiz 61; admission US$1.90; ☻ 10am-noon & 3-5pm Mon-Fri, 10am-noon Sat) holds one of Bolivia's best collections of religious relics. There are four sections, ritually unlocked as your visit progresses. In the entry room is a series of fine religious paintings from the colonial era. Next, a chapel has relics of saints, and fine gold and silver chalices. The highlight, however, comes in the **Capilla de la Virgen de Guadalupe**, which was completed in 1625. Encased in the altar is a painting

Antonio José de Sucre inflicted a final defeat at the Battle of Ayacucho. Peru, which included Alto Perú, had been liberated and the war was over. On August 6, 1825, the first anniversary of the Battle of Junín, Bolivia declared independence from Peru at Chuquisaca (Sucre), and the new republic was christened 'Bolivia,' after the liberator.

But, as Bolívar well knew, freedom means just that and, although he had grand dreams for a unified state in the north of South America, they would prove difficult to realize. 'I fear peace more than war,' he wrote perceptively in a letter.

Establishing Gran Colombia (which comprised modern-day Venezuela, Colombia, Panamá and Ecuador) was easy, but holding it together as president was impossible for Bolívar. Clinging stubbornly to his dream of the union, although it was rapidly slipping from his hands, he lost influence, and his glory and charisma faded. He then tried to set up a dictatorship, saying 'Our America can only be ruled through a well-managed, shrewd despotism'; he still saw himself (perhaps correctly) as the best steward of the young nations. After surviving an assassination attempt in Bogotá, he resigned in 1830, disillusioned, and in poor health. Almost at once, his Gran Colombia dissolved.

Venezuela broke away in 1830, approved a new congress and banned Bolívar from his homeland. A month later, Antonio José de Sucre, Bolívar's closest friend, was assassinated in southern Colombia. These two news items reached Bolívar just as he was about to board a ship for France. Depressed and ill, he accepted the invitation of a Spaniard, Joaquín de Mier, to stay in his home in Santa Marta, Colombia.

Bolívar died on December 17, 1830, of pulmonary tuberculosis. A priest, a doctor and a few officers were by his bed, but none of these were close friends. Joaquín de Mier donated one of his shirts to dress the body, as there had been none among Bolívar's humble belongings. Perhaps the most important figure in the history of the South American continent had died. 'There have been three great fools in history: Jesus, Don Quixote and I.' So he summed up his own life shortly before his death.

That Bolívar died lonely and abandoned is scarcely believable when you see the extent to which he is idolized in South America today. He is a symbol of South American freedom and, crucially, a symbol free of party-political connotations. Today, the Libertador is a hero once more.

One of the final remarks in Bolívar's diary reads, 'My name now belongs to history. It will do me justice.' It has.

of the Virgin, the city's patron, and a woman of means. She was originally painted by Fray Diego de Ocaña in 1601. The work was subsequently coated with highlights of gold and silver and adorned in robes encrusted with diamonds, amethysts, pearls, rubies and emeralds donated by wealthy colonial parishioners. The jewels alone are worth millions of dollars.

IGLESIA DE LA MERCED

Contrary to its ordinary exterior, this **church** (☎ 645-1483; Pérez 512; admission US$0.75; ⏰ 10am-noon & 3-5pm Mon-Fri) is blessed with the most beautiful interior of any church in Sucre and possibly in Bolivia. Because the order of La Merced left Sucre for Cuzco in 1826, taking its records with it, the church's founding date is uncertain, but it's believed to be sometime in the early 1550s. The building was completed no later than the early 1580s.

The Baroque-style altar and carved mestizo pulpit are decorated with filigree and gold inlay. Several paintings by the esteemed artist Melchor Pérez de Holguín are on display – notably *El Nacimiento de Jesús, El Nacimiento de María* and a self-portrait of the artist rising from the depths of Purgatory. There are also sculptures by other artists. The views from the bell tower are splendid.

MUSEO DE LA RECOLETA

Overlooking the city of Sucre from the top of Calle Polanco, **La Recoleta** (☎ 645-1987; Plaza Pedro Anzures; admission US$1.25; ⏰ 8:30-11:30am & 2:30-4:30pm Mon-Fri) was established by the Franciscan Order in 1601. It has served not only as a convent and museum but also as a barracks and prison. In one of the stairwells is a plaque marking the spot where, in 1829, General Pedro Blanco, who had assumed the role of president, was assassinated. Outside are courtyard gardens brimming with color and the renowned Cedro Milenario – the ancient cedar – a huge tree that was once even larger than its current size. It is the only remnant of the cedars that were once abundant around Sucre.

The museum is worthwhile for its anonymous sculptures and paintings from the 16th to 20th centuries, including numerous interpretations of St Francis of Assisi.

The highlight is the church choir and its magnificent wooden carvings dating back to the 1870s, each one intricate and unique. They represent the Franciscan, Jesuit and Japanese martyrs who were crucified in 1595 in Nagasaki.

MUSEO DE LOS NIÑOS TANGA-TANGA

On the same square as La Recoleta, and set in a beautiful building, this excellent interactive children's **museum** (☎ 644-0299; Plaza La Recoleta; adult/child US$1/0.65; 9am-noon & 2:30-6pm Tue-Sun) focuses on renewable energy sources. Highlights include the botanical gardens and explanations of Bolivian ecology. The museum also hosts cultural and environmental programs, including theater performances and ceramic classes. The attached Café Mirador (p251) is a great place to relax while enjoying the best view in town. The adjacent Ananay handicrafts store (p252) sells unique high-quality *artesanías*, including especially cute children's clothing.

CONVENTO DE SAN FELIPE NERI

A visit to the bell tower and tiled rooftop of the **San Felipe Neri convent** (☎ 645-4333; Ortiz 165; admission US$1.25; 4:30-6pm Mon-Fri, Sat in high season) more than explains Sucre's nickname of the 'White City of the Americas.'

In the days when the building served as a monastery, asceticism didn't prevent the monks from appreciating the view while meditating; you can still see the stone seats on the roof terraces. The church was originally constructed of stone but was later covered with a layer of stucco. Poinsettias and roses fill the courtyard, and an interesting painting of the Last Supper hangs in the stairwell.

In the catacombs there are tunnels where priests and nuns once met clandestinely and also where, during times of political unrest, guerrillas hid and circulated around the city. The building now functions as a parochial school.

To enter, you need to ring the bell; you may be able to visit outside the scheduled hours.

MUSEO DE SANTA CLARA

Located in the Santa Clara Convent, this **museum of religious art** (☎ 645-2295; Avaroa 290; admission US$1.25; 9am-noon & 3-5pm Mon-Fri, 9:30am-noon Sat), founded in 1639, contains several works by Bolivian master Melchor Pérez de Holguín and his Italian instructor, Bernardo de Bitti. In 1985 it was robbed and several paintings and gold ornaments were taken. One of the canvases, however, was apparently deemed too large to carry away, so the thieves sliced a big chunk out of the middle and left the rest hanging. The painting has been restored but you can still see evidence of the damage. Guides may also demonstrate the still-functional pipe organ, which was fabricated in 1664.

CONVENTO DE SANTA TERESA

This brilliant white **convent** (☎ 645-1986; San Alberto near Potosí; 10am-noon) belongs to an order of cloistered nuns. They sell homemade candied oranges, apples, figs and limes daily by way of a revolving wheel. The standard greeting and response to use with the nuns is '*Ave María purísima/Sin pecado concebida.*' Don't miss strolling down the charming adjacent **Callejón de Santa Teresa**, a lantern-lit alleyway. It was once partially paved with human bones laid out in the shape of a cross, which was intended to remind passersbys of the inevitability of death. In the 1960s it was repaved with its current cobbles.

IGLESIA DE SAN FRANCISCO

The **San Francisco church** (☎ 645-1853; Ravelo 1 at Arce; 7-9am & 4-7pm Mon-Fri, mass times only Sat-Sun) was established in 1538 by Francisco de Aroca soon after the founding of the city. It began as a makeshift structure; the current church wasn't completed until 1581. In 1809, when the struggle for Bolivian independence got under way, a law passed by Mariscal Sucre transferred San Francisco's religious community to La Paz and turned the building over to the army, to be used as a military garrison, market and customs hall. In 1838 the top floor collapsed, but it was rebuilt and later used as a military bunkhouse. It wasn't reconsecrated until 1925.

Architecturally, San Francisco's most interesting feature is its *mudéjar* ceiling. In the belfry is the Campana de la Libertad, Bolivia's Liberty Bell, which called patriots to revolution in 1825.

IGLESIA DE SANTA MÓNICA

The mestizo-style **Santa Mónica church** (Junín 601 at Arenales) was begun in 1574 and was originally intended to serve as a monastery for the Ermitañas de San Agustín. However the order ran into financial difficulties in the early 1590s, eventually resulting in its closure and conversion into a Jesuit school. The interior is adorned with mestizo carvings of seashells, animals and human figures; the ceiling features impressive woodwork; and the courtyard is one of the city's finest, with lawns and a variety of semitropical plants. The church now serves as a civic auditorium and is only open to the public during special events.

MUSEOS UNIVERSITARIOS & MUSEO GUTIÉRREZ VALENZUELA

The **Museos Universitarios** (☎ 645-3285; Bolívar 698; admission US$1.25; ☽ 8:30am-noon & 2:30-6pm Mon-Fri, 8:30am-noon Sat) are three separate halls housing colonial relics, anthropological artifacts and modern art. In the southeast corner of the main plaza, the university also runs the **Museo Gutiérrez Valenzuela** (☎ 645-3828; Plaza 25 de Mayo; admission US$1.35; ☽ 8:30am-noon & 2-6pm Mon-Fri, 8:30am-noon Sat), an old aristocrat's house with 19th-century decor. There's also a reasonably interesting natural history museum here.

CEMENTERIO MUNICIPAL

The enthusiasm surrounding Sucre's **cemetery** (admission free; ☽ 8:30am-noon & 2-5:30pm) seems disproportionate to what's there. There are some arches carved from poplar trees, as well as picturesque palm trees and the mausoleums of wealthy colonial families, but it's a mystery why it should inspire such local fervor. To enliven the experience, visit on a weekend when it's jam-packed with families, or hire one of the enthusiastic child guides for a few bolivianos. You can walk the eight blocks from the plaza south along Junín, or take a taxi or *micro* A.

Courses

Sucre is a popular place to learn Spanish; prices are fair, and the climate is wonderful. The **Instituto Cultural Boliviano Alemán** (ICBA; ☎ /fax 645-2091; www.icba-sucre.edu.bo; Avaroa 326) offers recommended Spanish lessons with homestay options; they also run Quechua classes. The **Academia Latinoamericana de Español** (☎ 646-0537; www.latinoschools.com; Dalence 109) has a compre-hensive program featuring cultural classes and homestay options. **Fox Language Academy** (☎ 644-0688; www.foxacademysucre.com; San Alberto 30) has a high turnover of teachers, but learning Spanish or Quechua there subsidizes English classes for underprivileged local kids.

There are plenty of private teachers who provide good one-to-one classes (US$4 to US$5 per hour). Reader-recommended **Patricia de Roo** (☎ 7116-0848; Potosí 237) combines lessons with trips around the city, putting you in practical situations, as does **Sofía Sauma** (☎ 645-1687; fsauma@hotmail.com; Loa 779).

Tours & Activities

While Sucre traditionally has been visited for its sublime colonial architecture and wealth of museums, there's an increasing amount on offer in the surrounding area, whether your interests are indigenous culture or adrenaline-fuelled adventure.

There are numerous agencies in town, and nearly all offer trips to Tarabuco (p253; around US$3 per person) for the Sunday market; many hotels and *hostals* can also arrange this trip. Many also offer daytrips to the Cordillera de los Frailes (p254), but you will contribute more to the local communities by going for longer (see boxed text p257).

Several operators offer half-day to multi-day excursions on horseback, mountain bike or Shanks' pony. These typically visit parts of the Cordillera de los Frailes (p254); expect to pay US$15 to US$25 for full day hiking, US$20 to US$30 for biking, or US$25 to US$50 for horsing around; somewhat more if you are by yourself.

Operators include:

Bolivia Specialist (☎ 643-7389; www.boliviaspecialist .com; Bolívar 525) Reliable agent that can organize things around Sucre or anywhere in Bolivia.

Candelaria Tours (☎ 646-1661; www.candelariatours .com; Audiencia 1) Intelligent and reliable agency running many types of trips. Particularly recommendable for trips to Tarabuco and Candelaria.

Eclipse Travel (☎ /fax 644-3960; eclipse@mara.scr .entelnet.bo; Avaroa 310) Reliable agent and tour operator.

Joy Ride Bolivia (☎ 642-5544; www.joyridebol.com; Ortiz 14) Popular hikes, bikes and horses, with groups leaving almost daily. Also offer paragliding; both tandem jumps and courses. Bookings and inquiries at the café of the same name (p250).

Locot's Aventura (☎ 691-5958; www.locotsadventure .com; Bolívar 465) Hiking, biking, horse-riding and paragliding.

Solarsa Tour (☎ 644-0839; asolares@entelnet.bo; Arenales 212) Reliable travel agent; also run culturally-sensitive trips to Jalq'a villages (see boxed text p257).

Sur Andes (☎ 645-3212; surandeses@hotmail.com; Junín 855) City tours and good treks.

Unlimited Adventure Tours (☎ 7116-0848; www .unlimited-adventure.com; Potosí 237) Recommended for its hiking, biking and horseback excursions, and have also pioneered a great two-day tour to the village of Icla, which combines several activities including floating downriver in an inner-tube with a chance to interact with local people.

Festivals & Events

On the evening of September 8, local *campesinos* celebrate the **Fiesta de la Virgen de Guadalupe** with songs and poetry recitations. The following day, they dress in colorful costumes and parade around the main plaza carrying religious images and silver arches.

Each September there's the **Festival de la Cultura**, featuring many organized and impromptu performances from both local and international artists in various disciplines including dance, theater and music. On November 2 **Todos Santos** is celebrated with much fervor.

Sleeping

Accommodations in Sucre are among the country's most expensive, but, on the upside, most of the choices are in typical, attractive whitewashed adobe buildings built around a pretty central courtyard.

BUDGET

Most places that charge in bolivianos rather than US currency are clustered near the market, and along Calles Ravelo and San Alberto.

Alojamiento San José (☎ 645-1475; Ravelo 86; r per person US$2.50) A basic choice in an interesting old building. Caters more for the market traders than travelers.

Alojamiento El Turista (☎ 645-3172; Ravelo 118; s/d US$2.50/3.70) Tucked away behind a quick chicken joint, the friendly Turista is musty and mediocre, but it's good value for strict budgets. Request a room on the top floor – unless you feel the need to be close to the shared bathrooms (which are also open to the general public for a pittance).

Casa de Huéspedes San Marcos (☎ 646-2087; Arce 233; r per person US$3.10, with bathroom US$4.40) This place gets a good rap from travelers, who appreciate its friendly owners, clean, quiet

rooms as well as kitchen and laundry access. The mattresses aren't the best, but that's life.

HI Sucre Hostel (☎ 644-0471; www.hostellingbolivia .org; Loayza 119; dm US$3.50, s/d US$4.90/9.80, with bathroom US$12.50/20; 🖳) Set in a building with attractive original features, Sucre's well maintained full-service hostel is very handy for the bus station (from the terminal, cross the street, head left, then take the first right). It's clean and friendly and has a shared kitchen and even some private rooms with spa baths and cable TV. It's one of Bolivia's few purpose-built hostels and thus has excellent amenities.

Hostal Cruz de Popayán (☎ 644-0889; www.bolivia hostels.com; Loa 881; dm US$3.50, s/d US$4.50/8, with bathroom US$15/20; 🖳) In a lovely 17th-century building that encloses three patios, this offers several types of accommodations in a very attractive setting. Many readers love this hostel, and it does offer decent value despite somewhat chilly rooms, but lackluster staff and reports of overcharging have let it down in recent times.

Casa de Huéspedes Colón 220 (☎ 645-5823; colon220@bolivia.com; Colón 220; r per person US$3.75, s/d with bathroom & breakfast US$10/14) A peaceful little place built around a creeper-draped courtyard, this offers decent, spotless rooms with beds that are a little on the concave side. English, German and Italian are spoken.

Hostal Veracruz (☎ 645-1560; Ravelo 158; s/d US$3.75/6.25, with bathroom US$8.75/12.50; 🖳) A central choice and consistently popular, this has a fair variety of rooms, some nice and sunny, some a little echoey from the central vestibule. Breakfast and laundry are available; staff can sometimes be vague about bookings made by phone.

Residencial Bolivia (☎ 645-4346; res_bol@cotes .net.bo; San Alberto 42; s/d US$4.40/7.50, with bathroom US$7.50/12.50) This helpful and handily located spot is friendly and used to making traveling types feel welcome. The rooms are set around a triple courtyard; some are markedly nicer than others, but all offer value, spotlessness and bright bedcovers. A simple breakfast is included, and guests also have use of a kitchen.

Hostal Charcas (☎ 645-3972; hostalcharcas@yahoo .com; Ravelo 62; s/d US$5/8.10, with bathroom US$8.10/12.50) The central location and helpful, friendly service make the Charcas, right opposite the market, a well-deserved travelers' favorite. Welcome services like a Tarabuco market bus, laundry service and 24-hour hot water, not to mention simple but clean and attractive rooms with or without bath, mean it's a reliable bet, and more than the sum of its parts. Breakfast is available, there's a curious parrot, and the staff will gladly help you with anything they can.

Villa de la Plata (☎ 642-2577; isis208@yahoo.com; Arce 369; r per person US$5) Tired of eating out? This *casa de huéspedes* (guesthouse) provides long-term language school students and visiting local professionals with modern apartments with spacious living rooms and shared full kitchens. The breezy rooftop terrace is a brilliant place to stargaze. The owner seems to enjoy taking in stray travelers almost as much as she enjoys taking in stray cats.

Casa de Huéspedes Finita (☎ 645-3220; Padilla 233; r per person US$5) A welcoming, homey choice offering good value and warm hospitality. There's hot water, and a good kitchen for guests' use. They can also offer full-board rates if you're staying for a while.

Ten minutes from town on *micro* A are a couple of decent places directly opposite the bus terminal:

Austria Hostal (☎ 645-4202; Ostria Gutiérrez 506; r per person US$4.40-5.60) Smart and comfortable. Good value.

Residencial Gloria Sur (☎ 645-2847; r US$2.50 per person)

MIDRANGE

Hostal Las Torres (☎ 644-2888; www.lastorreshostal.com; San Alberto 19; s/d US$12.50/18.75) This brand new place is very light and pleasant, and is entered down a little alleyway. The rooms have comfy beds with cutesy frilly coverings and heart-shaped cushions as well as cable TV and good bathroom. Breakfast is included.

Grand Hotel (☎ 645-1704; grandhotel_sucre9@hotmail .com; Arce 61; s/d with bath, breakfast & TV US$12.50/17.50) With an extremely central location and really excellent staff, this is a deserved favorite among travelers of all budgets. There's a decent restaurant here, a beautiful, plant-filled courtyard, and comfortable rooms with a patina of age. Some rooms have their own separate lounge area.

Hostal Libertad (☎ 645-3101; www.hostallibertad -bo.com; Arce 99; s/d/ste with bathroom US$18/20-25/30; 🖳) Central but tucked away, this spacious place is accessed via an arcade and offers good rooms with minibar, cable TV and piped music. Many of the rooms are suite-like, with a separate lounge area. Some suffer from a bit of traffic noise, but others are surprisingly

quiet. It's run by welcoming people and also has restaurant service.

Hostal Sucre (☎ 645-1411; www.hostalsucre.com; Bustillos 113; s/d/tr with bathroom US$19/25/32; 🖳) This pleasant typically white hotel has a particularly beautiful double courtyard, complete with well and fountain. Rooms, with attractive if faded old furniture, don't quite live up to it, being a little dingy, but are acceptable. It's very popular with travelers for its attentive service. Breakfast is served in an antique dining room.

Casa Kolping (☎ 642-3812; www.grupo-casas-kolping .net; Pje Iturricha 265; s/d US$22/30; 🖳) High on a hill by Plaza Recoleta, with great views over town, this new hotel caters mostly for conferences but is an appealing place to stay. As well as efficient service and a good restaurant, it boasts clean, well-equipped rooms – on the smallish side but very comfortable. For an extra US$5, you get a minibar and a view – well worth the spend. It's also a good place for the kids, with family apartments, plenty of space and a ping-pong table. The hotel is a fundraiser for the charitable Catholic foundation Kolping Verein.

Hostal Patrimonio (☎ 644-8101; www.hostalpatri monio.com.bo; Grau 154; s/d US$25/35) A central, recently renovated choice with lovely patio and attractive wooden beds.

Premier Hotel (☎ 645-2097; premierhotel@hotmail .com; San Alberto 43; s/d/ste US$25/40/50; 🖳) A handsome modern option catering for the local business-traveler market, this has a central courtyard and is sparklingly clean, with leather armchairs, and rooms with inviting beds and minibars. It's in the heart of town but pretty quiet.

Hostal Colonial (☎ 644-0312; www.hostalcolonial -bo.com; Plaza 25 de Mayo 3; s/d/tr/ste US$27/38/45/55) Handsome and welcoming, the Colonial exudes a restrained stylishness befitting its location among the plaza's noble buildings. The carpeted suites and rooftop terrace overlook the plaza, and the interior fireplace keeps things toasty in the foyer.

Hostal de Su Merced (☎ 644-2706; www.bolivia web.com/companies/sumerced; Azurduy 16; s/d/tr/ste US$30/45/60/60) In true Sucre style, this charming hotel is decorated with antiques and paintings, with rooms around an intimate, tiled courtyard. Room No 7 is particularly nice and the view from the rooftop terrace is stunning. The staff are English-speaking and especially helpful. There's also a restaurant.

La Posada (☎ 646-0101; www.laposadahostal.com; Audiencia 92; s/d US$30/50; 🖵) This comfortable and classy place has spacious, uncluttered rooms with a very appealing colonial ambience and wooden trimmings. There are views over town, a stylish and intimate feel, and a good family suite. The courtyard restaurant is also a recommendable spot. Excellent service adds to the package.

TOP END

Hotel Real Audiencia (☎ 646-0823; www.hotelreal audiencia.com; Potosí 142; s/d/ste with bath & breakfast US$45/55/65; 🛎 🖵) This welcoming place in an appealing part of Sucre has a mixture of the old and new. It's attractively set-out, with a pool area and Mediterranean-style balustrades. Rooms are spacious and have cable TV, but the 'executive' suites in a more modern wing are significantly better, with beautiful furniture and a minibar for not much more cash.

Parador Santa María la Real (☎ 691-1920; www .parador.com.bo; Bolívar 625; s/d/ste US$55/65/70-90; 🖵) This new and extremely stylish colonial hotel looks set to take over Sucre's 'top place to stay' mantle. Magnificently elegant, it boasts an arcaded courtyard, antique furniture, a spa bath with a view, and a curious historical underground section. Beds are lovely and inviting.

Eating

Sucre has a pleasant variety of quality restaurants and is a great place to spend time lolling around cafés while observing Bolivian university life.

RESTAURANTS

Freya (☎ 642-1928; Loa 751; 🕙 noon-2pm Mon-Sat) This likeable place serves up tasty vegetarian lunches (US$1.25) to local workers. Get there early for more choice.

Chifa New Hong Kong (☎ 644-1776; San Alberto 242; mains US$1.50-3) An expensive Chinese choice, but the best of several in town.

El Germen (San Alberto 231; mains US$2-3; 🕙 8am-10pm) This simply decorated, service-with-a-smile spot is a favorite for its tasty vegetarian dishes; they also do decent goulash and roast meat, as well as cracking curries and tempting cakes. There's a book exchange; you might need it, as you can often finish a novel (reading one, not writing one – quite) waiting for your meal.

Restaurant La Plaza (☎ 645-5843; Plaza 25 de Mayo; mains US$2-4) The mostly meat-based meals are filling and the outdoor balconies are a great place for a beer on a lazy Sunday afternoon.

Pizza Napolitana (☎ 645-1934; Plaza 25 de Mayo 30; set lunch US$3, pizza US$2-4; 🕙 11am-11pm) Enjoy US and British tunes over decent pizza and pasta or an ice-cream sundae at this cheerful and popular plaza hangout. The meal deals are good value but drinks and coffee are a bit on the expensive side.

Locot's (☎ 691-5958; Bolívar 465; mains US$2-4.50; 🕙 7am-late; 🖵) Relaxed and attractive, this bar-restaurant is in an interesting old building, and has original art on the walls. It offers a choice of Bolivian, Mexican and international food, including vegetarian, and a gringo-friendly vibe. Look out for the cocktails named after Bolivian presidents, and regular live music.

Arco Iris (☎ 7713-0396; Bolívar 567; mains US$2-5) Follow the rainbow to where a decent attempt (unless you are Swiss) is made of fondues and *rösti*. There are also simple vegetarian choices, desserts, and often live music and dancing. In truth, the atmosphere is perhaps better than the food.

Joy Ride Café (☎ 642-5544; Ortiz 14; mains US$2-4.25; 🕙 7:30am-2am Mon-Fri, 9am-2am Sat & Sun) A wildly popular gringo-tastic café, restaurant and bar with a bit of everything, from dawn espressos to midnight vodkas, from nightly movies to wild weekend dancing on tables. It's a spacious, well-run spot, albeit with high levels of self-promotion, and boasts decent food (salads, 'hangover eggs,' steaks), a book exchange, patio seating and an cozy upstairs lounge. Look out for the range of imported beers, but also for Ted's homebrews – tasty indeed.

La Repizza (La Casa del Flaco; ☎ 645-1506; Ortiz 78; pizza US$1.50-5, mains US$4-5; 🕙 10am-3pm, 5:30pm-2am) Welcoming Bolivian spot with a backyard, and popular for its pizzas, steaks and good-quality four course *almuerzos* (US$2.50). It's a popular place for a drink on Friday and Saturday nights too.

La Taverne (☎ 7193-1640; Arce 35; mains US$3-4.50) With a quiet sophisticated atmosphere, the restaurant of the Alliance Française (p240) is a delight to visit. The short, select menu has a French touch – tongue with chili and chocolate will appeal to adventurous palates – and there are excellent daily specials – a teriyaki beef went down well at time of research. There's live music every Friday night; films are also screened here several times a week.

La Posada (☎ 646-0101; Audiencia 92; mains US$3-4.50; ✪ 7am-10:30pm Mon-Sat, 7am-3pm Sun) This comfortable hotel (opposite) also has one of Sucre's most appealing spots for a meal or a drink, offering elegant indoor and outdoor seating around its stone-flagged courtyard. There are tasty fish and meat dishes, pastas and salads, various set meals, and good-natured service.

El Huerto (☎ 645-1538; Cabrera 86; mains US$3-6; ✪ lunch & dinner) Set in a lovely secluded garden, this is a favorite spot for Sucre's people in the know. It's got the atmosphere of a classy lawn party, with sunshades and grass underfoot; there's great service and stylishly presented traditional plates that don't come much better anywhere in the country. Sunday lunch (US$3.10) is a special treat too.

Churrasquería Cumaná (☎ 643-2273; Plaza Cumaná, Barrio Petrolero; full portion US$5-6; ✪ 6:30-11pm Tue-Thu, 11:30am-10:30pm Fri-Sun) A Sucre secret, this carnivore's delight is in the Barrio Petrolero, a cab ride from the center. The full portions of exquisitely-grilled meat can comfortably feed two; the courtyard is also a pleasant place to drink wine or cocktails. There's great service too.

CAFÉS

Kulturcafé Berlin (Avaroa 340; mains US$1-3; ✪ 8am-midnight Mon-Sat; 🖳) This dark and atmospheric spot is affiliated with the ICBA (p240), and offers German-language newspapers and magazines, a book exchange and filling dishes; try the *papas rellenas* (spicy filled potatoes). It's also a fine spot for an evening beer, with some German choices.

Café Mirador (Plaza la Recoleta; mains US$1.50-3; ✪ 9am-7pm Tue-Sun) The café of the Museo de los Niños Tanga-Tanga (p246) overlooks a botanical garden that exhibits a range of foliage from around the country. The panoramic views are a sunset treat and worth the hike up the hill, and it's a sweet place to linger over juice, sandwiches, cocktails or the rich desserts.

Bibliocafé (☎ 644-5002; Ortiz 42 & Ortiz 50; mains US$2-3; ✪ closed Mon) With two adjacent locations, this has something for everyone; one side is dark and cozy, the other a little smarter. There's good service, a menu of pasta and Mexican-Bolivian food, and drinks until late in a cheerful and unpretentious atmosphere. There's regular live music.

Café Tertulias (☎ 642-0390; Plaza 25 de Mayo; mains US$2-3) Writers, artists and journalists convene at this intimate hangout for chats over coffee, beer or food, which is principally pizza, salads and lasagna. It's a welcoming, quirky spot that also does decent mixed drinks.

QUICK EATS

Pastelería Amanecer (off Junín btwn Colón & Olañeta) Tucked away in a dead-end alley behind the police station, this petite, four-table, non-profit bakery has delightful homemade goodies, breakfast, coffee and fresh juices. Proceeds benefit local children's projects.

Good *salteñerías* include **Anita** (Siles at Arce) and the simple, unnamed place at Olañeta 39, opposite the police station. Thanks to Sucre's status as Bolivia's chocolate capital, there are plenty of stores that cater to sweet tooths. The best is **Para Ti Chocolates** (☎ 645-5689; Arenales 7), where tasty Breick bonbons are only the tip of the iceberg.

GROCERIES

The central **market** (✪ 7am-7:30pm Mon-Sat, Sun morning only) is home to some gastronomic highlights. Don't miss the fresh juices and fruit salads – they are among the best in the country. The vendors and their blenders always come up with something indescribably delicious – try *jugo de tumbo* (unripe passion-fruit juice). Upstairs, you'll find good, filling, cheap meals in sanitary conditions (for a market, anyway).

Super Abasto Sur (Bustillos at Colón) is the best stocked central grocery store.

Drinking

Places mentioned in Eating (opposite), such as Joy Ride, Locot's, Bibliocafé and La Repizza, are popular spots for a drink, and get pretty lively.

Salfari (☎ 644-5002; Bustillos 237) This little gem of a pub has friendly service, a loyal local crowd, and lively games of poker and *cacho* usually going on. Try their tasty but potent homemade fruit liqueurs; the passion fruit is our favorite.

One of the best *discotecas* is **Mitos** (Cerro s/n; admission women/men US$0.60/1.25; ✪ 10pm-late Fri & Sat), a spacious basement spot a 15-minute walk from the centre. It really fills up around 1am and plays well-loved local and international hits. Another that was due to open at time of research was nearby **Kon-Tiki Beach Club** (Junín 71), which promised more up-to-date sounds.

Entertainment

The **Centro Cultural los Masis** (☎ 645-3403; Bolívar 561; ☺ 10am-noon & 3:30-9pm Mon-Fri) hosts concerts and other cultural events, and has a small museum of local musical instruments. It also offers Quechua classes.

Southeast of the center, the Teatro al Aire Libre is a wonderful outdoor venue for musical and other performances. **Teatro Gran Mariscal de Ayacucho** (Plaza Pizarro), is an opulent old opera house. The tourist office and the Casa de la Cultura (p240) both distribute a monthly calendar of events. The most central cinema is **Cine Universal** (Plaza 25 de Mayo).

Shopping

The best place to learn about traditional local weavings is the Museo Textil-Etnográfico (p241), but to buy them you are best off going direct to the villages (see p254 and p257). Prices are steep by Bolivian standards, but the items are high quality. Plan on US$80 to US$150 for a fine Jalq'a or Candelaria weaving.

A trip to the Mercado Americano, around the junction of Mujía and Reyes, will keep clothes-junkies busy for hours, while nearby on Aguirre, the Mercado Campesino is a fascinating traditional food market with a really authentic feel.

Inca Pallay (☎ 646-1936; incapallay@entelnet.bo; cnr Grau & Bolívar) This weaver's and artisan's cooperative has an impressive array of high-quality handmade crafts, not all from the Sucre area. Prices are high, but this is the store that returns the highest percentage to the weavers themselves. You can sometimes see weavers at work in the patio.

Ananay (☎ 644-0299; www.bolivianhandicrafts.com; Museo de los Niños Tanga-Tanga, Plaza la Recoleta) This boutique features export-quality crafts, home furnishings and adorable children's clothing. It's not cheap, but the designs are unique and the quality is high.

Doña Máxima (Junín 411, Centro Comercial Guadalupe No 8) After some bargaining, you'll find excellent deals on less decorative and more utilitarian Candelaria and Jalq'a weavings in this jam-packed cubbyhole.

Getting There & Away

AIR

The domestic departure tax is US$1.90. **Aero-Sur** (☎ 645-4895; Arenales 31) operates one daily flight from La Paz, one to Cochabamba and a couple to Santa Cruz. At time of research, troubled **LAB** (☎ 691-3184; España 105) was operating one flight from Sucre to La Paz via Cochabamba, but none in the reverse direction. **TAM** (Airport ☎ 645-1310, Office ☎ 696-0944; Junín 744) flies on Friday to Cochabamba and Santa Cruz and on Sunday to La Paz. There are mooted plans to replace Sucre's inadequate, borderline dangerous **airport** (☎ 645-4445) with a new, international one. Note that the airport is frequently shut in bad weather, so check with the airline before heading out there.

BUS & SHARED TAXI

The **bus terminal** (☎ 644-1292) is a 15-minute walk uphill from the centre, and most easily accessed by *micros* A or 3 from along Calle España, or by taxi (as the *micros* are too crowded for lots of luggage). Unless you're headed for Potosí, it's wise to book long-distance buses a day in advance, in order to reserve a good seat. There's a terminal tax of US$0.40 here; services include a good information kiosk but no ATM.

One of the bus companies, **Trans Real Audiencia** (☎ 644-3119; San Alberto 73; ☺ 8:30am-9pm), has a central office where you can purchase tickets, which saves a trip to the bus station. They also run Sunday trips to Tarabuco.

Daily buses run to Cochabamba (around US$8, 12 hours), which all depart at around 6:30pm. There are also afternoon (4pm to 6pm) services to Santa Cruz (US$9 to US$11, 15 to 20 hours), mostly via the rough but scenic Samaipata route.

Lots of *flotas* have morning and evening departures for La Paz (US$11 to US$15, 14 to 16 hours) via Oruro (US$6 to US$8, 10 hours). There are around 40 departures a day for Potosí (US$2.50, three hours) from 7am until 6pm; some persevere to Tarija (US$9.50, 15 hours), Oruro and Villazón. You'll find daily connections to Uyuni (US$6, 10 to 12 hours), but they normally entail changing buses at Potosí.

Alternatively, you can take a shared taxi (US$16 for up to four people, 2½ hours), which is quicker and comfier, to Potosí. Most hotels can help arrange shared taxis. Try **Turismo Global** (☎ 642-5125), **Cielito Lindo** (☎ 644-1014) or **Infinito del Sur** (☎ 642-2277). Expect speed.

Whenever the road is passable, Flota Chaqueño does the beautiful-but-brutal trip to Camiri (US$13.50, 18 hours), with connections to the Argentine border at Yacuiba.

TRAIN

A recently implemented train service from Sucre to Potosí was, at time of writing, temporarily suspended but due to resume. Leaving from El Tejar siding near the cemetery, scheduled departures for this spectacular trip were at 8am Monday, Wednesday and Friday for the scenic six-hour journey (US$4.40 one-way), returning from Potosí at 8am on Tuesday, Thursday and Saturday. Call **Epifanio Flores** (☎ 7287-6280) to check whether the service is in operation.

Getting Around
TO/FROM THE AIRPORT

The airport, 9km northwest of town, is accessed by *micros* 1 or F (allow an hour to be safe) from Av Hernando Siles, by the *banderita blanca* taxi *trufi* from Av España, or by taxi (fixed tariff US$3.10).

BICYCLE

Several places rent bikes, including Unlimited, Locot's and Eclipse (see p247).

BUS & MICRO

Lots of buses and *micros* (US$0.15) ply circuitous routes around the city's one-way streets, and all seem to congregate at or near the market between runs. They're usually crowded, but fortunately, Sucre is a town of short distances. The most useful routes are those that climb the steep Av Grau hill to the Recoleta, and *micro* A, which serves the main bus terminal.

RENTAL CAR

Imbex (☎ 646-1222; Serrano 165) has 4WDs from US$29 a day.

TAXI

Taxis between any two points around the center, including the bus terminal, charge US$0.45 per person, a bit more after midnight.

TARABUCO
elevation 3200m

This small, predominantly indigenous village, 65km southeast of Sucre via a good paved road, enjoys a mild climate, just a bit cooler than Sucre's. Most *tarabuqueños* are involved in agriculture or textiles, and the textiles produced in the region are some of the most renowned in all of Bolivia. Tarabuco is best known for its Sunday market – which makes a popular daytrip from Sucre – and its March Phujllay celebrations.

Tarabuco's colorful, sprawling **Sunday market**, which features high-quality *artesanía* – pullovers, *charangos*, coca pouches, ponchos and weavings that feature geometric and zoomorphic designs – is one of Bolivia's most popular. By any standards, it's pretty touristy, which has meant the inevitable arrival of higher prices and lots of articles from well outside the local area. While there is some very high-quality work here, there's also a lot of generic stuff, and few bargains to be had. Sales tactics are somewhat less than passive, so it's not always a relaxing experience.

The colorful wares laid out in stalls around the plaza and on the side streets lend a festive and light-hearted atmosphere. Strolling, *charango*-playing *campesinos* model their local dress: the men wear distinctive *monteras* (also known as *morriones*), which are leather hats patterned after those worn by the conquistadores. You may also want to seek out the snake-oil vendors in the central market, who proffer the universal curative powers of leftover bits of snakes, dried starfish and toucan beaks.

On market days the **Centro Artesanal Inca Pallay** (Murillo 25), near the market, sells an array of local weavings and serves meals in its tourist-friendly restaurant. Several places put on exhibitions of *phujllay* dancing (see Festivals & Events below) while the market is on, for a small charge.

Festivals & Events

On March 12, 1816, Tarabuco was the site of the Battle of Jumbati, in which the villagers defended themselves under the leadership of a woman, Doña Juana Azurduy de Padilla, and liberated the town from Spanish forces. In commemoration of the event the village stages **Phujllay** ('amusement' or 'play' in Quechua) on the second or third weekend of March, when over 60 surrounding communities turn up in local costume. The celebration begins with a Quechua mass and procession followed by the **Pukhara** ceremony, a Bolivian version of Thanksgiving. Folkloric dancers and musicians perform throughout the two-day weekend fiesta. It's one of Bolivia's largest festivals, and is great fun.

Sleeping & Eating

During Phujllay, accommodations fill up quickly – so you may want to hedge your bets and carry camping gear. The nicest digs are at **Alojamiento Cuiza** (no phone; Bolívar s/n; r per person US$1.90), which has hot water. The price includes breakfast, and decent local meals can be added in for a pittance.

The plaza also has a couple of basic restaurants. Meals of chorizo, soup and *charquekan* (dried llama meat served with potatoes and corn) are available from street stalls during market hours.

Getting There & Away

The easiest way to get to Tarabuco is by charter bus (US$3.10 round-trip, 1½ hours each way) from Sucre, which leave from the center or pick up clients at their hotels around 7am. Hostal Charcas is one of several places that organize one. It's worth the early start, as things at the market are slowing down by midday. From Tarabuco, the buses return to Sucre anytime between 1pm and 3pm.

Alternatively, *micros* (US$0.75, 2½ hours) and *camiones* leave when full from Av de las Américas in Sucre on Sunday between 6:30am and 9:30am. Either walk from the center or take *micros* B or C. Transportation returning to Sucre departs from the main plaza in Tarabuco, and leaves anytime between 11am and 3:30pm.

CANDELARIA

While the Tarabuco Sunday market (see p253) is fairly touristy these days, to get a better idea of the Tarabuco culture and textiles you could visit the appealingly rustic indigenous village of Candelaria, which produces many of the finest weavings of the Candelaria/Tarabuco style. There's a very traditional way of life here, and it's far removed from the bustle of Sucre or Tarabuco. The community has established a weaving association, which owns a **museum** (US$0.60) and textile store, which explain the intricate weavings with displays depicting their culture. The store contains a large selection of the same high quality weaving found in Sucre but at lower prices, with 100% of the profits going to the association.

Some Sucre operators run tours leaving for Candelaria on Saturday, staying the night, and proceeding to Tarabuco's market on Sunday morning. Candelaria Tours (p247) runs a highly recommended one, overnighting in a beautiful colonial hacienda. The weaving association can also arrange stays in private homes.

There are buses from Sucre to Candelaria at 4pm on Tuesday, Thursday and Saturday. They are run by Flota Charcas and leave from the big clocktower on Av Mendoza (the ringroad). Several *camiones* pass through Candelaria daily, heading for Sucre.

CORDILLERA DE LOS FRAILES

The imposing serrated ridge forming Sucre's backdrop creates a formidable barrier between the departments of Chuquisaca and Potosí. It's home to the Jalq'a people, and offers a rich selection of scenery, activities and intriguing options for getting to know the Jalq'a culture.

Orientation

A recommended three- or four-day circuit taking in several Cordillera highlights and the villages at the heart of the community tourism project begins at Chataquila, on the ridge above Punilla, 25km northwest of Sucre. From here (with an optional side trip to the rock paintings at Incamachay) you descend to Chaunaca, then head to the Cráter de Maragua, before heading up to Potolo, from where there's daily transportation back to Sucre. (For more on these places, see Hiking below.)

You can do this circuit on foot or, combined hiking and public transportation. It's also a very enjoyable region to explore by bike – you can rent one in Sucre (see p253).

MAPS

There are numerous walking routes through the Cordillera de los Frailes, some of which are marked on the 1:50,000 topo sheets *Sucre*, sheet 6536-IV, and *Estancia Chaunaca*, sheet 6537-III (see Orientation & Maps p240).

Hiking

The best way to see this region is on foot. While hiking between the major villages is easy, a guide is highly recommended to increase your enjoyment of the region and communicate with the Quechua-speaking *campesinos*. A guide will also help to avoid misunderstandings, minimize your impact and help you get a better feeling for the local culture. It's easy to find a guide in any of the villages, or you

CORDILLERA DE LOS FRAILES

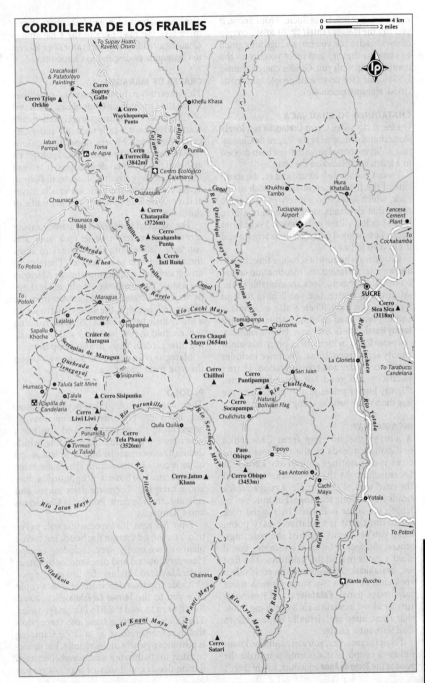

To Supay Huasi;
Ravelo; Oruro

Uracahuasi
& Patatoloyo
Paintings

Cerro Triqo ▲
Orkho

Cerro
Supray
Gallo

Cerro
Waykhopampa
Punta

Khellu Khasa

Jatun
Pampa

Toma
de Agua

Cerro
Torrecilla
(3842m)

Punilla

Río Cajamarca

Río Kollpa

Centro Ecológico
Cajamarca

Chaunaca

Inca Rd

Chataquila

Canal

Khukhu
Tambo

Hura
Khatalla

Fancesa
Cement
Plant

Chaunaca
Baja

Cerro
Chataquila
(3726m)

Cerro
Socabamba
Punta

Cerro
Inti Rumi

Río Quilwiqui Mayu

Tucsupaya
Airport

To
Cochabamba

To Potolo

Quebrada
Charco Khea

Cordillera de los Frailes

Río Ravelo

Canal

Río Tullma Mayu

SUCRE

To
Potolo

Maragua

Río Cachi Mayu

Tomapampa

Charcoma

Cerro
Sica Sica ▲
(3118m)

Lajalaja

Cemetery

Irupampa

Cerro Chaqui
Mayu (3654m)

Río Quirpinchaca

Sapallu
Khocha

Cráter de
Maragua

Serranías de Maragua

La Glorieta

To Tarabuco;
Candelaria

Quebrada
Cienegayaj

Sisipunku

Cerro
Chillhui

Cerro
Pantipampa

San Juan

Río Yotala

Humaca

Talula Salt Mine

Río Purunkilla

Cerro Socacampa

Río Chullchuta

Talula

Cerro Sisipunku

Cerro
Socacampa

Natural
Bolivian Flag

Capilla de
Candelaria

Cerro
Liwi Liwi

Chullchuta

Purunkilla

Cerro
Tela Phaqui
(3526m)

Quila Quila

Río Sayahua Mayu

Termas
de Talula

Paso
Obispo

Tipoyo

Río Pilcomayo

Cerro Jatun
Khasa

Cerro Obispo
(3453m)

San Antonio

Cachi
Mayu

Yotala

Río Cachi Mayu

To Potosí

Río Jatun Mayu

Río Wilakkota

Kanta Ñucchu

Chamina

Río Panti Mayu

Río Ayru Mayu

Río Rodeo

Cerro
Satari

Río Kaqui Mayu

0 ——— 4 km
0 ——— 2 miles

could arrange one from Sucre. From Sucre, if you call the **Maragua Entel** (☎ 693-8088) a couple of days in advance, you can arrange for a guide to come to the city and meet you, to do the complete trip with you. Guides charge around US$10 a day for up to four people, plus costs (food, transportation etc).

CHATAQUILA TO CHAUNACA

On the rocky ridge top at **Chataquila** is a lovely stone chapel dedicated to the Virgen de Chataquila, a Virgin-shaped stone that has been dressed in a gown and placed on the altar.

From Chataquila look around on the south side of the road for an obvious notch in the rock, which leads into a lovely pre-Hispanic route that descends steeply for 6km (three hours) to the village of **Chaunaca**, 39km from Sucre. Lots of good paved sections remain and it's easy to follow.

Chaunaca is home to a school, a tiny church, and an interpretation and information centre on the Jalq'a region. Beds are available in the information centre, but you'll have to fend for your own food. There's also a campsite, and the renovated colonial hacienda, **Posada Samay Huasi** (☎ 645-2935; samay_huasi43@yahoo.com; r per person US$30), which offers pricy but high-quality accommodations. The price includes three meals a day and transportation. There's electricity and good hot-water bathrooms. Slightly higher prices may apply if there are less than three people – ring to check.

INCAMACHAY

A worthwhile side trip from Chataquila or Chaunaca leads to the two sets of ancient rock paintings collectively known as Incamachay. At the first major curve on the road west of Chataquila, a rugged track heads north along the ridge. For much of its length the route is flanked by rugged rock formations, but it's relatively easy going until you've almost reached the paintings, where you face a bit of a scramble. You'll need a guide to find the paintings. The first set, **Uracahuasi**, lies well ensconced inside a rock cleft between two stone slabs. A more impressive panel, **Patatoloyo**, is 15 minutes further along beneath a rock overhang. Note that these sites are virtually impossible to find without a guide.

From Incamachay, you can continue downhill for a couple of hours until you strike the road at the **Tomo de Agua** aqueduct, where there's

drinking water and a good campsite. From there take the road 6km to the Chataquila–Chaunaca road, where you can either ascend to Chataquila or descend to Chaunaca.

CRÁTER DE MARAGUA

This unearthly natural formation, sometimes called the Ombligo de Chuquisaca (or Navel of Chuquisaca), features surreal settlements scattered across a 5-mile wide red-and-violet crater floor, and bizarre slopes that culminate in the gracefully symmetrical pale green arches of the Serranías de Maragua. It's one of the most visually striking places in all Bolivia. There's plenty to see here: waterfalls, caves and a picturesque cemetery in the middle of the crater.

The village of Maragua is an active weaving centre. The weavers have set up a store, and will take visitors into their homes to show them the creation of the textiles. There's also an agricultural museum planned. Maragua has a store, three *cabañas* (see boxed text opposite), and a campsite. A kilometer from the village, in Irupampa, the villagers have set up a lovely little **hostel** (dm US$1.25), with running water, a cold shower next door and an appealing little garden. You can also camp there.

Maragua is an easy three-hour walk along the road from Chaunaca.

POTOLO

The village of Potolo, 13km beyond Chaunaca, has some typically stunning weaving going on in the workshops, and also has a new museum of traditional medicine, which demonstrates vernacular healing practices and other aspects of the culture. There are three *cabañas* here (see boxed text opposite), a store and a campsite. There are daily *micros* and *camiones* from Sucre to Potolo via Chataquila and Chaunaca.

From Maragua, it's a spectacular walk to Potolo. You can get there in five hours, but there's plenty to see on the way, including *chullpa* (funerary towers) and dinosaur footprints at Niñu Mayu (add an hour for this side-trip).

A side trip from Hacienda Humaca could take you to the **Termas de Talula**, 5km away. You'll need to ford the Río Pilcomayo twice. The Talula hot springs issue into three pools that have temperatures up to 115°F. Camping is possible anywhere in the vicinity, but unfortunately the bathhouse was severely damaged during floods and it may or may not reopen

THE JALQ'A COMMUNITIES

The Cordillera de los Frailes is the home of the Quechua-speaking Jalq'a people, of whom there are some 10,000 in the area around Potolo and Maragua. They have traditionally made a living from farming potatoes, wheat and barley, and herding sheep and goats. The weaving of elaborately patterned *aqsus* (an apron-like skirt) is an important craft tradition, and these Escher-like red-and-black garments are instantly recognizable, being patterned with inventive depictions of *khurus* – strange, demon-like figures.

In 2001 the Jalq'a decided that they wanted to embrace tourism, but in a sustainable form that would benefit the community without destroying its traditions. They have developed a series of accommodations, cultural centers and guiding services, all involving maximal community participation. The villages receive 100% of profits.

To date, tailored accommodations and restaurant services have been set up in the villages of Maragua and Potolo. Sets of attractive thatched *cabañas* have been constructed using traditional methods and materials; they boast comfortable beds, hot water and attractive wooden furniture, and are decorated with local textiles. These cost US$8 per person per night; for US$16 per person, meals and cultural displays are included. These villages also have good camping areas. In Chaunaca, there's also a camping area, and six beds set up in the information center, but no restaurant service.

These are well-placed for a three-day circuit of the area, starting in Chataquila, heading to the rock paintings, and sleeping in Chaunaca. The next day you could head to Maragua (three hours), from where it's a spectacular six- to seven-hour walk – via *chullpa* (funerary towers) and with a short diversion to see the dinosaur footprints at Niñu Mayu – to Potolo.

On the way, you will eat traditional Bolivian *campesino* meals – such as *kala purca*, a maize soup cooked by immersing hot stones in it. Cultural activities that can be organized include demonstrations of *phujllay* dancing or traditional medicine. Weaving workshops can be found in all the villages mentioned, as well as some others, while Chaunaca has an interpretation center, and Potolo a museum of indigenous healing. Maragua has an agricultural museum in the pipeline. Note that the Jalq'a aren't fond of being photographed.

You can reach the area independently and organize guides, or take a pre-organized tour from Sucre. While many agencies offer day-trips to villages in the area, a longer trip that gives more back to the locals is recommended. There's a list of recommended Sucre agencies on p247.

To book the Maragua *cabañas,* call **Don Basilio** (☎ 693-8088; Entel office, Maragua). For Potolo, book via **ASUR** (☎ 645-3841; asur@asur.org.bo; Museo Textil-Etnográfico, San Alberto 413, Sucre).

as a public spa. Villagers have constructed temporary pools of rock.

From Talula it's 500m to the constricted passage that conducts the Río Pilcomayo between the steep walls of the Punkurani gorge. When the river is low, you can cross over to the Potosí shore and see the many rock-painting sites above the opposite bank.

SUPAY HUASI

Among the most interesting rock paintings in the Cordillera de los Frailes are those at Supay Huasi (House of the Devil). These unusual images in ocher, white and yellow include several animals, an ocher-colored 40cm man wearing a sunlike headdress, and several faded geometric figures and designs.

The paintings are south of Maragua – it's a longish day walk there and back. They are almost impossible to find without a local guide.

QUILA QUILA

Another worthwhile destination on the circuit is the beautiful village of Quila Quila, three hours south of Maragua by foot (guide recommended). It's a formerly deserted village that is being slowly repopulated. It has an elegant colonial church, and, nearby, the Marka Runi, three monoliths with pictographs. The area is rich in pre-Columbian archaeological artifacts; a villager, Don Román, has collected some of these in a small **museum** (admission US$0.60). You can also stay in a pleasant **room** (dm US$1.25) above his house, which has six beds in it. His wife makes tasty **meals** (US$0.60), they own a store, and he can act as a guide for the village and surrounding area.

CENTRAL HIGHLANDS

There's a daily *camión* to and from Sucre, passing through Quila Quila between noon and 2pm on its way back to the city (US$0.75, three to four hours).

Tours

Several Sucre travel agencies (see p247) offer quick jaunts into the Cordillera – for example, a two-day circuit from Chataquila to Incamachay and Chaunaca. It's important to go with an operator actually committed to giving something to the region – day trips aren't a great idea. Recommended agencies include Bolivia Specialist, Candelaria Tours, and Solarsa Tours. Others, such as Unlimited Adventure, offer trips that combine hiking and mountain biking. See p257 for opportunities to interact more with the Jalq'a culture.

Sleeping & Eating

See the boxed text p257 for details of *cabaña* and campsite accommodations in the villages of Chaunaca, Potolo and Maragua. Camping is possible in other places, but make sure you ask for permission and pay a small fee. The *cabañas* offer good meal services; those three villages also have simple stores.

Getting There & Away

A daily *micro* and a couple of *camiones* leave Sucre for Potolo (US$1 to US$1.50, three hours by *micro*, five by camión) via Chataquila and Chaunaca daily from the Yuraj Yuraj *camión* terminal on the road to the airport. The *micro* leaves at 9:30am, but get there plenty early to secure a seat. The *camiones* leave around 10am. To get there, take *micro* 1 or *trufi* 1 from the corner of Hernando Siles and Loa. For the return journey from Potolo, the *micros* leave between 8am and 11am, the *camiones* have no fixed departure time.

Daily *camiones* to Talula via Quila Quila (US$0.75, three to four hours) depart around 6am from Sucre's Barrio Aranjuez, returning the afternoon of the same day.

POTOSÍ

pop 149,200 / elevation 4070m

I am rich Potosí,
The treasure of the world…
And the envy of kings.

The conquistadors never found El Dorado, the legendary city of gold, but they did get their hands on Potosí and its Cerro Rico, a 'Rich Hill' full of silver. The quote above, from the city's first coat of arms, sums it up. The city was founded in 1545 as soon as the ore was discovered, and pretty soon the silver extracted here was bankrolling the Spanish empire.

Potosí's story is wholly tied to its silver. During the boom years, when the metal must have seemed inexhaustible, it became the largest and wealthiest city of the Americas. Even today, something very lucrative is said to *vale un Potosí* (be worth a Potosí). Then, once the silver more or less dried up, decline and poverty were the hard facts. The ore has been extracted by miners in some of the most abysmal conditions imaginable – a visit to see today's miners at work provokes disbelief at just how appalling the job is. But the rest of Potosí – its grand churches, ornate colonial architecture and down-to-earth, friendly inhabitants – is a real delight.

History

Noone is certain how much silver has been extracted from Cerro Rico over its four centuries of productivity, but a popular boast was that the Spanish could have constructed a silver bridge to Spain and still had silver left to carry across it. The Spanish monarchy, mortgaged to the hilt by foreign bankers, came to rely completely on the yearly treasure fleets which brought the Potosí silver. On the rare occasions when they were intercepted by storms or pirates, it was a national disaster.

Although the tale of Potosí's origins probably takes a few liberties with the facts, it's a good story. It begins in 1544 when a local Inca, Diego Huallpa, searching for an escaped llama, stopped to build a fire at the foot of the mountain known in Quechua as 'Potojsi' (meaning 'thunder' or 'explosion' in Quechua, although it might also have stemmed from *potoj,* 'the springs'). The fire grew so hot that the very earth beneath it started to melt, and shiny liquid oozed from the ground.

Diego immediately realized he'd run across a commodity for which the Spanish conquerors had an insatiable appetite. Perhaps he also remembered the Inca legend associated with the mountain, in which Inca Huayna Capac had been instructed by a booming voice not to dig in the hill of Potojsi, but to leave the metal alone, because it was intended for others.

Whatever the truth of this, the Spanish eventually learned of the enormous wealth buried

CORDILLERA DE LOS FRAILES

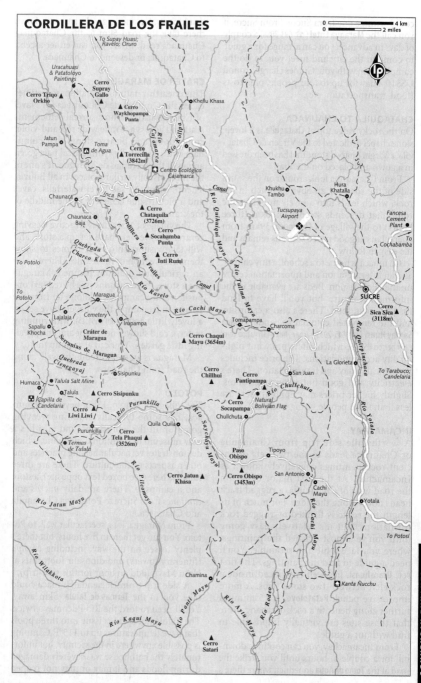

could arrange one from Sucre. From Sucre, if you call the **Maragua Entel** (☎ 693-8088) a couple of days in advance, you can arrange for a guide to come to the city and meet you, to do the complete trip with you. Guides charge around US$10 a day for up to four people, plus costs (food, transportation etc).

CHATAQUILA TO CHAUNACA
On the rocky ridge top at **Chataquila** is a lovely stone chapel dedicated to the Virgen de Chataquila, a Virgin-shaped stone that has been dressed in a gown and placed on the altar.

From Chataquila look around on the south side of the road for an obvious notch in the rock, which leads into a lovely pre-Hispanic route that descends steeply for 6km (three hours) to the village of **Chaunaca**, 39km from Sucre. Lots of good paved sections remain and it's easy to follow.

Chaunaca is home to a school, a tiny church, and an interpretation and information centre on the Jalq'a region. Beds are available in the information centre, but you'll have to fend for your own food. There's also a campsite, and the renovated colonial hacienda, **Posada Samay Huasi** (☎ 645-2935; samay_huasi43@yahoo.com; r per person US$30), which offers pricy but high-quality accommodations. The price includes three meals a day and transportation. There's electricity and good hot-water bathrooms. Slightly higher prices may apply if there are less than three people – ring to check.

INCAMACHAY
A worthwhile side trip from Chataquila or Chaunaca leads to the two sets of ancient rock paintings collectively known as Incamachay. At the first major curve on the road west of Chataquila, a rugged track heads north along the ridge. For much of its length the route is flanked by rugged rock formations, but it's relatively easy going until you've almost reached the paintings, where you face a bit of a scramble. You'll need a guide to find the paintings. The first set, **Uracahuasi**, lies well ensconced inside a rock cleft between two stone slabs. A more impressive panel, **Patatoloyo**, is 15 minutes further along beneath a rock overhang. Note that these sites are virtually impossible to find without a guide.

From Incamachay, you can continue downhill for a couple of hours until you strike the road at the **Tomo de Agua** aqueduct, where there's

drinking water and a good campsite. From there take the road 6km to the Chataquila–Chaunaca road, where you can either ascend to Chataquila or descend to Chaunaca.

CRÁTER DE MARAGUA
This unearthly natural formation, sometimes called the Ombligo de Chuquisaca (or Navel of Chuquisaca), features surreal settlements scattered across a 5-mile wide red-and-violet crater floor, and bizarre slopes that culminate in the gracefully symmetrical pale green arches of the Serranías de Maragua. It's one of the most visually striking places in all Bolivia. There's plenty to see here: waterfalls, caves and a picturesque cemetery in the middle of the crater.

The village of Maragua is an active weaving centre. The weavers have set up a store, and will take visitors into their homes to show them the creation of the textiles. There's also an agricultural museum planned. Maragua has a store, three *cabañas* (see boxed text opposite), and a campsite. A kilometer from the village, in Irupampa, the villagers have set up a lovely little **hostel** (dm US$1.25), with running water, a cold shower next door and an appealing little garden. You can also camp there.

Maragua is an easy three-hour walk along the road from Chaunaca.

POTOLO
The village of Potolo, 13km beyond Chaunaca, has some typically stunning weaving going on in the workshops, and also has a new museum of traditional medicine, which demonstrates vernacular healing practices and other aspects of the culture. There are three *cabañas* here (see boxed text opposite), a store and a campsite. There are daily *micros* and *camiones* from Sucre to Potolo via Chataquila and Chaunaca.

From Maragua, it's a spectacular walk to Potolo. You can get there in five hours, but there's plenty to see on the way, including *chullpa* (funerary towers) and dinosaur footprints at Niñu Mayu (add an hour for this side-trip).

A side trip from Hacienda Humaca could take you to the **Termas de Talula**, 5km away. You'll need to ford the Río Pilcomayo twice. The Talula hot springs issue into three pools that have temperatures up to 115°F. Camping is possible anywhere in the vicinity, but unfortunately the bathhouse was severely damaged during floods and it may or may not reopen

THE JALQ'A COMMUNITIES

The Cordillera de los Frailes is the home of the Quechua-speaking Jalq'a people, of whom there are some 10,000 in the area around Potolo and Maragua. They have traditionally made a living from farming potatoes, wheat and barley, and herding sheep and goats. The weaving of elaborately patterned *aqsus* (an apron-like skirt) is an important craft tradition, and these Escher-like red-and-black garments are instantly recognizable, being patterned with inventive depictions of *khurus* – strange, demon-like figures.

In 2001 the Jalq'a decided that they wanted to embrace tourism, but in a sustainable form that would benefit the community without destroying its traditions. They have developed a series of accommodations, cultural centers and guiding services, all involving maximal community participation. The villages receive 100% of profits.

To date, tailored accommodations and restaurant services have been set up in the villages of Maragua and Potolo. Sets of attractive thatched *cabañas* have been constructed using traditional methods and materials; they boast comfortable beds, hot water and attractive wooden furniture, and are decorated with local textiles. These cost US$8 per person per night; for US$16 per person, meals and cultural displays are included. These villages also have good camping areas. In Chaunaca, there's also a camping area, and six beds set up in the information center, but no restaurant service.

These are well-placed for a three-day circuit of the area, starting in Chataquila, heading to the rock paintings, and sleeping in Chaunaca. The next day you could head to Maragua (three hours), from where it's a spectacular six- to seven-hour walk – via *chullpa* (funerary towers) and with a short diversion to see the dinosaur footprints at Niñu Mayu – to Potolo.

On the way, you will eat traditional Bolivian *campesino* meals – such as *kala purca*, a maize soup cooked by immersing hot stones in it. Cultural activities that can be organized include demonstrations of *phujllay* dancing or traditional medicine. Weaving workshops can be found in all the villages mentioned, as well as some others, while Chaunaca has an interpretation center, and Potolo a museum of indigenous healing. Maragua has an agricultural museum in the pipeline. Note that the Jalq'a aren't fond of being photographed.

You can reach the area independently and organize guides, or take a pre-organized tour from Sucre. While many agencies offer day-trips to villages in the area, a longer trip that gives more back to the locals is recommended. There's a list of recommended Sucre agencies on p247.

To book the Maragua *cabañas*, call **Don Basilio** (☎ 693-8088; Entel office, Maragua). For Potolo, book via **ASUR** (☎ 645-3841; asur@asur.org.bo; Museo Textil-Etnográfico, San Alberto 413, Sucre).

as a public spa. Villagers have constructed temporary pools of rock.

From Talula it's 500m to the constricted passage that conducts the Río Pilcomayo between the steep walls of the Punkurani gorge. When the river is low, you can cross over to the Potosí shore and see the many rock-painting sites above the opposite bank.

SUPAY HUASI

Among the most interesting rock paintings in the Cordillera de los Frailes are those at Supay Huasi (House of the Devil). These unusual images in ocher, white and yellow include several animals, an ocher-colored 40cm man wearing a sunlike headdress, and several faded geometric figures and designs.

The paintings are south of Maragua – it's a longish day walk there and back. They are almost impossible to find without a local guide.

QUILA QUILA

Another worthwhile destination on the circuit is the beautiful village of Quila Quila, three hours south of Maragua by foot (guide recommended). It's a formerly deserted village that is being slowly repopulated. It has an elegant colonial church, and, nearby, the Marka Runi, three monoliths with pictographs. The area is rich in pre-Columbian archaeological artifacts; a villager, Don Román, has collected some of these in a small **museum** (admission US$0.60). You can also stay in a pleasant **room** (dm US$1.25) above his house, which has six beds in it. His wife makes tasty **meals** (US$0.60), they own a store, and he can act as a guide for the village and surrounding area.

There's a daily *camión* to and from Sucre, passing through Quila Quila between noon and 2pm on its way back to the city (US$0.75, three to four hours).

Tours

Several Sucre travel agencies (see p247) offer quick jaunts into the Cordillera – for example, a two-day circuit from Chataquila to Incamachay and Chaunaca. It's important to go with an operator actually committed to giving something to the region – day trips aren't a great idea. Recommended agencies include Bolivia Specialist, Candelaria Tours, and Solarsa Tours. Others, such as Unlimited Adventure, offer trips that combine hiking and mountain biking. See p257 for opportunities to interact more with the Jalq'a culture.

Sleeping & Eating

See the boxed text p257 for details of *cabaña* and campsite accommodations in the villages of Chaunaca, Potolo and Maragua. Camping is possible in other places, but make sure you ask for permission and pay a small fee. The *cabañas* offer good meal services; those three villages also have simple stores.

Getting There & Away

A daily *micro* and a couple of *camiones* leave Sucre for Potolo (US$1 to US$1.50, three hours by *micro*, five by camión) via Chataquila and Chaunaca daily from the Yuraj Yuraj *camión* terminal on the road to the airport. The *micro* leaves at 9:30am, but get there plenty early to secure a seat. The *camiones* leave around 10am. To get there, take *micro* 1 or *trufi* 1 from the corner of Hernando Siles and Loa. For the return journey from Potolo, the *micros* leave between 8am and 11am, the *camiones* have no fixed departure time.

Daily *camiones* to Talula via Quila Quila (US$0.75, three to four hours) depart around 6am from Sucre's Barrio Aranjuez, returning the afternoon of the same day.

POTOSÍ

pop 149,200 / elevation 4070m

I am rich Potosí,
The treasure of the world…
And the envy of kings.

The conquistadors never found El Dorado, the legendary city of gold, but they did get their hands on Potosí and its Cerro Rico, a 'Rich Hill' full of silver. The quote above, from the city's first coat of arms, sums it up. The city was founded in 1545 as soon as the ore was discovered, and pretty soon the silver extracted here was bankrolling the Spanish empire.

Potosí's story is wholly tied to its silver. During the boom years, when the metal must have seemed inexhaustible, it became the largest and wealthiest city of the Americas. Even today, something very lucrative is said to *vale un Potosí* (be worth a Potosí). Then, once the silver more or less dried up, decline and poverty were the hard facts. The ore has been extracted by miners in some of the most abysmal conditions imaginable – a visit to see today's miners at work provokes disbelief at just how appalling the job is. But the rest of Potosí – its grand churches, ornate colonial architecture and down-to-earth, friendly inhabitants – is a real delight.

History

Noone is certain how much silver has been extracted from Cerro Rico over its four centuries of productivity, but a popular boast was that the Spanish could have constructed a silver bridge to Spain and still had silver left to carry across it. The Spanish monarchy, mortgaged to the hilt by foreign bankers, came to rely completely on the yearly treasure fleets which brought the Potosí silver. On the rare occasions when they were intercepted by storms or pirates, it was a national disaster.

Although the tale of Potosí's origins probably takes a few liberties with the facts, it's a good story. It begins in 1544 when a local Inca, Diego Huallpa, searching for an escaped llama, stopped to build a fire at the foot of the mountain known in Quechua as 'Potojsi' (meaning 'thunder' or 'explosion' in Quechua, although it might also have stemmed from *potoj*, 'the springs'). The fire grew so hot that the very earth beneath it started to melt, and shiny liquid oozed from the ground.

Diego immediately realized he'd run across a commodity for which the Spanish conquerors had an insatiable appetite. Perhaps he also remembered the Inca legend associated with the mountain, in which Inca Huayna Capac had been instructed by a booming voice not to dig in the hill of Potojsi, but to leave the metal alone, because it was intended for others.

Whatever the truth of this, the Spanish eventually learned of the enormous wealth buried in the mountain of Potojsi and determined that it warranted immediate attention. On April 1 (according to some sources, April 10), 1545, the Villa Imperial de Carlos V was founded at the foot of Cerro Rico and large-scale excavation began. In the time it takes to say 'Get down there and dig,' thousands of indigenous slaves were pressed into service and the first of the silver was already headed for Spain.

The work was dangerous, however, and so many workers died of accidents and silicosis pneumonia that the Spanish imported literally millions of African slaves to augment the labor force. The descendants of the very few to survive mainly live in the Yungas (see boxed text p146).

In order to increase productivity, in 1572 the Viceroy of Toledo instituted the Ley de la Mita, which required all indigenous and African slaves over age 18 to work in shifts of 12 hours. They would remain underground without seeing daylight for four months at a time, eating, sleeping and working in the mines. When they emerged from a 'shift,' their eyes were covered to prevent damage in the bright sunlight.

Naturally these miners, who came to be known as *mitayos*, didn't last long. Heavy losses were also incurred among those who worked in the *ingenios* (smelting mills), as the silver-smelting process involved contact with deadly mercury. In all, it's estimated that over the three centuries of colonial rule – 1545 to 1825 – as many as eight million Africans and indigenous Bolivians died from the appalling conditions.

Inside the mines, silver was smelted in small ovens known as *huayrachinas,* which were fueled with wood and the spiky grass *paja brava*. The silver was then transported by llama train to Arica (Chile), along the Camino de Plata, or to Callao (now Lima, Peru) on the Pacific coast. From there it was taken to Spain.

In 1672 a mint was established to coin the silver, reservoirs were constructed to provide water for the growing population, and exotic European consumer goods found their way up the llama trails from Arica and Callao. Amid the mania, more than 80 churches were constructed, and Potosí's population grew to nearly 200,000, making it one of the largest cities in the world. One politician of the period put it succinctly: 'Potosí was raised in the pandemonium of greed at the foot of riches discovered by accident.'

As with most boom towns, Potosí's glory was not to last. The mines' output began to decline in the early 19th century, and the city was looted in the independence struggles in Alto Perú. The population dropped to less than 10,000, and the mid-19th century drop in silver prices dealt a blow from which Potosí has never completely recovered.

In the present century only the demand for tin has rescued Potosí from obscurity and brought a slow but steady recovery. Zinc and lead have now taken over from tin as Bolivia's major metallic exports. Silver extraction continues only on a small scale, but reminders of the city's grand colonial past are still evident.

Most of the operations in Cerro Rico today are in the control of miner-owned cooperatives, which operate under conditions that have changed shamefully little from the colonial period. There's little prospect of change in sight, as the miners barely extract enough ore to keep them in bread. The dream of the lucky strike (there are still a few) keeps them going.

In 1987 Unesco named Potosí a World Heritage Site in recognition of its rich and tragic history and its wealth of colonial architecture.

Orientation

Most things are in easy walking distance, except the observation tower, the mines and the bus station. The lack of oxygen can be disorienting, so take it easy if you are arriving from the lower areas.

MAPS

The tourist office periodically give out a city map; many of the tour agencies also include a useful map on the reverse of their brochure. **Instituto Geográfico Militar** (IGM; Chayanta btwn 10 de Abril & Litoral) sells topo sheets of all areas of Potosí department.

Information

EMERGENCY

Tourist police (☎ 622-7404; Ayacucho & Bustillos) Helpful; on the ground floor of the Torre de la Compañia de Jesús building.

IMMIGRATION

Migración (☎ 622-5989; Linares 35) For visa extensions etc.

INTERNET ACCESS

There are numerous places to get online, including **Café Internet Candelaria** (Ayacucho 5), and

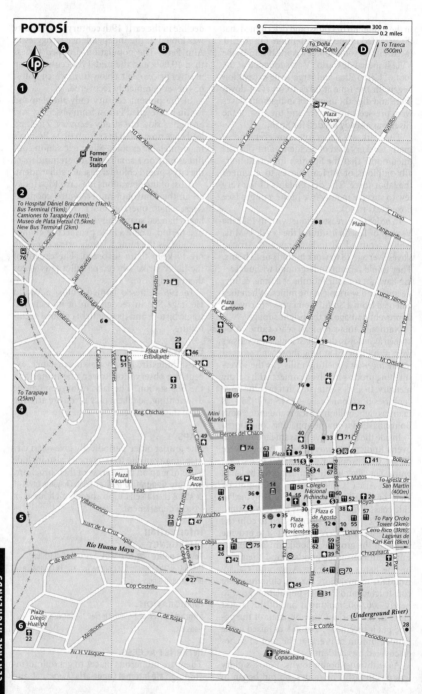

POTOSÍ

0   300 m
0   0.2 miles

To Doña
Eugenia (50m);
To Tranca
(500m)

Plaza
Uyuni

Former
Train
Station

To Hospital Daniel Bracamonte (1km);
Bus Terminal (1km);
Camiones to Tarapaya (1km);
Museo de Plata Herzul (1.5km);
New Bus Terminal (2km)

Plaza
Campero

Plaza
del
Estudiante

To Tarapaya
(25km)

Mini
Market

Héroes del Chaco

Plaza
Vacuñas

Plaza
Arce

Colegio
Nacional
Pichincha

To Iglesia de
San Martín
(400m)

Plaza
10 de
Noviembre

Plaza 6
de Agosto

To Pary Orcko
Tower (2km);
Cerro Rico (3km);
Lagunas de
Kari Kari (8km)

Río Huana Mayu

Plaza
Diego
Huallpa

(Underground River)

Iglesia
Copacabana

INFORMATION
Acces Computer.........................**1** C4
Banco de Crédito (ATM).............**2** D4
Banco Mercantil........................**3** D5
Banco Nacional..........................**4** D5
Café Internet Candelaría............**5** C5
Clinica/Optica Esculapio............**6** A3
Dirección de Turismo.................**7** C5
Instituto Geográfico Militar........**8** D2
Janus Limpieza..........................**9** C4
Migración.................................**10** D5
Prodem...................................**11** C4
Tourist Police.....................(see 7)

SIGHTS & ACTIVITIES
Altiplano Tours.......................(see 5)
Andes Salt Expeditions............ **12** D5
Arcos de Cobija.........................**13** B5
Casa de las Tres Portadas....(see 41)
Casa Nacional
  de Moneda..........................**14** C5
Cathedral.................................**15** C5
Don Antonio
  Villa Chavarría....................**16** C4
El Cabildo.................................**17** C5
Esquina de las
  Cuatro Portadas..................**18** D3
Hidalgo Tours...........................**19** C4
Iglesia de la Merced.................**20** D5
Iglesia de San Agustín.............**21** C4
Iglesia de San Benito...............**22** A6
Iglesia de San Bernardo...........**23** B4
Iglesia de San Juan de Dios.......**24** D5
Iglesia de San Lorenzo
  de Carangas.......................**25** C4
Iglesia de Santo Domingo........**26** C5
Ingenio Dolores.......................**27** B6

Ingenio San Marcos.................**28** D6
Koala Tours.........................(see 35)
La Capilla de Nuestra
  Señora de Jerusalén............**29** B3
Marco Polo Tours.................(see 36)
Miner Truck.............................**30** C5
Museo & Convento
  de San Francisco.................**31** D6
Museo & Convento
  de Santa Teresa..................**32** B5
Pasaje de Siete
  Vueltas.............................**33** D4
Portón Mestizo.....................(see 4)
Silver Tours.............................**34** C5
South American Tours.............**35** C5
Sumaj Tours.......................(see 46)
Torre de la Compañía
  de Jesús............................(see 7)
Turismo Claudia.......................**36** C5
Victoria Tours.....................(see 42)

SLEEPING 🏠
Alojamiento San José...............**37** B4
Hostal Colonial........................**38** D5
Hostal Compañía de Jesús........**39** D5
Hostal Felimar.........................**40** C4
Hostal Las Tres Portadas..........**41** D4
Hostal María Victoria...............**42** C5
Hostal Santa María...................**43** C3
Hotel Cima Argentum..............**44** B2
Hotel El Turista........................**45** C6
Hotel Jerusalén.......................**46** B3
Hotel Santa Teresa...................**47** B5
Koala Den................................**48** D4
Macuquina Dora Hotel..............**49** B4
Residencial Felcar....................**50** C3
Residencial Sumaj....................**51** B4

EATING 🍴
4060..**52** D5
Abya-Yala................................**53** C4
Aries..**54** C5
Café Cultural Kaypichu............**55** D5
Café de la Merced.................(see 20)
Cafe de la Plata........................**56** D5
Café-Restaurant Potocchi........**57** D5
Chaplin Café............................**58** C5
Cherry's Salon de Té................**59** D5
Confitería Capricornio.............**60** D5
El Fogón..................................**61** C5
El Mesón.................................**62** D5
Imma Sumac............................**63** C4
Los Azogueros.........................**64** D5
Manzana Mágica......................**65** C4

DRINKING 🍷
La Casona Pub.........................**66** C5
La Chatarra..............................**67** D5
Sumaj Orcko............................**68** C5

ENTERTAINMENT 🎭
Cine Universitario....................**69** D4
Imperial Cinema......................**70** D5

SHOPPING 🛍
Arte Nativo.............................. **71** D4
Artesanía Andina.....................**72** D4
Artesanías Palomita's...............**73** B3
Market....................................**74** C4
Mercado Artesanal................(see 28)

TRANSPORT
Aerosur...................................**75** C5
Buses to Uyuni........................**76** A3
Micros to Sucre........................**77** D1

---

the speedy **Acces Computer** (Bustillos 869). All places charge US$0.25 to US$0.40 per hour.

INTERNET RESOURCES
www.potosi.bo In Spanish; well worth checking out.

LAUNDRY
Most hotels can organize laundry services for their guests. Failing that, try **Janus Limpieza** (Bolívar 773; US$1 per kilo).

MEDICAL SERVICES
If you need an English-speaking doctor visit the **Hospital Daniel Bracamonte** (☎ 622-3900).

MONEY
ATMs are common in the center of town. Lots of businesses along Bolívar, Sucre and in the market change US dollars at reasonable rates; stalls along Héroes del Chaco also change euros and Chilean and Argentine pesos. Cash advances are available at **Banco de Crédito** (Bolívar & Sucre), **Banco Mercantil** (Paseo Blvd) and **Prodem** (cnr Bolívar & Junín), who also change US dollars.

POST & TELEPHONE
The central **post office** (Lanza & Chuquisaca) is close to the main square. There are numerous call centers with cheap international rates.

TOURIST INFORMATION
Dirección de Turismo (☎ 622-5288; Ayacucho near Bustillos; 🕑 8:30am-noon, 2-6pm) Located up the stairs in the beautiful Torre de la Compañía de Jesús. Very helpful; making a big effort to improve the standard of Potosí's services.

Sights & Activities
Such was the wealth of colonial Potosí that more than 80 churches were constructed here. But if it's a glimpse of hell you're after, see p265.

CASA NACIONAL DE MONEDA
The **National Mint** (☎ 622-2777; www.casanacional demoneda.org.bo; Ayacucho at Bustillos; admission US$2.50 for mandatory 2-3hr guided tour; 🕑 9am-noon & 2:30-6:30pm Tue-Sat, 9am-noon Sun) is Potosí's star attraction and one of South America's finest museums. Potosí's first mint was constructed on the

present site of the Casa de Justicia in 1572 under orders from the Viceroy of Toledo. This, its replacement, is a vast, elegant and strikingly beautiful building that takes up a whole city block. It was built between 1753 and 1773 to control the minting of colonial coins; legend has it that when the king of Spain saw the bill for its construction, he exclaimed 'that building must be made of silver' (expletive presumably deleted). These coins, which bore the mint mark 'P,' were known as *potosís*.

The building has walls that are more than a meter thick, and it has not only functioned as a mint but also done spells as a prison, a fortress and, during the Chaco War, as the headquarters of the Bolivian army. As visitors are ushered into a courtyard from the entrance, they're greeted by the sight of a stone fountain and a mask of Bacchus, hung there in 1865 by Frenchman Eugenio Martin Moulon for reasons known only to him. In fact, this aberration looks more like an escapee from a children's fun fair, but it has become a town icon (known as the *mascarón*).

Apart from the beauty of the building itself, there's a host of historical treasures here. There's a fine selection of religious paintings from the Potosí school, culminating in *La Virgen del Cerro*, a very famous anonymous work from the 18th century. It depicts the Virgin Mary as a Pachamama-like figure, actually within the earth, in this case represented by the Cerro Rico. It's full of symbols relating to the union of traditional Andean religion with Catholicism.

Perhaps the highlight of the visit are the immense assemblies of mule-driven wooden cogs that served to beat the silver to the width required for the coining. These were replaced by steam-powered machines in the 19th century. The last coins were minted here in 1953.

The guided tour is long, and the temperatures inside the building are chilly, so rug up. Although there are English and French tours available on request, the quality of the Spanish one is much higher and the visit more comprehensive, so it's well worth doing even if your levels are fairly limited.

CATHEDRAL

Construction of **La Catedral** (Plaza 10 de Noviembre; ☯ 3-6:30pm Mon-Fri) was initiated in 1564 and finally completed around 1600. The original building lasted until the early 19th century, when it mostly collapsed. Most of what is now visible is the neoclassical construction, and the building's elegant lines represent one of Bolivia's best exemplars of that style.

The interior décor represents some of the finest in Potosí. Note the bases of the interior columns, which still bear colonial-era tiles, the mid-17th century works of sculptor Gaspar de la Cueva titled *Señor de las Ánimas* and *Cristo de la Columna*, and the mausoleum, which holds the remains of colonial notables. At time of research, the cathedral was closed for

---

RHYTHMS OF LIFE

Australian artist Andrew Rogers, not content with sculpture on a conventional scale, has included Potosí as one of the sites for his fascinating global 'Rhythms of Life' project, where enormous, fluid, powerful, stone forms have been built in sites as diverse as Sri Lanka, Australia and Israel.

Rogers has endowed Potosí with three geoglyphs. Two adjacent ones, Circles and Presence, have their inspiration in ancient rock art found in the Potosí area. The third, on a hill near Cerro Rico, and the artistic centerpiece, is a complex, inspirational abstract figure named Rhythms of Life and derived from a Rogers bronze sculpture in Melbourne. But on a massive scale – the structure covers an area of 10,000 sq m.

The project was created with over 500 locals from an impoverished miners' barrio, using vernacular drystone-wall techniques. 'It was wonderful to see a community embrace and remember their heritage, and work together to perpetuate it for their children and grandchildren,' enthused Rogers.

While the geoglyphs are best viewed from a distance (and in the morning) – you have to climb up to them to really appreciate their scale and construction. The first two can be easily (if you've adapted to the altitude!) climbed to from near the *tranca* (highway police post) on the Oruro road at the edge of town; the third can be reached from the southwest of the city (you can get most of the way there by taxi).

a facelift, so opening hours may change once it re-opens in 2007.

CALLE QUIJARRO & ESQUINA DE LAS CUATRO PORTADAS

North of the Iglesia de San Agustín, **Calle Quijarro** narrows as it winds between a wealth of colonial buildings, many with doorways graced by old family crests. It's thought that the bends in Calle Quijarro were an intentional attempt to inhibit the cold winds that would otherwise whistle through and chill everything in their path. This concept is carried to extremes on the **Pasaje de Siete Vueltas** – 'the passage of seven turns' – which is an extension of Calle Ingavi, east of Junín. During colonial times Calle Quijarro was the street of potters, but it's now known for its hat makers. One millinery worth visiting is that of **Don Antonio Villa Chavarría** (Quijarro 41). The intersection of Calles Quijarro and Modesto Omiste, further north, has been dubbed the **Esquina de las Cuatro Portadas** because of its four decorative colonial doorways.

MUSEO & CONVENTO DE SAN FRANCISCO

The **San Francisco Convent** (☎ 622-2539; Tarija & Nogales; admission US$1.90, photo US$1.25; 🕘 9-11am & 2:30-5pm Mon-Fri, 9-11am Sat) was founded in 1547 by Fray Gaspar de Valverde, making it the oldest monastery in Bolivia. Owing to its inadequate size, it was demolished in 1707 and reconstructed over the following 19 years. A gold-covered altar from this building is now housed in the Casa Nacional de la Moneda. The statue of Christ that graces the present altar features hair that is said to grow miraculously.

The museum has examples of religious art, including various paintings from the Potosí School, such as *The Erection of the Cross* by Melchor Pérez de Holguín, various mid-19th century works by Juan de la Cruz Tapia, and 25 scenes from the life of St Francis of Assisi.

The highlight of the obligatory tour (ask for an English-speaking guide) comes at the end, when you're ushered up the tower and onto the roof for a grand view of Potosí.

MUSEO & CONVENTO DE SANTA TERESA

The fascinating **Santa Teresa Convent** (Santa Teresa at Ayacucho; admission by guided tour US$2.60, photo permit US$1.25; 🕘 9am-12:30pm & 3-6:30pm, last tour 5pm) was founded in 1685 and is still home to a small community of Carmelite nuns. One of them is an architect, and has directed a superb restoration project that has converted part of the sizeable building into a museum.

The excellent guided tour (Spanish & English) explains how girls of 15 from wealthy families entered the convent, getting their last glimpse of parents and loved ones at the door. Entry was a privilege, paid for with a sizeable dowry; a good portion of these offerings are on display in the form of religious artwork.

There are numerous fine pieces, including a superb Madonna by Castilian sculptor Alonso Cano, and several canvases by Melchor Pérez de Holguín, Bolivia's most famous painter. There's a room of fine painted wooden Christs (and a cracking Crucifixion by Ignacio del Río, a painter heavily influenced by Zurbarán and Velásquez). Some of the artworks verge on the macabre, as does the skull sitting in a bowl of dust in the middle of the dining room, and a display of wire whisks that some of the nuns used for self-flagellation.

As impressive as the works of art on show is the building itself, with two pretty cloisters housing numerous cacti and a venerable apple tree, and the glimpse into a cloistered world that only really changed character in the 1960s, with the reforms of the Second Vatican Council.

The guided tour lasts about two hours, and some of the rooms are particularly chilly. There's also a café and store, where you can buy *quesitos* (fried cheese and honey cakes) made by the nuns.

TORRE DE LA COMPAÑÍA DE JESÚS

The ornate and beautiful bell tower, on what remains of the former Jesuit church (☎ 622-7408; Ayacucho near Bustillos; mirador admission US$1.25; 🕘 8am-noon & 2-6pm Mon-Fri), was completed in 1707 after the collapse of the original church. Both the tower and the doorway are adorned with examples of Baroque mestizo ornamentation. The tourist office is in the same building.

MUSEO DE PLATA HERZUL

A silversmith has set up his home **workshop** (☎ 624-2736; Ecuador 880, btwn Manríquez & Gareca; US$1.90; 🕘 9am-12:30pm, 2:30-6pm Mon-Sat, 10am-12:30pm Sun) to accept visitors, and demonstrates every aspect of the craft, from forging to filigree. It's an interesting visit with plenty of chance to have a go yourself but it's wise to ring ahead to check that it's open. It's located in the Ciudad Satélite barrio 1km or so from the centre. You can also buy some of his work.

PARY ORCKO TOWER

This bizarre-looking observation **tower** (Barrio San Benito; US$1.90; ☉ 9am-10pm) makes a curious addition to the Potosí skyline. The viewing level revolves slowly and there's a restaurant here. It can't be denied that it's a great view! A bus heads to the tower on the hour from 9am to 6pm (no bus at 1pm) from in front of the Colegio Nacional 'Pichincha' on Plaza 6 de Agosto near the cathedral.

CHURCHES

The rather ordinary-looking **Iglesia de San Martín** (☎ 622-3682; Hoyos near Almagro; US$0.75; ☉ 3-6:30pm Mon-Fri, Sat by arrangement) was built in the 1600s and is today run by the French Redemptionist Fathers. Inside is an art museum, with at least 30 paintings beneath the choir depicting the Virgin Mary and the 12 Apostles. The Virgin on the altarpiece wears clothing woven from silver threads. However, San Martín is outside the center and is sometimes closed, so phone before traipsing out here.

La Capilla de Nuestra Señora de Jerusalén (☎ 623-0250; Camacho at Oruro; joint admission with Iglesia de la Merced US$1.25; ☉ 10am-noon, 3-6pm) is a little-known Potosí gem. Originally built as a humble chapel in honor of the Virgen de Candelaria, it was rebuilt more lavishly in the 18th century. It houses a fine gilt Baroque *retablo* – the Virgin has pride of place – and a magnificent series of paintings of Biblical scenes by anonymous artists of the Potosí school. The impressive pulpit has small paintings by Melchor Pérez de Holguín. Entry is by enthusiastic and well-informed guided tour.

The ornate Baroque mestizo portal of **Iglesia de San Lorenzo de Carangas** (Héroes del Chaco at Bustillos; ☉ 10am-noon Mon-Sat) is probably one of the most photographed subjects in Bolivia. It was carved in stone by master indigenous artisans in the 16th century, but the main structure wasn't completed until the bell towers were added in 1744. Inside are two Holguín paintings and handcrafted silverwork on the altar. The church was renovated in 1987.

Iglesia de San Agustín (Bolívar at Quijarro), with its elegant Renaissance doorway, is known for its eerie underground crypts and catacombs. At time of research, it was being equipped to open to the public.

Building began on the **Iglesia de San Benito** (Plaza Diego Huallpa) in 1711 and it's laid out in the form of a Latin cross and features Byzantine domes and a distinctive mestizo doorway. Other churches of note include **Iglesia de San Juan de Dios** (Chuquisaca at La Paz), which has stood since the 1600s despite its adobe construction. Restored **Iglesia de La Merced** (Hoyos at Millares; joint admission with Capilla de Jerusalén US$1.25; ☉ 11am-12:30pm, 3-6pm) is also lovely, with its carved pulpit and a beautiful 18th-century silver arch over the altarpiece. It was constructed between 1555 and 1687. The recently renovated **Iglesia de Santo Domingo** (Oruro at Cobija) contains an ornate portal, an unusual paneled ceiling and one of the eight original panels from the life of Santa Rosa de Lima, by Juan Díaz and Juan Francisco de la Puente. As well, there are other colonial paintings and sculptures located here. To gain admission to the church, visit on Sunday prior to the mass.

The former church and convent of **Iglesia de San Bernardo** (Plaza del Estudiante) is most notable for its spectacular facade of undressed boulders. The cavernous interior now houses a Spanish-sponsored school of art restoration.

HISTORIC BUILDINGS

Potosí's elaborate colonial architecture merits a stroll around the narrow streets to take in the ornate doorways and facades, as well as the covered wooden balconies that overhang the streets. Architecturally notable homes and monuments include **El Cabildo** (Old Town Hall; Plaza 10 de Noviembre), the pretty **Casa de las Tres Portadas** (Bolívar 1052) and the **Arcos de Cobija** (Arches of Cobija) on the street of the same name.

On Calle Junín, between Matos and Bolívar, is an especially lovely and elaborate **portón mestizo** doorway, flanked by twisted columns. It once graced the home of the Marqués de Otavi, but now ushers patrons into the Banco Nacional.

LOS INGENIOS

On the banks (*la ribera*) of the Río Huana Mayu, in the upper Potosí barrios of Cantumarca and San Antonio, are some fine ruined examples of the *ingenios*, or smelters. These were formerly used to extract silver from the ore hauled out of Cerro Rico. There were originally 82 *ingenios* along 15km of the stream. Some remaining ones date back to the 1570s and were in use until the mid-1800s.

Each *ingenio* consists of a floor penetrated by shallow wells (*buitrones*) where the ore was mixed with mercury and salt. The ore was then ground by millstones that were powered by water that was impounded in the 32 artificial Lagunas de Kari Kari (p272).

The **Ingenio San Marcos** (San Marcos Smelter; La Paz near Periodista) is the most interesting, but was closed at time of research, and its future is in doubt.

The **Ingenio Dolores** (Mejillones) continues to operate – or rather, the modern version does. Inside, however, you'll find the ruins of the colonial-era mill. It's open during business hours.

Most tours of the Cerro Rico mines include a stop at a working *ingenio* as part of the trip.

COOPERATIVE MINES

A visit to the cooperative mines will almost surely be one of the most memorable experiences you'll have in Bolivia, providing an opportunity to witness working conditions that are among the most grueling imaginable. You may be left stunned and/or ill (see the boxed text below).

Dozens of Potosí operators (see p266) offer guided tours through the mines. The best tour guides tend to be ex-miners, who know the conditions and are friendly with the men at work.

Mine visits aren't easy, and the low ceilings and steep, muddy passageways are best visited in your worst clothes. You'll feel both

---

THE JOB FROM HELL

In the cooperative mines on Cerro Rico, all work is done with primitive tools, and underground temperatures vary from below freezing – the altitude is over 4200m – to a stifling 115°F on the fourth and fifth levels. Miners, exposed to all sorts of noxious chemicals and gases, normally die of silicosis pneumonia within 10 to 15 years of entering the mines.

Contrary to popular rumor, women are admitted to many cooperative mines; only a few miners hang on to the tradition that women underground invite bad luck, and in many cases, the taboo applies only to miners' wives, whose presence in the mines would invite jealousy from Pachamama. At any rate, lots of Quechua women are consigned to picking through the tailings, gleaning small amounts of minerals that may have been missed.

Since cooperative mines are owned by the miners themselves, they must produce to make their meager living. All work is done by hand with explosives and tools they must purchase themselves, including the acetylene lamps used to detect pockets of deadly carbon monoxide gas.

Miners prepare for their workday by socializing and chewing coca for several hours, beginning work at about 10am. They work until lunch at 2pm, when they rest and chew more coca. For those who don't spend the night working, the day usually ends at 7pm. On the weekend, each miner sells his week's production to the buyer for as high a price as he can negotiate.

When miners first enter the mine, they offer propitiation at the shrine of the miners' god Tata Kaj'chu, whom they hope will afford them protection in the harsh underground world. Deeper in the mine, visitors will undoubtedly see a small, devilish figure occupying a small niche somewhere along the passageways. As most of the miners believe in a god in heaven, they deduce that there must also be a devil beneath the earth in a place where it's hot and uncomfortable. Since hell (according to the traditional description of the place) must not be far from the environment in which they work, they reason that the devil himself must own the minerals they're dynamiting and digging out of the earth. In order to appease this character, whom they call Tío (Uncle) or Supay – never Diablo – they set up a little ceramic figurine in a place of honor.

On Friday nights a *cha'lla* (offering) is made to invoke his goodwill and protection. A little alcohol is poured on the ground before the statue, lighted cigarettes are placed in his mouth and coca leaves are laid out within easy reach. Then, as in most Bolivian celebrations, the miners smoke, chew coca and proceed to drink themselves unconscious. While this is all taken very seriously, it also provides a bit of diversion from an extremely harsh existence. It's interesting that offerings to Jesus Christ are only made at the point where the miners can first see the outside daylight.

In most cooperative operations there is a minimal medical plan in case of accident or silicosis (which is inevitable after seven to 10 years working underground) and a pension of about US$15 a month for those so incapacitated. Once a miner has lost 50% of his lung capacity to silicosis, he may retire, if he so wishes. In case of death, a miner's widow and children collect this pension.

cold and hot at times, there will likely be a bit of crawling through narrow shafts and the altitude can be extremely taxing. On some tours, you'll end up walking 3km or 4km inside the mountain. You'll be exposed to noxious chemicals and gases, including silica dust (the cause of silicosis), arsenic gas and acetylene vapors, as well as asbestos deposits. Anyone with doubts or medical problems should avoid these tours. The plus side is that you can speak with the friendly miners, who will share their insights and opinions about their difficult lot. The miners are proud of their work in such tough conditions, and generally happy for visitors to observe their toil.

Tours begin with a visit to the miners' market, where miners stock up on acetylene rocks, dynamite, cigarettes and other essentials. In the past, gifts weren't expected, but with the growing number of tourists, you'd be very unpopular if you didn't supply a handful of coca leaves and a few cigarettes – luxuries for which the miners' meager earnings are scarcely sufficient. Photography is permitted. The tours then generally visit an *ingenio* (see p264), before heading up to the Cerro Rico itself. There's often a demonstration of a dynamite

explosion; the force is like a hammer blow to the chest even at some distance.

Mine tours run in the morning or afternoon and last from three to six hours; you tend to get longer in the mine on the morning visits. The standard charge is US$10 per person; lower rates may be available during periods of low demand. This price includes a guide, transportation from town and equipment: jackets, helmets, boots and lamps. Wear sturdy clothing and carry plenty of water and a handkerchief/headscarf to filter some of the noxious substances you'll encounter. There is less activity in the mines on Saturdays, Sundays and Mondays.

Tours

In addition to mine tours, there are many guided tours offered by many agencies. Other popular options include Tarapaya (p274; US$7.50) and trekking and camping trips around the Lagunas de Kari Kari (p272; US$20 to US$25 per day). Reliable agencies include:

Altiplano Tours (☎ 622-5353; www.altiplano.com; Ayacucho 19) Standard tours plus *tinku* excursions.

Andes Salt Expeditions (☎ 622-5175; www.andes -salt-uyuni.com.bo; Plaza Alonso de Ibañez 3) Guarantees at least one dynamite detonation.

Hidalgo Tours (☎ 622-5186; www.salardeuyuni.net; Bolívar at Junín) One of the best upmarket options.

Koala Tours (☎ 622-4708; www.koalatoursbolivia .com; Ayacucho 5) Runs some of the best mine tours, with an ex-miner as guide (US$10), plus mountain biking and excursions to local fiestas that feature *tinku* fighting.

Marco Polo Tours (☎ 623-1385; marcopoloagency@ hotmail.com; Bustillo 1036) Reader recommended; boss Wily is a former miner who speaks good English.

Miner Truck (☎ 7241-7272) An old truck picks up from the cathedral at 9am, noon and 3pm Monday to Saturday for a mine visit that's shorter and less strenuous than most.

Silver Tours (☎ 622-3600; silvertoursreservas@hotmail .com; Quijarro 12) All the standard tours around Potosí and adventure tours to the *salares*.

South American Tours (☎ 622-8919; osmedtur@ hotmail.com; Ayacucho 11) Visits the mine San Miguel la Poderosa and also does the standard tours.

Sumaj Tours (☎ 622-2600; hoteljer@cedro.pts.entelnet. bo; Oruro 143) Friendly agency at the Hotel Jerusalén.

Turismo Claudia (☎ 622-5000; jacky_gc@yahoo.com; Bustillos 1078) Reliable agency; local excursions and mine tours in French, English and Spanish.

Victoria Tours (☎ /fax 622-2132; Chuquisaca 148) Budget agency running mine and city tours, plus Tarapaya, Lagunas de Kari Kari and hot springs trips. Located at Hostal María Victoria.

WARNING!

The cooperatives are not museums, but working mines are fairly nightmarish places. Anyone planning to take a tour needs to realize that there are risks involved (see above). People with medical problems – especially claustrophobia, asthma and other respiratory conditions – should avoid these tours. While medical experts including the NHS note that limited exposure from a few hours' tour is extremely unlikely to cause any lasting health impacts, if you have any concerns whatsoever about exposure to asbestos or silica dust, you should not enter the mines. Accidents can also happen – explosions, falling rocks, runaway trolleys, etc. For these reasons, all tour companies make visitors sign a disclaimer absolving them completely from any responsibility for injury, illness or death – if your tour operator does not, choose another. Visiting the mines is a serious decision. If you're undeterred, you'll have an eye-opening and unforgettable experience.

Festivals & Events

FIESTA DEL ESPÍRITU

Potosí's most unusual event takes place on the last three Saturdays of June and the first Saturday of August. It's dedicated to the honor of Pachamama, the earth mother, whom the miners regard as the mother of all Bolivians.

Campesinos bring their finest llamas to the base of Cerro Rico to sell to the miners for sacrifice. The ritual is conducted to a meticulous schedule. At 10am, one miner from each mine purchases a llama and their families gather for the celebrations. At 11am, everyone moves to the entrances of their respective mines. The miners chew coca and drink alcohol from 11am to precisely 11:45am, when they prepare the llama for Pachamama by tying its feet and offering it coca and alcohol. At noon, the llama meets its maker. As its throat is slit, the miners petition Pachamama for luck, protection and an abundance of minerals. The llama's blood is splashed around the mouth of the mine to ensure Pachamama's attention, cooperation and blessing.

For the next three hours, the men chew coca and drink while the women prepare a plate of grilled llama. The meat is served traditionally with potatoes baked along with *habas* (fava beans) and oca in a small adobe oven. When the oven reaches the right temperature, it is smashed in on the food, which is baked beneath the hot shards. The stomach, feet and head of the llama are buried in a 3m hole as a further offering to Pachamama, then the music and dancing begin. In the evening, celebrants are taken home in transportation provided by the miner who bought his mine's llama.

FIESTA DE SAN BARTOLOMÉ (CHU'TILLOS)

This rollicking celebration takes place on the final weekend of August or the first weekend of September and is marked by processions, student exhibitions, traditional costumes and folk dancing from all over the continent. In recent years it has even extended overseas and featured musical groups and dance troupes from as far away as China and the USA. Given all the practicing during the week leading up to the festival, you'd be forgiven for assuming it actually started a week early. Booking accommodations for this period is essential.

EXALTACIÓN DE LA SANTA VERA CRUZ

This festival, which falls on September 14, honors Santo Cristo de la Vera Cruz. Activities occur around the church of San Lorenzo and the railway station. Silver cutlery features prominently, as do parades, dueling brass bands, dancing, costumed children and, of course, lots of alcohol.

Sleeping

Usually only the top-end hotels have heating, and there may be blanket shortages in the cheapies, so you'll want a sleeping bag.

BUDGET

Alojamiento San José (☎ 622-4394; Oruro 171; r per person US$2.50-3.75) This cheap place has a cheery welcome and decent location. For an extra US$1.25 per person, you get a significantly better (although still somewhat depressing) room: more warmth, an electric socket, and a bigger bed, with mattresses that are less lumpy.

Residencial Sumaj (☎ 622-3336; Gumiel 12; s/d with shared bathroom US$3.75/6.90) This long-time budget standby has small rooms. It's only worth staying on the top floor, which is lit by skylights; those downstairs are dreadfully dingy. There's an adequate kitchen for guests, but you have to pay (US$1.25) for the privilege. The shared showers are hot, and off-street parking is available. There's a 10% discount for HI members.

Hostal María Victoria (☎ 622-2132; Chuquisaca 148; s/d US$3.75/6.25, with bathroom US$6.25/9) This agreeable and attractive hostel occupies an old home at the end of a quiet lane. The rooms surround a classic whitewashed and tree-shaded courtyard; there's also a roof terrace with views. There are rooms with and without bathroom available, breakfast (US$1) and a tour agency.

Koala Den (☎ 622-6467; ktours_Potosi@hotmail .com; Junín 56; dm US$3.75-5, s/d US$7.50/15) Although not the best value in town, the cheerily colored Koala is a favorite for its traveler-friendly facilities and backpacker-social vibe. The dorms and rooms are cozy, with bedspreads ranging from Dr Seuss to Garfield; there's a kitchen, book exchange, 24-hour hot showers, and a bright and pleasant central lounge area. Management don't exactly bend over backwards, but it's clean and well-maintained.

Hostel Compañía de Jesús (☎ 622-3173; Chuquisaca 445; s/d US$6/10, with bath, breakfast & TV US$7/12) For sparkling clean rooms, firm mattresses, lots of blankets and a friendly atmosphere, stay in this old Carmelite monastery. It's a lovely building, but not for people who feel the cold too much. There are a couple of triple rooms and room No 18 is especially nice.

Residencial Felcar (☎ 622-4966; Serrudo 345; r per person US$3.10; s/d with bathroom US$10/15) This friendly, if slightly scattily run, place makes a sound, welcoming option. Clean, simple rooms with shared bathroom are great for the price, but you'll want a sleeping bag. New rooms with bathroom are very attractive, with typical modern Latin-American furniture and heaters. There are reliable hot showers throughout. Breakfast is available for US$0.75.

Hostal Felimar (☎ /fax 622-4357; Junín 14; s/d US$5/8.75, with bathroom US$10/15) This pleasant and centrally located, solar-powered hostel has some very nice upstairs rooms with balconies affording views over the colonial street below. Breakfast is included and there's a great suite on the top floor (US$27.50).

Hostal Santa María (☎ 622-3255; Serrudo 244; s/d with bathroom US$7.50/11.25) This clean and decent option has carpeted rooms with OK beds, TV and private bathroom. There are flowers around the courtyard, piping-hot showers and phones, but no heating.

Hotel El Turista (☎ 622-2492; Lanza 19; s/d with bathroom US$10/16) This offers spacious and fairly comfortable rooms with electric showers and superb views from the top floor. It's pretty good value and well maintained.

MIDRANGE & TOP END

Hotel Jerusalén (☎ 622-4633; hoteljer@entelnet.bo; Oruro 143; s/d US$15/26.25) Popular with visiting groups, this relaxed hotel is a reliable choice. Nobody would really claim that it's great value for money, but comfort counts; the staff can arrange all sorts of tours, and the rooms have quality gas showers and cable TV. Rates vary significantly by season, so be sure to confirm prices. A buffet breakfast is included, served in a café with a view.

Macuquina Dora Hotel (☎ 623-0257; www.macuquinadorahotel.com; Camacho 243; s/d with breakfast US$20/35; 🖳) This pleasant if slightly faded modern hotel is in a handy central location. There's cordial service, and clean, attractive heated rooms with heart-shaped cushions on the frilly beds. The front rooms (ending in 01–03) have miles more light and space than the others; try to bag one. There's also a sauna, restaurant and roof terrace.

Hostal Las Tres Portadas (☎ 622-4450; tresportadas@hotmail.com; Bolívar 1092; s/d/ste US$20/30/45; 🖳) This newly opened spot is situated in one of Potosí's most characterful buildings and is based around two pretty patios. It's a well-run place, and adequately heated; the rooms all have comfortable beds and come with minibar and excellent bathroom. The family suite is particularly appealing, but some of the ground floor rooms might be a little dark for some tastes; try for one of the lighter ones. The staff are helpful, and there's a good café-bar space.

Hotel Santa Teresa (☎ 622-5270; www.hotelsantateresa.com.bo; Ayacucho 43; s/d US$25/40; 🖳) This well-appointed hotel is by the convent of the same name, in a quiet part of central Potosí. Built around a whitewashed courtyard, it has smallish rooms but is a nice place to stay nonetheless. The restaurant, Rosicler, is one of the city's best.

Hostal Colonial (☎ 622-4265; www.hostalcolonialpotosi.com; Hoyos 8; s/d/ste US$33/43/60) In a well-kept colonial building near the main plaza, this warm, whitewashed retreat has smallish rooms with windows onto a central courtyard; all have minibars and cable TV, and some have bathtubs. It's a longstanding favorite with midrange travelers, but perhaps feels in need of a little facelift. Nevertheless, it still boasts very helpful English-speaking staff and a great location. Breakfast is available (US$2 to US$3).

Hotel Cima Argentum (☎ 622-9538; www.hca-potosi.com; Villazón 239; s/d/ste with breakfast US$33/46/52-60; 🖳) This professionally run place is a handsome, somewhat formal choice with decent facilities, including safes in every room, minibars in some, and off-street parking. The suites are a good choice for families, and all the rooms have good bathrooms and heating. The international restaurant offers room service.

Eating

There are several appealing restaurants in Potosí; good spots to ward off the nighttime chill with a hearty meal.

RESTAURANTS

Doña Eugenia (☎ 626-2247; cnr Santa Cruz & Ortega; dishes US$0.75-2.50; 🕙 9am-1pm) Potosí residents swear by this convivial local restaurant at the northern end of town. Head there early (around 10am is best) to make sure you get some of the legendary *kala purca* (thick maize soup with a hot rock in it). Other specialties include a hearty pork stew, *fricasé*.

Café-Restaurant Potocchi (☎ 622-2759; Millares 13; lunch US$1.50; 🕙 8am-midnight) A pleasant and inexpensive place serving a range of meals, with plenty of vegetarian choice. It also hosts a *peña* (folk music program; US$1.50 cover) a couple of nights a week.

Manzana Mágica (☎ 7183-6312; Oruro 239; meals US$2; ⏱ 8:30am-3pm, 5:30-10pm Mon-Sat) This is a worthwhile, strictly vegetarian spot known for its breakfast – muesli, juice, eggs and brown bread, and tasty soy steaks. Lunch is ultra-healthy and à la carte dinners are assertively spiced and portions are big.

Aries (☎ 622-1094; cnr Cobija & Oruro; mains US$2-2.50; ⏱ 10am-10pm) This attractive little local is run by a friendly boss and serves a good set lunch and tasty, spicy Bolivian dishes like *picante de pollo* (chicken with a hot sauce served with potatoes and rice) and *pique* (a spicy mix of beef, sausages and peppers on a pile of chips).

4060 (☎ 622-2623; Hoyos 1; mains US$2-3; ⏱ 6pm-1am) It took us a while to work out the name, but we blamed the altitude (of Potosí in meters). This spacious contemporary café-bar is a newcomer on the scene and earning plaudits for its pizzas, burgers and Mexican food (and paella, if you order it in advance) and as a sociable spot for a drink. There's a good beer selection, but mixing lager with blue curaçao in a cocktail struck us as highly dubious!

El Fogón (☎ 622-4969; Oruro & Frías; mains US$2-4.50; ⏱ noon-11pm) This spacious, brightly-lit central restaurant is popular with travelers for its range of international and Bolivian food, including llama steaks. In truth, it's not what it was – portions aren't huge, and the service is poor.

El Mesón (☎ 622-3087; cnr Tarija & Linares; mains US$3-5) This romantic, vaulted restaurant on a corner of the plaza has air heavy with smells of warm garlic. The menu is somewhat French, and has many choices. The food (steak, pasta, salads) is a tad overpriced but nonetheless excellent, and the attractive ambience adds to the experience.

Los Azogueros (☎ 622-8277; Padilla 40; mains US$3-5; ⏱ 11:30am-11pm) This smart restaurant opposite the Imperial cinema is where local lawyers lunch on their clients' bill. It's fairly formal, with excellent service and well-sourced ingredients. The fish dishes are particularly tasty.

CAFÉS

Cherry's Salon de Té (☎ 622-2352; Padilla 8; mains US$1-2; ⏱ 7:30am-10pm) Open all afternoon, this café makes a nice but very slow pit stop while you're out exploring the town. The apple stru-

del, chocolate cake and lemon meringue pie are superb, but the coffee is mediocre. They also serve light meals.

Confitería Capricornio (Pje Blvd 11; mains US$1-2; ⏱ 9am-10pm) Packed with students in the evening, this cheery quick-bite option serves soup, fast food, pizza, spaghetti, coffee and juices.

Abya-Yala (Junín near Bolívar; snacks US$1-2; ⏱ 10am-10pm) A simple but atmospheric place with rough wooden chairs, an indigenous theme, snacks, mediocre coffee and a friendly feel. There's often folk music at nights on the stage.

Chaplin Café (Matos near Quijarro; meals US$1.50-2.50; ⏱ 7am-noon, 4-10:30pm) Friendly and comfortable, this place serves mostly Bolivian fare with a few international, including Mexican, dishes. They do decent breakfasts too.

Café de la Merced (Iglesia de la Merced; Hoyos s/n; light meals US$2; ⏱ 9am-7:30pm) You couldn't ask for a better location than this rooftop café: atop the Iglesia de la Merced, right by the bells, with views all around the city. They serve very tasty juices, adequate coffee, delicious cakes and light meals; you may have to wait for a table though, as it's a small space.

Café de la Plata (☎ 622-6085; Plaza 10 de Noviembre; mains US$2-3; ⏱ 9:30am-11pm) This handsome place is cozy and chic in a restored sort of way, and a good place to hang out. There are rich espressos, magazines to read and wine served by the glass. Pastas, cakes, salads, sandwiches; it's all pretty tasty. Service can be grumpy, but there's no malevolence behind it.

Café Cultural Kaypichu (☎ 622-6129; Millares 24; mains US$2-3; ⏱ 7:30am-9pm Tue-Sun) A peaceful and relaxed mainly vegetarian spot, good at any time of day, starting with healthy breakfasts, and heading through generous set lunches (US$1.40), pasta and pizza dinners, and regular nighttime entertainment.

Stalls in the market *comedor* (dining hall) serve inexpensive breakfasts of bread, pastries and coffee. Downstairs there are some excellent juice stands.

Most Bolivians acknowledge, when pushed, that Potosí does the best *salteñas* – juicy, spicy, and oh-so-tasty. Go no further than **Imma Sumac** (Bustillos 987; ⏱ 9am-5pm), where one of these delicious items goes for US$0.30; there's a courtyard space to eat in. Cheese or meat empanadas are sold around the market until early afternoon, and in the evening, street vendors sell cornmeal and cheese *humitas*.

CENTRAL HIGHLANDS

Drinking

The atmospheric **La Casona Pub** (☎ 622-2954; Frías 41; ☺ 10am-12:30pm & 6pm-midnight Mon-Sat), is tucked away in the historic 1775 home of the royal envoy sent to administer the mint. It's a memorable friendly watering hole with pub grub and decent set lunches (US$2). On Friday it stages live music performances. **Sumaj Orcko** (☎ 622-3703; Quijarro 46) is a popular restaurant with a low-lit, comfortable bar on the corner that opens late. On the pedestrian street, **La Chatarra** (Pje Blvd 35; ☺ 6pm-late) is a lively local pub.

Entertainment

Café-Restaurant Potocchi (p268) hosts *peñas* (US$1.50) on Wednesday and Friday nights. Another atmospheric place for traditional music is Abya-Yala (p269).

Potosí has two cinemas, the **Imperial** (☎ 622-6133; Padilla 31) and **Cine Universitario** (Bolívar 893), which both screen relatively recent releases.

Real Potosí, the local soccer team, is one of Bolivia's best, and play at the town stadium. When they make the Libertadores Cup, a South American club championship, even the best Brazilian sides dread drawing them and having to play at this altitude!

Shopping

Favored Potosí souvenirs include silver and tin articles available in stands near the market entrance on Calle Oruro; many of them were produced in the village of Caiza, 80km south of Potosí, which now has its own co-op store featuring naturally dyed wool items. Here, small dangly earrings, hoop earrings, spoons and platters cost between US$1 and US$5.

A recommended store is **Arte Nativo** (☎ 622-3544; Sucre 30), selling indigenous handiwork and so improving the economic condition of rural women. **Proyecto Social Yanapahuay** (Lanza 4), in the post-office building, is another charitable concern with decent postcards and *artesanía*. **Artesanía Andina** (Sucre 92) is another option. The **Mercado Artesanal** (Omiste at Sucre) caters specifically to tourists. **Artesanías Palomita's** (Museo Etno-Indumentario; ☎ 622-3258; Serrudo 148-152; ☺ 9am-noon & 2-6pm Mon-Fri, 9am-noon Sat) is half shop, half museum and has costumes and weavings from each of the 16 provinces of Potosí department.

Getting There & Away

AIR

Potosí boasts the world's highest commercial airport, Aeropuerto Capitán Rojas. In the early 1990s the runway was extended to 4000m to accommodate larger planes. **AeroSur** (☎ 622-8988; Cobija 25) had flights for a while, but no more. At time of research, TAM were planning flights to La Paz from here; check at Turismo Claudia, their agent. In any event, Sucre isn't so far away.

BUS & SHARED TAXI

All road routes into Potosí are quite scenic, and arriving by day will always present a dramatic introduction to the city. The **bus terminal** (☎ 624-3361) is about 15 minutes on foot downhill (1km) from the center, and *micros* and minibuses (US$0.15) run every minute or two. By the time you read this, the more inviting new terminal should be open on the northwestern edge of town, in the barrio of Las Lecherías.

Numerous *flotas* offer a daily overnight service to La Paz (US$5 to US$7, 11 hours) via Oruro (US$3 to US$4, eight hours) departing around 7pm or 8pm; you can also opt for a *bus cama* (US$12, 10 hours).

Buses leave for Tupiza (US$3 to US$5, seven hours) and Villazón (US$6 to US$8, 10 to 12 hours) daily in the morning and evening. Buses to Tarija (US$5 to US$7, 14 hours) run at least three times daily, and there are numerous nighttime services to Cochabamba (US$7 to US$9, 12 to 15 hours). Several *flotas* also have daily services to Santa Cruz (US$8, 16 to 20 hours), but it's a long, arduous trip.

Quite a few *flotas* leave for Sucre (US$2, 3½ hours) between 7am and 6pm. Alternatively, you can take a shared taxi (US$16 for up to four people, 2½ hours), which is quicker and comfier, to Potosí. Most hotels can help arrange shared taxis. Try **Expreso Turismo Global** (☎ 624-5171), **Cielito Lindo** (☎ 624-3381) or **Auto Expreso Infinito del Sur** (☎ 624-5040). Expect high velocity.

If you prefer to take the least expensive route, *micros* (US$1.35, five hours) leave from the *tranca* 500m north of Plaza Uyuni all day when full.

Buses to Uyuni (US$2 to US$3.50, six to seven hours) depart between 9:30am and noon from just below the railway line, higher up on Av Antofagasta, but these services may switch to the new terminal once it opens. The rugged route is quite spectacular.

TRAIN

A recently implemented train service between Potosí and Sucre was, at time of writing,

TINKU – THE ART OF RITUAL MAYHEM

Native to the northern part of Potosí department, *tinku* fighting ranks as one of the few Bolivian traditions that has yet to be commercialized. This bizarre practice lies deeply rooted in indigenous tradition and is thus often misunderstood by outsiders, who can make little sense of the violent and often grisly spectacle.

Tinku may be best interpreted as a type of ritualized means of discharging tensions between different indigenous communities. Fights between *campesinos* are very rare in these communities in daily life. Festivities begin with singing and dancing, but participants eventually drink themselves into a stupor. As a result, celebrations may well erupt into drunken mayhem and frequently violence, as alcoholically charged emotions are unleashed in hostile encounters.

A *tinku* usually lasts two or three days, when men and women in brightly colored traditional dress hike in from surrounding communities. The hats worn by the men strongly resemble those originally worn by the Spanish conquistadores, but are topped Robin-Hood-style with one long, fluorescent feather.

On the first evening, the communities parade through town to the accompaniment of *charangos* and *zampoñas* (a type of pan pipe). Periodically, the revelers halt and form two concentric circles, with women on the inside and the men in the outer circle. The women begin singing a typically repetitious and cacophonous chant while the men run in a circle around them. Suddenly, everyone stops and launches into a powerful stomping dance. Each group is headed by at least one person – normally a man – who uses a whip to urge on any man whom he perceives isn't keeping up with the rhythm and the pace.

This routine may seem harmless enough, except that alcohol plays a significant and controlling role. Most people carry bottles filled with *puro* (rubbing alcohol), which is the drink of choice if the intent is to quickly become totally plastered. By nightfall, each participating community retreats to a designated house to drink *chicha* until they pass out.

This excessive imbibing inevitably results in social disorder, and by the second day the drunk participants tend to grow increasingly aggressive. As they roam the streets, they encounter people from other communities with whom they may have some quarrel, either real or imagined. Common complaints include anything from land disputes to extramarital affairs to the theft of farm animals, and may well result in a challenge to fight.

The situation rapidly progresses past yelling and cursing to pushing and shoving, before it turns into a rather mystical – almost choreographed – warfare. Seemingly rhythmically, men strike each other's heads and upper bodies with extended arms (in fact, this has been immortalized in the *tinku* dance, which is frequently performed during Carnaval *entradas* – entrance procession – especially in highly traditional Oruro). To augment the hand-to-hand combat, the fighters may also throw rocks at their opponents, occasionally causing serious injury or death. Any fatalities, however, are resignedly considered a blood offering to Pachamama in lieu of a llama sacrifice for the same purpose.

The best known and arguably most violent *tinku* takes place in the village of Macha during the first couple of weeks of May, while the villages of Ocurí and Toracarí, among others, also host *tinkus*.

As you'd imagine, few foreigners aspire to witness this private and often violent tradition, and many people who have attended insist they'd never do it again. For the terminally curious, however, Koala Tours and Altiplano Tours in Potosí conduct culturally sensitive – and patently less-than-comfortable – visits to several main *tinku* festivities. Note, however, that if you do go it will be at your own risk. Keep a safe distance from the participants and always remain on the side of the street to avoid being trapped in the crowd. When walking around the village, maintain a low profile, speak in soft tones and ignore any taunting cries of 'gringo.' Also, bear in mind that these traditional people most definitely do not want hordes of foreign tourists gawking at them and snapping photos; avoid photographing individuals without their express permission and do not dance or parade with the groups unless you receive a clear invitation to do so.

temporarily suspended, but due to resume. Scheduled departures for this spectacular trip were at 8am Tuesday, Thursday, and Saturday for the scenic six-hour journey (US$4.40 one-way), returning from Sucre at 8am on Monday, Wednesday and Friday. Call **Epifanio Flores** (☎ 7287-6280) to check whether the service is in operation.

Getting Around

Micros and minibuses (US$0.15) shuttle between the center and the Cerro Rico mines, as well as the bus terminal. Taxis charge US$0.40 per person around the center and to the bus terminal.

LAGUNAS DE KARI KARI

The artificial lakes of Kari Kari were constructed in the late 16th and early 17th centuries by 20,000 indigenous slaves to provide water for the city and for hydropower to run the city's 82 *ingenios*. In 1626 the retaining wall of Laguna San Ildefonso broke and caused an enormous flood that killed 2000 people and destroyed operations along La Ribera de los Ingenios. Of the 32 original lakes, only 25 remain and all have been abandoned – except by waterfowl, which appreciate the incongruous surface water in this otherwise stark region.

Lagunas de Kari Kari Hike

The easiest way to visit Lagunas de Kari Kari is with a Potosí tour agency (p266). If you prefer to strike out on your own, carry food, water and warm clothing. In a long day, you can have a good look around the *lagunas* and the fringes of the Cordillera de Kari Kari, but it may also be rewarding to camp overnight in the mountains.

Access is fairly easy. Take a *micro* heading toward Cerro Rico (Pailaviri or Calvario) and get off at the Tupiza turnoff. Follow that road until the pavement ends at a *tranca*, then head southeast along a stream. Any of the numerous uphill tracks will lead onto an open plain, where you should bear left and climb past a llama pasture and onto a ridge, which has a superb view of the **Lagunas San Sebastián**. At this point, you're about 4km southeast of central Potosí. Continue along this ridge until you cross a track, which will lead you through a hamlet and along the Río Masoni into the mountains.

Alternatively, cross the Masoni valley and scramble up the ridge on the other side and climb to the summit of **Cerro Masoni** for an excellent view of **Lagunas San Ildefonso** and **San Pablo**. Descending along the same ridge will lead you back to Potosí.

Another option is to descend to Laguna San Ildefonso, then follow the track around its northern shore and continue up the valley or strike off eastward into the hills. The higher you go, the more spectacular the views become. The area is riddled with open mine entrances, mining detritus and remains of mining equipment.

Those prepared for an overnight stay can travel even further into the mountains, since there are no difficult summits in the area. As long as you can catch sight of Cerro Rico, the route back to Potosí will be obvious. Remember, however – as if you could forget – that the altitude hereabouts ranges from 4400m to 5000m. The Cordillera de Kari Kari is included on the IGM topo sheet *Potosí (East) – sheet 6435* (see Maps p259).

HACIENDA CAYARA

For a peaceful retreat or some comfortable hill walking, visit Hacienda Cayara, which lies 25km down the valley northwest of Potosí. Set amid lovely hills at 3550m, this beautiful working farm produces vegetables and milk for the city. It dates back to colonial times, when it was owned by the Viceroy of Toledo. In the name of King Felipe II, its title was later handed to Don Juan de Tendones and was then transferred to the Marquez de Otavi, whose coat of arms the ranch still bears.

In 1901 it was purchased by the English Aitken family, who still own it. The family converted it into a hostel in 1992. The hostel is like a museum: an opulent colonial mansion furnished with original paintings and period furniture. Guests have the use of the fireplace and extensive library, which includes works dating from the 17th century.

For bookings, contact **Señora Luisa Serrano** (☎ /fax 622-6380; cayara@cotepnet.com.bo; r per person US$5; day use US$5; meals US$7).

Transportation can be arranged in Potosí at the time of booking the hostel, but it's cheaper to go by taxi, especially if you're in a group; have the driver take the left fork to La Palca instead of heading through the canyon toward Tarapaya. Otherwise, *micros* (US$0.50) that pass the turnoff depart from Mercado Quichimi daily around noon.

AROUND POTOSÍ

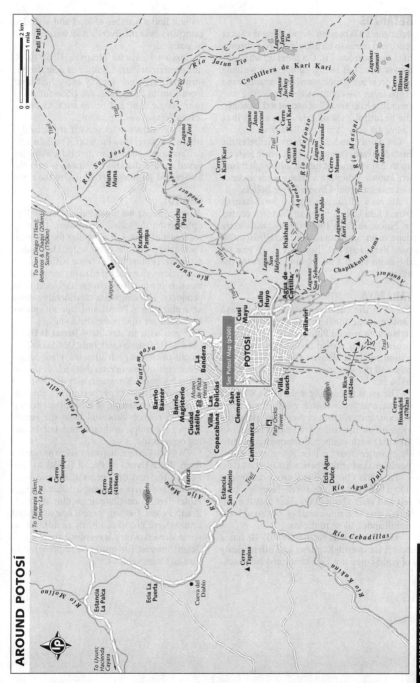

BETANZOS

Betanzos is 47km from Potosí along the Sucre road, and seems to blend into the rusty brown hills that surround it. On Sunday, when the **market** is in full swing, *campesinos* wearing local dress bring their weavings, ceramics and crops from the countryside to sell. The surrounding hills are full of **ancient rock paintings**; the beautiful sites of Lajas-Mayu and Inca Cueva are only 5km from Betanzos.

On April 4 and 5, Betanzos celebrates the **Fiesta de la Papa** (Potato Festival), which features up to 200 varieties of tubers. Although it isn't well known, it does attract major Andean dance and musical groups from all over Bolivia.

Micros and *camiones* leave for Betanzos from Plaza Uyuni, north of the town centre, in Potosí early in the morning, with extra departures on Sunday. All Sucre buses also pass Betanzos, but they may drop you on the main road, a 10-minute walk from the village itself.

TARAPAYA

Belief in the curative powers of Tarapaya (3600m), the most frequently visited **hot-springs** area around Potosí, dates back to Inca times. It even served as the holiday destination for Inca Huayna Capac, who would come all the way from Cuzco (now in Peru) to bathe.

The most interesting sight is the 85°F **Ojo del Inca**, a perfectly round, green lake in a low volcanic crater, 100m in diameter. Along the river below the crater are several *balnearios* (resorts) with medicinal thermal pools utilizing water from the lake. *Remolinos* (whirl-pools) make bathing here a hazardous affair.

To reach Ojo del Inca, cross the bridge 400m before the Balneario de Tarapaya, turn left and walk about 200m. Just past the waterfall on the right, a washed-out road leads uphill about 400m to the lake.

The **Balneario El Paraíso** (s/d US$5/10) has a hostel for overnight guests and offers plenty of good company. Self-contained backpack-ers will find a number of level and secluded campsites near the river, but all water should be purified.

Camiones leave for Tarapaya (US$0.40, 30 minutes) from Plaza Chuquimia near the bus terminal in Potosí roughly every half hour from 7am to 7pm. Taxis are US$6 for up to four people. The last *micro* back to Potosí leaves Tarapaya around 6pm.

Ask the driver to let you off at the bridge where the gravel road turns off. The Balneario de Tarapaya is 400m from the bridge along the paved road. Balneario El Paraíso is over the bridge and 400m down the road to the right.

CHAQUI

Another major **hot spring** bubbles away 3km uphill from the village of Chaqui, 45km by road east of Potosí. It's popular for the anti-rheumatic properties of the water. On Sunday, *potosiños* (Potosí locals) come with loads of sugar, flour, rice and bread to exchange in the markets for potatoes, cheese and local farm products. The climate is considerably more agreeable than in Potosí, and superior-quality **handicrafts** are sold in the small villages.

If you wish to stay, **Hotel Termas de Chaqui** (☎ 622-6112; Chuquisaca 587 in Potosí; s/d US$12.50/20) is an out-of-the-way but attractive place, with a restaurant and room rates that include the use of the hot pools. Nonguests may use the pools and sauna (US$1.25 per person). Chaqui village also has a couple of basic *alojamientos,* but they're 3km downhill from the resort. There are a couple of cheaper non-hotel soaking options too.

To get to Chaqui, hop on a *micro* or *camión* from Plaza Uyuni in Potosí (US$0.40, two hours); the first one leaves at around 8am. Alternatively, arrange transportation through Hotel Termas de Chaqui; inquire at its office in Potosí. Getting there is one thing, but returning to Potosí can be more difficult, as some drivers won't leave until there's sufficient interest (or until you're prepared to hire an entire vehicle).

South Central Bolivia & The Chaco

Famed for its dances, wines and an almost Mediterranean character, the isolated Tarija department is a Bolivia that not many travelers know. It shows the country in a guise of tranquility, with steely blue skies stretching above the gnarled vines that braid the windswept, dry land.

The culture here gravitates towards neighboring Argentina and dreams of being closer to faraway Andalucía. The references to the region's resemblance to the south of Spain were started by Tarija's founder, Luis de Fuentes, who seemingly tried to lend a bit of home to a foreign land. He thus named the river flowing past the city of Tarija the Guadalquivir (after Andalucía's biggest river), and left the *chapacos* – as *tarijeños* (Tarija locals) are otherwise known – with a lilting dialect of European Spanish.

Tarija's far eastern regions are full of petroleum-rich scrublands, backed by stark highlands and surrounded by the red earth of the Gran Chaco. This is where you'll find Bolivia's hottest town – Villamontes can reach up to 120°F in the relentless summer sun. Further down, reaching as far south as you can go before you hit the Argentine border, lie the lush sugarcane-producing valleys and oil-pumping veins that feed the prosperous town of Bermejo.

HIGHLIGHTS

- Taste the world's highest-grown wines in **Tarija** (p277)

- Hike the fascinating Inca Trail in the **Reserva Biológica Cordillera de Sama** (p287) and discover wildlife on the way

- Discover endangered Chaco wildlife in the **Parque Nacional y Área Natural de Manejo Integrado Aguaragüe** (p291) and the **Corvalán** (p291) and **Tariquía** (p288) **Reserves**

- Have a go on the rough **Trans-Chaco Road** (p290) if you think you're hard enough

- Get down and party Tarija-style at the **Fiesta de San Roque** (p281)

- TELEPHONE CODE: 4
- POPULATION: 391,200
- ELEVATION: 380M TO 2200M

History

Bolivian territory was vastly bigger before the 1932–1935 Chaco War. It encompassed most of Paraguay, an area of about 240,680 sq km stretching northeast of the Paraguay and Pilcomayo Rivers, and the 168,765-sq-km chunk of Argentina north of the Río Bermejo. The dispute between Bolivia and Paraguay that led to the war started when Paraguay formally declared its independence in 1842, thus bringing into question its official border demarcation with Bolivia.

The marking of the Río Pilcomayo as the boundary between Paraguay and Argentina in 1878 by the Hayes Arbitration was duly accepted, but the empty land to the north became a matter of conflict between Paraguay and Bolivia. Attempts at arbitration between the two countries failed, and Bolivia began pressing for a settlement.

After losing the War of the Pacific in 1884, Bolivia was desperate to have the Chaco as an outlet to the Atlantic via the Río Paraguay, so, hoping that physical possession would be interpreted as official sovereignty, the Bolivian army set up a fort at Piquirenda on the Pilcomayo river. Bolivia then refused to relinquish rights to Fuerte Vanguardia, its only port on the Paraguay river. In 1928 Paraguay responded by sending its army to seize the fort, and although things got heated, both sides maintained a conciliatory attitude, hoping that a peaceful solution might be possible.

Things, however, didn't go as planned. During settlement talks in Washington, the Bolivian army tried to seize land without authorization, triggering full-scale warfare. While casualties on both sides were heavy, the highland Bolivians fared exceptionally badly, finding they had to cope with the subtropical terrain. No decisive victory was reached, but despite the fact that Bolivia's most successful battle was fought in the town of Villamontes in 1934, the peace negotiations, held four years later, awarded most of the disputed territory to Paraguay.

Climate

This is the area of Bolivia where you most feel the country's proximity to the equator and its distance from the sea. Tarija's

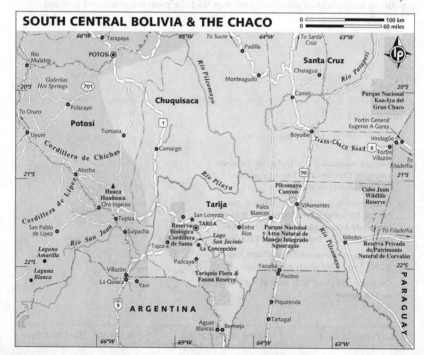

Mediterranean climate quickly disappears as soon as you head downhill, and Villamontes proudly claims the title of the country's hottest spot. The dry season lasts from April to November.

National Parks & Reserves

Remote, wild and off the beaten track, South Central Bolivia's parks and reserves are perfect for hardcore adventure seekers. Infrastructure is almost nonexistent, but a visit to any of the reserves will make a lasting impression. Those covered in this chapter include Reserva Biológica Cordillera de Sama (p287), Reserva Nacional de Flora y Fauna Tariquía (p288), Parque Nacional y Área Nacional de Manejo Integrado Aguaragüe (p291) and Reserva Privada de Patrimonio Natural de Corvalán (p291).

Getting There & Around

Most people visit Bolivia's far south on the way to or from somewhere else. Overland connections from Argentina and Paraguay and other regions within the country involve long bus rides. The Trans-Chaco Rd (see the boxed text p290) from Paraguay has improved in recent years but is still an arduous journey. Tarija has the biggest airport in the area and scheduled flights to La Paz, Sucre and other major towns go several times a week.

Public transportation runs frequently between towns, but you'll need a 4WD to get almost anywhere else. Few roads are paved so prepare yourself for hauls that take longer than they should.

SOUTH CENTRAL BOLIVIA

The region's capital is a quiet provincial town, with few visitors and some quality Argentine-style meat houses. The mild climate has attracted a few foreign settlers in the recent years, so tourist facilities and activities may develop more in the future. The wine country surrounding Tarija city offers some good tasting opportunities. Despite the fact that the Bolivians from bigger cities regard South Central Bolivia as a half-civilized backwater, and that 'chapaco' is the butt of tasteless jokes told in La Paz, Tarija is a pleasant place to stop off on your way to Argentina.

TARIJA

pop 132,000 / elevation 1850m

This little city is as laid-back as they get, with palm-lined squares, sizzling Argentine barbecues, sprawling bar and café terraces, and local vocal talents wailing from karaoke bars. Nothing much happens in Tarija, but the city does have some interesting, colonial architecture that can warrant a day's walking around. If you have time, go around some of the surrounding wineries and try Bolivian vino or get your throat heated on some *singani* (distilled grape spirit).

History

Tarija was founded as La Villa de San Bernardo de Tarixa, by Don Luis de Fuentes y Vargas on July 4, 1574, under the orders of Viceroy Don Francisco de Toledo. In 1810 the region declared independence from Spanish rule. Although the breakaways weren't taken seriously by the Spanish, the situation did erupt into armed warfare on April 15, 1817. At the Batalla de la Tablada, the *chapacos* won a major victory over the Spanish forces. In the early 19th century, Tarija actively supported Bolivia's struggle for independence. Although Argentina was keen to annex the agriculturally favorable area, Tarija opted to join the Bolivian Republic when it was established in 1825.

Orientation

Street numbers are preceded by an O (*oeste* – west) for those addresses west of Calle Colón and an E (*este* – east) for those east of Colón; addresses north of Av Victor Paz Estenssoro (Av Las Américas) take an N.

Information

Between 1pm and 4pm Tarija becomes a virtual ghost town. Conduct all your business in the morning or you'll have to wait until after the siesta.

EMERGENCY

Hospital San Juan de Dios (☎ 664-5555; Santa Cruz s/n)
Police (☎ 664-2222; cnr Campero & 15 de Abril)

IMMIGRATION

Migración (☎ 664-3450; Bolívar at Ballivián) Get entry/exit stamps or to extend your stay.

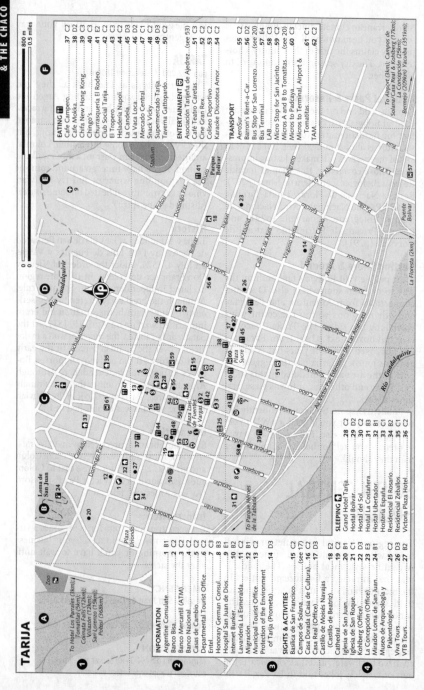

TARIJA

INFORMATION

Argentine Consulate	1	B1
Banco Bisa	2	C2
Banco Mercantil (ATM)	3	C2
Banco Nacional	4	C2
Casas de Cambio	5	C2
Departmental Tourist Office	6	C3
Entel	7	C3
Honorary German Consul	8	B3
Hospital San Juan de Dios	9	E1
Internet Bunker	10	B2
Lavandería La Esmeralda	11	C2
Migración	12	B1
Municipal Tourist Office	13	C2
Protection of the Environment of Tarija (Prometa)	14	D3

SIGHTS & ACTIVITIES

Basílica de San Francisco	15	C2
Campos de Solana	(see 17)	
Casa Dorada (Casa de Cultura)	16	C2
Casa Real (Office)	17	D3
Castillo de Moisés Navajas (Castillo de Beatriz)	18	E2
Cathedral	19	C2
Iglesia de San Juan	20	B1
Iglesia de San Roque	21	C1
Kohlberg (Office)	22	D3
La Concepción (Office)	23	E3
Mirador Loma de San Juan	24	B1
Museo de Arqueología y Paleontología	25	C2
Viva Tours	26	D3
VTB Tours	27	B2

SLEEPING

Grand Hotel Tarija	28	C2
Hostal Bolívar	29	D2
Hostal del Sol	30	C2
Hostal La Costañera	31	B3
Hostal Libertador	32	B1
Hostería España	33	C1
Residencial El Rosario	34	B2
Residencial Zeballos	35	C1
Victoria Plaza Hotel	36	C2

EATING

Café Campero	37	C2
Café Mokka	38	D2
Chifa New Hong Kong	39	C3
Chingo's	40	C3
Churrasquería El Rodeo	41	E2
Club Social Tarija	42	C2
El Tropero	43	C3
Heladería Napoli	44	D3
La Candela	45	C3
La Vaca Loca	46	D2
Mercado Central	47	C1
Snack Vicky	48	C2
Supermercado Tarija	49	D3
Taverna Gattopardo	50	C2

ENTERTAINMENT

Asociación Tarijeña de Ajedrez	(see 53)	
Café Teatro Caretas	51	C2
Cine Gran Rex	52	C2
Coliseo Deportivo	53	C3
Karaoke Discoteca Amor	54	C2

TRANSPORT

AeroSur	55	C2
Barron's Rent-a-Car	56	D2
Bus Stop for San Lorenzo	(see 20)	
Bus Terminal	57	E4
LAB	58	C3
Micro Stop for San Jacinto	59	C2
Micros A and B to Tomatitas	(see 20)	
Micros to Padcaya	60	C3
Micros to Terminal, Airport & Tomatitas	61	C1
TAM	62	C2

To Hotel Los Parrales (3km); Tomatitas (5km); Coimata Falls (12km); San Lorenzo (15km); Potosí (368km)

To Airport (3km); Campos de Solana/Casa Real & Kohlberg (17km); La Concepción (25km); Bermejo (209km) Yacuiba (351km)

To La Floresta (2km)

0   800 m
0   0.5 miles

INTERNET ACCESS
Internet Bunker (Saracho 456; per hour US$0.50; 🕑 until 1pm Sat & Sun)

LAUNDRY
Lavandería La Esmeralda (☎ 664-2043; La Madrid 0-157) Does a quick machine wash and dry service for US$1 per kilo.

MONEY
ATMs are numerous around the plaza. **Casas de cambio** (Bolívar) change US dollars and Argentine pesos. Banco Bisa and Banco Nacional, both on Sucre, will change up to US$1000 of traveler's checks for US$6 commission.

POST & TELEPHONE
The main **post office** (cnr Sucre & Lema) and **Entel** (cnr Lema & Campos) are conveniently located.

TOURIST INFORMATION
Departmental tourist office (☎ 663-1000; cnr 15 de Abril & Trigo; 🕑 8:30am–noon & 3-6pm Mon-Fri) Distributes basic town maps (US$1) and is reasonably helpful with queries regarding sites within and around town.
Municipal tourist office (☎ 663-8081; cnr Bolívar & Sucre; 🕑 8:30am–noon & 3-6pm Mon-Fri) Not much material or information, but friendly staff.

Sights
You can see everything the town has to offer in an afternoon. Wandering around Tarija's squares and checking out the remaining colonial atmosphere are the main attractions.

MUSEO DE ARQUEOLOGÍA Y PALEONTOLOGÍA
The free university-run **Archaeology & Paleontology Museum** (cnr Lema & Trigo; admission free; 🕑 9am–noon & 3-6pm) provides a good overview of the prehistoric creatures and the early peoples that once inhabited the Tarija area.

Downstairs you'll see the well-preserved remains of several animals: *megatherium,* a giant ground sloth; *glyptodon,* a prehistoric armadillo; *lestodon,* which resembled a giant-clawed aardvark; *scelidotherium,* a small ground sloth; *smilodon,* the saber-toothed tiger; and *toxodon,* a large and dozy-looking creature with buck teeth.

Particularly interesting are the *glyptodon* carapace, and the tail and a superb hand of a *megatherium.* Displays are accompanied by artistic representations of how the animals appeared in the flesh. The archaeological

section displays ancient tools, weapons, copper items, textiles and pottery from all over southern Bolivia.

The rooms upstairs focus on history, geology and anthropology, containing displays of old household implements, weapons, an old piano and various prehistoric hunting tools, including a formidable cudgel known as a *rompecabezas* (head-breaker). You might chuckle at the odd bit of presidential stationery bearing the letterhead 'Mariano Melgarejo, President of the Republic of Bolivia, Major General of the Army, etc, etc, etc,' topped by a hideous representation of the Antichrist made from nuts, seeds, grass, wool, hair, shells, flowers, wood and lichen.

CASA DORADA (CASA DE CULTURA)
The **Gilded House** (☎ 664-4606; Ingavi 0-370; 🕑 8am–noon & 2:30-6:30pm Mon-Fri) dates back to 1930, when it was one of the several properties of the wealthy Tarija landowner Moisés Navajas (often described as Bolivia's Teddy Roosevelt) and his wife, Esperanza Morales. The building appears imposing and impressive on tourist brochures, but in reality the exterior is sloppily splashed with gold and silver paint, and the roof is topped with a row of liberating angels. The interior is done with equally poor skill.

The ground floor is painted a scintillating shade of purple and the frescoes could have been the work of precocious preschoolers. There's also a winning kitsch collection of lamps: rose lamps, peacock lamps, morning glory lamps and, of course, crystal chandeliers that sprout light bulbs. Perhaps the most worthwhile relic is the *funola,* an early type of player piano that produced music by forcing air through a strip of perforated paper. The building now belongs to the university and houses the Casa de la Cultura. Brief guided tours are sometimes offered for a small donation.

CHURCHES
Architecturally, Tarija's most unusual church and major landmark is the bright, white 1887 **Iglesia de San Roque**. Dedicated to the city's patron saint, the church sits on the hill at the end of General Bernardo Trigo, lording over town. Its balcony once served as a lookout post.

The rather dull-looking **cathedral** (cnr Campero & La Madrid) contains the remains of prominent *chapacos,* including Tarija's founder, Don Luis

IDENTITY ON THE GRAPEVINE

The Tarija region prides itself on the fact that its vines are grown at some of the highest altitudes in the wine-producing world. The grapevines, first brought to the region by 17th-century missionaries, are grown at the staggering 1900m and 2100m altitude and only 22 degrees south of the equator. They ripen quicker than their sea-level brethren (because they are closer to the sun, apparently), and the wine is given a head start in the maturing process, making rich reserves easier to produce.

The grapes grown here are a mix of Muscat of Alexandria and Californian, but Bolivian wine growers are trying to come up with a new concept: determining and establishing the 'identity' of Bolivian wine. The dilemma: should the wine try to imitate the exclusive rich noses and bouquets of the French *vin*, the utilitarian, fast-produced Californian wine or should it look closer to home, to neighboring Chile's highly esteemed wines? We headed down to the valley of Concepción to visit two very different wineries, hoping they would provide some answers.

The first on the list was the Pineda family winery and one of Bolivia's best: **Bodega de Concepción** (see below). When asked what direction the family thinks Bolivia's wine should take in deciding on its influences, the Pinedas emphatically answer that the winemakers should follow no one. The wine should, instead, says owner and winemaker Sergio Pineda, 'reflect the uniqueness of Bolivia.' Their award-winning *Cepas de Altura* (literally, 'Vine from the Altitude') isn't matured in oak or any type of wood, and its taste is surprisingly fresh, fine and elegant. 'It's a powerful wine' says Sergio, 'but gentle at the same time, and able to carry itself on its own. It's not asking for meat, olives or cheese to be palatable. It's good on its own.'

Searching further to relieve our Bolivian wine identity crisis, we head for **Casa Vieja** (see below), a working man's bodega and a former Jesuit convent, 350 years old. The house owner, Doña Vita, is an affable lady with a row of golden teeth decorating her big smile. 'We started making wine by accident 15 years ago' she says, 'a man owed my father money and paid him back with a pair of barrels. We didn't know what to do with them, so we picked some of the grapes growing behind the house and stomped on them in the barrels, and we haven't stopped since,' laughs Doña Vita, patting the bloated barrels. When asked what she thinks of Bolivian wine, she answers: 'I think Bolivian wine should be simple and close to the earth, reflecting the nature of its people. The real strength of Bolivia's wine is its diversity. It's as individual as the country's inhabitants themselves.'

de Fuentes y Vargas. It was constructed in 1611 and expanded and embellished in 1925 and has some vaguely interesting stained glass depicting harvest scenes.

The **Basílica de San Francisco** (cnr Campos & La Madrid) was founded in 1606 and is now a national monument. The 16th-century convent library and archives, which may conjure up images from *The Name of the Rose*, can be used only by researchers who have been granted permission by the Franciscan order. Inside the basilica, the free **Museo Franciscano Frey Francisco Miguel Mari** (8am-6pm Mon-Fri) displays ecumenical paintings, sculptures and artifacts.

The **Iglesia de San Juan** at the top of Bolívar, was constructed in 1632. Here the Spanish signed their surrender to the liberation army after the Batalla de la Tablada. The garden serves as a *mirador* (lookout) of Tarija and its dramatic backdrop of brown mountains.

WINERIES

To visit the wineries of the Tarija region and sample the wines, inquire at the individual offices in Tarija. All offices sell bottles at factory prices (US$1.50 to US$10).

Bodega La Concepción (☎ 664-5040; www.bodegas laconcepcion.com, in Spanish; O'Connor N-642), the region's best, exports and promotes its vintages as the 'world's highest wines'; see the boxed text above. La Concepción is worth a visit for oenophiles. It is found 25km south of Tarija, just before the village of Concepción (Map p286).

The best *patero* (foot-stamped) wine is found at **Casa Vieja** (☎ 664-8877; Belgrano 2038/B Juan XXIII). Its atmospheric **Bodega Casa Vieja** (admission free; photo permission US$0.70) is in the village of Concepción, about 30km from Tarija town. You can have lunch in its lovely **restaurant** (lunch only; mains US$1-2), which is decorated with adobe arches, large fish heads and hanging plant pots. The restaurant hosts traditional Chaco dances during the Carnaval. Check at the Tarija office for updates on opening times. There are buses heading to Concepción every two or three hours from Plaza Sucre in Tarija (US$0.30; 30 minutes).

The most modern winery is **Campos de Solana/Casa Real** (☎ 664-8481; www.csolana.com, in Spanish; 15 de Abril E-259), with little atmosphere, but big vaults of wine. The oldest is the ubiquitous **Kohlberg** (☎ 663-6366; 15 de Abril E-275). Both Kohlberg and Casa Real are in Santa Ana, 17km southeast of Tarija via an indirect route that passes the Campos de Solana bodega (see Map p286).

Most bodegas also produce *singani*, a distilled grape spirit (40% alcohol) of varying quality. If you're interested in trying *singani*, there are three types: *Mi Socio*, the cheapest and harshest, marked by a blue label; the red-label *Special de Oro*, of medium price and quality; and the best, *Colecion Privada*, a flowery, fresh, fragrant spirit, marked by a green label. The cheaper types are usually drunk mixed with soda and lemon, but *Colecion Privada* can be enjoyed on its own. Bodega La Concepción produces the region's best *singani*.

Travelers without transportation could approach the in-town offices and see if they may be able to organize lifts. Alternatively, both Viva Tours and VTB Tours (right) offer excellent half-day and day-long wine-tasting tours.

In Tarija the best places to sample local vintages are the wine bar at Taverna Gattopardo (p283) and at Viva Tours.

MIRADOR LOMA DE SAN JUAN

This park area above the tree-covered slopes of San Juan hill provides a grand city view and is a favorite with smooching students. Climb uphill to the end of Calle Bolívar, then turn right behind the hill and follow the footpath up the slope that faces away from the city.

CASTILLO DE MOISÉS NAVAJAS

The exterior of this oddly prominent and deteriorating **private mansion** (Castillo de Beatriz; Bolívar E-644) is worth a look for its garish extravagance. It's still inhabited but is occasionally open for informal tours. Check at the tourist office.

Tours

For wine tours and adventurous ecotrips to Tarija's hinterlands – including four nearby national reserves – it's tough to beat **Viva Tours** (☎ /fax 663-8325; vivatour@cosett.com.bo; cnr 15 de Abril & Delgadillo), which charges around US$15 per person or US$25 per person for half or full-day tours. **VTB Tours** (☎ 664-3372; vtb@olivo.entelnet.bo; Ingavi 0-784) also runs trips to most sites of interest around the city and the region.

Festivals & Events

Tarija is one of Bolivia's most festive towns, especially around Carnaval (see the boxed text p282). If you're in town during the last week of March, check out the Fiesta de Leche y Queso outside of town in Rosillas (p287).

APRIL

In keeping with its gaucho heritage, Tarija stages an annual rodeo in Parque Héroes de la Tablada, beginning on the departmental holiday. **Rodeo Chapaco** (April 15-21) includes all the standard cowboy events. Take *micro* C from the center.

AUGUST

Tarija's well-known **Fiesta de San Roque** (August 16) features canines parading through the street in festive dress (San Roque is the patron saint of dogs). The main celebration however, doesn't begin until the first Sunday of September and then continues for eight days. It features traditional musical performances and a Chuncho (an indigenous tribe) procession. During the procession, participants wear costumes highlighted with bright feathers, ribbons and glittering sequins, symbolizing the conversion of the Chaco tribes to Christianity.

OCTOBER

The annual **Fiesta de las Flores** (2nd Sunday in October) is a religious celebration dedicated to the Virgin of Rosario. It begins with a procession, which sets off from the Iglesia de San Juan. Along the route, spectators shower participants with petals. The highlight of the day is a colorful fair and bazaar in which the faithful spend lavishly for the benefit of the Church.

Ask around about the arts fair in October and about the Serrano Ham & Cheese Festival.

HOW TO PARTY CHAPACO-STYLE

Tarija is Bolivia's music and dance region, famous for its unique traditions and loud, colorful festivals, especially during Carnaval, when all *tarijeños* (Tarija locals) come out to dance, sing and party the days away. If you find yourself in the region during a fiesta, here's what to expect.

The folk music of Tarija features unusual woodwind instruments, such as the *erque* and *quenilla*, the *caña* and the *camacheña*. The song that accompanies the music is called a *copla* – a direct import from Spain – with comic verses, sung in a duet, and the dance that tops it all off, is the traditional Chuncho. Dancers wear colorful outfits, feathered headgear and masks, symbolizing the Chiriguano tribes and their long-term resistance of the conquerors.

Tarija's **Carnaval** is one of the most animated in Bolivia and brilliant fun. To launch the festivities, two Thursdays before Carnaval, Tarija celebrates the **Fiesta de Compadres**. The unique **Fiesta de Comadres**, celebrated the following Thursday, is Tarija's largest pre-Carnaval festival. It is assumed that the celebration, originating in the village of Pola de Siero, in the northern Spanish region of Asturias, was inspired by the wives of Spanish colonial authorities and soldiers, who saw to it that social customs and morals were strictly followed. It was eventually adopted by the local indigenous population and is now celebrated by the entire community with music, dancing and special basket tableaux constructed of bread known as *bollus preñaus*. There are flowers, fruits, tubers, small cakes and other gifts, all passed between female friends and relatives.

Throughout the Carnaval season, the streets fill with dancing, original *chapaco* (local Tarijan) music and colorfully costumed country folk who turn up to town for the event. There's a Grand Ball in the main plaza after the celebration and the entire town comes out for dancing and performances by folkloric groups, bands and orchestras. Beware: water balloons figure prominently in the festivities.

On the Sunday after Carnaval, the barrio near the cemetery enacts a 'funeral' in which the devil is burned and buried in preparation for Lent. Paid mourners lend the ritual a morose air – although we suspect they're actually lamenting that they must remain free of vice for the 40 days until Easter.

Sleeping

BUDGET

Hostería España (☎ 664-1790; Corrado O-546; s without/ with bathroom US$3/5, d without/with bathroom US$6/10) A decent budget option, with helpful staff, though the rooms are pretty cold in winter. The hot showers and a pleasant flowery patio keep it popular with long-term university student residents.

Residencial El Rosario (☎ 664-3942; Ingavi 777; s without/with bathroom US$3/5.60, d without/with bathroom US$6/10) Small, freshly painted and clean rooms look onto a quiet patio. There are reliable gas-heated showers, laundry sinks and a common cable TV room. Breakfast is available for US$1.

Residencial Zeballos (☎ 664-2068; Sucre N-966; per person US$3.35, with bathroom & breakfast US$6.35) Dozens of potted plants in the bright patio lend this place an attractive look, but make sure you see the room before you commit: the basement ones are grim and dark, so go for something upstairs. The TV and laundry service add to the value.

MIDRANGE

Hostal Bolívar (☎ 664-2741; Bolívar N-256; s US$5.60-9, d US$10-15) Black-and-white chequered floors lead you to the cozy rooms decorated with old-fashioned, baby-blue telephones, velvety pink drapes and shoddy walls. There's a big, warm and quiet courtyard, and the hot showers work. All rooms have their own bathrooms, but the cheapest ones lack TV.

Hostal Libertador (☎ 664-4231; Bolívar O-649; s/d US$9/16) This central and welcoming place has en suite rooms with phones and cable TV. Breakfast costs an additional US$0.75.

Costanera (☎ 664-2851; cnr Estenssoro & Saracho; s US$15-20, d with bathroom & cable TV US$25-30; 🖳 🛇) One of Tarija's best options, the rooms here are elegant and decorated in caramels and sandy shades, with spacious bathrooms and possibly Bolivia's best showers (in this price range). There are phones, bar refrigerator, heaters (upon request) and parking, plus the staff is super friendly, there's a full buffet breakfast and free internet. Lower rates may be negotiated for longer stays or in the low season. A good vegetarian buffet *almuerzo* (set lunch; US$1.75) is served daily except Sunday.

Hostal del Sol (☎ 666-5259; hostaldelsol@entelnet .bo; cnr Sucre N-782 & Bolívar; s/d US$20/30; ☐) A brand new place, and among the nicest in town, Hostal del Sol has coffee walls, flat screen TVs, marble floors and a bright, modern design all round. Though there's an unfortunate lack of air conditioning or fans in the rooms, the friendly service, good breakfasts and free internet make this a great place to stay.

Grand Hotel Tarija (☎ 664-2893; fax 664-4777; Sucre N-770; s/d with breakfast & cable TV US$20/30) One of the town oldies that gets busy for lunch when the locals flood in to the hotel restaurant. The spacious, ocher-colored rooms breathe a bit of age and neglect, but are comfortable and central. Don't go for the patio-facing rooms, or you'll have to have your curtains drawn all day.

Victoria Plaza Hotel (☎ 664-2600; hot_vi@entelnet .bo; cnr La Madrid & Sucre; s/d US$25/35; ☐) A charming, four-star place right on the main plaza, with lovely 1950s rooms decked on with gleaming wooden floors, comfy beds and retro furnishing. All rooms are en suite, with cable TVs, and there's free internet for guests. A stylish café-bar, La Bella Epoca, is downstairs.

TOP END

Hotel Los Parrales (☎ 664-8444; www.losparraleshotel .com; Urbanización Carmen de Aranjuez; s/d with full breakfast US$95/115; ☒) In a relaxed setting 3.5km from the center, Tarija's only five-star option offers you a complimentary cocktail when you arrive, has a spa and a giant Jacuzzi, and a lovely open-air dining area overlooking the countryside. The rooms are colonial-style luxury, with very comfy beds. Transfers from the center cost US$10 for up to three people. Taxis are US$1. Significant discounts (up to 45%) are available for stays of more than one night during the low season.

Eating

RESTAURANTS

Club Social Tarija (☎ 664-2108; 15 de Abril E-271; ☺ lunch only Mon-Fri; lunch US$1) Old-fashioned *almuerzos* are the favorite of the loyal crowd of monthly meal-plan subscribers.

Chingo's (☎ 663-2222; Plaza Sucre; ☺ 11am-midnight; snacks US$1-2, meals US$3-4) Juicy steaks are the name of the game here, specializing in hefty Argentine beef *parrillada* (barbecued or

grilled) with all the standard trimmings – rice, salad and potatoes. Delivery is available for a nominal fee.

La Vaca Loca (☎ 666-0102; Bolivar O-233; mains US$2-3) Sister cow to the Samaipata mad cow ('Vaca Loca' means 'Mad Cow'), this is a more stylish version with cow-skin chairs, pleasant low lighting and good food. Go for the juicy chicken sandwiches and superb salads, and finish with an ice cream.

Taverna Gattopardo (☎ 663-0656; mains US$2-5, wine tasting US$6-10) On the north side of the main plaza, this welcoming European-run tavern is Tarija's most popular hangout. There are good espressos and cappuccinos in the morning; well-prepared salads, burgers and *ceviche* (Peruvian citrus-marinated fish dish) at midday, and chicken fillets and fish to fondue bourguignonne in the evening. A cozy, stone-lined alcove at the back hides a social bar and a wine-tasting area where you can sample a flight of the region's best vintages between bites of local Serrano ham.

Chifa New Hong Kong (☎ 663-7076; Sucre N-235; lunch US$2.25, mains US$2.50-4) Adjacent to a busy Chinese store, this places offers good food, cheap cocktails, huge lunches and an extensive Chinese menu.

La Floresta (☎ 664-2894; Carretera a San Jacinto, Barrio Germán Busch; buffet lunch US$2.50-3.50) A great place for pitchers of fresh lemonade and all-you-can-eat buffets of pork, chicken and salads, served in a lovely, leafy garden with a large swimming pool. Local families stream in on weekends when the atmosphere is particularly lively. It's a bit out of town, so get a taxi here and the staff will call one for the return journey (US$1).

Churrasquería El Rodeo (Oruro E-749; meals US$4) With Argentina so close, it's not surprising that big slabs of red meat are popular. This sparkling choice also has a salad bar.

El Tropero (Lema O-226; meals US$4) This rustic spot is another good choice for hungry carnivores. Steak is all that's for dinner with a salad bar to complement it.

QUICK EATS

Mercado Central (Sucre & Domingo Paz) At the northeast corner of the market, street vendors sell snacks and pastries unavailable in other parts of Bolivia, including delicious crêpe-like *panqueques*. Breakfast is served out the back, other cheap meals are upstairs and fresh juices are in the produce section. Don't miss the huge bakery and sweets section off Bolívar.

Heladería Napoli (Campero N-630; US$0.20) Serves simply divine scoops of ice cream until 8pm.

Snack Vicky (La Madrid near Trigo; mains & meals US$1-1.50) A local favorite for a quick bite; also serves steaks, sandwiches and *almuerzos*.

Café Mokka (Plaza Sucre; meals US$1-2) A stylish place with a pavement terrace overlooking the square, with not-amazing coffee, decent cocktails and good, light grub.

Café Campero (Campero near Bolívar; US$1-2) Dive into the fabulous range of breads, cakes and pastries, including French-style baguettes, chocolate cake and *cuñapes* (cassava and cheese rolls).

La Candela (☎ 664-9191; Plaza Sucre; ☺ 9am-midnight Mon-Fri, 9am-2am Sat & Sun; snacks & mains under US$2) In between owners and menus at the time of research, La Candela promises pizza, pasta and snacks, and live music upstairs, so watch this space.

GROCERIES
Supermercado Tarija (cnr 15 de Abril & Delgadillo) Tarija's best supermarket is well-stocked with imported foodstuffs and a good wine selection.

Entertainment
Earplug alert: karaoke runs rampant around Plaza Sucre, which is Tarija's youth hangout.

Café Teatro Caretas (Suipacha & Carpio; admission varied) A bohemian, all-ages cultural center, presenting live music, theater, chess lessons and art exhibitions. There is something happening most nights and the cover is minimal. Drinks and snacks are served and late-night burger stands wait outside.

Karaoke Discoteca Amor (La Madrid near Sucre) If you're familiar with Latin American pop hits, try this hip joint.

Cine Gran Rex (La Madrid) Screens double-feature, first-run flicks for a couple of bucks.

Keep an eye out for flyers advertising *peñas* (folk-music programs), usually held at restaurants on weekends. Entertaining basketball, *futsal* (*futból de salon*, five-vs-five minisoccer) and volleyball games are played at the **Coliseo Deportivo** (Campero). After 6pm, chess heads can pick up a game next door at the **Asociación Tarijeña de Ajedrez** (Campero), where you can play for free if you respect club rules: no smoking and quiet, please.

Getting There & Away
AIR
The Oriel Lea Plaza Airport is 3km east of town off Av Victor Paz Estenssoro. **LAB**

(☎ 664-2195; Trigo N-329) supposedly has regular services to Cochabamba and a couple of flights a week to Santa Cruz. **TAM** (☎ 664-2734; La Madrid O-470) has Saturday flights to Santa Cruz (US$55) and Sunday flights to La Paz (US$75) via Sucre (US$40). **AeroSur** (☎ 663-0893; cnr Ingavi & Sucre) flies three times a week to La Paz (US$90) and Santa Cruz (US$65).

BUS & CAMIÓN
The **bus terminal** (☎ 663-6508) is at the east end of town, a 20-minute walk from the center along Av Victor Paz Estenssoro. Several *flotas* (long-distance bus companies) run buses to Potosí (US$6.50, 12 to 15 hours), with connections to Uyuni (US$8, 20 hours), Oruro (US$9, 20 hours), Cochabamba (US$12, 26 hours) and Sucre (US$9, 18 hours); most leave daily in the afternoon.

Buses to Tupiza (US$4 to US$5, nine to 10 hours) and Villazón (US$4 to US$5, 10 hours) depart daily in the evening. Buses leave every morning to Yacuiba (US$4, 12 hours); this is a lovely journey. Daily buses for La Paz (US$15, 24 hours) leave at 7:30am. There are also daily services to Camiri (US$8, 14 hours), with connections to Santa Cruz (US$11, 24 hours) and numerous buses head daily for Bermejo (US$3.50, six hours).

You can also travel directly to most Argentine cities daily, including Buenos Aires (US$50, 32 hours). There is a daily service to Santiago, Chile (US$65, 34 hours), via Mendoza, Argentina, as well. International services to Asunción (Paraguay), Iquique (Chile) and Montevideo (Uruguay) are also regular.

To go to Yacuiba or Villamontes, the best place to wait for a *camión* is at the *tranca* (highway police post) east of town. Although it's an uncomfortable ride, you'll pass through some fabulous scenery, especially the stretch between Entre Ríos and Palos Blancos, and through the Pilcomayo Gorge. Use the north *tranca* for Villazón and Potosí and the southeast *tranca* for Yacuiba and Bermejo.

Getting Around
TO/FROM THE AIRPORT
Taxis from the airport to the center cost around US$1, but if you walk 100m past the airport gate (visible from outside the terminal), you'll pay as little as US$0.40 per person. Otherwise, cross the main road and take a passing *micro* A or *trufi* (US$0.20), which passes by the Mercado Central.

BUS

City *micros* and *trufis* cost US$0.20 per ride. Routes are clearly marked on the front windows of the vehicles.

CAR

Barron's Rent-a-Car (☎ 663-6853; Ingavi E-339)

TAXI

Although you can walk just about anywhere in Tarija (including the airport), taxis cost US$0.50/0.75 per person for day/night trips around the center, including the bus terminal. For a radio taxi, ring **4 de Julio** (☎ 664-6555/7676).

SAN JACINTO RESERVOIR

If you're hot in Tarija and after some aquatic refreshment, go to the 1700-hectare reservoir, 7km southwest of town. There's a tourist complex with little *cabañas* (cabins) serving *dorado* (a delicious local fish), a place to rent canoes, and nice walks along the shore and surrounding ridges. It's popular with *chapacos* on Sunday afternoons. *Micro* H and the *trufi* Línea San Jacinto (US$0.20, 10 minutes) leave every 20 minutes from the corner of Ingavi and Campos (outside the Palacio de la Justicia) in Tarija.

SAN LORENZO

pop 21,400

San Lorenzo, 15km north of Tarija along the Tupiza road, is a quaint colonial village with cobbled streets, carved balconies, a church built in 1709 and a flowery plaza. It's best known, however, as the home of one José Eustaquio 'Moto' Méndez, the hero of the Batalla de la Tablada, whose home now houses the **Museo Moto Méndez** (admission free; ☺ 9am-12:30pm & 3-5pm Mon-Sat, 10am-noon Sun). His personal belongings have been left exactly as they were when he died. Méndez left everything he owned to the people of Tarija. The popular **Fiesta de San Lorenzo** takes place here on August 10 and features *chapaco* musical instruments and dancing.

After seeing the museum, head 2km north to the **Capilla de Lajas**, a delicate chapel of exquisite proportions and a fine example of colonial architecture. It was once the Méndez family chapel and remains in private ownership. Just to the north is the former home of **Jaime Paz Zamora**, with an adjacent billboard paying homage to the ex-president.

Micros and *trufis* (US$0.35, 30 minutes) leave from Plaza Guemes (Iglesia de San Juan) in Tarija approximately every 20 minutes during the day.

EL VALLE DE LA CONCEPCIÓN

The Concepción Valley, or simply 'El Valle,' is the heart of Bolivian wine (see the boxed text p280) and *singani* production. La Concepción still bears many picturesque colonial elements and the plaza sports some lovely endemic flowering ceibo trees. To visit the valley's wineries, contact Viva Tours or VTB Tours (p281) or the winery offices in Tarija (see p280). The **Fiesta de la Uva** (Grape Festival) is held here for three days in March, corresponding with the grape harvest.

El Valle lies off the route toward Bermejo; take the right fork at the *tranca* east of Tarija. *Trufi* Línea V leaves for La Concepción from Tarija's Plaza Sucre (US$0.40, 30 minutes) approximately every half-hour during the day.

PADCAYA

pop 19,300

Visiting Padcaya brings full meaning to the old saying that 'it's better to travel than to arrive.' About all that remains of Padcaya's touted colonial heritage are a couple of buildings on the plaza and one other edifice (now a truck-repair shop) with a plaster colonial facade peeling to its adobe innards. While the town does enjoy a nice setting, nestled in a hollow with lots of eucalyptus trees, what makes Padcaya worthwhile is the trip itself – 50km of lovely mountainous desert with green river valleys.

For an interesting walk from Padcaya, continue southwest along the road toward Chaguaya (not toward Bermejo – turn right at the *tranca*) for 3km to a hamlet known as **Cabildo**. Tanning seems to be an important cottage industry here, done the old-fashioned way with pits of vile-looking liquids and hides strung on lines.

At Cabildo turn right on a llama track, then walk 5km further until you reach a **cave** with petroglyphs. This is a popular field trip for Tarija students. You'll probably need help to find the paintings, but don't ask a child to guide you: locals believe the devil inhabits this enchanting spot and they don't allow their own children to go near it.

If you're up for something totally off the beaten track, check out the annual **Fiesta de**

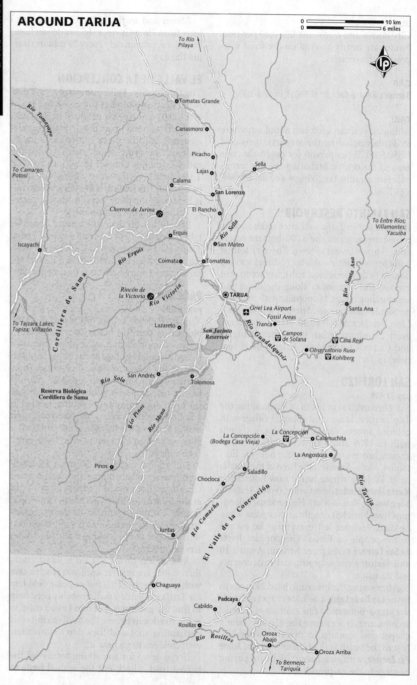

AROUND TARIJA

0 — 10 km
0 — 6 miles

To Río Pilaya

To Camargo; Potosí

Río Tomayapo

Tomatas Grande

Canasmoro

Picacho

Lajas

Sella

Calama

San Lorenzo

El Rancho

Chorros de Jurina

Erquis

San Mateo

Río Sella

To Entre Ríos; Villamontes; Yacuiba

Iscayachi

Río Erquis

Coimata

Tomatitas

Rincón de la Victoria

Río Victoria

TARIJA

Oriel Lea Airport

Santa Ana

Río Santa Ana

Cordillera de Sama

Lazareto

San Jacinto Reservoir

Fossil Areas

Tranca

Campos de Solana

Río Guadalquivir

Casa Real

Observatorio Ruso

Kohlberg

To Tajzara Lakes; Tupiza; Villazón

Río Sola

San Andrés

Tolomosa

Reserva Biológica Cordillera de Sama

Río Pinos

Río Mena

La Concepción (Bodega Casa Vieja)

La Concepción

Calamuchita

La Angostura

Río Tarija

Pinos

Chocloca

Saladillo

Río Camacho

El Valle de la Concepción

Juntas

Chaguaya

Padcaya

Cabildo

Rosillas

Río Rosillas

Oroza Abajo

Oroza Arriba

To Bermejo; Tariquía

Leche y Queso (Festival of Milk & Cheese) in **Rosillas** (population 1000), west of Padcaya. It takes place during the last week of March and celebrates the contributions of local cows.

Micro P leaves for Padcaya (US$1, 30 minutes) hourly from Plaza Sucre, at the intersection of Colón and 15 de Abril.

CHAGUAYA

In Chaguaya, 51km south of Tarija near Padcaya, you'll find the pilgrimage shrine Santuario de la Virgen de Chaguaya. The **Fiesta de la Virgen de Chaguaya** begins on August 15; celebrations follow on the subsequent Sunday. Alcohol is forbidden at this time. Pilgrims from all over Bolivia arrive during the following month, some on foot (including the annual 12-hour, 45km procession from Tarija). *Micros* (US$0.75) from Tarija to Chaguaya leave from the main bus terminal at 4pm daily.

RESERVA BIOLÓGICA CORDILLERA DE SAMA

The **Sama Biological Reserve** protects representative samples of both the Altiplano and the inter-Andean valley ecosystems. In the highland portion of the reserve (3400m above sea level) one can visit the Tajzara lakes, which serve as a stop for over 30 species of migrating aquatic birds, including three of the world's six flamingo species and the rare horned coot and giant coot. Temperatures in the highlands stay quite chilly year-round but are slightly more comfortable in the drier winter months (May to August). The best time to visit the lower elevations is in the summer, when it's warm enough to swim.

The reserve is jointly administered by **Servicio Nacional de Áreas Protegidas** (Sernap; Map pp72-3; ☎ 2-243-4420/243-4472; www.sernap.gov.bo; Loayza, Edificio Full Office, btwn Mariscal Santa Cruz & Camacho, La Paz) and **Protection of the Environment of Tarija** (Prometa; Map p278; ☎ 4-663-3873; www.prometa.org; Carpio E-659 in Tarija). They are developing an ecotourism trail in order to help fund and protect the reserve. Check their website or Tarija office for updates.

Tajzara Section

The area known as Tajzara lies high on the cold and windy *puna* (high open grasslands) of western Tarija department. Here, several shallow flamingo-filled lagoons appear like jewels in the harsh Altiplano, vegetated only by *thola* (a small desert bush of the Altiplano) and *paja brava* (spiky grass of the high Altiplano). Tarija's New Agers consider Tajzara to be a natural power site and indeed, it could easily be mistaken for an estranged corner of Tibet. Highland people believe the lakes are haunted by spirit voices that call out at night, and that to be out after dark would invite disaster. The night air does produce some eerie voice-like cries, but unimaginative people have ascribed the phenomenon to winds rushing through the *thola*.

Along the eastern shores of the lagoons, the wind has heaped up large *arenales* (sand dunes). An interesting climb takes you to the symmetrical peak of **Muyuloma**, which rises about 1000m above the plain. The summit affords views across the lagoons and beyond to the endless expanses of the southern Altiplano. The return climb takes the better part of a day.

Near the Tajzara visitors' center, Prometa has built an **albergue** (under/over 25 years old US$10/13) with hot showers, communal kitchen and an observatory where bird-watchers are able to spot the 45 resident species including the three flamingo species. Hikers can spend a very enjoyable six to eight hours on the wonderful **Inca Trail** as it descends 2000m to the valley below. With luck, you may see vicuñas, condors, the rare Andean deer or mysterious petroglyphs of unknown origin. Arrive the night before you intend to hike and bring all your food from elsewhere.

Inter-Andean Valleys

During the summertime, there are several places in the valley to go swimming in the rivers, including Tomatitas, Coimata and Chorros de Jurina.

Tomatitas, with its natural swimming holes, three lovely rivers (the Sella, Guadalquivir and Erquis) and happy little eateries, is popular with day-trippers from Tarija. The best swimming is immediately below the footbridge, where there's also a park with a campground and barbecue sites. From here you can walk or hitch the 5km to **Coimata**. From Tarija, turn left off the main San Lorenzo road. After less than 1km, you'll pass a cemetery on the left, which is full of flowers and brightly colored crosses. Just beyond it, bear right toward Coimata. Once there, turn left at the soccer field and continue to the end of the road. Here you'll find a small cascade of water and a **swimming**

hole that makes a great escape, as lots of Tarijeño families can attest. There's also a choice of small restaurants serving *misquinchitos* and *doraditos* (fried local fish with white corn), as well as *cangrejitos* (small freshwater crabs). From this point, you can follow a walking track 40 minutes upstream to the base of the two-tiered **Coimata Falls**, which has a total drop of about 60m.

Another swimming hole and waterfall are found at **Rincón de la Victoria**, 6.5km southwest of Tomatitas in a green plantation-like setting. Instead of bearing right beyond the colorful cemetery, as you would for Coimata, follow the route to the left. From the fork, it's 5km to Rincón de la Victoria.

The twin 40m waterfalls at **Chorros de Jurina** also make an agreeable destination for a day trip from Tarija. Set in a beautiful but unusual landscape, one waterfall cascades over white stone while the other pours over black stone. In late winter, however, they may diminish to a mere trickle or even be dry.

The route from Tarija to Jurina passes through some impressive rural landscapes. From near the flowery plaza in San Lorenzo, follow the Jurina road, which turns off beside the Casa de Moto Méndez. After 6km, you'll pass a school on the left side. Turn left 200m beyond the school and follow that road another 2.5km to the waterfalls. From the end of the road, it's a five-minute walk to the base of either waterfall. The one on the left is reached by following the river upstream; for the other, follow the track that leads from behind a small house.

Getting There & Away

From Tarija, **Viva Tours** (Map p278; ☎/fax 4-663-8325; vivatour@cosett.com.bo; cnr 15 de Abril & Delgadillo) organizes overnight trips to several areas of Sama. It is possible to reach Tajzara by local transportation, but often only at night. From Tarija take a bus toward Villazón and ask the driver to point out the Tajzara visitors' center, a 20-minute walk from the road. Otherwise, you can get off at **Pasajes**, 7km from the visitors' center. Contact Prometa (p287) about other transportation options.

Micros A and B to Tomatitas leave frequently from the western end of Av Domingo Paz in Tarija, and on weekends occasional *trufis* go all the way to Coimata. A taxi from Tomatitas to Coimata costs US$2 with up to four people; all the way from Tarija to

Coimata costs US$4. Trufis San Lorenzo leave for Jurina from near the Iglesia de San Juan in Tarija around 8:30am, 2:45pm and 5pm. Get off near the school and then walk the rest of the way. Hitchhiking is only feasible on weekends.

RESERVA NACIONAL DE FLORA Y FAUNA TARIQUÍA

The lovely and little-known 247,000-hectare **Tariquía Flora & Fauna Reserve** (created in 1989) protects a large portion of the dense cloud-forest ecosystem on the eastern slopes of Tarija department's mountains. Ranging in altitude from 400m to 1500m, it houses such rare animals as the spectacled bear, jaguar, tapir, collared peccary and Andean fox, as well as hundreds of bird species. Visitors to the reserve's southern sector are charged US$10 if they want to fish.

The only way to see this largely wild reserve is on foot, but hiking can be challenging and is most comfortably done with a guide. The best time to visit Tariquía is during the dry winter months (May to September), since river crossings become treacherous during the rainy season. In winter the climate is generally mild and sometimes even quite warm, especially at the lower altitudes.

Prometa (Map p278; ☎ 663-3873; www.prometa.org; Carpio E-659, Tarija) operates seven camps in Tariquía, including a simple **albergue** (US$15-20) with cooking and free camping facilities, and the Tariquía Community Center in the heart of the reserve. From the road it's a two-day hike to the center, but allow six days to fully explore the area on foot. You'll need to bring camping gear.

Transportation may be organized through Prometa, which does day trips and sometimes sponsors guided hikes. Alternatively, you can go with **Viva Tours** (Map p278; ☎/fax 4-663-8325; vivatour@cosett.com.bo; cnr 15 de Abril & Delgadillo) in Tarija.

BERMEJO

pop 1500 / elevation 415m

The hot, muggy and dusty town on Bolivia's southernmost tip lies on the banks of the Río Bermejo. The country's southwest end of the country's oil-bearing geological formation provides most of Bermejo's residents with a living – many work at the Yacimientos Petrolíferos Fiscales Bolivianos (YPFB) petroleum plant – while others opt to work for the sugarcane refinery. There isn't any reason a tourist may venture to Bermejo, unless wanting to cross to **Aguas Blancas** in Argentina from here, across the international bridge, 5km upriver from the town. Note that Bolivia is always one hour behind Argentine time.

Thanks to its border location, Bermejo has plenty of *casas de cambio* (exchange houses) that change cash. Check email at **Café Internet Cotabe** (cnr Arce & Ameller; per hr US$0.50). Both the Bolivian and Argentine border posts are open the same hours: from 7am to 4pm (though it could vary) in Bolivia and a more reliable 8am to 5pm in Argentina. *Chalanas* (ferries) over the river (US$0.15) leave every few minutes. Be sure to pick up an exit stamp before crossing.

There's a surprising choice of places to stay in Bermejo, but note that there is no accommodations in Aguas Blancas. **La Casona del Turista** (☎ 696-3342; carello@cotabe.com; Barranqueras 147; r per person with bathroom US$5) has clean rooms, hot showers and a good restaurant downstairs.

Plush little **Hotel Paris** (☎ /fax 696-4562; cnr Tarija & La Paz; s/d US$10/20; 🖳) offers a Jacuzzi, cable TV and air conditioning.

Right on the plaza, **Don Javier** (mains US$1) serves standard Bolivian favorites for equally standard prices. Nothing outstanding – just *lomo* (beef), chicken, soup and rice.

The bus terminal is eight blocks southeast of the main plaza. Hourly buses connect Bermejo and Tarija (US$3.50, six hours). From Aguas Blancas, Argentine buses to Orán (US$1.50, one hour) depart hourly from the terminal opposite the immigration office. From Orán, you can connect to Argentina's Salta, Jujuy, Tucumán and Tartagal (the connection to Pocitos and Yacuiba) and Asunción (Paraguay).

THE CHACO

Flat and sparsely populated, the Chaco is a vast expanse of thorn scrub where dispersed ranchers, isolated indigenous villages and Mennonite communities farm plots of land, dotted by police and military troops guarding their posts. This silent, flat land covers most of southeastern Bolivia and western Paraguay and stretches into neighboring Argentina.

Though you might not think it at first sight, the Chaco is South America's second most diverse ecosystem, after the Amazon Basin.

As opposed to the relatively rare humans, animal and plant life is abundant. There are armies of butterflies and birds, and mammals such as the tapir, jaguar and peccary have their stronghold here. The thorny scrub that characterizes the Chaco's unusual flora, apart from being prickled by various species of cacti, is enlivened by brilliant flowering bushes and trees, such as the yellow *carnival* bush; the white-and-yellow *huevo* (egg) tree; the pink or white thorny bottle tree, locally known as the *toboroche* or *palo borracho* (drunken tree); and the red-flowering, hard *quebracho* (break-axe) tree, whose wood, too heavy to float, is one of the Chaco's main exports.

YACUIBA

pop 83,500 / elevation 625m

There's only one reason to visit Yacuiba – crossing the border into Argentina, or indeed into Bolivia. Tiny **Pocitos**, 5km south, is the easternmost Bolivia–Argentina border crossing. Most people won't even spend the night here, but if you are unfortunate enough to be stranded in this border town, you can explore the town's abundance of old, dysfunctional, commercial goods, and join the Yacuibans in shopping sprees.

Yacuiba straddles the transition zone between the Chaco and the Argentine Pampa and is the terminus for both the railway from Santa Cruz and the YPFB oil pipeline from Camiri. The railway line was constructed with Argentine capital according to the terms of a 1941 treaty in which Bolivia agreed to export surplus petroleum to Argentina in exchange for a 580km rail approach from Buenos Aires. Although construction began immediately, it wasn't completed until the 1960s.

Information

Yacuiba's main north–south street is flanked by several *casas de cambio*, which only deal in cash. Calculate the amount you're to receive before leaving the window and beware of counterfeit US bills. Pickpocketing and petty theft have been reported, especially in crowded shopping areas. There's no consulate here for either Bolivia or Argentina.

Sleeping & Eating

The only thing Yacuiba has going for it is that there are lots of hotels here.

Hotel Valentín (☎ 682-2645; San Martín 1153; s/d US$4.50/7, d with bathroom US$14) Best value in town,

THE TRANS-CHACO ROAD

One of South America's great journeys stretches across the vast Gran Chaco between Filadelfia in Paraguay and Boyuibe in Bolivia. Now that several bus lines have taken up the Santa Cruz–Asunción challenge, the route has lost some of its romanticism, but most of the old uncertainties remain, and you can be assured that it's still an exciting haul through raw, wild and thorny country. Travelers describe amazing landscapes, swarms of gorgeous butterflies, biting bugs and pushing very heavy buses out of mud, among other things. Between Filadelfia and La Patria on the Paraguayan side, the road is good gravel, but from there it's little more than deep, parallel sand ruts. You can choose between buses, *camiones* and private 4WD vehicles – however you go, expect lots of jolts and bounces. During the wet season, the road becomes impassable quicksand and slimy mud. The Trans-Chaco Rd is also fraught with bureaucracy and there are repeated immigration, customs, police and military checkpoints.

In Bolivia your best bet for picking up exit stamps is in Tarija or Santa Cruz. At the Bolivian border post at Ibibobo, your passport will be checked. (There is another border post at Boyuibe, but some travelers have reported this closed; you'll need to ask around.) The Paraguayan border post is at Fortín Infante Rívarola, a few kilometers further along. Between there and Mariscal Estigarribia there are a couple more checkpoints, one at a remote police post and another at La Patria.

Coming from Paraguay, you must obtain your entry stamp within 72 hours of entering the country.

---

opposite the railway station, with an attached bar/restaurant.

Hotel Paris (☎ 682-2182; Comercio at Campero; s/d US$15/20; ❄) A pleasant option, with private bathrooms and air-con.

If you're on a tight budget, try any of the three basic but clean options:

Alojamiento Ferrocarril (☎ 682-2784; Comercio 145; r per person US$2)

Residencial San Martín (☎ 682-2532; San Martín 10; r per person US$2)

Residencial Aguaragüe (☎ 682-2704; Campero 165; s/d US$2.50/3)

For a taste of Argentina north of the border – most notably huge racks of meat – try any of the several *churrasquerías*. There are also numerous snack stands peppered around the shopping district.

Getting There & Around

TAM (☎ 682-3853) flies to Santa Cruz on Saturday afternoons and to La Paz on Sunday mornings, via Tarija and Sucre from around US$50.

There are morning and evening buses to Tarija (US$4, 12 hours) and numerous *flota* buses leave every evening for Santa Cruz (US$9, 15 hours) via Villamontes and Camiri. You can purchase Veloz del Norte Argentine bus tickets in Yacuiba at TVO Expreso Café.

Shared taxis (US$0.75 per person) shuttle between Yacuiba and Argentine immigration

at Pocitos. After crossing the border on foot, you can connect with onward Argentine bus services to Tartagal and Embarcación every couple of hours, where you can make connections to Salta, Jujuy, Orán and Buenos Aires.

Yacuiba's **railway station** (☎ 682-2308) ticket window opens in the morning on the day of departure; line up early. A reasonably quick and comfortable *ferrobus* (passenger rail bus) service to Santa Cruz (3rd/2nd/1st class US$4/5.50/12.50, nine hours) leaves on Wednesday and Sunday at 8pm.

Localiza Rent-a-Car (☎ 682-5600; Comercio at Juan XXIII) rents ordinary cars as well as 4WD vehicles.

VILLAMONTES

pop 23,800 / elevation 380m

As the mercury rises above the 120°F mark, and the hot, dry winds coat everything with a thick layer of red dust, you can see pride rising in the sweaty residents of Villamontes, who boast the fact that this is Bolivia's hottest town. Despite the heat, this is a welcoming place, and the majority indigenous Guaraní population means that lovely woven baskets and furniture made from natural Chaco materials can be found at the town's market. Like the rest of the Chaco, Villamontes is famous for its wildlife, particularly small buzzing varieties like flies and mosquitoes, so bring repellent. If you are nearby, don't miss the annual August **fishing festival** on the Río Pilcomayo or the **cattle fair** held at the end of August or beginning of September.

History

During Inca times Guaraní tribes emigrated here from present-day Paraguay. Their descendants now make up most of the town's indigenous population. Villamontes remained a lonely outpost until it emerged as a strategic Chaco War stronghold. The Paraguayans considered Villamontes their key to undisputed victory over the Bolivian resistance, but the Bolivian army saw its most significant victory here in the 1934 Battle of Villamontes. The momentum gained in that battle allowed them to recapture portions of the eastern Chaco and some of the Santa Cruz department's oil fields.

Sleeping & Eating

Hotel El Rancho (☎ 684-2049; r per person with bathroom US$8) An appealing hotel opposite the railway station, with bungalows that come with TVs. There are cheaper rooms in the hotel's older section, and a pleasant restaurant sits by the side.

Gran Hotel Avenida (☎ 684-2297; s/d with bathroom & breakfast US$12/15; ⊠) The best place in the center with decent rooms and cable TV.

There are a couple of good *churrasquerías* near the plaza.

Getting There & Away

Buses run several times daily to Yacuiba, Tarija and Santa Cruz. The Trans-Chaco Rd (see the boxed text opposite) heads out southeast along the Río Pilcomayo. *Camiones* line up near the northern end of the market. By train, Villamontes is two hours north of Yacuiba and 10 hours south of Santa Cruz. Taxis (per person US$0.40) frequent the railway station, 2km north of town. Inquire at **TAM** (☎ 684-2135) to see if they have resumed Saturday flights to Yacuiba, Santa Cruz and Tarija.

PARQUE NACIONAL Y ÁREA NATURAL DE MANEJO INTEGRADO AGUARAGÜE

The long and narrow 108,000-hectare Aguaragüe National Park takes in much of the mountains of **Serranía de Aguaragüe**, which divides the vast Gran Chaco and the highlands of Tarija department. The region is also well known as having Bolivia's hottest climate, with summer temperatures as high as 115°F, so it's best to visit in the cooler, winter months (May to October).

Although it lacks visitor facilities, the **Cañón del Pilcomayo** is easily accessible from Villamontes. The Guaraní name of the park means 'the lair of the jaguar,' because the range is famous for being home to this lovely, spotty (and scary) cat. Foxes, tapir, anteater, lynx, assorted parrots, numerous plant species and 70% of the region's potable water sources also live here. **Viva Tours** (Map p278; ☎ /fax 4-663-8325; vivatour@cosett.com.bo; cnr 15 de Abril & Delgadillo) conducts guided hikes and visits.

Cañón del Pilcomayo

In the beautiful Pilcomayo Canyon at **El Chorro Grande** waterfall, fish are prevented from swimming further upstream. Abundant *surubí, sábalo* and *dorado* are easily caught, making the area a favorite with anglers from all over the country. The prized *dorado* is particularly interesting because it has an odd hinge at the front of its jawbone that allows the mouth to open wide horizontally.

There are great views from the restaurants 7km to 10km west of town where you can sample local fish dishes.

To reach the gorge, take any Tarija-bound transportation, or taxi to the *tranca* and hitch or walk from there (as usual, weekends are the best time to hitchhike). Where the road forks, bear right and continue another 2km to the mouth of the gorge.

RESERVA PRIVADA DE PATRIMONIO NATURAL DE CORVALÁN

This private 4500-acre reserve on the Paraguayan border was established in 1996 to protect an ideal slice of the Gran Chaco. In addition to jaguar, puma, tapir, giant anteater and armadillo, it's also home to *ñandu* (rhea), iguana, alligator and all the classic Chaco vegetation. The only access route is the poor road from Villamontes, which takes at least four hours with a good vehicle. If you plan to visit, accommodations is limited to a simple park rangers' camp, and you'll need to bring your own food, water and other supplies. The only commercial access is with **Viva Tours** (Map p278; ☎ /fax 4-663-8325; vivatour@cosett.com.bo; cnr 15 de Abril & Delgadillo).

BOYUIBE

Tiny Boyuibe sits on the outskirts of the Chaco along the Santa Cruz–Yacuiba railway line. The town serves mainly as a transit point. Roads head north to Camiri and Sucre, south to Argentina and east into Paraguay.

SOUTH CENTRAL BOLIVIA & THE CHACO

Boyuibe's two crash pads, **Hotel Rosedal** (r US$3) and **Hotel Guadalquivir** (r US$3), are both on the main street. For meals the best bet is **Pensión Boyuibe** (mains US$1-2) also on the main street.

A motley assortment of *movilidades* (anything that moves!) to Camiri (US$1.25, one hour), Villamontes and Yacuiba wait in front of the Tránsito office on the main drag. All Yacuiba- and Santa Cruz–bound trains stop here.

CAMIRI

pop 35,000 / elevation 825m

Perhaps now most famous as the starting point of the much-advertised Ché Trail, the real revolutionary growth of the cobble-stoned streets of Camiri's occurred in the 1990s, when the town became the center for the production of petroleum and gas for the national oil company, YPFB (known more simply as 'Yacimientos'). The town is so proud of its oily role, it bills itself as the Capital Petrolífero de Bolivia (Oil Capital of Bolivia).

On a less capitalist note, the Ché Trail in Camiri has yet to take root as it has on its northern point in La Higuera (p318), and planned sites include the cell where the French intellectual Regis Debray was held during his trial for having been part of Ché's guerrilla group. The trial attracted world-wide attention and drew scores of international correspondents to Camiri, and Ché Trail organizers are keen to restore Debray's cell to how it looked in 1967.

Information

Visitors arriving from Paraguay must register with **immigration** (1 de Mayo s/n), downhill from Calle Tarija. Librería Ramirez changes cash and traveler's checks. Hotel Ortuño changes US dollars at decent rates and will sometimes change traveler's checks. Entel and internet places are near the plaza. The friendly **post office** (Santa Cruz) is a relic from the days when people had a lot more time than they do now.

Sights & Activities

Camiri may not be well endowed with attractions, but it's damn proud of its **YPFB plant**. There's no formal tour, but if you're keen to visit (weirdo!), get up at the crack of dawn and roll up at 8am. If you appear to be interested enough in oil, you may get a look around. Even if you're not into oil, don't miss the **Petrolero (Oil Worker) monument** in the middle of Av Petrolero.

There are also a couple of nice **walks**. One will take you up to the statue of **St Francis of Assisi** on the hill behind the market for a super view over town. Another heads down Av Mariscal Sucre to the **Río Parapeti**. On the bank, turn south and walk several hundred meters downstream, where you'll find a clean sandy beach and a good, deep **swimming hole**.

Sleeping & Eating

Residencial Las Mellizas (☎ 952-2614; Manchego 300; r per person with bathroom US$4) A friendly, clean and simple budget choice.

Residencial Premier (☎ 952-2204; Busch 60; per person with fan US$4, with bathroom & fan US$6.50; 🏊) A block from the plaza and more elaborate than Las Mellizas, with cable TVs, air-con and hot showers in some rooms. Particularly nice are the bright and spacious upstairs rooms that open onto a leafy patio.

Hotel JR (☎ 952-2200; Sánchez 247; s/d with bathroom US$12/20; 🏊) If you fancy hanging out with oil barons, check out the friendly JR, possibly named after the *Dallas* soap character. All rooms have telephones, heating and cable TVs, and there's a good restaurant, a bright sitting area and fine views.

Tasty breakfasts can be had near the **market** (cnr Bolívar & Comercio), where street vendors sell hot drinks, delicious *licuados* (fruit shakes made with either milk or water), bread and basic Bolivian grub. Restaurant choice is limited.

El Palacio del Pollo (mains US$1-2) For chicken, chicken and more chicken, come to this place, near the plaza.

La Estancia (cnr Comercio & Busch; mains US$1-3) *Almuerzos* for US$1.35 and evening à la carte meals.

Getting There & Away

There's no central bus terminal, but most buses leave from the corner of Bolívar and Cochabamba. After 7pm, numerous *flotas* have nightly services to Santa Cruz (US$8, seven to eight hours); buses coming from Yacuiba via Villamontes normally pass in the middle of the night. When the road is passable, Flota El Chaqueño leaves for Sucre (US$15, 24 hours) several times a week in the morning. The road to Boyuibe (US$1.25, one hour) passes through some beautiful hilly Chaco scrub; *micros* leave from Bolívar, four blocks uphill from the main market. *Camiones* to Santa Cruz and Sucre leave when full from Calle Comercio near the market.

Santa Cruz & Eastern Lowlands

The Bolivian Oriente is not what you generally see in Bolivian tourist brochures. This tropical region, the country's most prosperous, has a palpable desire to differentiate itself from Bolivia's renowned highland image. It has an odd mixture of conservatism, cosmopolitanism and provincialism, with a business head and a multicultural population. The region's agriculture boom in recent years brought about a rise in income and a standard of life that isn't matched by any other Bolivian province. Threatened by Evo Morales' 2006 proposals of land nationalization, the population of Santa Cruz cast an overwhelming 'yes' vote in a referendum for regional autonomy. It remains to be seen what changes this will bring to Santa Cruz.

Despite the fact that Santa Cruz is Bolivia's most populous city, it still has a small-town atmosphere, peppered with international restaurants, trendy youth, and Japanese, German, Italian, Eastern European, Arabic, Indian Sikh and German-Canadian Mennonite communities. From here you can visit the charming Jesuit mission towns, which contain the country's loveliest and most fascinating examples of Jesuit architecture. Pre-Inca ruins hide near the small town of Samaipata, and there are miles of trekking and tons of wildlife at the little-disturbed Parque Nacional Amboró. Revolutionaries can check out where Ché Guevara met his maker at the northern end of the work-in-progress Ché Trail in Higuera and Vallegrande.

Culturally and economically, the Oriente looks toward Brazil, and the Death Train, the region's lifeline, transports goods between Santa Cruz and Quijarro on the Brazilian border. If you want a look into a part of Bolivia that defies the stereotype, this is the place to be.

HIGHLIGHTS

- Check out the international cuisine of **Santa Cruz** (p301) and wander around the city's streets
- Trek the still-untouched wilderness and spot rare wildlife at **Parque Nacional & Área de Uso Múltiple Amboró** (p307)
- Explore the pre-Inca ruins in **Samaipata** (p312) and relax in this lovely village
- Get revolutionary on the **Ché Trail** in Vallegrande (p317) and La Higuera (p318)
- Admire the restored architecture around the wonderful **Jesuit missions circuit** (p320)

■ TELEPHONE CODE: 2   ■ POPULATION: 1.1 MILLION   ■ ELEVATION: 0M TO 1300M

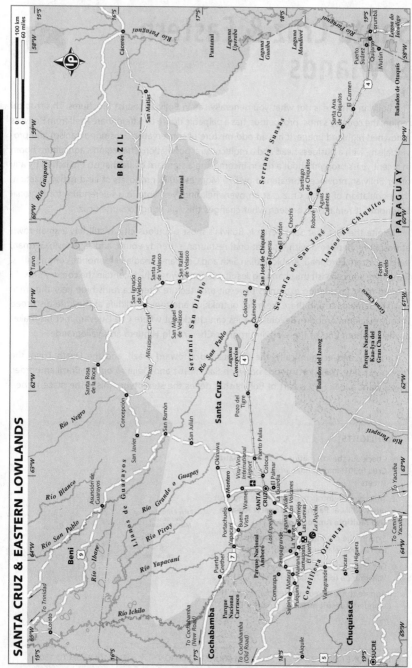

SANTA CRUZ & EASTERN LOWLANDS

Climate

The Oriente's overall climate is tropical, but because it occupies the transition zone between the Amazon rainforest, the highlands and the dry Chaco plains, Santa Cruz enjoys more sun and less stifling temperatures than the humid Amazon Basin further north and west. Winter rainfalls mean little more than 10-minute downpours, but a single summer deluge can last for days. Santa Cruz also experiences heavy winds that rarely subside and, at times during winter, *surazos* (chilly winds) blow in from Patagonia and the Argentine pampas. Outside of Santa Cruz, the Lowlands experience hot sunny days and an occasional afternoon shower to cool things off and settle the dust.

National Parks

Parque Nacional Amboró (p307) is an unquestionable highlight of the region. The remote Parque Nacional Kaa-Iya del Gran Chaco (p327) is Latin America's largest park. It includes the vast Bañados del Izozog wetlands and will be another highlight when access is improved.

Getting There & Away

Santa Cruz is the country's most connected city. Many flights from Europe and neighboring countries come direct to Santa Cruz and are worth considering if you're arriving from sea level and don't want to spend days acclimatizing in La Paz. Direct flights depart daily for Buenos Aires, Miami, São Paulo and Rio de Janeiro.

Trains trundle south to Argentina and east to the Brazilian Pantanal, and there are long-distance buses running along paved roads to the west and south, as well as frequent domestic flights.

SANTA CRUZ

pop 1.5 million / elevation 415m

Bolivia's largest city may surprise you with its small-town feeling, lack of high-rise blocks and a lightly buzzing, relaxed tropical atmosphere. Many arrive here expecting to find a city of businesspeople and throbbing traffic, but in truth, though Santa Cruz is the country's business center and most affluent city, it has kept its tameness. The locals still lounge on the main square, restaurants close for siesta and little stores line the porch-fronted houses and sell cheap local products.

Santa Cruz is certainly not where you'll find the Bolivia you see in pictures, and you won't brush shoulders with a llama (apart from in a zoo or on your plate), but this is the place with the largest population diversity in the country – from the overall-wearing Mennonites strolling the streets past local Goth kids, to a Japanese community, Altiplano immigrants, Cuban doctors, descendants of ex-Nazi runaways, Brazilian immigrants, bearded Russians, and fashionable *cruceños* (Santa Cruz locals) turning sharp corners in their SUVs.

The *cruceños* are an independent lot. They voiced their overwhelming desire for the region's autonomy in 2006, reflecting their wish to carry on the city's growth – both physical and economic. Once a cattle-producing backwater on the edge of wilderness, Santa Cruz is now Bolivia's most populous city and a trade and transportation hub.

It's worth spending a few days here, wandering the city's streets, eating at the many international restaurants and checking out the rich kids' play area, Equipetrol, where nightlife is rife with naughtiness. Alternatively, simply chill out at the town square before moving on to explore the rest of the region.

History

Santa Cruz de la Sierra was founded in 1561 by Ñuflo de Chavez, a Spaniard who hailed from present-day Paraguay. The town originated 220km east of its current location, but around the end of the 16th century it moved to its present position, 50km east of the Cordillera Oriental foothills, after the original location proved too vulnerable to attack from local tribes.

The city's main aim was to supply the rest of the colony with products such as rice, cotton, sugar and fruit. Its prosperity lasted until the late 1800s, when transportation routes opened up between La Paz and the Peruvian coast, making imported goods cheaper than those hauled from Santa Cruz over mule trails.

During the period leading up to Bolivia's independence in 1825, the eastern regions of the Spanish colonies were largely ignored. Although agriculture was thriving around Santa Cruz, the Spanish remained intent upon extracting every scrap of mineral wealth that could be squeezed from the rich and more hospitable highlands.

In 1954 a highway linking Santa Cruz with other major centers was completed, and the city

SANTA CRUZ

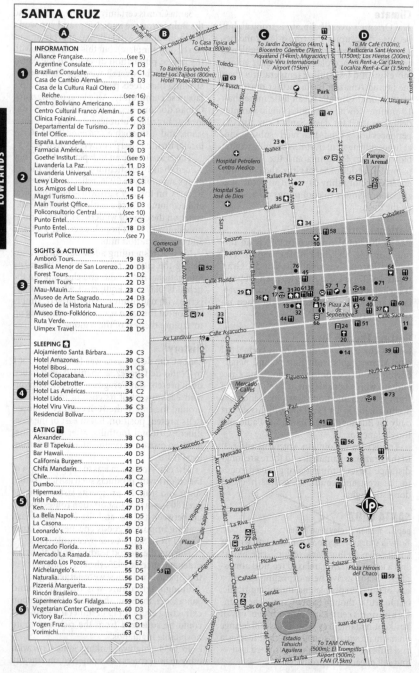

INFORMATION
Alliance Française...........................(see 5)
Argentine Consulate............................1 D3
Brazilian Consulate..............................2 C1
Casa de Cambio Alemán......................3 D3
Casa de la Cultura Raúl Otero
  Reiche..(see 16)
Centro Boliviano Americano................4 E3
Centro Cultural Franco Alemán............5 D6
Clínica Foianini....................................6 C5
Departamental de Turismo..................7 D3
Entel Office..8 D4
España Lavandería...............................9 C3
Farmacia América...............................10 D3
Goethe Institut...................................(see 5)
Lavandería La Paz..............................11 D3
Lavandería Universal..........................12 E4
Lewy Libros..13 C3
Los Amigos del Libro..........................14 D4
Magri Turismo....................................15 E4
Main Tourist Office............................16 D3
Policonsultorio Central......................(see 10)
Punto Entel..17 C3
Punto Entel..18 D3
Tourist Police....................................(see 7)

SIGHTS & ACTIVITIES
Amboró Tours.....................................19 B3
Basílica Menor de San Lorenzo............20 D3
Forest Tours..21 D2
Fremen Tours......................................22 D3
Mau-Mauín...23 C2
Museo de Arte Sagrado......................24 D3
Museo de la Historia Natural..............25 D5
Museo Etno-Folklórico........................26 D2
Ruta Verde..27 C2
Uimpex Travel.....................................28 D5

SLEEPING
Alojamiento Santa Bárbara.................29 C3
Hotel Amazonas..................................30 C3
Hotel Bibosi..31 C3
Hotel Copacabana...............................32 C3
Hotel Globetrotter...............................33 C3
Hotel Las Américas.............................34 C2
Hotel Lido...35 C2
Hotel Viru Viru....................................36 C3
Residencial Bolívar..............................37 D3

EATING
Alexander..38 C3
Bar El Tapekuá....................................39 D4
Bar Hawaii...40 D3
California Burgers................................41 D4
Chifa Mandarín....................................42 E5
Chile..43 C2
Dumbo...44 C3
Hipermaxi..45 C3
Irish Pub..46 D3
Ken..47 D1
La Bella Napoli....................................48 D5
La Casona..49 D3
Leonardo's...50 E4
Lorca...51 D3
Mercado Florida...................................52 B3
Mercado La Ramada.............................53 B6
Mercado Los Pozos..............................54 E2
Michelangelo's.....................................55 D5
Naturalia..56 D4
Pizzería Marguerita.............................57 D3
Rincón Brasileiro..................................58 D2
Supermercado Sur Fidalga...................59 D6
Vegetarian Center Cuerpomonte.........60 D3
Victory Bar..61 C3
Yogen Fruz...62 D1
Yorimichi...63 C1

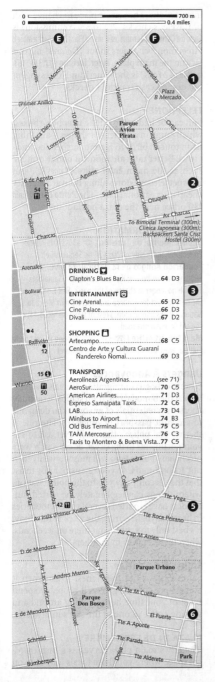

SANTA CRUZ & EASTERN LOWLANDS

DRINKING 🍷		
Clapton's Blues Bar	64	D3
ENTERTAINMENT 🎭		
Cine Arenal	65	D2
Cine Palace	66	D3
Divali	67	D2
SHOPPING 🛍		
Artecampo	68	C5
Centro de Arte y Cultura Guaraní		
Ñandereko Ñomai	69	D3
TRANSPORT		
Aerolíneas Argentinas	(see 71)	
AeroSur	70	C5
American Airlines	71	D3
Expreso Samaipata Taxis	72	C6
LAB	73	D4
Minibus to Airport	74	B3
Old Bus Terminal	75	C5
TAM Mercosur	76	C3
Taxis to Montero & Buena Vista	77	C5

sprang back from its 100-year economic lull. The completion of the railway line to Brazil in the mid-1950s opened trade routes to the east, after which time tropical agriculture boomed and the city grew as prosperously as the crops. It has continued to grow to the present day.

Orientation

Roughly oval in shape, Santa Cruz is laid out in *anillos* (rings), which form concentric circles around the city center, and *radiales*, the 'spokes' that connect the rings. Radial 1, the road to Viru-Viru airport, runs roughly north–south; the *radiales* progress clockwise up to Radial 27.

Most commercial enterprises, hotels and restaurants lie within the *primer* (first) *anillo*, which is centered on the Plaza 24 de Septiembre. The street of the same name becomes Av Monseñor Rivero, a stretch full of restaurants, cafés and bars. The railway station is within the third *anillo* but is still only a half-hour walk from the center. The second to seventh *anillos* are mainly residential and industrial.

Within the *primer anillo,* Junín is the street with most banks, ATMs and internet cafés, and Av René Moreno has loads of souvenir stores. Av San Martin, otherwise known as Equipetrol, has tons of bars and clubs.

MAPS

The best city map, *Multiplano Santa Cruz City Guide,* covers the first to fourth *anillos* and is available free from larger hotels or for a couple of dollars from the tourist office.

Information
BOOKSTORES

Near the plaza, **Los Amigos del Libro** (☎ 332-7937; Ingavi 114) and **Lewy Libros** (☎ 332-7937; lewylibros@cotas .com.bo; Junín 229) have limited selections of foreign-language books for sale or trade.

International periodicals are sold at street kiosks around the plaza.

CULTURAL CENTERS

Casa de la Cultura Raúl Otero Reiche (west side of Plaza 24 de Septiembre) Hosts free music and modern art exhibitions plus theater performances.
Centro Boliviano Americano (CBA; ☎ 342-2299; Cochabamba 66) Has an English-language library.
Centro Cultural Franco Alemán (Velarde 200; ⏰ 9am-noon & 3-8pm Mon-Fri) Houses the Alliance Française (☎ 333-3392) and Goethe Institut (☎ 332-9906; icbasc@sccbs-bo.com), and offers courses in French,

German, Spanish and Portuguese. Facilities include a trilingual multimedia library, the outdoor Kulture Café and an art exhibition gallery; it also sponsors lectures and screens foreign films.

EMERGENCY

Private ambulance (Foianini; ☎ 336-2211, 7162-7647)

Tourist police (☎ 322-5016; north side of Plaza 24 de Septiembre)

IMMIGRATION

Migración (☎ 333-2136; ✆ 8:30am-4:30pm Mon-Fri) is north of the center, opposite the zoo entrance. Visa extensions are available and overland travelers from Paraguay must pick up a free entry stamp here. There's an office at the **train station** (✆ supposedly 10am-noon & 1:30-7pm), which is more convenient but which is plagued by phony officials and thus should be a last-ditch resort. The most reliable office is at the airport. For those braving the Death Train, exit stamps are reportedly only available at the Brazilian frontier – ask around before departing.

INTERNET ACCESS

There are many internet places on Junín. **Punto Entel** (Junín 140; per hr US$0.50; ✆ 8am-11pm) has good speedy connections, printing facilities and webcams on some computers.

LAUNDRY

Central, efficient wash-and-dry places offering same-day service (with drop-off before noon) for around US$1 per kilo:

España Lavandería (España 160)

Lavandería La Paz (La Paz 42)

Lavandería Universal (cnr Ballivián & Quijarro)

MEDICAL SERVICES

The best pharmacy is the efficient and inexpensive **Farmacia América** (Libertad 333). Next door is the Policonsultorio Central, with the recommended Dr Ana María López, who trained in the USA and speaks English.

Clínica Foianini (☎ 336-2211; Irala 468) Hospital used by embassies, but travelers have reported unnecessary tests and longer stays than needed.

Clínica Japonesa (☎ 346-2031) On the third *anillo*, east side; recommended for inexpensive and professional medical treatment.

MONEY

Cash advances are available at most major banks, and ATMs line Calle Junín and most major intersections. The easiest place to change cash or traveler's checks (2% to 3% commission) is **Casa de Cambio Alemán** (east side of Plaza 24 de Septiembre). Street moneychangers shout '¡*Dolares!*' in your face on the main plaza. **Magri Turismo** (☎ 334-5663; cnr Warnes & Potosí) is the American Express agent but doesn't cash traveler's checks.

TELEPHONE

Fun can be had using public telephone boxes, which come in a variety of shapes – anything from toucan birds to jaguars suspended mid-growl. Better rates are found at phone centers, such as the main **Entel office** (Warnes 82), and internet telecom stores along Bolívar that offer cheap international calls. The **Punto Entel** (Junín 284) office near the plaza has landlines.

TOURIST INFORMATION

Departamental de Turismo (☎ 336-8901; Palacio Prefectural, north side of Plaza 24 de Septiembre)

Fundación Amigos de la Naturaleza (FAN; ☎ 355-6800; www.fan-bo.org; Km 7.5, Carretera a Samaipata) Though no longer in charge of the parks, FAN is still the best contact for Amboró and Noel Kempff Mercado National Parks information. West of town (minibus 44) off the old Cochabamba road.

Main tourist office (☎ 336-9595; Ground fl, Casa de la Cultura, west side of Plaza 24 de Septiembre)

Dangers & Annoyances

Beware of bogus immigration officials, particularly at the bimodal bus-train station – carefully check the credentials of anyone who demands to see your passport or other ID. The rule is that no real police officer will ever ask to see your documents in the street; be especially wary of 'civilian' police who will most certainly turn out to be frauds. If you're suspicious, insist that they accompany you to the police station, where things can legitimately be sorted out. Readers have reported several violent robberies in broad daylight during the week at Río Piray; it's best only to venture out there on weekends, when there's safety in numbers.

Sights & Activities

Santa Cruz is not the richest town when it comes to sightseeing. You'll probably spend most of your time here strolling around and sipping coffee in one of the city's many cafés.

PLAZA 24 DE SEPTIEMBRE

The city's main plaza serves as a lush tropical space where you'll see locals lounging on benches and strolling, and families bringing their kids to play. Once there were resident jaywalking sloths here, but they were relocated to the zoo in an effort to protect them from electrocution and increasing traffic hazards in the city center. The price of progress, eh?

BASÍLICA MENOR DE SAN LORENZO & MUSEO DE LA CATEDRAL

Although the original cathedral on Plaza 24 de Septiembre was founded in 1605, the present structure dates from 1845 and wasn't consecrated until 1915. Inside, the decorative woodwork on the ceiling and silver plating around the altar are worth a look. There are good views of the city from the **belltower** (admission US$0.50; 8:30am-noon & 2:30-6pm Tue-Sun).

The cathedral's air-conditioned **Museo de Arte Sagrado** (admission US$0.65; 8:30am-noon & 2:30-6pm Tue & Thu) has a collection of religious icons and artifacts but very little typical religious art. Most interesting are the many gold and silver relics from the Jesuit Guarayos missions. There's also a collection of religious vestments and medallions, as well as one of the world's smallest books, a thumbnail-sized volume containing the Lord's Prayer in several languages.

MUSEO DE LA HISTORIA NATURAL

The **Natural History Museum** (336-6574; Irala 565; admission by donation; 9am-noon & 3-6pm) gives you the lowdown on the flora, fauna and geology of eastern Bolivia. Exhibits include pickled frogs and the usual stuffed animals, fish and birds, as well as information on seeds, wood, fruit, gardening and other lowland pursuits. The bug collections include specimens large enough to keep many people out of rainforests forever.

PARQUE EL ARENAL & MUSEO ETNO-FOLKLÓRICO

Locals relax around the lagoon at Parque El Arenal, but it's best not to dawdle here at night. On an island in the lagoon, a bas-relief mural by renowned Bolivian artist Lorgio Vaca depicts historic and modern-day aspects of Santa Cruz. On a peninsula, the **Ethno-Folkloric Museum** (admission US$0.80; 9:30am-noon & 2:30-5:30pm Mon-Fri) has a small collection of traditional art and artifacts from several *camba* (lowland) cultures.

JARDÍN ZOOLÓGICO

Santa Cruz' **zoo** (342-9939; adult/child US$0.65/0.40; 9am-7pm) has a wild collection of South American birds, mammals and reptiles, who all appear to be humanely treated (although the llamas are a bit overdressed for the climate). If you're not into going to the jungle, this is a good place to see endangered and exotic species such as tapirs, pumas, jaguars and spectacled bears. Sloths laze about in the trees.

Take *micro* (minibus) 58 or 55 from Vallegrande, 76 from Calle Santa Bárbara or anything marked 'Zoológico.' Taxis for up to four people cost around US$1.35.

BIOCENTRO GÜEMBE

A great place for a day out of Santa Cruz, **Güembe** (370 0541; www.biocentroguembe.com; Km 7, Camino Porongo, Zona Los Batos) has a butterfly farm, orchid exhibitions, 10 natural pools, fishing and trekking in the surrounding forest. There's a restaurant with international cuisine, so you won't go hungry. The best way to get here is by taxi from Santa Cruz; expect to pay around US$5.

AQUALAND

For a real splash, dive into this **water park** (385-2500; half day US$5-8, full day US$7.50-10; 10am-6pm Thu-Sun May-Sep) near the airport. The best way to get here is by taxi (around US$5 to US$6).

Tours

Numerous companies offer organized tours, but it's hard to vouch for quality, particularly for those with cheap rates. Recommended agencies:

Amboró Tours (314-5858; www.amborotours.com; 1st fl, Ayacucho 19) Trips to Amboró and Noel Kempff Mercado National Parks and Jesuit missions.

Forest Tours (337-2042; www.forestbolivia .com; Cuéllar 22) Professional, English-speaking agency offering excellent custom-made tours and trips around the region.

Neblina Forest (/fax 3-347-1166; www.neblina forest.com; Paraguá 2560) Bird-watching and natural-history tours to Noel Kempff Mercado, Amboró and Madidi National Parks, along with the Beni region and the Pantanal.

Ruta Verde (339-6470; www.rutaverdebolivia.com; 21 de Mayo 332) Great for local information and tours to the Pantanal, Jesuit missions, Parques Nacional Amboró and Noel Kempff Mercado, Amazon riverboat trips and more.

Uimpex Travel (333-6001; Moreno 226) A long-established agency that runs tours to the Bolivian Pantanal, Jesuit missions and imaginative city sights.

Festivals & Events

If you're in Santa Cruz in February during **Carnaval**, you should most certainly head for the paintball-plagued streets and join in the collective chaos. See p370 for more on Carnaval. Alternatively, check out the Mau-Mauin, the auditorium on the corner of Ibáñez and 21 de Mayo. It attracts over 10,000 people with its dancing, music shows and coronation of the Carnaval queen.

Other festivals:

International Theater Festival Theater groups from all over the world perform in venues around the city. Held from April 14 to 24 (odd years only), it's a great time to be in Santa Cruz.

International Festival of Baroque Music A 10-day festival, held from the end of April to the beginning of May (even years only), with concerts in Santa Cruz and the Jesuit mission towns.

International Festival of Cheese & Wine A relatively recent festival, held in August, where locals showcase their best offerings. Great opportunity to taste Bolivian wine from Tarija.

ExpoCruz (www.fexpocruz.com.bo) Every year in mid- to late September, Santa Cruz hosts this enormous two-week fair where you can buy anything from a toothbrush or clothing to a new house, a combine harvester or a 20-ton truck. It's worthwhile even if you're not shopping, especially at night when it takes on a carnival atmosphere as local families stroll, browse, listen to music, eat, drink and be merry.

Sleeping

BUDGET

Backpackers Santa Cruz Hostel (☎ 334-0025; Irala 696; dm US$2-2.50) A basic backpacker crash pad, this place is very close to the bus station.

Alojamiento Santa Bárbara (☎ 332-1817; alojsta barbara@yahoo.com; Santa Bárbara 151; r per person US$2.65) This is a low-key place with a courtyard and bare rooms with hospital-like beds. It's much loved by backpackers and young Bolivians for being cheap and central.

MIDRANGE

Santa Cruz has a growing number of midrange hotels, all with private bathrooms and reasonable prices.

Residencial Bolívar (☎ 334-2500; Sucre 131; dm US$6, s/d US$9/15, d with bathroom US$19) This superior budget option has leafy tropical patios, two gorgeous toucans snoozing on a branch, and clean rooms and showers. You can laze in the hammocks or read in the courtyard. Breakfast is included.

Hotel Amazonas (☎ 333-4583; leanch@bibosi.scz .entelnet.bo; Junín 214; s/d with bathroom & TV US$10/14) If you're stuck for a room, you could spend a night here under neon strips.

Hotel Bibosi (☎ 334-8548; bibosi@scbbs-bo.com; Junín 218; s/d with breakfast & cable TV US$13/20) The Bibosi is all Amazonian style, with a shadowy interior, small cool rooms hung with paintings of rainforest wildlife, and whirring ceiling fans. The staff is friendly and helpful and there's a great rooftop view.

Hotel Copacabana (☎ 336-2770; Junín 217; s/d US$14/22, with air-con US$20/26; ☒ ▢) The small, 1970s disco-style rooms here are wood-paneled, with ceiling fans or air-con, firm beds and cable TVs. Avoid the noisy ground-floor rooms and bargain during slow periods. Breakfast is included.

Hotel Globetrotter (☎ 337-2754; Sara 49; s/d US$22/25; ☒) This is a lovely traditional Santa Cruz house converted into a hotel, with a long courtyard laden with plants, bright comfortable rooms, cable TV and a big back garden full of bunnies. The friendly multilingual owner is a well of local information who can book plane tickets and help with your itinerary.

Hotel Viru Viru (☎ 333-5298; Junín 338; s/d US$24/27; ☒ ▢ ☒) Great for stifling hot Santa Cruz days, Viru Viru has a pool in the center to cool off in. The rooms and rates are decent, with good beds, breakfasts, TVs and free internet access for guests, and the location is great.

Hotel Lido (☎ 336-3555; www.lido-hotel.com; 21 de Mayo 527; s/d US$30/40; ☒ ▢) A nice but relatively simple upmarket choice in the center, above a Chinese restaurant, the Lido has comfortable rooms with TVs, and access to laundry facilities. There's also a weight-lifting gym on the ground floor.

Hotel Las Américas (☎ 336-8778; www.lasamericas -hotel.com.bo; cnr 21 de Mayo & Seoane; s/d US$35/45; ☒ ▢) This old-fashioned four-star hotel has flowery bed covers, bright and spacious rooms, good large bathrooms with power showers, excellent service and a terrace restaurant with wide views. It's a favorite with business travelers. You get US$10 off the room price if you have AeroSur ticket stubs.

TOP END

Santa Cruz' five-star hotels are away from the center and are more like resorts than hotels. Many were built during the oil boom, but things went bust in the mid-1990s when the casinos were closed due to political wrangling.

Hotel Los Tajibos (☎ 342-1000, 800-10-2210; www .lostajiboshotel.com; San Martín 455, Barrio Equipetrol; s/d/ste with breakfast US$155/175/185; 🛇 🖃 🏊) If you stay at Los Tajibos you won't want to go out to see the city. There's a nightclub to go wild in and a health club to recover in, while muscle flexing can go on at the racquetball courts, followed by a massage or relaxing in the lush tropical gardens. Weekend package rates (from US$60 per person) are often available.

Hotel Yotaú (☎ 336-7799; www.yotau.com.bo; San Martín 7, Barrio Equipetrol; s/d US$159/179; 🛇 🖃 🏊) This beautiful tropical-style high-rise has fitness facilities and a sauna, as well as executive and family rooms for up to six people (US$300). Lunches and dinners cost US$7 each.

Eating
RESTAURANTS
The international population has rolled up its sleeves and opened some fine restaurants, so what Santa Cruz lacks in sightseeing it makes up in gastronomic offerings. There are delicious bites of sushi, fork-whirling spaghetti houses, artsy restaurants and per kilo Brazilian helpings.

Vegetarian Center Cuerpomonte (☎ 337-1797; Aroma 54; buffet per kg US$2; ⏱ 9am-7pm Mon-Sat) Basic and simple, this place has a buffet selection, including quinoa cake, mashed sweet potato, salad bar goodies, veggie soups and lots of other nice wholesome things to keep your body healthy.

Rincón Brasileiro (☎ 333-1237; Libertad 358; buffet per kg US$2-3) Brazilian food served by the kilo – it's a *feijoada* (pork and bean stew) lover's dream. There are delicious salads and desserts such as guava mousse, all eaten in a working-man's warehouse space while watching kitsch Brazilian TV.

Chile (Libertad; mains US$2-5) Mexican food is hard to come by in Santa Cruz, but Chile keeps the spice-loving locals happy. Barbecued lamb, tacos, fajitas and *enchiladas de mole* (corn wraps with chicken, covered in chocolate sauce) are all dished out and enjoyed in this little diner.

Chifa Mandarín (☎ 334-8388; Potosí 793; mains US$2-5) You'll find decent Chinese food done pagoda-style here. Phone ahead for pick-up or send a cab for delivery.

Lorca (☎ 334-0562; Moreno 20; mains US$2-7; ⏱ 8am-late) Santa Cruz' top restaurant, bar, theater and general hangout, Lorca has several worldly cuisines, and its llama steak, drib-

bled with a blue-cheese sauce, is top class. Vegetarians will rejoice in the salads, where olives are strewn liberally over fresh greenery. There's also falafel and hummus, and various tapas offerings, all served to live music and a great atmosphere.

Alexander (☎ 337-8653; Junín s/n; mains US$2.50-3.50) This is a haven for delicious breakfasts and good coffee. Part of a chain, Alexander is excellent for sampling local Madidi coffee and any range of breakfasts, including *huevos rancheros* (spicy scrambled eggs) and granola with yogurt. There's a small but superb range of Mexican wraps and quesadillas, plus good sandwiches.

Ken (☎ 333-3728; Uruguay 730; mains US$3-5; ⏱ 11:30am-2:30pm & 6-11pm Thu-Tue) We may have discovered the world's cheapest and tastiest Japanese eatery. The *yaki udon* (a thick-noodle dish) is massive, laden with chicken and cashews, and there's a great choice of daily dishes to be savored. Just check out all the folk from the Japanese community licking their whiskers in satisfaction.

Casa Típica de Camba (☎ 342-7864; www.casadel camba.com; Mendoza 539; mains US$3-8) You're likely to end up at this lively, sprawling landmark if you ask Bolivian friends where to find the 'most typical' *cruceña/camba* experience. Bolivian and Argentine meat comes sizzling off the grill while live crooners holler traditional tunes to the accompaniment of a Casio keyboard.

La Bella Napoli (☎ 332-5402; Independencía 635; pizzas & mains US$4-6) In a rustic barn six blocks south of the plaza, this place serves fine pizza and pasta dishes – including ravioli, cannelloni and lasagna – on chunky hardwood tables, some outside. It's a short taxi ride (or dark walk) back to the center at night.

Los Hierros (☎ 337-1309; Monseñor Rivero 300; mains US$4.50) The Argentine *parrilla* (grill) sizzles and tickles the taste buds of hungry carnivores amid the hunting-lodge decor and guns hanging on the walls here. The meat is good and fresh, and there's a salad bar to choose your greens.

Pizzería Marguerita (☎ 337-0285; north side of Plaza 24 de Septiembre; mains US$5) Long known for its high-quality pizza, pasta and salads, this well-located place is good for a casual meal.

Yorimichi (☎ 334-7717; Busch 548; mains US$5-7; ⏱ 11:30am-2:30pm & 6-11pm) An upmarket Japanese restaurant with bamboo screens separating eating spaces and traditional music tinkling from the speakers, this is the place to come for brilliant sushi, sashimi, tempura and heart-warming sips of sake. It's a favorite of upmarket *cruceños*, who come here to relish the fresh salmon slices.

La Casona (☎ 337-8495; Arenales 222; mains US$5-7; ☉ closed Sun) One of Santa Cruz' best places to eat, this German-run splash of California gourmet has seating in a shady courtyard or inside under peachy lighting. The food is diverse, with a variety of salads, chicken basted in a balsamic vinaigrette, or pasta in a spicy, palate-biting *arrabiatta* (a spicy tomato sauce).

Michelangelo's (☎ 334-8403; Chuquisaca 502; mains US$5-10) Located in a classy house, complete with fireplaces and marble floors, this is a good choice for a romantic evening or a little Italian self-indulgence.

Leonardo's (☎ 333-8282; Warnes 366; mains US$5-10) Continuing with the Italian Renaissance art theme, you can enjoy another cozy candlelit dinner of pasta or shellfish in this beautiful old converted mansion.

CAFÉS

Irish Pub (☎ 333-8118; east side Plaza 24 de Septiembre; ☉ 9am-midnight) A travelers' second home in Santa Cruz, this place has great beers, delicious soups and comfort food, plus tasty local specialties. It serves breakfast, lunch and dinner and, helped along by the excellent service and music, many people while the hours away drinking beer, relaxing and watching the goings-on in the plaza below.

Victory Bar (Galería Casco Viejo, cnr Junín & 21 de Mayo; lunch US$4) The palm-shaded terrace of this popular bar is a lovely place to enjoy boozy lunches. Offers Western breakfasts in the morning.

Bar El Tapekuá (☎ 334-5905; cnr La Paz & Ballivián; ☉ from 6pm Wed-Sat) This casual yet upscale Swiss and Bolivian–owned hangout serves good, earthy food and has live music most nights (US$1.20 cover).

QUICK EATS

As Bolivia's most modern, hustle-and-bustle town, Santa Cruz also boasts more fast-food outlets than you can shake a happy meal at.

California Burgers (☎ 333-4054; Independencia 481; donuts US$0.35, tacos US$1) This place serves coffee, burgers, tacos, burritos and sticky donuts.

Dumbo (☎ 336-7077; Ayacucho 247; ice creams US$0.50) Dumbo serves gourmet frozen yogurt in the usual flavors plus *maracuya* (passion fruit),

papaya, *guayaba* (guava), almond, tangerine and so on.

Mr Café (Monseñor Rivero 260; snacks US$1) Sandwiches, juices, cakes, light meals and ice cream to complement its rich espressos all make this place a favorite local hangout.

Pasticceria Sant Honorè (☎ 333-4410; Monseñor Rivero 328; cakes US$1-2) Sweet tooths gather here for the delicious cakes that glimmer beneath the glass counter, perfect for an afternoon bite or after-dinner dessert.

Yogen Fruz (☎ 337-7221; Rivero at Cañada Strongest; frozen yogurts US$1-2) It's cold, sweet and good for you, so hit the frozen-yogurt flavors before you hit the streets.

Bar Hawaii (Sucre at Beni; meals US$3) An expansive cross between an ice-cream joint and a fast-food eatery, this spot is popular for sundaes, cakes, light meals and good coffee.

GROCERIES

For simple, cheap eats, try Mercado La Ramada or the mall-like Mercado Los Pozos with food stalls on the top floor. The latter is especially good for unusual tropical fruits. It's hard to tear yourself away after only one glass of *licuado de papaya* (blended papaya with water or milk) or *guineo con leche* (banana with milk) – both are whipped in a blender, served cold and cost US$0.35. Mercado Florida is wall-to-wall blender stalls serving exquisite juices and fruit salads for US$0.50.

For a good variety of (relatively expensive) fixings to prepare meals yourself, try minimart **Hipermaxi** (cnr 21 de Mayo & Florida). **Supermercado Sur Fidalga** (east side Plaza Héroes del Chaco) is the best stocked, cheapest option for groceries. The **Naturalia** (Independencia 452) organic grocery store has a wide selection of locally produced healthy goodies.

Drinking

The hippest nightspots are along Av San Martin, between the second and third *anillos* in Barrio Equipetrol, a US$1 to US$2 taxi ride from the center. Hot spots change frequently so it's best to dress to impress and cruise the *piranhar* (strip; literally 'to go piranha fishing') and see what catches your fancy. Local kids line up with their cars along the pavements and play unbelievably loud music out of their gigantic car-boot speakers in competition with the music booming from neighboring cars, while drinking beer, dancing and chatting till late.

Cover charges run from US$2 to US$10 and drinks are expensive; most places start selling drinks between 6pm and 9pm but don't warm up until 11pm; they then continue until 3am or 4am.

North of the plaza between the first and second *anillos*, Av Monseñor Rivero is, according to the locals, 'the Equipetrol for the older generations,' with fewer discos but more see-and-be-seen cafés and trendy late-night restaurants with sidewalk seating. Near the university, Av Busch is lined with places catering to more serious, mostly male drinkers.

Lorca (☎ 334-0562; Moreno 20; admission for live music US$1.50; ☼ 8am–late) The meeting place of the city's arty crowd and those loving diversity, Lorca is positively one of the most innovative and happening places in town. It's perfect for chilled *caipirinha* and *mojito* cocktails while you enjoy the live music, be it jazz, samba, rumba, the sounds of the Middle East or a local rock band. Before the music starts, short films are screened and there is an art gallery in the back, right next to the little theater.

Clapton's Blues Bar (Murillo at Arenales; admission US$2; ☼ Sat & Sun) This is a tiny, dark jazz and blues bar with local bands playing to a sparse drinking audience till very late. There can be good jazz here (and very bad rock), so check what's playing by asking at the bar.

Entertainment

Santa Cruz has a number of discos and karaoke bars, which reflects the young city's liberal and cosmopolitan character. The bars and clubs close and open monthly, so ask around for what's hot.

The city also has a number of cinemas, and the films are generally better and more recent than elsewhere in Bolivia. For movie schedules and other venues, see the daily newspapers *El Mundo* and *El Deber*.

Lorca (☎ 334-0562; Moreno 20) Here you'll find live music and anything from local talent to international starlets.

El Rincón Salteño (☎ 353-6335; 26 de Enero at Charagua; ☼ from 10pm Fri, Sat & Sun) Traditional *peñas* (folk-music programs) are scarce in modern Santa Cruz, but this is an excellent choice. Positioned on the second *anillo,* there's a great variety of musical styles, from Argentine guitarists to Cuban village drummers, local singers and dancers in costume.

Divali (24 de Septiembre; admission women/men free/US$7) At the time of research, this was one of the more popular discos. The girls are groomed and boys muscular. Note that admission prices will go up a lot if you're not looking right.

Cine Palace (west side of Plaza 24 de Septiembre; admission US$2.50) First-run flicks are shown nightly here.

Cine Arenal (Beni 555; admission US$2) This building faces Parque El Arenal and screens older releases.

Shopping

Wood carvings made from the tropical hardwoods *morado* and the more expensive *guayacán* (from US$20 for a nice piece) are unique to the Santa Cruz area. Relief carvings on *tari* nuts are also interesting and make nice portable souvenirs. Locals also make beautiful macramé *llicas* (root-fiber bags).

Av René Moreno is the place for souvenir shopping. Be aware that prices are much higher here than in La Paz for llama and alpaca wool goods, so perhaps save your pennies by shopping in the capital.

Artecampo (☎ 334-1843; Salvatierra 407) The best place to find fine *artesanía* (locally handcrafted items), this store provides an outlet for the work of 1000 rural *cruceña* women and their families. The truly inspired and innovative pieces include leatherwork, hammocks, weavings, handmade paper, greeting cards and lovely natural-material lamp shades.

Centro de Arte y Cultura Guaraní Ñandereko Ñomai (☎ 337-6285; Junín 229) You'll find lovely wooden carvings and textiles from Guaraní villages here, created by indigenous families who benefit from the sales. It's well worth checking out.

Getting There & Away

AIR

Viru-Viru international airport (VVI; ☎ 181), 15km north of the center, handles domestic and international flights. Both **AeroSur** (☎ 336-4446; Irala at Colón) and **LAB** (☎ 334-4896; Chuquisaca 126) have daily services to Cochabamba, La Paz and Sucre, as well as several other Bolivian cities.

American Airlines (☎ 334-1314; Beni 167) flies direct daily to Miami, **Aerolíneas Argentinas** (☎ 333-9776; Junín 22) flies several times a week to Buenos Aires, and **TAM Mercosur** (☎ 337-1999; 21 de Mayo at Florida) flies to Asunción Monday to Saturday, with connections to Miami, Buenos Aires and several Brazilian cities.

TAM (☎ 353-2639) flies direct to La Paz (US$70) on Monday morning and about a couple more times a week from the military's El Trompillo airport, just south of the center. It also runs popular direct flights to Puerto Suárez (US$65) a couple of times a week.

BUS, MICRO & SHARED TAXI

The full-service **bimodal terminal** (☎ 348-8382; terminal fee US$0.40), the combo long-distance bus and train station, is 1.5km east of the center, just before the third *anillo* at the end of Av Brasil.

There are plenty of daily services morning and evening to Cochabamba (US$4 to US$6, 10 to 12 hours), from where there are connections to La Paz, Oruro, Sucre, Potosí and Tarija. Cosmos has a direct daily service to La Paz (US$6.50 to US$12.50, 16 to 25 hours).

Several companies offer daily evening services to Sucre (US$4 to US$14, 16 to 25 hours), with connections for Potosí. Most services to Camiri (US$8.50, seven to eight hours) and Yacuiba (US$9.50, 15 hours) depart in the mid-afternoon. Buses to Vallegrande (US$5.50, six hours) leave in the morning and afternoon.

To the Jesuit missions and all of Chiquitanía, Misiones del Oriente buses leave in the morning and afternoon. Buses run to San Ramón (US$3, 2¾ hours), Asunción de Guarayos (US$4, five hours), San Javier (US$4, three hours), Concepción (US$4.50, six hours), San Ignacio de Velasco (US$8.50, nine hours), San Miguel de Velasco (US$10.50, 10 hours) and San Rafael de Velasco (US$11.50, 11 hours). Several other companies do the same routes but may be less comfortable.

To Trinidad (US$4.50 to US$10.50, at least 12 hours) and beyond, a number of buses leave every evening. Although the road is theoretically open year-round, at least to Trinidad, the trip gets rough in the rainy season and is frequently canceled for weeks on end.

Several companies also offer international services. Daily services connect Santa Cruz with Buenos Aires (US$62, 42 hours). In the dry season, you can attempt the Trans-Chaco Rd (see the boxed text p290) to and from Asunción, Paraguay (around US$52, 30 hours minimum).

Smaller *micros* and *trufis* (collective taxis or minibuses that follow a set route) to Viru-Viru airport, Montero (with connections to Buena Vista and Villa Tunari), Samaipata and other communities in Santa Cruz department leave regularly from outside the old bus terminal. To Buena Vista (US$2.75, 1½ hours), they wait along Izozog (Isoso). To Samaipata (US$3.50, three hours), *trufis* leave on the opposite side of Av Cañoto, about two blocks from the old bus terminal. Alternatively, ring **Expreso Samaipata Taxis** (☎ 333-5067; Ortíz 1147), which charges US$14 for up to four passengers.

TRAIN

The *Expreso del Oriente* (the infamous Death Train) runs to Quijarro, on the Brazilian border, daily except Sunday at around 3pm (2nd-/1st-/Pullman-class US$8/16/21). It takes at least 21 hours and in the wet season may not run at all. The train chugs through soy plantations, forest, scrub and oddly shaped mountains to the steamy, sticky Pantanal region on the Brazilian frontier. Bring plenty of food and water and mosquito repellent for long stops in swampy areas. About halfway, the train stops in San José de Chiquitos (p324) on the mission circuit, a good place to layover before continuing to Brazil.

Trains arrive the following day in Quijarro (p327), from where taxis shuttle passengers to the Brazilian border town of Corumbá, 2km away. Don't pay more than US$2 per person for the taxi – rip-offs are common. Once on the Brazilian side, get a yellow *colectivo* (minibus) from the kiosk at the border to Corumbá. The person inside the kiosk knows what time the buses leave, but they go frequently between 6am and 11pm (ticket to Corumbá US$1). You can change dollars or bolivianos into *reais* (*hay*-ice) on the Bolivian side, but rates are poor. Note that there's no Brazilian consulate in Quijarro, so if you need a visa, get it in Santa Cruz. Don't be surprised if an official asks for money for an exit stamp at Quijarro. From Corumbá there are good bus connections into southern Brazil, but no passenger trains.

Train tickets can be scarce and carriages are often so jammed with people and contraband that there's nowhere to sit. Ticket windows (supposedly) open at 8am, and you can only buy your ticket on the day of departure, when lines reach communist proportions. A funkier alternative is to stake out a place in the *bodegas* (boxcars) of a mixed train and purchase a 2nd-class ticket on board (for 20% over the ticket-window price). The upmarket option is to buy a 1st-class ticket through a Santa Cruz travel agent. You must pay a US$1.50/4.50 national/international departure tax after purchasing your ticket.

Rail service to Yacuiba, on the Argentine border, is a reasonably quick and comfortable *ferrobus* (passenger rail bus; 2nd-/1st-/Pullman-class US$5.50/7/14, nine hours), which supposedly departs at 5pm on Monday, Wednesday and Friday, returning on Wednesday and Sunday at 8pm.

Getting Around
TO/FROM THE AIRPORT
Handy minibuses leave Viru-Viru for the center (US$0.60, 30 minutes) when flights arrive. Minibuses to the airport leave every 20 minutes starting at 5:30am from Av Cañoto at stops along the first *anillo*. Taxis for up to four people cost US$5 to US$6.

TO/FROM THE BUS & TRAIN STATION
The bimodal bus-train station is beyond easy walking distance, but you can get to the center in about 10 minutes on *micros* 12 or 20.

BUS
Santa Cruz' handy system of city *micros* (US$0.20) connects the transportation terminals and all the *anillos* with the center. *Micros* 17 and 18 circulate around the first *anillo*. To reach Av San Martin in Barrio Equipetrol, take *micro* 23 from anywhere on Vallegrande.

CAR
American Rent-a-Car (☎ 334-1235; Justiniano 28 at Uruguay)
Avis Rent-a-Car (☎ 343-3939; www.avisbolivia.com; Carretera al Norte km 3.5)
Barron's Rent-a-Car (☎ 342-0160; www.rentacarbolivia.com; Alemania 50 at Tajibo) Also at Viru-Viru airport.
Localiza Rent-a-Car Carretera al Norte (☎ 343-3939; Banzer km 3.5); Viru-Viru airport (☎ 385-2190)

TAXI
Generally, taxis charge the official rate of US$1 to anywhere in the first *anillo* for one person, plus US$0.25 for each additional person and about US$0.25 for each additional *anillo*. If you have lots of luggage, however, drivers may try to extract up to 50% more. Overcharging is common on the way to and from the airport; it's better to ask the price in advance for any city trip to avoid arguments.

BUENA VISTA
pop 13,300
Buena Vista welcomes you with a jaguar phone box and a bizarre Irish pub on the town square, while the mosquitoes rejoice and waste no time exploring new flesh (so bring repellent). This sweet little town is two hours (100km) northwest of Santa Cruz and serves as an ideal staging point for trips into Parque Nacional Amboró's forested lowland section. Though most foreigners now prefer Samaipata (p312) for national park exploration, Buena Vista still has some of the best places to view wildlife, observe birds and see local traditions.

Information
The municipal government is planning to open its own tourist office on the plaza. For information on Parque Nacional Amboró, visit the **Sernap office** (Servicio National de Areas Protegidas; ☎ 932-2054; www.sernap.gov.bo in Spanish), two blocks southwest of the plaza, where you can pick up an entry permit and inquire about current park regulations and accommodations options.

There's no bank or ATM here, so bring cash from elsewhere. Dial-up internet connections (per hour US$2) are available after 7pm during the week and all day on weekends at a couple of places around the plaza.

English-speaking **Amboró Tours** (☎ 932-2093, in Santa Cruz 358-5383; www.vektron.net/amborotours), off the northeast corner of the plaza, runs adventurous trips to the northern section of

the park, starting at US$50 per person per day for two people, including transportation, a guide and food.

Sights & Activities

IGLESIA DE LOS SANTOS DESPOSORIOS

Buena Vista's Jesuit mission was founded in 1694 as the fifth mission in the Viceroyalty of Perú. The need for a church was recognized, and 29 years later, after a search for a high-standing location with sufficient water and potential cropland, the first building was finally constructed.

By the mid-1700s, 700 Chiraguano people had been converted to Christianity. The Swiss Jesuit missionary and architect Padre Martin Schmid built a new church to replace the dilapidated 17th century one, completing the current structure in 1767. When the Jesuits were expelled from Bolivia later that year, the administration of the church passed to the bishop of Santa Cruz. Although the building is deteriorating, it has a lovely classic form.

CURICHI MARSH

This beautiful marshy wetland, a 30-minute walk south of the main plaza, is a municipal **reserve** (admission without/with guide US$1.35/4). It provides Buena Vista's water supply and serves as a habitat and breeding site for both migratory and native birds. There is an elevated boardwalk and two viewing towers. It's best to visit at dawn or dusk, but don't forget to bring insect repellent. You can set up a guided visit with any of the tour companies around the plaza.

RÍO SURUTÚ, SANTA BÁRBARA & EL CAIRO

Río Surutú is a popular excursion for locals, and there's a pleasant sandy beach ideal for picnics, swimming and camping during the dry season. There have been attempts to make more sandy beaches along the river, but the attempts failed when the river rose in the rainy season and washed the sand away. From Buena Vista it's an easy 3km walk to the river bend nearest town. The opposite bank is the boundary of Parque Nacional Amboró.

A good longer option is the six-hour **circuit walk** through the community of Santa Bárbara and partially forested tropical plantation country. From Buena Vista, follow the unpaved road to Santa Bárbara and ask for the track that leads to an idyllic river beach on the Río Ucu-

rutú. After a picnic and a dip, you can return to Buena Vista via the Huaytú road.

An even better swimming hole is at El Cairo, which is an hour's walk from town. To get there, pass Los Franceses and follow the unpaved road as it curves to the right. About 2km from town, take the left fork and cross over a bridge. After passing El Cairo, on your right, keep going until you reach the river.

Festivals & Events

The local fiesta, **Día de los Santos Desposorios** (November 26), features bullfights, food stalls and general merrymaking. Culinary festivals include: the **Chocolate Festival** (last Sunday in January), the **Coffee Festival** (third Sunday in April) and the **Rice Festival** in early May after the harvest.

Sleeping

Residencial Nadia (☎ 932-2049; Sevilla 186; r per person US$3, with bathroom US$4) Just off the main square, rooms at this family home surround a patio. There are firm beds and the owner is a good source of park information. All rooms have fans. The main drawback is the blaring disco across the street – try for a room out the back.

La Casona (☎ 932-2083; western cnr of plaza; d with bathroom US$9) This is a new place on the plaza, with a friendly owner and a nice patio with sagging hammocks. The rooms are in baby blues, have good beds and all should now have en suite bathrooms.

Cabañas Quimorí (☎ 932-2081, in Santa Cruz 342-7747; hamel@cotas.com.bo; r incl breakfast US$10) Another good-value option is this German and Bolivian–run place just off the road toward Santa Bárbara. The simple individual cabins are spread over a large area with a great view over Amboró. It charges a bit more on weekends.

Hotel Amboró (☎ 932-2104; hotelamboro@cotas .com.bo; s/d US$20/30; ✷ ▣) Newly refurbished, this hotel has en suite bathrooms, air-conditioned rooms, hammocks and a restaurant. There are opportunities for exploring the park, plus a swimming pool and water games for children.

Hacienda El Cafetal (☎ 935-2067; www.anditrade coffee.com; s/d US$20/35; ✷ ▣) Part of a community ecoproject set up to support Bolivian coffee growers and their families, this place warms your heart with its conscientiousness and gives you a caffeine rush with all the delicious, fresh coffee produced here. The accommodations are good, with stylish, self-catering *cabañas* (cabins) and suites, all with good views. You can go around the plantations and see how coffee is produced, taste different types of the strong black stuff, and then, caffeine-pumped, ride horses and go bird-watching.

Hotel Flora & Fauna (Double F; ☎ 710-43706; amboroadventures@hotmail.com; r per person, all-inclusive US$50) British ornithologist and entomologist Robin Clarke runs this modern, utilitarian collection of cabins that sits atop a breezy, bird-rich ridge overlooking Amboró, surrounded by 200 acres of primary forest. Pluses include wildlife-viewing platforms, an extensive book exchange and guided walks (for guests only) from US$10. Access is by car/moto-taxi (US$2.65/1.35) from Buena Vista. It's 4km south of the plaza off Huaytú. Book before getting here, as the owner is planning to spend more time in Santa Cruz.

Amboró Eco-Resort (☎ 932-2048, in Santa Cruz 342-2372; www.amboro.com; s/d/ste US$80/90/140; 🍽 🏊) A good 20- to 25-minute walk from the center, this place is surrounded by its own tropical forest complete with walking paths and fenced-in forest animals. Amenities include a swim-up bar in the pool, a sauna, a disco and several sporting options. It's not the world's quietest place, but it's fun if you're with children. It also runs the Mataracú Tent Camp, a relatively luxurious complex on the edge of Parque Nacional Amboró (see p310).

A couple of the cheaper places allow camping on their grounds.

Eating

La Tranquera Kaffee Pub (northwest side of plaza; mains US$3-4) This is an excellent choice, with a jolly owner who prepares exotic rainforest juices (US$3 per jug). Go for beef and chicken dishes, accompanied by fried yucca, potatoes, rice and tomato salad. There's wild game – agouti, peccary and armadillo – but in the interest of wildlife, you might want to avoid these.

El Bibosi (western cnr of plaza; mains US$3-4) Next door to La Casona, the offerings here are similar, with plenty of meat and rice, and plaza-watching opportunities.

In a kiosk in the middle of the plaza, the Irish Pub is open all day for coffee, muffins, juice, wine and cocktails. There are several other cheap family-run places on the plaza

and along the highway serving burgers and specials.

Shopping

The Jipijapa store (one block northwest of the plaza) sells lamp shades, handbags, boxes and panama hats made from *jipijapa*, the fronds of the *cyclanthaceae* fan palm tree; the use of these fronds for making *artesanía* is specific to Buena Vista. Up the street, the recommended Artecampo store also sells *jipijapa* products, plus other local creations.

Getting There & Away

From Santa Cruz, shared taxis (per person US$2.75) leave for Yapacaní from behind the old long-distance bus terminal. Make it clear that you want to get off at Buena Vista.

To return to Santa Cruz, wait for a shared taxi coming from Yapacaní, which will cruise around the plaza in search of passengers with its horn blaring.

Getting Around

Car- and moto-taxis (US$0.20) wait at one corner of the plaza; there's also another taxi stand along the road to Santa Bárbara for Cabañas Quimorí and Hotel Flora & Fauna.

PARQUE NACIONAL & ÁREA DE USO MÚLTIPLE AMBORÓ

This 430,000-hectare park lies in a unique geographical position at the confluence of three distinct ecosystems: the Amazon Basin, the northern Chaco and the Andes.

The park was originally created in 1973 as the Reserva de Vida Silvestre Germán Busch, with an area of 180,000 hectares. In 1984, thanks to the efforts of British ornithologist Robin Clarke and Bolivian biologist Noel Kempff Mercado, it was given national park status and in 1990 was expanded to 630,000 hectares. In late 1995, however, amid controversy surrounding *campesino* (subsistence farmer) colonization inside park boundaries, it was pared down to its current size (see the boxed text p308).

The park's range of habitats means that both highland and lowland species are found here. All species native to Amazonia, except those of the Beni savannas, are represented, including the elusive spectacled bear. Jaguars, capybaras, river otters, agoutis, tapirs, deer, peccaries and various monkeys still exist in relatively large numbers, and more

---

THE STRUGGLE FOR AMBORÓ

The location of Parque Nacional Amboró is a mixed blessing; although it's conveniently accessible to visitors, it also lies practically within spitting distance of Santa Cruz and squarely between the old and new Cochabamba–Santa Cruz highways. Considering the fact that even the remote parks of the Amazon Basin are coming under threat, Amboró is in an especially vulnerable position.

The first human settlers in the area were Chiriguano and Yuracare people, who occupied the lowlands, while Altiplano people, such as the Aymará, settled in the highland areas. Although agriculture was introduced after the arrival of the Spanish in the late 16th century, the remote Amboró region remained untouched until the late 20th century, when unemployed opportunity-seekers began migrating from the highlands in search of land.

When Parque Nacional Amboró was created in 1973, its charter included a clause forbidding settlement and resource exploitation. Unfortunately for naturalists and conservationists, hunters, loggers and *campesino* (subsistence farmer) settlers continued to pour in – many of them displaced from the Chapare region by the US Drug Enforcement Agency. The northeastern area is already settled, cultivated and hunted out. For poor farmers, cultivation practices have changed little since the 1500s, and slash-and-burn is still the prevailing method of agriculture.

Although NGOs (nongovernmental organisations) have attempted to train committed *guarda-parques* (park rangers) and educate people about the value of wilderness, more land is lost every year and the park's future is far from certain. In 1995 conflicts between colonists and authorities heated up, and as a result the park was informally redefined to include only land that lay 400m beyond the most remote cultivated field. This effectively shrank the protected area by about 200,000 hectares.

In July of the same year, *campesinos* pressed for official recognition of their rights to occupy the land, and prevented tourists and researchers from entering the park. The following October, with regional elections coming up, the government abandoned the struggle and issued an official decree reducing the park by over 200,000 hectares. The decommissioned area was then redesignated as the Área de Uso Múltiple Amboró, which effectively opened it up for settlement. The affected portion includes a band across the southern area from Comarapa to Samaipata, all of the eastern bit up to the headwaters of the Surutú tributaries, and parts of the far north.

---

than 700 species of birds have been identified. The unfortunately tasty *mutún* (razor-billed curassow), is still native to the area, and even rare quetzals have been spotted. The park is also one of the only remaining habitats of the rare and endangered blue-horned curassow, also known as the unicorn bird.

To see most of these wild creatures, however, you will have to spend several days getting deep into the park.

Buena Vista Section

Access to the eastern part of the reserve requires crossing over the Río Surutú, either in a vehicle or on foot. Depending on the rainfall and weather, the river may be anywhere from knee- to waist-deep. For details on huts and campsites throughout the park, contact the Sernap office in Buena Vista (p305). For a list of companies running guided excursions into this section of the park, see Tours in Santa Cruz, p299.

RÍO MACUÑUCU

The Río Macuñucu route is the most popular into the Área de Uso Múltiple Amboró and begins at **Las Cruces**, 35km southeast of Buena Vista. It's a US$4 taxi ride from Buena Vista. From there it's 7km to the Río Surutú, which you must drive or wade across; just beyond the opposite bank you'll reach **Villa Amboró**. Be aware that villagers may illegally try to charge an entrance fee to any tourist who passes their community en route to Macuñucu, regardless of whether you intend to stay there or not. The park administration doesn't yet charge an admission fee, and most tour operators and agencies pay a fee to the Macuñucu villagers, who threaten to block the road if a fee is not paid to them. It remains to be seen whether this fee will become legalized or a new one imposed.

A track that continues several kilometers through the trees and homesteads starts here and heads past a few cattle gates to the banks of the **Río Macuñucu**. The track continues upriver through thick forest for about two hours, then disappears into the river course. Continue upstream another hour or so, hopping over river stones past beautiful red rocks, cliffs and overhangs. Beyond a particularly narrow canyon, which confines hikers to the river, you'll reach a large rock overhang accommodating up to 10 campers. If you have a tent, the sandy river beaches also make pleasant campsites.

At this point, the upriver walk becomes increasingly difficult, and entails negotiating some large and slippery river boulders and scrambling past obstructing landslides. After several hours of heavy slogging upstream from the cave you reach a nice **waterfall** and another potential campsite. The daring can continue the treacherous boulder-hopping

to more overhangs further upstream. The terrain becomes more rugged, so a guide is recommended for overnight or extended trips above the waterfall.

RÍO ISAMA & CERRO AMBORÓ
The Río Isama route turns off at the village of **Espejitos**, 28km southeast of Buena Vista, and provides access to the base of 1300m Cerro Amboró, the bulbous peak for which the park is named. It's possible to climb to the summit, but it is a difficult trek and a guide is essential.

UPPER SAGUAYO
The objective of this route is the study site on the upper Río Saguayo, where researchers

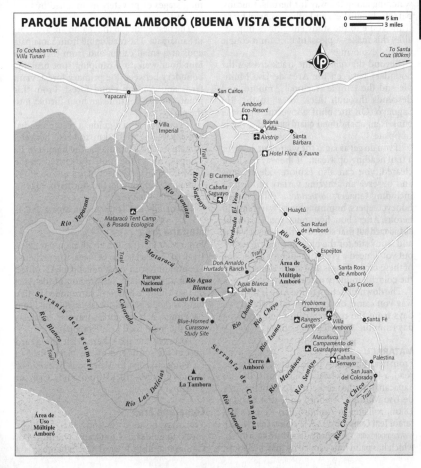

PARQUE NACIONAL AMBORÓ (BUENA VISTA SECTION)

0 — 5 km
0 — 3 miles

rediscovered the rare blue-horned curassow, once thought to be extinct. It's very rough-going in places, so prospective hikers need a guide and a good machete. Without a 4WD to take you to the end of the motorable track, the return trip requires about five days.

The hike begins at the mouth of the **Río Chonta**. To get there, take a taxi or *micro* from Buena Vista to Huaytú. Here, turn right (southwest) and walk 5km to the Río Surutú. In the dry season, you can ford the river by vehicle or on foot. From the opposite bank it's 12km along the 4WD track to the end of the motorable track at Don Arnaldo Hurtado's ranch.

From the ranch, keep going a short distance along the track to the **Agua Blanca Cabaña**, watching along the way for herons, toucans, parrots, kingfishers and other colorful birds. If the route to the study site proves impassable, this makes a pleasant base for a couple of days' exploring.

Beyond the *cabaña,* the track crosses the boundary between the Área de Uso Múltiple and the Parque Nacional Amboró, and descends through thick forest to the Río Saguayo. On the bluff above the opposite bank is an abandoned **guard hut** and a viable campsite.

If you do get as far as the guard hut, look for a trail heading upstream. If the way has been cleared, you can also explore side streams and observe an amazing variety of birdlife, including tanagers, *orpendolas* (blackbirds), honeycreepers, hummingbirds, warblers and herons. After about five hours, you'll reach the **abandoned hut** that served as the research base and study site for the blue-horned curassow, but you'll need a great deal of luck to see one of these birds. This is also an ideal habitat for the colorful military macaw.

The downhill return to the road is the same way you came; on foot, this takes about two days from the research camp and one long day from the Agua Blanca Cabaña.

MATARACÚ

From near Yapacaní, on the main Cochabamba road, a 4WD track heads south across the Río Yapacaní into the northern reaches of the Área de Uso Múltiple Amboró and, after a rough 18km, rolls up to Amboró Eco-Resort's **Mataracú Tent Camp** (☎ 932-2048, in Santa Cruz 342-2372; www.amboro.com; r per person incl breakfast & lunch US$92), which has palm huts capped by thatched roofs,

and *cabañas* on stilts. There is also the community-run **Posada Ecologica** (☎ 716-74582; dm/d US$4/5.35), which offers all-you-can-eat meals (breakfast/lunch US$1/2) and can be booked through any agency in Buena Vista. This is the only Sernap *cabaña* accessible by motor vehicle; however, crossing the Río Yapacaní may be a problem except in the driest part of the year.

Samaipata Area

Samaipata sits just outside the southern boundary of the Área de Uso Múltiple Amboró and is the best access point for the Andean section of the former park. There's no real infrastructure, and public facilities and walking tracks are still largely in the planning stages or privately maintained by local guides.

The best guides to the region are available in Samaipata. The road uphill from Samaipata ends at a small cabin, and from there it's a four-hour walk to a camping spot near the boundary between the primary forest, giant ferns and Andean cloud forest. From this point, you can continue an hour further into the park.

If you can't find a guide, a recommended **two-day walk** is the 23km traverse between Samaipata and Mairana via the hamlet of La Yunga. Most of the route is depicted on the IGM 1:50,000 topo sheet *Mairana – 6839-IV*. Samaipata appears at the northern edge of *Samaipata – 6839-III*.

For details, see Tours in Samaipata, p314.

Mairana Area

From Mairana, it's 7km uphill along a walking track (or take a taxi) to **La Yunga**, where there's a community-run guest hut and a FAN office. It's in a particularly lush region of the Área de Uso Múltiple Amboró, surrounded by tree ferns and other cloud-forest vegetation. From La Yunga, a 16km forest traverse connects with the main road near Samaipata.

To enter the park here, visit the guard post at the south end of the soccer field in La Yunga. Access to Mairana is by *micro* or *camión* (flatbed truck) from Santa Cruz or Samaipata.

Comarapa Area

You may be able to find local Spanish-speaking guides in Comarapa. Northwest of Comarapa, 4km toward Cochabamba, is a little-used entrance to the Área de Uso Múltiple Amboró. After the road crosses a pass between a hill and a ridge with a telephone tower, look for the minor road turning off to the northeast (right) at the settlement of **Khara Huasi**. This road leads uphill to verdant stands of cloud forest, which blanket the peaks.

Other worthwhile visits in this area include the 36-sided **Pukhara de Tuquipaya**, a set of pre-Inca ruins on the summit of **Cerro Comanwara**, 1.5km outside of Comarapa; and the colonial village of **Pulquina Arriba**, several kilometers east of Comarapa.

Sleeping

Inside the park are five wilderness *cabañas* for around US$3 per person per day. For bookings and information, contact **Sernap** (☎ in Buena Vista 932-2054; www.sernap.gov.bo in Spanish). The *cabañas* are very basic, so you'll need your own sleeping bag. The most popular and accessible *cabaña* is the one on the Río Macuñucu – the Macuñucu Campamento de Guardaparques. It's 4km upstream, with a sleeping loft and rudimentary cooking facilities. The main camp activity is sitting beside the river and waiting for wildlife to wander past. Jaguar and puma tracks are frequently seen along the riverbank, but large cats are rarely observed. Other *cabañas* can be found on the lower Río Semayo, above the Río Matarací, on the Río Agua Blanca and on the lower Río Saguayo.

Situated at Villa Amboró, near the mouth of the Macuñucu, the nongovernment organisation (NGO) **Probioma** (☎ 343-1332; www .probioma.org.bo; Córdova 7 Este No 29, Barrio Equipetrol, Santa Cruz) helped start a community-run camp site with clean showers, toilets and several hiking trails. There is a two-hour route to a lovely 50m-high waterfall and a four-hour return hike to a gorgeous viewpoint over Cerro Amboró. Local Spanish-speaking guides can provide information on the flora and fauna, and the community can organize meals and arrange horse transportation for visitors who might not want to walk or have children. A two-day stay, including guides, horses, camping gear and meals costs around US$30 per person. With your own food and camping equipment, you'll pay half price.

Getting There & Away

Every morning a *micro* heads south from Buena Vista through Huaytú, San Rafael de Amboró, Espejitos, Santa Rosa de Amboró, Santa Fé and Las Cruces. This boundary provides access to several rough routes and tracks that lead southwest into the interior, following tributaries of the Río Surutú. Note that all access to the park along this road will require a crossing of the Río Surutú. In Buena Vista you can hire a 4WD vehicle to reach Macuñucu camp.

SANTA CRUZ TO SAMAIPATA

Thirty kilometers west of Santa Cruz on the road to Samaipata and 1km north up a valley in the village of El Torno, **Tapekuá Le Mayen** (☎ 382-2925; Warnes 999; mains US$4-8; ☺ Sat & Sun 11:30am-6pm) serves gourmet Swiss-French fare in a lovely rural setting and has four charming, rustic *cabañas* (one night US$50 to US$70, additional nights US$4 to US$5), which are superb value for extended stays.

Los Espejillos

The name of this popular retreat – 'the little mirrors' – comes from the sparkling smooth black rock that surrounds the park, polished by a small mountain river. **Espejillos Park** has several waterfalls and natural swimming pools, with lovely, clean and refreshing water. It stands across the Río Piray 18km north of the highway.

About 400m beyond the free public site, the mediocre **Hotel Espejillos** (☎ 333-0091; camping weekdays/weekends US$5/6, d US$45/55) has a clean private stretch of the river for bathing, an unremarkable restaurant, a bar that's good for a beer in the sun and a disco.

Catch any *micro* or *trufi* going toward Santiago del Torno, Limoncito, La Angostura or Samaipata and get off just beyond the village of San José. From here, Los Espejillos is a long walk or hitch north along the 4WD track (which isn't passable by vehicle at all during the rainy season). Weekends are the most crowded and chaotic but are also the best for finding taxis or catching lifts from the turnoff.

Bermejo & Volcanes Region

Bermejo, 85km southwest of Santa Cruz on the Samaipata road, is marked by a hulking slab of red rock known as **Cueva de los Monos**, which is flaking and chipping into nascent natural arches.

The **Laguna Volcán**, an intriguing crater lake 6km up the hill north of Bermejo, was once a popular stopover for migrating ducks, but the birds dispersed in the late 1980s when a *cruceño* developer cleared all the vegetation with the idea to build condos here. His time-share scheme failed and the foliage and wildlife are returning, so it makes a pleasant walk from the highway. A lovely **walking track** climbs from the lake to the crater rim; it begins at the point directly across the lake from the end of the road. Coming from Santa Cruz, take a *micro* or *trufi* toward Samaipata and get off 1km beyond Bermejo.

The beautiful nearby region known as **Los Volcanes**, north of the main road, features an otherworldly landscape of tropical sugarloaf hills. If you're in the area, it's not to be missed. In the dry season, it's worth spending the night at **Refugio Volcanes** (☎ 337-2042; www .forestbolivia.com; r per person all-inclusive US$65), where ecofriendly *cabañas* have hot showers, and transportation from the main road is offered, as well as guided hikes through the impossible landscapes. This wonderfully wild slice of paradise is 4km off the main road (two hours on foot or 45 minutes from the end of the easily motorable section of the side road into the complex). In addition to more than 10km of **hiking trails** through the tropical forests,

you'll find heavenly natural pools to swim in, fascinating flora, including several unusual species of wild orchids, and some of Bolivia's most interesting bird-watching.

Las Cuevas
One hundred kilometers southwest of Santa Cruz and 20km east of Samaipata lies **Las Cuevas** (admission US$1). If you walk upstream on a clear path away from the road, you'll reach two lovely waterfalls that spill into eminently swimmable lagoons bordered by sandy beaches. Camping is also possible here for a small fee.

SAMAIPATA
pop 9700 / elevation 1650m
Samaipata has developed into one of the top gringo-trail spots over the last few years. This sleepy village in the foothills of the Cordillera Oriental is brimming with foreign-run, stylish hostels and restaurants. Visitors flock to see the pre-Inca site of El Fuerte, which – some might say – is solely responsible for the influx of foreigners who come in search of the ancient site's mystical energy. But it's not just

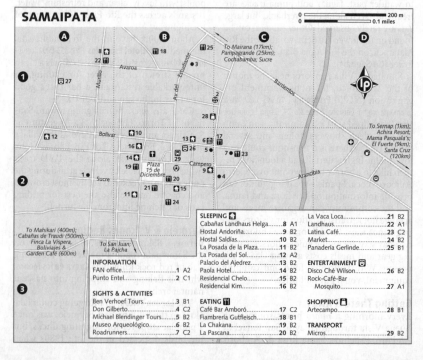

SAMAIPATA

0 _____ 200 m
0 _____ 0.1 miles

To Mairana (17km);
Pampagrande (25km);
Cochabamba; Sucre

To Sernap (1km);
Achira Resort;
Mama Pasquala's;
El Fuerte (9km);
Santa Cruz
(120km)

To Mahikari (400km);
Cabañas de Traudi (500m);
Finca La Víspera,
Boliviajes &
Garden Café (600m)

To San Juan;
La Pajcha

INFORMATION	
FAN office	1 A2
Punto Entel	2 C1

SIGHTS & ACTIVITIES	
Ben Verhoef Tours	3 B1
Don Gilberto	4 C2
Michael Blendinger Tours	5 B2
Museo Arqueológico	6 B2
Roadrunners	7 C2

SLEEPING	
Cabañas Landhaus Helga	8 A1
Hostal Andoriña	9 B2
Hostal Saldías	10 B2
La Posada de la Plaza	11 B2
La Posada del Sol	12 A2
Palacio del Ajedrez	13 B2
Paola Hotel	14 B2
Residencial Chelo	15 B2
Residencial Kim	16 B2

EATING	
Café Bar Amboró	17 C2
Fiambrería Gutfleisch	18 B1
La Chakana	19 B2
La Pascana	20 B2

La Vaca Loca	21 B2
Landhaus	22 A1
Latina Café	23 C2
Market	24 B2
Panadería Gerlinde	25 B1

ENTERTAINMENT	
Disco Ché Wilson	26 B2
Rock-Café-Bar Mosquito	27 A1

SHOPPING	
Artecampo	28 B1

TRANSPORT	
Micros	29 B2

foreigners who come up here; Samaipata is a popular weekend destination for *cruceños* too. The Quechua name, meaning 'Rest in the Highlands,' could hardly be more appropriate. If you're coming from the lowlands, it's also a good place to begin altitude acclimatization by degrees.

Samaipata is also the jumping-off point for forays to Parque Nacional Amboró (p307) and to the site of Ché Guevara's last stand outside Vallegrande (p317).

Information

There are no banks or ATMs in Samaipata. It's best to bring cash with you, even though some upmarket places might accept, or even cash, traveler's checks.

A new tourist office is projected to open in 2007–08 at the corner of the main plaza and Campero. In the meantime, you can check Samaipata's website (www.samaipata .info), and reliable tourist information is also available at Café Bar Amboró (p316) and the restaurant La Chakana (p316). Sernap has an office 1km outside of town on the road to Santa Cruz. The **FAN office** (Sucre & Murillo) can arrange trips to the community of La Yunga at the edge of the park.

Several telecom places near the plaza are working on getting the internet going (per hour US$2); try **Roadrunners** (☎ 944-6153/93; dustyroad99@hotmail.com). There are a couple of Punto Entel offices for phone calls. The post office only delivers mail; it can't accept outgoing post (and if it did, the mail would probably never be seen again).

Sights
EL FUERTE

The mystical site of El Fuerte exudes such pulling power that visitors from all over the world make their way to Samaipata just to climb the hill and see the remains of this pre-Inca site.

Designated in 1998 as a Unesco World Heritage site, **El Fuerte** (adult/child US$4/2; ☺ 9am-5pm) occupies a hilltop about 10km from the village with breathtaking views across the rugged transition zone between the Andes and lowlying areas further east. There are two observation towers allowing visitors to view the ruins from above. Allow at least two hours to fully explore the complex, and take sunscreen and a hat with you. There is a kiosk with food and water next to the ticket office.

The purpose of El Fuerte has long been debated, and there are several theories. Early conquerors assumed the site had been used for defense, hence its Spanish name, 'the fort,' though there is no actual fort on the site. In 1832 French naturalist Alcides d'Orbigny proclaimed that the pools and parallel canals had been used for washing gold. In 1936 German anthropologist Leo Pucher described it as an ancient temple to the serpent and the jaguar. Recently the place has gained a New Age following; some have claimed that it was a take-off and landing ramp for ancient spacecraft.

But the exact purpose of El Fuerte continues to mystify and feed imaginations. The site has been radiocarbon-dated at approximately 1500 BC. There are no standing buildings, but the remains of 500 dwellings have been discovered in the immediate vicinity and ongoing excavation reveals more every day. The main site, which is almost certainly of religious significance, is a 100m-long stone slab with a variety of sculpted features: seats, tables, a conference circle, troughs, tanks, conduits and *hornecinos* (niches), which are believed to have held idols. Zoomorphic designs on the slab include a raised relief of a puma and numerous serpents, which probably represented fertility. Most intriguing are the odd parallel grooves that appear to shoot off into the sky, inspiring alien and spaceshuttle theories.

About 300m down an obscure track behind the main ruin is **El Hueco**, a sinister hole in the ground that appears all the more menacing by the concealing vegetation and sloping ground around it. It's almost certainly natural, but three theories have emerged about how it might have been used: that it served as a water-storage cistern; that it functioned as an escape-proof prison; and that it was part of a subterranean communication system between the main ruin and its immediate surroundings. El Hueco has been partially explored, but the project was abandoned when excavators heard mysterious sounds emanating from the walls. Openings of suspected side passages are now shut tight.

Hitchhiking from Samaipata is easiest on weekends – especially Sunday – but the 20km round-trip walk also makes a fine day-long journey. Better yet, taxi up and walk back down. Follow the main highway back toward Santa Cruz for 3.5km and turn right at the sign pointing uphill. From here it's a scenic

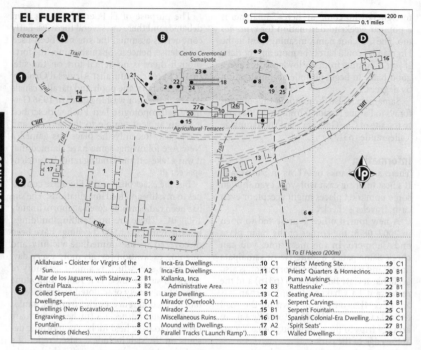

EL FUERTE

Akllahuasi - Cloister for Virgins of the		Inca-Era Dwellings...............................10 C1		Priests' Meeting Site............................19 C1
Sun...1 A2		Inca-Era Dwellings...............................11 C1		Priests' Quarters & Hornecinos........20 B1
Altar de los Jaguares, with Stairway...2 B1		Kallanka, Inca		Puma Markings....................................21 B1
Central Plaza..3 B2		Administrative Area........................12 B3		'Rattlesnake'...22 B1
Coiled Serpent.......................................4 B1		Large Dwellings...................................13 C2		Seating Area...23 B1
Dwellings...5 D1		Mirador (Overlook).............................14 A1		Serpent Carvings.................................24 B1
Dwellings (New Excavations)..............6 C2		Mirador 2...15 B1		Serpent Fountain................................25 C1
Engravings...7 C1		Miscellaneous Ruins...........................16 D1		Spanish Colonial-Era Dwelling.........26 C1
Fountain...8 C1		Mound with Dwellings........................17 A2		'Spirit Seats'...27 B1
Hornecinos (Niches).............................9 C1		Parallel Tracks ('Launch Ramp').......18 C1		Walled Dwellings................................28 C2

5km to the summit. Watch for condors, and in the morning and afternoon for the flocks of commuting parakeets that chatter overhead.

Taxis for the round-trip, including a one-hour stop (negotiate for more time) at the ruins, charge US$8 for up to four people from Samaipata.

MUSEO ARQUEOLÓGICO

Samaipata's small **archaeological museum** (Bolívar; admission US$0.65; 8:30am-12:30pm & 2:30-6:30pm) makes an interesting visit, but offers little explanation of El Fuerte. It does have a few Tiahuanaco artifacts and some local pottery. Admission to the ruins also covers the cost of the museum.

Tours

Several agencies organize trips to nearby attractions (US$10 to US$50 per person per day). Longer guided overnight trips on foot and horseback start around US$70 per person per day.

In addition to Amboró adventure tours, the recommended **Boliviaje** (/fax 944-6082; www .lavispera.org; Finca La Víspera) offers several exciting

hiking, horseback and 4WD trips into wonderfully remote places south of Samaipata.

Biologist **Michael Blendinger** (944-6227; www .discoveringbolivia.com; Bolívar s/n) is best for orchid, birding and full-moon tours in English and German. **Ben Verhoef Tours** (944-6365; www.ben verhoeftours.com; Estudiante s/n), run by Dutch couple Ben and Susanne, can organize a variety of tours around Samaipata, such as a six-hour 'condor hike'. It also offers a Ché Guevara tour.

Visit Olaf and Frank at German and English–speaking **Roadrunners** (944-6153/93; dustyroad99@hotmail.com; Bolívar) for self-guided hikes with GPS, and guided hikes to Amboró's waterfalls and cloud forests, and El Fuerte.

Spanish-speaking Samaipata native **Don Gilberto** (944-6050; Sucre 2) lived inside what is now the national park for many years and runs tours to his own simple encampment inside the park.

Sleeping

You're spoiled for choice when it comes to accommodations in Samaipata. From basic dorms to lush campsites, rustic hostels and organic farms, it's all here.

BUDGET

Hostal Saldías (☎ 944-6023; Bolívar s/n; r per person US$1.35, with bathroom US$2) There are some very basic sleeping choices in Samaipata; this is the funkiest acceptable cheapie.

Paola Hotel (☎ 944-6903; northwest cnr of plaza; r per person US$2, with bathroom & breakfast US$3.50) This is a basic, family-run place with clean, uneventful rooms and decent beds, plus a shared kitchen, laundry sinks, cheap meals, a sunny *mirador* (lookout) reading room and a terrace overlooking the plaza. Note that no alcohol is allowed in the rooms.

Mama Pasquala's (camping US$3.50, cabins US$5) Basic camping and simple cabins are available in this beautiful valley near some great swimming holes. It's 500m upstream from the river crossing en route to El Fuerte.

Achira Resort (☎ 352-2288; bolivia.resort@scbbs-bo.com; km 112; camping US$4, cabañas US$6; ☻) Bolivia's leap into European-style camping begins 8km east of Samaipata. This family-style complex has *cabañas*, campsites, baths, showers and washing sinks, as well as a social hall with a restaurant and games room.

Residencial Kim (☎ 944-6161; d US$6, with bathroom US$7.50) Near the northern end of the plaza, this is a family home with some cozy rooms, where yellow walls are topped with wooden beams and beds are covered with flowery bedspreads. There's a big shared kitchen where you can cook your own meals, and the rooms have TVs.

La Posada de la Plaza (☎ 944-6218; www.bolivianromance.net; Ruben Terrazas; d US$7) One of the two *posadas* (inns), this is the more central choice. The place is reminiscent of a mountain lodge, with incredibly creaky floorboards in the pleasant attic rooms, and wood-paneled walls in the dining area. Breakfasts are good and there's a relaxing, peaceful garden out the back.

MIDRANGE

Hostal Andoriña (☎ 944-6333; www.andorina-samaipata .blogspot.com; Campero s/n; dm US$4.50-6, s/d US$6/9, d with bathroom US$11-14) This is a new place run by a Dutch-Bolivian couple who are into rustic décor. The house and rooms are painted in earthy colors, the beds are comfy and the breakfasts (included in the price) big and healthy. There's a communal room downstairs, with a roaring fireplace in winter and a *mirador* on the top with great views of the valley, plus a rooftop Jacuzzi that'll give you

a special sense of luxury. One of the owners has a good photo gallery attached to the hostel that's worth checking out.

Cabañas Landhaus Helga (☎ 944-6033; www .samaipata-landhaus.com; Murillo; s/d US$5/8, with bathroom US$10/16, cabañas US$30-70; ☻) These tasteful *cabañas*, behind the Landhaus restaurant, have their own cooking and bathroom facilities. They accommodate up to seven people in three bedrooms, making it ideal for families. Breakfast costs an additional US$1 to US$2, and Finnish saunas are available with two hours' notice (US$20 for up to five people).

Cabañas de Traudi (☎ 944-6094; www.traudi.com; r per person US$5, s/d with bathroom US$10/15, cabañas US$30-70; ☻) Across from the Finca La Víspera retreat, this amenable Austrian-run spread has ample manicured grounds and horses for rent. It's set up as a family-oriented recreation center with ping-pong, tennis and equipment for other activities. The swimming pool is open to nonguests for US$2 per person.

Finca La Víspera (☎ /fax 944-6082; www.lavispera. org; camping with/without own tent US$4/5, cabins per person US$10-15) This relaxing organic farm and retreat run by a Dutch couple is a lovely place on the 'outskirts' of Samaipata. The owners rent horses (US$7 per hour or US$25 a day) and organize adventurous trips throughout the region. The attractive rooms with communal kitchens, and four self-contained guesthouses (for two to 12 people), are all warm and clean and enjoy commanding views across the valley. Camping includes hot showers and kitchen facilities. Bring a flashlight, as there's no street lighting between the village and the guesthouse, an easy 15-minute walk southwest of the plaza.

La Posada del Sol (☎ 944-6218; Zona Barrio Nuevo; d/tr US$10/12) A short walk off the square, this place has great views of the valley and even a glimpse of El Fuerte from its garden. The rooms are new, though characterless, and you can get triples with kitchenettes and self-catering *cabañas*.

Palacio del Ajedrez (☎ 944-6196; paulin-chess@cotas .com.bo; Bolívar s/n; s/d with bathroom US$10/15; ☻) An interesting place next to the archaeological museum, this hotel has a chess club (*ajedrez* means 'chess' in Spanish) that has created Bolivia's national chess champions. The rooms are reminiscent of student halls, with modern furniture in oranges and blues, and there's a small swimming pool under construction for guests and chess players to enjoy.

Eating

RESTAURANTS

La Vaca Loca (south side of plaza; snacks US$0.60-3.20) This is where Samaipatans go for ice cream, devoured either on the small porch overlooking the square or in the back garden. The food is not as great as the ice creams, but it's still a popular hangout for lunch and dinner.

La Chakana (☎ 944-6207; chakanabol@yahoo.com; west side of plaza; mains US$1.25-2.50) This is Samaipata's best and friendliest eatery, where you can get breakfast, sandwiches, vegetarian meals, excellent pizza, homemade sweets, cocktails and European specialties.

Garden Café (☎/fax 944-6082; Finca La Víspera; meals US$1.50-3) You can gaze at La Víspera's organic garden from its sunny, alfresco café and see kitchen staff running up and down to pick your salad fresh from the ground. There are good breakfasts and lunches, and special dietary needs are catered for on request.

Landhaus (☎ 944-6257; mains US$2-4; ☽ dinner Thu-Sun) If you are hankering for a European gourmet-style meal, this is the place to go. The food is superb, and it has veggie options and a salad bar. It's at the northern end of town.

Latina Café (☎ 944-6153; Bolívar 3; mains US$2.50-3; ☽ 6-10pm Mon-Fri, lunch & dinner Sat & Sun) One of Samaipata's most popular bar-restaurants, Latina serves pretty much anything your heart desires: juicy steaks, saucy pastas, vegetarian delights and gorgeous brownies. The lighting is intimate and the sunsets beautiful.

QUICK EATS

Panadería Gerlinde (☎ 944-6175; Estudiante; ☽ 8am-10pm) This place rules when it comes to baked goods, cheese, yogurt, muesli, organic produce, meats, healthy snacks and herbal remedies. It's run by a German woman who swears it's all *zehr gut!* She also has a stall at the market on Saturday and Sunday.

Café Bar Amboró (☎ 944-6220; Bolívar s/n; snacks US$1) Come here for coffee, snacks, ice cream and internet (US$2 an hour).

La Pascana (southeast cnr of plaza; almuerzos US$1) This is the local favorite for cheap and filling *almuerzos* (set lunches).

Fiambrería Gutfleisch (snacks US$1; ☽ 7am-6pm Mon-Fri) You'll find some of Bolivia's best cheese, salami and cold cuts at this factory during the week, and at the market (8am to 4pm) on weekends.

Mahikari (☽ 2-6pm Tue-Sun) Along the road to La Víspera, this Japanese religious sect sells organic vegetables fertilized with divine light. For under US$1 you can be blessed with the 'energy' of the Mahikari Luz Divina – go on, don't be shy.

Entertainment

A slice of Santa Cruz teenage nightlife is transported to Samaipata each weekend and revived at the popular **Disco Ché Wilson** (Bolívar). Anyone over 21 will probably prefer the Saturday disco at the Landhaus, which cranks up as the restaurant winds down, normally around 10pm.

Rock-Café-Bar Mosquito (☎ 944-6232; ☽ 7pm-late Tue-Sat) In the northwestern part of town, this is the most happening watering hole, with a full bar and a hell-for-leather theme.

Shopping

Saturday and Sunday are market days. You'll find locally produced ceramics at the Landhaus. Opposite the museum, **Artecampo** (☽ 8am-1pm) sells the work of women from around Santa Cruz department. Vendors show up on the plaza on weekends with homemade wine and food.

Getting There & Around

Four-passenger **Expreso Samaipata Taxis** (☎ in Santa Cruz 333-5067) leave Santa Cruz for Samaipata (per person US$3.50, 2½ hours) when full from the corner of Chávez Ortíz and Solis de Olguin, two blocks south of the old bus terminal. Alternatively, a *micro* (US$2, three hours) departs from Av Grigotá in the third *anillo* at 4pm daily.

From Samaipata, **shared taxis** (☎ 944-6133, 944-6016) depart for Santa Cruz from the gas station on the highway. *Micros* leave from near the plaza daily around 4:30am and between noon and 5pm on Sunday. You can also get *trufis* returning in the afternoon.

Finding a lift west to Mairana, Comarapa, Siberia, Vallegrande or Cochabamba is a bit trickier, but if you wait on the main highway, something will eventually come along. For a private taxi ring ☎ 944-6050.

AROUND SAMAIPATA

La Pajcha

A series of three beautiful waterfalls on a turbid mountain river, La Pajcha has a sandy beach for swimming and some inviting campsites. It's 42km (one to two hours by car) south of

Samaipata, toward San Juan, then 7km on foot off the main road. The site is privately owned and visitors are charged US$1 to visit and swim here. You'll occasionally find transportation from Samaipata, but unless you have a guaranteed ride back, take camping gear and plenty of food, or join a tour from Samaipata (p314).

Pampagrande

An especially nice spot is Pampagrande, which is surrounded by a desertlike landscape of cactus and thorny scrubland. There are no hotels, but the Dominican friar **Hermano Andres** (☎ 911-3155, in Samaipata 944-6011) operates a basic bunkhouse with cooking facilities. He also guides informal and highly worthwhile **tours** into the surrounding hills and imparts his extensive knowledge of the local flora and fauna (especially birds and snakes). The only charge for these tours is a donation to the church so, if you've enjoyed yourself, please don't skimp. For meals there's only the small eatery near the market, three blocks north of the plaza.

Micros to Pampagrande leave from Santa Cruz late in the afternoon; they leave Pampagrande for the return journey at 7am daily.

VALLEGRANDE

pop 16,800 / elevation 2100m

Vallegrande's claim to fame is that it was the spot where Ché Guevara's emaciated corpse was exhibited before its burial. Thanks to this fame, it is now the northern point of the developing 815km **Ché Trail** community-based tourism project, with Camiri (p292) anchoring the southern end. The route traces Ché's final movements on foot, mule, bicycle and boat, with basic, rustic accommodations at encampments and with local families, though most of it is still in development. For an update on the project's progress, contact America Tours in La Paz (p80).

After Ché Guevara was executed in La Higuera, south of Vallegrande, his body was brought to the now-dilapidated hospital laundry here, where graffiti pays homage to this controversial figure (see the boxed text p318). Visit the **Ché museum** (admission free), which features objects and artifacts that belonged to Ché's guerrilla group.

Most visitors to the town are passing through on a Ché pilgrimage, but Vallegrande is also a nice spot to relax and walk in the hills. It's a quiet little town set in the Andean foothills and enjoys a lovely temperate climate.

Information

Vallegrande's **alcaldía** (town hall; ☎ 942-2149) is keen to promote tourism and is happy to answer questions. For cultural or historical information, see the Casa de la Cultura, which has a small archaeological museum and a Ché Guevara room with a video in Spanish. For information on local rock paintings, fossils and archaeological sites, seek out Don Lalo Carrasco, president of the Grupo Yungauri; try first at Librería Acuarela.

Festivals & Events

The daily market begins in the plaza about 5am and a bigger weekly *fería* (market) is held every Sunday. Nearly every week, there's some sort of small festival at the sports ground featuring traditional music and dancing. Around February 23 the town marks its anniversary with various sporting and cultural events. Since the bodies of Ché and several of his comrades were recovered from the airport in 1997, the town has celebrated an annual **Ché Guevara festival** in October, featuring folk art and cultural activities.

Sleeping & Eating

Vallegrande has a growing number of hostelries, so you're unlikely to be without a bed.

Hostal Juanita (☎ 942-2231; hostaljuanita@cotas .net; Manuel María Caballero 123; r per person with bathroom US$5) This is a clean, family-run hotel just two blocks from the main square.

Hotel El Marques (☎ 942-2336; Pedro Montaño; r per person incl bathroom US$5) A new, clean and friendly place.

Café Galeria de Arte Santa Clara (cnr Plaza 26 de Enero & Florida; snacks US$0.50-1) Come here for good coffee and snacks.

El Mirador (☎ 942-2341; El Pichacu near La Cruz; mains US$3) Literally the top spot in town, with excellent views, and good fish and meat dishes, this restaurant is run by the German man who took the famous photo of dead Ché.

All charging around US$4 per person for accommodations are **Alojamiento Teresita** (☎ 924-2151; Escalante/Mendoza 107), **Hotel Copacabana** (☎ 942-2014; Escalante/Mendoza 100) and **Residencial Vallegrande** (☎ 942-2281; Santa Cruz 125).

Getting There & Away

From the terminal in Santa Cruz, buses leave for Vallegrande (US$5, six hours) from around 9am to 2pm. There may also be a later bus, but don't count on it. From Samaipata,

HASTA SIEMPRE, COMANDANTE

As you travel around Bolivia, the iconic image of Ché – the revolutionary with a popularity status reached only by rock stars, and remembered in Cuban songs like *Hasta Siempre Comandante* (Forever with You, Commander) – will be staring at you from various walls, paintings, posters and carvings. Bolivia is where Ché went to his death and where his image is being fervently resurrected.

Ernesto 'Ché' Guevara de la Serna was born on June 14, 1928 in Rosario, Argentina, to a wealthy middle-class family. He qualified as a doctor at the University of Buenos Aires, and having gone on the famous motorcycle trip around Latin America that fired up his social consciousness, he decided to dedicate his life to the armed struggle against poverty and oppression.

Ché's first post was in Guatemala, where in 1954 he held a minor position in Jacobo Arbenz' communist government. The following year he fled to Mexico, after the CIA-aided overthrow of Arbenz, and had his first, fateful meeting with Fidel Castro. Guevara and Castro struck up a companionship and dedicated themselves to the overthrowing of Fulgencio Batista's government in Cuba. After much bloodshed on both sides, Castro became Cuba's new leader on January 2, 1959, and Ché held many important positions in the government.

Having accomplished what he saw necessary in Cuba, the untiring Guevara decided to take his struggle to Africa in 1965. Before he left, Castro required him to sign a letter of resignation and, by making Guevara's resignation public, indicated that Ché's African activities were not sanctioned by the Cuban government. Ché returned to Latin America and set up a base in Bolivia in 1966 at the farm Ñancahuazú, 250km southwest of Santa Cruz. He was hoping to convince the *campesinos* (subsistence farmers) that they were oppressed, and to inspire them to social rebellion, but was met only with suspicion. Not even the local communist party would take up his cause.

Suffering from chronic asthma, arthritis and malnutrition, Guevara struggled to keep his belief in the cause. When he was captured on October 8, 1967, near La Higuera by the CIA-trained troops of Bolivian military dictator René Barrientos Ortuño, he was an emaciated, unrecognizable version of the handsome, cigar-puffing, beret-wearing young man depicted in countless photographs. He was taken to a schoolroom in La Higuera and, just after noon the next day, executed by the Bolivian army. Ché's body was flown to Vallegrande, where it was displayed until the following day in the hospital laundry room. Local women noted an uncanny resemblance to the Catholic Christ and took locks of his hair as mementos. His hands, cut off to prevent fingerprint identification, were smuggled to Cuba by a Bolivian journalist and remain there in an undisclosed location.

Having been buried in an unmarked grave for nearly 30 years, in 1997 one of the soldiers who carried out the burial revealed that the grave was beneath Vallegrande's airstrip. The Bolivian and Cuban governments called for exhumation, and Ché was officially reburied in Santa Clara de Cuba on October 17, 1997.

The Motorcycle Diaries is an excellent account of Ché's extraordinary trip around Latin America, and the basis for the 2005 film of the same name. *Bolivian Diary* was written by Ché during the final months of his life.

an unreliable Vallegrande bus leaves around 2pm and there's sometimes another one at 5pm. If you're hitchhiking, get off at Mataral, 55km north of Vallegrande, and wait there (praying) for something headed south. From Cochabamba (US$4, 11 hours), buses leave several times weekly in the morning. Buses return to Cochabamba from near the market several times a week; make sure you get your ticket in advance, as there have been cases of overbooking and long waits to get out of town.

PUCARÁ & LA HIGUERA

To reach La Higuera, the site of Ché Guevara's last struggle and execution, catch a taxi or *camión* from Vallegrande to Pucará. *Camiones* leave Vallegrande around 8am a couple of blocks uphill from the market. For a taxi, ask around on Pedro Montano, near the school.

On the plaza in Pucará, you can experience Bolivian hospitality at the local bar-*tienda* (small shop), run by a grizzled *campesino* and his daughter, who serve meals in a basic *comedor* (dining hall). They're both very kind, and if you buy the man a couple of beers, he'll probably share a few Ché tales or suggest people who rent horses to go to La Higuera. They also have a room to rent on the roof at the back of the house, with marvelous views over the mountains and the upper Río Grande.

From Pucará, the 15km trip to La Higuera requires a 4WD (try a car-rental agency in Santa Cruz, p305), seven or eight hours on foot, five hours on horseback or a fortuitous hitch or taxi ride. Along the route, signposts point out Ché-related sites of historic interest.

Approaching La Higuera, you'll see the long *barranca* (cliff) where Ché was captured. A bust of Ché lords over the dusty main plaza, witnessing the growing (though still small) attempts to attract tourists here. The **Museo Historico del Ché** (Historical Museum of Ché; admission US$1; ☯ Thu & Sun) is next to the schoolroom where Ché was taken after his capture, and displays photographs, newspaper cuttings and various Ché memorabilia (such as the machete he used to get around the jungle). There's also a **mausoleum** with the tombstones of Ché and his revolutionary comrades, which you can visit if you get the key from the caretaker – ask for his whereabouts in the village. The schoolroom – now the local clinic – where Ché was kept before being executed is the yellow building just off the plaza, with a solar panel on the roof.

Most travelers come by horse or foot, so you'll probably have to stay the night in La Higuera, since the road back is long and painful. Built especially for Ché tourists, **La Posada del Telegrafista** (losnomadas@caramail.com; camping US$0.50, r per person US$6.20) offers straw beds, lunch (US$2) and romantic, candlelit dinners (because there's no electricity; US$2.50). You can also stay in the school for US$1 per person, but note that it's very basic and there's no shower.

There is a small bar-shop where you can buy a beer and chat with locals about historical events. Also seek out the woman who served Ché his last lunch – she hangs out on the town square and is happy to share her memories.

EASTERN LOWLANDS

The Bolivian Oriente is where the hostile, thorny Chaco scrubland and the low, tropical savannas of the Amazon Basin have a stand-off, watched by the foothills of the Cordillera Oriental to the west, the Llanos de Guarayos to the north and the international boundaries

of Paraguay and Brazil to the south and east. The two vastly different landscapes stand together, never making peace.

The flat landscapes of the lowlands are broken and divided by long, low ridges and odd monolithic mountains. Much of the territory lies soaking under vast marshes such as the Bañados del Izozog (part of the Parque Nacional Kaa-Iya del Gran Chaco) and the magnificent Pantanal on the Brazilian frontier. This is the land the Death Train runs through, past tranquil border towns; it's also the area of Jesuit mission towns, with their wide-roofed churches and fascinating history.

History

The captivating story of the Jesuit missions and their time in Latin America is for many a sad tale of how history could have been better on this vast continent.

In the days when eastern Bolivia was still unsurveyed and largely unorganized, the Jesuits established an autonomous religious state in Paraguay. From there they moved outwards, founding missions and venturing into territories previously unexplored by other Europeans. The northern parts of this area were inhabited by indigenous tribes, such as the Chiquitanos, Chiriguanos, Moxos and Guaranís, whose descendants still inhabit the region.

The missions were organized as an experiment in communal living between the Jesuits and the original indigenous inhabitants. The Jesuits established what they considered an ideal community hierarchy: each population unit, known as a *reducción*, was headed by two or three Jesuit priests, and a self-directed military unit was attached to each of these *reducciónes*. For a time the Jesuit armies were the strongest and best trained on the continent. This makeshift military force served as a shield for the area from both the Portuguese in Brazil and the Spanish to the west, creating what was in effect an autonomous theocracy.

Politically, the *reducciónes* were under the nominal control of the *audiencia* (judicial district) of Chacras, and ecclesiastically under the bishop of Santa Cruz, though the relative isolation of the settlements meant that the Jesuits were basically in control. Internally, the settlements were jointly administered by a few priests and a council of eight indigenous people representing specific tribes who met daily to monitor community progress. This was a rare example of colonial-era power sharing, and though the indigenous population was free to choose whether it lived within the missionary communities, a less altruistic motive for cooperation was that those who chose not to live in the missions faced the harsh *encomienda* system (the feudal land-owning system implemented by Spanish colonialists) or, worse still, outright slavery elsewhere.

The Jesuit settlements reached their apex under the untiring Swiss priest Father Martin Schmidt, who not only built the missions at San Javier, Concepción and San Rafael de Velasco, but also designed many of the altars, created the musical instruments, acted as the chief composer for the *reducciónes* and published a Spanish–Chiquitano dictionary. He was later expelled from the region and died in Europe in 1772.

Ironically, the Jesuits' growing strength proved their eventual undoing. By the mid-1700s, political strife in Europe had escalated into a power struggle between the Church and the governments of France, Spain and Portugal. When the Spanish in South America fully realized the extent of Jesuit influence and all the wealth being produced in the wilderness, they decided the Jesuits had usurped too much power from the state. Portuguese slave traders encroached westward, while Spanish imperial troops marched eastward to fortify the vague eastern border of Alto Perú. Caught in the cross fire, the lucrative missions proved easy pickings for the Spanish. In 1767, swept up in a whirlwind of political babble and religious dogma, the missions were disbanded, and King Carlos III signed the Order of Expulsion, which evicted the Jesuits from the continent.

In the wake of the Jesuit departure, the carefully managed balance between Europeans and local peoples shifted dramatically. The Spanish overlords, after realizing their newly acquired lands were sources of neither unlimited mineral wealth nor slave labor for the Potosí mines, essentially abandoned the settlements, leaving them to decline. Without the Jesuits' adeptness at integrating the two cultures, the indigenous people soon left, and the towns became little more than agricultural backwaters. Their amazing churches stand as mute testimony to the incredible experiment that ended so abruptly.

JESUIT MISSIONS CIRCUIT

The seven-town region of Las Misiones Jesuíticas hides some of Bolivia's richest cultural and historic accomplishments. To travel through the entire circuit takes five or six days, but for those with an interest in architecture or history, it's one of Bolivia's most rewarding excursions.

Forgotten by the world for more than two centuries, the region and its history captivated the world's imagination when the 1986 Palm d'Or winner *The Mission* spectacularly replayed the last days of the Jesuit priests in the region (with Robert de Niro at the helm). The growing interest in the unique synthesis of Jesuit and native Chiquitano culture in the South American interior resulted in Unesco declaring the region a World Heritage site in 1991. Thanks to 25 years of painstaking restoration work, directed by the late architect Hans Roth, the centuries-old mission churches have been restored to their original splendor.

The circuit can be traversed either clockwise or counterclockwise: that is, going by bus from Santa Cruz around the circuit to San José de Chiquitos (p324), or by train to San José de Chiquitos and then between the missions by bus or by hitchhiking.

TOURS
See Tours under Santa Cruz (p299) for a list of agencies that organize trips through the Jesuit missions circuit.

San Ramón
pop 5700

Dusty San Ramón serves as a crossroad between Santa Cruz, Trinidad, the missions and Brazil. There is no church here, and most people simply pass through. It may be the site of a gold mine, but anything taken out of the ground is quickly transported somewhere else.

Hotel Manguarí (☎ 965-6011; r per person US$5), two blocks from the plaza on the Trinidad road, has basic facilities. For meals, wander the few meters to the recommended **Boliche de Arturo** (meals US$1-2).

Buses to Trinidad pass between 10pm and midnight, as do those headed east to San Ignacio de Velasco. The first bus leaves for Santa Cruz at 7am, but *camiones* also run relatively frequently.

San Javier
pop 11,300

The first (or last, depending on which way you travel) settlement on the circuit, San Javier, founded in 1691, is the oldest mission town

THE JESUITS & THE TRANSFORMATION OF LOWLAND CULTURE

The Jesuit missionaries were possibly the only group of colonial-era settlers who practiced the integration of their own culture with that of the native people. Aside from economic and religious ventures, the Jesuits promoted cultural and educational expansion, cautiously avoiding the all-too-typical 'all-or-nothing' approach. They sought to incorporate the best of both cultures, and to an astonishing extent succeeded.

The native Chiquitano people, traditionally nomadic hunters and gatherers, were instructed in animal husbandry and European agricultural techniques, and successfully integrated into a predominantly agricultural economy; they, in turn, showed the Europeans how to adapt to the demanding tropical environment. Over the years a trade network was established between these communities and the Aymará and Quechua villages in the Altiplano. Beeswax, cotton, honey and indigenous textiles were exchanged for imported goods and raw silver mined in the highlands.

The indigenous people were also exposed to and inculcated with Christianity. Although subtle at first, the cumulative effect was that the new religion eventually obliterated any trace of their original tenets. To this day almost nothing is known of the beliefs and practices of these tribes prior to the arrival of the Jesuits.

With Jesuit training, the indigenous peoples became accomplished artisans, handcrafting the renowned harps and violins that still play a prominent role in traditional Paraguayan music. They also became formidable artists; at the height of this revolutionary cultural transition, the inhabitants of the missions were performing concerts, dances and plays that rivaled the best in Europe, playing sophisticated Italian Renaissance madrigals, and baroque masques and operas.

For those interested in learning more about this fascinating culture, two books, both in Spanish, are highly recommended: *Misiones Jesuíticas*, by Jaime Cisneros, and the pre-eminent *Las Misiones Jesuíticas de Chiquitos*, edited by Pedro Querejazu.

in the region. It's also a favorite holiday destination for wealthy *cruceño* families. Swiss priest Martin Schmidt arrived in 1730 and founded the region's first music school and a workshop to produce violins, harps and harpsichords. He also designed the present church, which was constructed between 1749 and 1752. It sits on a forested ridge with a great view over the surrounding low hills. Restoration work was completed in 1992 to beautiful effect and the newly restored building appears pleasantly old.

San Javier has some inviting **hot springs** (US$6.50 via moto-taxi) 14km northwest of town. A further 6km along is a natural pool and waterfall, **Los Tumbos de Suruquizo.**

SLEEPING & EATING

Ame Tauna (☎ 963-5018; Plaza 24 de Septiembre; r per person US$5.50) Right on the plaza, Ame Tauna means 'Welcome Friend' in Guaraní. The rooms are comfortable and cool, but bathrooms are shared.

Gran Hotel El Reposo del Guerrero (Warrior's Rest; ☎ 963-5022, in Santa Cruz 332-7830; Santa Cruz; r per person with bathroom & breakfast US$12) A good, central option a couple of blocks from the plaza,

the Reposo del Guerrero has pleasant, clean rooms with plenty of amenities, plus a good restaurant.

Cabañas Totaitú (☎ 963-5063; 4/6/8 people weekdays US$60/80/100, weekends US$80/100/120; ⚑) This four-star dairy farm, 4km northwest of town, is probably the mission circuit's loveliest place to stay, with a pool, golf course and tennis courts. You can go on lovely walks or rent horses and mountain bikes to explore the area.

El Turista (☎ 963-5063; San Javier; mains US$2-3) This place serves simple but good Bolivian food, mostly to mission-bound tour groups.

El Ganadero (San Javier; mains US$2-4) The tender, juicy scrumptious steaks here come highly recommended.

GETTING THERE & AWAY

All Santa Cruz–San Ignacio de Velasco buses pass through San Javier, 68km west of Concepción (US$1.50, 1½ hours) and 229km from Santa Cruz (US$4, five hours).

Concepción

pop 14,500

Sleepy Concepción is a dusty village with a friendly, quiet atmosphere in the midst of an agricultural and cattle-ranching area. It stands 182km west of San Ignacio de Velasco and is the center for all the mission restoration projects. The elaborately restored 1709 **Catedral de Concepción** (admission free; ☺ 7am-8pm), sitting on the east of the plaza, has an overhanging roof supported by 121 huge tree-trunk columns and a similar bell tower. It is decorated with golden baroque designs depicting flowers, angels and the Holy Virgin. The décor is unfortunately quite kitsch, though it gives some idea of the former opulence of the village.

Architectural aficionados should visit the **restoration workshops** (☺ 10:30am-3:30pm) behind the mission, where many of the fine replicas and restored artworks are crafted. The **Museo Misional** (south side of plaza; admission US$1; ☺ 8:30am-noon & 2:30-6:30pm Tue-Sat, 10am-12:30pm Sun), in the old Cabildo building, shows the progress of restoring the various churches in the area and sells interesting wood carvings made by the locals.

SLEEPING & EATING
Hotel Sede Ganaderos (☎ 964-3055; Capobianco; r per person with bathroom US$5) A block west of the plaza, this hotel is good value and has shaded hammocks in the courtyard.

Gran Hotel Concepción (☎ 964-3031; west side of plaza; s/d with bathroom US$28/43; ☒) The most upscale place to lay your head is this charming, three-star hotel with a pool, a quiet patio with a lush, pretty garden, and intricately carved wooden pillars.

El Buen Gusto (☎ 964-3117; south side of plaza; mains US$1.50-3) Great meat and massive *almuerzos* are served here, all enjoyed on the leafy, quiet patio.

Club Social Ñuflo de Chavez (west side of plaza; set menu US$2) This place delivers set meals, live music on Friday nights and bats in the rafters.

GETTING THERE & AWAY
All Santa Cruz–San Ignacio de Velasco buses (US$6, seven hours) pass through Concepción, stopping on the main road 1km from the plaza (only buses destined for Concepción actually enter the center). From Trinidad, take a Santa Cruz bus and get off at San Ramón, where you can pick up a bus to Concepción and other points east. *Micros* leave for San Javier (US$1.50, 1½ hours) and Santa Cruz (US$5, six hours) daily at 7:30am, 2pm and 6pm. Otherwise, wait near the gas station and flag down whatever may be passing (usually a *camión*).

San Ignacio de Velasco
pop 41,400

The first mission church at San Ignacio de Velasco, founded in 1748, was once the largest and most elaborate of all the mission churches. It was demolished in the 1950s and replaced by a modern abomination. Realizing they'd made a hash of it, the architects razed the replacement and designed a reasonable facsimile of the original structure. The new version is completed, and there is a beautiful altar and wooden pillars from the original church.

The village has a large indigenous population and remains the 'capital' and commercial center of the Jesuit missions. Along with San Javier, it has adopted Brazilian-influenced agribusiness, commercialization and development.

SIGHTS & ACTIVITIES
Several attractive, large **wooden crosses** (a trademark of Jesuit mission towns and villages) stand at intersections just off the plaza. Check out the wooden pillars in front of the **Casa Miguel Areijer** on the plaza; one pillar is beautifully carved with the image of a group of Bolivian musicians.

Attached to the Casa de la Cultura is a small **museum** (main plaza; admission US$1), which is noteworthy for its collection of musty, centuries-old musical instruments.

Only 700m from the church is the imposing **Laguna Guapomó**, where you can swim or rent a boat and putter around.

FESTIVALS & EVENTS
There's a big party celebrating the **election of Miss Litoral** during the last weekend in March. San Ignacio fetes its patron saint every July 31. Every summer, the Chiquitania hosts the **International Festival of Baroque Music** (see p300), which runs for several weeks and centers on San Ignacio de Velasco.

SLEEPING
Because San Ignacio de Velasco is the commercial heart of the mission district, there's a good choice of accommodations.

Plaza Hotel (☎ 962-2035; east side of plaza; r per person US$3, with bathroom US$6) This hotel has spotless rooms with fans, concentrated around a quiet patio.

Casa Suiza (7 blocks west of plaza; r per person with meals US$8.50) The helpful proprietor here speaks German and Spanish, has a wonderful library and can organize horseback riding, fishing trips and visits to surrounding haciendas.

Apart-Hotel San Ignacio (☎ 962-2157; 24 de Septiembre & Cochabamba; d with bathroom & breakfast US$17; ⏢ ⏢) The nicest place in town, this hotel has elegant and stylish rooms, a small pool and a relaxing garden.

Hotel Misión (☎ 962-2035; www.hotel-lamision.com; east side of plaza; s/d US$45/55; ⏢) For a bit of luxury, neocolonial style, try this place with stylish rooms, a little pool and opulent suites. There's also a good, upmarket restaurant serving an eclectic choice of dishes.

EATING
Unfortunately, eating options are quite poor here, and on Sunday everything is closed. All of the following are on the plaza.

Snack Marcelito (south side of plaza; mains US$1-3) This spot is good for *salteñas* (filled pastry shells) and burgers, plus fresh fruit juices and coffee.

Restaurant Acuario (west side of plaza; mains US$2-3) A great place for tasty Greek barbecues while you watch the plaza life.

Pizzería Pauline (south side of plaza; mains US$3-4) If you don't like pizza, try the meaty mains on offer here.

You'll also find decent meals at the market, one block west and three blocks south of the plaza.

GETTING THERE & AWAY
Bus travelers will want to cover their luggage to prevent it from arriving with a thick coating of red dust. Several Santa Cruz–based *flotas* (long-distance bus companies) serve San Ignacio de Velasco (US$5 to US$6, 11 hours) via San Javier, Concepción and Santa Rosa de la Roca. Some buses continue from San Ignacio to San Miguel (US$1.50, one hour). Most buses and *micros* leave San Ignacio from near the market.

Coming from Trinidad, take a Santa Cruz bus and get off at San Ramón (usually in the middle of the night); from there you can hitch or wait for an eastbound bus to San Ignacio.

In the dry season, several Santa Cruz bus companies operate services between the mission towns. A couple of Brazilian companies leave San Ignacio daily from early to mid-morning for San Matías, on the Brazilian border, where you'll find connections to the Brazilian towns of Cáceres and Cuiabá. The Flota Trans-Bolivia *micro* departs daily to San Miguel (US$1, 30 minutes), San Rafael (US$1, one hour) and Santa Ana around 8am.

San Miguel de Velasco
pop 10,300

Sleepy San Miguel hides in the scrub, 38km from San Ignacio. Its **church** was founded in 1721 and is, according to the late Hans Roth, the most accurately restored of all the Bolivian Jesuit missions. Its spiral pillars, carved wooden altar with a flying San Miguel, extravagant golden pulpit, religious artwork, toylike bell tower and elaborately painted façade are simply superb.

Although not designed by Martin Schmidt, the church does reflect his influence and is generally considered the most beautiful of Bolivia's Jesuit missions. During the restoration (1978–84), Hans Roth and his colleagues set up workshops and trained local artisans, probably much as the Jesuits did two centuries earlier. The restoration artisans remained and now work in cooperatives making furniture and carvings, such as small, carved-cedar chests painted in pastels.

The best time to photograph the church is in the morning light. The nightly mass at 7pm is a good time to visit.

SLEEPING & EATING
Alojamiento Pascana (☎ 962-4220; Plaza Principal; r per person US$3) On the plaza, this place has basic and clean rooms, and an attached restaurant that serves cold drinks and simple meals (mains US$1 to US$3).

Alojamiento Pardo (☎ 962-4209; Sucre; r per person US$3) Just off the plaza, this is another simple but sparkling option.

If you'd prefer to camp, speak with the nuns at the church, who can direct you to a suitable site.

GETTING THERE & AWAY
A *micro* leaves daily at 8:30am for San Ignacio de Velasco and returns, then leaves at about 10am for San Rafael. Next it travels back through San Miguel at around noon before returning to San Ignacio. It's also easy to get to San Ignacio with the *camionetas* (pickup trucks) that buzz around town honking for passengers in the early morning and after lunch.

Santa Ana de Velasco
The mission at this tiny Chiquitano village, 24km north of San Rafael de Velasco, was established in 1755. The **church**, with its earthen floor and palm-frond roof, is more rustic than the others and recalls the first churches

constructed by the Jesuit missionaries upon their arrival. In fact the building itself is post-Jesuit, but the interior contains exquisite religious carvings and paintings.

Given its age, the original structure was in remarkable condition and the church has been recently restored. During renovations a diatonic harp, more than 1.5m tall, was found; it's displayed in the church and is a lovely complement to the local children's music practice.

You shouldn't have problems finding transportation from either San Ignacio or San Rafael. Most days, *micros* run between San Ignacio and San Rafael via Santa Ana. Because most traffic now uses this route, hitchhiking is also a possibility.

San Rafael de Velasco
pop 5000

San Rafael de Velasco, 132km north of San José de Chiquitos, was founded in 1696. Its **church** was constructed between 1740 and 1748, the first of the mission churches to be completed in Bolivia. In the 1970s and 1980s, the building was restored, along with the churches in Concepción and San José de Chiquitos.

The interior is particularly beautiful, and the original paintings and wood work remain intact. The pulpit is covered with a layer of lustrous mica, the ceiling is made of reeds and the spiral pillars were carved from *cuchi* (ironwood) logs. It's the only mission church to retain the original style, with cane sheathing. Most interesting are the lovely music-theme paintings in praise of God along the entrance wall, which include depictions of a harp, flute, bassoon, horn and maracas.

At the corner of the main road and the street running south from the church, the unsigned **Alojamiento San Rafael** (r per person US$3) has basic rooms, good enough for a night's stay. On the plaza, **Alojamiento La Pascana** (r per person US$3) has basic rooms with shared bathrooms.

The best place to wait for rides south to San José de Chiquitos (five to six hours) or north to Santa Ana, San Miguel or San Ignacio is on the main road in front of Alojamiento San Rafael. In the morning, buses run in both directions. To reach Santa Ana, use the right fork north of town.

San José de Chiquitos
pop 16,600

An atmospheric and beautiful place, San José de Chiquitos has the appeal of an old Western film set. The frontier town, complete with dusty streets straight out of *High Noon* and footpaths shaded by pillar-supported roofs, is flanked on the south by a low escarpment and on the north by flat, soggy forest.

This most accessible Jesuit mission town was named after the indigenous Chiquitano inhabitants of the area. Santa Cruz city started 4km to the west of here, but moved to its present location soon after its founding in 1561. The Jesuits arrived sometime in the mid-1740s, and began construction of the magnificent town church in 1750.

Cattle ranching is popular and after Evo Morales' nationalization of natural resources, it remains to be seen what will happen with the oil-exploration business, a growing concern here.

INFORMATION
The bank on the plaza may change cash US dollars if it has sufficient bolivianos on hand. Most businesses will accept cash dollars for purchases and a few will change small amounts for noncustomers. Check around the plaza for telecom and internet services.

SIGHTS & ACTIVITIES
Jesuit Mission Church
San José has one of the most unique and beautiful stone Jesuit mission churches, which merits a visit even if you miss all the others. Although the main altar is nearly identical to those in other nearby missions and has vague similarities to churches in Poland and Belgium, there is no conclusive evidence about the source of its unusual exterior design.

The Jesuits could not find a ready source of limestone for making cement mortar, so they used wood and mud plaster. The church compound consists of four principal buildings arranged around the courtyard and occupying an entire city block. The bell tower was finished in 1748, the *funerario* (death chapel) is dated 1752 and the *parroquio* (living area) was completed in 1754. It is believed, however, that only the façades were finished before the Jesuits were expelled in 1767. All construction work was done by the Chiquitano people under Jesuit direction. The doors, some of the altar and one magnificent bench seat were handcarved in wood by expert Chiquitano artisans.

It's taking a long time to complete the massive renovations and restorations (which have been going on for over a decade), so many details are still incomplete, but the restored altar and front pews are especially noteworthy.

Phone the **church rectory** (☎ 972-2156) for up-to-date information on what's open, closed or under renovation. Chances are the person answering will speak not only Spanish but German, French, English or Portuguese.

Plaza 26 de Febrero

The church is fronted by the **toboroche trees** on the town's huge plaza, where once a family of sloths lazed their time away, but a flowering of the trees several years ago sent them off to search for leafier pickings. The trees now house noisy green parrots, and during the rainy season the ground beneath hops with thousands of frogs and large toads. Note also the **bust of Ñuflo de Chavez**, founder of Santa Cruz, and the erotic **fountain** off to one side of the plaza; it's a safe bet you won't see anything like it in highland Bolivia.

Santa Cruz la Vieja Walk

Just south of town, the road passes beneath an **archway** supported by bizarre, bikini-clad concrete nymphs beckoning you to step down the old Santa Cruz highway. About 1km further along, through dusty ranchland, you'll pass an abandoned schoolhouse, and after around 3km the road enters more junglelike vegetation, home to throngs of squawking green parrots.

Along this road is the **Parque Histórico Santa Cruz la Vieja** (admission US$1.80), on the site of the original Santa Cruz de la Sierra. The only thing left behind of the old city is an abandoned guardhouse. In the forest nearby is a **waterfall**, the source of San José's drinking water; it's a cool spot sheltered from the tropical heat, but swarms of biting insects may limit you to a fleeting visit. Carry insect repellent and wear good shoes and pants to protect your feet and legs from ferocious ants.

If you continue another 2km to 3km up the switchbacks onto the escarpment, you'll get a good view of San José and the surrounding plains. Further along are some nice eroded landscapes and a series of lovely waterfalls known as the **Cascadas del Suruquizo**.

SLEEPING

Hotel Denisse (☎ 972-2230; Monseñor Carlos Gerike s/n; r per person US$4) Basic and clean, with whirling fans overhead, Denisse isn't bad for a night or two.

Hotel Raquelita (☎ 972-2037; west side of plaza; r per person US$4.50, with bathroom US$6.50; 🕸) With cooling fans, you-can-lick-the-floor clean rooms, a laundry service and a little bar, this is the most attractive place to stay in town, and the owners are well informed on transportation times.

If you prefer to camp, ask the priest at the mission church whether you can pitch a tent in the courtyard.

EATING

Hotel Raquelita (☎ 972-2037; west side of plaza; mains US$1-2) This is a good, clean snack bar serving breakfast, lunches and delicious homemade ice cream.

La Choza de Don Pedro (☎ 972-2292; Circunvalación lado Norte; mains US$1-3) Hearty *almuerzos* are all the rage in this place, as are its steaks. La Choza is beyond the railway line, on the north road to San Ignacio.

On Monday, the Mennonites come into town from the colonies and sell homemade cheese, butter, bread and produce.

GETTING THERE & AWAY

On Monday, Wednesday and Friday morning, *micros* leave from San Ignacio for San José (via San Rafael and San Miguel); they return on Tuesday, Thursday and Saturday afternoon.

If you prefer to take your chances with a *camión*, wait at the *tranca* (highway police post) beyond the railway line 300m north of town. In the dry season, *camiones* go to San Ignacio at least a couple of times daily. Plan on about US$4 per person as far as San Ignacio.

There is a *ferrobus* from Santa Cruz to Quijarro that goes through San José (sleeper/semisleeper US$23/20) on Tuesday, Thursday and Sunday, leaving Santa Cruz at 7:30pm and arriving at San José Terminal Bimodal around 1am. It goes back to Santa Cruz from Quijarro on Monday, Wednesday and Friday, arriving in San José in the middle of the night.

The eastbound *Expreso del Oriente* (aka the Death Train) to Quijarro passes through daily, except Sunday, at 9:30pm; the westbound train to Santa Cruz passes through daily except Sunday at 2am (tickets US$5 to US$13). The *tren mixto* (very slow goods train) leaves Santa Cruz on Monday and Friday at 7:15pm and arrives in San José de Chiquitos at around 5am; it leaves less than an hour later and arrives in Quijarro at around 3pm the next day.

Freight trains run at any time; in theory you can simply hop into the passenger *bodega* and pay the 2nd-class fare to either Santa Cruz or Quijarro, although polite inquiries beforehand are appreciated. The ticket window opens whenever the ticket seller rolls up and feels ready to work, which may be anytime between 6am and 3pm.

Buying train tickets is a slow process, and you need to show a passport for each person traveling (to forestall ticket scalping). Intermediate stations such as San José de Chiquitos receive only a few allotted tickets, and these are sold only on the day of departure (or, in the case of departures in the wee hours, on the previous day).

FAR EASTERN BOLIVIA

Between Roboré and San José de Chiquitos, the railway line passes through a bizarre and beautiful wilderness region of hills and monoliths. Further east, along the Brazilian border, much of the landscape lies soaking beneath the wildlife-rich swamplands of the Pantanal, while the southern area of the region is dominated by the equally soggy Bañados del Izozog. This latter wetland is part of the Parque Nacional Kaa-Iya del Gran Chaco (opposite), which is the largest national park in Latin America.

Roboré & Santiago de Chiquitos

There ain't much fun to be had in Roboré, but the landscape surrounding the town is spectacular. The town began in 1916 as a military outpost, and there's still an overwhelming military presence. A good reason to stop here is to go to nearby Santiago de Chiquitos, a lovely Jesuit mission village with good accommodations. In Roboré itself, it's best to keep a low profile since, apparently, the soldiers can get a bit rowdy when they see outsiders.

SIGHTS & ACTIVITIES

A pleasant day-trip from Roboré will take you to **El Balneario**, a mountain stream with a waterfall and natural swimming hole. It's a two-hour walk each way from town; you'll need a local guide to find it. There's another closer swimming hole that is accessible by taxi (US$1.50 round-trip).

Culturally, the Jesuit mission at **Santiago de Chiquitos**, 20km from Roboré, is more interesting than San José de Chiquitos. It's set in the hills, and the cooler climate provides

a welcome break from the tropical heat of the lowlands. Its church is well worth a look, and there are some great excursions from Santiago, such as **El Mirador**, a 15-minute walk from the village, with dizzy views of the Tucavaca valley. The round-trip taxi fare from Roboré is US$10 for up to four people. *Camiones* and military vehicles occasionally do the run from the east end of town for US$1 per person one way.

The 105°F thermal baths at **Aguas Calientes**, 31km east of Roboré, are popular with Bolivian visitors who believe in their curative powers. The Santa Cruz–Quijarro train stops in Aguas Calientes, and *camiones* (US$1 per person) leave from the eastern end of Roboré. Taxis charge US$12 for up to four passengers. There are no accommodations, so the baths are best visited on a day trip.

If you're keen to see the best of the landscape between Roboré and San José de Chiquitos, the most convenient station is **El Portón**, which lies immediately west of the spectacular and oft-photographed rock pillar of the same name. There are no tourist facilities, so carry food and camping gear.

SLEEPING & EATING

Hotel Pacheco (☎ 974-2074; 6 de Agosto s/n; d US$5, with bathroom US$7) This is Roboré's best sleeping option, with simple but bright and clean rooms at decent prices.

Hotel Beulá (☎ 313-6274; s/d US$25/35) On the plaza in Santiago de Chiquitos, the stylish Beulá has big breakfasts and dinners, but they need to be arranged in advance. You can also hire local guides here.

Pollo de Oro (meals US$1-2) Apart from the hotels, you can check out this place near the railway station for a meal. It's a bit grim, but the alcohol-assisted celebrators provide some diversion from the inevitable wait for the evening *tren atrasado* (late train).

GETTING THERE & AWAY

Buses go to Roboré (sleeper/semisleeper US$25/22) from Santa Cruz on Tuesday, Wednesday and Friday at 5pm, going back to Santa Cruz after midnight. Buses to Quijarro (sleeper/semisleeper US$13.50/11.50) go on Monday, Wednesday and Friday after midnight, though you might be better off traveling by train. Roboré is about four hours west of Quijarro by train (tickets from US$10) and the same distance (time-wise) east of San

José de Chiquitos. **TAM** (☎ in Santa Cruz 974-2035) flies from Santa Cruz to San Matías on Friday morning, returning via Roboré.

Parque Nacional Kaa-Iya del Gran Chaco

In the late 1990s, the Guaraní people, in conjunction with the Bolivian Ministerio de Desarrollo, the World Bank, the Swiss government, the Wildlife Conservation Society and the Armonía Foundation, succeeded in having their ecological treasure protected in this two-million-hectare reserve, now Latin America's largest national park. The huge and enigmatic **Bañados del Izozog** wetland, in the heart of this vast wilderness, lies buried in a wild and relatively inaccessible expanse of territory between San José de Chiquitos and the Paraguayan border.

Of the total area, 800,000 hectares belong to the Guaraní people and 300,000 hectares to the neighboring Ayoreos. The only access into this fabulous region is by 4WD or on foot from El Tinto (on the railway line west of San José de Chiquitos) but organized tours from Santa Cruz may begin some day. This is a true wilderness and there are no facilities or services in the area. If you enjoy places that recall the Brazilian Pantanal and have a way to get into the area, a visit is emphatically recommended.

PUERTO SUÁREZ

pop 20,100

Puerto Suárez is one of those places that is too far away to be visited unless you're passing through on your way to Brazil, so there isn't much in the way of facilities, but it provides a unique opportunity to witness illicit dealings in stolen cars from Brazil. Its plus side is that it's set in a watery wilderness with some of the densest wildlife populations on the continent.

A simple, budget sleeping choice is **Hotel Sucre** (☎ 976-2069; Bolívar 63; r per person US$4). **Hotel Bamby** (☎ 976-2015; 6 de Agosto s/n; d US$8.50) offers the best value.

TAM (☎ 976-2205) runs popular Tuesday and Saturday morning flights from Santa Cruz to Puerto Suárez (US$59), returning the same afternoon. These flights actually land in Corumbá, but passengers intending to cross into Brazil must first return to Bolivia to exit the country before checking into Brazil at the Policía Federal in Corumbá.

Puerto Suárez is also on the railway line, 15km west of Quijarro.

QUIJARRO

pop 12,900

The eastern terminus of the Death Train has its home in Quijarro, a border town comprising a muddy collection of shacks, and the crossing point between Bolivia and Corumbá (Brazil). Visitors heading east will glimpse a wonderful preview of Corumbá: it appears on a hill in the distance, a dream city of sparkling white towers rising above the vast green expanses of the Pantanal.

Sights & Activities

Hotels in Quijarro can organize boat tours through the wetlands of the **Bolivian Pantanal**, an alternative to the well-visited Brazilian side. A comfortable three-day excursion, including transportation, food and accommodations (on the boat) should cost around US$100 per person.

Sleeping & Eating

There are *alojamientos* (basic accommodations) on the left as you exit from the railway station.

Hotel Bilbosi (☎ 978-2113; s/d with bathroom US$10/16; ✷) This friendly hotel is two blocks from the railway station and has clean aircon rooms.

El Pantanal Hotel Resort (☎ 978-2020, in Santa Cruz 355-9583; www.elpantanalhotel.com; r per person US$50; ✷ ✷) This five-star place is in the beautiful Arroyo Concepción, 12km from Puerto Suárez and 7km from Corumbá. It offers wide-ranging luxury, 600 hectares of grounds and several restaurants. Standard two-day, three-night packages, with meals and airport transfers, cost around US$120 per person.

Lots of good inexpensive restaurants are lined up along the street perpendicular to the railway station entrance.

Getting There & Away

TRAIN

By rail the trip between Quijarro and Santa Cruz takes anywhere from 16 to 23 hours, depending on which train you take. The *Expreso del Oriente* leaves Quijarro in the afternoon daily except Sunday (2nd-/1st-/Pullman-class US$7/15.50/20), but departure times depend entirely on when the train arrives from Santa Cruz. The slow, cumbersome and slightly cheaper *tren mixto* chugs out on Wednesday and Saturday. You'll pay the same to ride in a bodega on a freight train. The ticket office opens around 7am and only sells tickets on the day of departure; depending on the lines, you may be better off buying tickets for a few dollars more from an agency on the Bolivian side of the frontier.

TO BRAZIL
When the train pulls into Quijarro, a line of taxis waits to take new arrivals to the border. The border post is just 2km from the station, so if you can't bargain the drivers down to something reasonable – say US$0.70 per person – it's a pretty easy walk to the border. Travelers report being charged up to US$10 for Bolivian exit stamps, but this is entirely unofficial; politely explain that you understand there is no official charge for the stamp, and appear prepared to wait until they get real.

Over the bridge, you pass through Brazilian customs. From there, yellow *comunales* (city buses) will take you into Corumbá (US$1). Brazilian entry stamps are given at the Polícia Federal at the *rodoviária* (haw-doo-*vyahr*-ya; bus terminal); it's open until 5pm.

Travelers arriving in Brazil from Bolivia need a yellow-fever vaccination certificate. Officials don't always ask for one, but when they do, the rule is inflexibly enforced. In a pinch, a clinic in Corumbá provides the vaccine. You can change US dollars in cash or traveler's checks at the Banco do Brasil, two blocks from Praça Independência.

To reach the Bolivian border from Corumbá, catch a bus from Praça Independência, opposite the cathedral. If you're entering Bolivia, you can change Brazilian *reais* and US dollars at the frontier.

SAN MATÍAS
The border town of San Matías is the main Bolivian access point into the northern Brazilian Pantanal. Travelers between Cáceres (Brazil) and Bolivia must pick up Brazilian entry or exit stamps from the Polícia Federal office at Rua Antônio João 160 in Cáceres. On the Bolivian side, you'll have to hunt up the immigration officer; otherwise, pick up your entry or exit stamp in Santa Cruz (p298).

For accommodations you're limited to the basic, stifling rooms at **Hotel San José** (US$3). The best restaurant, which serves a very limited menu, is **BB's** (mains US$1-2).

TAM (☎ 968-2256) may offer an occasional unscheduled flight between Santa Cruz and San Matías. In the dry season, a Trans-Bolivia bus leaves from Cáceres to Santa Cruz (US$26, 30 hours), via San Matías (US$5.50, four hours), between 5am and 6am daily.

Coming from Brazil, get your exit stamp the night before; in San Matías, the bus will stop and wait while you visit immigration (US$0.80 by taxi from the bus terminal). It's possible to change dollars or *reais* to bolivianos at the Trans-Bolivia bus office.

Amazon Basin

The Amazon Basin is one of Bolivia's largest and most mesmerizing parts. The rainforest is raucous with wildlife (the flora and fauna include rare species), and spending a few days roaming the sweaty jungle (and minding the bugs) is an experience you're unlikely to forget. This is where you'll find the deep and mysterious lushness that has drawn adventurers and explorers since the beginning of time. And it's not only the forests that are enchanting: it's also the richness of indigenous cultures, traditions and languages that exist in the region.

While Brazilian rainforests continue to suffer heavy depredation, the Amazon forests of northern Bolivia remain relatively intact, though, unfortunately, the region continues to face the serious problems of road construction and highland immigration that have led to an upsurge in logging and slash-and-burn agriculture.

Mossy hills peak around the town of Rurrenabaque, most people's first point of entry into the region and the place from where to visit the fascinating Parque Nacional Madidi. This is home to a growing eco- and ethnotourism industry that looks to help local communities. The village of San Ignacio de Moxos has a kicking July fiesta where indigenous traditions, mixed with a strong Jesuit missionary influence, are vigorously celebrated. Trinidad, the region's biggest settlement and an active cattle ranching center, is a transit point toward Santa Cruz.

All of the Amazon Basin's main rivers are Amazon tributaries that would be considered great rivers in their own right in any smaller country. You can indulge in long journeys down these jungle waterways, using hotel-like riverboats, cargo boats, canoes or barges.

AMAZON BASIN

HIGHLIGHTS

- Glide down the long **Río Mamoré** (p349) on a boat trip between Trinidad and Guayaramerín
- Take part in responsible tourism, discover the rainforest and peek into the life of a local community on a tour from **Rurrenabaque** (p336)
- Party with the locals at the Amazon's best village fiesta in **San Ignacio de Moxos** (p346)
- Discover the little-explored forests of **Parque Nacional Noel Kempff Mercado** (p354) and see fascinating wildlife and landscapes
- Dive into the rainforest at the community-run Chalalán Ecolodge, deep inside **Parque Nacional Madidi** (p341)

Parque Nacional Madidi ★ ★ Río Mamoré

Rurrenabaque ★ ★ San Ignacio de Moxos

★ Parque Nacional Noel Kempff Mercado

- TELEPHONE CODE: 3
- POPULATION: 187,400 (CHAPARE REGION); 362,500 (BENI REGION)
- ELEVATION: 0M TO 200M

History

The Bolivian Amazon has always oozed mystery. The Incas believed that a powerful civilization lived in the great rainforest, and tried to conquer the area in the 15th century. The indigenous peoples of the western Bolivian Amazon, mainly the Moxos tribe, are said to have posed such a mighty resistance to the invading army, that once they realized they were unable to beat them, the Incas asked for an alliance and settled among the Moxos.

The tale of the Incas' experience fired up the imagination of the Spanish conquerors a century later – they too were chasing a legend in search of a rich and powerful civilization in the depths of the Amazonian forest. The name of the kingdom was El Dorado (the Golden One) or Paitití (the land of the celestial jaguar), thought to have existed east of the Andean Cordillera, near the source of the Río Paraguai. The Spanish spent the entire 16th century trying to discover the elusive kingdom, but, unfamiliar with the rainforest environment, found nothing but death and disease. By the 17th century they moved their search elsewhere.

Though the Spanish were disappointed with their search in the Moxos region, the Jesuits saw their opportunity to 'spread the word' to the highly spiritual *moxeños*. The tough missionaries were the first Europeans to significantly venture into the lowlands. They founded their first mission at Loreto, in the Moxos region, in 1675. While they imposed Christianity and European ways, the Jesuits also recognized the indigenous peoples' expertise in woodwork, which eventually produced the brilliant carvings now characteristic of the missions. They imported herds of cattle and horses to some remote outposts, and the descendants of these herds still thrive throughout most of the department.

After the expulsion of the Jesuits in 1767, the Franciscan and Dominican missionaries, as well as the opportunistic settlers who followed, brought slavery and disease. Otherwise, the vast, steamy forests and plains of northern Bolivia saw little activity for decades.

Climate

The seasons are less pronounced here than in other parts of Bolivia, and temperatures are high year-round. Most of the rain falls during the summer in unrelenting downpours and, during wet times, the streets fill with mud and the sound of croaking frogs. Although winter is drier than summer, it also sees a good measure of precipitation. If you're unlucky you may experience the unpredictable *surazo*, a cold wind blowing from Patagonia and the Argentine pampas, which produces a dramatic drop in temperature and frost even in the hottest parts of the jungle.

National Parks & Reserves

The Bolivian Amazon is blessed with some of the richest wildlife habitats on earth and the country's best-known national parks and reserves. For bird-watchers, monkey lovers and jaguar seekers, this region is heaven. You can choose between the jungles and wild rivers of Parque Nacional Madidi (p341), the less-frequented, wildlife-rich Reserva Biosférica del Beni (p344) and the virtually unexplored 'lost world' of Parque Nacional Noel Kempff Mercado (p354). Conservation International is attempting to raise awareness of the need for protection of the headwaters of several major Amazon tributaries with their ambitious Vilcabamba-Amboró Conservation Corridor initiative.

Getting There & Around

Rurrenabaque is the Amazon's most popular settlement. Flying is the best way of getting here, though many choose to take the treacherous bus ride from La Paz, part of which is down the 'World's Most Dangerous Road' (see p78). Buses going back to La Paz from Rurrenabaque are less crowded – many people decide to wing it (or take a faster Jeep) after surviving the initial bus ride.

Transportes Aéreos Militares (TAM) and Amaszonas fly daily between La Paz and Rurrenabaque. Their low-flying planes afford great glimpses of Lake Titicaca after takeoff before squeezing past Chacaltaya and soaring over the Yungas. You can see the landscape change from desolate, rugged highlands to lush, forested lowlands. And the grass landing strip in Rurrenabaque is worthy of more than one post-trip tale.

Generally, 4WDs are necessary to reach most off-road spots, but there are regular bus services between major towns. Boat travel is big here, especially in the rainy season, when it is usually the only real option. Riverboat travel isn't for everyone: it's relaxing but slow going and there are no real schedules. While the scenery can be mesmerizing, it

THE AMAZON BASIN

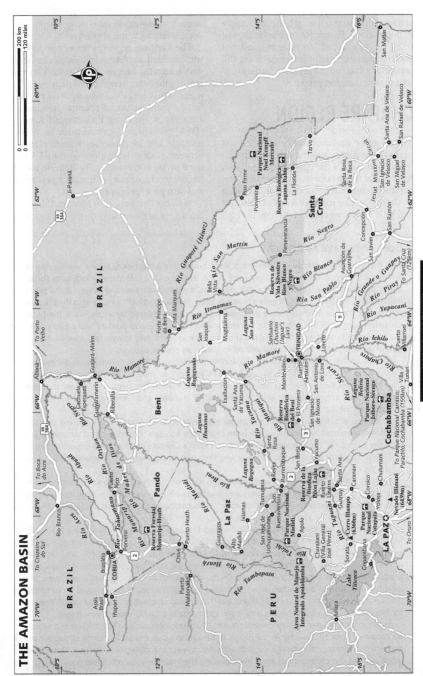

changes little, so you'll want to bring a couple of books along. Passenger comfort is the last thing cargo-boat builders have in mind, but Bolivian accommodations standards are still superior to those on the Brazilian 'cattle boats' that ply the Amazon proper.

CHAPARE REGION

The Chapare stretches out beyond the last peaks of the Andes into the dramatically different landscape of the upper Amazon Basin, where lush, moist rainforest replaces the dry, barren mountains. The contrast is breathtaking on the spectacular road between Cochabamba and Villa Tunari, where twists around the high peaks and mountain lakes drop steeply into deep, steaming tropical valleys.

The Chapare region is heavily populated with highland *campesinos* (subsistence farmers) who emigrated here in the 1970s and started growing the controversial coca-leaf, turning the region into Bolivia's main source of coca grown for the manufacture of cocaine. Subsequent attempts by the Drug Enforcement Agency (DEA) to eradicate coca have made the region unstable, with frequent messy confrontations between *cocaleros* (coca growers), the DEA and the Bolivian government. The Bolivian media frequently expose cases of human-rights abuse and disregard for property.

With the election of Evo Morales, things are looking to improve slightly for the *cocaleros*

DOES COCA HAVE A FUTURE?

Less than a century after the rubber boom went bust in the early 1900s, Bolivia saw the rise of another industry: cocaine production. Coca – the leaf revered by Altiplano inhabitants for its ability to stave off the discomforts of altitude, thirst, hunger, discontent and stress – is the prime ingredient of the class-A drug. It grows primarily in the Yungas, north of La Paz, and in the Chapare region. The Yungas produces more palatable leaves that are chewed by locals, while the bitter Chapare variety suffers a different fate: dried, soaked in kerosene and mashed into a pasty pulp, the leaves are treated with hydrochloric and sulfuric acids until they form a foul-smelling brown base. Further treatment with petrol and other chemicals creates cocaine.

It's been estimated that between 30% and 40% of Bolivia's GDP is derived from the cocaine industry. By the mid-1980s, US yuppiedom was snorting so much Bolivian coke that the US government decided something had to be done about it. With President Ronald Reagan at the helm, the USA proposed some joint cleaning up of the Beni and Chapare, aided by Bolivian President Victor Paz Estenssoro.

Since the '80s, the Drug Enforcement Agency's war on coca growth has persisted and the Bolivian government and military have been repeatedly accused of human-rights violations. But with the election of Evo Morales in 2006, himself from a Chapare *cocalero* (coca growing) family, the life of *cocaleros* is looking to improve and the stigmatized international image of the plant might yet get a better reputation.

Morales intends to encourage production of coca goods, such as food and cosmetics, while continuing to combat cocaine producers and smugglers. He has vowed to decriminalize Bolivia's coca leaf internationally by 2008, hoping to bring his campaign to a head at the fourth convention of the UN held in Vienna in the same year.

Since October 2004, the legal size of land allowed for coca growing has been 1 *cato* (131 sq ft, less than half an acre), which brings the *cocalero* family an average income of US$80 to US$120 per month, and legal crops have increased from 88,967 acres in 1983 to 370,658 acres in 2005 in the Chapare region. Morales is under growing pressure from the *cocaleros* to increase coca production and thus improve their income. On the other hand, he faces criticism from Caban, the local banana growers' association, which produces the region's second-largest crop. It claims the president is ignoring the success of Caban's alternative crop program (financed by the US Agency for International Development) because it will cast a shadow on his pro-coca message.

In the meantime, the military presence in the Chapare continues, and the soldiers still search for cocaine laboratories hidden in the jungle. It remains to be seen what will come of this debate and whether Morales can manage the difficult balancing act of fulfilling the demands of the poor inhabitants in this controversial area, while bearing the pressure of international governments.

of the Chapare: he has sworn to protect the growth of coca and to encourage the making of coca products, such as tea, cookies and other edible goodies, while at the same time continuing to target cocaine production and smuggling.

Although things may improve in the years to come, road blockades still occur and independent adventurers should inquire locally about safety before straying too far off the Cochabamba–Santa Cruz highway.

VILLA TUNARI

pop 2000 / elevation 300m

Villa Tunari is a quiet spot to relax, hike and swim in cool rivers, and a lovely warm-up place for frozen highlanders. This tropical town was once the playground of drug barons, and the large houses with their lush gardens bear witness to better days. The local authorities have been making an effort to promote Villa Tunari as a tourist destination, but the town has yet to develop its tourist appeal – the coca debate and drug wars will no doubt be crucial to when it can start to reinvent itself.

Information

There's no ATM here yet, so bring cash with you or get advances at Prodem bank. Some hotels may change cash. There are several telecom places along the highway, and two internet spots in town: **Puma con Cháki** (Plazuela Los Pioneros; per hr US$0.50) and **El Gaucho** (Plaza El Colonizador; per hr US$0.50).

Sights & Activities

Swimming holes, or *pozos*, are the main source of fun in Villa Tunari. In addition to Hotel El Puente's Los Pozos (p334), there are several free *pozos* in town along the Río San Mateo. Great opportunities for **fishing**, **kayaking** and **whitewater rafting** abound in the surrounding rivers, but it's always better to ask around to see what's safe before heading out anywhere in the forest on your own.

A good, independent **hike** will take you to the friendly village of **Majo Pampa**. Follow the route toward Hotel El Puente and turn right onto the walking track about 150m before the hotel. After crossing the Valería Stream, it's 8km to the village.

PARQUE MACHÍA (INTI WARA YASSI)

This 36-hectare **wildlife sanctuary** (☎ 413-6572; www.intiwarayassi.org; admission US$0.75, photo/video

permit US$2/$3.35) houses over 200 poached or injured animals, including abandoned tropical pets, former zoo inhabitants, old circus animals and other abused critters. All this is done with the help of an international crew of volunteers.

It's a relaxing place to **camp** (US$2) and wander through the forest, taking in the sights, sounds and tranquility. The name Inti Wara Yassi means 'sun,' 'moon,' and 'stars' in Quechua, Aymará and Guaraní, respectively.

It's best to watch the animals at noon and 5pm, at feeding time. Tours for prospective volunteers are conducted daily at 10am. Volunteers must stay for a minimum of 15 days and can choose between rustic camping and the hostel, both of which cost US$70 for the first two weeks, including showers and cooking facilities.

ORCHIDEARIO VILLA TUNARI

Lovingly tended by German botanists, Villa Tunari's **orchid nursery** (☎ 413-4153) is a beautiful garden that's home to over 70 species of tropical orchids. There's also a small **museum**, El Bosque restaurant and a couple of *cabañas* (cabins) for rent. It's just north of the highway, 2km west of town near the *tranca* (highway police post).

Tours

Villa Tunari is the main focus for Cochabamba-based **Fremen Tours** (☎ 425-9392; www.andes-amazonia.com; Tumusla N-245, Cochabamba), which arranges all-inclusive tours, accommodations, river trips and other activities at out-of-the-way sites. It also offers live-aboard riverboat cruises around Trinidad and adventure tours in Parque Nacional Isiboro-Sécure (when it's safe to do so).

Festivals & Events

The festival of **San Antonio**, the town's patron saint, is celebrated in the first week of June. The first week of August has delicious and unique Amazonian fish dishes served up at the **Feria Regional del Pescado**.

Sleeping & Eating

BUDGET

Hotel Las Vegas (Arce S-325; per person US$2.50) While not much like Las Vegas in terms of glitz, in fact quite the opposite, this place is nevertheless friendly and has some good food served in its restaurant.

AMAZON BASIN

La Querencia (☎ 413-4189; Beni 700; per person US$3) This is a simple, basic place with clean rooms, fresh (cold) showers, laundry facilities and some rooms facing the river. Unexciting but edible food is served in the downstairs restaurant.

Hotel Villa Tunari (☎ 413-6544; per person US$3, d with bathroom US$9) Villa Tunari's top budget option, this hotel has clean, bright rooms and hot water occasionally. The owner is friendly and home-proud and does his best to please the crowds. The place is above a corner store opposite Alojamiento Pilunchi.

Camping is possible at Parque Machía and also at the sporting ground, north of the center. Other *alojamientos* (basic accommodations) may allow emergency camping when they are full.

MIDRANGE & TOP END

Residencial San Martín (☎ 413-4115; s/d US$16/26; 🖭) This is a friendly place with modern, en suite rooms and a gorgeous garden with a pool. It's on the southern side of the main road leading into town.

Hotel El Puente (☎ in Cochabamba 425-9392; Integración; s/d/tr/q US$19/27/38/45; 🖭) This gorgeous place in a remnant island of rainforest 4km outside Villa Tunari, near the Ríos San Mateo and Espíritu Santo confluence, has huts that gravitate around a courtyard and hammocks on the top floor. You can go on a wonderful walk around Los Pozos, 14 idyllic natural swimming holes (US$2 for nonguests) deep in the forest, where you're guaranteed to see blue morpho butterflies. The hotel is run by Fremen Tours. To get here, catch a *micro* (minibus) heading east from Villa Tunari, get off at the first turnoff after the second bridge, turn right and walk for 2km. Taxis from the center charge around US$3 for up to four people.

Las Araras (☎ 413-4116; s/d with breakfast US$20/30) This modern hotel in a tropical garden setting is an HI affiliate. It's just over the first bridge east of the highway and offers good midweek package discounts.

Los Tucanes (☎ 413-4108; s/d with breakfast US$25/35; 🍽 🖭) Famous for their luxurious appeal, the five-star *cabañas* here have good beds, elegant décor and a pool to lounge around. It's a great spot for total holiday surrender. The hotel is on the Cochabamba–Santa Cruz highway, opposite the turn-off for Hotel El Puente.

Hotel/Restaurant Las Palmas (☎ 413-4163, in Cochabamba 427-7762; s/d/tr US$30/40/45; 🍽 🖭) This is another tropical hotel with a refreshing swimming pool and spacious rooms. Though the air-con rooms aren't the most luxurious, considering the price, the cheaper rooms with fans and the family *cabañas* are a good option for big groups. The open-air restaurant (mains US$1.50 to US$4) serves well-prepared locally caught fish and great fresh tropical juices.

For eating, the restaurants mentioned at the various accommodations are your best bet. Otherwise, a rank of food stalls along the highway sells all manner of inexpensive tropical fare. The *comedores* (dining halls) in the market are also worth a look.

Getting There & Away

The bus and *micro* offices are sandwiched amid the line of food stalls along the main highway. From Cochabamba (US$2.20, four to five hours), *micros* leave in the morning from the corner of 9 de Abril and Oquendo; some continue on to Puerto Villarroel (US$1, two hours). From Villa Tunari to Santa Cruz, several services operate in the early afternoon, but most Santa Cruz traffic departs in the evening. To Cochabamba, *micros* leave at 8:30am.

PARQUE NACIONAL CARRASCO

Created in 1988, this 622,600-hectare park has some of Bolivia's most easily explored cloud forest. It skirts a large portion of the road between Cochabamba and Villa Tunari, and also includes a big lowland area of the Chapare region. The rainforest hides a vast variety of mammal species, together with a rainbow of birds, crawling reptiles, amphibians, fish and insects.

The easiest way to visit is with Fremen Tours (p333). Tour programs include the **Cavernas del Repechón** (Caves of the Night Birds), where you'll see the rare nocturnal *guáchero* (oilbird) and six bat species. Access is from the village of Paractito, 8km west of Villa Tunari. This half-day excursion involves a short slog through the rainforest and a zippy crossing of the **Río San Mateo** in a cable-car contraption.

Another interesting option is the Conservation International–backed **Camino en las Nubes** (Walk in the Clouds) project, a three-day trek through the park's cloud forests, descending with local guides from 4000m to 300m along the old Cochabamba–Chapare road. For details, contact **Conservation International** (CI; ☎ 717-3527; Hans Gretel 10, Villa Tunari) or Fremen Tours.

PUERTO VILLARROEL

pop 2000

This muddy tropical port on the Río Ichilo is a small settlement with tin-roofed houses raised off the ground to defend themselves from the mud and wet-season floods. There isn't much to look forward to here – unless you're excited by tumbledown wooden hovels, a military installation, a petroleum plant and a loosely defined port area – but if you fancy gliding down the river toward Trinidad (p347), then Puerto Villarroel, a vital transportation terminal and gateway to the Amazon lowlands, is a good place to start. For a quick look at the rainforests, it makes an easy two-day round-trip from Cochabamba. Bring lots of insect repellent and wear strong old shoes with lots of tread. Even in the dry season, the muddy streets will submerge your ankles and devour your footwear.

The best sleeping option is the 10-room **Amazonas Eco-Hotel** (☎ 424-2431; tombol@hotmail.com; s/d US$3/6, with bathroom US$7.50/12.50), which also serves meals. Those who are using river transportation will normally be permitted to sleep on the boat. Apart from this, there are a couple of very basic places to stay around the central plaza, costing around US$3 per person.

Half a dozen restaurant shacks opposite the port captain's office serve up fish and chicken dishes. For good empanadas, snacks, hot drinks and fresh juices, try the market on the main street.

Micros from Cochabamba to Puerto Villarroel, marked 'Chapare' (US$2, seven hours), leave from the corner of Av 9 de Abril and Oquendo, near Laguna Alalay. The first one sets off around 6:30am, and subsequent buses depart when full. The first *micro* back to Cochabamba leaves around 7am from the bus stop on the main street. *Camiones* (flatbed trucks) leave from the same place at any hour of the day, especially when there are boats in port. Note that transportation between Cochabamba and Santa Cruz doesn't stop at Puerto Villarroel.

Two types of boats run between Puerto Villarroel and Trinidad. The small family-run cargo boats that putter up and down the Ríos Ichilo and Mamoré normally only travel by day and reach Trinidad in around six days. Larger commercial crafts travel day and night and do the run in three or four days.

In Puerto Villarroel the Capitanía del Puerto and other related portside offices can provide sketchy departure information on cargo transporters. Unless military exercises or labor strikes shut down cargo services, you shouldn't have more than a three- or four-day wait.

The average fare to Trinidad on either type of boat is US$15 to US$20, including food (but it's still wise to carry emergency rations), a bit less without meals. The quality of food varies from boat to boat, but overall the shipboard diet consists of fish, dried meat, *masaco* (mashed yucca or plantain) and fruit; avoid endangered turtle eggs if they're offered. Few boats along the Ichilo have cabins. Most passengers sleep in hammocks (sold in Cochabamba markets for around US$3 to US$5) slung out in the main lounge.

PARQUE NACIONAL ISIBORO-SÉCURE

Created in 1965, this 1.2-million-hectare national park occupies a large triangle between the Ríos Isiboro and Sécure and the Serranías Sejerruma, Mosetenes and Yanakaka. It encompasses mountains, rainforest and savanna and provides habitat for profuse wildlife in its more remote sections. An obscure 1905 resolution opened the region to settlers and much of the park has been overrun by squatters since, with no way to halt the influx. As a result, the natural environment and the once-prevalent indigenous population, which consisted of Yuracarés, Chimanes, Sirionós and Trinitarios, have been compromised.

The park also lies along drug-running routes, so independent visitors must exercise extreme caution. The DEA activity means that locals might regard any foreigner as an anti-*cocalero* and hence fair game for abuse. If you wish to venture anyway, it is wise to carry letters of introduction from the coca growers' association.

The only truly safe way to visit the park is with Fremen Tours (p333). Its worthwhile seven-day boat trip from Trinidad to Laguna Bolivia, the park's best-known destination, includes stops at riverside settlements, rainforest walks, horseback riding, wildlife viewing and a canoe trip on the Río Ichoa.

Owing to seasonal flooding, the park is inaccessible between November and March. For more information, contact **Sernap** (☎ 448-6452/3) in Cochabamba.

WESTERN BOLIVIAN AMAZON

This is the Amazon as it's meant to be. Rich with wildlife, flora and indigenous culture, you may never want to leave. In the midst of the tropical lushness is the lovely town of Rurrenabaque, a primary gringo trail hangout. Pampas, jungle and ethno-ecotourism options are innumerable here, but vary significantly in quality and price. Parque Nacional Madidi, one of South America's and the world's most precious wilderness gems, sits on Rurrenabaque's doorstep.

For background reading, pick up *Phoenix: Exploration Fawcett* (2001), by early explorer Colonel Percy Harrison Fawcett, or *Back from Tuichi* (1993; also published as *Heart of the Amazon*, 1999), about the 1981 rescue of Israeli Yossi Ghinsberg, whose expedition was lost in the rainforest and rescued by locals.

RURRENABAQUE

pop 15,000

The relaxing 'Rurre,' as the town is endearingly known, has a fabulous setting, sliced by the deep Río Beni that gives the region its name. Surrounded by mossy green hills, the town's mesmerizing sunsets turn the sky a burnt orange, and a dense fog sneaks down the river among the lush, moist trees. Once darkness falls, the surrounding rainforest comes alive, and croaks, barks, buzzes and roars can be heard from a distance.

Rurre is a major traveler base. Backpackers fill the streets, and restaurants, cafés and hotels cater mainly to Western tastes. Some travelers spend their days relaxing in the ubiquitous hammocks, but the majority go off on riverboat adventures into the rainforest.

The area's original people, the Tacana, were one of the few lowland tribes that resisted Christianity. They are responsible for the name Beni, which means 'wind,' as well as the curious name of 'Rurrenabaque,' which is derived from 'Arroyo Inambaque,' the Hispanicized version of the Tacana name 'Suse-Inambaque,' the 'Ravine of Ducks.'

Information

BOOKSTORES

For reading material, try the **Deep Rainforest Tour Agency** (Comercio; 8:30am-7pm), where

there's a book exchange (loan/purchase per book US$0.65/US$4). Otherwise, check the popular hotels.

IMMIGRATION

Extend your stay by visiting **Migración** (892-2241; 8:30am-4:30pm Mon-Fri) on the plaza's northeast corner.

INTERNET ACCESS

Access is more expensive here than anywhere else in the country and can sometimes be slow. Try **Camila's** (Santa Cruz at Avaroa; per hr US$1) or **Internet** (Comercio; per hr US$1.60; 9am-10pm).

LAUNDRY

Recommended Laundry Service Rurrenabaque and neighboring Number One promise same-day machine-wash-and-dry service (US$1.35 per kilo).

MONEY

There's no ATM here, so beware. You can get cash advances at **Prodem Bank** (Comercio; 8am-6pm Mon-Fri, to 2pm Sat), but only on Visa and MasterCard (including Visa debit cards). It also does Western Union transfers and changes cash. Some tour agencies and hotels change traveler's checks (4% to 5% commission). Tours can usually be paid for with credit cards, and some bars, agencies and hotels may be willing to facilitate cash advances.

TELEPHONE

Punto Entel (892-8510; Comercio & Santa Cruz; 7am-10pm) Cheaper for calls than the main Entel office.

TOURIST INFORMATION

The municipal **tourist office** (cnr Vaca Diez & Avaroa) is happy to answer questions. Sernap's main **Parque Nacional Madidi office** (892-2540), where independent visitors must register and pay the US$10 entrance fee, is across the river in San Buenaventura. Inquire at **Conservation International** (CI; 892-2015, 892-2495; www.conservation.org.bo; south side of Plaza 2 de Febrero) about new community ecotourism developments in the region.

Sights & Activities

Rurrenabaque's appeal is in its surrounding natural beauty. It's easy to pass a day or three here while waiting to join a tour. Behind town

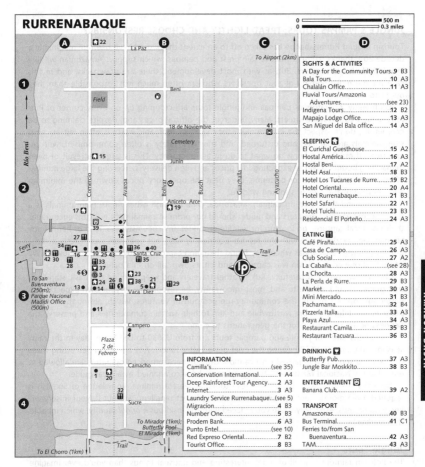

RURRENABAQUE

0 — 500 m
0 — 0.3 miles

SIGHTS & ACTIVITIES
A Day for the Community Tours...9 B3
Bala Tours.............................10 A3
Chalalán Office......................11 A3
Fluvial Tours/Amazonia
   Adventures......................(see 23)
Indigena Tours......................12 B2
Mapajo Lodge Office...............13 A3
San Miguel del Bala office........14 A3

SLEEPING
El Curichal Guesthouse............15 A2
Hostal América......................16 A3
Hostal Beni...........................17 A2
Hotel Asaí............................18 B3
Hotel Los Tucanes de Rurre.....19 B2
Hotel Oriental........................20 A4
Hotel Rurrenabaque................21 B3
Hotel Safari..........................22 A1
Hotel Tuichi..........................23 B3
Residencial El Porteño.............24 A3

EATING
Café Piraña...........................25 A3
Casa de Campo......................26 A3
Club Social...........................27 A3
La Cabaña..........................(see 28)
La Chocita............................28 A3
La Perla de Rurre....................29 A3
Market.................................30 A3
Mini Mercado........................31 B3
Pachamama..........................32 B4
Pizzería Italia.........................33 A3
Playa Azul............................34 A3
Restaurant Camila..................35 B3
Restaurant Tacuara................36 B3

DRINKING
Butterfly Pub.........................37 A3
Jungle Bar Moskkito...............38 B3

ENTERTAINMENT
Banana Club..........................39 A2

TRANSPORT
Amazonas.............................40 B3
Bus Terminal.........................41 C1
Ferries to/from San
   Buenaventura....................42 A3
TAM....................................43 A3

INFORMATION
Camilla's............................(see 35)
Conservation International..........1 A4
Deep Rainforest Tour Agency.....2 A3
Internet.................................3 A3
Laundry Service Rurrenabaque...(see 5)
Migracion..............................4 B3
Number One...........................5 B3
Prodem Bank..........................6 A3
Punto Entel.........................(see 10)
Red Expreso Oriental................7 B2
Tourist Office..........................8 B3

---

is a low but steep **mirador** that affords a view across the seemingly endless Beni lowlands; it's reached by climbing up the track at the southern end of Bolívar. Near here is the Butterfly Pool El Mirador, a fabulous spot where you can swim and sigh over the beautiful views of the Beni lowlands. Reservations can be made at the **Butterfly Pub** (☎ 7111-5324; cnr Comercio & Vaca Diez; admission US$2.50).

Another nice excursion is **El Chorro**, an idyllic waterfall and pool 1km upstream. You can reach this place by boat only; enquire at the harbor. On a rock roughly opposite El Chorro is an ancient **serpentine engraving**, which was intended as a warning to travelers: whenever the water reached serpent level, the Beni was considered unnavigable.

Tours
JUNGLE & PAMPAS
Jungle and pampas tours are Rurrenabaque's bread and butter, and operators mushroom at incredible speed. When choosing an operator, your best bet is to speak to other travelers who've been on some of the trips – you will find that some operators' track records are less than impressive. For more on jungle and pampas tours, see the boxed text p338.

Most agencies have offices on Avaroa. The following agencies have received more positive reports:

Bala Tours (☎ 892-2527; www.mirurrenabaque.com; Santa Cruz at Comercio) Has its own jungle camp and comfortable pampas lodge on Río Yacumo.

JUNGLE & PAMPAS TOURS: TREAD LIGHTLY AND CHOOSE RESPONSIBLY

Tourism around Rurrenabaque has taken off to an extent that would have been unimaginable a decade ago, thanks to the attractive rainforest and pampas, which support Amazonian wildlife in relatively large numbers. But, as with most development, there are drawbacks, and in this case it's the mushrooming of tour operators who are often much less responsible than they ought to be.

'Ecofriendly' operators of pampas and jungle tours are cropping up on every corner of Rurrenabaque's cobblestone streets. Many undercut the official prices and, despite claiming to be ecofriendly, don't respect the environment they work in. Inorganic waste is often left at camp sites, animals are handled and disturbed, and travelers' safety is often compromised, with inexperienced guides not knowing what to do in an emergency. This is largely a result of overdemanding budget travelers expecting low prices and high delivery: perceiving the large number of operators as fair game for bartering, they beat the operators' prices down to the minimum and demand guarantees of spotting wildlife.

Bear in mind that spotting caiman, anaconda, piranhas and other Amazonian animals is a privilege, not a right. Operators and guides should not promise animal sightings (this encourages their unethical capture), go looking for wildlife or, under any circumstances, feed or handle any animals. One reader wrote with this report: 'Ecofriendly-wise, our operators were pretty awful – grabbing hold of anacondas when they found them and capturing baby caimans to show us. We heard that one adult caiman was captured and bit its own tail off in a panic.'

Choose your operator carefully. Talk to other travelers and keep in mind the basic standards that guides should adhere to and, most importantly, be responsible in your own expectations. Better still, opt for one of the community-run ecotourism ventures, which, although more expensive, are definitely more worthwhile and aim to help sustain communities and preserve the richness of the rainforests for the generations to come.

The official rates for jungle and pampas tours are from US$30 to US$40 per day in the rainy season and US$25 to US$30 during the drier period after June 1. Any agency undercutting these official rates should be regarded with caution. Only Sernap-authorized operators are allowed to enter Parque Nacional Madidi and foreigners must be accompanied by a local guide.

Note that to get the most out of these tours, at least a minimal knowledge of Spanish is required. Even more essential, however, is a strong insect repellent; without it, your misery will know no bounds, especially when you're faced with the insidious *marigui* sandfly, which inhabits the riverbanks.

Jungle Tours

The Bolivian rainforest is full of more interesting and unusual things than you'd ever imagine. Local guides, most of whom have grown up in the area, are knowledgeable about the fauna, flora and forest lore; they can explain animals' habits and habitats and demonstrate the uses of some of the thousands of plant species, including the forest's natural remedies for colds, fever, cuts, insect bites (which come in handy!) and other ailments.

Most trips are by canoe upstream along the Río Beni, and some continue up the Río Tuichi, camping and taking shore and jungle walks along the way, with plenty of swimming opportunities and hammock time. Accommodations are generally in agencies' private camps.

Rain, mud and badass insects make the wet season (especially January to March) particularly unpleasant for jungle tours, but some agencies have jungle camps set up for good wildlife watching at this time.

Pampas Tours

It's often easier to see wildlife in the wetland savannas northeast of town, but the sun is more oppressive, and the bugs can be worse, especially in the rainy season. Bring binoculars, a good flashlight, extra batteries and plenty of strong anti-bug juice. Highlights include spotting pink river dolphins, horseback riding and nighttime canoe trips to spot caimans from a distance.

Fluvial Tours/Amazonia Adventures (☎ 892-2372; www.megalink.com/rurrenabaque; Hotel Tuichi, Avaroa s/n) This is Rurrenabaque's longest-running agency.

Indigena Tours (☎ 892-2091; indigenaecologico6@ hotmail.com; Avaroa s/n) A frequently recommended agency.

OTHER TOURS

See the boxed text p342 for information on community ecotourism options around Rurrenabaque.

Sleeping

The sleeping scene in Rurrenabaque's is ruled by one thing: the hammock. The sagging sack can be the sole factor in deciding whether a business does well here or not, so expect there to be many hammocks and enjoy the laziness. The town has good sleeping choices and you should always be able to find a bed.

BUDGET

Hotel Tuichi (☎ /fax 892-2372; Avaroa s/n; s/d US$2/3, with bathroom US$4/5.50) The backpacker scene is most evident here. There is a laundry service, cooking facilities and hammocks, all in a pleasant garden.

El Curichal Guesthouse (☎ 892-2647; elcurichal@ hotmail.com; Comercio 1490; per person US$2.50, with bathroom US$4.30) A new place located at the end of Comercio, this guesthouse has clean, comfortable rooms that come with hot showers. The owners are super-friendly and reside in the house attached. There are also several hammocks swinging seductively in the shade.

Hostal América (☎ 892-2413; Santa Cruz near Comercio; per person US$2.65) This slightly dingy, run-down hotel has fabulous river views from its top floor rooms.

Hotel los Tucanes de Rurre (☎ 892-2039; tucanesderurre@hotmail.com; Bolivar at Aniceto Arce; s/d US$3/6, with bathroom US$4/8) This big, thatched-roof house offers a sprawling garden, a roof terrace and sweeping views over the river. There are hammocks swinging on the patio and the clean and simple rooms are painted in gentle colors. Breakfast is included in the price.

Residencial El Porteño (☎ 892-2558; Comercio at Diez; per person US$3.35, with bathroom US$4.65) Run by a motherly *dueña* (proprietor), the sprawling El Porteño features a prolific carambola tree that provides delicious free juice for hammock-lounging guests.

Hotel Rurrenabaque (☎ 892-2481, in La Paz 279-5917; Diez near Bolívar; s/d US$4.50/9, with bathroom & breakfast US$8/12.50) On a nice quiet street far from the whooping late-night disco crowd, this place has comfortable rooms where you can relax in peace. A restaurant is opening by the hotel, so things might get a bit more noisy.

Hotel Asaí (☎ 892-2439; Diez near Busch; s/d US$6.25/10) All rooms here have their own bathroom and encircle a shaded courtyard. The friendly woman who runs the place is welcoming and proud of the comfy beds and hot showers. There are several obligatory hammocks under a *palapa* (palm-thatched umbrella).

MIDRANGE

Hostal Beni (☎ 892-2408; fax 892-2273; Comercio; s/d US$4/6.65, d with bathroom US$9.35, d with bathroom & air-con US$20; 🖳) The quiet rooms here face away from the busy central street and the decor is cozy, with firm beds, whirling fans and TVs.

Hotel Oriental (☎ 892-2401; Plaza 2 de Febrero; s/d US$9/13) If you meet people who are staying at the Oriental, right on the plaza, they'll invariably be raving about what an excellent place it is – and it is. Comfy rooms, great showers, garden hammocks for snoozing and big breakfasts are included in the price.

Hotel Safari (☎ /fax 892-2210; Comercio Final; s/d with bathroom & breakfast US$25/35; 🖳) Rurre's poshest option sits by the riverfront, away from the town center. It's a quiet, Korean-run place with simple but comfortable rooms with fans. Amenities, catering to tour groups, include a restaurant and karaoke bar.

Eating

Rurre's eating options are numerous and varied, from good market meals and quick chicken to fresh river fish and decent international cooking. Freshly brewed Yungas coffee is widely available.

Several fish restaurants line the riverfront: basic La Chocita, candlelit La Cabaña and Playa Azul grill or fry up the catch of the day for around US$2 to US$3. In addition to the Beni standard, *masaco*, try the excellent *pescado hecho en taquara*, fish baked in a special local pan, or *pescado en dunucuabi*, fish wrapped in a rainforest leaf and baked over a wood fire.

AMAZON BASIN

Restaurant Tacuara (Santa Cruz at Avaroa; mains US$1-3) This open-air eatery with shaded sidewalk seating has an ambitious breakfast through dinner menu. It's friendly and popular, especially for its lasagna.

Restaurant Camila (Santa Cruz at Avaroa; mains US$1-4; 🖳) Camila's gets more popular by the year and has the best value breakfasts in town. The walls are plastered with photos of happy punters, matched by smiling real-life customers. Choose from muesli breakfasts, juices, salads, pasta, burgers, vegetarian lasagna, burritos and chicken dishes, plus unbeatable milkshakes.

Club Social (Comercio near Santa Cruz; lunch US$1.25, dinner US$2-4) With an atmospheric, open-air riverfront setting, Club Social is a good place to enjoy a cocktail. It serves up meat, chicken and à la carte international dishes for dinner.

Pachamama (☎ 892-2620; Avaroa; mains US$1-2.50; 🕐 noon-midnight) This fabulous place occupying an old house has a lounging area on the ground floor, and two movie rooms (US$1.20 per film) and a billiard table upstairs. There's also a book and music exchange and you can leaf through old issues of *National Geographic*. The food is good, be it meaty or vegetarian, and there's great coffee to be sipped. You can even have a barbecue with your friends in the garden. What else could you want?

Café Piraña (Santa Cruz near Comercio s/n; mains US$1.50; 🕐 7am-midnight) This Piraña has bite, with a great chill-out area, delicious vegetarian and meat dishes, yummy breakfasts, lovely fresh juices, a library and film screenings every night in the back garden. Run by the friendly and informed Daniel and his father, you can get lots of local info here too.

La Perla de Rurre (Bolívar at Diez; mains US$2-3) Everyone in Rurre will tell you that this is their favorite restaurant and 'The Pearl' does indeed serve some mean fresh fish and chicken dishes. The service is excellent.

Pizzería Italia (Comercio near Santa Cruz; pizzas US$2-4) The most popular thing about this hangout is the pool tables, but the pizza and pasta are pretty poor. Wine is available as are vegetarian options. It shares the *palapa* with the Jungle Bar Moskkito.

Casa de Campo (☎ 7199-3336; Diez at Avaroa; mains US$2.50-3; 🕐 6:30am-10:30pm) Healthy food is the name of the game here, with all-day breakfasts, homemade pastries, vegetarian dishes, soups, salads, you name it. The friendly owner is keen to make her guests happy, but her breakfast is the priciest in town.

For groceries, try the *tiendas* (small shops) along Comercio or the **Mini Mercado** (Santa Cruz at Busch), where you'll find a selection of canned rations, snacks and alcohol.

Drinking & Entertainment

Rurre doesn't see a lot of action, but there are a couple of bars and discos.

Banana Club (Comercio; admission US$1.20) If you want to try salsa dancing or Bolivian-style grooving, this slightly sleazy club has Cuban doctors shaking their booty, locals getting drunk and gringos joining in.

Club Social (Comercio near Santa Cruz) This is a pleasant place for a quiet drink after dinner; the river slides by as the beer slides down.

Jungle Bar Moskkito (☎ 892-0267; moskkito@terra .com; Comercio s/n; drinks US$2-3) Still the undisputed travelers' favorite, this bar is a good spot to form tour groups. It's Peruvian-run, English is spoken and there's a positive vibe, cheery service and a wide selection of tropical cocktails. Throw some darts, shoot pool and choose your music – the extensive menu of CDs is played by request. Happy hour runs from 7pm to 9pm.

It's hard to miss the thumping, locals-only discos and karaoke bars full of off-duty soldiers on weekends – especially if they're near your hotel. The welcome to gringos at these places usually takes the form of a collective death-stare, so you're better off at Hotel Safari's karaoke bar. The billiards halls along Comercio are mellower, more gringo-friendly options.

Shopping

The cheap clothing stalls near the market and on Comercio are a good place to pick up *hamacas* (hammocks; single/double US$5/10) and finely woven cotton and synthetic *mosquiteros* (mosquito nets; from US$5). Café Piraña has the best selection of local handicrafts.

Getting There & Away

Rurre tries to make the most of its visitors by charging foreigners a 'tourist tax' of US$1 at the airport. That's in addition to the bus terminal tax and the US$0.80 airport tax.

AIR

Rurre's humble airport is a grassy landing strip a few kilometers north of town. The number of flights to Rurre is increasing all the time, but tickets still sell out fast in the high season. Even when the windows are hopelessly scratched, the glorious flights from La Paz afford superb views of 6000m peaks as they climb over the Cordillera Real, then pass over the Yungas, where the land dramatically drops away and opens onto the forested expanses of the Amazon Basin. Have your tour agency purchase your return ticket in advance. If you're stuck, try using the Reyes airport, an hour northeast by bus or shared taxi.

In theory, **TAM** (☎ 892-2398; Santa Cruz) flies between La Paz and Rurre (US$50, one hour) daily except Tuesday. In reality, flights are often canceled or diverted to Reyes in the rainy season. Note that TAM tickets are standby; reserving a seat does not guarantee a place on the return flight, so be sure to confirm your return booking at the in-town office as soon as you arrive.

Amaszonas (☎ 892-2472; Santa Cruz near Avaroa) has four daily flights to La Paz (US$60), but whether the plane will take off is never entirely certain. Make sure you reconfirm your ticket the day before your flight otherwise you may find yourself without a seat. It also flies daily to Trinidad (US$50) via La Paz, and Santa Cruz (US$80), though the latter flight (via La Paz and Trinidad) takes eight hours, so you might be better off getting a flight to La Paz and then catching a direct AeroSur flight to Santa Cruz.

BOAT
Thanks to the Guayaramerín road, there's little cargo transportation down the Río Beni to Riberalta. There's no traffic at all during periods of low water. If you do find something, plan on at least four or five days at around US$7 per day, including meals, for the 1000km trip. Going upstream to Guanay, the journey takes as many as 10 days (on a cargo boat). Except at times of low water, motorized canoe transportation upriver (US$15, 12 hours) may be occasionally available; ask around at the port or larger tour agencies.

BUS & JEEP
The bus terminal is a good 20-minute walk northeast of the center. Minibuses and shared taxis to Reyes (US$1.35, 30 minutes) leave when full from the corner of Santa Cruz and Comercio. When the roads are passable, **Totaí** and **Yungueña** (☎ 892-2112) run daily buses between Rurrenabaque and La Paz (US$6.50, 18 hours), via Yolosa (US$6, 15 hours), 7km

from Coroico. There are also Thursday and Saturday dry-season runs to Trinidad (normal/*bus cama,* or sleeper, US$17/22, 17 hours) via Yucumo, San Borja and San Ignacio de Moxos. Dry-season services sometimes reach Riberalta (US$18, 17 to 40 hours) and Guayaramerín (US$22, 18 hours to three days).

Getting Around
TAM and Amaszonas *micros* (US$0.65, 10 minutes) shuttle between the airport and in-town airline offices; the quicker and breezier moto-taxis (US$0.65) require that you carry all your luggage on your back. Moto-taxis around town cost US$0.35 per ride. Taxi ferries to San Buenaventura (US$0.15) set sail frequently from the riverbank, but the last boat goes across at 6pm.

SAN BUENAVENTURA
Sleepy San Buenaventura sits across the Río Beni watching all the busy goings-on in Rurre, content with its own slower pace. Most Rurre visitors cross over for a stroll, and the residents cross to Rurre daily to conduct their business. The only access is via ferry across the Río Beni from Rurre.

If you're looking for fine Beni leather goods, visit the well-known store of leather artisan Manuel Pinto on the main street, but avoid purchasing anything made from wild rainforest species. The **Centro Cultural Tacana** (☎ 892-2394; west side of plaza; admission US$0.50; ⌚ Sun-Thu) has a handicrafts store and celebrates the Tacana people's unique cosmovision. Sernap's **Parque Nacional Madidi headquarters** (☎ 892-2540) and a tourist information office staffed by agencies authorized to conduct tours in the park provide visitor information.

PARQUE NACIONAL MADIDI
The Río Madidi watershed is one of South America's most intact ecosystems. Most of it is protected by the 1.8 million–hectare Parque Nacional Madidi, which takes in a range of wildlife habitats, from the steaming lowland rainforests to 5500m Andean peaks. This little-trodden utopia is home to an astonishing variety of Amazonian wildlife: 44% of all New World mammal species, 38% of tropical amphibian species, more than 10% of all bird species known to science and more protected species than any park in the world.

The populated portions of the park along the Río Tuichi have been accorded a special

COMMUNITY-BASED ECOTOURISM

This is what many hope the future of Amazonian tourism will look like: responsible operators and customers; respect for culture, environment and wildlife; and benefits for local communities. You can choose from one-day tours to longer stays, incorporating walks in the rainforest with visits to indigenous communities, where you can peek into local lifestyles and traditions. Make sure you don't give sweets or presents to children, no matter how cute they look, as this builds unrealistic expectations. Whether choosing a brief or longer visit, you're bound to have a great experience.

Chalalán Ecolodge (Map p337; ☎ 892-2419, in La Paz ☎ 2-223-1145; www.chalalan.com; Comercio near Campero, Rurrenabaque) is Bolivia's leading community-based ecotourism project. Set up in the early 1990s by the inhabitants of the remote Amazonian village, San José de Uchupiamonas, it has become the lifeline for villagers, and has so far generated money for a school and a small clinic. Built entirely from natural rainforest materials by the enthusiastic San José youth, the lodge surrounds the idyllic oxbow lake, Laguna Chalalán, with simple, elegant huts. Chalalán is Parque Nacional Madidi's only formal visitor accommodations and it provides the opportunity to amble through relatively untouched rainforest and appreciate the richness of life. While the flora and fauna are lovely, it's the sounds that provide the magic here: the incredible dawn bird chorus, the evening frog symphony, the collective whine of zillions of insects, the roar of bucketing tropical rainstorms and, in the early morning, the thunderlike chorus of every howler monkey within a 100km radius.

Your trip (once you're in Rurre) starts with a six-hour canoe ride upstream on the misty Río Beni, and moves onto the smaller tributary, Río Tuichi. Once you're at Chalalán, you can go on long daytime treks or on nocturnal walks, when jaguars are most easily spotted and spiders, surreptitious snakes and colorful tree frogs come out to play. Boat excursions on the lake are a delight, when you can see different types of monkeys who come to feed and drink water. Swimming in the lake among docile caiman is a must, especially at dusk when the light is heavenly. On nights prior to departures from the lodge, the guides throw parties, with windpipe-playing, coca-chewing and general merriment. The village of San José (below) is another three hours upstream by boat, so if you wish to visit it from Chalalán, you'll need to arrange it in advance. For a high-season stay in a simple, comfortable lodge, you'll pay US$295 per person (all-inclusive) for two nights and three days; there are longer options too. Rates include transfers to and from the airport (if you're coming

Unesco designation permitting indigenous inhabitants to utilize traditional forest resources, but the park has also been considered for oil exploration and as a site for a major hydroelectric scheme in the past. In addition, illicit logging has affected several areas around the park perimeter and there's been talk of a new road between Apolo and Ixiamas that would effectively bisect the park. Though the hydroelectric scheme has been abandoned, the debate continues over whether road building and oil exploration will take place and many suspect that the illicit loggers will use the opportunity to benefit from these projects. It is very difficult, however, to distinguish facts from rumors, and the only thing to do is to watch this space and hope for the best.

The US$10 admission fee is payable via tour agencies or at the Sernap office in San Buenaventura. An excellent publication for visitors is *A Field Guide to Chalalán*, sold at the project's office in Rurre.

San José de Uchupiamonas

This lovely traditional village operates Chalalán Ecolodge (see boxed text above), the Bolivian Amazonia's most successful community-based ecotourism project. The village alone merits a visit, and both jungle walks and boat trips are available with local guides. San José celebrates its patron saint with a weeklong **fiesta** around May 1.

You can visit the village independently (though you have to be tough), or on day-long tours through Chalalán. Be aware that village seniors prefer organized visits, though they are always friendly to respectful individual travelers. If you want to get here by yourself, you can take a ferry from Rurre to San Buenaventura, from where *vagonetas* (vans) depart daily from around 8am for Ixiamas. Get off at the village of Tumupasa (US$2, 1½ hours), which has an *alojamiento* half a block from the plaza. From here, it's a relatively easy 30km, eight-hour hike along a rough dry-

from La Paz), one night in Rurre, three great meals per day, a well-trained English-speaking guide, excursions, canoe trips on the lake, plus local taxes and a community levy.

A Day for the Communities Tours (Map p337; ☎ 7128-9884; turismoecologicosocial@hotmail.com; Santa Cruz & Avaroa, Rurrenabaque) provides a fascinating day-long visit to unique Altiplano immigrant communities and alternative sustainable development projects, including a women's *artesanía* (locally handcrafted items) co-op, a sustainable agroforestry experiment, a carpentry workshop and a tropical fruit processing plant. Transportation to the colonies recently settled by Aymará and Quechua refugees fleeing harsh economic conditions is in open trucks and can be dusty and rough, but is reportedly worth the hassle. Rates include transportation, visits to four communities, lunch and a guide, and the community receives 21% of the US$25 per person fee.

Mapajo Lodge (Map p337; ☎ 892-2317; www.mapajo.com; Comercio btwn Santa Cruz & Vaca Diez, Rurrenabaque), an outstanding example of community-run, responsible tourism, offers all-inclusive overnight visits to the Mosetén-Chimane community of Asuncíon, three hours upriver from Rurre inside the Reserva de la Biosfera Pilón Lajas. The project takes in six traditional communities of Tacana, Chimane and Mosetén peoples. Since lumbering was stopped in 1998, the ecosystem is relatively intact and wildlife is quickly returning. The visits include bow-and-arrow fishing, rainforest hiking and unchoreographed community visits. The cost is around US$65 per person per day. The individual *cabañas* are comfy, the hosts are friendly and the food is good and plentiful. Guides mostly speak Spanish. The project's profits finance community health and education projects.

San Miguel del Bala (Map p337; ☎ 892-2394; www.sanmigueldelbala.com; Comercio btwn Vaca Diez & Santa Cruz, Rurrenabaque) is a glorious community ecolodge in its own patch of paradise right on Madidi's doorstep, 40 minutes upstream by boat from Rurre. Accommodations are in cabins with mahogany wood floors, separate bathrooms and beds covered by silky mosquito nets. There are several guided walks, including a visit to the San Miguel community. This Tacana community consists of around 230 inhabitants who'll be happy to show you their traditional agricultural methods or weaving and wood-carving. Guests can also chill in hammocks in the communal hut. What the guides lack in English, they make up for in their enthusiasm and knowledge. If you go for the three-days, two-nights arrangement, you can have a day's visit into Parque Nacional Madidi. The price (per person per day US$65) includes transportation, accommodations, food and guided tours.

AMAZON BASIN

season road to San José de Uchupiamonas; throw in rocks or slap the water with a stick before crossing the numerous river fords to disperse the stingrays.

REYES & SANTA ROSA

The area of Reyes and Santa Rosa is awash with lovely lagoons and myriad birds, alligators and other local wildlife. Though Reyes is less than an hour east of Rurre, Santa Rosa, with its attractive **Laguna Rogagua**, is two rough hours further along. Both places are best visited on a good pampas tour (see p337). Most wildlife sightings are by the Río Yacuma, and the best way to see animals is to travel on a canoe from Santa Rosa. You'll be able to spot caiman, capybara, turtles and birds such as kingfishers, storks, hoatzin and herons, but what most people are hoping for are the pink river dolphins, or *bufeos*, that play on the river bends.

Should you wish to stick around, Reyes' best place to stay is **Alojamiento Santa Tereza** (24 de Septiembre at Fernandez; r US$2), which has a beautiful garden and clean, though spartan rooms. In Santa Rosa, recommended places include **Hotel Oriental** (r US$2) and the more basic **Residencial Los Tamarindos** (r US$2), both along the main street. For meals, try **Bilbosi** (mains US$1) or **Restaurante Triángulo** (mains US$1-2) in Santa Rosa.

TAM (☎ 825-2168, 825-2083) flies to Reyes around once a week, though its schedule changes frequently, so it's wise to check in advance. *Micros* between Santa Rosa and Rurre (US$4.50, four hours) normally leave in the morning.

YUCUMO

This frontier town is basically a stretch of dusty road, populated by development-crazed settlers. You'll be dying to get out of here as soon as you step off the bus. In fact, most buses make a lunch or dinner break here and find passengers queuing impatiently and elbowing each other to get back on the bus. It's at the intersection of the La Paz–Guayaramerín road and the Trinidad turnoff.

The Rurrenabaque–Yucumo road passes through a devastated environment of cattle ranches and logged-out forest. If biding your time here, a decent hike leads along the road south of town; after the bridge, turn left and follow the walking track to a scarlet macaw colony.

If you're stuck here overnight, try the **Hotel Palmeras** (US$2) or **Hotel Tropical** (r US$6, with bathroom US$8), both on the main street. All transportation between Rurre and La Paz or Trinidad passes through Yucumo. Once in Yucumo, connect with a *camioneta* (pickup truck), which will take you through the savanna to San Borja (US$1.75, two hours), from where there are onward connections to Reserva Biosferíca del Beni, San Ignacio de Moxos and Trinidad.

SAN BORJA

Much like Yucumo, San Borja is a bus- and truck-stop destination and few wander into the wilderness beyond the bus terminal. Many visitors sense unsettling vibes here, but it's only really dangerous to those involved in drug smuggling. The town's prosperity is revealed in the palatial homes that rise on the block behind the church. A long day's walk along the relatively little-traveled road west of town will take you through a wetlands area where you can see numerous tropical bird species. At night, San Borja comes alive with motorcycles buzzing, revving and zipping, when life literally revolves around the plaza.

Sleeping & Eating

Hotel San Borja (☎ 848-3313; r US$3.35, with bathroom US$5) This is a clean and friendly place facing the plaza, with higher-end rooms catering to the more plush visitor and cheaper ones providing a crash pad for the night. Note that there is a 6am gospel wakeup call courtesy of the nearby Catholic church.

Hotel Manara (r US$6; ❄) Just off the plaza, this place has en suite rooms, some with air-conditioning.

Hostal Jatata (☎ 895-3103; r US$9) Two blocks off the plaza, Jatata offers good, comfy rooms and a lovely patio with drooping hammocks.

Meals are available at both Hotel Manara and Hostal Jatata. *Lomo* (loin of meat) and *pollo* (chicken) are king at the simple eateries near the plaza on the way to the airport.

Getting There & Away

In the dry season buses pull out several times daily from the bus terminal (3km south of the plaza; US$0.40 by moto-taxi) for the Reserva Biosférica del Beni (US$1.50, 1½ hours), San Ignacio de Moxos (US$3, five hours), Trinidad (US$6.75, eight to 12 hours) and Santa Cruz (US$15, 20 to 24 hours). There are daily services to Rurrenabaque (US$5, five to eight hours) and masochists can travel several times weekly to La Paz (US$20, 23 to 27 hours). The best spot to wait for infrequent *camiones* is at the gas station at the south end of town.

If you're Trinidad-bound, note that the Mamoré *balsa* (raft) crossings close at 6pm, and you need five to six hours to reach them from San Borja. There are no accommodations on either side of the crossing, so give yourself plenty of time. Between San Borja and San Ignacio de Moxos, watch for birds and wildlife. You may also spot capybaras and pink river dolphins at small river crossings.

Amaszonas (☎ 895-3185; Bolívar 157) has daily round-trip flights between La Paz, San Borja and Trinidad. **TAM** (☎ 895-3609) sometimes makes a surprise landing, but doesn't have any regularly scheduled flights.

RESERVA BIOSFÉRICA DEL BENI

Created by Conservation International in 1982 as a loosely protected natural area, the 334,200-hectare Beni Biosphere Reserve was recognized by Unesco in 1986 as a 'Man & the Biosphere Reserve,' and received official recognition the following year through a pioneering debt swap agreement with the Bolivian government.

The adjacent **Reserva Forestal Chimane**, a 1.15-million-hectare buffer zone and indigenous reserve, has been set aside for sustainable subsistence use by the 1200 Chimane people living there. The combined areas are home to at least 500 tropical bird species as well as more than 100 mammal species, including monkeys, jaguars, deer, two species of peccary, river otters, foxes, anteaters and bats.

The Chimane reserve was threatened in 1990, when the government decided to open the area to loggers. Seven hundred Chimanes and representatives of other tribes staged a march from Trinidad to La Paz, in protest of the decision that would amount to the wholesale destruction of their land. Logging concessions were changed but not altogether revoked and the problems continue.

The increasing pressure of immigration has meant that the degraded western 20% of the reserve was lopped off and sacrificed to settlement and exploitation in hopes that the remaining pristine areas can be more vigilantly protected. Though this project has been reasonably successful in recent years, the environmental and cultural impact of the continuing cutting and burning of timber in the area is still a pressing issue.

Information

The reserve is administered by the **Bolivian Academy of Sciences** (☎ in La Paz 235-2071). Admission to the **reserve** (☎ 895-3385, in San Borja 885-3898) costs US$5 per person. Horse rentals are available for US$8 per eight-hour day.

When to Visit

The best months to visit the reserve are June and July, when there's little rain and the days are clear; bring warm clothing to protect against the occasional *surazo*. During the rainy season, days are hot, wet, muggy and miserable with mosquitoes, so bring plenty of repellent. In August and September the atmosphere becomes somber thanks to El Chaqueo smoke (see the boxed text p48).

Tours

The reserve headquarters, El Porvenir, is in the savannas and quite a distance from the true rainforest, so walks around the station will be of limited interest. The station organizes everything in the reserve: accommodations, food, guides and horseriding. The best way to observe wildlife is to hire a guide at the station and go for a hike through the savannas and the primary and secondary-growth rainforests, though the heat might be easier to take if you hire a horse (US$8 per day).

El Porvenir station offers several tours: a four-hour canoe trip to see the black caimans in **Laguna Normandia** (per person US$8.50) at 4pm daily; a four-hour savanna hike to several monkey-rich rainforest islands (US$12); and a full-day **Las Torres tour** (incl food US$21) on horseback to three wildlife-viewing towers where you can observe both savanna and rainforest ecosystems and fish piranha for dinner. When flocks of white-eyed parrots pass through the reserve, you can take the **Loro tour** (US$11) on foot or horseback to see the colorful spectacle – or you can check them out in the palms at El Porvenir, where they provide a raucous 6am wakeup call.

To go into the rainforest beyond Laguna Normandia, you'll need to organize a tour from El Porvenir. It's a four-hour walk from the lake to the margin of the secondary-growth rainforest. A further four hours' walk takes you into the primary forest. Along the way, a 6m viewing tower provides a vista over an island of rainforest, and a 4m tower along the Río Curiraba provides views over the forest and savanna in the remotest parts of the reserve.

Perhaps the most interesting option is the four-day **Tur Monitoreo** (per person without/with food US$81/91), during which visitors accompany park rangers on their wildlife monitoring (and anti-logging) rounds into the reserve's furthest reaches to search for monkeys, macaws and pink river dolphins. You will need your own camping gear for this and, of course, plenty of insect repellent.

Laguna Normandia

This savanna lake, an hour's walk from El Porvenir, is the reserve's most popular destination. The sight of the crawling, rare black caimans – at least 400 – is astounding. The reptile-amphibians are the descendants of specimens originally destined to become unwilling members of the fashion industry, by providing shoe and bag material for a leather company. When the caiman breeder's business failed, the animals were left behind, and the majority perished from neglect, crowding and hunger. The survivors were rescued by Bolivian authorities and airlifted to safety.

Fortunately, caimans have little interest in humans, so it's generally safe to observe them at close range while rowboating around with a guide. If you find them too scary to get up close and personal, climb the 11m **viewing tower**.

Totaizal & Reserva Forestal Chimane

A stone's throw from the road and a 40-minute walk from El Porvenir is Totaizal. This friendly and well-organized village of 140 people lies hidden in the forest of the Chimane reserve. The Chimane, traditionally a nomadic forest tribe, have been facing expulsion from their ancestral lands by lumber companies and highland settlers over the last few years, though things have settled down somewhat recently. The Chimane people are skilled hunters and have a fascinating way of fishing, using natural poisons to kill their

AMAZON BASIN

prey. They are also highly skilled at collecting wild honey and avoiding ballistic bees. People living in the settlement of **Cero Ocho**, a four-hour walk from Totaizal, trudge into the village to sell bananas, while others provide guiding services for visitors. You can visit the village of Totaizal, but you'll have to make prior arrangements through El Porvenir.

Sleeping & Eating

Accommodations at El Porvenir are in airy bunk-bed rooms (including three simple meals) that cost US$13 per person. Amenities include a library, a researchers' workshop, an interpretive center and a small cultural and biological museum. There's plenty of potable water but you'll want to bring snacks and refreshments as there's nothing available for miles around. Thanks to its isolation and relative anonymity, it's quite likely you'll have this peaceful place all to yourself.

Getting There & Away

Don't blink or you'll miss El Porvenir, which is 200m off the highway, 90 minutes east of San Borja, and is accessible via any *movilidad* (anything that moves) between Trinidad and San Borja or Rurrenabaque. On the way out, Trinidad-bound buses pass by between 9:30am and 10:30am. Buses heading for San Borja pass by anytime between 4pm and 7pm. Otherwise, there's surprisingly little traffic. The San Borja–Trinidad bus drivers are usually happy to drop you off at the reserve entrance at El Porvenir.

SAN IGNACIO DE MOXOS

San Ignacio de Moxos is a friendly, tranquil indigenous Moxos village, 89km west of Trinidad, that dedicates itself to agriculture and oozes an ambience quite distinct from any other Bolivian town. The people speak an indigenous dialect known locally as Ignaciano, and their lifestyle, traditions and food are unique in the country. The best time to visit San Ignacio is during the annual festival at the end of July. This is when the villagers let their hair down and get their feather headgear up, and don't stop drinking, dancing and letting off fireworks for three days (see the boxed text below).

San Ignacio was founded as San Ignacio de Loyola by the Jesuits in 1689. In 1760 the village suffered pestilence and had to be shifted to its present location on higher and healthier ground. Although the Jesuits were expelled from South America in 1767, they are now returning to work with the Moxos, and attempting to create an understanding between them, the dispossessed Chimane people and the newly arriving settlers and loggers.

WHEN THE VILLAGE GOES WILD

Annually, July 31 is the first day of the huge Fiesta del Santo Patrono de Moxos, held in honor of San Ignacio, the sacred protector of the Moxos. This is one of the best festivals in the Amazon and if you're in Bolivia during this time, you'd be crazy to miss it.

The celebration includes processions of *macheteros*, local youths dressed as Amazon-style hunters, traditional dancing, music, fireworks and lots of drinking. The festivities begin at noon on the first day of the fiesta, when dancers led by El Machetero proceed from the church, accompanied by drumming, enormous bamboo pan-pipes and flutes. Fresh river fish is eaten in abundance, plenty of drinking takes place (as you'll see by the number of booze-casualties sleeping in the streets) and local *artesania* (locally handcrafted items) are displayed around the village. The processions go on all of the first day, and traditional indigenous dancing takes place in the large warehouse around the corner from the church. There's also a funny local tradition of a man wearing a wooden mask pretending to be a bull chasing the kids in the warehouse courtyard.

The evening of the first day starts with huge fireworks, let off by two rich local families outside the church, who 'compete' with each other through the lavishness of their displays. The pinnacle of the day, though, is the spectacle of the *chasqueros:* men and women wearing large, high-topped leather hats with firecrackers fizzling on the top. The *chasqueros* run through the crowd, while everyone shrieks and runs away from them, laughing and screaming – children have a particularly good time. (It's a good idea to shield your clothes from sparks flying around.)

The second and third days are filled with bull-teasing, when the (drunk) locals attempt to get the bulls' attention, often to little avail. A few days later, San Ignacio goes back to its quiet life, only to go wild again the following year.

Sights & Activities

In the main plaza is a **monument** to Chirípieru, El Machetero Ignaciano, with his crown of feathers and formidable-looking hatchet, a look that's recreated extensively during the village festival. The modern-day **church** (☉ 8am-7pm) on the plaza was rebuilt in 1997, and hides a small museum of local art and Ignaciano religious artifacts at the back. If you get a small group together, one of the church workers will take you around for US$1.20.

At the **museum** (admission US$0.50) in the Casa Belén, near the northwest corner of the plaza, you'll see elements of both the Ignaciano and Moxos cultures, including the *bajones*, or immense flutes introduced by the Jesuits.

North of town at the large **Laguna Isirere**, you can go fishing and swimming, observe the profuse bird life and watch the gorgeous sunset (take insect repellent). It's accessible on a 30-minute walk or by hitchhiking from town.

The greater area also boasts a number of obscure – and hard-to-reach – sights of interest: the **Lomas de Museruna**, several **archaeological ruins**, and the ruins of the **missions** San José and San Luis Gonzaga.

Sleeping & Eating

Note that prices double during the fiesta, but visitors can camp at established sites just outside town during the festivities.

Residencial 31 de Julio (r US$3) A block off the plaza, this friendly place maintains clean and basic rooms.

Plaza Hotel (☎ 482-2032; r US$3, with bathroom US$5) On the plaza, a cheery option with bright, spacious doubles with fans.

Residencial Don Joaquín (☎ 482-8012; Montes; r US$5, with bathroom US$7.50) At the corner of the plaza near the church, offers a nice patio and clean, simple rooms.

Doña Anita (☎ 482-2043; Ballivián; mains US$1) The *doña* is famed for her icy fruit juices and massive burgers topped with cheese, egg and tomato.

Restaurant Don Chanta (mains US$1-1.50) A wonderfully friendly place on the plaza, serving local dishes. Ignaciano specialties include *chicha de camote* (sweet potato *chicha*) and the interesting *sopa de joco* (beet and pumpkin soup).

Getting There & Away

From Trinidad, *micros* and *camionetas* leave for San Ignacio (US$3, three hours) when full from the terminals on Calle La Paz, and *cami-ones* leave in the morning from the east end of La Paz, near the river. There's good forest scenery all along the way, but prepare for heat and dust, as well as delays at the Río Mamoré *balsa* crossing between Puerto Barador and Puerto Ganadero. There are also buses from Trinidad going to San Ignacio (US$3.70, four hours) around 9am every morning, though you'll have to turn up earlier to get your ticket. From March to October, it's four hours from Trinidad to San Ignacio, including the *balsa* crossing, but this route is impassable during the summer rainy season.

Note that the *balsa* shuts down at 6pm (it may stay open later at times of heavy traffic) and there are no accommodations on either side, so check the timing before setting out.

To get to San Borja (US$5, four to five hours), a bus passes through town every day between 1pm and 3pm; make sure you get your ticket in advance from the **bus station restaurant** (San Isteban), otherwise you might find it difficult to get out of town. Buses to Rurrenabaque (US$7.50, 10 hours) go on Monday, Wednesday and Friday between 1pm and 3pm; again, buying a ticket in advance is highly recommended. It's easy to catch a *micro* from San Borja to Rurrenabaque, if there's no direct bus. You can get lunch at the station restaurant for US$1 while you wait.

EASTERN BOLIVIAN AMAZON

The eastern side of the Amazon hides the spectacular Parque Nacional Noel Kempff Mercado, still considered one of Bolivia's least accessible parks, visited mainly by serious adventurers, bird watchers and wildlife enthusiasts who want to feel they are still able to tread little-explored lands. Trinidad, Bolivian Amazon's population center, is still very much a frontier settlement, though it's also an access point for dozens of smaller communities, wild rivers and remote jungle reserves.

TRINIDAD

pop 86,500 / elevation 235m

Trinidad's the place you'll come to if you're after a trip down the long and deep Río Mamoré, or on your way between Santa Cruz and Rurrenabaque. The town's massive, green, tropical main square (Trinidad is only

AMAZON BASIN

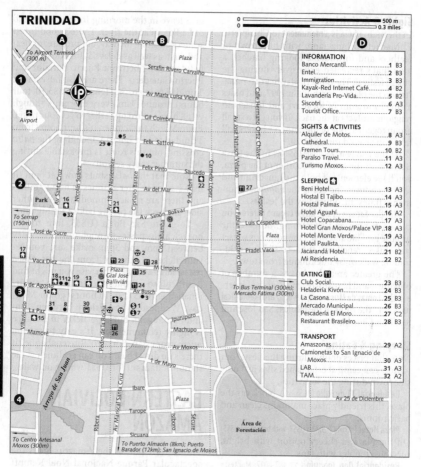

TRINIDAD

INFORMATION
Banco Mercantil.................1 B3
Entel............................2 B3
Immigration......................3 B3
Kayak-Red Internet Café..........4 B2
Lavandería Pro-Vida..............5 B2
Siscotri.........................6 A3
Tourist Office...................7 B3

SIGHTS & ACTIVITIES
Alquiler de Motos................8 A3
Cathedral........................9 B3
Fremen Tours....................10 B2
Paraíso Travel..................11 A3
Turismo Moxos...................12 A3

SLEEPING
Beni Hotel......................13 A3
Hostal El Tajibo................14 A3
Hostal Palmas...................15 A3
Hotel Aguahí....................16 A2
Hotel Copacabana................17 A3
Hotel Gran Moxos/Palace VIP.....18 A3
Hotel Monte Verde...............19 A3
Hotel Paulista..................20 A3
Jacarandá Hotel.................21 B2
Mi Residencia...................22 B2

EATING
Club Social.....................23 B3
Heladería Kivón.................24 B3
La Casona.......................25 B3
Mercado Municipal...............26 B3
Pescadería El Moro..............27 C2
Restaurant Brasileiro...........28 B3

TRANSPORT
Amazonas........................29 A2
Camionetas to San Ignacio de
  Moxos.........................30 A3
LAB.............................31 A3
TAM.............................32 A2

14 degrees south of the equator) greets you with a freshness that, unfortunately, doesn't extend to the rest of the town. The streets of Beni's growing tropical capital are dusty, pot-holed and lined with open sewage canals, which will make your appetite shrivel significantly.

The city of La Santísima Trinidad (the Most Holy Trinity) was founded in 1686 by Padre Cipriano Barace as the second Jesuit mission in the flatlands of the southern Beni. It was originally constructed on the banks of the Río Mamoré 14km from its present location, but floods and pestilence along the riverbanks necessitated relocation. In 1769 it was moved to the Arroyo de San Juan, which now divides the city in two.

Information

Trinidad's helpful municipal **tourist office** (☎ 462-1722; Santa Cruz at La Paz) is inside the Prefectura. Several Enlace ATMs near the main plaza accept international cards – this is a good spot to get some cash before heading out to the ATM-less San Ignacio de Moxos and Rurrenabaque. Moneychangers gather on Av 6 de Agosto between Suárez and Av 18 de Noviembre. You can change traveler's checks at Banco Mercantil.

For telephone calls, see **Entel** (Cipriano Barace 23-A). Fast internet access is available at Siscotri, on the west side of the plaza, **Kayak-Red Internet Café** (cnr Bolívar & Cochabamba) and at several other places; all charge between US$0.30 and US$0.60 per hour. **Lavandería Pro-Vida** (☎ 462-

0626; Sattori at Suárez) charges US$1.20 per dozen stinky items. The provincial **immigration office** (Busch) may grant length-of-stay extensions.

Dangers & Annoyances
Although mud is the biggest problem for pedestrians, the open sewers will make anyone nauseous – except perhaps the 3m boa constrictors sometimes seen swimming in them! Take special care at night.

Sights & Activities
Trinidad's loveliest feature is **Plaza Gral José Ballivián**, with its tall tropical trees, lush gardens and community atmosphere. You can spend an evening eating ice cream and watching hundreds of motorbikes orbiting around the square with more urgency than would seem necessary. Often, entire families ride snuggled on one bike. In the past, the traffic was refereed by a police officer who sat in a big wooden chair and conjured up red, yellow and green traffic lights by touching an electric wire against one of three nails. Alas, technology has prevailed and this stalwart public servant has now been replaced by automatic traffic lights.

On the south side of the plaza, the **cathedral**, built between 1916 and 1931 on the site of an earlier Jesuit church, is an unimpressive build-ing that doesn't even have its own bells – the on-the-hour bell ringing is played off a cassette and tends to sound like a cockerel on fire.

There's a new **ethno-archaeological museum** (admission US$0.60; ☺ 8am-noon & 3-6pm) at the university, 1.5km out of town, which is Spanish-funded and exhibits artifacts from the Trinidad region, including traditional instruments and tribal costumes.

Motorbikes are a great way to while the day away – for US$1.20 per hour you can rent a bike and join the general public in whizzing around the square, or go for a trip out of town. Pick one up from **Alquiler de Motos** (La Paz; from 8am to 6pm US$8, 24hr-hire US$10).

Festivals & Events
The mid-June town **founding fiesta** is a big loud drunken party at the Plaza de la Tradición, and features the climbing of greased poles for prizes and a *hocheadas de toros* (teasing of bulls).

Tours
Several agencies run tours into the city's hinterlands. **Turismo Moxos** (☎ 462-1141; turmoxos@sauce.ben.entelnet.bo; 6 de Agosto 114) organizes three-day cruises on the Río Ibare, visits to Sirionó villages, four-day canoe safaris into the jungle and one-day horseback trips

DOWN THE LAZY RIVER
River trips from Trinidad will carry you to the heart of Bolivia's greatest wilderness area along the Mamoré river, where you'll experience the mystique and solitude for which the Amazonian rainforests are renowned. For optimum enjoyment, go during the dry season, which lasts roughly from May or June to October.

Although the scenery along the northern rivers changes little, the diversity of plant and animal species along the shore picks up any slack in the pace of the journey. The longer your trip, the deeper you'll gaze into the forest darkness and the more closely you'll scan the riverbanks for signs of movement. Free of the pressures and demands of active travel, you'll have time to relax and savor the passing scene.

In general, the riverboat food is pretty good, but meals consist mainly of *masaco* (mashed yucca or plantain), *charque* (dried meat), rice, noodles, thin soup and bananas in every conceivable form. After a couple of days you'll probably start dreaming of pizza, so bring along some treats to supplement the daily fare. It's also wise to carry your own water or some form of water purification.

Be sure to discuss sleeping arrangements with the captain before setting out. Passengers must usually bring their own hammocks (available in Trinidad), but you may be allowed to sleep on deck or on the roof of the boat. You'll also need a sleeping bag or a blanket, especially in winter, when jungle nights can be surprisingly chilly. If you're fortunate enough to be on a boat that travels through the night, a mosquito net isn't necessary, but on one that ties up at night passengers without a mosquito net will find the experience ranges from utterly miserable to unbearable. See the Boat section of Getting There & Away (p351) for how to arrange a boat trip. For a more lush, hotel-boat river trip, see Fremen Tours (p333).

into remote areas. **Paraíso Travel** (☎ /fax 462-0692; paraiso@sauce.ben.entelnt.bo; 6 de Agosto 138) offers four-day bird-watching safaris, jungle camping trips, day cruises on the Rio Mamoré and excursions to Laguna Suárez.

Fremen Tours (☎ /fax 462-1834; www.andes-amazonia.com; Barace 332) specializes in all-inclusive river cruises on its posh hotel-boat *Flotel Reina de Enin*. Cabins include private baths and there's an excellent dining room and bar. It also owns the houseboat *Ebrio*, with four berths and hammock space, which does the run down into Parque Nacional Isiboro-Sécure (p335).

Sleeping

BUDGET

Hotel Paulista (☎ 462-0018; 6 de Agosto & Suárez; r per person US$3, s/d with bathroom US$9/14) Tattered but friendly and central, the Paulista is decent enough for a night.

Hostal Palmas (☎ 462-6979; La Paz 365; s US$3-6.20, d US$6.20-10; ✷) Choose your room carefully at this friendly place – some don't have windows and can get ultra stuffy. The ceilings are high and walls made of exposed brick, but the showers are on the wrong side of clean. Rooms range from shared bathrooms and fans, to en suites with TVs and air-con.

Hotel Copacabana (☎ 462-2811; Villaviencio 627; r US$4, with bathroom US$9) This is a friendly, good-value place with basic rooms with fans.

MIDRANGE

Beni Hotel (☎ 462-2788; benihotel@latinmail.com; 6 de Agosto 68; s/d with bathroom US$10/14) Try for the airy rooms on the first floor in this bright place, though the décor can't get much more basic. There's no breakfast.

Hotel Monte Verde (☎ 462-2750; fax 462-2044; 6 de Agosto 76; s/d with fan US$10/17, with air-con US$20/25; ✷) Musty rooms with little light make this place rather overpriced (especially the air-conditioned rooms). There are TVs and phones in each room, but no breakfast.

Hostal El Tajibo (☎ 462-2324; Santa Cruz 423 & 6 de Agosto; s/d US$12.50/17.50, with air-con US$25/30; ✷) A new place and Trinidad's best-value midrange option, this hotel has attractive, almost stylish rooms and comfortable beds. Some rooms have balconies overlooking the street and breakfast is included in the price.

Hotel Gran Moxos/Palace VIP (☎ 462-2462; moxostdd@sauce.ben.entelnet.bo; 6 de Agosto 146; r with bathroom US$35; ✷) This was once Trinidad's

best hotel, but it's been closed for 10 years and reopened in 2006. The friendly management hopes to make this the town's pride and joy once again, but at the time of research the place was in a shabby state, with peeling paint and plastic furniture. Rooms do come with cable TV, and breakfast is included.

Mi Residencia (☎ 462-1543; fax 462-2464; Saucedo 555; s/d US$35/46.50; ✷ ✷) A flashy entrance through a wooden gate takes you into the smooth, glass-fronted reception here. The large rooms are decked out in loud, kitsch designs, and each has a TV and fridge. A pool was under construction at the time of research in the nice, leafy garden at the back. The hotel is a 10-minute walk from the main plaza. There is parking available.

Jacarandá Hotel (☎ 462-1659; hoteljacaranda@yahoo.es; Bolívar 229; s/d with bathroom & breakfast US$35/50; ✷ ▢) Trinidad's loveliest hotel is a modern, three-star choice with good firm beds plus air-con, phones. cable TV and minibar. The patio has good-looking plants and trees, and there are stylish wooden chairs to lounge on. Children under 12 stay free of charge.

Hotel Aguahí (☎ 462-5569; aguahi@sauce.ben.entelnet.bo; Bolívar at Santa Cruz; s/d with bathroom & breakfast US$35/50; ✷ ▢ ✷) Don't be fooled by the gloomy reception – this hotel is very handsome indeed. The rooms are large, the beds comfortable and quite luxurious, and there are two pools in the spacious, tropical garden. Aguahí is a five-minute walk from the center.

Eating

Since Trinidad is the heart of cattle country, it's the place to indulge in beef; all the major hotel dining rooms feature it on the menu.

Heladería Kivón (east side Plaza Gral José Ballivián; snacks US$1-2) Light meals, full breakfasts, ice cream, cakes, sweets, pastries, sandwiches, coffee and juice are all on offer at this family hangout. It's open when everything else is closed, including mornings and Saturday afternoons. Sit upstairs for good views of the cruising scene.

La Casona (east side Plaza Gral José Ballivián; mains US$1-3) Trinidad's main restaurant has green walls and high ceilings, though it's more attractive during the day than at night when the dull bulbs barely light up the place. There is a daily *almuerzo* (set lunch) and Chinese dishes, as well as rubbery pizza to indulge in.

Club Social (18 de Noviembre; lunch & dinner US$1.20) Right on the plaza, in a shady, breezy courtyard, the lovely social club is a local family favorite. The generous two-course menus include soup, meat, rice and veg, plus a drink.

Pescadería El Moro (Bolívar at Velasco; mains US$2-4) Feeling fishy? Drop anchor here, after a short hike from the center. After dark, the path is badly lit, so you may want to catch a taxi.

Restaurant Brasileiro (Limpias s/n; per kilo US$4) A help-yourself Brazilian food extravaganza, food here is priced by the kilo. Enjoy dodgy TV chat shows while you eat.

Head out to Puerto Barador (p352) on weekends, when *palapa* restaurants serve up the catch of the day.

If budget is a major concern, head for the Mercado Municipal. For a pittance, you can pick up tropical fruits or sample the local specialty, *arroz con queso* (rice with cheese), as well as *pacumutu* (shish kebabs), yucca, plantains and salad. The main plaza is home to plenty of popcorn, ice cream and *refresco* (refreshment) vendors.

Shopping

Local Beni crafts, including weavings, woodwork and ceramics, are sold at the **Centro Artesanal Moxos** (☎ 462-2751; Bopi s/n).

Getting There & Away

AIR

In addition to the US$1.35 Aasana tax, departing air travelers must pay US$0.40 to support senior citizens and finance public works. Note that the inter-Beni flights are frequently suspended for long periods.

Amaszonas (☎ 462-2426, 462-7575; 18 de Noviembre 267) shuttles daily between La Paz, San Borja, Riberalta and Guayaramerín, and **TAM** (☎ 462-2363; Bolívar at Santa Cruz) has a couple of flights a week to Cobija (US$65), Cochabamba (US$38), Guayaramerín (US$57), La Paz (US$55) and Riberalta (US$57). **LAB** (☎ 462-1277; La Paz 322) flies to Cochabamba, if it flies at all.

BOAT

Trinidad isn't actually on the bank of a navigable river; Puerto Almacén is on the Ibare, 8km southwest of town, and Puerto Barador is on the Río Mamoré, 13km in the same direction. Trucks charge around US$1 to Puerto Almacén and US$2 to Puerto Barador.

If you're looking for river transportation north along the Mamoré to Guayaramerín, or south along the Mamoré and Ichilo to Puerto Villarroel, inquire at La Capitania, the port office in Puerto Almacén. Speak to the captain for the boat schedule and ask around for Lidia Flores Dorado, the current *sub-alcaldeza* (town mayor), who will confirm the boat captain's reliable reputation. The Guayaramerín run takes up to a week (larger boats do it in three to four days) and costs around US$30 to US$35, including food. To Puerto Villarroel, smaller boats take 10 days and cost US$15 to US$25, normally including meals.

For a more plush river affair, get on Fremen Tours' posh hotel-boat *Flotel Reina de Enin* (see p333).

BUS & CAMIÓN

The rambling bus terminal is a 10-minute walk east of the center. Road conditions permitting, several *flotas* (long-distance bus companies) depart nightly between 6pm and 9pm for Santa Cruz (normal/*bus cama* US$3.70/7.40, eight to 10 hours). Several companies serve Rurrenabaque (US$10, 12 hours) daily via San Borja. Flota Copacabana beelines direct to La Paz (*bus cama* US$24, 30 hours) daily at 5:30am. There are also daily dry-season departures to Riberalta, Guayaramerín and Cobija. Buses (US$3) and *camionetas* (US$2.50) run to San Ignacio de Moxos (three to four hours) when full; the buses leave the bus terminal at around 9am, though you should get there at least an hour before to make sure you get a seat, and the *camionetas* leave from opposite the Municipality.

Getting Around

TO/FROM THE AIRPORT

Taxis to and from the airport charge around US$1.20 per person (beware of overcharging), but if you don't have much luggage, moto-taxis charge US$0.70 – you'll be surprised how much luggage they can accommodate with a bit of creativity.

MOTORCYCLE

Moto-taxi drivers are normally happy to take the day off and rent out their vehicles, but you'll need a regular driving license from home. Plan on US$1.20 per hour or around US$10 for a 24-hour day. Idle moto-taxi drivers hang out around the southwest corner of the plaza. Alternatively, you can rent motorbikes at Alquiler de Motos (see p349).

TAXI

Moto-taxis around town cost US$0.25, while car taxis charge an outrageous US$1.20. A taxi to the bus terminal costs US$1.20. For rides to outlying areas, phone **Radio Taxi Progreso Beniano** (☎ 462-2759). It's important to know the distances involved and to bargain well for a good rate, which should be no more than US$4 per hour for up to four people. Be sure to include any waiting time you'll need to visit the sights.

PUERTOS ALMACÉN & BARADOR

Puerto Almacén is best known for its lineup of rickety fish restaurants, which provide excellent lunch options. Otherwise, this pointless little place is the proud home of a massive concrete bridge, and vehicles no longer have to be shunted across on *balsas*.

You may prefer to continue 5km to Puerto Barador, where you can observe pink river dolphins in small Mamoré tributaries or sample fresh fish at one of several pleasant portside restaurants. One of the best is El Pantano, which serves excellent *surubí* fish for US$2. It's very popular with locals, especially on Sunday.

Taxis from Trinidad to either port cost about US$8 each way and moto-taxis charge US$3 round-trip. *Camiones* and *camionetas* leave frequently from Av Santa Cruz, one and a half blocks south of Pompeya bridge in Trinidad. All transportation to San Ignacio de Moxos also passes both Puerto Almacén (US$0.75) and Puerto Barador (US$1). For information on boat travel from Puerto Barador, see p351.

SANTUARIO CHUCHINI

The Santuario Chuchini (Jaguar's Lair), 14km northwest of Trinidad, is one of the few easily accessible Paititi sites. This **wildlife sanctuary** sits on an 8-hectare *loma* (artificial mound), one

THE AMAZONIAN EL DORADO

In the Llanos de Moxos, between San Ignacio de Moxos and Loreto, the heavily forested landscape is crossed with more than 100km of canals and causeways and dotted with hundreds of *lomas* (artificial mounds), embankments and more fanciful prehistoric earthworks depicting people and animals. One anthropomorphic figure measures over 2km from head to toe – a rainforest variation on Peru's famed Nazca Lines. The original purpose of the earthworks was probably to permit cultivation in a seasonally flooded area, but inside the mounds were buried figurines, pottery, ceramic stamps, human remains and even tools made from stone imported into the region.

The discovery of the *lomas* has caused scientists to look at the Beni region with entirely new eyes: what was previously considered to be a wilderness never touched by humans, save for a few dispersed tribes who inhabited the region, is now thought to have been an area where a vast, advanced civilization farmed, worked and lived in a highly structured society with sophisticated cities.

It is believed that the ceramic mounds came from the large numbers of people who lived on them and who ate and drank from pots, which were then destroyed and buried to improve soil stability. Archaeologists say that the sheer amount of pots indicates the complexity of this lost society. Charles C Mann, author of *1491: New Revelations of the Americas Before Columbus* (Knopf, 2005) writes, according to archaeologist Clark Erickson, based at the University of Pennsylvania:

...beginning as much as three thousand years ago, this long-ago society...created one of the largest, strangest, and most ecologically rich artificial environments on the planet. These people built up the mounds for homes and farms, constructed the causeways and canals for transportation and communication, created the fish weirs to feed themselves, and burned the savannas to keep them clear of invading trees. A thousand years ago their society was at its height. Their villages and towns were spacious, formal and guarded by moats and palisades. In Erickson's hypothetical reconstruction, as many as a million people may have walked the causeways of eastern Bolivia in their long cotton tunics, heavy ornaments dangling from their wrists.

Some believe that the prehistoric structures of the Beni were constructed by the Paititi tribe 5500 years ago, and that this ancient Beni civilization was the source of popular Spanish legends of the rainforest El Dorado known as Gran Paititi. Archaeologists continue their research into this fascinating part of history, but one thing is for sure: once you know what lies here in terms of world history, you'll never look at the forests of the Beni in the same way again.

of many dotted throughout the surrounding forest. From the camp, you can take short walks in the rainforest to lagoons with caimans, other larger animals and profuse bird life.

The camp has shady, covered picnic sites, trees, children's swings and a variety of native plants, birds and animals. There's also an **archaeological museum** displaying articles excavated from the *loma,* including bizarre statues with distinctly Mongol pigtails and slanted eyes as well as a piece that appears to be a female figure wearing a bikini (it's actually thought to be an identification of and homage to specific body areas rather than an article of clothing).

For a day visit, including admission, a three-hour cruise and a meal, the price is US$50, and to stay overnight it's US$100. Package tours booked in Trinidad may work out a bit cheaper. Further information is available from **Lorena or Efrém Hinojoso** (☎ 462-1968, 462-1811) or travel agencies in Trinidad.

Unless you organize a tour, which will include transportation, you'll have to hitch here. It's easiest to get a ride on Sunday, though you may have to walk the last 5km from Loma Suárez. It's also a good destination for those who've rented motorbikes. Boat transportation may be possible in the wet season.

Bungalows, with meals included, cost US$55 per person. If you're not staying, exotic dishes are available in the restaurant; the food is great but pricey. If you just want a snack, try the tasty *chipilos* (fried green plantain chips).

MAGDALENA

The small and charming settlement of Magdalena presides over the Iténez province, in the heart of vast, low-lying forest and pampa, beside the Río Itonamas and 220km northeast of Trinidad. An abundance of birds and wildlife inhabits the area, and tourism is still a long way away, so if you like the undiscovered, Magdalena is a perfect proposition. Founded by the Jesuits in 1720, the small town was the northernmost of the Bolivian missions. Today, coming here is like stepping back a few centuries: most of the local transportation still consists of carts pulled by rugged horses and tough oxes.

Activities

About 7km upstream is the inviting **Laguna Baíqui**, which is excellent for swimming, picnics and fishing, and is accessible by boat from town (US$1 per person, 30 minutes). Another pleasant excursion will take you to **Bella Vista**, which is considered one of the Beni's most charming villages – and one of its finest fishing venues. It's at the junction of the Ríos San Martín and Blanco. In the dry season, minibuses do the two-hour trip, passing en route through the old-fashioned village of **Orobayaya**.

Magdalena's biggest festival, **Santa María de Magdalena**, takes place on July 22.

Sleeping & Eating

Budget choices, both in the center near the plaza, are **Hotel Ganadero** (r US$6, with bathroom US$8), a clean, spartan place, and **Hotel San Carlos** (r US$6.50, with bathroom US$10) with en suite, fan-cooled rooms.

The town's best accommodations are at the lovely **Hotel Internacional** (☎ 886-2210; s/d with bathroom & breakfast US$30/45; 🖭), offering a surprising amount of comfort in the midst of old-fashioned Magdalena. There is a good restaurant-bar and two pools to refresh yourself in the tropical heat. The rooms are stylishly tropical, bright and airy. The friendly management is happy to help guests organize excursions through the surrounding region.

Getting There & Away

TAM lands here once a week, though its schedule changes and days vary. The Oasis del Aire air-taxi service shuttles daily between Trinidad and Magdalena (US$35 to US$40 one way). The poor dry-season-only road from Trinidad is served by hardy *camiones* and an occasional bus, but realistically it should only be tackled in a 4WD.

RESERVA DE VIDA SILVESTRE RÍOS BLANCO Y NEGRO

This 1.4-million-hectare reserve, created in 1990, occupies the heart of Bolivia's largest wilderness area and contains vast tracts of undisturbed rainforest with myriad species of plants and animals. These include giant anteaters, peccaries, tapirs, jaguars, bush dogs, marmosets, river otters, capuchin monkeys, caimans, squirrel monkeys, deer and capybaras. The diverse bird life includes curassows, six varieties of macaw and over 300 other bird species.

The area's only settlement, the privately owned *estancia* (extensive ranch) of

AMAZON BASIN

Perseverancia, is 350km north of Santa Cruz. It started as a rubber production center in the 1920s, working until the last *seringueros* (rubber tappers) left in 1972. When the airstrip was completed, professional hunters went after river otters and large cats. By 1986 the *estancia* had again been abandoned, and it remained so until tourism – albeit scanty – began to be promoted in 1989.

In the mid-1990s Moira logging concerns began encroaching on the eastern portion of the reserve and USAID recommended that loggers clear a section of the forest rather than cut selective trees. The extent of logging is hard to establish, especially since the park was privatized in the late 1990s, when it lost its protected status and Fundación del Amigos de la Naturaleza (FAN) administration. With the government of Evo Morales planning to introduce a national park 'nationalization,' which will see parks administered through Sernap's cooperation with local communities, it remains to be seen what status the reserve will have in the future.

Tours

Check in Santa Cruz' tourist office (p299) whether any reputable agency runs tours to the park. At the time of research, agencies running this tour were thin on the ground.

Getting There & Away

The privately owned *estancia* of Perseverancia is most easily accessible by a 1½-hour charter flight from El Trompillo airport in Santa Cruz. There's a 100km 4WD track between Asunción de Guarayos and Perseverancia that's passable year-round – with considerable perseverance.

PARQUE NACIONAL NOEL KEMPFF MERCADO

The wonderfully remote **Noel Kempff Mercado National Park** is a real Amazonian highlight and one of South America's most spectacular parks. It is home to a broad spectrum of Amazonian flora and fauna and has a wide range of dwindling habitats, lending it world-class ecological significance and making it a fabulous place to explore. It is estimated that mammal species number at 130, birds at 630, reptiles 75, frogs 63 and fish 260. The park also supports over 4000 plant species.

There is an abundance of animals that can be spotted here, and if you're extremely lucky you may even see a jaguar (you have to be really lucky: even professional researchers see them on average only twice a year). You're more likely to see the maned wolf, the most endangered species in the park.

The rivers hide alligators, caimans, pink river dolphins and rare river otters, and peccaries, tapirs and spider monkeys often come to the river banks to feed and drink water in the evenings. You're more likely to hear the horrific wail of howler monkeys than to actually see them, since they too are considered an endangered species, along with giant anteaters, bush dogs, short-eared dogs and giant armadillos.

Bird-watchers are in for a serious treat. You might glimpse any of these: the rusty-necked piculet, Zimmer's tody tyrant, collared crescent-chest, ocellated crake, rufous-winged antshrike, rufous-sided pygmy tyrant, campo miner, yellow-billed blue finch, black and tawny seed-eater and a host of others.

The park lies in the northernmost reaches of Santa Cruz department, between the Serranía de Huanchaca (aka Meseta de Caparú) and the banks of the Ríos Verde and Guaporé (Río Iténez on Bolivian maps). It encompasses 1.5 million hectares of the most dramatic scenery in northern Bolivia, including rivers, rainforests, waterfalls, plateaus and rugged 500m escarpments.

History

Originally known as Parque Nacional Huanchaca, the lovely park was created in 1979 to protect the wildlife of the Serranía de Huanchaca. Many of the people living around the fringes are descended from rubber tappers who arrived here during the 1940s. When synthetic rubber was developed, their jobs disappeared and they turned to hunting, agriculture, logging and the illegal pet trade.

The park's name was officially changed to its current one in 1988, in honor of its de facto founder, the distinguished Bolivian biologist Noel Kempff Mercado, who had originally lobbied for the creation of the park, but was murdered by renegades at a remote park airstrip east of the Río Paucerna on September 5, 1986. The pilot Juan Cochamanidis and guide Franklin Parada also lost their lives. In 1995 two Brazilians and a Colombian were convicted of the murders. In 2000 the park was inscribed by Unesco as a World Heritage site.

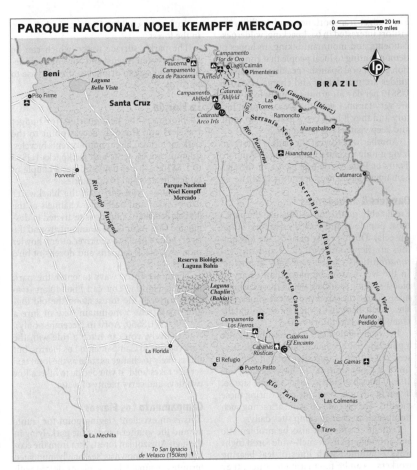

PARQUE NACIONAL NOEL KEMPFF MERCADO

When to Go

There's no wrong season to visit the park. The wet season is great for river travel, especially if you want to boat up to the two big waterfalls. The wettest months are from December to March. The dry season is obviously better for vehicles, but in the late winter months smoke from forest burning can obliterate the scenery, especially from mid-August to October. March to June is pleasant and not overly hot or rainy, and from October to December the spring blooms add another fabulous dimension.

Information

The park is administered by **Sernap** (☎ 243-4429; www.sernap.gov.bo; 20 de Octubre 2659) in La Paz, and though **Fundación Amigos de la Naturaleza**

(FAN; ☎ 355-6800; www.fan-bo.org; Km 7.5, Carretera a Samaipata) in Santa Cruz is no longer an official administrator, it still runs tours and is a great source of information on the park.

Every prospective visitor to the park must first visit a park information office in either Santa Cruz, Concepción or on San Ignacio de Velasco's main plaza; this is in order to ensure that park personnel will be available to accompany travelers on their visit. Visit www .noelkempff.com for an excellent overview of what makes the park so special and for details about the park's ongoing, award-winning Climate Action carbon sequestration program.

The park administration and the Noel Kempff Mercado section at the Natural History Museum (p299) in Santa Cruz organize low-budget transportation and facilities for visitors interested in backpacking, wilderness canoeing and mountain biking, in hopes of demonstrating to local people that conservation pays. Local Spanish-speaking Chiquitano guides are mandatory and charge US$10 to US$15 per day for groups of up to four. They are very familiar with the area's natural history and they'll help carry gear, set up camp and keep visitors out of danger.

Another way to visit the park is by organizing a tour in Santa Cruz through Amboró Tours or Ruta Verde (see p299), or through Samaipata-based tour operators (p314).

Dangers & Annoyances

Predictably, guard yourself against the park's most populous and varied creatures: *bichos* (insects). During rainy periods, the mosquitoes are fierce and voracious and tiny *garapatilla* ticks can be especially annoying. In the wet season, be particularly wary of blood-sucking sandflies, which carry leishmaniasis. These flies are a real pest at some camp sites, particularly in the high forest around the Huanchaca I laboratory ruins.

Between September and December there's a phenomenal bee hatch-out, when the bees seek out human camp sites for salt. At such times it's not unusual to have as many as 10,000 bees hanging around a single site so, if you're allergic, avoid the park during these months. The best way to avoid attracting such numbers is to change camp sites daily.

Leafcutter ants can also be problematic and although their six-inch-wide forest highways – jammed with lines of leaf-bearing workers – can be fascinating to watch, they also often attack the rip-stop nylon of tents. They line their nests with the leaves, which produce fungus for food, and by confusing nylon for leaves the ants do double damage: they can destroy your tent in less than an hour – even while you're sleeping in it – and lose their precious food by lining their nests with plastic. So, don't set up camp anywhere near an ant trail. If that isn't enough, termites have a taste for backpacks that have been left lying on the ground.

Fire is also a concern. The main natural fire season in the park is from July to November and, since the savanna doesn't burn every year, the amount of dead vegetation is substantial. Never cook or even camp in grassland habitat, no matter how flat and inviting, and

never leave a cooking fire unattended, even in the forest.

The park's surface water, which can be scarce between August and November, is delicious and safe to drink, but it's still wise to purify it.

La Florida

La Florida is the headquarters for budget travelers and the only access point to the park's interior. The community rents bicycles, dugout canoes, tents and backpacks (US$5 to US$10 each per day) and has a couple of budget hostels and basic eateries.

By canoe, you can visit the blackwater oxbow lakes and backwater channels of the **Río Bajo Paraguá**. Camping is restricted to designated sites. Wildlife is abundant around the river: you're likely to see river otters, howler monkeys, black caimans and dozens of bird species.

There are three ways to enter the park from La Florida. You can hike 40km (two days) through the forest along the old logging road, rent a mountain bike or hire a 4WD taxi (US$50; April to December only). Alternatively, you can hitch a ride with the park rangers to Campamento Los Fierros, but this is likely to change as soon as the local taxi service takes hold. If you decide to hike, allow two days and carry plenty of water.

Campamento Los Fierros

This is an excellent staging point for jaunts around the southern end of the park, lying in the high Amazonian forest, 2km from the ecological habitat known as 'seasonally inundated termite savanna' (that is, plains dotted with termite mounds). Nearby excursions include bicycle trips to **Laguna Chaplin** and **Catarata El Encanto** and steep hikes up onto the wild **Huanchaca Plateau**.

There's superb bird-watching along the forested roads near Los Fierros, and a nearby creek for cooling off or watching fish-eating bats at night. An early morning visit to the termite savanna will frequently yield glimpses of rare wildlife: maned Andean wolves, crab-eating foxes and even the odd jaguar.

CATARATA EL ENCANTO

The spectacular 150m **waterfall** that spills off the Serranía de Huanchaca is the main objective of most visitors to Los Fierros, making for an enchanting three-day hike. With a mountain bike, it's a long and tiring day-trip; with a vehicle, it can be done in a day, with lots of time for stops along the way.

The excursion begins along the 4WD track that heads east from Los Fierros. Along the way you'll pass through high Amazonian forest, seasonally inundated termite savanna and the threatened *cerrado* (gallery forest) savanna.

Once you've crossed the savanna area, continue until you reach a fork in the road; take the left fork. This abandoned logging road passes through some attractive forest, and you're almost guaranteed to observe – or at least hear – spider monkeys.

Eventually you'll reach a brook with potable water. Here the logging road ends and you follow a trail running alongside the stream to the foot of the waterfall. Camping is allowed along the stream below the trailhead, but not along the trails to the waterfall. In the evening ask your guide to take you to the *salitrals* (natural salt licks) that attract tapirs, peccaries and other large mammals.

SERRANÍA DE HUANCHACA (LA SUBIDA DE LAS PELADAS)

This excursion begins the same as the trip to Catarata El Encanto but, while crossing the seasonally inundated termite savanna, you'll see a small track that turns left (northeast) off the road and leads through the *cerrado* and forest to the foot of the escarpment. From here it's a steep 500m climb up a footpath that crosses three bald hills known as **Las Peladas**. On the way you'll pass through dry forest on the lower slopes, and *cerrado* and bamboo groves on the upper slopes. Once at the top you're ushered onto a spectacular grassy plain dotted with unusual rock outcrops that lent it the name **Campo Rupestre** (Rocky Landscape). There are also plenty of islands of gallery forest with some excellent camp sites.

From the escarpment on a clear day you can see the Amazon forests, termite savannas, Laguna Chaplin and the gallery forests of the Río Bajo Paraguá. It's also a good vantage point to watch hawks and vultures riding the thermals and flocks of blue and yellow macaws migrating between their nesting sites in the highland palm groves and their feeding grounds in the forests below.

On the plateau you can hike for two or three days north to a spectacular unnamed **waterfall** or south to the escarpment overlooking

the Catarata El Encanto. Along the way watch for the endangered *gama* (white-tailed deer), which has its last stronghold here. You'll also pass numerous **crystalline ponds** that make for refreshing swimming holes; at least one species of fish here is found nowhere else on earth and, although it may nip at your legs, it's not dangerous.

Those with adequate financial resources can fly into one of two remote airstrips at the abandoned drug-processing laboratories **Huanchaca I** (now used as an overnight camp on FAN's extension tour) and **Las Gamas**, a beautiful place at the southern end of the escarpment. The former lies on the northern end of the plateau amid *cerrado* savanna dotted with islands of Amazonian forest. From there it's a short day hike to the upper reaches of the **Río Paucerna**, which is a fast-running blackwater river. Strong swimmers will be OK, but drag yourself out before you reach the **Arco Iris waterfall**!

Flor de Oro

FAN runs a comfortable lodge at the airstrip for its package visitors. Around the camp you'll find examples of periodically inundated termite savanna, degraded *cerrado,* oxbow lakes and riverine flooded forests, all of which afford superb bird-watching opportunities. More than 300 bird species have been recorded here, and sightings of pink river dolphins are almost guaranteed. It's a 30-minute motorboat ride or four-hour hike upstream to **Lago Caimán**, a superb spot for bird-watching and seeing caimans. The lagoon is the trailhead for **Allie's Trail**, which climbs up through dry forest to the **Mirador de los Monos** for great scenery along the edges of the escarpment.

Two spectacular **waterfalls** tumble down the Río Paucerna above the Campamento Boca de Paucerna ranger station. From December to late June, the boat trip from Flor de Oro to the rustic **Campamento Ahlfeld** takes about five hours each way, depending on water levels. From the *campamento* (camping grounds) it's an easy 30-minute walk to the spectacular 35m **Catarata Ahlfeld** and its lovely swimming hole. The more adventurous can hike four hours beyond to the fabulous **Catarata Arco Iris**.

Tours

FAN (☎ in Santa Cruz 355-6800; www.fan-bo.org) offers a variety of package tours to the park, including both wet- and dry-season options, as well as other tours that run year-round. All include guides, accommodations, food and local transportation (but not transportation to/from Santa Cruz). In the rainy season a five-/seven-day package at Flor de Oro costs around US$700/1100 per person with two people and US$550/900 with four people. In the dry season a seven-day excursion to both Los Fierros and Flor de Oro costs around US$1100/800 with two/four people. A 10-day bird-watching expedition costs around US$2000/1500. Special four-day, three-night discount trips (from US$465 per person) run several times a year during Bolivian holiday weekends – contact FAN for the current schedule.

Otherwise, contact tour agencies in Santa Cruz (p299) who also run trips to the park.

Sleeping & Eating

In the park's southwest sector, 10km directly west of the escarpment, Campamento Los Fierros provides dorm beds (US$20) and private *cabañas* (US$65). Camping in your own tent is free. In addition, there is running water and showers, meals and kitchen facilities. There are also rustic *cabañas* just below Catarata El Encanto.

The Campamento Flor de Oro in the park's northwest sector is a collection of plush, elegantly furnished en suite huts, with solar-powered lighting and fans. An excellent innovation is the mosquito net–covered patio, with swinging hammocks overlooking the river. You'll pay US$70 per person per day, including delicious Brazilian and Bolivian meals.

The simple Campamento Ahlfeld is a 45-minute walk downstream from the waterfall of the same name. It is accessible by boat from Flor de Oro during periods of high water – normally from December to June.

Getting There & Away

AIR

The easiest – and most expensive – way into the park is via one of FAN's private Cessna aerotaxis. Round-trip charter flights for up to five passengers from Santa Cruz cost US$1200 to Los Fierros (two hours) and US$1300 to Flor de Oro (2¾ hours) and are the major costs of package tours.

BOAT

From the pleasant little Bolivian village of Piso Firme (which has several humble *alojamientos*

and restaurants as well as a small store selling staples), there's an infrequent barge service upriver to Pimenteiras, Brazil (12 hours). From there it's a 30-minute boat ride upstream to Flor de Oro. Otherwise you'll have to negotiate a hired motorboat (up to US$200 one way) or, failing that, swim! There's also a fair amount of Brazilian cargo transportation along the Ríos Mamoré and Guaporé between Guajará-Mirim and Costa Marques, in the Brazilian state of Rondônia. If coming from Brazil, there's no immigration officer in the park, so afterwards you'll have to return to Brazil or make a beeline for immigration in Santa Cruz.

BUS & CAMIÓN

Without your own transportation, reaching the park independently overland will require a great deal of effort, patience and a good measure of your own steam. In any case, it is not generally advisable to visit the park on your own, since many underestimate the tough conditions.

When the roads are driest (normally from June to November), **Trans-Bolivia** (☎ 336-3866; Arana 332) buses depart Santa Cruz every Thursday at 7pm, passing Concepción, San Ignacio de Velasco and La Mechita en route to Piso Firme (US$16, 18 hours). For La Florida, get off at La Mechita, a wide spot in the road 55km west. This is a popular route so book well in advance.

If you're traveling this route, it's wise to speak with the FAN office in San Ignacio and see if a 4WD taxi can meet you in La Mechita. Alternatively, you can try to hitch a ride with the park rangers or a passing logging truck. There are also plans to provide bicycle rental in La Mechita.

At other times take an overnight bus from Santa Cruz to San Ignacio de Velasco (US$7, 10 to 12 hours) – most companies leave between 6pm and 8pm. Once there visit the FAN office and see if anyone can help you find a 4WD taxi service. Similar arrangements can be made in Concepción, where the taxi stand is just off the plaza. Costs are negotiable, but drivers tend to charge by the kilometer (note that it's 250km to the park). You can minimize costs by sharing transportation with four or five travelers.

Alternatively, take the Santa Cruz–San Ignacio de Velasco bus to Santa Rosa de la Roca (US$6.50, nine hours), or take a *micro* there from San Ignacio. After you've secured a good supply of food and drink, find the restaurant El

Carretero, five minutes' walk from Santa Rosa de la Roca along the road toward San Ignacio, and look for a *camión* headed north toward La Mechita. If you're unsuccessful – which will be rare – you can always stay overnight in Santa Rosa, which has a couple of *alojamientos*.

At La Mechita you'll find a couple of *alojamientos* but, with luck, your *camión* may be passing the La Florida turnoff, 20km away, where it's possible to camp. From the turnoff you'll probably have to walk the remaining 35km to La Florida. After 34km from the turnoff, turn right and continue the last kilometer into the village. Here it's possible to camp. On the next day, register at the park rangers' office and embark on the 40km hike to Los Fierros.

CAR & MOTORCYCLE
The easiest way to reach the park is via 4WD (US$75 to US$100 per day) from Santa Cruz. From Santa Cruz it takes at least 14 hours to reach Los Fierros, so most people take two days for the trip, spending the night in Concepción en route.

TO BRAZIL
A more radical alternative is the Brazilian connection to Flor de Oro. After picking up a visa in Santa Cruz, take a bus to San Matías (on the Brazilian border) and then on to Cáceres, four hours into Brazil. From there catch another bus to Vilhena (with a federal police post for entrance stamps) in the southern part of Rondônia state. From there daily buses leave for the village of Pimenteiras, 25 minutes by boat downstream from Flor de Oro. Alternatively, from San Ignacio de Velasco (exit stamps sporadically available), you can catch a direct Trans Joao bus into Brazil via San Vincente to La Cerda (US$17, 10 hours) and change buses for Vilhena (US$10, 4½ hours). If stuck overnight Vilhena has a couple of hostelries near the *rodoviária* (bus terminal).

THE NORTHERN FRONTIER

The isolated, once-untouched rainforests of northern Bolivia's frontier attract only the intrepid, the renegading and the logging. Fire, chainsaws and cattle are guzzling the wilderness at increasing speed, but the rare visitor in search of the unexplored and untamed will have their sense of adventure tickled. Facilities are scarce and travel is slow: perfect for those who really want to evade the gringo trail.

GUAYARAMERÍN
pop 14,000 / elevation 130m

Knocking on Brazil's back door, Guayaramerín is twinned with the Brazilian town of Guajará-Mirim on the other side of the Río Mamoré. This lively town thrives on all kinds of trade (legal and illegal) with Brazil and its streets are full of dusty motorcycle tracks and markets heaving with synthetic garments.

AMAZON BASIN

THE RAIL TO NOWHERE

Guayaramerín is often dubbed 'a rail town where the railway never arrived.' The ill-fated plans to build a railway line that would have connected the Río Beni town of Riberalta and the Brazilian city of Porto Velho started in 1872, with US journalist George Church at the helm of the grand project.

Following a series of disasters, Church abandoned his plans, only to resuscitate and abandon them again in 1882. Brazil picked up the building plans in 1903 and constructed the line only as far as Guajará-Mirim, never reaching Bolivian territory. German, Jamaican and Cuban workers, and even Panama Canal hands, were brought in to work on the project, and by the time the track was finished in 1912, more than 6000 workers had perished from malaria, yellow fever, gunfights and accidents, and the railway came to be known as A Via do Diabo (The Devil's Line).

The railway started working just as the rubber market collapsed, making the effort and deaths involved in the project all the more tragic. The Brazilian side of the railway drew its final chug in 1972, letting the jungle swallow up the rusty rails.

Márcio Souza chronicles the brutal story in *Mad María* (1985), out-of-print but mandatory reading for anyone interested in how humanity briefly conquered this small parcel of the Green Hell.

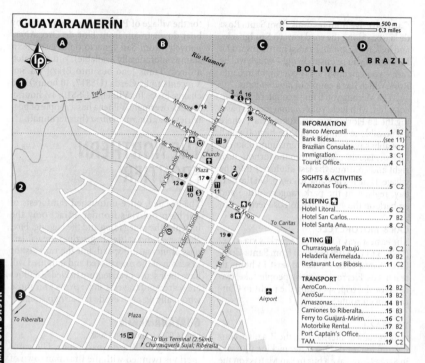

GUAYARAMERÍN

INFORMATION
Banco Mercantil	**1** B2
Bank Bidesa	(see 11)
Brazilian Consulate	**2** C2
Immigration	**3** C1
Tourist Office	**4** C1

SIGHTS & ACTIVITIES
Amazonas Tours	**5** C2

SLEEPING
Hotel Litoral	**6** C2
Hotel San Carlos	**7** B2
Hotel Santa Ana	**8** C2

EATING
Churrasquería Patujú	**9** C2
Heladería Mermelada	**10** B2
Restaurant Los Bibosis	**11** C2

TRANSPORT
AeroCon	**12** B2
AeroSur	**13** B2
Amazonas	**14** B1
Camiones to Riberalta	**15** B3
Ferry to Guajará-Mirim	**16** C1
Motorbike Rental	**17** B2
Port Captain's Office	**18** C1
TAM	**19** C2

It is now the northern terminus for river transportation along the Río Mamoré.

Information

The makeshift tourist office is happy to answer questions, though it can't provide any literature. A block east of the plaza, the relatively efficient **Brazilian consulate** (☎ /fax 855-3766; Beni & 24 de Septiembre; ⏰ 9am-1pm & 3-5pm Mon-Fri) issues visas in two days. Exchange US dollars at the Banco Mercantil, Hotel San Carlos or the *casas de cambio* (exchange bureaus) around the plaza. For traveler's checks, try Bank Bidesa. Moneychangers hanging around the port area deal in US dollars, Brazilian *reais* and bolivianos.

Tours

Amazonas Tours (☎ /fax 855-4000; Román 680) conducts five-hour city tours of Guayaramerín and Guajará-Mirim, as well as La Ruta de la Goma (The Rubber Trail) to Cachuela Esperanza. You can also arrange one-day cruises on the Río Yata or fishing trips to Rosario del Yata, and four-day tours that include hiking and fishing at the Lago Santa Cruz and a cruise along the Río Guaporé to Brazil's Forte Principe da Beira.

Camping equipment is available for rent if you are planning a multi-day trip.

Sleeping

Hotel Santa Ana (☎ 855-3900; 25 de Mayo 611; r US$2.65, with bathroom US$3.50) This shady little hotel has quiet, clean rooms and sprinkling, cool showers.

Hotel Litoral (☎ 855-2016; 25 de Mayo; r per person US$3) Relax in the clean rooms of this budget place, or chill out in front of Brazilian soaps in its courtyard snack bar.

Hotel San Carlos (☎ 855-3555; San Carlos & 6 de Agosto; s/d with bathroom & breakfast US$18/37; ✦ ✦) The choice for anyone here on business, this hotel has a restaurant, redundant sauna, hydromassage, billiards room and 24-hour hot water.

Eating & Drinking

Heladería Mermelada (Central Plaza; ice cream US$1) Mermelada (literally, marmelade) is renowned for its mountainous fruit and ice cream creations.

Churrasquería Patujú (6 de Agosto s/n; mains US$1-2) This place serves up tasty, good-value steak-oriented meals.

Churrasquería Sujal (mains US$1-3) This out-of-town steak house is a nice, quiet place most readily accessible by motorbike taxi.

Restaurant Los Bibosis (Central Plaza; beer & juice US$0.20) Get yourself a beer or a juice here and watch the square.

Shopping

Thanks to its designation as a duty-free zone (authorities couldn't fight the illicit trade, so they decided to sanction it), Guayara is a shopper's mecca. There's nothing of exceptional interest, but it's a good place to pick up brand-name knock-off shoes and clothes, and fake brand-name electronic goods. For *artesanía*, visit Caritas, near the airfield, which sells locally produced wooden carvings for reasonable prices.

Getting There & Away

AIR
The airport is on the edge of town. **Amaszonas** (☎/fax 855-3731; Mamoré 100) and **AeroCon** (☎ 855-3882; Oruro s/n) both shuttle daily between La Paz, San Borja, Trinidad, Riberalta and Guayaramerín. **TAM** (☎ 855-3924) flies twice a week from La Paz (US$88), Riberalta (US$20) and Trinidad (US$57), and once a week from Cochabamba (US$85) and Santa Cruz (US$94). **AeroSur** (☎ 855-3731) serves Cobija a couple of times a week.

BOAT
Cargo boats up the Río Mamoré to Trinidad (around US$25 with food) leave almost daily. The notice board at the port captain's office lists departures. For details, see p351.

OVER THE RIVER & INTO BRAZIL

Popping into Brazil for the day is really easy from Guayaramerín. Day visits are encouraged, and you don't even need a visa.

Between early morning and 6:30pm, frequent motorboat ferries cross the river between the two ports; they cost US$0.75 from Bolivia and US$1.50 from Brazil. After hours there are only express motorboats (US$4 to US$5 per boat) making the crossing. Once you are across the river, the Portuguese words *'onde fica'* (*awn*-jee *fee*-ca), meaning 'where is,' will go a long way, and *'gracias'* is replaced by *'obrigado'* (bree-*gah*-doo) if you're a man or *'obrigada'* (bree-*gah*-dah) if you're a woman.

While you're here, check out the free **Museo Histórico Municipal de Guajará-Mirim** (☯ 8am-noon & 2:30-6:30pm Mon-Fri, 9am-noon & 3-7pm Sat & Sun) in the old Madeira-Mamoré railway station, which focuses on regional history and contains the remains of some of Rondônia's fiercely threatened wildlife. Note the tree full of moth-eaten dead animals, the brilliant butterfly collection, the hair-raising assortment of enormous bugs, the huge anaconda that stretches the length of the main salon, the *sucurí* (the snake of your nightmares) and an informative history of Brazilian currency inflation. The collection of historical photographs includes an intriguing portrayal of an indigenous attack taken in the 1960s. Also check out the classic steam locomotives in the square outside – especially the smart-looking *Hidelgardo Nunes*.

To travel further into Brazil or to enter Bolivia, you'll have to complete border formalities. The Bolivian **immigration office** (☯ 8am-8pm) is at the port in Guayaramerín. On the Brazilian side you pass through customs and have your passport stamped at the port in Guajará-Mirim. They may also ask you to visit the Polícia Federal, on Av Presidente Dutra, five blocks from the port. Leaving Brazil you may also need to pick up a stamp at the Bolivian consulate in Guajará-Mirim.

Although officials don't always check, technically everyone needs to have a yellow-fever vaccination certificate to enter Brazil. If you don't have one, head for the convenient and relatively sanitary clinic at the port on the Brazilian side. For more information, check out Lonely Planet's *Brazil*.

For onward travel, at least eight daily buses connect Guajará-Mirim and Porto Velho (US$10, 5½ hours) along an excellent road, commonly known as the Trans-Coca highway. In addition, Brazilian government boats ply the Ríos Mamoré and Guaporé from Guajará-Mirim to the military post at Forte Príncipe da Beira in two to three days. They then continue to nearby Costa Marques, where food and accommodations are available. Enquire about schedules at the Capitânia dos Portos in Guajara-Mirim.

BUS, CAMIÓN & TAXI

The bus terminal is on the south end of town, beyond the market. With the exception of Riberalta, the only bus services to and from Guayaramerín operate during the dry season – roughly June to October. Buses run to Riberalta (US$2.50, three hours) several times daily. Foolhardy Flota Yungueña departs daily in the morning for Rurrenabaque (US$18, 14 to 36 hours) and La Paz (US$23, 30 to 60 hours) via Santa Rosa and Reyes. There are four brave buses weekly to Cobija (US$14, 16 hours) and Trinidad (US$25, 22 hours). Beware that if enough tickets aren't sold, any of these runs may be summarily canceled.

Shared taxis to Riberalta (US$4.50, two hours) leave from the terminal when they have four passengers. *Camiones* to Riberalta leave from opposite the 8 de Diciembre bus terminal. *Camiones* charge the same as buses but make the trip in less time. To Cobija, YPFB gasoline trucks and a Volvo freight carrier depart occasionally from the same place as the *camiones* to Riberalta.

Getting Around

Guayaramerín is small enough to walk just about anywhere. Motorbike taxis and auto rickshaws charge US$0.40 to anywhere in town. To explore the area, you can hire motorbikes from the plaza for US$1.35 per hour or negotiate all-day rentals – figure US$15 for 24 hours.

RIBERALTA

pop 60,000 / elevation 115m

Despite being a major town in Bolivia's northern frontier region, Riberalta has very little going for it, unless you count the exciting fact that this is one of the world's top Brazil nut production sites. The only reason to stop here is if you're going to Brazil via Cobija and need to take a break. The rather smelly open sewers don't do much for your appetite, especially in the stifling heat, but the plaza can look pretty during orange sunsets. The town sits on the banks of the Río Beni near its confluence with the Río Madre de Dios.

Information

There are no ATMs in town. Get cash advances on Visa and MasterCard and change US dollars at **Prodem** (☎ 857-2212; Suárez 1880). As a service to travelers, Brother Casimiri at the vicarage changes US dollars and traveler's checks. The post office and Entel are near the main plaza and there is an **internet café** (per hr US$1) on the plaza itself.

Keep in mind that the town's municipal water supply is contaminated; the heat and open sewers create a rather pungent atmosphere. Stick to bottled or thoroughly purified water.

Sights & Activities

Riberalta is a pleasant enough town, but it doesn't cater to visitors. In the paralyzing heat of the day, strenuous activity is suspended and you'll find yourself clambering into the nearest hammock. Cool down in the Club Náutico's sparkling **riverside pool** (two blocks north of the plaza), a favorite local activity.

Riberalta's **cathedral** is a wonderful structure in classic Missionary style, wide and elegant, built using red brick and cedar. It sits on the main square and was built on the same spot as the old, less grandiose church, and it cost over half a million US dollars to build.

Parque Mirador La Costañera, on Riberalta's river bluff, overlooks a broad, sweeping curve of the Río Beni and affords the standard Amazonian view over water and rainforest.

At **Puerto Beni-Mamoré**, within walking distance of the center, you can watch the hand-carving and construction of small boats and dugouts by skilled artisans. Two kilometers east of the plaza along Ejército Nacional, you can visit an **old rubber plantation**, watch coffee beans being roasted and visit a **carpentry workshop**.

Sleeping

Residencial Los Reyes (☎ 852-8018; r US$3, with bathroom US$4) The town's best-value place is close to the airport and has a lovely, cool garden courtyard and sparkling rooms. Iced water and hot coffee are always available.

Residencial Las Palmeras (☎ 852-8353; s/d US$12.50/17, with air-con US$23/25; ⌘) Salmon pinks shimmer in this quiet, family home-cum-B&B, 15 minutes' walk from the center. The rooms are cozy and have their own baths. Rates include breakfast.

Hotel Colonial (☎ 852-8212; Baptista; s/d US$25/35; ⌘) Riberalta's loveliest and most expensive hotel is a beautifully renovated colonial home dotted with antique furniture and backed by a delightfully fresh garden where you can relax in a hammock.

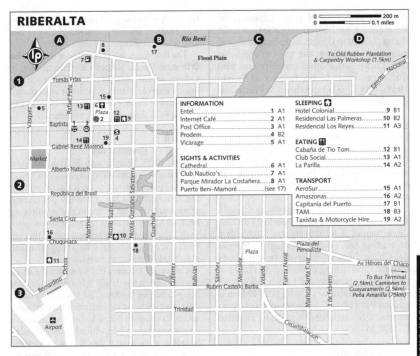

RIBERALTA

0 — 200 m
0 — 0.1 miles

Río Beni

Flood Plain

To Old Rubber Plantation
& Carpentry Workshop (1.5km)

To Old Rubber Plantation & Carpentry Workshop (1.5km)

INFORMATION	
Entel	1 A1
Internet Café	2 A1
Post Office	3 A1
Prodem	4 B2
Vicarage	5 A1

SIGHTS & ACTIVITIES	
Cathedral	6 A1
Club Nautico's	7 A1
Parque Mirador La Costañera	8 A1
Puerto Beni-Mamoré	(see 17)

SLEEPING	
Hotel Colonial	9 B1
Residencial Las Palmeras	10 B2
Residencial Los Reyes	11 A3

EATING	
Cabaña de Tío Tom	12 B1
Club Social	13 A1
La Parilla	14 A2

TRANSPORT	
AeroSur	15 A1
Amaszonas	16 A2
Capitanía del Puerto	17 B1
TAM	18 B3
Taxistas & Motorcycle Hire	19 A2

Plaza del Periodista

Av Héroes del Chaco

To Bus Terminal
(2.5km); Camiones to
Guayaramerín (2.5km);
Peña Amarilla (75km)

Plaza

Airport

AMAZON BASIN

Eating

The market is the best place for a classic breakfast of *api* (a syrupy beverage made from sweet purple corn, lemon, cinnamon and lots of white sugar), juice and empanadas. There are several ice-cream places on the plaza. For an unforgettable Riberalta specialty, sample its famous *almendras* (Brazilian nuts), which are roasted in sugar and cinnamon and sold by children around the bus terminals and the airport for US$0.15 per packet.

Club Social (Dr Martinez; set lunch US$1.20) This place serves inexpensive set lunches, superb filtered coffee, drinks and fine desserts.

La Parilla (Dr Martinez; mains US$2.20) This is highly recommended by the locals for slabs of juicy barbecued meat.

Cabaña de Tío Tom (Baptista; mains US$2.20-2.70) Come here for great traditional meals, coffee, ice cream, juices, shakes and sandwiches, as well as fish and Beni beef. What's more, the sidewalk seating provides a front-row view of the nightly Kawasaki derby. It also does breakfast, but doesn't get going until at least 8:30am.

Getting There & Away

AIR

The airport is a 15-minute stroll south of the main plaza. Departing flights are subject to an airport tax of US$1 and a US$0.60 municipal tax. In the rainy season, however, flights are often canceled and you may be stuck awhile.

AeroSur (☎ 852-2798) and **AeroCon** (☎ 852-2870; airport) fly several times weekly to Trinidad, with connections to La Paz, Santa Cruz and Cochabamba. **TAM** (☎ 852-2646) flies from La Paz to Riberalta (US$88) on Tuesday and Thursday, returning to La Paz on Wednesday and Saturday. **Amaszonas** (☎ 852-3933; Chuquisaca at Sucre) shuttles daily between La Paz, San Borja, Trinidad, Riberalta and Guayaramerín.

BOAT

The Río Beni passes through countless twisting kilometers of virgin rainforest and provides Bolivia's longest single-river trip. Unfortunately, boats upriver to Rurrenabaque are now rare and, in any case, they normally only run when the road becomes impassable (October to May). For information on departures, check the notice board at the Capitanía del Puerto at the northern end of Calle Guachalla. Budget US$20 to US$30 (including meals and hammock space) for the five- to eight-day trip. Lucky Peru-bound travelers may also find cargo boats to the frontier at Puerto Heath, which has onward boats to Puerto Maldonado.

BUS & CAMIÓN
During the soggy rainy season (November to at least March), the mucky Riberalta–Guayaramerín road opens sporadically but, at such times, the La Paz road is closed. The bus terminal is 3km east of the center, along the Guayaramerín road.

In the dry season, several *flotas* do daily runs to and from Guayaramerín (US$2.75, three hours). Alternatively, try hitchhiking or waiting for a *camión* along Av Héroes del Chaco. This typically dusty trip passes through diminishing rainforest. All *flotas* between Guayaramerín and Cobija (US$12, 12 hours), Rurrenabaque (US$18, 17 to 40 hours) and La Paz (US$28, 35 to 60 hours) stop at Riberalta. Several *flotas* also go to Trinidad (US$20 to US$25, 17 hours) daily.

Getting Around
Motorbike taxis (US$0.40) will take you anywhere, but *colectivos* (collective taxis; US$0.40) are scarce. With a driver's license from home, you can rent motorbikes (US$15 per 24 hours) from *taxistas* (taxi drivers) at the corner of Nicolás Suárez and Gabriel René Moreno.

RIBERALTA TO COBIJA
Not so long ago, the route between Riberalta and Cobija was negotiated only by hardy 4WD vehicles and high-clearance *camiones*. Nowadays, it's a high-speed gravel track that connects the once-isolated Pando department with the rest of the country. In the years it has been open, the road has attracted unprecedented development and large parts of virgin rainforest have been cleared at a frightening rate.

At Peña Amarilla, two hours outside Riberalta, the route crosses the **Río Beni** by *balsa*. On the western bank you can find stands selling empanadas and other snacks.

The most interesting crossing on the trip, however, traverses the **Río Madre de Dios**. From the eastern port, the 45-minute crossing begins with a 500m cruise along a backwater

tributary onto the great river itself. Along the way listen for the intriguing jungle chorus that characterizes this part of the country.

The last major *balsa* crossing is over the **Río Orthon**, at Puerto Rico. From Puerto Rico to Cobija, development is rampant. The scene is one of charred giants, a forest of stumps and smoldering bush; often the sun appears like an egg yolk through the dense smoke.

COBIJA
pop 15,000 / elevation 140m
Capital of the Pando and Bolivia's wettest (1770mm of precipitation annually) and most humid spot, Cobija sits on a sharp bend of the Río Acre and has a healthy population of mosquitoes who thrive in the smothering heat, so beware. Cobija means 'blanket' and, with a climate that makes you feel as though you're being smothered with a soggy blanket, it certainly lives up to its name.

Cobija was founded in 1906 under the name 'Bahía,' and in the 1940s it boomed as a rubber-producing center. The town's fortunes dwindled with the shriveling of that industry and it has been reduced to little more than a forgotten village, albeit with a Japanese-funded hospital, a high-tech Brazil-nut processing plant and a pork-barrel international airport.

Information
There is an unreliable Pando tourist office on the plaza that might be able to help you if it's open. The **Brazilian consulate** (☎ 842-2110; ☒ 8:30am-12:30pm Mon-Fri) is on the corner of Beni and Fernández Molina. **Bolivian immigration** (☒ 9am-5pm Mon-Fri) is in the Prefectural building on the main plaza.

There are no ATMs in town. **Prodem** (☎ 842-2800; Febrero 186) gives cash advances on Visa and MasterCard and changes US dollars. *Casas de cambio* Horacio and Horacio II change *reais*, bolivianos and US dollars at official rates, and will occasionally change traveler's checks, for an arm and a leg. The post office is on the plaza and Entel is a block away toward the river.

Sights & Activities
The town rambles over a series of hills, giving it a certain desultory charm. If you spend a day here, take a look at the remaining **tropical wooden buildings** in the center, and the lovely avenues of royal palms around the plaza. The **cathedral** has a series of naive paintings from the life of Christ.

The Pando's biggest annual bash, the **Fería de Muestras** (August 18 to 27), features local artisans and is held at the extreme western end of town, near the Río Acre.

Sleeping & Eating

Residencial Frontera (☎ 842-2740; 9 de Febrero s/n; r US$4, s/d with bathroom US$8/10) The nice, quiet rooms here, some with bathrooms, overlook the patio.

Hostería Sucre (☎ 842-2797; Cornejo & Suárez; s/d with bathroom US$9/13) Just off the plaza, the Sucre includes breakfast and has pleasant rooms.

Esquina de la Abuela (Molina s/n; mains US$2-4) This is Cobija's nicest eatery with alfresco tables and fresh, well-cooked chicken and meat dishes.

Churrasquería La Cabaína del Momo (Molina s/n; mains US$2-4) Dine on cheap *churrasco* (steak) on the balcony here, five minutes' walk from the center.

In the early morning, the market sells chicken empanadas, fresh fruit and vegetables and lots of canned Brazilian products. Unfortunately, nothing stays fresh very long in this sticky climate, and most people won't touch the meat. For a tropical treat, head for the juice bar on the plaza.

Getting There & Away

AIR

For some bizarre reason, Cobija has two airports. Despite the fact that the white elephant Aeropuerto Internacional Anibal Arab (CIJ) can accommodate 747s, most flights use the domestic airport just outside the town. Flights are sporadic at best, and it's largely a matter of luck to connect with something. You'll generally have the best luck flying with TAM or heading to Riberalta.

TAM (☎ 842-2267) flies directly to and from La Paz (US$85) on Wednesday and Friday morning. **AeroSur** (☎ 842-3132; Molina 41) is a block away.

BUS & CAMIÓN

In the dry season, buses to Riberalta (US$12, 12 hours) and Guayaramerín (US$16, 14 hours) leave at 6am daily. There you can connect with services to Rurrenabaque, Trinidad and La Paz. Three times daily Flota Cobija heads 30km south to Porvenir (US$0.80, one hour). In the dry season, *camiones* travel 'direct' to La Paz (around US$30 after bargaining). In the wet, *camiones* may still get through, but plan on at least three hot, wet days.

TO BRAZIL

Entry/exit stamps are available at immigration in Cobija and from Brasiléia's Polícia Federal. A yellow-fever vaccination certificate is required to enter Brazil, but there's no vaccination clinic in Brasiléia, so you'll have to chase up a private physician.

It's a long, hot slog across the bridge to Brasiléia. With some negotiation, taxis will take you to the Polícia Federal in Brasiléia, wait while you clear immigration, then take you on to the center or to the bus terminal. Alternatively, take the rowboat ferry (US$0.40) across the Río Acre. At the Brazilian landing, you're greeted by a topiary turkey, from where it's a 1km hike to the *rodoviária* and another 1.5km to the **Polícia Federal** (8am-noon & 2-5pm). Dress neatly (no shorts!) or you may be refused entry. Check official rates before changing money in Brasiléia. None of Brasiléia's banks accept traveler's checks.

From Brasiléia's *rodoviária*, several daily buses leave for Rio Branco (US$14, six hours), where there are many buses and onward flights.

Getting Around

Motorbike and automobile taxis charge a set US$0.40 to anywhere in town, including the domestic airport. Taxis charge US$0.85 to Brasiléia and US$2.50 to the international airport.

Directory

CONTENTS

Accommodations	366
Activities	367
Business Hours	367
Children	368
Climate Charts	368
Customs	368
Dangers & Annoyances	368
Discount Cards	369
Embassies & Consulates	369
Festivals & Events	370
Food	371
Gay & Lesbian Travelers	371
Holidays	371
Insurance	372
Internet Access	372
Legal Matters	372
Maps	372
Money	373
Photography & Video	373
Post	374
Shopping	374
Solo Travelers	374
Telephone	375
Time	377
Toilets	377
Tourist Information	377
Travelers with Disabilities	377
Visas	377
Women Travelers	378
Work & Volunteering	378

ACCOMMODATIONS

Bolivian accommodations are among South America's cheapest, though price and value are hardly uniform. Be aware that with the exception of the international chains of hotels, the star ratings for hotels are not based on the recognized international rating.

The Bolivian hotel-rating system divides accommodations into *posadas*, *alojamientos*, *residenciales*, *casas de huéspedes*, *hostales* and *hoteles*. This subjective zero- to five-star rating system reflects the price scale and, to some extent, the quality. (Note that *hostales* are not necessarily hostels as you might normally think; some are in fact upmarket hotels.)

Prices in this chapter reflect high-season rates (late June to early September); prices can double during fiestas. Room availability is only a problem during fiestas (especially Carnaval in Oruro) and at popular weekend getaways. The accommodations sections in this book are organized into budget, midrange and top-end categories. Budget typically means less than US$9 per person per night with a shared bathroom (exceptions to this are noted). Midrange is usually around US$10 to US$40 per person (most often with private bathroom and breakfast). The top-end tag is applied to places charging more than US$40 per person. Of course, in bigger cities like La Paz and Santa Cruz, prices may be slightly higher, and top-end places can fetch upwards of US$100 per night. We've noted where accommodations provide bathrooms and/or breakfast.

Camping

Bolivia offers excellent camping, especially along trekking routes and in remote mountain areas. Gear (of varying quality) is easily rented in La Paz and popular trekking base camps like Sorata. There are few organized campsites, but you can pitch a tent almost anywhere outside population centers. Remember, however, that highland nights are often freezing. Theft and assaults have been reported in some areas – always inquire locally about security before heading off to set up camp.

HI Hostels

Hostelling International (HI; www.hostellingbolivia.org) is affiliated with a nascent network of 14 accommodations. Atypical of other 'hostelling' networks, members range from two-star hotels to camping places, but few offer traditional

---

BOOK ACCOMMODATIONS ONLINE

For more accommodations reviews and recommendations by Lonely Planet authors, check out the online booking service at www.lonelyplanet.com. You'll find the true, insider lowdown on the best places to stay. Reviews are thorough and independent. Best of all, you can book online.

PRACTICALITIES

■ Use the metric system for weights and measures – except when buying produce at street markets, where everything is sold in *libras* (pounds; 1lb = 0.45kg).

■ Buy or watch videos on the VHS system.

■ Most electricity currents are 220V AC, at 50Hz. Most plugs and sockets are the two-pin, round-prong variety, but a few anomalous American-style two-pin, parallel flat-pronged sockets exist.

■ Most locals take their coca tea or *cafécito* ('little' coffee) with **La Razón** (www.la-razon.com), the nation's biggest daily newspaper. In Sucre seek out *El Correo del Sur;* in Santa Cruz, *El Deber.* International periodicals are sold at Los Amigos del Libro outlets in bigger cities.

■ In La Paz, tune into noncommercial 96.5FM for folk tunes or 100.5FM for a catchy English-Spanish language pop mix. In Cochabamba Radio Latina 97.3FM spins a lively blend of Andean folk, salsa and rock. For a 24/7 stream of Andean artists, browse **Bolivia Web Radio** (www.boliviaweb.com/radio).

■ Switch on the TV to watch the government-run Canal 7 or the private ATB TV network. Cable (with BBC, CNN, ESPN and other international stations) is available in most upmarket hotels.

amenities like dorm beds or shared kitchens. HI membership cards may be for sale at the flagship hostel in Sucre (p248), although rumor has it that some are yet to learn about offering the 10% discount to members.

Hostales & Hotels

Bolivia has pleasant midrange places and five-star luxury resorts, although these are generally limited to the larger cities and popular vacation and weekend resort destinations. Standard hotel amenities include breakfast, private bathrooms with 24/7 hot showers (gas- or electric-heated), phones and color TV, usually cable. Luxury accommodations are a great bargain where they exist.

Posadas, Alojamientos, Residenciales & Casas de Huéspedes

Quality varies little at the bottom of the range, except at the worst *posadas* (US$1 to US$2 per person) where shared facilities can be smelly, showers scarce and hot water unheard of. Most *alojamientos* (US$2 to US$5 per person) have communal bathrooms with electric showers. Most travelers end up at *residenciales*, which charge US$5 to US$20 for a double with private bathroom, about 30% less without. *Casas de huéspedes* (guesthouses) sometimes offer a more midrange, B&B-like atmosphere. Warning: several readers have alerted us to instances of improper use of propane heaters in Bolivia. Propane heaters are sometimes offered in cheaper accommodations, but these heaters are not meant to be used in enclosed spaces and can have deadly consequences. In

May 2007, two Canadian backpackers died of carbon monoxide poisoning from a faulty propane heater at a hostel in Uyuni.

ACTIVITIES

Want to get the heart pumping and the lungs gasping? Bolivia offers a smorgasbord of activities for the adventure-seeker: from mountaineering to horseback riding, single-track mountain-bike rides to climbing. Hiking and trekking are arguably the most rewarding Bolivian activities; the country rivals Nepal in trekking potential, and awesome climbing opportunities abound. There's riveting river rafting and even basic seasonal skiing (admittedly, on a retreating glacier).

Those who simply prefer chilling out can head off for pleasant jungle strolls or countryside meanders. Fauna and flora fanatics rejoice – Bolivia abounds with rarely visited, world-class, wildlife-watching destinations. Alternatively, you can absorb a few archaeological sites, slide across the salt plains in a 4WD, soak in a hot spring, or visit vineyards. For more, see the Outdoors chapter, p49.

BUSINESS HOURS

Usual business hours are listed inside the front cover. Exceptions to these have been noted in individual listings in this book. Few businesses open before 9am, though markets stir as early as 6am. Banks are open between 8:30am and 4pm. Cities virtually shut down between noon and 2pm or 3pm, except markets and restaurants serving lunch-hour crowds. Hours between eateries vary – this book indicates where restaurants and cafés are open for breakfast, lunch and/or dinner. Most businesses remain open until 8pm or 9pm. If you have urgent business to attend to, don't wait until the weekend as most offices will be closed.

CHILDREN

Few foreigners visit Bolivia with children, but those who do are usually treated with great kindness; Bolivians love babies and children in tow will do wonders to breaking down cultural barriers.

Civilian airlines allow children under the age of 12 to fly at a reduced rate (currently 67% of the full fare), but on long-distance buses, those who occupy a seat will normally have to pay the full fare. Most hotels have family rooms with three or four beds. Restaurants rarely advertise children's portions, but will often offer a child-sized serving at a lower price, or will allow two kids to share an adult meal.

Safety seats, diaper-changing facilities and child-care services are only available in the finest hotels. Breast feeding in public is widespread. Formula milk is available in modern supermarkets in big cities, as are disposable diapers.

There is a fantastic children's museum in La Paz (p80) and in Sucre (p246), and a water park in Santa Cruz (p299), but most Bolivians spend Sunday afternoons picnicking with the family in parks and zoos or strolling the traffic-less Prados of La Paz and Cochabamba.

For more information, advice and anecdotes, check out Lonely Planet's *Travel with Children*.

CLIMATE CHARTS

The following climate charts provide an indication of temperature and rainfall around the country. Note that for La Paz, the airport (where temperature rates are recorded) is 400m higher than the city centre, so official temperature recordings are around 40°F (5°C) cooler than that experienced on the street. For more on Bolivia's climate and the best times to visit, see p14.

CUSTOMS

When entering Bolivia you can bring in most articles duty-free provided that you can convince customs that they are for personal use. There's also a loosely enforced duty-free allowance of 200 cigarettes and 1L of alcohol per person.

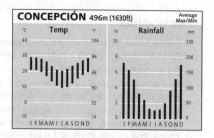

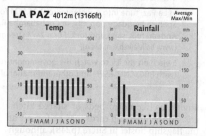

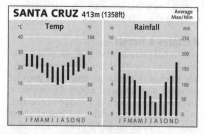

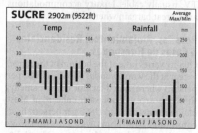

DANGERS & ANNOYANCES

Sadly, Bolivia no longer lives up to its reputation as one of the safest South American countries for travelers. Crime against tourists is on the increase, especially in La Paz and, to a lesser extent, Cochabamba, Copacabana and Oruro (especially during festival times). Scams are commonplace and fake police, false tourist police and 'helpful' tourists are on the rise. Be aware, too, of circulating counterfeit banknotes. See p69 for a detailed rundown of *en vogue* cons.

There is a strong tradition of social protest in Bolivia: demonstrations are a regular occurrence and this can affect travelers. While generally peaceful, in the past few years these have been more threatening in nature at times: agitated protestors throw stones and rocks and police occasionally use force and tear gas to disperse crowds. *Bloqueos* (roadblocks) and strikes by transportation workers often lead to long delays. Be careful using taxis during transportation strikes – you may be at the receiving end of a rock which people pelt at those who are not in sympathy with them.

The rainy season means flooding, landslides and road washouts, which in turn means more delays. Getting stuck overnight behind a landslide can happen; you'll be a happier camper with ample food, drink and warm clothes on hand.

DISCOUNT CARDS

The **International Student Travel Confederation** (ISTC; www.istc.org) is an international network of specialist student travel organizations. It's also the body behind the International Student Identity Card (ISIC), which gives carriers discounts on a few services in Bolivia. La Paz-based **et-n-ic** (Map pp72-3; ☎ 2-246-3782; Illampu 863) sells cards.

Some Bolivian airlines offer 5% student discounts, but they may not be available to foreigners. AeroSur has more generous discounts for passengers over 65 (20% at time of research).

EMBASSIES & CONSULATES

The website of the **Ministerio de Relaciones Exteriores y Culto de Bolivia** (Bolivian Ministry of Exterior Relations & Culture; www.rree.gov.bo in Spanish) has a full listing of Bolivian diplomatic missions overseas, as well as a complete listing of foreign diplomatic representation in Bolivia.

Bolivian Embassies & Consulates

Australia Honorary Consul (☎ 02-9247-4235; Suite 305, 4 Bridge St, Sydney)
Canada Embassy (☎ 613-236-5730; fax 613-236-8237; Suite 416, 130 Albert St, Ontario K1P 5G4)
France Embassy (☎ 01-42 24 93 44; embolivia.paris@ wanadoo.fr; 12 Ave du President Kennedy, F-75016)
Germany Embassy (☎ 030-2639-150; www.bolivia.de, in German & Spanish; Wichmannstr. 6, Berlin PLZ-10787)

GOVERNMENT TRAVEL ADVICE

The following government websites offer travel advisories and information on current hot spots.
Australian Department of Foreign Affairs (☎ 06-6261-3305; www.dfat.gov.au/consular /advice)
British Foreign Office (☎ 0870-606-0290; www.fco.gov.uk)
Canadian Department of Foreign Affairs (☎ 1-800-267-6788; www.dfait-maeci.gc.ca)
US State Department (☎ 202-647-5225; http://travel.state.gov)

UK Embassy (☎ 020-7235 4248/2257; www.embassyof bolivia.co.uk; 106 Eaton Sq, London SW1W 9AD)
USA Embassy (☎ 202-483-4410; 202-328-3712; www .bolivia-usa.org in Spanish; 3014 Massachusetts Ave NW, Washington, DC 20008); Consulate General (☎ 202-232-4828, 202-232-4827; bolivianconsulatewdc@starpower .net; Suite 335, 2120 L St NW, Washington, DC 20037)

Embassies & Consulates in Bolivia

Argentina La Paz (Map pp66-7; ☎ 2-241-7737; Aspiazu 497); Cochabamba (Map p212; ☎ 4-422-9347; fax 4-425-5859; Blanco 0-929); Villazón (Map p206; Saavedra 311); Santa Cruz (Map pp296-7; ☎ 3-334-7133; Junín 22) Above Banco de la Nación Argentina facing Plaza 24 de Septiembre); Tarija (Map p278; ☎ 4-664-2273; Ballivián N-699)
Australia La Paz (Map pp66-7; ☎ 2-243-3241, 211-5655; Aspiazu 416)
Brazil La Paz (☎ 2-244-0202; fax 2-244-0043; Arce, Edificio Multicentro); Cochabamba (Map p212; ☎ 4-425-5860; fax 4-411-7084; 9th fl, Edificio Los Tiempos II, Plaza Quintanilla); Guayaramerín (Map p360; ☎ /fax 3-855-3766; Beni & 24 de Septiembre); Santa Cruz (Map pp296-7; ☎ 3-334-4400; Busch 330); Sucre (Map pp242-3; ☎ 4-645-2661; Arenales 212)
Canada La Paz (Map pp66-7; ☎ 2-241-5021; fax 2-241-4453; 2nd fl, Edificio Barcelona, Sanjinés 2678)
Chile La Paz (☎ 2-279-7331; fax 2-212-6491; Calle 14, 8024, Calacoto); Santa Cruz (☎ 3-343-4272; Calle 5 Oeste 224, Barrio Equipetrol)
Colombia La Paz (☎ 2-278-6841; Calle 9 No 7835, Calacoto)
Ecuador La Paz (Map pp72-3; ☎ 2-231-9739, fax 2-233-1588; 14th fl, Edificio Herrmann, 16 de Julio s/n); Sucre (☎ 4-646-0622, Ceibos 2, Barrio Tucsupaya)
France La Paz (☎ 2-278-6114; Siles 5390 at Calle 8, Obrajes); Santa Cruz (☎ 3-341-0022, fax 3-341-0040); Sucre (☎ 4-645-3018; Bustillos 206)
Germany La Paz (Map pp66-7; ☎ 2-244-0066, 244-1133/66; www.embajada-alemana-bolivia.org; Arce 2395);

Cochabamba (Map p212; ☎ 4-425-4024; fax 4-425-4023; 6th fl, Edificio La Promontora, cnr España & Heroínas); Sucre (Map pp242-3; ☎ 645-2091; www.icba-sucre.edu .bo; Avaroa 326)

Italy La Paz (Map pp66-7; ☎ 3-243-4955/29, fax 2-243-4975; 6 de Agosto 2575, Sopocachi); Santa Cruz (☎ 3-353-1796; 1st fl, Edificio Honnen, El Trompillo); Sucre (Map pp242-3; ☎ 4-645-1514; Avaroa 546)

Netherlands La Paz (Map pp66-7; ☎ 2-244-4040, fax 2-244-3804; 7th fl, Edificio Hilda, 6 de Agosto 2455); Santa Cruz (☎ 3-358-1866; Aguilera 300, 3rd Anillo)

Paraguay La Paz (Map pp66-7; ☎ 2-243-3176; Edificio Illimani, 6 de Agosto); Cochabamba (Map p212; ☎ /fax 4-425-0183; Edificio El Solar, Achá O-107)

Peru La Paz (Map pp66-7; ☎ 2-244-0631, fax 2-244-4149; Edificio Hilda, 6 de Agosto); Cochabamba (Map p212; ☎ 4-448-6556; Edificio Continental, Pedro Blanco N-1344); Santa Cruz (☎ 3-336-8979; 2nd fl, Edificio Oriente); Sucre (Map pp242-3; ☎ 4-645-5592; Avaroa 462)

Spain La Paz (☎ 243-0118, fax 2-243-2752; Av 6 de Agosto 2827); Santa Cruz (☎ 3-332-8921; Santiesteban 237)

UK La Paz (Map pp66-7; ☎ 2-243-3424, fax 2-243-1073; www.embassyofbolivia.co.uk; Arce 2732)

USA La Paz (Map pp66-7; ☎ 2-216-8216; http://lapaz .usembassy.gov; Arce 2780); Cochabamba (Map p212; ☎ /fax 4-425-6714; Rm 601, Torres Sofer, Oquendo E-654)

It's important to realize what your own embassy can and can't do for you. Generally speaking your embassy won't be much help in emergencies if the trouble you're in is remotely your own fault. Remember that while in Bolivia you are bound by Bolivian laws. Your embassy will not be sympathetic if you end up in jail after committing a crime locally, even if such actions are legal in your own country.

In genuine emergencies you might get some assistance, but only if other channels have been exhausted. For example if you need to get home urgently, a free ticket home is exceedingly unlikely – the embassy would expect you to have insurance. If you have all your money and documents stolen, embassy staff might assist with getting a new passport, but a loan for onward travel is out of the question.

FESTIVALS & EVENTS

Bolivians love to party, and celebrations and rituals are integral to their culture. Fiestas are invariably of religious or political origin, and typically include lots of music, drinking, eating, dancing, processions, rituals and general unrestrained behavior. Sometimes water balloons (gringos are sought-after targets!) and fireworks (all too often at eye-level) figure prominently. On major holidays and festive occasions, banks, offices and other services are closed, and public transportation is often bursting at the seams; book ahead if possible.

August is an important month for Pachamama, the Earth Mother, especially in traditional communities, with ceremonies and rituals taking place in her honor. Occasionally you might witness a *cha'lla* (ritual blessing), including the burning of *mesa blanca* (literally 'white table') offerings and incense.

The following is a snapshot of nationwide festivals and events. See the destination chapters for city- and town-specific festivals or events that are held around Bolivia during the year; dates are subject to change.

JANUARY
Día de los Reyes 'Kings' Day' (Epiphany) is celebrated on January 6 as the day the three wise kings visited the baby Jesus after his birth. The largest celebrations are in Reyes (Beni); Sucre; Tarija; and rural villages in Oruro, Cochabamba and Potosí departments.

FEBRUARY/MARCH
Fiesta de La Virgen de Candelaria This weeklong festival is held during the first week of February in Aiquile (Cochabamba); Samaipata (Santa Cruz); Angostura (Tarija) and Cha'llapampa (Oruro). The biggest celebration, however, is at Copacabana in La Paz department.

Carnaval Celebrations are held nationwide the week before Lent. They start with enthusiastic processions with wonderful dancing and booming brass bands, but – with the addition of alcohol – crescendo into madness. In most parts of the world, Lent grinds to a halt with the dawning of Ash Wednesday. In Bolivia, hair-of-the-dog celebrations may continue for several days later than the Catholic Church would consider appropriate.

MARCH/APRIL
Semana Santa One of the most impressive of the nationwide Holy Week activities is the Good Friday fiesta in Copacabana, when hundreds of pilgrims arrive on foot from La Paz.

MAY
Fiesta de la Cruz The Festival of the Cross (May 3) commemorates the cross on which Christ was crucified (or the Southern Cross, in pagan circles). Despite the somber theme, the celebrations are quite upbeat. The greatest

revelry takes place in Tarija, with two weeks of music, parades, and alcohol consumption. The fiesta is also big in Vallegrande (Santa Cruz), Cochabamba and Copacabana.

Día de la Madre Mother's Day celebrations (May 27) are held nationwide. In Cochabamba the festivities are known as Heroínas de la Coronilla in honor of the women and children who defended their cities and homes in the battle of 1812.

JUNE
San Juan Bautista Held nationwide (June 24) but the largest bash takes place in Santa Cruz.

AUGUST
Independence Day Fiesta Held August 6, this highly-charged anniversary provides inspiration for excessive raging nationwide. The largest celebration is held at Copacabana.

OCTOBER
Vírgen del Rosario This celebration is held on different days during the first week of the month and in different locations, including Warnes (Santa Cruz); Tarata, Morochata and Quillacollo (Cochabamba); Tarabuco (Chuquisaca); Viacha (La Paz) and Potosí.

NOVEMBER
Día de Todos los Santos All Saints' Day (November 1) sees nationwide cemetery visits, with much mourning and celebrating, and colorful decoration of graves.

DECEMBER
Christmas Celebrated throughout Bolivia from midnight December 24. Some of the most unique festivities take place in San Ignacio de Moxos (Beni) and Sucre.

FOOD
It might not have the reputation for the spices of Asia, the panache of French cuisine, or the profile of Italian food, but Bolivian food is equally as delicious. The more you learn about Bolivian cuisine, the more you'll appreciate it. This includes knowing how to consume dishes (heartily, and often with condiments), when to consume them (there are special dishes for specific festivals), and where to consume (don't miss the regional or local specialties). Bolivian dishes are made of fresh ingredients, are served in generous helpings and are satisfying and filling. See the Food & Drink chapter (p55) for more specific information.

The eating recommendations provided in this book for larger cities are often broken down by style of eatery. For those who aren't shy to try, the best-value meals are found at midday in and around markets (often under US$1) and at nicer restaurants, where four courses run from US$2 to US$5. A meal at one of the best cosmopolitan restaurants with internationally trained chefs starts at around US$10 a head with wine.

Formal tipping is haphazard except in nicer restaurants. Elsewhere, locals leave coins amounting to a maximum of 10% of the total in recognition of good service.

GAY & LESBIAN TRAVELERS
Homosexuality is legal in Bolivia. In 2004, parliament attempted (unsuccessfully) to introduce Law 810, allowing homosexual couples to marry and foster children.

Gay bars and venues are limited to the larger cities. As for hotels, sharing a room is no problem – but discretion is still in order.

Gay rights lobby groups are active in La Paz (MGLP Libertad), Cochabamba (Dignidad) and most visibly in progressive Santa Cruz. In June 2003 Santa Cruz' La Comunidad Gay, Lésbica, Bisexual y Travestí (GLBT) replaced their fourth annual Marcha de Colores on Día del Orgullo Gay (Gay Pride Day, June 26) with a health fair called Ciudadanía Sexual in an effort to gain wider public acceptance. La Paz is known for La Familia Galan, the capital's most fabulous group of cross-dressing queens who aim to educate Bolivians around issues of sexuality and gender through theater performances. The feminist activist group Mujeres Creando is based in La Paz and promotes the rights of oppressed groups.

HOLIDAYS
Public Holidays
Public holidays vary from province to province. The following is a list of the main national and provincial public holidays; for precise dates (which vary from year to year), check locally.
Nuevo Año (New Year's Day) January 1
Carnaval February/March
Semana Santa (Easter Week) March/April
Día del Trabajo (Labor Day) May 1
Corpus Christi May
Día de la Independencia (Independence Day) August 6
Día de Colón (Columbus Day) October 12
Día de los Muertos (All Souls' Day) November 2
Navidad (Christmas) December 25

Departmental Holidays

Not about to be outdone by their neighbors, each department has its own holiday.

Beni November 18
Chuquisaca May 25
Cochabamba September 14
La Paz July 16
Oruro February 10
Pando & Santa Cruz September 24
Potosí November 10
Tarija April 15

INSURANCE

A good travel-insurance policy to cover theft, loss and medical mishaps is important. Nothing is guaranteed to ruin your holiday plans quicker than an accident or having that brand new digital camera stolen.

There is a wide variety of policies available: shop around and scrutinize the fine print. Some policies specifically exclude 'dangerous activities,' which can include skiing, motorcycling, mountain biking, even trekking. Check that the policy covers ambulances and emergency airlift evacuations. You may prefer a policy which pays doctors or hospitals directly, rather than you having to pay on the spot and claim later. If you have to claim later, make sure you keep all documentation. For more on health insurance, see p391.

INTERNET ACCESS

Nearly every corner of Bolivia has a cybercafé. Rates run from US$0.25 to US$3 per hour. In smaller towns check the local Entel office for access.

Most travelers make constant use of internet cafés and free web-based email such as **Yahoo!** (www.yahoo.com) or **Hotmail** (www.hotmail.com). If you're traveling with a notebook or handheld computer, be aware that your modem may not work once you leave your home country. The safest option is to buy a reputable 'global' modem before you leave home, or buy a local PC-card modem if you're spending an extended time in any one country. For more information on traveling with a portable computer, see www.teleadapt.com.

For a list of useful Bolivia-savvy websites, see 'Internet Resources,' p17.

LEGAL MATTERS

Bolivia may be the land of cocaine, but you'd be a fool to seek the 'Bolivia experience.' Refined cocaine is highly illegal in Bolivia – the standard sentence for possession of cocaine in Bolivia is eight years – so it's clearly best left alone. The big guys get away with processing and exporting because they're able to bribe their way around the regulations. Backpackers and coca farmers become statistics to wave at foreign governments as proof, if you will, that Bolivia is doing something about the drug problem. It's still unwise to carry drugs of any kind, as the consequences are just too costly.

If the worst happens – you're caught with drugs and arrested – the safest bet is to pay off the arresting officer(s) before more officials learn about your plight and want to be cut in on the deal. It's best not to call the payoff a bribe per se. Ask something like '¿Cómo podemos arreglar este asunto?' ('How can we put this matter right?'). They'll understand what you mean.

Foreign embassies should be contacted immediately but note, they don't have the power to resolve the legalities (or illegalities) of the situation.

Be aware that more recently incidences of fake police have been on the rise; see p368.

MAPS

Maps are available in La Paz, Cochabamba and Santa Cruz through Los Amigos del Libro and some bookstores. Government 1:50,000 topographical and specialty sheets are available from the Instituto Geográfico Militar (IGM), with two offices in La Paz (p65) and in other most major cities.

The superb *New Map of the Cordillera Real*, published by O'Brien Cartographics, is available at various gringo hangouts including the postcard kiosks within the La Paz post office. O'Brien also publishes the *Travel Map of Bolivia*, which is one of the best country maps. Walter Guzmán Córdova also produces a range of colored contour maps. Freddy Ortiz' widely available, inexpensive *Journey Routes* map series covers the major touristic regions including La Paz and Lake Titicaca. The **South American Explorers** (www.samexplo.org) has maps of major cities.

An excellent general map of Bolivia is published by Nelles, or Berndston & Bernsdton does a slightly less detailed one. The perfect map of the country for cyclists (because it's plastic) is published by World Mapping Project.

International sources for hard-to-find maps include the US-based **Maplink** (www.maplink.com) and **Omnimap** (www.omnimap.com) and the

UK-based **Stanfords** (www.stanfords.co.uk). In Germany, try **Deutscher Alpenverein** (www.alpenverein.de), which publishes its own series of climbing maps.

MONEY
ATMs
Sizeable towns have *cajero automaticos* (ATMs) – usually Banco Nacional de Bolivia, Banco Mercantil and Banco de Santa Cruz. They dispense bolivianos in 50 and 100 notes (sometimes US dollars as well) on Visa, Plus and Cirrus cards, but in the past, many Europeans have reported trouble using their cards. In smaller towns, the local bank Prodem is a good option for cash advances on Visa and MasterCard (3% to 5% commission charged) and many are meant to be open on Saturday mornings; the hours and machines are often unreliable.

Change
Finding change for bills larger than B$10 is a national pastime as change for larger notes is scarce outside big cities. When exchanging money or making big purchases, request the *cambio* (change) in small denominations. If you can stand the queues, most banks will break large bills.

Credit Cards & Cash Advances
Brand-name plastic, such as Visa, MasterCard and (less often) American Express, may be used in larger cities at better hotels, restaurants and tour agencies. Cash advances (according to your limit at home) are available on Visa (and less often MasterCard), with no commission, from most Banco Nacional de Bolivia, Banco Mercantil and Banco de Santa Cruz branches. In smaller towns, Prodem Bank is your best bet for Visa advances, although normally charges a 3% to 5% commission. Some travel agencies in towns without ATMs will sometimes provide cash advances for clients for 3% to 5% commission.

Currency
Bolivia's unit of currency is the boliviano (B$), which is divided into 100 centavos. Bolivianos come in 10, 20, 50, 100 and 200 denomination notes, with coins worth 10, 20 and 50 centavos. Often called pesos (the currency was changed from pesos to bolivianos in 1987), bolivianos are extremely difficult to unload outside the country.

Prices throughout this book are quoted in US dollars.

Exchanging Money
Visitors fare best with US dollars (travelers have reported that it's difficult to change euros). Currency may be exchanged at *casas de cambio* (exchange bureaux) and at some banks in larger cities. You can often change money in travel agencies and sometimes stores selling touristy items. *Cambistas* (street moneychangers) operate in most cities but only change cash dollars, paying roughly the same as *casas de cambio*. They're convenient after hours, but guard against rip-offs and counterfeit notes. The rate for cash doesn't vary much from place to place, and there is no black-market rate. Currencies of neighboring countries may be exchanged in border areas and at *casas de cambio* in La Paz. Beware, too, mangled notes: unless both halves of a repaired banknote bear identical serial numbers, the note is worthless.

International Transfers
The fastest way to have money transferred from abroad is with **Western Union** (www.westernunion.com). A newer, alternative option is through **Money Gram** (www.moneygram.com), which has offices in all major cities – watch the hefty fees, though. Your bank can also wire money to a cooperating Bolivian bank; it may take a couple of business days.

Traveler's Checks
Changing traveler's checks in smaller towns is often impossible. You'll usually be charged a commission of up to 5% (slightly lower in La Paz). American Express is the most widely accepted brand, though with persistence you should be able to change other major brands.

PHOTOGRAPHY & VIDEO
Bolivian landscapes swallow film, so don't be caught without a healthy supply. Keep in mind, however, that the combination of high-altitude ultraviolet rays and light reflected off snow or water will conspire to fool both your eye and your light meter.

A polarizing filter is essential when photographing the Altiplano, and will help to reveal the dramatic effects of the exaggerated UV element at high altitude. In the lowlands, conditions include dim light, humidity, haze and leafy interference. For optimum shots you need either fast film or a tripod for long exposures.

La Paz is generally the best place to pick up film and for repairs; see p93. As always, avoid exposing your equipment to sand and water.

Photographing People

While some Bolivians are willing photo subjects, others may be superstitious about your camera, suspicious of your motives or interested in payment. Many children will ask for payment, often after you've taken their photo. It's best to err on not taking such shots in the first place. Be sensitive to the wishes of locals, however photogenic. Ask permission to photograph if a candid shot can't be made; if permission is denied, you should neither insist nor snap a picture.

POST

Even the smallest towns have post offices – some are signposted 'Ecobol,' (Empresa Correos de Bolivia). From major towns, the post is generally reliable, but when posting anything important, it's better to pay extra to have it registered.

Parcels

To mail an international parcel in La Paz, take it downstairs in the Central Post Office (p69; the stairs are halfway along the ground floor and to the right). You may be charged a small fee to have the belongings wrapped or your box officially labeled. You'll need two copies of your passport – one will be included in your package. Complete the necessary forms (at the time of research these included a customs declaration form and list of contents, known as a CN-23: Declaracion de Aduana and CP-71 Boletin de Expedicion). Take your parcel to the office marked 'Encomiendas.' If your package is less than 2kg it's easier to send by regular mail. Pay the cost of postage and complete the CN-23. A 2kg parcel to the USA will cost around US$80 by air, US$50 economy rate; to Australia it's US$150.

In some cities, you might have your parcels checked by customs at the post office; in cities without inhouse customs agents, you may have to trek across town to the *aduana* (customs office). A parcel's chances of arriving at its destination are inversely proportional to its declared value, and to the number of 'inspections' to which it is subjected.

Postal Rates

Airmail *postales* (postcards) or letters weighing up to 20g cost around US$0.80 to the USA, US$1.30 to Europe and US$1.55 to the rest of the world. Relatively reliable express-mail service is available for rates similar to those charged by private international couriers.

Receiving Mail

Reliable free *lista de correos (poste restante)* is available in larger cities. Mail should be addressed to you c/o Poste Restante, Correo Central, La Paz (or whatever city), Bolivia. Using only a first initial and capitalizing your entire LAST NAME will help avoid confusion. Mail is often sorted into foreign and Bolivian stacks, so those with Latin surnames should check the local stack. La Paz holds *poste restante* for two months.

SHOPPING

Each town or region has its own specialty *artesania*. For traditional musical instruments, head for Tarija or Calle Sagárnaga in La Paz. For weavings, head for the Cordillera Apolobamba or the environs of Sucre. Ceramics are a specialty around Cochabamba and lowland arts in tropical woods are sold in Santa Cruz, Trinidad and the Amazon Basin.

You'll find a range of reasonably priced work from all over the country in La Paz and Copacabana, but prices are generally lower at the point of original production. All sorts of clothing are available in llama and alpaca wool. Wool from vicuñas is the finest and most expensive. Some pieces are hand-dyed and woven or knitted while others are mass-produced by machine.

Many articles are made by cooperatives or profit companies with ecofriendly and culturally responsible practices. See shopping in La Paz (p92) for more.

SOLO TRAVELERS

As always when traveling, safety is in numbers; solo travelers should remain alert when traveling alone, especially at night. On the whole, however, being alone can open up many doors to meeting local people, and other travelers. The benefits can be huge.

On the more well-trodden gringo circuit, solo travelers should have little trouble meeting up with others. Some hostels and hotels have notice boards for those wanting to form groups to do activities, and in places like

---

TOP BOLIVIAN SOUVENIRS

- *Bolivianita stone* – this stunning yellow-pink semiprecious stone is unique to Bolivia (p92).

- *Chulla* – this traditional hat (the knitted one with patterns and ear flaps) is great for keeping your ears warm. It's got 'I've been to South America' written all over it.

- Irupana chocolate – where else can you buy top-quality, organic chocolate for US$0.15 per bar? (p90)

- Wall hanging – a stunning touch for any abode. The best hail from the Jalq'a region around Sucre.

- Bowler hat – these felt hats go for only US$5 in the section of market along Max Paredes, La Paz (Map pp72–3).

- Ekeko figure – this little lucky man of abundance (see boxed text p81) may look after you – whether a silver trinket or larger ornament.

- *Sampaña* or *charango* – take a stroll and a strum to Sagárnaga for some top-quality musical instruments (see p40 and p92).

- Alpaca and llama designer wear – go animal and kit yourself out in some stunning international fashions with a local touch (p92).

- Wine – connoisseurs rate La Concepción as up there with the world's best (p280).

Uyuni, it's relatively easy to meet other travelers around town to make up the numbers.

Hostel prices are often based on a per-person rate, although more upmarket hotels have separate prices for single and double, with the latter being more economical.

The recent increase in tourism to Bolivia has meant that locals are becoming more accustomed to seeing Western travelers, including unaccompanied women. This has significantly reduced the incidence of sexual harassment and concept of the 'loose gringa,' but in some places you may still face unwanted attention.

If you are traveling without a male companion and/or alone, it's wise to avoid such male domains as bars, sports matches, mines and construction sites. It's all right to catch a lift on a *camión* (flatbed truck), especially if there are lots of other people waiting; otherwise, women should never hitchhike alone. Especially in urban areas and at night, women – even in groups – should use caution, and avoid isolating situations. Hiking alone is discouraged under any circumstances. See also Women Travelers p378.

TELEPHONE

Numerous carriers – such as Entel, Viva, Boliviatel, Cotel and Tigo – offer local and long-distance rates on both landlines and cellular phones. Bolivia's first company, Empresa Nacional de Telecomunicaciones (Entel), is still the most prevalent in smaller towns, with offices usually open 7am to 11:30pm daily, but other companies are making an entrance. Local calls cost just a few bolivianos from these offices. *Puntos*, run by all of the above companies, are small privately run outposts offering similar services. Alternatively, street kiosks are often equipped with telephones that charge B$1 for brief local calls.

In some tiny villages you'll find card-phone telephone boxes – phones take both magnetic and computer chip varieties. Both card types come in denominations of B$10, B$20, B$50 and B$100. Touts in fluorescent jackets with cellular phones chained to themselves offer calls for B$1 per minute.

Cellular SIM cards are cheap and available from larger carrier outlets. Make sure your cellular has tri-band network capabilities (similar to the US system). To top up your call amount, buy cards (ask for *credito*, ie credit) from the numerous *puntos* in any city or town.

Phone Codes

The boxed text p376 has detailed instructions on making calls. In a nutshell, one-digit area codes change by province: 2 for La Paz, Oruro and Potosí; 3 for Santa Cruz, Beni

DIALING IN TO THE TELEPHONE NETWORK

Even Bolivians struggle with their own telephone network, thanks to the recent changes in the system. With patience, dialing is easy once you get your head – and ears – around it. The following should help you tap into the network.

Líneas fijas (landlines) numbers have seven digits; cellular numbers have 8 digits.

Numerous telecommunications carriers include, among others, Entel, Cotel, Tigo, Boliviatel and Viva. Each carrier has an individual code between 10 and 21.

Each department (region) has its own single-digit area code which must be used when dialing from another region or to another city, regardless of whether it's the same area code as the one you're in. The department codes are: (2) La Paz, Oruro, Potosí; (3) Santa Cruz, Beni, Pando; (4) Cochabamba, Chuquisaca, Tarija.

Public phone booths and phone boxes

Dialing landlines from public phone shops is easy; ask the cashier for advice. To make a call to another landline **within the same city**, simply dial the number seven-digit number. If you're calling from **to another region**, dial '0' plus the one-digit area code followed by the seven-digit number eg 02-123-4567. If calling a **cell phone**, ask the cashier for instructions; most *puntos* have different phones for calls to cellular and landlines, so you may have to swap cabins if calling both.

Private landlines

If dialing from landline to landline **within the same city**, dial the seven-digit number. If dialing **another region or city**, enter 0 + 2-digit carrier code + single-digit area code, followed by the number.

Cellular phones

Cellular to cellular calls within the same city are simple – just dial the eight digits. A recorded message (in Spanish) may prompt you for a carrier number, indicating that the person is either not within the same city or region (or has a SIM card from another region), in which case you must then redial using a 0 + 2-digit carrier number plus the eight-digit cellular number.

For **cellular to landline calls within the same city**, in most cases you must dial the single-digit area code, and then the seven-digit number.

For **cellular to landline calls to another region**, in most cases you must dial a 0 + 2-digit carrier code, followed by the single-digit area code, and then the seven-digit number, eg if dialing Sucre from La Paz, dial 0 + 10 (or any one of the carrier codes – 10 is Entel's network carrier) + 4 (Sucre's area code) + the seven-digit number.

International calls

For international calls, you must first dial 00 followed by a country code, area code (without the first 0) and the telephone number.

and Pando; and 4 for Cochabamba, Sucre and Tarija. If you're calling outside your city or region from a *punto*, you must add a '0' plus the initial code. If calling from abroad, do not dial a '0' before the code. If you're calling from a private landline to another city or region, you must dial '0,' plus a two digit-carrier code (10-21), plus the seven-digit number. If ringing a local cellular phone, dial the eight-digit number; if the cellular is from or in another city or province, you must first dial a 0 plus a two-digit carrier code (10 through 21).

In this book, when the given phone number is in another city or town (eg some rural hotels have La Paz reservation numbers), the single-digit telephone code is provided along with the number.

International Calls

Bolivia's country code is ☎ 591. The international direct-dialing access code is 00. Calls from telephone offices are getting cheaper all the time, especially now that there's competition between the carriers. These can vary between US$0.20 and US$1 per minute.

In La Paz the cheapest of cheap calls can be made from international calling centers around Calle Sagárnaga for around US$0.20 per minute.

Some Entel offices accept reverse-charge (collect) calls; others will give you the office's number and let you be called back. For reverse-charge calls from a private line, ring an international operator: for the **USA** (AT&T toll-free ☎ 800-10-1110; MCI ☎ 800-10-2222), **Canada** (Teleglobe ☎ 800-10-0101) or **UK** (BT ☎ 800-10-0044) – be aware that these calls can be bank-breakers.

INTERNET CALLS

Much cheaper Net2Phone internet call centers, charging as little as US$0.05 a minute to the USA and less than US$0.50 a minute to anywhere in the world, exist in major cities, but in many cases connections are shaky at best.

TIME

Bolivian time is four hours behind Greenwich Mean Time (GMT). When it's noon in La Paz, it's 4pm in London, 11am in New York, 8am in San Francisco, 4am the following day in Auckland and 2am the following day in Sydney.

TOILETS

Toilet humor becomes the norm in Bolivia. First and foremost, learn to live with the fact that facilities are nonexistent in nearly all buses (except for a few of the luxury ones). Smelly, poorly maintained *baños publicos* abound and charge around US$0.15 (B$1). Carry toilet paper with you wherever you go at all times! Toilet paper isn't flushed down any Bolivian toilet – use the wastebaskets provided. In an emergency, you can always follow the locals' lead and drop your drawers whenever and wherever you feel the need. Some of the most popular spots seems to be below '*No Orinar*' (Don't Urinate) signs threatening *multas* (fines) equal to the average Bolivian monthly wage. Whatever you do, wash your hands when you are finished and think about using the facilities at your hotel before heading out.

TOURIST INFORMATION

Despite the fact that tourism has taken off in recent years, the Bolivian tourist industry is still in its formative stages, and government tourist offices still concentrate more on statistics and bureaucratic spending than on promotion of the country's attractions. Most real development and promotion have been courtesy of the private sector and it is they who produce brochures and promotional programs.

Tourism now seems to be on the political agenda, which means that tourist offices change with new presidents. The previous national office Secretaría Nacional de Turismo (Senatur) no longer exists, having been replaced by the Vice-Ministero de Turismo with the inception of the Morales government. There are offices covering the *prefectura* (departments), and *alcaldea* (local municipalities) or particular city. The major cities, such as Santa Cruz and La Paz have offices for both, although the different tourism bodies range from helpful to useless. Most municipal offices can provide street plans and answer specific questions about local transportation and attractions. The most worthwhile are those in La Paz, Santa Cruz and Oruro, while those in other major cities seem to be considerably less useful. There are no tourist offices abroad.

As with many Bolivian operations, posted opening hours are not always followed.

TRAVELERS WITH DISABILITIES

The sad fact is that Bolivia's infrastructure is ill-equipped for travelers with disabilities. You will, however, see locals overcoming myriad obstacles and challenges while making their daily rounds. If you encounter difficulties yourself, you'll likely find locals willing to go out of their way to lend a hand.

VISAS

Passports must be valid for six months beyond the date of entry. Entry or exit stamps are free, and attempts at charging should be met with polite refusal; ask for a receipt if the issue is

---

NEW US VISA REQUIREMENTS

In January 2007, the Morales government announced that from March 2007 all US citizens visiting Bolivia will require a visa. At the time of writing the details were still to be worked out; check with the **Bolivian embassy** (☎ 202-483-4410, 202-328-3712; www .bolivia-usa.org in Spanish; 3014 Massachusetts Ave NW, Washington, DC 20008) for the latest.

pressed. Personal documents – passports and visas – must be carried at all times, especially in lowland regions, but it's safest to carry photocopies rather than originals.

Bolivian visa requirements can be arbitrarily changed and interpreted. (At the time of research, there had been three Directors of Migration in six months, since the inception of the Morales Government.) Regulations, including entry stays, are likely to change. Each Bolivian consulate and border crossing may have its own entry requirements, procedures and idiosyncrasies.

Citizens of most South American and Western European countries can get a tourist card on entry for stays up to 90 days, depending on the nationality. Citizens of Canada, Australia, New Zealand and Japan are granted 30 days while citizens of USA and Israel are granted 90 days. This is subject to change; always check with your consulate prior to entry. If you want to stay longer, you have to extend your tourist card (easily accomplished at the immigration office in any major city; those nationalities who have 30 day entries must pay US$21 for extensions). The maximum time travelers are permitted to stay in the country is 180 days in one year. Alternatively, you can apply for a visa. Visas are issued by Bolivian consular representatives, including those in neighboring South American countries. Costs vary according to the consulate and the nationality of the applicant.

Overstayers can be fined US$1.25 per day – which is payable at the migration office or airport – and may face ribbons of red tape at the border or airport when leaving the country. See the website of the **Ministerio de Relaciones Exteriores y Culto** (Bolivian Ministry of Exterior Relations & Culture; www.rree.gov.bo, in Spanish) for a complete list of overseas representatives and current regulations.

In addition to a valid passport and visa, citizens of many Communist, African, Middle Eastern and Asian countries require 'official permission' from the Bolivian Ministry of Foreign Affairs before a visa will be issued.

Vaccination Certificates

Anyone coming from a yellow-fever infected area needs a vaccination certificate to enter Bolivia. Many neighboring countries, including Brazil, also require anyone entering from Bolivia to have proof of a yellow-fever vaccination. If necessary, a jab can often be administered at the border. For more on yellow fever, see p395.

WOMEN TRAVELERS

Women's rights in Bolivia are nearing modern standards and cities are more liberal than country regions. But despite the importance of women in Bolivian society and the elevation of females in public life (including a female president, women mayors and many female members of the 2006 Constitutional Assembly), the machismo mind-set still pervades in Bolivia. As a female traveling alone, the mere fact that you appear to be unmarried and far from your home and family may cause you to appear suspiciously disreputable.

Bear in mind that modesty is expected of women in much of Spanish-speaking Latin America. Local women who wear Western dress in the warmer and lower areas tend to show more flesh than elsewhere in the country. That said, as a foreigner, avoid testing the system alone in a bar in a miniskirt. Conservative dress and confidence without arrogance are a must for gringas, more so to be respectful than anything else. Men are generally more forward and flirtatious in the lowlands than in the Altiplano. The best advice is to watch the standards of well-dressed Bolivian women in any particular area and follow their example. See also Solo Travelers p374.

WORK & VOLUNTEERING

There are hundreds of voluntary and nongovernmental organizations (NGOs) working in Bolivia, but travelers looking for paid work on the spot shouldn't hold their breath.

For paid work, qualified English teachers can try the professionally run **Centro Boliviano-Americano** (CBA; ☎ 243-0107; www.cba.edu.bo; Parque Zenón Iturralde 121) in La Paz; there are also offices in other cities. New, unqualified teachers must forfeit two months' salary in return for their training. Better paying are private school positions teaching math, science or social studies. Accredited teachers can expect to earn up to US$500 per month for a full-time position.

Unpaid work is available in several places, and in others, you pay for the privilege of working on a project. (Be aware that some profit organizations offer 'internship' or 'volunteer' opportunities, when in reality it's unpaid work in exchange for free trips or activities.)

There are a few options to do genuine volunteer work. Government-sponsored organizations or NGOs such as the Peace Corps offer longer term programs (usually two years) for which you receive an allowance, predeparture briefings and ongoing organizational support; church-affiliated or religious organizations offer short-term opportunities, often on a group basis; and smaller volunteer organizations (often profit-based) offer independent travelers the opportunity to work in community projects. These usually have a two- or four-week minimum for which you pay. This covers a language immersion course, a local homestay and administrative costs.

Some popular volunteer options include:

Animales S.0.S (☎ 2-230-8080; www.animalessos.org) An animal welfare group caring for mistreated or abused stray animals.

Parque Machía (☎ 4-413-6572; www.intiwarayassi.org; Parque Machía, Villa Tunari, Chapare) Volunteer-run wild animal refuge; minimum commitment is 15 days and no previous experience working with animals is required. See p333.

Volunteer Bolivia (Map p212; ☎ 4-452-6028; www .volunteerbolivia.org; Ecuador 342, Cochabamba) Arranges short- and long-term volunteer work, study and homestay programs throughout Bolivia.

For longer-term volunteering assignments, you're better off contacting international NGOs in your country or region, including **Peace Corps** (www.peacecorps.gov) in the USA and **Centre d'Etude et de Coopération Internationale** (CECI; www.ceci.ca) in Canada.

Interested wannabe volunteers and workers can make a start by looking up the following websites of profit and not-for-profit organizations and NGOs.

- www.amizade.org
- www.earthwatch.org.uk
- www.freiwilliger-weltweit.de (in German)
- www.globalcrossroad.com
- www.gvi.co.uk
- www.i-to-i.com
- www.realgap.co.uk
- www.teaching-abroad.co.uk
- www.transitionsabroad.com
- www.unv.org
- www.vivabolivia.org/bcmission
- www.volunteerabroad.com (this site features a broad selection of short and longer term opportunities)
- www.volunteeradventures.com
- www.worldvolunteerweb.org

Transportation

CONTENTS

Getting There & Away	**380**
Entering the Country	380
Air	380
Land & River	383
Getting Around	**385**
Air	385
Bicycle	385
Boat	386
Bus	386
Car & Motorcycle	387
Hitchhiking	388
Local Transportation	388
Train	389
Tours	389

GETTING THERE & AWAY

A landlocked country, Bolivia has numerous entry/exit points. Some are easier and more accessible than others; the more remote borders are recommended for intrepid travelers only – those with time and lust for unpredictable adventure.

Flights, tours and rail tickets can be booked online at www.lonelyplanet.com/travel_services.

ENTERING THE COUNTRY

If you have your documents in order and you are willing to answer a few questions about the aim of your visit, entry into Bolivia should be a breeze. If crossing at a smaller border post, you might be asked to pay an 'exit fee.' Unless otherwise noted in the text, these fees are strictly unofficial. Note that

---

DEPARTURE TAX

The international departure tax, payable in cash only at the airport, is US$25, no matter how long you've been in Bolivia. There's also a 15% tax on international airfares purchased in Bolivia.

Bolivian border times can be unreliable at best; always check with a *migración* office in the nearest major town. Also, if you plan to cross outside these hours, or at points where there is no border post, you can usually do so by obtaining an exit/entry stamp from the nearest *migración* office on departure/arrival.

AIR

There are only a few airlines offering direct flights to Bolivia, so air fares are as high as the altitude. There are direct services to most major South American cities; the flights to/from Chile and Peru are the cheapest. Santa Cruz is an increasingly popular entry point from Western European hubs. Due to altitude-related costs, flying into La Paz is more expensive than into Santa Cruz. High season for most fares is from early June to early September, and mid-December to mid-January.

Airports & Airlines

Bolivia's principal international airports are La Paz's **El Alto** (LPB; ☎ 2-281-0240); formerly known as John F Kennedy Memorial, and Santa Cruz' **Viru-Viru International** (VVI; ☎ 181).

At the time of research, Bolivia's national carrier, **Lloyd Aéreo Boliviano** (LAB; ☎ 2-237-1024; www.labairlines.com.bo), was having some financial turbulence and was unreliable at best. **AeroSur** (☎ 2-15-2431; www.aerosur.com), the nation's other airline, is more reliable.

AIRLINES FLYING TO/FROM BOLIVIA

Airlines with international flights and offices in La Paz include the following:
AeroSur (airline code 5L; ☎ 2-231-1333; www.aerosur.com)
American Airlines (airline code AA; ☎ 2-235-1360; www.aa.com)
Aerolíneas Argentinas (airline code AR; ☎ 2-235-1711; www.aerolineas.com.ar)
Gol Airlines (airline code EH; ☎ 800-10-01-21; www.voegol.com.br)
Grupo Taca (airline code TA; ☎ 2-231-3132; www.taca.com)
Lloyd Aéreo Boliviano (LAB; airline code LB; ☎ 2-237-1024; www.labairlines.com.bo)

CLIMATE CHANGE & TRAVEL

Climate change is a serious threat to the ecosystems that humans rely upon, and air travel is the fastest-growing contributor to the problem. Lonely Planet regards travel, overall, as a global benefit, but believes we all have a responsibility to limit our personal impact on global warming.

Flying & Climate Change

Pretty much every form of motor transport generates CO_2 (the main cause of human-induced climate change) but planes are far and away the worst offenders, not just because of the sheer distances they allow us to travel, but because they release greenhouse gases high into the atmosphere. The statistics are frightening: two people taking a return flight between Europe and the US will contribute as much to climate change as an average household's gas and electricity consumption over a whole year.

Carbon Offset Schemes

Climatecare.org and other websites use 'carbon calculators' that allow travellers to offset the greenhouse gases they are responsible for with contributions to energy-saving projects and other climate-friendly initiatives in the developing world – including projects in India, Honduras, Kazakhstan and Uganda.

Lonely Planet, together with Rough Guides and other concerned partners in the travel industry, supports the carbon offset scheme run by climatecare.org. Lonely Planet offsets all of its staff and author travel.

For more information check out our website: www.lonelyplanet.com.

Lan Airlines (airline code LA; ☎ 2-235-8377; www .lan.com)

TAM Mercosur (airline code PZ; ☎ 2-244-3442; www .tam.com.py in Spanish)

Tickets

World aviation has never been so competitive, making air travel better value than ever. Research your options carefully to get yourself the best deal. Online ticket sales work well if you are doing a simple one-way or return trip on specified dates. However, whiz-bang online fare generators are no substitute for a knowledgeable travel agent. Note that ticket prices in this chapter do not include taxes or fuel levies, which can significantly increase costs.

If you're time-rich and money-poor, try an air-ticket auction site such as **Priceline. com** (www.priceline.com) or **Skyauction.com** (www .skyauction.com), where you bid on your own fare. The restrictions are not crippling, but read the fine print.

Some of the better international online ticketing sites include:

Expedia (www.expedia.msn.com) Microsoft's USA travel site has links to sites for Canada, the UK and Germany.

Flight Centre (www.flightcentre.com) Respected operator for direct flights with sites for Australia, New Zealand, the UK, USA and Canada.

Flights.com (www.eltexpress.com) A truly international site for flight-only tickets; cheap fares and an easy-to-search database.

STA Travel (www.sta.com) The leader in world student travel but you don't necessarily have to be a student.

Travelocity (www.travelocity.com) This US site allows you to search fares (in US dollars) to/from practically anywhere.

INTERCONTINENTAL (RTW) TICKETS

Round-the-world (RTW) tickets can be real bargains if you are coming to South America from the other side of the world. They are generally put together by the airline alliances, and give you a limited period (usually a year) in which to circumnavigate the globe.

An alternative type of RTW ticket is one put together by a travel agent. These tickets are more expensive than airline RTW fares, but you choose your itinerary. Travel agents, by combining tickets from two low-cost airlines, can also offer multiple destination fares which are cheaper than a RTW ticket, and allow for two stops on the way to and from South America.

Some online ticket sites for intercontinental tickets include:

Airbrokers International (www.airbrokers.com) A US company specializing in cheap RTW tickets.

Oneworld (www.oneworld.com) Airline alliance of eight major airlines.

TRANSPORTATION

Roundtheworldflights.com (www.roundtheworld flights.com) An excellent site that allows you to build your own trip from the UK.

Star Alliance (www.staralliance.com) Another airline alliance.

Australia & New Zealand

Travel between Australasia and South America ain't cheap, so it makes sense to think in terms of a RTW ticket, or a ticket via Buenos Aires or Santiago. Round-trip fares from Sydney to La Paz via Auckland and Santiago start at around A$2500/3000 in low/high season. Fares via the USA are considerably more expensive, starting at around A$3000 return in the low season. RTW tickets including La Paz start at about A$3100/3300. The most direct routes are from Sydney to Santiago on Qantas and its partners, or to Buenos Aires with Aerolineas Argentinas. The best RTW ticket is probably from the Oneworld alliance, which has two different options: one restricted by the number of continents you visit, the other restricted by mileage. Fares start at around A$3200. The Visit South America Airpass offered by LAN Airlines and its partners, is around US$85 per sector.

For discount fares check **STA Travel** (☎ 1300-733 035; www.statravel.com.au) or **Flight Centre** (☎ 1300-133 133; www.flightcentre.com.au). For online bookings try www.travel.com.au or www.goholidays .com.nz. **Destination Holidays** (☎ 03-9725-4655, 800-337 050; www.south-america.com.au) and **South American Travel Centre** (☎ 03-9642 5353; www.satc.com.au) specialize in Latin American travel. Also check the ads in Saturday editions of newspapers, such as the *Age* or the *Sydney Morning Herald*.

Continental Europe

The best places in Europe for cheap airfares are student travel agencies (you don't have to be a student to use them). If airfares are expensive where you live, try contacting a London agent. The cheapest flights from Europe are typically charters, usually with fixed outward and return flight dates.

Some fares include a stopover in the USA. Note that passengers through New York (JFK) or Miami must pass through US immigration procedures, even if they won't be visiting the USA. That means you'll either need a US visa or be eligible for the Visa Waiver Program, which is open to Australians, New Zealanders and most Western Europeans, unless they're traveling on a nonaccredited airline (which includes most Latin American airlines).

From Europe, you can search for cheap airfares at **DiscountAirfares.com** (www.etn.nl).

There are bucket shops by the dozen in Western European capitals. Many travel agents in Europe have ties with STA Travel, where you'll find cheap tickets that may be altered once without charge. Other discount outlets in major transportation hubs include:

Alternativ Tours (☎ 030-212-3419; www.alternativ -tours.de in German; Berlin)

CTS Viaggi (☎ 06 462 0431; www.cts.it in Italian; Rome)

Kilroy Travel (☎ 036-822-2203; www.kilroytravel.com; Amsterdam)

NBBS Reizen (☎ 0900-10 20 300; www.nbbs.nl in Dutch; Amsterdam)

SSR/STA (☎ 0900 450-402; www.statravel.ch; Zürich)

USIT (☎ 01-602-1904; www.usitworld.com; Dublin)

Voyages Wasteel (☎ 825-887-070; www.wasteels.fr in French; Paris)

South America

LAB connects La Paz to Rio de Janeiro, Buenos Aires, Lima, Santiago, Arica and Iquique several times a week. Aerolíneas Argentinas flies daily between Santa Cruz and Buenos Aires and Gol Airlines flies between Santa Cruz and Rio de Janeiro (amongst other destinations). AeroSur has a new weekly flight between La Paz and Miami.

LanChile connects La Paz with Iquique and Santiago. Passengers departing Chile are subject to a departure tax of US$30, and Australians, Canadians and US citizens landing in Santiago must pay an 'entry tax' of US$30 to US$60 per person according to their nationality.

Brazilian-owned TAM Mercosur connects Asuncíon with La Paz and Santa Cruz.

LanPeru flies daily to Cusco (often via Lima) from La Paz.

The UK

Discount air travel is big business in London. Advertisements for many agencies appear in the travel pages of the weekend broadsheet newspapers, in *Time Out,* the *Evening Standard* and in the free magazine *TNT.*

There are no direct flights to La Paz from Europe. From London, all flights go via the US or other South American countries. Expect to pay from around £400. RTW tickets from London that take in South America (Santiago and Rio de Janeiro) start from around £1400.

London-based South American specialists include **Journey Latin America** (JLA; ☎ 020-8747 3108; www.journeylatinamerica.co.uk); **South American Experience** (☎ 020-7976 5511; www.southamericanexperience.co.uk); and **Austral Tours** (☎ 020-7233 5384; www.latinamerica.co.uk).

Recommended travel agencies include:
ebookers.com (☎ 0800 082 3000; www.ebookers.com)
Flight Centre (☎ 0870 499 0040; flightcentre.co.uk)
North-South Travel (☎ 01245 608 291; www.northsouthtravel.co.uk) Donates profits to projects in the developing world.
Quest Travel (☎ 0871 423 0135; www.questtravel.com)
STA Travel (☎ 0871 630 026; www.statravel.co.uk)
Trailfinders (Long-haul line ☎ 0845 058 5858; www.trailfinders.co.uk)
Travel Bag (☎ 0800 082 0500; www.travelbag.co.uk)

The USA & Canada

Inexpensive tickets from North American gateways (Miami is cheapest) usually have restrictions. Often there's a two-week advance-purchase requirement, and usually you must stay at least one week and no more than three months (prices often double for longer periods). For an idea of what's available, peruse the Sunday travel sections of major newspapers and free alternative weeklies.

Look for agencies specializing in South America, such as **exito** (☎ 800-655-4053; www.exitotravel.com), which has an expert staff and is superb for anyone traveling with special interests.

The following are recommended internet-only consolidators:
airtech (www.airtech.com)
airtreks.com (www.airtreks.com)
American Express Travel (www.itn.net)
CheapTickets (www.cheaptickets.com)
Expedia (www.expedia.com)
lowestfare.com (www.lowestfare.com)
Orbitz (www.orbitz.com)
Travelocity (www.travelocity.com)

Most flights from Canada involve connecting via a US gateway such as Miami or Los Angeles. Canada's national student travel agency, **Travel CUTS** (☎ Canada & USA 800-667-2887; www.travelcuts.com), offers great deals for students and those under 26. There are good fares for the general public as well. It has offices in several US cities. Owned by Travel Cuts, the **Adventure Travel Company** (☎ Canada & USA 1-888-238-2887; www.atcadventure.com) deals with the general public as much as it does with students, and offers some excellent prices.

LAND & RIVER

Bus

Depending on which country you enter from, some agency-booked, intercountry buses might carry you for the complete route; at other times you'll change into an associated bus company once you cross the border. If going with local buses, you'll usually need to catch onward buses once you've made your border crossing.

Car & Motorcycle

You can enter Bolivia by road from any of the neighboring countries. The routes from Brazil and Chile are poor, and those from Paraguay should be considered only with a 4WD. The routes from Argentina and Peru pose no significant problems.

Foreigners entering Bolivia from another country need a *hoja de ruta* (circulation card), available from the Servicio Nacional de Tránsito at the frontier. This document must be presented and stamped at all police posts – variously known as *trancas, tránsitos* or *controles* – which are spaced along highways and just outside major cities. *Peajes* (tolls) are often charged at these checkpoints and vehicles may be searched for contraband.

For details about driving in Bolivia, see p387.

Argentina

Two major overland crossings between Argentina and Bolivia include: **Villazón/La Quiaca** and **Yacuiba/Pocitos** (⏰ 7am-4pm).

You can arrive or depart Villazón by train from Oruro or Tupiza (see p205 for timetable information) or by regular buses. Entry and exit stamps are obtained from Bolivian

TRANSPORTATION

immigration, at the Villazón border post. A few meters down on the other side of the road is the Argentine Immigration Office. Formalities are minimal, but you may be held up on the Argentine border by thorough custom searches (mainly for locals and their contraband goods). Expect more checkpoints about 20km further on in Argentina. If you are not intending to stay in La Quiaca, you can purchase bus tickets to Argentina from the Villazón terminal. Alternatively, catch a taxi to the terminal at La Quiaca.

The Yacuiba/Pocitos crossing is 5km from Yacuiba, reached by taxi (US$1 per person) and crossed on foot. Buses further into Argentina go every couple of hours.

The minor border crossing at **Bermejo/Aguas Blancas** (⊙ Bolivian side 7am-4pm, Argentinean side 8am-5pm) is at an international bridge which goes onto a highway further into Argentina. It's 5km up the river from Bermejo and ferries take passengers every few minutes for US$0.20. An exit stamp can be obtained from the Bolivian immigration at the border post.

Brazil

Note: A yellow fever vaccine is needed when crossing into Brazil.

Bolivia can be reached or departed via **Quijarro/Corumbá**. On arrival in Brazil, taxis shuttle passengers to the Brazilian border town of Corumbá, 2km away. You can change dollars or bolivianos into *reais* (pronounced hay-ice) on the Bolivian side, but the boliviano rate is poor. Note that there's no Brazilian consulate in Quijarro, so if you need a visa, get it in Santa Cruz. From Corumbá there are good bus connections into southern Brazil, but no passenger trains. See p327 for more details on getting to and from Quijarro.

Frequent motorboats (US$1.50) provide a novel water entry/exit via Río Mamoré at **Guayaramerín/Guajará-Mirim** (⊙ 8am-8pm). There are no restrictions entering Guajará-Mirim for a quick visit, but if you intend to travel further into Brazil, you must pick up an entry/exit stamp. For departure stamps from Bolivia, head to the Polícia Federal in Bolivian immigration by the dock. If arriving into Guayaramerín, Bolivia, you can fly to Trinidad, Santa Cruz or La Paz, or travel the long and dusty bus routes to Riberalta and on to Cobija, Rurrenabaque or La Paz.

Alternative ferry options facilitate short hops across borders in the Amazon Basin at

far flung locales such as Parque Nacional Noel Kempff Mercado and Pimienteras, Brazil, and Cobija and Brasiléia, Brazil; see p365.

Chile

Note that meat, fruit and food produce (including coca leaves) cannot be carried from Bolivia into Chile and will be confiscated at the border. The most popular route between Chile and Bolivia is via bus from La Paz to Arica through the border at **Chungará/Tambo Quemado** (⊙ 8am-8pm). A convenient alternative for those doing the 4WD Southwest Circuit tour is to get dropped off on the last day at **Hito Cajón** (⊙ 8am-11pm) and head to San Pedro, Chile, from where you can pick up buses (note the latter cannot be done in the reverse order). Alternatively, there is a lesser used road route between Oruro and Iquique with a border at **Pisiga/Colchane** (⊙ 8am-8pm); see p177 for bus details. A novel crossing can be done via train from Uyuni (to Calama; see p189), whose border crossing is **Ollagüe/Avaroa** (⊙ 8am-8pm). This is also a road crossing.

Paraguay

The easiest route between Paraguay and Bolivia is to cross from Pedro Juan Caballero (in Asuncion, Paraguay) to Ponta Porã (Brazil), and then travel by bus or train to Corumbá (Brazil) and Quijarro (Bolivia).

The three-day overland Trans-Chaco bus trip (p290) between Santa Cruz, Bolivia, and Asunción, Paraguay, now has a daily bus service, but it's still not a breeze.

In Bolivia your best bet for picking up exit stamps is in Santa Cruz. At the Bolivian border post at Ibibobo, your passport will be checked. (There is another border post at Boyuibe, but some travelers have reported this closed; you'll need to ask around.) The Paraguayan border post is at Fortín Infante Rívarola, a few kilometers further along and the **immigration and customs office** (⊙ 24hr) is at Mariscal Estigarribia. Coming from Paraguay, you must obtain your entry stamp within 72 hours of entering Bolivia.

For the adventurous, river transportation between Asunción, Paraguay and Bolivia (via Corumbá, Brazil) is likely to involve a series of short journeys and informal arrangements with individual boat captains. From Asunción, there's a regular – albeit leisurely – river service to Concepción (Paraguay). Beyond Concepción is where the informal boat arrangements begin. You'll probably wind up doing it in two stages: Concepción to Bahía Negra (northern Paraguay), then Bahía Negra to Corumbá.

Peru

Bolivia is normally reached overland from Peru via Lake Titicaca. If you've got time, the border crossing at **Kasani/Yunguyo** (☺ 8am-6pm) via Copacabana is more appealing than the faster, less secure and least interesting crossing at **Desaguadero** (☺ 9am-9pm). There is a rarely used route at **Puerto Acosta** (see p125).

If departing Bolivia direct from La Paz, the easiest way is to catch an agency bus to Puno (Peru); the bus breaks in Copacabana and again for immigration formalities in Yunguyo. Similar buses go direct to Cuzco. A cheaper way from Copacabana is via minibus from Plaza Sucre to the Kasani/Yunguyo border (US$0.50, 30 minutes); there's onward transportation to Puno, changing buses in Yunguyo.

Crillon Tours (☎ 2-233-7533; www.titicaca.com; Camacho 122, La Paz) sells tickets for all-inclusive hydrofoil tours between La Paz and Puno, Peru.

An adventurous riverboat route is possible through the rainforest from Bolivia's Riberalta to Puerto Maldonado in Peru, via the Puerto Heath/Puerto Prado border crossing.

GETTING AROUND

Bolivia boasts an extensive transportation system which covers most parts of the country in varying degrees of comfort and ease. Despite the remoteness of many places in Bolivia, locals are creative in the ways they get from one place to another taking a variety of *movilidades* (anything that moves!) including buses, trucks and boats. Interruptions to travel plans are usually not caused by lack of transportation, but by protests in the form of road blockades, floods, damaged roads (especially in the lowlands during rainy season) and, in the Amazon, low river levels. In the major tourist destinations, regular bus transportation usually ensures efficient travel.

AIR

Air travel in Bolivia is inexpensive and it's the quickest and most reliable means of reaching out-of-the-way places. It's also the only means of transportation that isn't washed out during the wet season. Although weather-related disruptions definitely occur, planes eventually get through even during summer flooding in northern Bolivia.

Airlines in Bolivia

Bolivia's national carrier **LAB** (☎ 2-237-1024; www.labairlines.com.bo) and private carriers **AeroSur** (☎ 2-231-1333; www.aerosur.com), **Amazonas** (www.amazonas.com) and **Aerocon** (www.aerocon.info) connect the country's major cities and remote corners. They all charge similar fares and allow 15kg of luggage, excluding 3kg of carry-on luggage. With LAB you must reconfirm your reservations 72 hours before the flight or your reservations may be canceled.

The military airline, **Transportes Aéreos Militares** (TAM; Map pp72-3; ☎ 212-1582/212-1585, TAM airport ☎ 2-284-1884; Montes 738), operates domestic flights in smaller planes that fly closer to the landscape. Prices are as much as 40% lower than other airlines, but schedules can change without notice and reservations can only be made in the town of departure. They are strict with the 15kg baggage limit; each additional kilo costs around US$0.50, depending on the length of the flight.

Air Passes

AeroSur offers a four-flight, 45-day air pass (around US$250) between any of the main cities. The only catch is that you can't pass through the same city twice, except to make connections. Check out the latest offers and restrictions at www.aerosur.com.

Departure Tax

AASANA, the government agency responsible for airports and air traffic, charges a US$1 to US$2 domestic departure tax, which is payable at its desk after check-in. Some airports also levy a municipal tax of up to US$1.

BICYCLE

For cyclists who can cope with the challenges of cold winds, poor road conditions, high altitude and steep terrain, Bolivia is a paradise. Traffic isn't a serious problem, but intimidating buses and *camiones* (flatbed trucks) may leave cyclists lost in clouds of dust or embedded in mud. However, finding supplies may prove difficult, so cyclists in remote areas must carry ample food and water. Given these challenges, many prefer to leave the work to a tour company. Mountain-biking hubs and hotspots include La Paz, Sorata and the Yungas.

Bolivia has its fair share of inexpensive bikes – mostly supermarket beaters from China. However, quality new wheels are few and far between. Your best bet for purchasing a used, touring-worthy stead is through agencies in La Paz. Try **Gravity Assisted Mountain Biking** (Map pp72-3; ☎ 2-231-3849; www.gravitybolivia .com; 16 de Julio 1490, Edificio Avenida, No 10) for spare parts and help with repairs. Bringing your own bicycle into the country is generally hassle-free. For information on mountain biking, see p52.

BOAT
Ferry
The only public ferry service in Bolivia operates between San Pedro and San Pablo, across the narrow Estrecho de Tiquina (Straits of Tiquina) on Lake Titicaca. To visit any of Lake Titicaca's Bolivian islands, you can travel by launch or rowboat. To the Huyñaymarka islands in the lake's southernmost extension, boats and tours are available in Huatajata. To visit Isla del Sol, you can take a tour, hire a launch or catch a scheduled service in Copacabana, or look for a lift in Yampupata or the villages on the way here. Cruises by motorboat or hydrofoil are provided by a couple of well-established tour companies.

River Boat
The most relaxing way to get around the Amazon is by river. There's no scheduled passenger service, so travelers almost invariably wind up on some sort of cargo vessel. The most popular routes are from Puerto Villarroel to Trinidad and Trinidad to Guayaramerín. There are also much less frequented routes from Rurrenabaque or Puerto Heath to Riberalta. It is also possible to get to Rurrenabaque from Guanay by boat.

BUS
Buses and their various iterations are the most popular form of Bolivian transportation. It's relatively safe and cheap, if a bit uncomfortable or nerve-wracking at times. Long-distance bus lines in Bolivia are called *flotas*, large buses are known as *buses* and three-quarter (usually older) ones are called *micros* and minibuses are just that. If looking

for a bus terminal, ask for *la terminal terrestre* or *la terminal de buses*.

Thankfully, the Bolivian road network is improving as more kilometers are paved. Modern coaches use the best roads, while older vehicles sometimes still ply minor secondary routes.

It's safer and the views are better during the day. Drunken driving is illegal, but bus drivers have been known to sip the hard stuff on long nighttime hauls. There have been numerous reports of items disappearing from buses' internal overhead compartments. Hold on tight to your day packs and bags if they are with you in the bus. Backpacks and bags are generally safe when stored in the baggage compartment. You will be given a baggage tag which you must show when reclaiming your bag.

Except on the most popular runs, most companies' buses inexplicably depart at roughly the same time, regardless of the number of competitors. Between any two cities, you should have no trouble finding at least one daily bus. On the most popular routes you can choose between dozens of daily departures.

Classes & Costs
The only choices you'll have to make are on major, long-haul routes, where the better companies offer *coche* (or *'bus'*) *cama* (sleeper) service for around double the *común* or normal going rate. The VCR on the newest buses will be in better shape than the reclining seats, heaters *may* function and toilets (yes, toilets) *may* work. Whether you will actually be able to sleep is another matter.

Prices vary according to the different standards of buses – from the more luxurious *bus cama* service to the ancient Bluebird-style buses – and the length of trip – whether overnight or short day hop. An overnight trip from La Paz to Cochabamba costs between US$3.15 and US$7.50 and from La Paz to Potosí costs between US$7 and US$13.

Reservations
To be safe, reserve bus tickets at least several hours in advance. For the lowest fare, purchase immediately after the driver starts the engine. Many buses depart in the afternoon or evening and arrive at their destination in the wee hours of the morning. Often you can crash on these buses until sunrise. On

most major routes there are also daytime departures.

CAR & MOTORCYCLE

The advantages of a private vehicle include schedule flexibility, access to remote areas and the chance to seize photo opportunities. More Bolivian roads are gradually being paved (most recently, that between La Paz and Potosí) but others are in varying stages of decay, so high-speed travel is impossible (unless, of course, you're a Bolivian bus driver) and inadvisable. The typically narrow and winding mountain roads often meander along contours and rocky riverbeds.

The undaunted should prepare their expeditions carefully. Bear in mind that spare parts are a rare commodity outside cities. A high-clearance 4WD vehicle is essential for off-road travel. You'll need a set of tools, spare tires, a puncture repair kit, extra gas and fluids, and as many spare parts as possible. For emergencies, carry camping equipment and plenty of rations.

Low-grade (85-octane) gasoline and diesel fuel are available at *surtidores de gasolina* (gas dispensers) – also known as *bombas de gasolina* (gas pumps) – in all cities and major towns. Gas costs around US$0.45 to US$0.50 per liter.

In lowland areas, where temperatures are hot and roads are scarce, motorbikes are popular for zipping around the plazas, as well as exploring areas not served by public transportation. They can be rented for around US$12 to US$15 per 24 hours from moto-taxi stands. Gringo-run agencies offering motorcycle tours through the rugged highland are popping up like mushrooms in the larger cities. Bear in mind that many travel insurance policies will not cover you for injuries arising from motorbike accidents, so check your policy carefully.

For details on bringing your own vehicle into Bolivia, see p383.

Automobile Association

Bolivia's automobile association is the **Automovil Club Boliviano** (ACB; ☎ 2-431-132/2-432-136; 6 de Agosto 2993, La Paz).

Driver's License

Most Bolivian car-rental agencies will accept your home driver's license, but if you're doing a lot of driving, it's wise to back it up with an International Driver's License. Bolivia doesn't require special motorcycle licenses, but neighboring countries do. For motorcycle and moped rentals, all that is normally required is a passport.

Private Drivers

Hiring a driver can be a more comfortable and efficient alternative to being squished in a bus on bad roads for long periods. Alternatively, many people just want transportation to trailheads or base camps rather than a tour.

Examples of one-way transportation prices from La Paz with a *chofer* (private driver), regardless of the number of passengers (six to eight maximum), include the following: Refugio Huayna Potosí US$50; Estancia Una (for Illimani climb) US$120 to US$140; Curva (for the Cordillera Apolobamba trek) US$250 to US$350; Chuñavi or Lambate (for the Yunga Cruz trek) US$150; Sajama US$300; and Rurrenabaque US$300. Private Salar de Uyuni and Southwest Circuit tours cost from US$150 per day.

Several La Paz drivers are recommended for their value, and are listed below. Club Andino also have a recommended list of drivers, while another option is **Minibuses Yungueña** (☎ 221-3513), which contracts drivers and 2WD minibuses.

Carlos Aguilar (☎ 7152-5897) Bolivian Climbing Federation secretary; speaks some English and provides safe, informative and inexpensive jeep trips. He also works as a climbing guide and is especially popular with mountaineers.

Juan Carlos Mujiano Centellas (☎ 2-273-0382) Recommended by Club Andino; offers transportation in a 4WD or 14-seater minibus.

Oscar L Vera Coca (☎ 2-223-0453; 7156-1283) Speaks some English.

Romero Ancasi (☎ 2-283-1363; 7192-1318) Offers experienced driving in well-maintained Toyota Landcruisers.

Rental

Few travelers in Bolivia rent self-driven vehicles. Only the most reputable agencies service vehicles regularly, and insurance bought from rental agencies may cover only accidental damage – breakdowns may be considered the renter's problem.

You must be over 25 years, have a driver's license from your home country, have a major credit card or cash deposit (typically around US$1000) and accident insurance. You'll be charged a daily rate and a per-kilometer rate (some agencies allow a set number of free kilometers). They'll also want you to leave your passport as a deposit.

Costs vary widely but the average daily rate for a small VW or Toyota starts at around US$36, plus an additional US$0.20 to US$0.40 per kilometer. For the least expensive 4WD, companies charge around US$40 per day plus US$0.40 to US$0.60 per kilometer. Weekly rates (with up to 1600km free) start around US$350 for a compact and US$600 for a 4WD pickup.

For listings of better-known agencies, see the Getting Around section in the major cities.

Road Rules

Traffic regulations aren't that different from those in North America or Europe. Speed limits are infrequently posted, but in most cases the state of the road will prevent you from exceeding them anyway.

Bolivians keep to the right. When two cars approach an uncontrolled intersection from different directions, the driver who honks (or gets there first) tends to have right of way if passing straight through – but be aware, this can be a bit hit and miss. In La Paz, those going up the hill have right of way at an intersection. When two vehicles meet on a narrow mountain road, the downhill vehicle must reverse until there's room for the other to pass.

HITCHHIKING

Thanks to relatively easy access to *camiones* and a profusion of buses, hitchhiking isn't really necessary or popular in Bolivia. Still, it's not unknown and drivers of *movilidades* – *coches* (cars), *camionetas* (pickup trucks), NGO vehicles, gas trucks and other vehicles – are usually happy to pick up passengers when they have room. Always ask the price, if any, before climbing aboard; if they do charge, it should amount to about half the bus fare for the equivalent distance.

Please note that hitchhiking is never entirely safe in any country. If you decide to hitchhike, you should understand that you are taking a small but potentially serious risk. Travel in pairs and let someone know where you're planning to go.

LOCAL TRANSPORTATION
Camión

Prior to the current expansive bus network, *camiones* were often the only way for travelers to venture off the beaten track. Nowadays, in the more populated areas, you might consider a *camión* trip more for the novelty than necessity, although it is how many *campesinos* (subsistence farmers) choose to travel. *Camiones* generally cost around 50% of the bus fare. You'll need time and a strong constitution; travel can be excruciatingly slow and rough, depending on the cargo and number of passengers. A major plus is the raw experience, including the best views of the countryside.

On any *camión* trip – especially in the highlands – day or night, be sure to take plenty of warm clothing as night temperatures can plunge below freezing; at best they can be chilly.

Most towns have places where *camiones* gather to wait for passengers, and some may have scheduled departures.

Micros, Minibuses & Trufis

Micros – half-size buses – are used in larger cities and serve as Bolivia's least expensive form of public transportation. They follow set routes, and the route numbers or letters are usually marked on a placard behind the windshield. This is often backed by a description of the route, including the streets that are followed to reach the end of the line. They can be hailed anywhere along their routes. When you want to disembark, move toward the front and tell the driver or assistant where you want them to stop.

Minibuses and *trufis* (which may be either cars or minibuses) are prevalent in the larger towns and cities, and follow set routes that are numbered and described on placards. They are always cheaper than taxis and nearly as convenient. As with *micros*, you can board or alight anywhere along their route.

Taxis

Urban taxis are relatively inexpensive. Few are equipped with meters, but in most cities and towns there are standard per-person fares for short hauls. In some places taxis are collective and behave more like *trufis*, charging a set rate per person. However, if you have three or four people all headed for the same place, you may be able to negotiate a reduced rate for the entire group.

Radio taxis, on the other hand, always charge a set rate for up to four people; if you squeeze in five people, the fare increases by a small margin. When using taxis, try to have enough change to cover the fare; drivers often like to plead a lack of change in the hope that you'll give them the benefit of the difference. As a general rule, taxi drivers aren't tipped, but if an individual goes beyond the call of duty, a tip of a couple bolivianos wouldn't be amiss.

TRAIN

Since privatization in the mid-1990s, passenger rail services have been cut back. The western network operated by the **Empresa Ferroviaria Andina** (FCA; www.fca.com.bo) runs from Oruro to Villazón (on the Argentine border); a branch line runs southwest from Uyuni to Avaroa, (on the Chilean border).

In the east, there's a line from Santa Cruz to the Brazilian frontier at Quijarro, where you cross to the Pantanal. An infrequently used service goes south from Santa Cruz to Yacuiba on the Argentine border.

Reservations

Even in major towns along the routes, tickets can be reserved only on the day of departure. At smaller stations tickets may not be available until the train has arrived. Larger intermediate stations are allotted only a few seat reservations, and tickets go on sale quite literally whenever employees decide to open up. The best info is usually available from the *jefe de la estación* (stationmaster).

When buying tickets, make sure you have a passport for each person for whom you're buying a ticket. This is a remnant from the days when ticket scalping was profitable.

TOURS

Many organized tours run out of La Paz or towns closest to the attractions that you wish to visit. Tours are a convenient way to visit a site when you are short on time or motivation; they are frequently the easiest way to visit remote areas. They can also be relatively cheap, depending on the number of people in your group and the mode of transportation.

There are scores of outfits offering trekking, mountain-climbing and rainforest-adventure packages around Bolivia. For climbing in the Cordilleras, operators offer customized expeditions. They can arrange anything from just a guide and transportation right up to equipment, porters and even a cook. Some also rent trekking equipment.

For biking companies, see p77. The following is a list of recommended agencies around the country.

Adventure Climbing & Trekking Company of South America (☎ 2-241-4197; Jaimes Freyre 2950, Sopocachi, La Paz) Carlos Escobar is a UIAGM/UIAA certified international mountain guide (who recently climbed Mount Everest) and runs serious climbing expeditions to Illampu, Jancohuma, Chearoco, Chacacomani, Huyana Potosí (including the East face) and others.

America Tours (Map pp72-3; ☎ 2-237-4204; www .america-ecotours.com; No 9, Edificio Avenida, 16 de Julio 1490, La Paz) Warmly recommended English-speaking agency that organizes trips to anywhere in the country. Specializes in new routes and community-based ecotourism in such places as Parque Nacional Madidi, Parque Nacional Sajama, Rurrenabaque and the Salar de Uyuni.

Andean Summits (☎ 2-242-2106; www.andean summits.com; Aranzaes 2974, Sopocachi, La Paz) Mountaineering and trekking all over Bolivia, plus adventure tours and archaeology trips.

Calacoto Tours (Map pp72-3; ☎ 2-211-5592; www .calacototours-bolivia.com in Spanish; office 20, Galería Doryan, Sagárnaga 189, La Paz) Tours to Lake Titicaca and the islands (including Pariti), and horseback-riding trail rides in the Valle de las Animas and beyond.

Candelaria Tours (Map pp242-3; ☎ 4-646-0289; www.candelariatours.com; Audiencia 1, Sucre) One of the most established and professional travel agencies in Sucre offering a variety of tours around Bolivia. Arranges travel and accommodations.

Colibri (☎ 2-242- 3246; www.colibri-adventures.com; 4th fl 4B, cnr Alberto Ostria & Juan Manuel Caceres San Miguel, La Paz) Offers comprehensive trekking, mountaineering, mountain biking, jungle trips and 4WD tours; rents gear.

Crillon Tours (☎ 2-233-7533; www.titicaca.com; Camacho 122, La Paz) An upmarket option offering a range of tours, including the hydrofoil services in Lake Titicaca.

Forest Tours (Map pp296-7; ☎ 3-372-042; www .forestbolivia.com; Cuéllar 22, Santa Cruz) English-speaking, knowledgeable and extremely helpful, offering tours in the Santa Cruz region and elsewhere, including the Ché Trail and Parque Nacionales Amboró.

Fremen Tours (Map pp72-3; ☎ 2-240-7995; www .andes-amazonia.com; No 13, Galeria Handal, cnr Santa Cruz & Socabaya, La Paz) Upmarket agency with offices in Cochabamba, Santa Cruz and Trinidad. Specializes in soft adventure trips in the Amazon and Chapare.

Inca Land Tours (pp72-3; ☎ 2-231-3589; www .incalandtours.com; No 10, Sagárnaga 213, La Paz) Established Peruvian budget operation running tours out of Rurrenabaque and Coroico; it arranges its own charter flights to Rurre and will book tickets in advance with TAM – at a premium.

TRANSPORTATION

Magri Turismo (Map pp72-3; 2-244-2727; www
.magri-amexpress.com.bo; Capitan Ravelo 2101 at
Montevideo) Established agency and American Express
representative offering tours to the eastern, southern and
La Paz regions of Bolivia including soft adventure and
harder-core climbing activities.

Michael Blendinger Tours (Map p312; (/fax
3-944-6227; www.discoveringbolivia.com; Bolívar s/n,
Samaipata) Based in Samaipata, biologist Michael Blendinger specializes in tours to the southern Amboró and
surrounding region. Also does birding tours. English and
German spoken.

Neblina Forest (/fax 3-347-1166; www.neblina
forest.com; Paraguá 2560, Santa Cruz) Specializes in
bird-watching and natural-history tours throughout Bolivia,
especially to Noel Kempff Mercado, Amboró and Madidi National Parks, along with the Beni region and the Pantanal.

Travel Tracks (Map pp72-3; 2-231-6934; www
.travel-tracks.com; Sagárnaga 213, La Paz) This English-
speaking agency is an excellent choice for guided hikes as
well as customized trips around the country.

Turisbus (Map pp72-3; 2-245-1341; www
.travelperubolivia.com; Hotel Rosario, Illampu 702, La Paz)
Upmarket agency specializing in Lake Titicaca tours.

Health

CONTENTS

Before You Go	**391**
Insurance	391
Medical Checklist	391
Online Resources	391
Further Reading	392
In Transit	**392**
Deep Vein Thrombosis	392
Jet Lag & Motion Sickness	392
In Bolivia	**393**
Availability & Cost of Healthcare	393
Infectious Diseases	393
Travelers' Diarrhea	396
Environmental Hazards	396
Traveling with Children	398
Women's Health	398

Prevention is the key to staying healthy while abroad. Travelers who receive the recommended vaccines and follow common-sense precautions usually come away with nothing more than a little diarrhea.

BEFORE YOU GO

Since most vaccines don't produce immunity until at least two weeks after they're given, visit a physician four to eight weeks before departure. Ask your doctor for an International Certificate of Vaccination, containing a list of your vaccinations. This is mandatory for countries, such as Brazil, Bolivia and Venezuela, that require proof of yellow fever vaccination on entry, but it's a good idea to carry it wherever you travel.

Bring medications in their original containers, clearly labeled, and a signed, dated letter from your physician describing all medical conditions and medications. If carrying syringes or needles, carry a physician's letter documenting their medical necessity.

INSURANCE

If your health insurance does not cover you for medical expenses abroad, consider supplemental insurance. Check the Bookings & Services section of the **Lonely Planet website** (www.lonelyplanet.com/travel_services) for more information. Find out in advance if your insurance plan will make payments directly to providers or reimburse you later for overseas health expenditures. Most private-practice providers in Bolivia expect cash payment and should provide receipts for your insurance company claims and reimbursement. Credit cards are usually not accepted for medical services.

MEDICAL CHECKLIST
- antibiotics
- antidiarrheal drugs (eg loperamide)
- acetaminophen (Tylenol) or aspirin
- anti-inflammatory drugs (eg ibuprofen)
- antihistamines (for hay fever and allergic reactions)
- antibacterial ointment (eg Bactroban) for cuts and abrasions
- steroid cream or cortisone (for poison ivy and other allergic rashes)
- bandages, gauze, gauze rolls
- adhesive or paper tape
- scissors, safety pins, tweezers
- thermometer
- pocket knife
- DEET-containing insect repellent for the skin
- permethrin-containing insect spray for clothing, tents and bed nets
- sun block
- oral rehydration salts
- iodine tablets (for water purification)
- syringes and sterile needles
- acetazolamide (Diamox) for altitude sickness

ONLINE RESOURCES
There is a wealth of travel health advice on the internet. For further information, the **Lonely Planet website** (www.lonelyplanet.com) is a good place to start. The **World Health Organization** (www.who.int/ith) annually publishes *International Travel and Health*, which is revised annually and is available online at no cost. Another website of general interest is **MD Travel Health** (www.mdtravelhealth.com), which provides complete travel health recommendations for every country and is updated daily.

HEALTH

Consult your government's travel health website before departure:

Australia (www.dfat.gov.au/travel)
Canada (www.hc-sc.gc.ca/english/index.html)
UK (www.doh.gov.uk/traveladvice)
US (www.cdc.gov/travel)

FURTHER READING

For further information see *Healthy Travel Central & South America*, also from Lonely Planet. If you are traveling with children, Lonely Planet's *Travel with Children* might well be useful. The *ABC of Healthy Travel*, by E Walker et al, is another valuable resource.

IN TRANSIT

DEEP VEIN THROMBOSIS

Blood clots may form in the legs (deep vein thrombosis) during plane flights, chiefly because of prolonged immobility. The longer the flight, the greater the risk. Though most blood clots are reabsorbed uneventfully, some may break off and travel through the blood vessels to the lungs, where they could cause life-threatening complications.

The chief symptom of deep vein thrombosis is swelling or pain of the foot, ankle or calf, usually but not always on just one side. When a blood clot travels to the lungs, it may cause chest pain and difficulty breathing. Travelers with any of these symptoms should immediately seek medical attention.

To prevent deep vein thrombosis on long flights, walk about the cabin, perform isometric compressions of the leg muscles (ie contract the leg muscles while sitting), drink plenty of fluids, and avoid alcohol and tobacco.

JET LAG & MOTION SICKNESS

Jet lag is common when crossing more than five time zones, resulting in insomnia, fatigue, malaise or nausea. To avoid jet lag try drinking plenty of fluids (nonalcoholic) and eating light meals. On arrival get exposure to natural sunlight and readjust your schedule (for meals, sleep, etc) as soon as possible.

Antihistamines such as dimenhydrinate (Dramamine) and meclizine (Antivert, Bonine) are usually the first choice for treating

RECOMMENDED VACCINATIONS

The only required vaccine for Bolivia is yellow fever, and that's only if you're arriving in Bolivia from a yellow fever–infected country in Africa or the Americas. However, a number of other vaccines are recommended:

Vaccine	Recommended for	Dosage	Side effects
Chickenpox	Travelers who have never had chickenpox	Two doses one month apart	Fever; mild case of chickenpox
Hepatitis A	All travelers	One dose before trip; booster six to 12 months later	Soreness at injection site, headaches, body aches
Hepatitis B	Long-term travelers in close contact with the local population	Three doses over a six-month period	Soreness at injection site, low-grade fever
Measles	Travelers born after 1956 who have had only one measles vaccination	One dose	Fever, rash, joint pains, allergic reactions
Rabies	Travelers who may have contact with animals and may not have access to medical care	Three doses over a three- to four-week period	Soreness at injection site, headaches, body aches
Tetanus/diphtheria	All travelers who haven't had a booster within 10 years	One dose lasts 10 years	Soreness at injection site
Typhoid	All travelers	Four capsules by mouth, one taken every other day	Abdominal pain, nausea, rash
Yellow fever	Travelers to Beni, Cochabamba, Santa Cruz, La Paz, possibly other areas	One dose lasts 10 years	Headaches, body aches; severe reactions are rare

motion sickness. Their main side effect is drowsiness. A herbal alternative is ginger.

IN BOLIVIA

AVAILABILITY & COST OF HEALTHCARE

Good medical care is available in the larger cities, but may be difficult to find in rural areas. Many doctors and hospitals expect payment in cash, regardless of whether you have travel health insurance. For a medical emergency in La Paz, call **SAMI ambulance** (☎ 2-279-9911) or go directly to the **Clinica del Sur emergency room** (☎ 2-278-4001/02/03; cnr Hernando Siles & Calle 7, Obrajes). In Cochabamba, call the **Medicar Emergency Ambulance Service** (☎ 4-453-3222) or go to the emergency room of **Centro Medico Boliviano Beluga** (☎ 4-422-9407, 425-0928, 423-1403; Antezana, btwn Venezuela & Paccieri N-0455). In Santa Cruz, go to the emergency room of **Clinica Angel Foianini** (☎ 3-336-2211, 336-6001/02/03/04; Irala 468). A taxi may get you faster to the emergency room than an ambulance.

For the names of physicians, dentists, hospitals and laboratories for routine medical problems, the **US Embassy** (http://bolivia.usembassy.gov/english/consular/medicalresources.htm) provides an online directory of medical resources.

If you develop a life-threatening medical problem, you'll probably want to be evacuated to a country with state-of-the-art medical care. Since this may cost tens of thousands of dollars, be sure you have insurance to cover this before you depart. You can find a list of medical evacuation and travel insurance companies on the **US State Department website** (travel.state.gov/medical.html).

Bolivian pharmacies offer most of the medications available in other countries. In general it's safer to buy pharmaceuticals made by international manufacturers rather than local companies; buy the brand name prescribed by your doctor, not the generic brand drugs that may be offered at lower prices. These medications may be out of date or have no quality control from the manufacturer. For a list of pharmacies, see the US Embassy website.

INFECTIOUS DISEASES
Cholera

Cholera is an intestinal infection acquired through ingestion of contaminated food or water. The main symptom is profuse, watery diarrhea, which may be so severe that it causes life-threatening dehydration. The key treatment is drinking oral rehydration solution. Antibiotics are also given, usually tetracycline or doxycycline, though quinolone antibiotics such as ciprofloxacin and levofloxacin are also effective.

Cholera sometimes occurs in Bolivia, but it's rare among travelers. Cholera vaccine is no longer required. There are effective vaccines, but they're not available in many countries and are only recommended for those at particularly high risk.

Dengue Fever

Dengue fever is a viral infection found throughout South America. Dengue is transmitted by Aedes mosquitoes, which bite preferentially during the daytime and are usually found close to human habitations, often indoors. They breed in artificial water containers, such as jars, barrels, cans, cisterns, metal drums, plastic containers and discarded tires. As a result, dengue is especially common in densely populated, urban environments.

Dengue causes flu-like symptoms, including fever, muscle aches, joint pains, headaches, nausea and vomiting, often followed by a rash. The body aches may be quite uncomfortable, but most cases resolve uneventfully in a few days. Severe cases usually occur in children under age 15 who are experiencing their second dengue infection.

There is no specific antivirus (antibiotics) treatment for dengue fever except to take analgesics such as acetaminophen/paracetamol (Tylenol) and drink plenty of fluids. Severe cases may require hospitalization for intravenous fluids and supportive care. There is no vaccine. The cornerstone of prevention is insect protection measures (see p397).

Hepatitis A

Hepatitis A is the second most common travel-related infection (after travelers' diarrhea). It's a viral infection of the liver that is usually acquired by ingestion of contaminated water, food or ice, or by direct contact with infected persons. The illness occurs throughout the world, but the incidence is higher in developing nations. Symptoms may include fever, malaise, jaundice, nausea, vomiting and abdominal pain. Most cases resolve without complications, though hepatitis A occasionally causes severe liver damage. There is no treatment.

The vaccine for hepatitis A is extremely safe and effective. A booster six to 12 months later lasts for at least 10 years. It is encouraged for Bolivia. A vaccine has not been established for pregnant women or children under two years – instead, they should be given a gammaglobulin injection.

Hepatitis B

Like hepatitis A, hepatitis B is a liver infection that occurs worldwide but is more common in developing nations. Unlike hepatitis A, the disease is usually acquired by sexual contact or by exposure to infected blood, generally through blood transfusions or contaminated needles. The vaccine is recommended only for long-term travelers (on the road more than six months) who expect to live in rural areas or have close physical contact with the local population. Additionally, the vaccine is recommended for anyone who anticipates sexual contact with the local inhabitants or a possible need for medical, dental or other treatments while abroad, especially if a need for transfusions or injections is expected.

Hepatitis B vaccine is safe and highly effective. However, a total of three injections are necessary to establish full immunity. Several countries added hepatitis B vaccine to the list of routine childhood immunizations in the 1980s, so many young adults are already protected.

Malaria

Malaria occurs in every South American country except Chile, Uruguay and the Falkland Islands. It's transmitted by mosquito bites, usually between dusk and dawn. The main symptom is high spiking fevers, which may be accompanied by chills, sweats, headache, body aches, weakness, vomiting or diarrhea. Severe cases may involve the central nervous system and lead to seizures, confusion, coma and death.

Taking malaria pills is strongly recommended for areas below 2500m (8202 ft) in the departments of Beni, Santa Cruz and Pando, where the risk is highest. Falciparum malaria, which is the most dangerous kind, occurs in Beni and Pando. No malaria is currently present in the cities of these departments.

There is a choice of three malaria pills, all of which work about equally well. Mefloquine

(Lariam) is taken once weekly in a dosage of 250mg, starting one to two weeks before arrival, and continuing through the trip and for four weeks after return. The problem is that a certain percentage of people (the number is controversial) develop neuropsychiatric side effects, which may range from mild to severe. Stomach ache and diarrhea are also common. Atovaquone/proguanil (Malarone) is taken once daily with food, starting two days before arrival and continuing daily until seven days after departure. Side effects are typically mild. Doxycycline is relatively inexpensive and easy to obtain, but it is taken daily and can cause an exaggerated sunburn reaction.

For longer trips it's probably worth trying mefloquine; for shorter trips, Malarone will be the drug of choice for most people.

Protecting yourself against mosquito bites is just as important as taking malaria pills (for recommendations see p397), since none of the pills are 100% effective.

If you may not have access to medical care while traveling, you should bring along additional pills for emergency self-treatment, which you should take if you can't reach a doctor and you develop symptoms that suggest malaria, such as high spiking fevers. One option is to take four tablets of Malarone once daily for three days. However, Malarone should not be used for treatment if you're already taking it for prevention. An alternative is to take 650mg quinine three times daily and 100mg doxycycline twice daily for one week. If you start self-medication, see a doctor at the earliest possible opportunity.

If you develop a fever after returning home, see a physician, as malaria symptoms may not occur for months.

Plague

Small outbreaks of the plague sometimes occur in Bolivia, most recently in the town of San Pedro (department of La Paz) in the mid-1990s. The plague is usually transmitted to humans by the bite of rodent fleas, typically when rodents die off. Symptoms include fever, chills, muscle aches and malaise, associated with the development of an acutely swollen, exquisitely painful lymph node, known as bubo, most often in the groin. Most travelers are at extremely low risk for this disease. However, if you might have contact with rodents or their fleas, you should bring along a bottle of doxycycline, to be taken prophylactically during periods of exposure. Those less than eight years old or allergic to doxycycline should take trimethoprim-sulfamethoxazole instead. In addition, you should avoid areas containing rodent burrows or nests, never handle sick or dead animals, and follow the guidelines in this chapter for protecting yourself from insect bites (see p397).

Rabies

Rabies is a viral infection of the brain and spinal cord that is almost always fatal. The rabies virus is carried in the saliva of infected animals and is typically transmitted through an animal bite, though contamination of any break in the skin with infected saliva may result in rabies. Rabies occurs in all South American countries. In Bolivia most cases are related to dog bites. Risk is greatest in the southeastern part of the country.

Rabies vaccine is safe, but a full series requires three injections and is quite expensive. Those at high risk for rabies, such as animal handlers and spelunkers (cave explorers), should certainly get the vaccine. In addition, those at lower risk for animal bites should consider asking for the vaccine if they might be traveling to remote areas and might not have access to appropriate medical care if needed. The treatment for a possibly rabid bite consists of rabies vaccine with rabies-immune globulin. It's effective, but must be given promptly. Most travelers don't need rabies vaccine.

All animal bites and scratches must be promptly and thoroughly cleansed with large amounts of soap and water, and local health authorities contacted to determine whether or not further treatment is necessary (see p397).

Typhoid Fever

Typhoid fever is caused by ingestion of food or water contaminated by a species of salmonella known as salmonella typhi. Fever occurs in virtually all cases. Other symptoms may include headache, malaise, muscle aches, dizziness, loss of appetite, nausea and abdominal pain. Either diarrhea or constipation may occur. Possible complications include intestinal perforation, intestinal bleeding, confusion, delirium or (rarely) coma.

A typhoid vaccine is a good idea. It's usually given orally, but is also available as an injection. Neither vaccine is approved for use in children under age two.

It is not a good idea to self-treat for typhoid fever as the symptoms may be indistinguishable from malaria. If you show symptoms for either, see a doctor immediately – treatment is likely to be a quinolone antibiotic such as ciprofloxacin (Cipro) or levofloxacin (Levaquin).

Yellow Fever

Yellow fever is a life-threatening viral infection transmitted by mosquitoes in forested areas. The illness begins with flu-like symptoms, such as fever, chills, headache, muscle aches, backache, loss of appetite, nausea and vomiting. These symptoms usually subside in a few days, but one person in six enters a second, toxic phase characterized by recurrent fever, vomiting, listlessness, jaundice, kidney failure and hemorrhage, leading to death in up to half of the cases. There is no treatment except for supportive care.

Yellow fever vaccine is strongly recommended for all those visiting areas where yellow fever occurs, which at time of publication included the departments of Beni, Cochabamba, Santa Cruz and La Paz. For the latest information on which areas in Bolivia are reporting yellow fever, go to the 'Blue Sheet' on the website of **Centers for Disease Control & Protection** (CDC; www.cdc.gov/travel/blusheet.htm).

Proof of vaccination is required from all travelers arriving from a yellow fever–infected country in Africa or the Americas.

Yellow-fever vaccine is given only in approved yellow fever vaccination centers, which provide validated International Certificates of Vaccination (yellow booklets). The vaccine should be given at least 10 days before any potential exposure to yellow fever, and remains effective for approximately 10 years. Reactions to the vaccine are generally mild and may include headaches, muscle aches, low-grade fevers, or discomfort at the injection site. Severe, life-threatening reactions have been described but are extremely rare. In general the risk of becoming ill from the vaccine is far less than the risk of becoming ill from yellow fever, and you're strongly encouraged to get the vaccine.

Taking measures to protect yourself from mosquito bites (p397) is an essential part of preventing yellow fever.

Other Infections
BARTONELLOSIS
Bartonellosis (Oroya fever) is carried by sandflies in the arid river valleys on the western

slopes of the Andes in Peru, Bolivia, Colombia and Ecuador between altitudes of 800m and 3000m. (Curiously, it's not found anywhere else in the world.) The chief symptoms are fever and severe body pains. Complications may include marked anemia, enlargement of the liver and spleen, and sometimes death. The drug of choice is chloramphenicol, though doxycycline is also effective.

BOLIVIAN HEMORRHAGIC FEVER
Bolivian hemorrhagic fever has been reported from the Beni Department in the northeastern part of the country. The causative organism, known as Machupo virus, is thought to be acquired by exposure to rodents.

CHAGAS' DISEASE
Chagas' disease is a parasitic infection that is transmitted by triatomine insects (reduviid bugs), which inhabit crevices in the walls and roofs of substandard housing in South and Central America. In Bolivia most cases occur in temperate areas, especially in the departments of Cochabamba, Chuquisaca and Tarija. The triatomine insect lays its feces on human skin as it bites, usually at night. A person becomes infected when he or she unknowingly rubs the feces into the bite wound or sore. Chagas' disease is extremely rare in travelers. However, always protect yourself with a bed net and a good insecticide if in mud, adobe or thatched houses. Do not accept blood transfusions if in these areas – local incidence of the disease is high.

HIV/AIDS
HIV/AIDS has been reported from all South American countries. Be sure to use condoms for all sexual encounters.

LEISHMANIASIS
Leishmaniasis occurs in the mountains and jungles of all South American countries except for Chile and Uruguay. The infection is transmitted by sandflies, which are about one-third the size of mosquitoes. In Bolivia, risk is greatest in the forested foothill regions east of the Andean Cordillera. Most cases of leishmaniasis are limited to the skin, causing slowly growing ulcers over exposed parts of the body. The more severe type, which disseminates to the bone marrow, liver and spleen, occurs only in the Yungas. Leishmaniasis may be particularly severe in those with

HIV. There is no vaccine. To protect yourself from sandflies, follow the same precautions as for mosquitoes (see opposite), except that netting must be finer-mesh (at least 18 holes to the linear inch).

TYPHUS
Typhus may be transmitted by lice in mountainous areas near La Paz.

TRAVELERS' DIARRHEA
To prevent diarrhea, avoid tap water unless it has been boiled, filtered or chemically disinfected (with iodine tablets); only eat fresh fruits or vegetables if peeled or cooked; be wary of dairy products that might contain unpasteurized milk; and be highly selective when eating food from street vendors.

If you develop diarrhea, be sure to drink plenty of fluids, preferably an oral rehydration solution containing lots of salt and sugar. A few loose stools don't require treatment but if you start having more than four or five stools a day you should start taking an antibiotic (usually a quinolone drug) and an antidiarrheal agent (such as loperamide). If diarrhea is bloody, or persists for more than 72 hours or is accompanied by fever, shaking chills or severe abdominal pain, you should seek medical attention.

ENVIRONMENTAL HAZARDS
Altitude Sickness
Altitude sickness may develop in those who ascend rapidly to altitudes greater than 2500m (8100 feet). In Bolivia this includes La Paz (altitude 4000m). Being physically fit offers no protection. Those who have experienced altitude sickness in the past are prone to future episodes. The risk increases with faster ascents, higher altitudes and greater exertion. Symptoms may include headaches, nausea, vomiting, dizziness, malaise, insomnia and

---

FOLK MEDICINE

Problem	Treatment
Altitude sickness	Gingko; coca leaf tea
Jet lag	Melatonin
Motion sickness	Ginger
Mosquito-bite prevention	Oil of eucalyptus; coconut oil

loss of appetite. Severe cases may be complicated by fluid in the lungs (high-altitude pulmonary edema) or swelling of the brain (high-altitude cerebral edema).

The best treatment for altitude sickness is descent. If you are exhibiting symptoms, do not ascend. If symptoms are severe or persistent, descend immediately.

To protect yourself against altitude sickness, take 125mg or 250mg acetazolamide (Diamox) twice or three times daily, starting 24 hours before ascent and continuing for 48 hours after arrival at altitude. Possible side effects include increased urinary volume, numbness, tingling, nausea, drowsiness, myopia and temporary impotence. Acetazolamide should not be given to pregnant women or anyone with a history of sulfa allergy.

For those who cannot tolerate acetazolamide, the next best option is 4mg dexamethasone taken four times daily. Unlike acetazolamide, dexamethasone must be tapered gradually on arrival at altitude, since there is a risk that altitude sickness will occur as the dosage is reduced. Dexamethasone is a steroid, so it should not be given to diabetics or anyone for whom steroids are contraindicated. A natural alternative is gingko, which helps some people.

When traveling to high altitudes, it's also important to avoid overexertion, eat light meals and abstain from alcohol.

If your symptoms are more than mild or don't resolve promptly, see a doctor immediately. Altitude sickness should be taken seriously; it can be life-threatening when severe.

Animal Bites

Do not attempt to pet, handle or feed any animal, with the exception of domestic animals known to be free of any infectious disease. Most animal injuries are directly related to a person's attempt to touch or feed an animal.

Any bite or scratch by a mammal, including bats, should be promptly and thoroughly cleansed with large amounts of soap and water, followed by application of an antiseptic such as iodine or alcohol. The local health authorities should be contacted immediately for possible post-exposure rabies treatment, whether or not you've been immunized against rabies. It may also be advisable to start an antibiotic, since wounds caused by animal bites and scratches frequently become infected. Or use one of the newer quinolones,

such as levofloxacin (Levaquin), which many travelers carry in case of diarrhea.

Snakes and leeches are a hazard in some areas of South America. In Bolivia there are two species of poisonous snakes: pit vipers (rattlesnakes) and coral snakes. These are found chiefly in the sugar and banana plantations, and in the dry, hilly regions. In the event of a venomous snake bite, place the victim at rest, keep the bitten area immobilized and move the victim immediately to the nearest medical facility. Avoid tourniquets, which are no longer recommended.

Insect Bites & Stings

To prevent mosquito bites, wear long sleeves, long pants, hats and shoes (rather than sandals). Bring along a good insect repellent, preferably one containing DEET, which should be applied to exposed skin and clothing, but not to eyes, mouth, cuts, wounds or irritated skin. Products containing lower concentrations of DEET are as effective, but for shorter periods of time. In general, adults and children over 12 should use preparations containing 25% to 35% DEET, which usually lasts about six hours. Children between two and 12 years of age should use preparations containing no more than 10% DEET, applied sparingly, which will usually last about three hours. Neurologic toxicity has been reported from DEET, especially in children, but appears to be extremely uncommon and generally related to overuse. DEET-containing compounds should not be used on children under age two.

Insect repellents containing certain botanical products, including oil of eucalyptus and soybean oil, are effective but last only 1½ to two hours. DEET-containing repellents are preferable for areas where there is a high risk of malaria or yellow fever. Products based on citronella are not effective.

For additional protection you can apply permethrin to clothing, shoes, tents and bed nets. Permethrin treatments are safe and remain effective for at least two weeks, even when items are laundered. Permethrin should not be applied directly to skin.

Don't sleep with the window open unless there is a screen. If sleeping outdoors or in accommodations that allow entry of mosquitoes, use a fine-mesh bed net, preferably treated with permethrin, with edges tucked in under the mattress. If the sleeping area is not protected, use a mosquito coil, which will fill the room with insecticide through the night. Repellent-impregnated wristbands are not effective.

Sunburn & Heat Exhaustion

To protect yourself from excessive sun exposure, stay out of the midday sun, wear sunglasses and a wide-brimmed sun hat, and apply sunscreen with SPF 15 or higher, with both UVA and UVB protection. Sunscreen should be generously applied to all exposed parts of the body approximately 30 minutes before sun exposure and should be reapplied after swimming or vigorous activity. Travelers should also drink plenty of fluids and avoid strenuous exercise in high temperatures.

Water

Tap water in Bolivia is not safe to drink. Vigorous boiling for one minute is the most effective means of water purification. At altitudes greater than 2000m (6500 ft), boil for three minutes.

Another option is to disinfect water with iodine pills such as Globaline, Potable-Aqua and Coghlan's, available at most pharmacies. Instructions are enclosed and should be carefully followed. Or you can add 2% tincture of iodine to one quart or liter of water (five drops to clear water, 10 drops to cloudy water) and let it stand for 30 minutes. If the water is cold, longer times may be required. The taste of iodinated water may be improved by adding vitamin C (ascorbic acid). Iodinated water should not be consumed for more than a few weeks. Pregnant women, those with a history of thyroid disease and those allergic to iodine should not drink iodinated water.

A number of water filters are on the market. Those with smaller pores (reverse osmosis filters) provide the broadest protection, but they

are relatively large and are readily plugged by debris. Those with larger pores (microstrainer filters) are ineffective against viruses, although they remove other organisms. Manufacturers' instructions must be carefully followed.

TRAVELING WITH CHILDREN

When traveling with young children, be particularly careful about what you allow them to eat and drink, because diarrhea can be especially dangerous in this age group and because the vaccines for hepatitis A and typhoid fever are not approved for use in children under two years.

Since there's little information concerning the medical consequences of taking children to high altitudes, it's probably safer not to do so. Also, children under nine months should not be brought to areas where yellow fever occurs, since the vaccine is not safe in this age group.

The two main malaria medications, Lariam and Malarone, may be given to children, but insect repellents must be applied in lower concentrations.

WOMEN'S HEALTH

There are English-speaking obstetricians in Bolivia, listed on the **US Embassy website** (http://bolivia.usembassy.gov/english/consular/medicalresources .htm). However, medical facilities will probably not be comparable to those in your home country. It's safer to avoid travel to Bolivia late in pregnancy, so that you don't have to deliver there.

If pregnant, you should avoid travel to high altitudes. The lower oxygen levels that occur at high altitudes can slow fetal growth, especially after the 32nd week. Also it's safer not to visit areas where yellow fever occurs, since the vaccine is not safe during pregnancy.

If you need to take malaria pills, mefloquine (Lariam) is the safest during pregnancy.

Language

CONTENTS

Spanish	399
Pronunciation	399
Gender & Plurals	400
Accommodation	400
Conversation & Essentials	401
Directions	401
Emergencies	402
Health	402
Language Difficulties	402
Numbers	402
Shopping & Services	403
Time & Dates	403
Transport	404
Travel With Children	404
Aymará & Quechua	405

The official language of Bolivia is Latin American Spanish, but only 60% to 70% of the people speak it, and then often only as a second language. The remainder speak Quechua (the language of the Inca conquerors) or Aymará (the pre-Inca language of the Altiplano). In addition, a host of other minor indigenous tongues are used in small areas throughout the country. English in Bolivia won't get you very far, but fortunately it's not difficult to learn the basics of Spanish. You mightn't be able to carry on a deep and meaningful philosophical or political discussion after a short course or self-teaching program, but you'll have the tools you need for basic communication.

SPANISH

Spanish courses in Bolivia are available in La Paz (p79), Cochabamba (p225) and Sucre (p247) for those who want to learn the language in greater depth while in the country.

For a more comprehensive guide to the Spanish of Bolivia than we can offer here, pick up a copy of Lonely Planet's *Latin American Spanish Phrasebook*. Another useful resource is the compact *University of Chicago Spanish Dictionary*. For words and

phrases for use when ordering at a restaurant, see p59.

PRONUNCIATION

Spanish spelling is phonetically consistent, meaning that there's a clear and consistent relationship between what you see in writing and how it's pronounced. In addition, most Spanish sounds have English equivalents, so English speakers should not have much trouble being understood if the rules listed below are adhered to.

Vowels

a	as in 'father'
e	as in 'met'
i	as in 'marine'
o	as in 'or' (without the 'r' sound)
u	as in 'rule'; the 'u' is not pronounced after **q** and in the letter combinations **gue** and **gui**, unless it's marked with a diaeresis (eg *argüir*), in which case it's pronounced as English 'w'
y	at the end of a word or when it stands alone, it's pronounced as the Spanish **i** (eg *ley*); between vowels within a word it's as the 'y' in 'yonder'

Consonants

As a rule, Spanish consonants resemble their English counterparts, with the exceptions listed below.

While the consonants **ch**, **ll** and **ñ** are generally considered distinct letters, **ch** and **ll** are now often listed alphabetically under **c** and **l** respectively. The letter **ñ** is still treated as a separate letter and comes after **n** in dictionaries.

b	similar to English 'b,' but softer; referred to as 'b larga'
c	as in 'celery' before **e** and **i**; otherwise as English 'k'
ch	as in 'church'
d	as in 'dog,' but between vowels and after **l** or **n**, the sound is closer to the 'th' in 'this'
g	as the 'ch' in the Scottish *loch* before **e** and **i** ('kh' in our guides to pronunciation); elsewhere, as in 'go'

LANGUAGE

h   invariably silent. If your name begins with this letter, listen carefully if you're waiting for public officials to call you.

j   as the 'ch' in the Scottish *loch* (written as 'kh' in our guides to pronunciation)

ll   as the 'y' in 'yellow'

ñ   as the 'ni' in 'onion'

r   a slap of the tongue against the palate (like the 'd' in 'ladder'); at the beginning of a word or after **l**, **n** or **s**, it's strongly rolled, though some Bolivians pronounce it as the 's' in 'pleasure'

rr   very strongly rolled

v   similar to English 'b', but softer; referred to as 'b corta'

x   as in 'taxi' except for a very few words, when it's pronounced as **j**

z   as the 's' in 'sun'

Word Stress

In general, words ending in vowels or the letters **n** or **s** have stress on the next-to-last syllable, while those with other endings have stress on the last syllable. Thus *vaca* (cow) and *caballos* (horses) both carry stress on the next-to-last syllable, while *ciudad* (city) and *infeliz* (unhappy) are both stressed on the last syllable.

Written accents will almost always appear in words that don't follow the rules above, eg *sótano* (basement), *América* and *porción* (portion). When counting syllables, be sure to remember that diphthongs (vowel combinations, such as the 'ue' in *puede*) constitute only one. When a word with a written accent appears in capital letters, the accent is often not written, but is still pronounced.

GENDER & PLURALS

In Spanish, nouns are either masculine or feminine, and there are rules to help determine gender (there are of course some exceptions). Feminine nouns generally end with **-a** or with the groups **-ción**, **-sión** or **-dad**. Other endings typically signify a masculine noun. Endings for adjectives also change to agree with the gender of the noun they modify (masculine/feminine **-o**/**-a**). Where both masculine and feminine forms are included in this language guide, they are separated by a slash, with the masculine form first, eg *perdido/a*.

If a noun or adjective ends in a vowel, the plural is formed by adding **s** to the end. If it ends in a consonant, the plural is formed by adding **es** to the end.

ACCOMMODATIONS

I'm looking for …	*Estoy buscando …*	e·stoy boos·*kan*·do …
Where is …?	*¿Dónde hay …?*	*don*·de ai …
a hotel	*un hotel*	oon o·*tel*
a boarding house	*una pensión/ residencial/ un hospedaje*	oo·na pen·*syon*/ re·see·den·*syal*/ oon os·pe·*da*·khe
a youth hostel	*un albergue juvenil*	oon al·*ber*·ge khoo·ve·*neel*
I'd like a … room.	*Quisiera una habitación …*	kee·*sye*·ra oo·na a·bee·ta·*syon* …
double	*doble*	*do*·ble
single	*individual*	een·dee·vee·*dwal*
twin	*con dos camas*	kon dos *ka*·mas
How much is it per …?	*¿Cuánto cuesta por …?*	*kwan*·to *kwes*·ta por …
night	*noche*	*no*·che
person	*persona*	per·*so*·na
week	*semana*	se·*ma*·na
full board	*pensión completa*	pen·*syon* kom·*ple*·ta
private/shared bathroom	*baño privado/ compartido*	*ba*·nyo pree·*va*·do/ kom·par·*tee*·do
too expensive	*demasiado caro*	de·ma·*sya*·do *ka*·ro
cheaper	*más económico*	mas e·ko·*no*·mee·ko

MAKING A RESERVATION

(for phone or written requests)

To …	*A …*
From …	*De …*
Date	*Fecha*
I'd like to book …	*Quisiera reservar …* (see the list under 'Accommodations' for bed/ room options)
in the name of …	*en nombre de …*
for the nights of …	*para las noches del …*
credit card …	*tarjeta de crédito …*
number	*número*
expiry date	*fecha de vencimiento*
Please confirm …	*Puede confirmar …*
availability	*la disponibilidad*
price	*el precio*

May I see the room?
¿Puedo ver la | pwe·do ver la
habitación? | a·bee·ta·*syon*
I don't like it.
No me gusta. | no me *goos*·ta
It's fine. I'll take it.
OK. La alquilo. | o·*kay* la al·*kee*·lo
I'm leaving now.
Me voy ahora. | me voy a·o·ra
Does it include breakfast?
¿Incluye el desayuno? | een·*kloo*·ye el de·sa·*yoo*·no

CONVERSATION & ESSENTIALS

In their public behavior, South Americans are very conscious of civilities, sometimes to the point of ceremoniousness. Never approach a stranger for information without extending a greeting and use only the polite form of address, especially with the police and public officials. Young people may be less likely to expect this, but it's best to stick to the polite form unless you're quite sure you won't offend by using the informal mode. The polite form is used in all cases in this guide; where options are given, the form is indicated by the abbreviations 'pol' and 'inf.'

Hello. | Hola. | o·la
Good morning. | Buenos días. | bwe·nos dee·as
Good afternoon. | Buenas tardes. | bwe·nas tar·des
Good evening/ | Buenas noches. | bwe·nas no·ches
night.
Goodbye. | Adiós. | a·dyos
Bye/See you soon. | Hasta luego. | as·ta lwe·go
Yes. | Sí. | see
No. | No. | no
Please. | Por favor. | por fa·vor
Thank you. | Gracias. | gra·syas
Many thanks. | Muchas gracias. | moo·chas gra·syas
You're welcome. | De nada. | de na·da
Pardon me. | Perdón. | per·don
Excuse me. | Permiso. | per·mee·so
(used when asking permission)
Forgive me. | Disculpe. | dees·kool·pe
(used when apologizing)
How are things? | ¿Qué tal? | ke tal

What's your name?
¿Cómo se llama? | ko·mo se ya·ma (pol)
¿Cómo te llamas? | ko·mo te ya·mas (inf)
My name is ...
Me llamo ... | me ya·mo ...
It's a pleasure to meet you.
Mucho gusto. | moo·cho goos·to

The pleasure is mine.
El gusto es mío. | el goos·to es mee·o
Where are you from?
¿De dónde es/eres? | de don·de es/e·res (pol/inf)
I'm from ...
Soy de ... | soy de ...
Where are you staying?
¿Dónde está alojado? | don·de es·ta a·lo·kha·do (pol)
¿Dónde estás alojado? | don·de es·tas a·lo·kha·do (inf)
May I take a photo?
¿Puedo sacar una foto? | pwe·do sa·kar oo·na fo·to

DIRECTIONS

How do I get to ...?
¿Cómo puedo llegar | ko·mo pwe·do lye·gar
a ...? | a ...
Is it far?
¿Está lejos? | es·ta le·khos
Go straight ahead.
Siga/Vaya derecho. | see·ga/va·ya de·re·cho
Turn left.
Voltée a la izquierda. | vol·te·e a la ees·kyer·da
Turn right.
Voltée a la derecha. | vol·te·e a la de·re·cha
I'm lost.
Estoy perdido/a. | es·toy per·dee·do/a
Can you show me (on the map)?
¿Me lo podría indicar | me lo po·dree·a een·dee·kar
(en el mapa)? | (en el ma·pa)

north | norte | nor·te
south | sur | soor
east | este/oriente | es·te/o·ryen·te
west | oeste/occidente | o·es·te/ok·see·den·te
here | aquí | a·kee
there | allí | a·yee
block | cuadra | kwa·dra
street | calle/paseo | ka·lye/pa·se·o
mountain | montaña/cerro/ | mon·ta·nya/se·ro/
nevado | ne·va·do
mountain pass | paso/pasaje/ | pa·so/pa·sa·khe/
abra/portachuel | a·bra/por·ta·chwel

SIGNS	
Entrada	Entrance
Salida	Exit
Información	Information
Abierto	Open
Cerrado	Closed
Prohibido	Prohibited
Comisaria	Police Station
Servicios/Baños	Toilets
Hombres/Varones	Men
Mujeres/Damas	Women

LANGUAGE

EMERGENCIES

Help!	¡Socorro!	so·ko·ro
Fire!	¡Incendio!	een·sen·dyo
I've been robbed.	Me robaron.	me ro·ba·ron
Go away!	¡Déjeme!/ ¡Váyase!	de·khe·me/ va·ya·se
Call ...!	¡Llame a ...!	ya·me a
the police	la policía	la po·lee·see·a
a doctor	un médico	oon me·dee·ko
an ambulance	una ambulancia	oo·na am·boo·lan·sya

It's an emergency.
Es una emergencia.   es oo·na e·mer·khen·sya
Could you help me, please?
¿Me puede ayudar, por favor?   me pwe·de a·yoo·dar por fa·vor
I'm lost.
Estoy perdido/a.   es·toy per·dee·do/a
Where are the toilets?
¿Dónde están los baños?   don·de es·tan los ba·nyos

HEALTH

I'm sick.
Estoy enfermo/a.   es·toy en·fer·mo/a
I need a doctor.
Necesito un médico.   ne·se·see·to oon me·dee·ko
Where's the hospital?
¿Dónde está el hospital?   don·de es·ta el os·pee·tal
I'm pregnant.
Estoy embarazada.   es·toy em·ba·ra·sa·da
I've been vaccinated.
Estoy vacunado/a.   es·toy va·koo·na·do/a

I'm allergic to ...	Soy alérgico/a a ...	soy a·ler·khee·ko/a a ...
antibiotics	los antibióticos	los an·tee·byo·tee·kos
penicillin	la penicilina	la pe·nee·see·lee·na
peanuts	los manies	los ma·nee·es

I'm ...	Soy ...	soy ...
asthmatic	asmático/a	as·ma·tee·ko/a
diabetic	diabético/a	dya·be·tee·ko/a
epileptic	epiléptico/a	e·pee·lep·tee·ko/a

I have ...	Tengo ...	ten·go ...
altitude sickness	soroche	so·ro·che
diarrhea	diarrea	dya·re·a
nausea	náusea	now·se·a
a headache	un dolor de cabeza	oon do·lor de ka·be·sa
a cough	tos	tos

LANGUAGE DIFFICULTIES

Do you speak (English)?
¿Habla/Hablas (inglés)?   a·bla/a·blas (een·gles) (pol/inf)
Does anyone here speak English?
¿Hay alguien que hable inglés?   ai al·gyen ke a·ble een·gles
I (don't) understand.
Yo (no) entiendo.   yo (no) en·tyen·do
How do you say ...?
¿Cómo se dice ...?   ko·mo se dee·se ...
What does ...mean?
¿Qué quiere decir ...?   ke kye·re de·seer ...

Could you please ...?	¿Puede ..., por favor?	pwe·de ... por fa·vor
repeat that	repetirlo	re·pe·teer·lo
speak more slowly	hablar más despacio	a·blar mas des·pa·syo
write it down	escribirlo	es·kree·beer·lo

NUMBERS

1	uno	oo·no
2	dos	dos
3	tres	tres
4	cuatro	kwa·tro
5	cinco	seen·ko
6	seis	says
7	siete	sye·te
8	ocho	o·cho
9	nueve	nwe·ve
10	diez	dyes
11	once	on·se
12	doce	do·se
13	trece	tre·se
14	catorce	ka·tor·se
15	quince	keen·se
16	dieciséis	dye·see·says
17	diecisiete	dye·see·sye·te
18	dieciocho	dye·see·o·cho
19	diecinueve	dye·see·nwe·ve
20	veinte	vayn·te
21	veintiuno	vayn·tee·oo·no
30	treinta	trayn·ta
31	treinta y uno	trayn·ta ee oo·no
40	cuarenta	kwa·ren·ta
50	cincuenta	seen·kwen·ta
60	sesenta	se·sen·ta
70	setenta	se·ten·ta
80	ochenta	o·chen·ta
90	noventa	no·ven·ta
100	cien	syen
101	ciento uno	syen·to oo·no
200	doscientos	do·syen·tos
1000	mil	meel

5000	*cinco mil*	seen·ko meel
10,000	*diez mil*	dyes meel
50,000	*cincuenta mil*	seen·kwen·ta meel
100,000	*cien mil*	syen meel
1,000,000	*un millón*	oon mee·yon

SHOPPING & SERVICES

I'd like to buy ...
Quisiera comprar ...   kee·sye·ra kom·prar ...
I'm just looking.
Sólo estoy mirando.   so·lo es·toy mee·ran·do
May I look at it?
¿Puedo mirar(lo/la)?   pwe·do mee·rar·(lo/la)
How much is it?
¿Cuánto cuesta?   kwan·to kwes·ta
That's too expensive for me.
Es demasiado caro   es de·ma·sya·do ka·ro
para mí.   pa·ra mee
Could you lower the price?
¿Podría bajar un poco   po·dree·a ba·khar oon po·ko
el precio?   el pre·syo
I don't like it.
No me gusta.   no me goos·ta
I'll take it.
Lo llevo.   lo ye·vo

Do you accept ...?	*¿Aceptan ...?*	a·sep·tan ...
American dollars	*dólares americanos*	do·la·res a·me·ree·ka·nos
credit cards	*tarjetas de crédito*	tar·khe·tas de kre·dee·to
travelers checks	*cheques de viajero*	che·kes de vya·khe·ro

less	*menos*	me·nos
more	*más*	mas
large	*grande*	gran·de
small	*pequeño/a*	pe·ke·nyo/a

I'm looking for (the) ...	*Estoy buscando ...*	es·toy boos·kan·do
ATM	*el cajero automático*	el ka·khe·ro ow·to·ma·tee·ko
bank	*el banco*	el ban·ko
bookstore	*la librería*	la lee·bre·ree·a
embassy	*la embajada*	la em·ba·kha·da
exchange house	*la casa de cambio*	la ka·sa de kam·byo
general store	*la tienda*	la tyen·da
laundry	*la lavandería*	la la·van·de·ree·a
market	*el mercado*	el mer·ka·do
pharmacy/ chemist	*la farmacia/ la botica*	la far·ma·sya/ la bo·tee·ka
post office	*el correo*	el ko·re·o

| **supermarket** | *el supermercado* | el soo·per·mer·ka·do |
| **tourist office** | *la oficina de turismo* | la o·fee·see·na de too·rees·mo |

What time does it open/close?
¿A qué hora abre/cierra? a ke o·ra a·bre/sye·ra
I want to change some money/travelers checks.
Quiero cambiar dinero/ kye·ro kam·byar dee·ne·ro/
cheques de viajero. che·kes de vya·khe·ro
What is the exchange rate?
¿Cuál es el tipo de kwal es el tee·po de
cambio? kam·byo
I want to call ...
Quiero llamar a ... kye·ro lya·mar a ...

airmail	*correo aéreo*	ko·re·o a·e·re·o
black market	*mercado (negro/ paralelo)*	mer·ka·do ne·gro/ pa·ra·le·lo
letter	*carta*	kar·ta
registered mail	*certificado*	ser·tee·fee·ka·do
stamps	*estampillas*	es·tam·pee·lyas

TIME & DATES

What time is it?	*¿Qué hora es?*	ke o·ra es
It's one o'clock.	*Es la una.*	es la oo·na
It's seven o'clock.	*Son las siete.*	son las sye·te
midnight	*medianoche*	me·dya·no·che
noon	*mediodía*	me·dyo·dee·a
half past two	*dos y media*	dos ee me·dya

now	*ahora*	a·o·ra
today	*hoy*	oy
tonight	*esta noche*	es·ta no·che
tomorrow	*mañana*	ma·nya·na
yesterday	*ayer*	a·yer

Monday	*lunes*	loo·nes
Tuesday	*martes*	mar·tes
Wednesday	*miércoles*	myer·ko·les
Thursday	*jueves*	khwe·ves
Friday	*viernes*	vyer·nes
Saturday	*sábado*	sa·ba·do
Sunday	*domingo*	do·meen·go

January	*enero*	e·ne·ro
February	*febrero*	fe·bre·ro
March	*marzo*	mar·so
April	*abril*	a·breel
May	*mayo*	ma·yo
June	*junio*	khoo·nyo
July	*julio*	khoo·lyo
August	*agosto*	a·gos·to
September	*septiembre*	sep·tyem·bre
October	*octubre*	ok·too·bre

| November | noviembre | no·*vyem*·bre |
| December | diciembre | dee·*syem*·bre |

TRANSPORTATION
Public Transportation

What time does	¿A qué hora	a ke o·ra
... leave/arrive?	sale/llega ...?	sa·le/ye·ga ...
the bus	el autobús	el ow·to·boos
the plane	el avión	el a·*vyon*
the ship	el barco/buque	el *bar*·ko/boo·ke
the train	el tren	el tren

airport	el aeropuerto	el a·e·ro·*pwer*·to
train station	la estación de	la es·ta·*syon* de
	ferrocarril	fe·ro·ka·*reel*
bus station	la estación de	la es·ta·*syon* de
	autobuses	ow·to·*boo*·ses
bus stop	la parada de	la pa·*ra*·da de
	autobuses	ow·to·*boo*·ses
luggage check	guardería/	gwar·de·*ree*·a/
room	equipaje	e·kee·*pa*·khe
ticket office	la boletería	la bo·le·te·*ree*·a

I'd like a ticket to ...
  Quiero un boleto a ...   kye·ro oon bo·*le*·to a ...
What's the fare to ...?
  ¿Cuánto cuesta hasta ...?   kwan·to *kwes*·ta a·sta ...

student's	de estudiante	de es·too·*dyan*·te
1st class	primera clase	pree·me·ra *kla*·se
2nd class	segunda clase	se·*goon*·da *kla*·se
single/one-way	ida	ee·da
return/round trip	ida y vuelta	ee·da ee *vwel*·ta
taxi	taxi	*tak*·see

Private Transportation

I'd like to	Quisiera	kee·*sye*·ra
hire a ...	alquilar ...	al·kee·*lar* ...
4WD	un todo terreno/	oon *to*·do te·*re*·no/
	un cuatro por	*kwa*·tro por
	cuatro	*kwa*·tro
car	un auto	oon ow·to
motorbike	una moto	oo·na mo·to
bicycle	una bicicleta	oo·na bee·see·
		kle·ta

pickup (truck)	camioneta	ka·myo·*ne*·ta
truck	camión	ka·myon
hitchhike	hacer dedo	a·ser de·do

Is this the road to (...)?
  ¿Se va a (...) por   se va a (...) por
  esta carretera?   es·ta ka·re·*te*·ra
Where's a petrol station?
  ¿Dónde hay una   don·de ai oo·na
  gasolinera/un grifo?   ga·so·lee·*ne*·ra/oon gree·fo

Please fill it up.
  Lleno, por favor.   ye·no por fa·*vor*
I'd like (20) liters.
  Quiero (veinte) litros.   kye·ro (vayn·te) lee·tros

| diesel | diesel | dee·sel |
| gas/petrol | gasolina | ga·so·*lee*·na |

(How long) Can I park here?
  ¿(Por cuánto tiempo)   (por kwan·to tyem·po)
  Puedo aparcar aquí?   pwe·do a·par·kar a·kee
Where do I pay?
  ¿Dónde se paga?   don·de se pa·ga
I need a mechanic.
  Necesito un   ne·se·*see*·to oon
  mecánico.   me·*ka*·nee·ko
The car has broken down (in ...).
  El carro se ha averiado   el ka·ro se a a·ve·*rya*·do
  (en ...).   (en ...)
The motorbike won't start.
  No arranca la moto.   no a·*ran*·ka la mo·to
I have a flat tire.
  Tengo un pinchazo.   ten·go oon peen·*cha*·so
I've run out of gas/petrol.
  Me quedé sin gasolina.   me ke·de seen ga·so·*lee*·na
I've had an accident.
  Tuve un accidente.   too·ve oon ak·see·*den*·te

TRAVEL WITH CHILDREN
I need ...
  Necesito ...   ne·se·*see*·to ...
Do you have ...?
  ¿Hay ...?   ai ...
  a car baby seat
  un asiento de seguridad   oon a·*syen*·to de se·goo·ree·da
  para bebés   pa·ra be·bes

(disposable) diapers/nappies
pañales (de usar y tirar)   pa·*nya*·les de oo·*sar* ee tee·*rar*
infant milk formula/powder
leche en polvo   *le*·che en *pol*·vo
a highchair
una trona   oo·na *tro*·na
a potty
una pelela   oo·na pe·*le*·la
a stroller
un cochecito   oon ko·che·*see*·to

Do you mind if I breast-feed here?
¿Le molesta que dé   le mo·*les*·ta ke de
de pecho aquí?   de *pe*·cho a·*kee*
Are children allowed?
¿Se admiten niños?   se ad·*mee*·ten nee·nyos

AYMARÁ & QUECHUA

Here's a brief list of Quechua and Aymará words and phrases. The grammar and pronunciation of these languages are quite difficult for native English speakers, but those who are interested in learning them will find language courses in La Paz (p79), Cochabamba (p225) and Sucre (p247).

Dictionaries and phrasebooks are available through Los Amigos del Libro and larger bookstores in La Paz, but to use them you'll first need a sound knowledge of Spanish.

Lonely Planet's *Quechua Phrasebook* provides useful phrases and vocabulary in the Cuzco (Peru) dialect, but it will also be of use in the Bolivian highlands.

The following list of words and phrases (with Aymará listed first, Quechua second) is obviously minimal, but it should be useful in the areas where these languages are spoken. Pronounce them as you would a Spanish word. An apostrophe represents a glottal stop, which is the 'non-sound' that occurs in the middle of 'uh-oh.'

Hi!
Laphi!   *Raphi!*
Hello.
Kamisaraki.   *Napaykullayki.*
Please.
Mirá.   *Allichu.*
Thank you.
Yuspagara.   *Yusulipayki.*
It's a pleasure.
Take chuima'hampi.   *Tucuy sokoywan.*

Yes/No.
Jisa/Janiwa.   *Ari/Mana.*
How do you say ...?
Cun sañasauca'ha ...?   *Imainata nincha chaita ...?*
It is called ...
Ucan sutipa'h ...   *Chaipa'g sutin'ha ...*
Please repeat that.
Uastata sita.   *Ua'manta niway.*
Where is ...?
Kaukasa ...?   *Maypi ...?*
How much?
K'gauka?   *Maik'ata'g?*

distant	*haya*	*caru*
downhill	*aynacha*	*uray*
father	*auqui*	*tayta*
food	*manka*	*mikiuy*
mother	*taica*	*mama*
lodging	*korpa*	*pascana*
near	*maka*	*kailla*
river	*jawira*	*mayu*
snowy peak	*kollu*	*riti-orko*
trail	*tapu*	*chakiñan*
very near	*hakítaqui*	*kaillitalla*
water	*uma*	*yacu*

1	*maya*	*u'*
2	*paya*	*iskai*
3	*quimsa*	*quinsa*
4	*pusi*	*tahua*
5	*pesca*	*phiska*
6	*zo'hta*	*so'gta*
7	*pakalko*	*khanchis*
8	*quimsakalko*	*pusa'g*
9	*yatunca*	*iskon*
10	*tunca*	*chunca*
100	*pataca*	*pacha'g*

Also available from Lonely Planet:
Latin American Spanish Phrasebook

Glossary

For a glossary of food and drink items, see the Food & Drink chapter on p59.

abra – opening; refers to a mountain pass, usually flanked by steep high walls

achachilas – Aymará mountain spirits, believed to be ancestors who look after their *ayllus* and provide bounty from the earth

aduana – customs office

aguayo – colorful woven square used to carry things on one's back, also called a *manta*

alcaldía – municipal/town hall

Altiplano – High Plain; the largest expanse of level (and, in places, arable) land in the Andes, it extends from Bolivia into southern Peru, northwestern Argentina and northern Chile

Alto Perú – the Spanish colonial name for the area now called Bolivia

anillos – literally 'rings'; the name used for main orbital roads around some Bolivian cities

apacheta – mound of stones on a mountain peak or pass; travelers carry a stone from the valley to place on top of the heap as an offering to the *apus*; the word may also be used locally to refer to the pass itself

apu – mountain spirit who provides protection for travelers and water for crops, often associated with a particular *nevado*

arenales – sand dunes

artesanía – locally handcrafted items, or a shop selling them

ayllus – loosely translates as 'tribe'; indigenous groups inhabiting a particular area

Aymará or Kolla – indigenous people of Bolivia; 'Aymará' also refers to the language of these people; also appears as 'Aymara'

azulejos – decorative tiles, so-named because most early Iberian *azulejos* were blue and white

bajones – immense flutes introduced by the Jesuits to the lowland indigenous communities; they are still featured in festivities at San Ignacio de Moxos

balsa – raft; in the Bolivian Amazon, *balsas* are used to ferry cars across rivers that lack bridges

barranca – cliff; often refers to a canyon wall

barranquilleros – wildcat gold miners of the Yungas and Alto Beni regions

barrio – district or neighborhood

bloqueo – roadblock

bodega – boxcar, carried on some trains, in which 2nd-class passengers can travel; or a wine cellar

bofedales – swampy alluvial grasslands in the *puna* and Altiplano regions, where Aymará people pasture their llamas and alpacas

boletería – ticket window

bolivianita – a purple and yellow amethyst

bolivianos – Bolivian people; also the Bolivian unit of currency

bombas de gasolina – gasoline pumps

bus cama – literally 'bed bus'; a bus service with fully reclining seats that is used on some international services, as well as a few longer domestic runs; it's often substantially more expensive than normal services

cabaña – cabin

cama matrimonial – double bed

camarín – niche in which a religious image is displayed

camba – a Bolivian from the Eastern Lowlands; some highlanders use this term for anyone from the Beni, Pando or Santa Cruz departments (oddly enough, the same term applies to lowlanders in eastern Tibet!)

cambista – street moneychanger

camino – road, path, way

camión – flatbed truck; a popular form of local transportation

camioneta – pickup truck, used as local transportation in the Amazon Basin

campesino – subsistence farmer

cancha – open space in an urban area, often used for market activities; soccer field

casilla – post-office box

cerrado – sparsely forested scrub savanna, an endangered habitat that may be seen in Parque Nacional Noel Kempff Mercado

cerro – hill; this term is often used to refer to mountains, which is a laughably classic case of understatement given their altitudes!

chacra – cornfield

cha'lla – offering

chalanas – ferries

chapacos – residents of Tarija; used proudly by *tarijeños* and in misguided jest by other Bolivians

chaqueo – annual burning of Amazonian rainforest to clear agricultural and grazing land; there's a mistaken belief that the smoke from the *chaqueo* forms clouds and ensures good rains

charango – a traditional Bolivian ukulele-type instrument

cholo/a – Quechua or Aymará person who lives in the city but continues to wear traditional dress

chompa – sweater, jumper

chullo – traditional pointed woolen hat, usually with earflaps

chullpa – funerary tower, normally from the Aymará culture

cocalero – coca grower

cochabambinos – Cochabamba locals

colectivo – minibus or collective taxi

Colla – alternative spelling for Kolla

comedor – dining hall

Comibol – Corporación Minera Boliviana (Bolivian Mining Corporation), now defunct

contrabandista – smuggler

cooperativos – small groups of miners who purchase temporary rights

cordillera – mountain range

corregidor – chief magistrate

cruce – turnoff

cruzeños – Santa Cruz locals

DEA – Drug Enforcement Agency, the US drug-offensive body sent to Bolivia to enforce coca-crop substitution programs and to apprehend drug magnates

denuncia – affidavit

derecho – a right; a privilege provided in exchange for a levy or tax

dueño/a – proprietor

edificio – building

EFA – Empresa Ferroviaria Andina; the new private railway company, also known as FVA, or 'Ferroviarias Andinas'

ejecutivo – executive

Ekeko – household god of abundance; the name means 'dwarf' in Aymará

enclaustromiento – landlocked status

Entel – Empresa Nacional de Telecomunicaciones (Bolivian national communications commission)

entrada – entrance procession

esquina – street corner, often abbreviated *esq*

estancia – extensive ranch, often a grazing establishment

feria – fair, market

ferretería – hardware shop

ferrobus – passenger rail bus

flota – long-distance bus company

frontera – border

futból – soccer

FVA – see EFA

garapatillas – tiny ticks that are the bane of the northern plateaus and savanna grasslands

guardaparque – national park ranger

hechicería – traditional Aymará witchcraft

hoja de ruta – circulation card

hornecinos – niches commonly found in Andean ruins, presumably used for the placement of idols and/or offerings

huemul – Andean deer

iglesia – church

Inca – dominant indigenous civilization of the Central Andes at the time of the Spanish conquest; refers both to the people and to their leader

ingenio – mill; in Potosí, it refers to silver smelting plants along the Ribera, where metal was extracted from low-grade ore by crushing it with a mill wheel in a solution of salt and mercury

jardín – garden

javeli – peccary

jefe de la estación – stationmaster

jipijapa – the fronds of the cyclanthaceae fan palm (*Carludovica palmata*)

jochi – agouti, an agile, long-legged rodent of the Amazon basin; it's the only native animal that can eat the Brazil nut

Kallahuayas – itinerant traditional healers and fortune-tellers of the remote Cordillera Apolobamba; also spelled 'Kallawaya'

koa – sweet-smelling incense bush (*Senecio mathewsii*), which grows on Isla del Sol and other parts of the Altiplano and is used as an incense in Aymará ritual; also refers to a similar smelling domestic plant *Mentha pulegium*, which was introduced by the Spanish

Kolla – the name used by the Aymará to refer to themselves; also spelt Colla

Kollasuyo – Inca name for Bolivia, the 'land of the Kolla,' or Aymará people; the Spanish knew the area as Alto Perú, 'upper Peru'

La Diablada – Dance of the Devils, frequently performed at festivals

LAB – Lloyd Aéreo Boliviano, the Bolivian national airline

lago – lake

laguna – lagoon; shallow lake

legía – alkaloid usually made of potato and quinoa ash that is used to draw the drug from coca leaves when chewed

licuados – fruit shake made with either milk or water

liquichiris – harmful spirits who suck out a person's vitality, causing death for no apparent reason

llanos – plains

llapa – see *yapa*

llareta – combustible salt-tolerant moss (*Azorella compacta*) growing on the *salares* of the southern Altiplano that oozes a turpentinelike jelly used by locals as stove fuel; also spelled *yareta*

loma – artificial mounds

lucha libre – freestyle wrestling matches

Manco Capac – the first Inca emperor

manta – shawl

mariguí – a small and very irritating biting fly of the Amazon lowlands; the bite initially creates a small blood blister and then itches for the next two weeks, sometimes leaving scars

mate – herbal infusion of coca, chamomile, or similar

menonitas – Mennonites of the Eastern Lowlands, Paraguay, northern Argentina and southwestern Brazil

mercado – market

mestizo – person of Spanish and indigenous parentage or descent; architectural style incorporating natural-theme designs

micro – small bus or minibus

minifundio – a small plot of land

mirador – lookout

mobilidad – any sort of motor vehicle

moto-taxi – motorbike taxi, a standard means of public transportation in the Eastern Lowlands and Amazon Basin

movilidades – anything that moves (in terms of transportation)

mudéjar – Spanish name for architecture displaying Moorish influences

ñandu – rhea, a large, flightless bird also known as the South American ostrich

nevado – snowcapped mountain peak

orureño/a – Oruro local

paceño/a – La Paz local

Pachamama – the Aymará and Quechua goddess or 'earth mother'

pahuichi – straw-thatched home with reed walls, a common dwelling in the Beni department

paja brava – spiky grass of the high Altiplano

parrilla – barbecue

parrillada plate of mixed grilled meats

peajes – tolls sometimes charged at a *tranca* or toll station

peña – folk-music program

piso – floor

pongaje – feudal system of peonage inflicted on the Bolivian peasantry; abolished after the April Revolution of 1952

pullman – 'reclining' 1st-class rail or bus seat; it may or may not actually recline

puna – high open grasslands of the Altiplano

punto – privately run phone offices

quebrada – ravine or wash, usually dry

Quechua – highland (Altiplano) indigenous language of Ecuador, Peru and Bolivia; language of the former Inca empire

quena – simple reed flute

queñua – dwarf shaggy-barked tree (*Polylepis tarapana*) that grows at higher altitudes than any other tree in the world; it can survive at elevations of over 5000m

quinoa – highly nutritious grain similar to sorghum, used to make flour and thicken stews; grown at high elevations

quirquincho – armadillo carapace used in the making of *charangos*; nickname for residents of Oruro

radiales – 'radials', the streets forming the 'spokes' of a city laid out in *anillos*, or rings; the best Bolivian example is Santa Cruz

reais – pronounced 'hey-ice'; Brazilian unit of currency (R$); singular is *real* pronounced 'hey-ow'

refugio – mountain hut

río – river

roca – rock

salar – salt pan or salt desert

salteña – filled pastry shell

sarape – poncho

saya – Afro-Bolivian dance that recalls the days of slavery in Potosí; it's featured at festivities

seringueros – rubber tappers in the Amazon region

Sernap – Servicio Nacional de Áreas Protegidas, government-run environment agency

singani – a distilled grape spirit (local firewater)

soroche – altitude sickness, invariably suffered by newly arrived visitors to highland Bolivia

surazo – cold wind blowing into lowland Bolivia from Patagonia and Argentine pampa

surtidores de gasolina – gas dispensers/stations

Tahuatinsuyo – the Inca name for their entire empire

tambo – wayside inn, market and meeting place selling staple domestic items; the New World counterpart of the caravanserai

tarijeños – Tarija locals

taxista – taxi driver

termas – hot springs

terminal terrestre – long-distance bus terminal

thola – small desert bush

tienda – small shop, usually family-run

tinku – traditional festival that features ritual fighting, taking place mainly in northern Potosí department; any blood shed during these fights is considered an offering to Pachamama

totora – type of reed, used as a building material around Lake Titicaca

tranca – highway police post, usually found at city limits

tranquilo – 'tranquil', the word most often used by locals to describe Bolivia's relatively safe and gentle demeanor; it's also used as an encouragement to slow down to the local pace of life

tren expreso – reasonably fast train that has 1st- and 2nd-class carriages and a dining car

tren mixto – very slow goods train; any passengers normally travel in *bodegas*

trufi – collective taxi or minibus that follows a set route

vicuña – a small camelid of the high puna or Altiplano, a wild relative of the llama and alpaca

viscacha – small, long-tailed rabbitlike rodent (*Lagidium viscaccia*) related to the chinchilla; inhabits rocky outcrops on the high Altiplano

Wara Wara – slow train on the Red Occidental that stops at most stations

yagé – a hallucinogenic drug used by certain tribes of the upper Amazon

yapa – bargaining practice in which a customer agrees to a final price provided that the vendor augments or supplements the item being sold

yareta – see *llareta*

yatiri – traditional Aymará healer/priest or witch doctor

zampoña – pan flute made of hollow reeds of varying lengths, lashed together side by side; it's featured in most traditional music performances

Behind the Scenes

THIS BOOK

This 6th edition of *Bolivia* was researched and written by Kate Armstrong, Vesna Maric and Andy Symington. Kate served as the coordinating author, writing all of the front and back chapters as well as researching and writing the La Paz and Lake Titicaca chapters. Vesna Maric covered South Central Bolivia & the Chaco, Santa Cruz & the Eastern Lowands and the Amazon Basin. Andy Symington covered the Cordilleras & Yungas, Southern Altiplano and Central Highlands. Brian Klupfel contributed boxed texts on soccer, musical instruments and Evo Morales. Dr David Goldberg MD wrote the Health chapter.

The 5th edition was written by Andrew Dean Nystrom and Morgan Konn. Deanna Swaney wrote editons 1 through 4. This guidebook was commissioned in Lonely Planet's Oakland office and produced by the following:

Commissioning Editor Kathleen Munnelly
Coordinating Editor Fionnuala Twomey
Coordinating Cartographer Karina Vitiritti
Coordinating Layout Designer Carol Jackson
Managing Editor Imogen Bannister
Managing Cartographer Adrian Persoglia
Assisting Editors Michelle Bennett, Michael Day, Trent Holden, Alison Ridgway, Laura Stansfeld, Phillip Tang
Assisting Layout Designer Cara Smith
Cover Designer Mary Nelson-Parker
Project Manager Kate McLeod
Language Content Coordinator Quentin Frayne

Thanks to Rebecca Dandens, Jessa Boanas-Dewes, Sin Choo, Sally Darmody, Ryan Evans, Dan Keane, Indra Kilfoyle, Celia Wood

THANKS
KATE ARMSTRONG

Mil gracias to so many wonderful Bolivians. First and foremost to Martin at La Cúlpula for his generosity of spirit, enthusiasm and friendship; likewise to Eduardo Zeballos, Vania, Adolfo, Fernando, Juan José and staff at Rosario Hotel; my Irish friends for their trekking knowledge; Todd for his downhill mountain bike thrills; Monica, Jaqui and Maria Theresa at the tourist office; Martin Cariega; Fundacion Cajias; Pablo and management at Calacoto Tours; Mario Ninos; Alistair and Karen Matthew of Gravity Assisted for their ongoing help; Dr Jordon, for getting me out of a stuffy situation; Fernando of Andes Amazon Adventures; Bernardo, André and Feli; Duncan at Flight Centre; Antonio Morón-Nava; Rob Wallace from Conservation International; and finally to Jazmin and David of America Tours for their professional advice and friendship. Lando, all my love for helping me dance my way through your culture. *Gracias* Stephen Taranto, Clea, Sr Paz (and Melina!) for their infectious enthusiasm and knowledge-sharing. In Sucre, three cheers to Jorge, ICBA and Domingo. An ultra final thanks to previous authors Andrew Dean Nystrom and Morgan Konn, fellow authors Andy Symington and Vesna Maric for their like-enthusiasm for Bolivia,

---

THE LONELY PLANET STORY

The story begins with a classic travel adventure: Tony and Maureen Wheeler's 1972 journey across Europe and Asia to Australia. There was no useful information about the overland trail then, so Tony and Maureen published the first Lonely Planet guidebook to meet a growing need.

From a kitchen table, Lonely Planet has grown to become the largest independent travel publisher in the world, with offices in Melbourne (Australia), Oakland (USA) and London (UK). Today Lonely Planet guidebooks cover the globe. There is an ever-growing list of books and information in a variety of media. Some things haven't changed. The main aim is still to make it possible for adventurous travelers to get out there – to explore and better understand the world.

At Lonely Planet we believe travelers can make a positive contribution to the countries they visit – if they respect their host communities and spend their money wisely. Every year 5% of company profit is donated to charities around the world.

editor Fionnuala Twomey for her amazing eye for detail and Kathleen Munnelly, commissioning ed, for making a *sueño* come true.

VESNA MARIC

Massive thanks go to my partner Rafael, as always, for providing fun and support, and taking all that time off to come along. Thanks also to our Bolivian friends Paola and Andres in Santa Cruz, as well as Ubaldo and Felipe, for their hospitality and company. Big thanks to our man at Hotel Globetrotter, who worked out so many complex schedules for us and gave us tea when we were ill. Great big hello and thanks to Julien Ureel, the most Bolivian of non-Bolivians. Thanks also to Daniel Manzaneda in Rurre, plus Pancho, Che and Peanut for taking us out on the town in Banana Club. Big thanks to Rolando at Chalalan for his hard work, help and information. Great big thanks to Kathleen Munnelly, the commissioning editor, for all her help and hard work, and to Kate Armstrong who was always so kind and helpful both as co-author and coordinating author, and to Andy Symington for his help. It was a pleasure to work on this book.

ANDY SYMINGTON

I owe thanks to numerous folk in Bolivia: local people for good company and wise counsel; people in tourist offices and travel agencies for information; and many travelers and volunteers for friendship, help and advice. Particular thanks go to a number of people who went above and beyond the call, with pages worth of helpful suggestions, generous hospitality and sound companionship. These are: Roberto de Urioste and his colleagues, Mike McCaffrey, Regine Zopf, Ramiro Becerra & Claudia Mendienta, Bärbel Junk, Amparo Miranda, Margarita Herrera, Xavier Sarabia, Hans & Patricia De Roo, Pete Good, Elba Alfaro, Fabiola Mitru, Jacqueline Gutiérrez, Travis Gray, and Petra Las Piedras. Thanks also to fellow authors Kate & Vesna, to the LP team, to my parents for their support and to Begoña García de León.

OUR READERS

Many thanks to the travelers who used the last edition and wrote to us with helpful hints, useful advice and interesting anecdotes:

A Ilze Aizsilniece, Juan Antonio Alegre, Ameling Algra, Daniel Alsen, Frida Andrae, Isabel Armbrust, Linda Armstrong, Sebastian Arnoldt, Troy Austin, Daniel Avital **B** Laura Louise Baker, Paul & Susana Balderrama, Dina Barile, Adrian Barnett, Bret Batchelor, Ronan Beasley, Christopher W Behr, Joanne Bell, Caryl Bergeron, Marc Berry, Antoine Beurskens, Liz & Mike Bissett, Camila Bjorkbom, Philippe Blank, Maaik Borst, Antonia Boulsien, Kerry Roanna Bray, Andrew Bresler, Arnold Brouwer, Louise Brown, Sam Brown, Joni Browne, Gerry Buitendag, Stuart Burton, Nick Buxton, Emily Byrne **C** Liz Callegari, Catherine Calver, Steve Camley, Marie Campbell, Brett Capron, Danielle Carpenter, Antonio Castro, Aymar Ccopacatty, Steve Chambers, Fabio Chiari, Peter Churchill, Claire Clapshaw, Michael Connellan, Patrick Corveleijn, Matthew Courtney, Eveline Coussens, Maxime Coutié, Ben Crichton, Gabor Csonka **D** Mark Dawes, Yigal Dayan, Ine de Bock, Bjorn de Boeck, Mario G de Mendoza III, Elmer de Ronde, Amber de Vries, Dominic Degrazier, Rowan Dellal, Kylie Dempsey, Jeff Dennis, Susanne Deyerler, Julian Dickinson, Roman Dietschi, Klaus Dons, Steve Downs, Dana Drake, Anna Draper, Frederique Duval **E** Charlie Earl, JC Eby, Dino Edwards, Robert Ehlert, Robert Elze, Matthieu en Marlous, Heiko Erner, April Evans, Hannah Evans, John Ewan **F** Marie-Andrée Fallu, Rossana Faoro, Tom Fertek, Camilla Freeth, Rosalind Fussell **G** Gordon Gaffney, Steven Gary, Didi Gepner, Jayson Gilbert, Heather Gill, Elizabeth Gledhill, Keat Goh, John Goodman, Wendy Goosen, Vera-Maria Graubner, Clare Green, Ruth Greenaway, Christoph Groenegress, Joanne Gullick **H** Ronald Haccou, Chris Hackney, Dennis Hamann, Clint Harris, Nadia Harrison, Claudia Hauser, Roger Hennekens, Gerald Henzinger, Keith Herndon, John & Romina Hilton, Tim Holding, Roy Hoogmoed, Helmut Hornik, Richard Hughes, Felix Hurter **I** Reynaldo Imana-Wendt, Rebecca Irani **J** Lisa Jacobson, Nick Jacobs, Anke Janssen, Rachel Jay, Markus Jirikovsky **K** Seth Kaplan, Marie Keiding, Barbara Kelly, Adam Kemmis Betty, Guido Kerbusch, Gavin Kerns, Ton Kersbergen, Julie Kiser, Anne-Marie Kleijberg, Michelle & Richard Knight, Renee Koenig, Martijn Kollen, TJ Komoly, John Koncki, I Kreutzer, Herbert Kroeg, Karen Kwok **L** Nancy Lanee, Christy Lanzl, Karla Leary, Eva Lerch, Farrel Lever, Manuel Lins, Annemarie Lopez, Esther López, Martin Lundgren **M** Bernhard Maierhofer, Maria Main, Tara Mallett, Outi Mannila, Sandra Martinez, Bruno Maul, Mike Mayer, Margaret Mcaspurn, Paul McCarthy, Ian McDonald, Mary Mcgrath Schwartz, Karl McGuigan, Emma McMahon, Maree McNicol, Sabrina Menzel, Elke Messner-Küttner, Roman Micairan, Tara Miller, Carolyn Miranda, Kjell Mittag, Irene Moser, Vicki Mountford, Chico Muerto **N** Andrew Nava, Erik Nennie, Jeff Newman, Ronnie Nielsen, Sabine Nonn **O** James O'Donnell, Stephanie & Paul O'Hagan, Stanislaw Orzel, Jolanda Oudeman **P** Christiana Papadopoullos, Robert Patterson, Emma Pearson, Karen Pereyra, Jan Peters, Steve Piercy, Núria Prat Orriols, Klara Prinz **R** Frederieke Rasenberg, Ian Reeves, Andy Richmond, Abad Rios, Isabelle Risom, David Rivel, Toby Rowallan, Amber Rowley, Sophie Rudent, Kate Rudkins, Arno & Karin Runge, Katrine Rydland **S** Beatriz Sainz de Vicuna, Raniah Salloum, Christian Sam, Tamara Samson, Judith Samuel, Sara Sangiovanni, Thomas Sarosy, Esther Schmid, Stephan Schneider, Jet & Collin Scholten, Reuven Schossen, Mark Schouten, Alayna Schroeder, Edwin Schuurman, Emma Scragg, Helen & Wolfe Sharp, Paul Sheen, Grace Shih, Kate Shower, Tom Shower, Lindsay Simmonds, Elisa Snel, Graham Snowdon, Jose Soliz, Martien Spanjer, Menno Staarink, Philip Starecky, Michael Stauch, Casper Steenbergen, Cheryl Stewart, Sandra Stortz, Heather Sunderland, Laura Sweeting, Emma Syme

T Tommie Teasdale, Ben Terry, Martin & Jacky Thomas, Robert Tocco, Ronny Tømmerbakke, Marie Travers, Paul Turner **V** Wouter van der Heijde, Jordan van der Schoot, Jef van Hout, Denise van Poppel, Oliver van Straaten, Dirk Verboven, Soeren Vinther, Eva Vosicka, Nander Vrees **W** Glenn Walker, Kai Walther, Alastair Warren, Anja Weber, Wolfgang Weber, Neil Weissenborn,

Christian Juergen Welz, Christian Wepf, Jack Westenburg, Sarah Westenburg, William Whelan, Mike White, Paul White, Jaap Wijdeveld, Mats Willer, Jeromie Williams, Kathleen & Terry Williams, Tim Wilson, Maik David Winteler, Jon Wirth, Jill Wright **Y** Yuval Yirmiyahu **Z** Botond Zalai, Tomas Zilinsky, Udi Zohar, Lincoln Zuks

---

SEND US YOUR FEEDBACK

We love to hear from travelers – your comments keep us on our toes and help make our books better. Our well-traveled team reads every word on what you loved or loathed about this book. Although we cannot reply individually to postal submissions, we always guarantee that your feedback goes straight to the appropriate authors, in time for the next edition. Each person who sends us information is thanked in the next edition – and the most useful submissions are rewarded with a free book.

To send us your updates – and find out about Lonely Planet events, newsletters and travel news – visit our award-winning website: **www.lonelyplanet.com/contact**.

Note: we may edit, reproduce and incorporate your comments in Lonely Planet products such as guidebooks, websites and digital products, so let us know if you don't want your comments reproduced or your name acknowledged. For a copy of our privacy policy visit www.lonelyplanet.com/privacy.

Index

4WD 53, 387

A
accommodations 366-7
Achacachi 125
achachilas 37, 108
activities 16, 49-54, 367, *see*
    also individual activities
Afro-Bolivian people 26, 146
Agua Blanca 165
Aguaragüe national park 275, 291
Aguas Calientes 326
AIDS 396
Aiquile 236
air travel
    to/from Bolivia 380-3
    within Bolivia 385
Alasitas 80, 112
alojamientos 367
alpacas 45, 56, 181
Altiplano 24, 44, 124, *see*
    also Southern Altiplano
altitude sickness 396-7
Amazon Basin 329-65, **331**, 217
    climate 328
    history 328
    jungle tours 337-9
    pampas tours 337-9
    travel to/from 328
Amboró national park 47, 293,
    307-11, **309**, 5
Ancohuma 159-60, 221
Ancoraimes 125
animals 45, *see also individual animals*
Anmin 47, 49, 162-3
Apa-Apa Reserva Ecológica 144
Apolobamba natural area 47, 162-3
Apolobamba national park 181
April Revolution 29, 30, 74
apus 37, 108
Árbol de Piedra 195
archeological sites, *see also* rock
    paintings
    Calacala 178
    Charazani 160-2
    Chincana ruins 120, 220

000 Map pages
000 Photograph pages

Copacabana 111
Coquesa 193
Curahuara de Carangas 182
El Fuerte 313
Horca del Inca 111
Incallajta 234-5
Inca Tribunal 112
Inca-Rakay 232-3
Isla de la Luna 122
Isla del Sol 118-20, 220
Isla Pariti 123
Iskanwaya 155
Kusijata 112
Llama Chaqui 238
Llanos de Moxos 352
Palacio del Inca 118-19
Pampa Aullagas 179
Pasto Grande 146
Pukara Monterani 182
Templo del Inca 120
Tiahuanacota Inca cemetery 116
Yaraque 182
architecture 41-2
Área Natural de Manejo Integrado
    Nacional (Anmin) Apolobamba 47,
    49, 162-3
Argentina 28, 205, 276, 277, 289
    travel to/from 207-8, 383-4
Arica 183
artesanía 39, 76, 92, 134-5, 151,
    160, 176, 253, 254, 256, 274,
    303, 375
arts 39-43
    architecture 41-2
    dance 41-3
    film 31, 42-3, 91
    literature 15, 28, 35, 43
    music 39-41
    painting 42
    textiles 39, 76, 92, 134-5, 151,
        160, 176, 253, 254, 256, 274,
        303, 375
Atahualpa 26
ATMs 373
Atocha 197
Aucapata 155
Aymará
    culture 34, 38, 81, 140
    language 405
    New Year 81, 104, 111, 7, 217

people 34, 36, 76, 140
    spirituality 37, 38, 81, 118, 140

B
Bañados del Izozog wetland 327
Banzer Suárez, Hugo 29, 31
bargaining 15
Barrancas 196
bartonellosis 395-6
basilicas, *see* churches & basilicas
bathrooms 377
Batea Cocha 238
beer 57
begging 35
Bella Vista 353
Benedicion de Movilidades 112
Beni biosphere reserve 344-6
Bermejo 288-9, 311
Betanzos 274
bicycling 385-6, *see also* mountain
    biking
bird-watching 45, 47, 54
    Apa-Apa Reserva Ecológica 144
    Área Natural de Manejo Integrado
        Nacional (Anmin) Apolobamba
        162
    books 45
    Buena Vista 305, 306
    Chulumani 143
    Curichi Marsh 306
    environmental groups 48
    Lagunillas 164
    Los Volcanes 312
    Magdalena 353
    Parque Nacional & Área de Uso
        Múltiple Amboró 308, 310
    Parque Nacional Carrasco 334
    Parque Nacional Madidi 54, 341
    Parque Nacional Noel Kempff
        Mercado 354, 356, 357
    Quebrada Seca 203
    Reserva Biológica Cordillera de
        Sama 287
    Reserva Biosférica del Beni 344
    Reserva de Vida Silvestre Ríos
        Blanco y Negro 353
    Reserva Nacional de Flora y Fauna
        Tariquía 288
    Reyes 343
    Samaipata 314

INDEX

San Borja 344
San Ignacio de Moxos 347
Santa Rosa 343
Santurio Cuchini
Yunga Cruz Trek 141
boat travel
river trips 156, 349, 363-4
to/from Bolivia 358, 361, 384-5
within Bolivia 386, *see also* river trips
Bolívar, Simón 27, 244-5
Bolivian hemorrhagic fever 396
bolivianita 44, 375
books
adventure 50, 51
bird-watching 45
health 392
history 27, 28
literature 15, 28, 35, 43
travel 17
Boyuibe 291-2
Brasiléia 365
Brazil 27, 28
travel to/from 304, 328, 358, 359, 361, 365, 384
Buena Vista 305-7, **305**, **309**
bus travel
to/from Bolivia 383
within Bolivia 386-7
business hours 367-8, *see also* inside front cover
butterflies 143, 144, 146, 289, 334

C
Cabeza del Cóndor 159
Cabildo 285
caimans 338, 342, 345
Calacala 178
camelids 181
camiones 388
Camiri 292
Campamento Los Fierros 356
camping 366
Candelaria 254
canoeing 53
Cañón de Palca 99-100
Cañón de Torotoro 238
Cañón del Pilcomayo 291
Capachos hot springs 178
car travel
to/from Bolivia 383
within Bolivia 387-8
Caranavi 156-7
Carlos Mesa 31
Carnaval 41, 167, 173, 282, 300, 370

Carrasco national park 47, 334-5
Casa de la Libertad 241
Casa Nacional de Moneda 261-2, **223**
casas de huéspedes 367
Cassidy, Butch 53, 190, 203, 204
Catarata El Encanto 356-7
cathedrals, *see also* churches & basilicas
Aiquile 236
Cobija 364
Cochabamba 216
Concepción 322
Copacabana 111, **6**
La Paz 70
Oruro 172
Potosí 262-3
Riberalta 362
Santa Cruz 299
Sucre 244
Trinidad 349
Catholicism 37
caves
Cavernas del Repechón 334
Ciudad Pétrea de Pumiri 182
Cráter de Maragua 256
Gruta de Lourdes 116
Gruta de San Pedro 147-8
Inca-Rakay 232
Padcaya 285
Parque Nacional Carrasco 334
Parque Nacional Torotoro 237
Cavour Aramayo, Ernesto 40, 76
cell phones 376
Central Highlands 209-74, **210**
climate 211
history 210-11
travel to/from 211
Cerro Calvario 111, **220**
Cerro Rico 258, 259, 265
Cerro Tunari 230
Chacaltaya 54, 78, 100-1
Chaco, the 29, 275, 289-92, **276**
Chaco War 28, 29
Chagas' disease 396
Chaguaya 287
Chalalán Ecolodge 342-3
Cha'lla 119
Cha'llapampa 119-20
Challapata 178
Chapare Region 332-5
Chaqui 274
charangos 40, 76, 236, **217**
Charazani 160-2
Chari 160
Chataquila 256
Chaunaca 256

Ché Guevara, *see* Guevara, Ernesto (Ché)
Ché Trail 292, 293, 317
Chicha people 198
children, travel with 368
health 398
La Paz 80
language 404-5
Chile 23, 27, 28, 182-3
travel to/from 183, 189-90, 384
Chimane people 344, 345-6, 346
Chimane reserve 344-6
Chincana ruins 120, **220**
Chipaya people 193
Chiquitano people 321
Chisi 118
cholas 34, 38
cholera 393
chullpares 178-9, 182, 256
Chulumani 143-6, **144**
Chuquisaca 27, *see* Sucre
Church, George 359
churches & basilicas, *see also* cathedrals
Basílica de San Francisco 280
Iglesia & Convento de San Francisco 216
Iglesia de la Merced 245
Iglesia de la Recoleta 216
Iglesia de los Santos Desposorios 306
Iglesia de San Agustín 264
Iglesia de San Francisco (La Paz) 74, **217**
Iglesia de San Francisco (Sucre) 246
Iglesia de San Lorenzo de Carangas 264
Iglesia de San Martín 264
Iglesia de San Pedro 234
Iglesia de San Roque 279
Iglesia de Santa Mónica 247
Iglesia de Santo Domingo 216
Jesuit mission churches 322-6
La Capilla de Nuestra Señora de Jerusalén 264
Santuario de la Virgen del Socavón 172
Cinemateca Boliviana 91
climate 14, 368, 369
climate change 381
climbing 49-51, 78, 174
Ancohuma 159-60, **221**
Cabeza del Cóndor 159
Condoriri Massif 159
Cordillera Quimsa Cruz 50, 165-6
Cordillera Real 127, 157-60, **221**

climbing *continued*
Huayna Potosí 157-8, **8**, **221**
Illimani 158-9
Cliza 234
clothing 38, 39, 92
cloud forests 310, 334-5
Cobija 364-5
coca 23, 25, 31, 32-3, 58, 71, 140,
332-3, 372
Coca Museum 71
cocaine 332, 372
Cochabamba 209, 211-30, **212-13**,
231
accommodations 225-7
attractions 215-25
courses 225
drinking 228-9
entertainment 229
festivals 225
food 227-8
history 213
medical services 214
shopping 229
tourist information 215
tours 225
travel to/from 229-30
travel within 230
Cochabamba Valley 232-4
Coimata 287-8
Colcha K 194
Colchani 190
comedores 58
Comibol 29, 171
Concepción 321-2
Condoriri Massif 159
condors 45, 162, 203, 314
conquistadores 26-7
Consata 155
consulates 369-70
Convento de San Felipe Neri 246
Convento de Santa Teresa
(Cochabamba) 216
Convento de Santa Teresa (Sucre) 246
Copacabana 108-16, **109**, **6**
accommodations 113-14
attractions 111-12
drinking 115
entertainment 115
festivals 111, 112-13
food 114-15
history 108

medical services 110
shopping 115
tours 112
travel to/from 116
Coquesa 193
cordilleras 127-8, 157-66, **139**
Cordillera Apolobamba 127,
160-5, **161**
Cordillera de los Frailes 49, 209,
254-8, **255**
Cordillera Quimsa Cruz 50, 165-6
Cordillera Real 127, 157-60, **221**
Coroico 127, 129-35, **131**
accommodations 132-4
activities 131-2
drinking 134
food 134
mountain biking 132
shopping 134-5
tourist information 131
travel to/from 135
Corvalán private reserve 275, 291
costs 15, 366
courses
language 79, 132, 225, 247
music 79
wellbeing 79-80
Cráter de Maragua 256
credit cards 373
crime 49, 69-70, 110-11, 368-9
Cuba 33
Cueva de los Monos 311
culture 34-43
Curahuara de Carangas 182
Curichi Marsh 306
Curva 164
customs regulations 368
cycling, *see* bicycling & mountain
biking

D
dance 41-3
de Almagro, Diego 26
Death Train 327
dengue fever 393
departure tax 380, 385
Desaguadero 126
Día de los Muertos 58, 81, 193
Diablada, La 176
diarrhea 396
dinosaur tracks 237, 238, 241-4,
256
disabilities, travelers with 377
dolphins, *see* pink river dolphins
Domingo Murillo, Don Pedro 71

drinks 57-8, *see also* water & wine
drugs 372, *see also* coca

E
Eastern Lowlands 319-28, **294**
climate 295
travel to/from 295
economy 30-1, 35-6
ecotourism 48, 342-3
Eduardo Avaroa national reserve
47, 191
Ekeko 37, 81, 375
El Alto 37, 76-7
El Camino del Oro (Gold Digger's Trail)
151-3, **151**
El Cañón 202
El Chaqueo 48
El Choro Trek 127, 135-7, **136**, **8**
El Chorro Grande 291
El Clásico 36
El Fuerte 312-14, **314**
El Gran Poder 81
El Sillar 202-3
El Valle de la Concepción 285
El Vergel 238
electricity 367
email services 372
embassies 369-70
employment 35
Empresa Nacional de Ferrocarriles 31
endangered animals 45, 308
ENFE 31
environmental groups 48
environmental issues 46-8, 50, 97,
342, 344-5, 354
Estrecho de Tiquina 125
etiquette 34, 59
Eustaquio Méndez, José 285

F
ferries 386
festivals 16, 58, 370-1
Alasitas 80, 112
Aymará New Year 81, 104, 111,
7, **217**
Benedicion de Movilidades 112
Carnaval 41, 167, 173, 282, 300,
370
cattle fair 290-1
charango 40, 236
Ché Guevara festival 317
Chicha Festival 233
Chocolate Festival 306
Cochabamba 225, 232
Coffee Festival 306

INDEX

Día de los Muertos 58, 81, 193
Día de los Santos Desposorios 306
Día de Todos los Santos 371
El Gran Poder 81
Exaltación de la Santa Vera Cruz 267
ExpoCruz 300
Fería de la Fruta 235-6
Fería de Muestras 365
Feria Regional del Pescado 333
Festival de la Cultura 248
Festival de la Wallunk'a 233
Fiesta de la Cruz 113, 370-1
Fiesta de la Papa 274
Fiesta de la Uva 285
Fiesta de la Virgen de Candelaria 112, 370
Fiesta de la Virgen de Chaguaya 287
Fiesta de la Virgen de Guadalupe 248
Fiesta de la Virgen de las Nieves 160
Fiesta de la Virgen de Urkupiña 225, 232
Fiesta de las Flores 281
Fiesta de las Ñatitis 38
Fiesta de Leche y Queso 285-7
Fiesta de San Andrés 235
Fiesta de San Bartolomé (Chu'tillos; Potosí) 267
Fiesta de San Bartolomé (Chulumani) 143
Fiesta de San Lorenzo 285
Fiesta de San Roque 275, 281
Fiesta de Santa Veracruz Tatala 225
Fiesta de Santiago 125
Fiesta del Espíritu 266-7
Fiesta del Santo Patrono de Moxos 346
Fiesta del Señor de Burgos 236
Fiesta del Señor Santiago 238
fishing festival 290-1
Flower Festival 233
Grape Festival 285
Heroínas de la Coronilla 225
Independence Day 81, 111, 113
International Festival of Baroque Music 300, 322
International Festival of Cheese & Wine 300
International Theater Festival 300
Miss Litoral 322
Phujllay 253-4, 223
Rice Festival 306
Rodeo Chapaco 281
Semana Santa 113, 370
tinku 271

Tiquipaya 233
Trout Festival 233
Vírgen del Rosario 371
film 31, 42-3, 91
flamingos 45, 195, 287
food 16, 55-62, 89, 371
fossils 237-8, *see also* dinosaur tracks
futból 36-7, 92

G
Garcia Meza Tejada, Luis 30
gas reserves 31, 33
gay travelers 371
geography 44
    Bolivia Cross Section **129**
geysers 179-81, 195
Gold Digger's Trail 151-3, **151**
golf 54
government 23, 27, 29-30, 32-3, 38
Gruta de San Pedro caves 147-8
Gruta de Umajalanta 238
Guajará-Mirim, Brazil 361
guanacos 181
Guanay 155-6
Guaqui 125-6
Guaraní people 290, 327
Guayaramerín 359-62, **360**
Guevara, Ernesto (Ché) 29, 30, 317, 318, 319
    Ché Trail 292, 293, 317
    festival 317
    museums 317, 319

H
Hacienda Cayara 272
health 391-8
    folk medicine 396
    language 402
    vaccinations 392
hepatitis A 393-4
hepatitis B 394
Heyerdahl, Thor 123
hiking 49-53, *see also* trekking
    Cañón de Palca 99-100
    Chacaltaya 78, 100-1
    Cordillera de los Frailes 49, 254-8
    Coroico 131-2
    Laguna Mamankhota 101
    Lagunas de Kari Kari 272
    Los Volcanes 312
    Muela del Diablo 98
    Parque Nacional & Área de Uso Múltiple Amboró 49, 308-11
    Parque Nacional Noel Kempff Mercado 49, 356-7

Quebrada Chua Keri 99-100
Reserva Biológica Cordillera de Sama 287
Reserva Nacional de Flora y Fauna Tariquía 288
Sorata 148
Valle de las Ánimas 98
history 24-33
    books 27, 28
    Early & Middle Horizons 24-5
    independence 27
    Late Horizon – the Inca 25-6
    political strife 29-30
    Spanish conquest 26-7
    territory loss 27-9, **28**
    Tiahuanaco 102
hitchhiking 388
HIV 396
holidays 15, 371-2
Horca del Inca 111
horseback riding 53-4, 132, 201
hostales 367
hostels 366-7
hot springs 54
    Aguas Calientes 326
    Capachos 178
    Chaqui 274
    Parque Nacional Sajama 179-81
    San Javier 321
    Tarapaya 274
    Termas de Charazani Phutina 160
    Termas de Obrajes 177-8
    Termas de Polques 196
    Termas de Talula 256-7
    Urmiri 105
hotels 367
Huaca Huañusca 203
Huari 178-9
Huarina 123
Huatajata 124-5
Huayna Potosí 50, 157-8, **8**, **221**

I
iglesias, see churches & basilicas
Illampu 51
Illampu circuit 148
Illimani 158-9
immigration 380
Inca empire 25-6, 108, 112, 118-20, 122, 124, 147, 182, 232, 234, 330
Inca sites 116, 146, 232-3, 234-5, 238
Inca trails 136, 138, 139, 141, 151, 153, 287, **8**
Incallajta 234-5
Incamachay 256

INDEX

Inca-Rakay 232-3
independence 27
indigenous Bolivians 32-3, 34
insurance 372, 391
internet access 372
internet calls 377
internet resources
   air tickets 381, 383
   climbing 49
   Copacabana 110
   film 42
   food 55, 59
   health 391-2
   La Paz 67
   planning 17
Irupana 146
Isiboro-Sécure national park
   335-6
Iskanwaya 155
Isla Cáscara de Huevo 192
Isla de la Luna 122
Isla del Sol 118-22, **117**, **220**
   accommodations 121
   food 121-2
   ruins 118-20
   tours 120-1
   travel to/from 122
Isla Incahuasi 192
Isla Kalahuta 122
Isla Pariti 123
Isla Suriqui 122
Islas de Huyñaymarka 122
itineraries 18-22

J
Jalq'a people 257
Jesuit missions 21, 165, 293, 306, 319,
   320-6, 330, 346, 348, 353
jungle tours 337-9

K
Kaa-Iya national park 47, 327
Kallawaya people 160, 163
kayaking 53-4, 333
Koati, see Isla de la Luna
Kolla people 26, 108

L
La Angostura 233
La Cumbre 78, 130
La Diablada 173

000 Map pages
000 Photograph pages

La Florida 356
La Higuera 318
La Pajcha 316-17
La Paz 63-105, **66-8**, **72-3**, **79**, **86-7**,
   96, **217**, **218**, **219**
   accommodations 82-5
   activities 77-8
   attractions 70-7
   children, travel with 80
   churches 70, 74
   courses 79
   drinking 90
   El Alto 76-7
   emergency services 67
   entertainment 91-2
   festivals & events 80-1
   food 85-90
   history 64
   itineraries 18, 65
   medical services 68
   shopping 92-3
   tourist offices 69
   tours 80
   travel to/from 93-5
   travel within 95-6
   walking tour 78-9, **79**
   Zona Sur 85, **86-7**
La Plata 26, see also Sucre
La Quiaca 207-8, **206**
Lago Chungará 182
Lago Poopó 178
Lago Uru Uru 178
Laguna Amarilla 196
Laguna Baíqui 353
Laguna Blanca 196
Laguna Celeste 196
Laguna Chillata 148
Laguna Colorada 195
Laguna Glacial 148, **221**
Laguna Guinda 196
Laguna Normandia 345
Laguna Verde 196
Laguna Volcán 311-12
Lagunas de Kari Kari 272
Lagunillas 163, 164
Laja 101
Lake Titicaca 106-26, **107**,
   220
   climate 107
   history 107
   travel to/from 108
   travel within 108
language 399-405, see also inside
   front cover
   accommodations 400-1

Aymará 405
   children, travel with 404-5
   courses 79, 132, 225, 247
   food vocabulary 59
   Quechua 34, 35, 405
   Spanish 399-405
Lauca national park 181, 182, **180**
Laza 146
legal matters 332, 372
leishmaniasis 396
lesbian travelers 371
literature 15, 28, 35, 43
Llama Chaqui 238
llamas 45, 56, 181
Llanos de Moxos 352
Llica 194
logging 344-5, 354, 359
lomas 352-3
Lorgio Vaca 299
Los Espejillos 311
Los Lípez 167
Los Volcanes 312
lucha libre 37, 76

M
Madidi national park 45, 47, 52, 329,
   341-3, **224**
Magdalena 353
malaria 394
Mallasa 97
Mallcu Villa Mar 197
Mamani Mamani 42
Mapiri Trail 49, 153-5, **153**
maps 50-1, 65, 372-3
Maragua 256, 257
markets
   Cochabamba 215-16
   La Paz 71, 74-5, 76
   Tarabuco 253-4
MAS 23, 32-3
measures 367, see also inside front
   cover
Mecapaca 97-8
medical services 393, see also health
Melgarej, Mariano 27, 234
Mercado de Hechicería (Witches'
   Market) 71
Mercado Negro 74
micros 388
Milluni 101
minibuses 388
mining
   cooperative mines 172-4, 265-6
   film 43
   gold 26, 165

INDEX

nationalization 29
Oruro 172-4
Potosí 26, 146, 209, 258-9,
    264-6
silver 26, 146, 169, 190, 209,
    258-9, 264-6
tin 165-6, 169-71, 174, 259
MIR 30
Mizque 235-6
MNR 29
mobile phones 376
Mollu people 155
money 15, 369, 373, see also inside
    front cover
monkeys 45, 307, 330, 342, 345, 353,
    354, 356
Morales Ayma, Juan Evo 23, 32-3, 34,
    171, 332-3
motorcycle travel
    to/from Bolivia 383
    within Bolivia 387-8
mountain biking 52-3, 77
    Chacaltaya 130
    Coroico 130, 132
    La Cumbre 78, 130
    La Paz 77, 78, 130
    Sorata 130, 149
    World's Most Dangerous Road
        52, 77, 78
    Zongo Valley 52, 130
mountaineering, see climbing
Movimiento al Socialismo (MAS)
    23, 32-3
Movimiento de la Izquierda
    Revolucionaria (MIR) 30
Movimiento Nacionalista
    Revolucionario (MNR) 29
Moxos people 330, 346
Muela del Diablo 98
museums
    Alcaldía museum 147
    Casa de la Libertad 241
    Casa de Murillo 71
    Casa Nacional de Moneda 261-2
    Centro Cultural Simón Patiño 216
    Ché museum 317
    Museo & Convento de San
        Francisco 263
    Museo & Convento de Santa
        Teresa 263
    Museo Antropológico Eduardo
        López Rivas 172
    Museo Arqueología y
        Antropológico de los Andes
        Meridionales 184

Museo Arqueológico
    (Cochabamba) 216
Museo Arqueológico (Samaipata)
    314
Museo Costumbrista Juan de
    Vargas 74
Museo de Arqueología y
    Paleontología 279
Museo de Arte Contemporaneo
    75-6
Museo de Aves Acuático 116
Museo de Etnografía y Folklore
    75
Museo de Instrumentos Musicales
    76
Museo de la Catedral 244-5
Museo de la Coca 71
Museo de la Historia Natural 299
Museo de la Recoleta 245-6
Museo de la Revolución Nacional
    74
Museo de los Niños Tanga-Tanga
    246
Museo de Metales Preciosos 71
Museo de Plata Herzul 263
Museo de Santa Clara 246
Museo de Textiles Andinos
    Bolivianos 76
Museo del Charango 236
Museo del Litoral 71
Museo del Poncho 112
Museo El Altiplano 124
Museo Etno-Folklórico 299
Museo Gutiérrez Valenzuela
    247
Museo Historico del Ché 319
Museo Mineralógico 172
Museo Misional 322
Museo Moto Méndez 285
Museo Nacional de Arqueología
    71
Museo Nacional del Arte 71
Museo Patiño 172
Museo Sacro, Folklórico,
    Arqueológico y Minero 172
Museo San Francisco 74
Museo Tambo Quirquincho 74
Museo Templo de Sol 119
Museo Textil-Etnográfico 241
Museos Universitarios 247
Templete Semisubterráneo (Museo
    al Aire Libre) 76
music 39-41
musical instruments 40, 76, 92
Muyuloma 287

N
National Mint 261-2
national parks & reserves 46
    Amazon Basin 330
    Apa-Apa Reserva Ecológica 144
    Área Natural de Manejo Integrado
        Nacional (Anmin) Apolobamba
        47, 162-3
    Central Highlands 211
    itineraries 22
    Parque Nacional & Área de Uso
        Múltiple Amboró 47, 293,
        307-11, **309**, 5
    Parque Nacional Apolobamba
        181
    Parque Nacional Carrasco 47, 334-5
    Parque Nacional Isiboro-Sécure
        335-6
    Parque Nacional Kaa-Iya del Gran
        Chaco 47, 327
    Parque Nacional Lauca 181-4, **180**
    Parque Nacional Madidi 45, 47, 52,
        329, 341-3, **224**
    Parque Nacional Noel Kempff
        Mercado 47, 329, 354-9, **355**
    Parque Nacional Sajama 47, 167,
        179-82, **180**
    Parque Nacional Torotoro 47, 209,
        236-40, **237**
    Parque Nacional Tunari 47, 230
    Parque Nacional y Área Natural de
        Manejo Integrado Aguaragüe
        275, 291
    Reserva Biológica Cordillera de
        Sama 275, 287-8
    Reserva Biosférica del Beni
        344-6
    Reserva de Vida Silvestre Ríos
        Blanco y Negro 353-4
    Reserva Forestal Chimane 344-6
    Reserva Nacional de Fauna Andina
        Eduardo Avaroa 47, 191
    Reserva Nacional de Flora y Fauna
        Tariquía 275, 288
    Reserva Privada de Patrimonio
        Natural de Corvalán 275, 291
    Santa Cruz & Eastern Lowlands
        295
    South Central Bolivia 277
    Southern Altiplano 169
nationalization 29, 33
Nevado Candelaria 191
newspapers 367
Nido de Cóndores 158, 159
Niño Calvario 111

Noel Kempff Mercado national park 47, 329, 354-9, **355**
Núñez del Prado, Marina 42, 71

O

Ocabaya 146
oil 29, 33
Oruro 169-77, **170**
accommodations 174-5
attractions 172-4
Carnaval 173
drinking 176
entertainment 176
food 175-6
history 169-71
medical services 171
shopping 176
tourist information 171
tours 174
travel to/from 177
travel within 177

P

Pachamama 37, 57
Pachamama Wasi 238
Padcaya 285-7
painting 42, see also rock paintings
paleontology 237-8, see also dinosaur tracks
Pampa Aullagas 179
Pampagrande 317
pampas tours 337-9
Pantanal 327
paragliding 54
Paraguay 28, 29, 276
travel to/from 290, 292, 298, 384-5
Parinacota 182-3
Parque Cretácico 241-4
parques nacionales, see national parks & reserves
passports 377-8
Pasto Grande 146
Patiño, Simón 169-71, 172, 216, 233
Paz Estenssoro, Victor 29, 30, 31
Paz Zamora, Jaime 30
Pazña 178
Pelechuco 165
peñas 91

people
Afro-Bolivian 26, 146
Aymará 34, 36, 76, 140
Chicha 198
Chimane 344, 345-6, 346
Chipaya 193
Chiquitano 321
Guaraní 290, 327
Jalq'a 257
Kallawaya 160, 163
Kolla 26, 108
Mollu 155
Moxos 330, 346
Quechua 36, 140
Peru 24, 25, 27
travel to/from 94, 116, 124, 125, 364, 385
petroleum 31, 288-9, 292
photography 93, 373-4
Phujllay 253-4, **223**
pink river dolphins 338, 352, 357
Pizarro, Francisco 26
plague 394
planning 14-17, 369
itineraries 18-22
plants 46
Pocitos 289
politics 23, 27, 29-30, 32-3, 38
Pongaje 29
population 36
posadas 367
postal services 374
potatoes 56, 274
Potolo 256-7
Potosí 43, 209, 258-72, **260-1**, **273**, **223**
accommodations 267-8
attractions 261-6
churches 264
drinking 270
entertainment 270
food 268-9
history 26-7, 258-9
medical services 261
mines 265-6
shopping 270
tourist information 261
tours 266
travel to/from 270-2
travel within 272
privatization 30-1, 32
protests 29, 31, 32, 35, 369
Pucará 318
Puerto Almacén 352
Puerto Barador 352

Puerto Pérez 123
Puerto Suárez 327
Puerto Villarroel 335
Pukara Monterani 182
Pulacayo 190
pumas 45
Punata 233-4

Q

Quebrada Chua Keri 99-100
Quebrada de Palala 201-2
Quebrada de Palmira 203
Quebrada Negra 99
Quebrada Seca 203
Quechua
language 34, 35, 405
people 36, 140
spirituality 37
Quetena Chico 196-7
Quijarro 327-8
Quila Quila 257-9
Quillacollo 232
quinoa 56

R

rabies 395
radio 367
rainforest 46, see also Amazon Basin
reed boats 122, 124
religion 37-9, 108
René Barrientos 234
reserves, see national parks & reserves
residenciales 367
responsible travel 338, 342-3, 381
restaurants 58
Reyes 343
Riberalta 362-4, **363**
Rincón de la Victoria 288
Río Beni 338, 342, 363
Río Choqueyapu 97
Río Coroico 132
Río Huarinilla 132
Río Macuñucu 308-9
Río Mamoré 329, 349
Río Ovejuyo 98
Río Paucerna 357
Río Solacama 146
Río Surutú 146
Río Umajalanta 238
Río Unduavi 146
Ríos Blanco y Negro reserve 253-4
river trips 156, 349, 363-4
road rules 388
Roboré 326-7
Rocas de Dalí 196

000 Map pages
000 Photograph pages

rock paintings 178, 197, 238, 256, 257, 274, 285
Rodeo Chapaco 281
Rosillas 285-7
rubber 27-8, 147, 354, 364
Rurrenabaque 329, 336-41, **337**, **224**
  accommodations 339
  attractions 336-7
  drinking 340
  entertainment 340
  food 339-40
  shopping 340
  tourist information 336
  tours 337-9
  travel to/from 340-1
  travel within 341

S
safe travel, see also crime
  drugs 372
  hitchhiking 388
  road rules 388
  women travelers 375, 378
Sajama national park 47, 167, 179-82, **180**
Salar de Chalviri 196
Salar de Chiguana 194
Salar de Coipasa 194, **192**
Salar de Uyuni 167, 190, 191-4, **192**, **8**
Salo 203
salt extraction 190, 191
salt hotels 191
salteñas 16, 55, 89
Sama biological reserve 275, 287-8
Samaipata 293, 310, 312-16, **312**
Sampaya 118
San Borja 344
San Buenaventura 341
San Cristóbal 197
San Ignacio de Moxos 329, 346-7, **7**
San Ignacio de Velasco 322-6
San Jacinto Reservoir 285
San Javier 320-1
San José de Chiquitos 324-6
San José de Uchupiamonas 342-3
San Juan 194
San Lorenzo 285
San Matías 328
San Miguel de Velasco 323
San Pablo de López 197
San Pedro de Quemez 194
San Pedro Prison 75

San Rafael de Velasco 324
San Ramón 320
San Vicente 203-4
Sánchez de Lozada, Gonzalo ('Goni') 30, 31, 33
Santa Ana de Velasco 323-4
Santa Cruz 23, 293-305, **296-7**
  accommodations 300-1
  attractions 298-9
  drinking 302-3
  entertainment 303
  festivals 300
  food 301-2
  history 295-7
  itineraries 20
  medical services 298
  shopping 303
  tourist information 298
  tours 299
  travel to/from 295, 303-5
  travel within 305
Santa Cruz department 293-319, **294**
  climate 295
Santa Rosa 343
Santiago de Chiquitos 326
Santuario Chuchini 352-3
Santuario de Quillacas 179
scams 70, see also crime
Schmidt, Martin 320
sea fossils 237-8
Semana Santa 113, 370
Sepulturas 178
Sernap 44, 46
shopping 374, 375
  language 403
Sicuani 116
Siles Zuazo, Hernán 30
silver mining 26, 146, 169, 190, 209, 258-9
Sipe Sipe 232
skiing 78, 100-1
slavery 259
soccer 36-7, 92
Sol de Mañana Geyser Basin 195, **222**
solo travelers 374-5, 378
Sorata 52, 127, 147-51, **148**
South Central Bolivia 275-89, **276**
  climate 276-7
  history 276
  travel to/from 277
Southern Altiplano 167, **168**
  climate 169
  history 169
  travel to/from 169
Southwest Circuit 185-7, 190-208

soybean crops 47, 57
Spanish Empire 26-7, 124, 258-9
spirituality 37, 108
sports 36-7
steam locomotives 190
Sucre 209, 240-53, **242-3**, **6**, **223**
  accommodations 248-50
  activities 247-8
  attractions 241-7
  churches 244, 247
  courses 247
  drinking 251
  entertainment 252
  festivals 248
  food 250-1
  history 210-11
  medical services 240
  museums 241, 244-5, 247
  shopping 252-74
  tourist information 241
  tours 247-8
  travel to/from 252-3
  travel within 253
Sundance Kid 53, 190, 203, 204
Supay Huasi 257

T
Tahua 194
Tajzara 287
Takesi (Taquesi) Trek 127, 138-40, **139**
Tarabuco 253-4, **223**
Tarapaya 274
Tarata 234
Tarija 275, 277-85, **278**, **286**
  accommodations 282-3
  attractions 279-81
  cathedrals 279-80
  entertainment 284
  festivals 281-2
  food 283-4
  history 277
  itineraries 18
  tourist information 279
  tours 281
  travel to/from 284
  travel within 284-5
  wineries 280-1
Tariquía national reserve 275, 288
taxis 388-9
telephone services 375-7
Templete Semisubterráneo
  La Paz 76
  Tiahuanaco 104
  Chisi 118

tennis 54
Termas de Charazani Phutina 160
Termas de Obrajes 177-8
Termas de Polques 196
Termas de Talula 256-7
territory loss 27-9, **28**
textiles 39, 76, 92, 134-5, 151, 160, 176, 253, 254, 256, 274, 303, 375
theater 92
theft, *see* crime
Tiahuanaco 24-5, 41, 102-5, 123, 124, 163, **103**, 6, 7, 217
time 377, 430
tin mining 165-6, 169-71, 174, 259
tinku 271
tipping 59
Tiquina Straits 125
Tiquipaya 233
titi monkey 45
Tiwanaku, *see* Tiahuanaco
toilets 377
Tomatitas 287
Torotoro national park 47, 209, 236-40, **237**
Totaizal 345-6
Totora 235
tourist information 377
tours 389-90
    4WD 53
    Candelaria 254
    Cochabamba 225
    Cordillera de los Frailes 258
    ecotours 342-3
    El Choro Trek 136
    Guayaramerín 360
    Incallajta 235
    jungle tours 337-9
    La Paz 78, 80
    Lake Titicaca 108, 112, 116, 120-1, 123, 124
    mine tours 265-6
    Oruro 174
    pampas tours 337-9
    Parque Nacional & Área de Uso Múltiple Amboró 305-6
    Parque Nacional Carrasco 334
    Parque Nacional Isiboro-Sécure 335
    Parque Nacional Lauca (Chile) 183

Parque Nacional Noel Kempff Mercado 357-8
Parque Nacional Torotoro 238
Parque Nacional Tunari 230
Parque Nacional y Área Natural de Manejo Integrado Aguaragüe 291
Potosí 265-6, 271
Reserva Biológica Cordillera de Sama 288
Reserva Biosférica del Beni 345
Reserva Nacional de Flora y Fauna Tariquía 288
Reserva Privada de Patrimonio Natural de Corvalán 291
Rurrenabaque 337-9
Salar de Uyuni 185-7
Samaipata 314
Santa Cruz 299
Southwest Circuit 185-7
Sucre 247-8
Tarija 281
Tiahuanaco 105
Trinidad 349-50
Tupiza 199-200
Uyuni 185-7
Villa Tunari 333
wineries 281
train travel 95, 389
Trans-Chaco Road 275, 290
transportation
    air travel 93-4
    bus travel 94-105
    itineraries 22
    train travel 95, 389
    travel to/from Bolivia 380-5
    travel within Bolivia 385-90
trekking 49-51, *see also* hiking
    Copacabana to Yampupata Trek 116, **117**
    Cordillera Apolobamba 160-5
    Cordillera Quimsa Cruz 166
    Cordillera Real 157
    El Camino del Oro 151-3, **151**
    El Choro Trek 127, 135-7, **136**, 8
    Gold Digger's Trail 151-3, **152**
    Lagunillas to Agua Blanca Trek 49, 163-6
    Mapiri Trail 49, 153-5, **153**
    Takesi Trek 127, 138-40, **139**
    Yunga Cruz Trek 127, 141-3, **141**
Trinidad 347-52, **348**

trufis 388
tubing 53-4
Tunari national park 47, 230
Tupiza 167, 197-201, **198**, **202**, 5
TV 367
typhoid fever 395
typhus 396

U
Unesco World Heritage sites 21, 240, 259, 313, 354
Urmiri 105
Uyuni 184-90, **185**
    accommodations 187-8
    attractions 184-5
    drinking 188
    food 188
    tours 185-7
    travel to/from 189-90

V
vacations 15, 371-2
vaccinations 378
Valencia 97-8
Valle de la Luna 96
Valle de las Ánimas 98
Vallegrande 317
Valles de Rocas 197
vegetarian travelers 59
vicuñas 39, 45, 162, 181, 191, **222**
video systems 367
Villa Albina 233
Villa Remedios 146
Villa Tunari 333-4
Villamontes 290-1
Villazón 204-7, **206**
visas 377-8
visual arts 42
Volcán Illimani 50
Volcán Licancabur 191, 196, 5
Volcán Ollagüe 191, 194
Volcán Sajama 50, 179, **222**
Volcán Tunupa 193, **222**
volunteering 378-9

W
War of the Pacific 27, 28
water
    drinking 47, 398
    pollution 97
    shortages 31
    Water War 31, 215
waterfalls
    Catarata el Encanto 356-7
    Coimata Falls 288

000 Map pages
000 Photograph pages

INDEX

La Pajcha 316-17
Los Espejillos 311
Los Tumbos de Suruquizo 321
Parque Nacional & Área de Uso
    Múltiple Amboró 309
San José de Chiquitos 325
weather 14, 368, 369
weights 367, *see also inside
    front cover*
whitewater rafting 53
    Chulumani 146
    Coroico 132
    Villa Tunari 333
wildlife-watching 45, 47, 53-4, *see
    also* bird-watching
    Amazon Basin 330, 343, 344-6,
        352-3, 354, 356
    Chaco, the 289, 291
    Cordillera Apolobamba 162, 163
    Parque Nacional & Área de Uso
        Múltiple Amboró 307
    Parque Nacional Lauca (Chile)
        182

Parque Nacional Noel Kempff
    Mercado 354, 356
Parque Nacional Sajama 179
Parque Nacional y Área Natural de
    Manejo Integrado Aguaragüe
    291
Reserva Biosférica del Beni 3
    44-6
Reserva Nacional de Flora y Fauna
    Tariquía 288
Reserva Privada de Patrimonio
    Natural de Corvalán 291
wine 58, 280, 375
wineries 280-1
Witches' Market 71
women in Bolivia 30, 34, 37,
    38-9
women travelers 375, 378
women's health 398
work 378-9
World's Most Dangerous Road 52,
    77, 78
wrestling 37, 76

Y
Yacimientos Petrolíferos Fiscales
    Bolivianos 31
Yacuiba 289-90
Yampupata 118
Yanacachi 140-1
Yani 153
Yaraque 182
yellow fever 378, 395
Yolosa 137-8
YPFB 31
Yucumo 343-4
Yumani 119
Yunga Cruz Trek 127, 141-3,
    141
Yungas 127-56, **128**
    climate 128
    history 128
    travel to/from 128

Z
Zona Sur 85, **86-7**
Zongo Valley 52, 101, 130